THE LEGAL
EFFECTS OF WAR

BY

LORD McNAIR, C.B.E., Q.C., LL.D., F.B.A.

AND

A. D. WATTS, M.A., LL.B.

OF GRAY'S INN, BARRISTER-AT-LAW

CAMBRIDGE

AT THE UNIVERSITY PRESS

1966

PUBLISHED BY
THE SYNDICS OF THE CAMBRIDGE UNIVERSITY PRESS

Bentley House, 200 Euston Road, London, N.W. 1
American Branch: 32 East 57th Street, New York, N.Y. 10022

THIS EDITION
©

CAMBRIDGE UNIVERSITY PRESS
1966

First edition 1920
Second edition 1944
Third edition 1948
Fourth edition 1966

Printed in Great Britain at the University Printing House, Cambridge
(Brooke Crutchley, University Printer)

CONTENTS

v

PREFACE TO THE FOURTH EDITION

A godson of Queen Elizabeth I, Sir John Harington (1561–1612), once remarked:

> Treason doth never prosper, what's the reason?
> For if it prosper, none dare call it Treason.

Today the term 'war' is out of fashion. Resort to armed force is widespread and constant, but none dare call it 'war'. So in producing a fourth edition of this book we have tried to include some assessment of the legal effects of this developing practice. At present they are tentative and scattered, but, if the practice continues, a new body of law will emerge governing armed conflict falling short of 'war', either in breach or in pursuance of the Charter of the United Nations or otherwise. In the main, however, this edition, like the editions of 1920, 1944 and 1948, is concerned with war *stricto sensu*, and its effects upon the legal position of private persons.

Furthermore, we are primarily concerned with English law (including what is gradually gaining recognition as a distinct branch of English law, namely, our foreign relations law), and the legal effects which ensue when the United Kingdom is a belligerent or a neutral. We are not qualified to deal with either Scots law or the law of any foreign country; international law we have had to touch upon occasionally in passing, but it would have been out of place in this book to have attempted more than a somewhat summary treatment. We have, however, from time to time cited particularly relevant Commonwealth, Colonial and foreign decisions, which since 1919 is made possible by the essential series known as the *Annual Digest (and Reports) of Public International Law Cases*, 1919–49, which in 1950 became the *International Law Reports*. We may mention that in considering a maritime or commercial question it is sometimes useful to look at the comprehensive *Lloyd's List Law Reports*, where cases are often reported at greater length than elsewhere, and some cases are only found there.

We draw particular attention to five chapters—chapter 1, 'War and Other Armed Conflicts', which considers the meaning of 'war' and describes various activities and situations which, while producing abnormal legal effects, fall short of 'war'; chapter 5, which deals with Frustration of Contracts and includes developments resulting from the Suez crisis of 1956; chapter 17, 'Effects of Belligerent Occupation of Territory; chapter 18, 'Acts of Governments Dispossessed by Belligerent Occupation'; and chapter 19, 'When the United Kingdom is Neutral'. One of the features of the war of 1939–45 was the wide extent of territory under belligerent occupation, the effect of which has been a mass of litigation in many parts of the world. The resulting output of judicial decisions has been enormous, and it is only now that the main lines of the law are beginning to emerge.

Citations of cases will be found in the *Table of Cases*, and not in the footnotes, except where it seems relevant to the argument to mention the date or the country or for some other reason. We are greatly indebted to Miss Gillian White, Fellow of New Hall, for preparing the index.

This book has once more had the great benefit of the constant care of the Cambridge University Press.

McN.
A.D.W.

April 1966

TABLE OF CASES CITED

(Numbers in heavy type refer to page numbers)

Yorkshire Dale Steamship Co. *v.* Minister of War Transport [1942] A.C. 691 **276** n.
Yrisarri *v.* Clement (1826) 3 Bing. 432 **449** n.
Yudsin *v.* Estate of Shanti, 19 I.L.R. (1952) p. 555 (Israel) **13** n.

Z. *v.* K., 18 I.L.R. (1951) No. 183 (France) **369** n., **382** n., **411**
Zarine *v.* Owners of S.S. *Ramava*: McEvoy *v.* Owners of S.S. *Otto* [1942] Irish Reports 148 **396** n.
Zbigniew G. *v.* Land and Building Company E. in Cracow, 26 I.L.R. (1958-II) p. 714 (Poland) **390** n.
Zeeuwsche Hypotheek-Bank Ltd *v.* Netherlands, 15 A.D. (1948) No. 188 (Holland) **385** n.
Zeiss, *see* Carl Zeiss...
Zenzo Arakawa, *Ex parte*, 15 A.D. (1948) No. 164 (U.S.A.) **12** n.
Zimmerman *v.* Hicks 3 A.D. (1925–6) No. 333 (U.S.A.) **139** n.
Zinc Corporation *v.* Hirsch [1916] 1 K.B. 541 (C.A.) **122** n., **124** n., **128** n. **131** n., **139, 264, 288, 301** n., **303**

TABLE OF STATUTES CITED

(Numbers in heavy type refer to page numbers)

1

ABBREVIATIONS

Oppenheim = Oppenheim, *International Law*, I, 8th ed. 1955; II, 7th ed. 1952.

Hyde = Hyde, *International Law*, 2nd rev. ed. (1945), vols. I, II and III.

Dicey = Dicey, *Conflict of Laws* (7th ed. 1958).

A.D. = *Annual Digest (and Reports) of Public International Law Cases*, 1919–49.

A.J. = *American Journal of International Law*.

B.Y. = *British Year Book of International Law*.

I.L.Q. or *I. and C.L.Q.* = *International Law Quarterly* or *International and Comparative Law Quarterly*.

I.L.R. = International Law Reports, 1950– .

L.Q.R. = *Law Quarterly Review*.

McNair, *Opinions* = McNair, *International Law Opinions* (3 vols.).

Pitt Cobbett = Pitt Cobbett, *Leading Cases in International Law* (5th ed.), vols. I and II.

T.S. = British Treaty Series.

I

WAR AND OTHER ARMED CONFLICTS

BIBLIOGRAPHY

(i) *War and Armed Conflict*

Baty and Morgan, *War: Its Conduct and Legal Results* (1915), pp. 3–17, 395–400.

Brierly, *The Law of Nations* (6th ed.), pp. 397–432.

Briggs, *The Law of Nations* (2nd ed.), pp. 947–86.

Brownlie, *International Law and the Use of Force by States.*

Calvo, *Le Droit International Théorique et Pratique*, III, §§ 1807–59, IV, §§ 1863–1910, 2411–90 and V, §§ 3115–68.

Fauchille, *Traité de Droit International Public* (8th ed.), §§ 971–94, 1000–43, 1248–67 and 1692–1711.

Hackworth, *Digest of International Law*, VI, §§ 560–3, 589 and 590.

Hall, *International Law* (8th ed.), §§ 118–23, 192 and 197–206.

Hindmarsh, *Force in Peace.*

Hyde, II, §§ 586–94, and III, §§ 596–603, 646–7A and 904–21.

Kelsen, *Principles of International Law*, pp. 18–70.

Moore, *Digest of International Law*, VII, §§ 1089–1107, 1162 and 1163.

Oppenheim, II, §§ 26–52aa, 53–8, 93–6, 231–40 and 261–84.

Phillimore, *International Law* (3rd ed.), III, pp. 1–113 and 770–91.

Pitt Cobbett, I, pp. 347–64, and II, pp. 1–25 and 290–7.

Rousseau, *Droit International Public*, §§ 695–703 and 723–30.

Schwarzenberger, *International Courts* (2nd ed.), chaps. 27, 28 and 38.

Stone, *Legal Controls of International Conflict*, pp. 285–317 and 635–47, and *Aggression and The World Order.*

Webber, *Effect of War on Contracts* (2nd ed.) (1946), chap. 1.

Holland, 19 *L.Q.R.* (1903), pp. 133–5.

McDougal and Feliciano, 67 *Yale Law Journal* (1958), pp. 771–845.

(ii) *United Nations Actions*

Bowett, *United Nations Forces.*

Burns and Heathcote, *Peace-Keeping by United Nations Forces.*

Halderman, 56 *A.J.* (1962), pp. 971–996.

Kelsen, *The Law of the United Nations*, chap. 18, and *Recent Trends in the Law of the United Nations.*

Oppenheim, II, §§ 52b–52fd, and 65.

Seyersted, 37 *B.Y.* (1961), pp. 351–475.

Stone, *Legal Controls of International Conflict*, pp. 191–200, 228–37 and 266–81.

(iii) *Civil War*

Briggs, *The Law of Nations* (2nd ed.), pp. 987–1004.

Green, 61 *Revue Générale de Droit International Public* (1962), p. 5.

Hyde, III, §§ 600 and 604.

McNair, *Opinions*, II, section XVI.

Moore, *Digest of International Law*, VII, §§ 1103 and 1108.

Oppenheim, II, §§ 59 and 59a.

Pitt Cobbett, I, pp. 56–63.

Rougier, *Les Guerres Civiles et le Droit des Gens.*

Schwarzenberger, *International Courts* (2nd ed.), chap. 37.

Wehberg, 63 *Receuil des Cours* (1938), p. 7.

It is the primary object of this book to consider the legal effects, in English municipal law, of the existence of a war, whether the United Kingdom is belligerent or neutral. Our inquiries will cover not only the legal consequences of war but also those of certain other situations of armed conflict (and even of quasi-hostility not involving armed operations) which fall short of war *stricto sensu*, of civil war and insurgency, and of the use of armed force by or under the authority of the United Nations. First, however, we must look more closely into what we mean by war and these other kinds of conflict, and this we shall do in this first chapter.

War and other forms of conflict raise problems of definition in international law as well as in municipal law. We shall first—briefly and without going into very much detail—outline the way in which wars and other conflicts are considered in international law, before we turn to the rules of municipal law with which we are primarily concerned.

A. INTERNATIONAL LAW

We shall consider international law under the following heads: (*a*) the state of war; (*b*) war; (*c*) conflicts not amounting to war; (*d*) conflicts involving forces acting under the authority of the United Nations; (*e*) civil war and insurgency.

(*a*) *The state of war*

Although the degree of armed force used by one State against another has ranged from isolated expeditions by a few men to full-scale conflicts of armed forces, international law has traditionally expressed the legal relationship between States in terms of a relatively clear cut dichotomy: a State has been considered as being either at peace with another State, or at war with it.[1] Being 'at war', however, is a technical concept referring to a state or condition of affairs, not mere acts of force. It is a state to which international law

---

[1] The dichotomy between peace and war, and the related notion (to which we shall refer later) of there being no intermediate legal state between them, has been much written about (not without criticism) in recent years. Among the extensive literature on this subject we should mention the following: Baxter, 16 *Revue Egyptienne de Droit International* (1960), p. 1; Borchard, 27 *A.J.* (1933), p. 114; Delbez, 57 *Revue Générale de Droit International Public* (1953), p. 177; Eagleton, *International Conciliation*, no. 291 (1933); Grob, *The Relativity of War and Peace*; Jessup, 48 *A.J.* (1954), p. 98, and 23 *Nordisk Tidsskrift for International Ret* (1953), p. 16; McDougal, 49 *A.J.* (1955), p. 63; McDougal and Feliciano, 52 *A.J.* (1958), p. 241 and 67 *Yale L.J.* (1958), p. 771; McNair, 11 *Transactions of the Grotius Society* (1926), p. 29; Ronan, 31 *A.J.* (1937), p. 642; Stone, *Legal Controls of International Conflict*, pp. 297–306; Schwarzenberger, 37 *A.J.* (1943), p. 460, and *Frontiers of International Law*, pp. 234–55; Tucker, 4 *I. and C.L.Q.* (1951), p. 11; Wright, *A Study of War*, p. 10.

attaches far-reaching consequences, and it confers upon States who might be affected by it a distinct legal status: this applies not only to the States parties to the war, but also to third States, since where a state of war exists it gives rise to the collateral status of neutrality for non-participants in the contest, with all its attendant rights and duties. This doctrine that war entails a special legal status is of long standing: Grotius writing in the early seventeenth century states that by 'bellum' is meant 'non actio sed status'.[1]

This *state* of war may perfectly well exist even if no armed force is being employed by the opposing parties and no actual hostilities between them are occurring.[2] Conversely, force may be used by one State against another without any state of war arising.[3] In this latter circumstance peace will, in law, still subsist[4] between the parties although their relations will be strained to a greater or lesser extent. This absence of identity between the state of war and actual hostilities has led to the adoption of various pairs of terms to point the difference, such as '*de jure* war' and '*de facto* war', 'war' and 'warlike acts',[5] 'legal war' and 'war in the material sense' (or 'actual war').

An associated element of the traditional concept of war in international law is that war and peace are alternatives between which no intermediate state[6] exists.[7] Again we can go back to Grotius: 'inter bellum et pacem nihil est medium.'[8] Thus in the absence of war, peace subsists: and vice versa.

Modern developments in international affairs have led to some criticism of the continued validity and utility of these traditional doctrines. This has, for example, shown itself in a tendency to avoid references to the concept of a state of war, particularly in treaties, a tendency which was considerably strengthened by the legal arguments which arose over the use of the term 'war' in the Covenant

---

[1] *De Jure Belli ac Pacis*, I, I, 2, I.

[2] As for example during an armistice, or where, as during the Second World War, some of the opposing belligerents are too distant from each other to be able to engage in hostilities.   [3] See below, p. 15.

[4] It will be noted that this implies that peace is the normal state of affairs which continues to exist until superseded by the abnormal state of war. For criticism of the doctrine of the normalcy of peace, see Schwarzenberger, *Frontiers of International Law*, pp. 240–2.

[5] On the meaning of 'acts of war' see Eagleton, 35 *A.J.* (1941), p. 321.

[6] This, of course, refers to an intermediate legal state, involving a distinct accompanying legal status for affected States, from their possession of which they are subject to a special legal regime with its own rights and duties. In a certain non-legal sense the use of armed force while a state of peace subsists is an intermediate stage in international relations: but this is a matter of politics rather than law.

[7] See in general on the question of an 'intermediate state' the works cited at p. 2, n. 1 above.

[8] *De Jure Belli ac Pacis*, 3, 21, 1, 1.

of the League of Nations and the Treaty for the Renunciation of War, 1928 (usually called the Kellogg-Briand Pact). As long ago as 1907, parties to Hague Convention II respecting the Employment of Force for the Recovery of Contract Debts agreed not to have recourse to 'armed force'. The Charter of the United Nations does not use the term 'war' in any of its operative provisions, but refers instead to terms such as 'use of force' and 'armed attack'.[1] Particularly significant are the Geneva Conventions of 1949 concerning various humanitarian aspects of the laws of war: they brush aside the terminological difficulties in stating that they apply not only in cases of declared war but also in 'any other armed conflict...even if a state of war is not recognised by one[2] of [the parties to the conflict]'.[3] Even where the term 'war' is used in a treaty, it has been suggested, and may indeed sometimes be appropriate, that a correct interpretation of the treaty requires that term to be given the wider meaning of armed hostilities whether or not giving rise to a state of war.[4] That there is sometimes justification for interpretations of this kind is as true of international legal instruments as it is in municipal law.[5] But it must not be overlooked that some treaties still need to be interpreted in terms of the traditional concept of a state of war, and even that some international instruments of recent years employ that concept.[6]

A further argument sometimes advanced is that the earlier view that the right to resort to war is an inherent right of a sovereign State has been replaced by a general outlawry of war which, in the light of the successive provisions of the Covenant of the League, the Kellogg-Briand Pact and the Charter of the United Nations,[7] has

[1] Although some provisions of the Charter also refer to breaches of international 'peace', there has been no inclination to apply those provisions by reference to the strict legal doctrine whereby peace only ceases to exist upon the outbreak of a state of war. But see Stone, *Legal Control of International Conflict*, p. 306, n. 47.

[2] Presumably the Conventions apply to an armed conflict even if a state of war is not recognized by both or all of the belligerents: see Baxter, 16 *Revue Egyptienne de Droit International* (1960), p. 5.

[3] Article 2, one of the articles common to all the Geneva Conventions of 1949.

[4] Brierly, *The Basis of Obligation in International Law*, pp. 235–6. The treaty may, of course, contain an express definition to this effect, as in Article v (9) (b) of the Anglo-American Agreement of 24 June 1960, concerning the establishment in the Bahama Islands of a LORAN Station (T.S. no. 64 (1960)).

[5] See below, p. 36. Such an interpretative approach cannot be pressed too far without the concept of a state of war being rendered meaningless for legal purposes.

[6] Thus the fifth reservation in the United Kingdom's Declaration of 27 November 1963, accepting the compulsory jurisdiction of the International Court of Justice, uses the term 'state of war' along with other terms denoting hostilities of various kinds.

[7] For a summary of the provisions of the Charter prohibiting the threat or use of force, see below, p. 17.

now led to the legal institution of war itself being incompatible with an international legal order based on those provisions.[1] Of course, the attempt to brand some wars as illegal is not a development of our own times, and the doctrines relating to *bellum justum* are of impressive antiquity. But whatever success there may have been in establishing satisfactory criteria for distinguishing the just from the unjust war (and it was not very great), it was never accepted that the unjust war was not nevertheless a war. Modern variants on this theme have scarcely been more successful. The existence of the Covenant and the Kellogg-Briand Pact did not prevent the 1939–45 war from being generally regarded as giving rise to a state of war.[2] States have invoked the concept of a state of war even after the entry into force of the Charter of the United Nations. Several of the Arab States did so in their relations with Israel, as did Pakistan against India[3]; the formal state of war between Germany and certain of the Allied States subsisted for several years after the entry into force of the Charter;[4] and the 1949 Geneva Conventions refer to a 'declared war' and a 'state of war'. In the *Corfu Channel* case the International Court accepted that Greece regarded herself as technically at war with Albania.[5] The General Assembly in a Resolution on the Duties of States in the event of the Outbreak of Hostilities[6] treated 'the outbreak of war' (as distinct from 'hostilities') as something which might still come about.

It thus seems to us to be, at the least, premature to conclude that the Covenant, the Kellogg-Briand Pact and the Charter have rendered obsolete the traditional concepts and doctrines relating to war and the state of war. There can be no doubt that those instruments have very significantly affected both the legality of resorting to war and some of the incidents previously attaching to the state of war and, more particularly, to its associated state of neutrality.[7] While as a result we may be in the process of relegating the traditional

[1] See Jessup, *A Modern Law of Nations*, pp. 53, 219; Baxter, 16 *Revue Egyptienne de Droit International* (1960), p. 8; Bloomfield, *Egypt, Israel and the Gulf of Aqaba*, pp. 53–8; Higgins, 37 *B.Y.* (1961), pp. 311–13; Hsu Mo, 35 *Transactions of the Grotius Society* (1950), p. 8; Feinburg, *The Legality of a 'State of War' after the Cessation of Hostilities, under the Charter of the United Nations and the Covenant of the League of Nations*; Scelle, 58 *Revue Générale de Droit International Public* (1954), p. 5.

[2] In a very few decisions municipal courts have been exceptional in holding that because of the 'criminal' nature of German attacks the ensuing conflict did not give rise to a state of war in international law: see two Polish decisions, *In re Greiser*, and *N. v. B.*

[3] See note at p. 455 below.

[4] See below, p. 42. But note Article 107 of the Charter.

[5] *I.C.J. Reports*, 1949, p. 29.   [6] Resolution 378 (V).

[7] Thus the conduct of neutrals may take account of the facts that one or more of the belligerents has violated its obligations under those instruments and has illegally resorted

concept of war to a subsidiary position, developing and raising up in its place the notion of armed conflicts which do not, even under the traditional doctrines, constitute a war, nevertheless there seems little doubt that at the present time the traditional doctrines associated with a state of war still properly form a significant part of international law. We still need, therefore, to know just what is meant by 'war'.

(b) War

Many definitions of 'war' have been put forward,[1] but while they adequately reflect the general nature of the state of war, the difficulties of pin-pointing the specific characteristics of war have hardly been surmounted. Indeed, the difficulties have seemed to some so great as to lead them to the conclusion that there is no one definition of war, but rather that each separate use of that term requires its own definition in the light of its particular purposes.[2] Such a multitude of particular definitions would seem to deprive the term of virtually any legal usefulness. So unhelpful a conclusion hardly

to war and also that States not participating in the war may have obligations to abide by decisions of competent organs of the United Nations (see Articles 2 (5), 2 (6), 25 and 49 of the Charter). Such inroads into the legal doctrines of neutrality match the developments in the nature of modern warfare whereby neutrality is less likely to lead to the result it professes to achieve, namely, the protection of a State from involvement in a war with which it is not primarily concerned: see Brierly, *The Basis of Obligation in International Law*, pp. 291–3. See in general on the role of neutrality in contemporary international law: Boye, 64 *Receuil des Cours* (1938), p. 219; Chaumont, 89 *ibid.* (1956), p. 5; Komarnicki, 80 *ibid.* (1952), p. 395, and 38 *Transactions of the Grotius Society* (1952), p. 77; Lalive, 24 *B.Y.* (1947), p. 72; Oppenheim, II, §§ 292A–292i; Whitton, 17 *Receuil des Cours* (1927), p. 453; Wright, 34 *A.J.* (1940), p. 391.

[1] The following is a selection of definitions which have been advanced: (i) 'War is a contention between two or more States through their armed forces, for the purpose of overpowering each other and imposing such conditions of peace as the victor pleases' (Oppenheim, II, p. 202); (ii) 'War is the state or condition of Governments contending by force' (Westlake, *International Law*, II, p. 1); (iii) 'cet état dans lequel on poursuit son droit par la force' (Vattel, *Droit des Gens*, Book III, ch. 1); (iv) 'the exercise of the international right of action, to which, from the nature of the thing and the absence of any common superior tribunal, nations are compelled to have recourse, in order to assert and vindicate their rights' (Phillimore, *Commentaries upon International Law*, III, paragraph 49); (v) 'un état de fait contraire à l'état normal de la communauté internationale qui est la paix, état de fait dont la résolution, la fin, le but ultime est cette paix elle-même' (Fauchille, *Droit International Public*, II, paragraph 1000); (vi) 'a condition of armed hostility between States' (Hyde, III, p. 1686); (vii) 'Powers are in a state of war with each other and of neutrality towards third States, if, subject to the limitations of international customary and treaty law, they choose to apply against each other power to the utmost, i.e. military as well as political and economic power' (Schwarzenberger, *The Frontiers of International Law*, p. 246); (viii) 'War is, in principle, an enforcement action involving the use of armed force performed by one state against another, constituting as it does an unlimited interference in the sphere of interests of the other state' (Kelsen, *Principles of International Law*, p. 32).

[2] See Grob, *The Relativity of War and Peace*, p. 204; Stone, *Legal Controls of International Conflicts*, p. 312.

seems necessary, however, and a more fruitful approach, for practical purposes, is to consider the circumstances in which a state of war may arise and may subsequently cease: for the period between these two events a state of war will subsist.

The commencement of war.[1] War may begin, first, by a declaration of war.[2] Such a declaration (which may take the form of a conditional ultimatum) was not required by customary international law, although since 1907 Hague Convention III[3] has required of all States who are parties thereto at the relevant time a previous and unequivocal warning, though without specifying any interval which must intervene before hostilities[4] begin. However, even for parties to that Convention the absence of a declaration, while it will involve the breach of a treaty obligation, will not of itself render the ensuing conflict any the less a war.[5] The declaration of war may itself specify the moment at which the state of war is to arise; if it does not, then war will arise immediately upon the communication of the declaration of war to the other party.

In the second place, a state of war will arise upon the commission of an act of force, under the authority of a State, which is done *animo belligerendi*,[6] or which, being done *sine animo belligerendi*, the State

---

[1] See McNair, 11 *Transactions of the Grotius Society* (1926), pp. 29–50, and comments thereon by Brierly, *The Basis of Obligation in International Law*, pp. 233–6, and H. Lauterpacht, 28 *A.J.* (1934), pp. 43 and 47, note 9. A state of war requires that the opposing parties be subjects of international law: for a purported declaration of war by an entity not constituting a State, see *Krishna Chettiar v. Subbiya Chettiar* and Green, 61 *Revue Générale de Droit International Public* (1962), p. 21; in the Rhodesian situation of 1965 some States purported to regard themselves as 'at war' with such an entity. Organized resistance movements may have some standing as belligerents: see J. A. C. Gutteridge, 26 *B.Y.* (1949), pp. 312–13. See also Schwarzenberger, *International Courts* (2nd ed.), pp. 369–70, on the status of Polish and Czechoslovak armies recognized as belligerent armies during the 1914–18 war.

[2] See Owen, *Declaration of War*; Eagleton, 32 *A.J.* (1938), p. 19; Brown, 33 *A.J.* (1939), p. 538. As to the position where a State declares war on another State which does not want to fight, see Pearce Higgins, *War and the Private Citizen*, p. 27; also *The Nayade*. For the interpretation of the term 'declared war' in a contract, in relation to the Suez incident in 1956, see *Navios Corporation v. The Ulyssees II*.

[3] 100 *B.F.S.P.* p. 326. See Pearce Higgins, *Hague Peace Conferences*, p. 198. As to the significance of the communications addressed by the United Kingdom to Israel and Egypt in 1956, see 6 *I. and C.L.Q.* (1957), pp. 331–3. It has been suggested that even non-signatories of Hague Convention III are bound by the substance of its provisions because the Convention is evidence of international law: see Baxter, 16 *Revue Egyptienne de Droit International* (1960), p. 3. See also General Assembly Resolution 378 (V) on the Duties of States in the event of the outbreak of hostilities.

[4] See Westlake, *Collected Papers*, p. 591, and Holland, *Letters on War and Neutrality*, p. 19.

[5] See Wright, 26 *A.J.* (1932), p. 363, and authorities cited in note 7 therein; Oppenheim, II, pp. 292 and 299. Undeclared wars have not been infrequent.

[6] As with an action which is only permissible on the assumption that a state of war exists: see Wright, 26 *A.J.* (1932), p. 364. *Animus belligerendi* may be implied, so that a state which while neither affirming nor denying an intention of embarking upon a state of war continues to engage in an armed conflict on a large scale may, by its acts, show

against which it is directed expressly or impliedly elects[1] to regard as creating a state of war,[2] such election having retroactive effect so that the state of war arises on the commission of the first act of force.[3] An election by an attacked State to treat an act of force as creating a state of war may be implied, for example, by that State choosing to repel force by force; but, as in other cases where an implication arises from conduct, no implication will arise if the actor can in all the circumstances be said to have denied it, and thus repelling force by force, while raising a presumption that the attacked State elects to regard war as having broken out, does not necessarily amount to such an election. So serious a matter as the existence of a state of war is not lightly to be implied. Furthermore, where leading political figures of a country engaged in hostilities refer to their country being 'at war', caution must be exercised before concluding therefrom that a state of war exists in any legal sense, since such references may prove to be more of emotional and political significance than legal.

It will be apparent that the existence of a state of war depends upon the determination of the parties to the conflict, and can arise where only one of the parties to the conflict asserts the existence of a state of war, even if the other denies it or keeps silence.[4] State practice has by and large accepted that for war to exist one at least of the contenders must so assert. Such a view has not proved without advantages. It has enabled conflicts, even if militarily extensive as between the parties, to stay essentially limited rather than to entail the overall dislocation, both international and municipal, both military and civil, which would accompany the escalation of those conflicts into a state of war. That so fundamental a concept of international law as war should depend upon the view of the parties

clearly an intention to make war: see Wright, *ibid.* p. 365. See also *The Cheref*, relating to the start of the war between France and Turkey in 1914. For the opening of the Russo-Japanese war in 1904 see Pitt Cobbett, ii, p. 12. On the question whether war broke out *ipso facto* between Japan and the U.S.A. the moment that Pearl Harbour was attacked, see cases cited by McDougal and Feliciano, 52 *A.J.* (1958), p. 251, n. 30, and also Borchard 41 *A.J.* (1947), p. 621, and Hill, 42 *A.J.* (1948), p. 355.

[1] The effect of such an election by a Government which is not recognized by the attacking State is uncertain, and it may be that the election can be disregarded—the United States persistently denied that a state of war existed with Mexico even after the Huerta Government of Mexico had stated that it regarded the attack by United States forces at Vera Cruz as 'the initiation of war against Mexico': see Wright, 26 *A.J.* (1932), p. 366, n. 17. A State may in advance bind itself not to elect to treat certain actions against it as acts of war: see Treaty of Versailles, Part viii, Sec. 1, Annex ii, paragraph 18.

[2] It is unnecessary for the State attacked, or, in the case of an attack *sine animo belligerendi*, the State electing to treat the attack as creating a state of war, to make a declaration of war—*per* Lord Hardwicke and Lord Talbot in 1726: McNair, *Opinions*, iii, p. 105.

[3] See Wright, 26 *A.J.* (1932), p. 365, especially n. 16.

[4] See below pp. 9 and 39.

8

involved—even of one of them alone—has been a principal reason for criticism[1] and for the attraction of other, more objective, concepts such as the 'threat or use of force' adopted in the Charter. However, the international legal order is still essentially decentralized, and even apparently more objective criteria are not in the last resort entirely free from subjective evaluation.

If, as we have seen, the existence of a state of war between two States depends upon at least one of them being of that opinion, to what extent is the determination of the parties to the conflict binding upon other States? If the parties have clearly asserted the existence of a state of war, it is difficult to accept that a third State against which one of them seeks to exercise a belligerent right can deny the existence of the right on the basis that the third State does not recognize that there is a state of war.[2] If the parties to a conflict have characterized it as a state of war, third States are bound thereby to the extent that they become neutrals and their relationship with the belligerents involves the rights and obligations of neutrality.[3] This will, in principle, we suggest, be the case even where the state of war is asserted by one contestant only, the other denying it.[4] Something approaching this kind of situation has arisen in recent years as between the United Arab Republic and Israel,[5] and between Pakistan and India,[6] although both situations display special features which allow room for argument as to the existence of a state of war. The denial by one of the parties to a conflict that a state of war exists seems primarily to serve as an indication that it neither claims any belligerent rights, nor holds third States to the obligations of the laws of neutrality; it might also serve, should there be any ambiguity in

[1] See Brownlie, *International Law and the Use of Force by States*, p. 399; Baxter, 16 *Revue Egyptienne de Droit International* (1960), pp. 4–6; Schwarzenberger, *The Frontiers of International Law*, pp. 248–51.

[2] But note the view expressed in Brownlie, *The Use of Force in International Law*, pp. 398–9, that a determination by the parties, while conclusive 'at least so far as the parties to a conflict are concerned...is not now regarded as conclusive when questions of general international law are being considered by third states'. For a rather special case see below, p. 11, n. 4.

[3] By Article 2 of the Hague Convention Relative to the Opening of Hostilities, 1907, a belligerent which is a party to the Convention must notify neutrals which are parties of the existence of a state of war, and the state of war affects them after receipt of the notification or, even before that, if it is established beyond doubt that they were in fact aware of the state of war.

[4] For the unwillingness of the third State (the United Kingdom) to admit a state of war between the United Arab Republic and Israel, see *Parliamentary Debates* (5th Series) (Commons), vol. 617 (1959–60), cols. 1264–7.

[5] See Baxter, 16 *Revue Egyptienne de Droit International* (1960), pp. 4–5, especially notes 14–19; and Bloomfield, *Egypt, Israel and the Gulf of Aqaba*, pp. 50–5.

[6] See note at p. 455 below.

the other party's attitude to the war, to justify a conclusion that no state of war exists.

In the converse situation, where the parties to a conflict, although engaged in armed hostilities, assert that a state of war does not exist and are not acting in a manner only supportable on the basis that a state of war does exist, difficulties are perhaps less likely to arise in practice. Where in such circumstances a third State purports to determine that a state of war exists in international law,[1] the effects thereof are limited:[2] it will do little more than give public notice that that State will conduct its relations with the participants to the conflict on the basis of the laws of neutrality as they would apply if the conflict were a war, and it may also estop that State from protesting against the exercise by the contestants of belligerent rights against itself. Of itself it will not give the contestants the rights and duties of belligerents as between themselves, or in respect of the world at large, nor impose on the relations between the contestants and other States the incidents of neutrality.[3]

Somewhat different, and very much a special case, is the position of a third State when a party to a conflict, while denying that a state of war exists, nevertheless acts towards a third State in a manner justifiable only on the basis of the existence of a state of war, as by exercising rights which are only enjoyed by a State which is at war. The third State may declare that it will regard the continuation of that conduct as an affirmation that the conflict between the other parties amounts to a state of war, and that it will only concede the right to exercise the rights in question on the basis that war exists.[4]

[1] A determination by a third State that a state of war exists for purposes of its municipal law (for example, in connection with the prohibition of enlistment in the forces of the belligerents) is different. While this will be binding internally, it is not necessarily effective internationally; furthermore, the concept of war may well bear a different meaning for purposes of municipal law from that which it bears in international law.

[2] But see Wright, 26 *A.J.* (1932), pp. 365–7, for an expression of the view that a war may exist as a result of the determination to that effect by third States.

[3] Even if there is a general recognition by third States that a state of war exists, it is difficult to accept that that signifies much more than that a large number of States will act as if there were a war, and that, in so far as those States are acting together in an international organization, their determination may also be effective for the purposes of the organization. A determination even by a majority of States that war exists could hardly, for example, impose upon a State which was not part of that majority the obligations of neutrality (except possibly as a result of a decision of the Security Council which is binding under Article 25 of the Charter), or, to take another example, give rise to the abrogation between the parties to the conflict of those treaties which are abrogated by war.

[4] As in 1884 in connection with the Franco-Chinese conflict: see Westlake, *Collected Papers*, pp. 582 and 599, and 76 *B.F.S.P.* p. 423. In connection with the blockade of Venezuelan ports in 1902, see Brierly, *Basis of Obligation in International Law*, p. 231, and for the French Blockade of Siam in 1893, see McNair, *Opinions*, II, pp. 412–15.

The termination of war.[1] War having arisen, the state of war continues until peace is resumed. It would seem to follow that if a state of war arises between two States at the moment when at least one of them determines that a state of war exists between them (i.e. at the moment when it cannot be said that they both agree that they are in a state of peace), a state of war will cease at the first moment when the continued existence of the state of war is maintained by neither party. This would appear to be the principle underlying the traditional enumeration of the circumstances in which a war may come to an end, and it is probably better to look always to the principle and to regard the enumeration as exemplary and not exhaustive. The circumstances of particular wars are so various, and their termination so frequently attended by great political complications, that it cannot be expected that the termination of all wars will fit tidily into any set of categories.

The more usual circumstances by which a state of war is terminated are:

(*a*) *By the conclusion of a treaty of peace.*[2] While the actual signature of a peace treaty, assuming it not to have been preceded by an armistice, may be assumed to be the signal for a cessation of hostilities[3] and, in general, to give the treaty a significance similar to that of an armistice, the state of war is not terminated by the treaty until it has entered into force in accordance with whatever procedure may be provided in the treaty: this will usually involve ratification.[4]

---

[1] In addition to works cited in the bibliography to this chapter, see Phillipson, *Termination of War and Treaties of Peace*. Note also the curious situation regarding the state of war between Siam and the United Kingdom during the Second World War, in which Siam declared war on the United Kingdom and this declaration was later declared 'null and void and not binding on the Thai people': see 145 *B.F.S.P.* p. 1172 and Treaty Series no. 10 (1951).

[2] The second and third editions of this book contained a chapter entitled 'The Effects of Treaties of Peace upon Private Rights', which dealt with Territorial Changes, Change in Nationality, Change in Domicil, Scope of a State's Power to Affect the Private Rights of its Nationals, Effect upon Nationals of Third States, How far a Peace Treaty Concluded by the British Crown involves Legislation, and Relation of the British Crown to its Subjects in regard to a Peace Treaty.

[3] The treaty itself may provide otherwise, as where communications are difficult and it is consequently stipulated that hostilities in distant or inaccessible parts should cease at a future date: see, e.g. Article II of the Treaty of Ghent, 1814, between the United Kingdom and the United States (2 *B.F.S.P.* p. 357). Where a future date is adopted, questions may arise in connection with hostile acts performed prior to that date but after receipt of notice of the peace treaty: see Phillimore, *International Law* (3rd ed.), III, pp. 779–82; Hall, *International Law* (8th ed.), § 202.

[4] On 11 August 1909, the Law Officers advised that at a time when a peace treaty between two foreign States had been ratified by both but ratifications had not been exchanged, the United Kingdom should not recognize that a state of war then existed.

(*b*) *By one belligerent subjugating the other.* The essence of subjugation is that the subjugated state ceases to exist as a State, so that the war is inevitably brought to an end through the disappearance of the enemy State. Subjugation has been defined as the 'extermination in war of one belligerent by another through annexation of the former's territory after conquest, the enemy's forces having been annihilated'.[1] While more frequently occurring before the twentieth century, subjugation is not unknown in modern times: the Italian annexation of Abyssinia in 1936 may be regarded as an example.[2] A more recent situation sometimes regarded[3] as amounting, at least temporarily, to subjugation is that which obtained in respect of Germany immediately after the unconditional surrender of Germany in May 1945, and the Berlin Declaration a month later whereby France, the United Kingdom, the United States and the Soviet Union assumed 'supreme authority' with respect to Germany without annexing her territory.[4]

(*c*) *By the belligerents abstaining from further acts of war and establishing peaceful relations without any formal peace treaty.* A state of war is not necessarily accompanied by active hostilities, and thus the mere cessation of hostilities does not in itself put an end to the state of war.[5]

[1] Oppenheim, II, p. 600.

[2] Rousseau, 45 *Revue Générale de Droit International* (1938), pp. 53–77; Strupp, 44 *ibid.* (1937), pp. 43–6. [3] Oppenheim, II, pp. 602–5.

[4] The status of Germany immediately after the cessation of hostilities has been a matter of some controversy and considerable difference of opinion: see, *inter alia*, Kelsen, 38 *A.J.* (1944), p. 689, and 39 *A.J.* (1945), p. 518; Jennings, 23 *B.Y.* (1946), p. 112; Mann, 33 *Transactions of the Grotius Society* (1947), p. 119; Potter, 43 *A.J.* (1949), p. 323; von Laun, 45 *A.J.* (1951), p. 267; Kunz, 46 *A.J.* (1952), p. 114; Wright, *ibid.* p. 299; Bathurst and Simpson, *Germany and the Atlantic Community* (1956). Judicial decisions of the courts of many countries upon the legal effects of the unconditional surrender of Germany and the Berlin Declaration, and particularly whether they involved the termination of the state of war, will be found in the volumes of the A.D. and I.L.R., particularly volumes 12–16, and attention is drawn to the following cases: *In re Hourigan* (New Zealand); *Occupation of Germany Case (Zurich)* (Switzerland); *Dawson v. The Commonwealth* (Australia); *Stinson v. New York Life Insurance Co.,* (U.S.A.); *Greenville Enterprise Inc. v. Jennings* (U.S.A.); *Grahame v. Director of Prosecutions* (Germany, British Zone of Control); *In re Altstotter; New York Life Insurance Co. v. Durham* (U.S.A.); *Ex parte Zenzo Arakawa* (U.S.A.); *Waller v. United States* (U.S.A.); *Ludecke v. Watkins* (U.S.A., Supreme Court); *Commune de Barvaux v. Preud'homme* (Belgium); *In re Lindemann de Melamet* (Argentine); *Public Prosecutor v. H.* (Holland); *In re Société Bonduelle et Cie* (France); *Acheson v. Wohlmuth* (U.S.A.); *Schering A.G. v. Pharmedica Property Ltd* (Australia); *German Civil Servant Case* (Germany). For British decisions arising out of the circumstances of the end of the 1939–45 war, see below, pp. 40–3.

[5] The actual cessation of hostilities may be of legal significance in its own right (e.g. Article 118 of the 1949 Geneva Prisoners of War Convention—'cessation of active hostilities'—and Article 6 of the 1949 Geneva Civilians Convention—'general close of military operations'); it may also be considered to be the situation with reference to which expressions such as 'the end of the war' should be interpreted. In connection with the exercise of rights of prize after an unconditional surrender, see *Schiffahrt-Treuhand G.m.b.H. v. H.M. Procurator-General,* and *The Eilenau (Norway).*

In addition to the cessation of hostilities, neither party to the prior conflict must maintain the continued existence of the state of war. It will be apparent that where a war ends in this way there will frequently be uncertainty as to the precise date on which the war ended. This will however be avoided if some suitable declaration is issued.[1] Such a declaration has in fact been resorted to in order to avoid the undue prolongation of a technical state of war long after the final cessation of hostilities but prior to the conclusion of a treaty of peace[2] (which, in such circumstances, would not itself put an end to the state of war but would be concerned with spelling out the relationship of the ex-belligerents and regulating matters arising out of the war). Thus in 1920 a Joint Resolution was passed by the Congress of the United States terminating the war with Germany;[3] in 1947 the United Kingdom notified the end of the formal state of war with Austria,[4] and in 1951 declared the end of the state of war with Germany.[5]

Armistice agreements require particular mention.[6] Armistices may be of varying extent, but they all have in common the fact that they involve a cessation of hostilities at least for the time being. The various limited armistices do not concern us here, since it is never seriously suggested that they result in the end of a war. Some armistices, however, are of a general character and bring to a halt the conduct of all hostilities between the belligerents. While such a total cessation of hostilities might appear to be tantamount to the termination of the war, it is in fact well established in international law that this is not so in any legal sense. The state of war continues,

[1] Since a state of war depends upon the intentions of both parties, a unilateral declaration would only terminate the war if accepted by—or at least not rejected by—the other party.

[2] See Hyde, III, pp. 2386–8; Ottensooser, 29 *B.Y.* (1952), p. 435; Transill, 38 *L.Q.R.* (1922), p. 26.

[3] Hyde, III, p. 2386. But see *United States* v. *Hicks* (U.S.A.) holding the war to have ended with the President's announcement of the armistice in 1918.

[4] 147 *B.F.S.P.* (1947, Pt I), p. 433. A peace treaty with Austria was concluded subsequently.

[5] 158 *B.F.S.P.* (1951), p. 67; see further, p. 42 below. No peace treaty with Germany has yet been concluded, but much of the substance of a peace treaty has been included in the Bonn Agreements of 1952 (T.S. nos. 10–14 (1959)) and the Paris Agreement of 1954 (T.S. no. 15 (1959)). The Paris Agreement has been held to be the instrument effecting the 'conclusion of peace': *Maturity of Bill of Exchange Case* (Germany); *Société des Etablissements Martin* v. *Clergé* (France).

[6] In addition to the works cited in the bibliography to this chapter, see Bloomfield, *Egypt, Israel and the Gulf of Aqaba*, pp. 24–35; Rosenne, *Israel's Armistice Agreements with the Arab States*; Levie, 50 *A.J.* (1956), p. 880; Sibert, 40 *Revue Générale de Droit International Public* (1933), p. 657; Gros, 51 *A.J.* (1957), p. 530, esp. pp. 543 ff.; Graham, 39 *A.J.* (1945), p. 286, and 40 *A.J.* (1946), p. 148.

and it is only the actual conduct of hostilities which is stopped.[1] Thus during an armistice the rights and duties of belligerents[2] (other than those suspended, expressly or by implication, by the armistice agreement in bringing about a cessation of hostilities) and of neutrals[3] remain in being.

While this view of the legal significance of an armistice is still generally held, it has been suggested that in contemporary international practice an armistice may in certain circumstances terminate the legal state of war.[4] Partly this is due to the development which has taken place in the nature of armistice agreements, so that, in concerning themselves with matters much wider than necessary merely to secure a cessation of hostilities, they now 'tend more and more to assume the character of a preliminary peace treaty'[5] and in part the suggestion also finds a basis in the apparent inappropriateness of treating an armistice which is clearly intended to put a permanent end to the hostilities pending the eventual conclusion of formal peace arrangements as having the same legal effects as an armistice which involves a cessation of hostilities which is essentially only temporary.[6]

It seems necessary to keep various aspects of this matter quite

---

[1] Several of the cases cited in n. 4, at p. 12 above, deal with the legal effects of the armistice agreements of the 1939–45 war: in addition, see *Société Industrielle et Commerciale des Marbres* v. *Sarfati* (France); *In re Suarez* (France); *The Abeille No. 24* (Germany); *Artel* v. *Seymand* (France); *Re Scarpato*, 18 *I.L.R.* (1951), no. 193 at p. 627 (Italy). In connection with the armistice agreements of the 1914–18 war, see *Düsseldorfer Allgemeine Versicherungs—A.G.* v. *L.* (Germany); *United States* v. *Hicks* (U.S.A.); *Ahmed Enim Bey* v. *United Kingdom*; *Dooley* v. *Johnson* (U.S.A.); *Spitz* v. *Secretary of State for Canada* (Canada). In connection with the Arab–Israel Armistice Agreement of 1949, see the works by Bloomfield and Rosenne cited at p. 13, n. 6, above; *Yudsin* v. *Estate of Shanti* (Israel); *Custodian of Absentee Property* v. *Samra* (Israel); *Jiday* v. *C.E.O. Haifa* (Israel); and nn. 2 and 6 below. As to the armistice which put an end to the fighting in the United Nations conflict in Korea, see below, p. 29, n. 1.

[2] As to rights of seizure in prize during an armistice, see *The Rannveig*; *Schiffahrt-Treuhand G.m.b.H.* v. *H.M. Procurator-General*; Colombos, *Law of the Sea* (5th ed.), §§ 686–7; and Rowson, 24 *B.Y.* (1947), pp. 171–4. Many decisions of the Prize Court of the United Arab Republic since the conclusion of the Egypt-Israel Armistice in 1949 are reported in the volumes of the *Revue Egyptienne de Droit International* from 1949 onwards (and in the A.D. and *I.L.R.*): for the United Nations practice relating to the exercise of rights of visit and search and seizure by Egypt and Israel during the armistice between them, see Higgins, 37 *B.Y.* (1961), pp. 311–12, and Anon., 1 *I. and C.L.Q.* (1952), pp. 85–92.

[3] See Oppenheim, II, p. 555, n. 1.

[4] See Starke, *An Introduction to International Law* (5th ed.), p. 429; Bloomfield, *Egypt, Israel and the Gulf of Aqaba*, pp. 24–35, 50–8.

[5] Fitzmaurice, *Receuil des Cours* (1948, II), p. 271. A consequence appears to be the elevation of truces into the position traditionally occupied by armistices: see Stone, *Legal Controls of International Conflict*, p. 636.

[6] The 'permanent' character of the armistice between Egypt and Israel has been considered by the Security Council: see Higgins, 37 *B.Y.* (1961), pp. 311–12. A further distinction is sometimes drawn between armistices concluded between belligerents on their own and those concluded under the auspices of the United Nations: see Bloomfield, *Egypt, Israel and the Gulf of Aqaba*, pp. 33, 36–40, 50–8.

distinct from each other. First, in so far as the conflict is an armed conflict not amounting to war, a general and permanent armistice will itself put an end to the conflict.[1] Second, an armistice may well be followed by the termination of the state of war by the parties gradually establishing peaceful relations:[2] but this is not to say that the armistice ended the state of war.[3] Third, an armistice agreement may be capable of interpretation as showing that both parties intended not only a cessation of hostilities but also the termination of the state of war between them: where such an intention is shown it would not seem right to deny that the state of war has ended, merely because the intention was made manifest in an 'armistice' agreement. Fourth, it is quite proper for the purposes of particular instruments to interpret terms connoting the end of a war, or peace, as bearing a meaning satisfied by the conclusion of an armistice, where this is required by the rules of interpretation applicable to the instruments.[4] Fifth, it is quite proper for a belligerent, if it so wishes, to waive during an armistice the exercise of its belligerent rights[5] or to adopt administrative measures giving rise to conditions approximating to those of a state of peace.[6]

(c) Conflicts not amounting to war

States have not always wanted to embark upon a full-scale state of war, the circumstances and consequences of which would perhaps be out of all proportion to the particular end to be achieved, but

[1] See below, p. 19, n. 6. This line of thought may be followed by those who contend that in view of the provisions of the United Nations Charter a state of war cannot exist between members of the United Nations, so that nothing more than an armistice is now needed to end a conflict between two Member States (see Bloomfield, *ibid.* pp. 37, 52–8).

[2] See above, p. 12.

[3] The fact that an armistice is shown by the passage of time to have been observed and to have been clearly applied as putting a permanent end to hostilities, and perhaps even as preventing a resumption of hostilities, cannot mean that the armistice ended the war, unless the legal effect of the armistice is to be held to be dependent upon events subsequent to the date of its conclusion.

[4] See above, p. 4, and below, p. 36.

[5] See *The Rannveig*, where a governmental agreement with Norway was considered in the light of the possibility that it amounted to a waiver, during the period between the signature of an armistice and the entry into force of a peace treaty, of the United Kingdom's belligerent rights. In *The Hermes and the Four Hulls*, [1951] P. 347, 361, Merriman P. did 'not doubt that short of the signing of a peace treaty victors may abrogate, expressly or impliedly, any rights that they have *jure belli*, including rights of prize', and this statement was affirmed by the Privy Council, [1953] A.C. 232, 266, on appeal: the Privy Council added that in certain circumstances unreasonable delay after an unconditional surrender in regulating the situation by a new declaration or arrangement may have a prejudicial effect on the victor's retention of his rights.

[6] Thus the United States in 1946, and the United Kingdom in 1949, authorized the resumption of commercial relations with Germany, although the state of war was not terminated until 1951. See below, p. 42.

have instead frequently had recourse to a limited degree of force. This has become accepted in international law as not necessarily giving rise to a state of war and as compatible with the continuation of a state of peace.

However, at the same time rules of international law developed to cover these situations, regulating and limiting the circumstances and manner in which armed force, even if not amounting to war, might exceptionally be lawfully used for coercive purposes. Thus recourse to armed force by way of reprisals[1] was only considered lawful if the State against which armed force was used had committed a violation of international law, if prior to recourse to reprisals an attempt had been made to obtain redress from that State and had failed, and if the armed force used was proportional to the wrong which occasioned it.[2] Recourse to armed force in self-defence was only justifiable where there was initially a necessity for self-defence, instant, overwhelming, leaving no choice of means and no moment for deliberation, and so long as the acts done in self-defence were not unreasonable or excessive but were kept within the limits of the necessity which occasioned them.[3] Other, and somewhat more doubtful and less clearly defined, circumstances justifying recourse to armed force were sometimes invoked, as where there is claimed to be a right of intervention[4] or of self-preservation.[5] The various acts or measures which constitute or accompany conflicts not amounting to war (such as laying an embargo, instituting a pacific blockade, landing armed forces,[6] and bombarding and occupying territory)[7] are usually just the particular methods adopted by States in exercising their exceptional rights, under one or other of these general headings, to have recourse to force.

Some of the more frequently used modes of peaceful conflict, such

---

[1] See Oppenheim, II, §§ 33–43; Hyde, II, pp. 1660–7; De la Brière, 22 *Receuil des Cours* (1928), p. 241; Venezia, 64 *Revue Générale de Droit International Public* (1960), p. 465. Distinguish *retorsion*, which involves taking action which while unfriendly is not unlawful: see Oppenheim, II, §§ 29–32; Hyde, II, pp. 1657–60.

[2] *The Naulilaa Case* (German-Portuguese Arbitral Tribunal).

[3] *The Caroline Incident* (see Moore, *Digest of International Law*, II, pp. 409–14; Jennings, 32 *A.J.* (1938), p. 82; and McNair, *Opinions*, II, pp. 221–30).

[4] See Oppenheim, II, §§ 50–1; Hyde, I, §§ 69–84; Winfield, 3 *B.Y.* (1922–3), p. 130; Potter, 32 *Receuil des Cours* (1930), p. 611; Stowell, 40 *ibid.* (1932), p. 91.

[5] See Hall, *International Law* (8th ed.), chap. VII; Bowett, *Self-Defence in International Law*, p. 10.

[6] For comment on the landing of United States troops in the Lebanon in 1958, see Potter, 52 *A.J.* (1958), p. 727, Wright, 53 *A.J.* (1959), p. 112, and E. Lauterpacht, 8 *I. and C.L.Q.* (1959), p. 148 (also dealing with the landing of British troops in Jordan). See also, in general, E. Lauterpacht, 7 *I. and C.L.Q.* (1958), p. 99.

[7] On non-belligerent military occupation of alien territory, see Jones, 9 *Transactions of the Grotius Society* (1924), p. 149.

as pacific blockade[1] and embargo,[2] have acquired a technical meaning, but in most cases the use of force has to be looked at in the light of the particular circumstances rather than in terms of precise definitions.[3] It would be a mistake to consider the permissible uses of force short of war as having to fall within certain fixed categories.

The Covenant of the League of Nations and the Kellogg-Briand Pact had little enough impact on the notion of war, and, being phrased primarily in terms of 'war', have had even less in the realm of armed conflicts short of war. With the Charter of the United Nations certain advances have been made.[4] By Article 2 (3), all member States are obliged to 'settle their international disputes by peaceful means in such a manner that international peace and security, and justice, are not endangered'. Article 2 (4) obliges them to 'refrain in their international relations from the threat or use of force against the territorial integrity or political independence of any State, or in any other manner inconsistent with the Purposes of the United Nations'. Article 33 imposes on the parties to any dispute, the continuance of which is likely to endanger the maintenance of international peace and security, the obligation to seek first of all a settlement by pacific means. Furthermore, the Security Council has

---

[1] See below, p. 20.   [2] See below, p. 21.

[3] The naval 'quarantine' of Cuba by the United States of America in 1962 displayed various unique characteristics: see in general Meeker, 57 *A.J.* (1963), p. 515; Christol and Davis, *ibid.* p. 525; Wright, *ibid.* p. 546; Oliver, *ibid.* p. 373; Fenwick, *ibid.* p. 588; MacChesney, *ibid.* p. 592; McDougal, *ibid.* p. 597; Rousseau, 67 *Revue Générale de Droit International Public* (1963), p. 144; Giraud, *ibid.* p. 523. The use of the word 'quarantine' by the United States Government to categorize their action would seem to have been intended to underline the very special nature of the measures taken, and in particular to get away from the ideas associated with 'pacific blockade'. In its medical sense quarantine connotes the temporary isolation of persons or property having been in contact with infectious diseases, as a means of preventing the spread of the infection; an essentially prophylactic and protective measure. It was in such a sense that the term was used in, for example, the Quarantine Act, 1825, which contained provisions whereby vessels were liable to medical quarantine, even on the high seas. Statutes protective of other interests, and equally involving interference with shipping on the high seas, have been passed by many countries in connection with, for example, customs and revenue matters—the so-called 'hovering acts' (see, in general, Briggs, *The Law of Nations* (2nd ed.), pp. 371 ff.). In view of such precedents for protective action on the high seas, it is not too unreasonable to regard the notion of sanitary quarantine as having been adapted to the Cuban situation in a way which, while retaining the essential prophylactic and protective elements of the measure, took into account the difference between infectious diseases and nuclear attack from the point of view of the nature of the isolation needed to ensure adequate protection.

[4] On the general question of the legal effects of the Covenant, the Kellogg-Briand Pact and the Charter upon recourse to force by States, see Brownlie, 8 *I. and C.L.Q.* (1959), p. 707; Oppenheim, II, §§ 52a–52aa; Tucker, 4 *I. and C.L.Q.* (1951), p. 11; Waldock, 81 *Receuil des Cours* (1952, II), p. 455; Wehberg, 78 *ibid.* (1951), p. 7. For the practice of the United Nations in connection with the use of force by States, see Higgins, 37 *B.Y.* (1961), p. 269; Giraud, 67 *Revue Générale de Droit International* (1963), p. 501.

certain extensive powers to investigate disputes, recommend methods for their adjustment, and, in respect of threats to the peace, breaches of the peace, and acts of aggression, it may make recommendations and decide on measures to maintain or restore international peace and security. These powers of the Security Council are, of course, given weight by the obligation of Member States under Article 25 to accept and carry out the Council's decisions.

One cannot, however, conclude that the provisions of the Charter have effectively put an end to the legitimate occurrence of armed conflicts between States, not even if both are members of the United Nations (and furthermore we must not forget that even unlawful recourse to force can still result in an armed conflict). The exercise of the Security Council's powers is subject to the political conditions in the Council, which have prevented the Council's powers from being exercised as rigorously as they might have been; and in any event the Security Council's powers operate on a somewhat different plane from those provisions which directly proscribe recourse to armed force. The obligations of Member States under Articles 2 (3), 2 (4), and 33 are not so tightly drawn that States may never resort to armed force otherwise than in violation of their obligations under those Articles. Most important of all, Article 51 expressly leaves unimpaired the inherent right of individual or collective self-defence if an armed attack occurs against a member of the United Nations.[1] Quite clearly the traditional rules of international law relating to the exceptional permissibility of recourse to armed force have now to be considered in the light of the terms of the Charter. The restrictions which customary international law places on recourse to armed force have not been displaced and superseded by the provisions of the Charter, but only extensively supplemented by them.[2] We may expect that further developments or refinements of existing customary concepts in connection with recourse to force will occur now that States must consider their actions with the additional restrictions imposed by the Charter in mind.

State practice since 1945 gives no ground for believing that resort to armed force is a thing of the past; the General Assembly has acknowledged this in adopting a resolution on the duties of States

[1] See, in general, Bowett, *Self-Defence in International Law*; Brownlie, 37 *B.Y.* (1961), p. 183, and *International Law and the Use of Force by States*, chap. XIII; Giraud, 49 *Receuil des Cours* (1934), p. 691; Higgins, 37 *B.Y.* (1961), p. 297.

[2] Thus, at the time of the Suez incident in 1956, the United Kingdom justified its action in terms of customary international law and the Kellogg-Briand Pact as well as in terms of the Charter: see 6 *I. and C.L.Q.* (1957), pp. 325–30, for the texts of statements made in Parliament.

in the event of the outbreak of hostilities.[1] Whether by taking advantage of those provisions of the Charter which in certain situations permit, or at least may be argued to permit, the use of armed force, or by committing a breach of their obligations under the Kellogg-Briand Pact or the Charter, States are likely to continue to resort to armed force and to do so in circumstances which do not result in a state of war. At the same time we should mention that States, in embarking upon some limited use of armed force, are not engaging upon action in respect of which they have an unfettered discretion. Both the justifications for a policy of armed force, and its manifestations, are justiciable matters.[2]

The most noticeable distinction[3] between a conflict not amounting to war and war itself is that the former is essentially limited, while the latter is not. For example, in contemporary practice, the strictly limited objectives of the British and French intervention in the Suez Canal in 1956[4] and of the United States quarantine in Cuba in 1962[5] were emphasized at the time.

Not only does armed conflict differ from war in its essentially limited nature but it also differs in that it gives rise to no separate and distinct legal state of affairs.[6] The rights and duties of States in connection with an armed conflict depend on the particular circumstances. The totality of their relations is not necessarily disrupted, and for them and their nationals the full rights and obligations of belligerency do not arise, although the circumstances may call for limited variations of the normal international law of peace and even occasionally confer upon the parties some particular right usually only belonging to a belligerent. As between the contestants and third States, problems will probably only infrequently arise: in some cases it is now accepted that rights of third parties may not be interfered with, and this may probably be regarded as the general rule. Diplomatic relations between the contestants may, or may not, be broken off.[7] Some, but probably not all, rules which

---

[1] Res. 378 (V).   [2] *The Corfu Channel Case*, I.C.J. Reports, 1949, p. 35.

[3] For other distinguishing features, see Oppenheim, II, pp. 132–3.

[4] On the Suez incident in general, see Bloomfield, *Egypt, Israel and the Gulf of Aqaba*, pp. 144–53; Wright, 51 *A.J.* (1957), p. 257; Finch. *ibid.* p. 376.

[5] For references to discussion of this quarantine, see n. 3, p. 17 above.

[6] An armed conflict being thus only a question of fact, its beginning and end also turn simply on matters of fact. Thus a general armistice, while not terminating a state of war, may well end an armed conflict not amounting to war since it would put an end to the actual use of armed force.

[7] To take two recent examples, diplomatic relations between China and India were not broken off during fighting between them in 1962 (see 67 *Revue Generale de Droit International Public* (1963), pp. 136, 143), but they were broken off between Egypt on the one

apply to the conduct of hostilities in time of war will probably apply. Nationals of one of the contestant States who are in the territory of the other may be subject to certain restraints and legal disabilities. An end will not automatically be put to the treaties between the contestants, although it may be that the occurrence of the armed conflict will justify their denunciation.[1]

A conflict in circumstances not giving rise to a state of war is often constituted by, or accompanied by, certain formal measures,[2] and it may be useful here to refer briefly to some of the more common of these—namely blockade, embargo, sequestration and blocking (or 'freezing') of property and assets, and boycott.

Blockade.[3] The essence of a blockade is that the blockading State prevents access to or exit from (or both) all or part of the territory of the State being blockaded. While blockade is usually thought of as a belligerent measure taking place in time of war, it has not infrequently been adopted in time of peace as a coercive measure, when it has come to be known as 'pacific blockade'. The practice of States has accepted the permissibility of such a measure, and has acknowledged that its employment does not *ipso facto* give rise to a state of war, although, even if the blockading State is acting *sine animo belligerendi*, it will amount to an act of force which the blockaded State may elect to regard as creating a state of war. As a general proposition it may be said that all those restrictions which regulate the powers and rights of a blockading State in time of war apply also to a blockade imposed in time of peace, so that, for example, a pacific blockade must be effective, and must be duly declared and notified. But a blockade as a measure short of war is, in addition, subject to further restrictions. Thus while it is clear that the blockading State may prevent access to and exit from the blockaded ports by ships of the blockaded and the blockading States, it is controversial—and probably very doubtful—whether it may also prevent such access

hand and the United Kingdom and France on the other at the time of the Suez incident in 1956.

[1] See Layton, 3 *University of Chicago Law Review* (1962), p. 105; McNair, 22 *Hague Receuil* (1928), pp. 512–13. For the consequences of the blockade of Venezuela in 1902–3 upon treaties between Venezuela and the United Kingdom (one of the blockading States), see McNair, *Law of Treaties* (1961), pp. 701–2. As a result of the Suez incident in 1956 a law was passed in Egypt (Law no. 1 of 1957) stating that the British 'aggression' had put an end to the Anglo-Egyptian Agreement of 1954.

[2] Some of these measures were included in the extensive range of measures taken by many States in 1965 against the rebellious regime in Southern Rhodesia.

[3] In addition to the works cited in the bibliography of this chapter, see Colombos, *International Law of the Sea* (5th ed.), §§ 484–8; Hogan, *Pacific Blockade* (1908); Westlake, *Collected Papers*, pp. 572–89; Falcke, *Le Blocus Pacifique*.

and exit by ships of third States. Furthermore, ships which are apprehended while breaking the blockade may not be confiscated or condemned, but may only be held temporarily until the end of the blockade when they must be returned (but without compensation for the mere fact of their seizure).

While the imposition of a pacific blockade in the classic nineteenth-century manner would nearly always constitute a threat or use of force in violation of the Charter, it would not be safe to conclude that non-war blockades are in all circumstances now prohibited[1] (indeed, Article 42 of the Charter expressly envisages their use).

Embargo[2] is a term which is very widely used with differing meanings.[3] In its more technical sense it involves the coercive measure in time of peace consisting of the seizure by the forces of one State of vessels of a foreign State, usually only if they are in the ports or waters of the State laying the embargo but sometimes also on the high seas. When the dispute or incident which gave rise to the embargo has been satisfactorily settled the embargo is lifted and the ships which have been seized are restored, but, again without payment of compensation for the mere fact of their detention. A leading illustration of an embargo is afforded by the British embargo against Naples in 1840, which was met by a counter-embargo on British vessels; no state of war ensued, and the British Envoy in Naples was not recalled. It would seem an embargo might be one of the measures which could be called for by the Security Council under Articles 41 or 42 of the Charter; and it is perhaps not to be altogether excluded that an embargo laid on foreign vessels in the ports of a State would be consistent with Article 2 of the Charter.

Apparently akin to the kind of embargo just discussed, but nevertheless to be distinguished from it, is the embargo which, while laid against the ships of a foreign State at a time of peace with that State, is laid in contemplation of war. Upon the subsequent outbreak of war, the prior seizure effected under the embargo is treated as a belligerent seizure. This kind of embargo may now be obsolete.[4] Of

---

[1] As to the significance of imposing a blockade in connection with the United Nations action in Korea, see Potter, 47 *A.J.* (1953), p. 273. The United States' quarantine of Cuba in 1962 occasioned considerable discussion of the rules relating to pacific blockade; see authorities cited in n. 3, p. 17, above. Note also the Security Council's Resolution of 9 April 1966, concerning the prevention of oil reaching the port of Beira.

[2] In addition to the works cited in the bibliography for this chapter, see Colombos, *International Law of the Sea* (5th ed.), §§ 481–3.

[3] For the meaning given to the term in a treaty of 1783 between Sweden and the United States, see *The Kronprins Gustav Adolf* and *The Pacific*.

[4] For an example just before the outbreak of the war between Greece and Turkey in 1912, see *Embiricos* v. *Sydney Reid & Co.*

a totally distinct nature is the embargo which is not an international embargo laid against foreign ships, but a municipal, civil embargo, imposed by a State against its own ships, forbidding them to leave its ports.[1]

In current usage, however, the term 'embargo' has lost its primarily maritime connotation, and now more often than not is used to refer to a prohibition of exports of goods (usually strategic and military) to a particular country. We may mention in particular that embargoes have been used not only by individual States pursuing their own ends, but also in the general interests of the community of States as a means of exerting pressure upon States whose conduct is inimical to the general interest. Thus in 1934 an embargo was adopted, with the backing of the League of Nations, on the sale of arms to Paraguay and Bolivia who at the time were engaged in hostilities against each other.[2] During the Korean conflict the General Assembly recommended that an embargo be imposed on shipments of war materials to Communist China and North Korea,[3] and more recently the Security Council has called for embargoes to be applied against South Africa,[4] Southern Rhodesia[5] and Portugal.[6]

Sequestration and blocking (or 'freezing') of property and assets. These measures when adopted in time of peace are in many ways the non-maritime equivalents of embargo. They are also the counterparts in time of peace to the measures usually imposed in the event of war under 'trading with the enemy' legislation. The lawfulness of adopting such measures in peacetime is perhaps still not clearly established, but, for example, if their imposition can properly be regarded as satisfying the conditions for reprisals it would seem difficult to deny that their adoption is in accordance with international law.

Sequestration and blocking do not involve the confiscation of the property and assets involved,[7] but rather the temporary loss of enjoyment of their use, the care, control and administration of the property

---

[1] See *Sands* v. *Child*; *France Fenwick & Co.* v. *Rex*; Holdsworth, 35 *L.Q.R.* (1919), pp. 12–42. For the distinction between civil and international embargoes, see *The Gertruyda* (1799) 2 C. Rob. 211, 219–21. The embargo which was considered in *Hadley* v. *Clarke* would appear to have been more in the nature of what would now be regarded as a 'trading with the enemy' prohibition.

[2] See Fenwick, 28 *A.J.* (1934), p. 534; Woolsey, *ibid.* p. 724.

[3] Res. 500/V.

[4] Resolutions of 7 August 1963, and 4 December 1963.

[5] Resolutions of 20 November 1965 and 9 April 1966.

[6] Resolution of 23 November 1965.

[7] They may prove to be the preliminaries to confiscation, but that then becomes another matter. On the distinction between sequestration and expropriation, see the remarks made in Parliament by the Lord President of the Council (Lord Hailsham) in 1958, quoted in 8 *I. and C.L.Q.* (1959), p. 184.

being for the duration of its sequestration the responsibility of the sequestering State. Upon the settlement of the difference which led to the adoption of such measures, the *status quo ante* should be restored and the owners of the property once again be able to enjoy the use of their property. Where the measures have been lawfully adopted, no compensation will be payable in respect of the sequestration or blocking itself; although if the sequestrating State has, while being justified in imposing sequestration, nevertheless not taken due care of the sequestrated property while in its care and control, and loss or damage has resulted, compensation for such loss or damage is probably payable. A recent and instructive example occurred in connection with the armed conflict at Suez in 1956, upon the outbreak of which Egypt sequestrated all British property in Egypt, while for its part the United Kingdom had already blocked Egypt's sterling balances in London, and later imposed certain other financial restrictions upon residents in Egypt. The Anglo-Egyptian Financial Agreement of 1959, by which the two States re-established normal relations, provided for the United Kingdom to unblock the sterling balances and to lift the financial restrictions, and for the United Arab Republic (of which Egypt then formed part) to return all sequestrated British property[1] and to pay compensation in respect of injury or damage to property as a result of the measures of sequestration.

A *boycott*[2] is a measure whereby relations, usually commercial and financial, with another State may be, to the extent specified, interrupted or prevented. Thus State *A* in declaring a boycott against State *B* may, for example, merely prohibit the import of goods from State *B*; or it may go further and also prohibit exports to State *B*; or it may forbid its own nationals or persons in its territory from having any dealings at all with persons in State *B*; or it may forbid the use of its territory for the passage of goods to State *B*, even if they emanate from a third State; it may possibly even provide certain penalties in its territory upon persons abroad who have dealings with State *B*. It is clear that a boycott has many affinities with the prohibition of intercourse with an enemy in time of war. Examples of a boycott currently imposed are those by Egypt against Israel

---

[1] Certain specified British property had been sold by the Egyptian authorities while it was under sequestration, and this property was not to be returned and compensation for it was paid.

[2] See Bouve, 28 *A.J.* (1934), p. 19; Friedmann, 29 *B.Y.* (1938), pp. 143–5 and 50 *A.J.* (1956), pp. 495–8; Hyde and Wehle, 27 *A.J.* (1933), pp. 1–10; H. Lauterpacht, 14 *B.Y.* (1933), pp. 125–40, and in Oppenheim, I, § 127a, p. 293, n. 1; Rousseau, 62 *Revue Générale de Droit International Public* (1958), p. 5. For references to some early United States legislation suspending commercial intercourse with specified foreign countries, see Hyde, II, p. 1675, n. 1.

(although we should note that in this case the boycotting State maintains that a state of war formally exists with Israel) and by India against South Africa.

The imposition of a boycott raises certain controversial questions as to its legality in general international law (apart from any treaty obligations, such as might flow from a commercial treaty). The limits within which it might be lawful are not clear, and at least in its more extensive forms some doubt must attend its legality in time of peace.

(d) Conflicts involving forces acting under the authority of the United Nations

Dr Bowett's recently published book, *United Nations Forces*, gives very comprehensive treatment to various aspects of conflicts in which United Nations forces are engaged, and the reader is referred to Dr Bowett's book for an exhaustive analysis of this subject. In the next few pages we shall only outline, in very general terms, some of the principal considerations bearing upon the place of armed conflicts involving United Nations forces in the wider context of international wars, conflicts and other hostilities. At the outset we may emphasize that the key to a proper understanding of the nature and consequences of such armed conflicts is an awareness that the feature which primarily distinguishes them from resort to armed force by States is that they are undertaken for 'the collective enforcement of the basic instrument of organized international society' and not to secure the interests of an individual State.[1]

The provisions of the Charter whereby United Nations forces may engage in an armed conflict are not free from difficulty.[2] Under the Charter the Security Council has the primary responsibility for the maintenance of international peace and security,[3] and the only provisions which expressly authorize the United Nations to establish armed forces are to be found in chapter VII: this express power is given to the Security Council. In respect of enforcement action taken under these provisions, the Council's competence is exclusive.[4] Article 42 provides that if the Security Council considers that measures not involving the use of armed force would be, or have proved to be, inadequate 'it may take such action by air, sea or land forces as

---

[1] Oppenheim, II, p. 224.

[2] For a general review of the relevant Charter provisions, see Bowett, *United Nations Forces*, p. 274. See also *Certain Expenses of the United Nations*, I.C.J. Reports, 1962, pp. 163–5, and Amerasinghe, 5 *Indian Journal of International Law* (1965), pp. 305–33. Note also Article 41 of the Charter relating to 'measures not involving the use of armed force', and the United Nations Act, 1946; see below, p. 51.   [3] Article 24.

[4] *Certain Expenses of the United Nations*, I.C.J. Reports, 1962, pp. 164–5.

may be necessary to maintain or restore international peace and security. Such action may include demonstrations, blockade and other operations by air, sea or land forces of Members of the United Nations'. Articles 43, 45 and 48 refer to the way in which such Security Council decisions shall be carried out and to the provision of armed forces for the purpose. However, it would seem that the Security Council has power to set up an armed force otherwise than in exercise of the express powers given under chapter VII.[1] Furthermore, the Security Council's responsibility for the maintenance of international peace and security is not exclusive, and the General Assembly also has certain responsibilities and competences in this field.[2] In particular, the General Assembly, recognizing that the existence of the veto in the Security Council much reduced the effectiveness of the Council, and also recognizing that the need to employ armed force on behalf of the collectivity of States acting through the United Nations should not be frustrated by the use of the veto in the Security Council, in 1950 adopted the so-called 'Uniting for Peace' resolution.[3] Under this resolution the General Assembly may in certain circumstances make 'appropriate recommendations to Members for collective measures, including in the case of a breach of the peace or act of aggression the use of armed force when necessary, to maintain or restore international peace and security'.

So far armed forces have been created under the authority of the United Nations on four occasions:[4] in Korea, in Egypt (UNEF), in the Congo (ONUC) and in Cyprus (UNFICYP). The force in Korea and ONUC were set up as the result of action initially taken by the Security Council,[5] although later action was taken by the

---

[1] Neither the United Nations force in Korea nor that in the Congo was set up by the Security Council under the express powers given in the Charter: see Seyersted, 37 *B.T.* (1961), pp. 437–40, and *Certain Expenses of the United Nations, supra*, pp. 175–7. The general proposition that the creation by the United Nations of an armed force not based on express provisions of the Charter is an inherent power of the Organization is developed by Seyersted, *loc. cit.* pp. 435–75.

[2] *Certain Expenses of the United Nations, supra*, pp. 163–5.

[3] Resolution 377 A (V). The literature on this resolution is extensive: see e.g. Bowett, *United Nations Forces*, p. 290; Kelsen, *Recent Trends in the Law of the United Nations*, p. 953; Seyersted, 37 *B.T.* (1961), p. 370; Stone, *Legal Controls of International Conflict*, p. 266.

[4] Other military units, such as truce supervisory and observer teams, have been established by the United Nations.

[5] The principal resolutions were: (i) for Korea—resolutions of 25 and 27 June, and 7 July 1950; (ii) for the Congo—resolutions of 14 and 22 July, 9 August, and 17 September 1960, and 21 February 1961. On the Korean conflict in general, see Baxter, 29 *B.T.* (1952), p. 332; Bowett, *United Nations Forces*, p. 29; Green, 4 *I.L.Q.* (1951), p. 462; Hoyt, 55 *A.J.* (1961), p. 45; Kelsen, *Recent Trends in the Law of the United Nations*, p. 927; Kunz, 45 *A.J.* (1951), p. 137; Potter, 44 *A.J.* (1950), p. 709; Seyersted, 37 *B.T.* (1961), p. 362; Stone, *Legal Controls of International Conflict*, p. 228. On the Congo operations, see Bowett,

General Assembly, UNEF was established by the General Assembly[1] under the 'Uniting for Peace' resolution, and UNFICYP was created by the Security Council.[2]

The four United Nations forces have all been engaged in very different roles. In Korea the immediate conflict had some of the elements of a civil war in which the north Korean forces were fighting against the legitimate Government of the Republic of Korea. However, the general circumstances of the conflict, culminating in the overt participation of non-Korean (namely, Chinese) armed forces,[3] have led to the conflict being generally regarded as essentially an international armed conflict in which the United Nations forces were resisting an international aggression against the Republic of Korea. The Congo operations similarly possessed a somewhat mixed character, although taken overall the conflict was in this case essentially one of internal civil strife in which the United Nations forces were engaged to assist the legitimate Government of the Congo in restoring and maintaining law and order, and to prevent foreign interference and the occurrence of civil war in the Congo. UNEF and UNFICYP, by way of contrast, have not really been engaged as parties to a conflict, but have been involved primarily in separating and keeping apart parties who might otherwise use armed force against each other; this essential nature of their role is not altered by the fact that with UNEF the parties being separated were States, while with UNFICYP they were factions within a State.

Since the development of United Nations forces is still in its early stages, and in view of the many dissimilarities between the four precedents, it is not possible to formulate any precise conclusions as to the place in international law of United Nations forces or armed conflicts in which they participate. Only some tentative observations will be made here, upon three of the broader issues of principle which arise in connection with the subject-matter of the present book.

(i) Are United Nations forces properly forces *of the United Nations itself* rather than merely a coalition army of the various participating

op. cit. p. 153; Draper, 12 *I. and C.L.Q.* (1963), p. 387; Schachter, 55 *A.J.* (1961), p. 1; Riad, 17 *Egyptian Review of International Law* (1961), p. 1; Seyersted, 37 *B.Y.* (1961), p. 390. For extensive discussion of many aspects of ONUC (as well as UNEF), see *Certain Expenses of the United Nations*, I.C.J. Reports, 1962, p. 151.

[1] Resolutions 998 (ES–I), 1000 (ES–I) and 1001 (ES–I). See, in general, Bowett, *op. cit.* p. 90; Seyersted, *loc. cit.* p. 374.

[2] Resolution of 4 April 1964. See Bowett, *op. cit.* p. 552.

[3] See the General Assembly's Resolution, 498 (V). The eventual Armistice Agreement was between, on the one hand, the Commander in Chief, United Nations Command, and, on the other, the Supreme Commander of the Korean People's Army and the Commander of the Chinese People's Volunteers (160 *B.F.S.P.* p. 433).

States? So far as such forces are established under express provisions of the Charter, the language of the relevant Articles provides no clear answer.[1] Where they are established on some other basis, the terms of the Charter can naturally give no guidance, nor is any given by the terms of the 'Uniting for Peace' resolution. The position would seem to be that nothing in the Charter prevents (and certain provisions allow) the creation of an armed force which could properly be considered a force of the United Nations itself, while, on the other hand, not every armed force established pursuant to a resolution of the General Assembly or Security Council is *necessarily* such a force, there being no legal reason why the use of the forces of several Member States should not be merely sanctioned by such a resolution without the forces in any way thereby becoming forces 'of the United Nations' in anything but the broadest political sense. The nature of the force will in each case turn on the particular circumstances of its creation and operation. Of the four armed forces which, so far, have been established under the authority of the United Nations UNEF, ONUC and UNFICYP would seem clearly to have been United Nations forces properly so called; the force in Korea was clearly a force constituted within the framework of, and for the achievement of the purposes of, the Charter, but while it is probably to be regarded as a force 'of the United Nations', it is still controversial to what extent it was so in a strict legal sense.

Whether or not an armed force is a force of the United Nations in a legal sense is of course very important in determining where legal responsibility for acts of the force resides and by whom claims for damage suffered by the force should be presented. In the case of a United Nations force *stricto sensu*, it would seem that claims should in principle be made by and addressed to the United Nations itself.[2] In connection with damage suffered by British subjects during the fighting in the Congo, the Joint Under-Secretary of State for Foreign Affairs said in Parliament that the United Nations might be one of the 'parties against whom claims might lie for damage which has taken place in Katanga' and that in 'cases where United Nations responsibility appears to be established, I certainly see no reason why the claims should not be taken up with them by the persons concerned'.[3]

---

[1] Articles 42–49 refer almost indiscriminately to forces being forces of the Security Council and to their being forces of the Member States.

[2] See *Reparations for Injuries suffered in the Service of the United Nations*, I.C.J. Reports, 1949, p. 175; Bowett, *United Nations Forces*, pp. 57, 85–6, 149–51 and 242–8; Seyersted, 37 *B.Y.* (1961), pp. 420–7.　　　　[3] House of Commons Debates, vol. 655, cols. 551–2.

(ii) Does an armed conflict between the armed forces of a State and those of the United Nations give rise to a state of war between that State and the United Nations?[1] Partly this is a question of definition and the extent to which such a conflict satisfies whatever definition of 'war' is adopted. It will be apparent that such a conflict would not amount to a war within the meaning of any definition which regards war as a relationship between States only.[2] But it is not simply a matter of definitions, and there are broader grounds for submitting that it is preferable to regard United Nations armed conflicts as *sui generis*. Although some of the consequences[3] attaching to a state of war between States may also apply to an armed conflict involving the United Nations as a participant (as indeed they may apply to certain other armed conflicts not constituting a war), it is hardly appropriate to apply the technical concept of war to action taken on behalf of the general community of States acting in pursuance of the general international interest. Such action is always likely to have essentially limited objectives.[4] Furthermore, in such a conflict the provisions of the Charter[5] could have the effect of largely restricting the application (at least by Members of the United Nations) of those laws of neutrality which would normally apply if the conflict were to be considered a war. The impropriety of regarding a state of war with the United Nations as arising out of a conflict conducted under the authority of the United Nations would seem to be as great in those cases where the United Nations merely sanctions

---

[1] This question is quite distinct from the question whether words such as 'war' and 'peace' used in treaties, contracts and other documents should be *interpreted* as covering such armed conflicts involving the United Nations. For several judicial decisions on the question whether there was a 'war' in Korea, see below, p. 51, nn. 3–5.

[2] Thus on this basis, where the United Nations forces are fighting against a non-State entity (e.g. rebels), there is a twofold absence of statehood as a reason for not regarding the conflict as a war in international law. In this light Mr Tshombe's proclamation of a state of war against the United Nations in the Congo (S/4750, paragraph 11) would seem to be largely devoid of legal significance. It is to be noted that it was not excluded by some writers that the League of Nations itself could be 'at war': see Seyersted, 37 *B.Y.* (1961), p. 357.

[3] One of the important consequences is the application of the laws of war: see Baxter, 29 *B.Y.* (1952), p. 352; Bowett, *United Nations Forces*, p. 488; Draper, *The Red Cross Conventions*, pp. 10, 69–70, and 12 *I. and C.L.Q.* (1963), p. 408; Jessup, *A Modern Law of Nations*, p. 188; H. Lauterpacht, 30 *B.Y.* (1953), p. 206; Marin, 92 *Receuil des Cours* (1957), p. 722; Stone, *Legal Controls of International Conflict*, p. 314; Taubenfeld, 45 *A.J.* (1951), p. 671. For the declarations made in 1950 by both sides in the Korean conflict, see Draper, *The Red Cross Conventions*, p. 10, n. 33.

[4] The United Nations forces in Korea, as well as UNEF, ONUC and UNFICYP all had strictly limited functions.

[5] See Articles 2 (5), 25 and 49; in virtue of Article 2 (6) non-Member States may also be affected. On the whole question of neutrality in international enforcement actions, see Lalive, 24 *B.Y.* (1947), p. 72; Stone, *Legal Controls of International Conflict*, p. 382; Taubenfeld, 47 *A.J.* (1953), p. 377.

the use of national armed forces in the interests of the United Nations as in those where the United Nations establishes its own forces. There was no disposition by States to consider the Korean conflict as amounting to a state of war in international law.[1]

(iii) To what extent does an armed conflict between the armed forces of a State and those of the United Nations affect the legal relationship between that State and the States Members of the United Nations? There is no support for the view that a state of war automatically arises.[2] There would seem to be no room for doubting this conclusion where it is armed forces 'of the United Nations' *stricto sensu* which are engaged, and it is thought that the conclusion is still sound, although there may be more room for argument, where the armed forces are clearly those of Member States but acting under the authority and on behalf of the United Nations. However, if the State against which the United Nations forces were employed were to regard the occasion as justifying a declaration of war against, say, States whose forces were participating in the United Nations forces, it would seem difficult to deny that a state of war existed, although the legal position would in that case clearly give rise to anomalies.

Even if the hostilities do not give rise to a state of war, however, they will not be entirely without legal effects on the relations between Members of the United Nations and the State against which they occur; the precise effects will vary both with the circumstances and also as between those Members of the United Nations who contribute forces and materials to the United Nations and those who do not. All Members of the United Nations are obliged by Article 2 (5) of the Charter to give the United Nations every assistance in any action it takes in accordance with the Charter, and to refrain from giving assistance to any State against which the United Nations is taking preventive or enforcement action. This obligation may be reinforced by specific decisions of the Security Council which would impose obligations on Member States under Articles 25 and 49 of the Charter. Furthermore, the hostilities might well be sufficient to bring into operation in Member States rules of their municipal law relating to matters such as treason and foreign enlistment.[3]

---

[1] Oppenheim, II, p. 224; see also Green, 4 *I.L.Q.* (1951), p. 462. Not constituting a war, the beginning and end of United Nations conflicts are questions of fact: and thus, like armed conflicts in general (see above, p. 19, n. 6), they may end with merely a formal armistice, as happened with the Korean conflict: see two United States decisions, *U.S. v. Sanders*, and *U.S. v. Shell*.

[2] Particularly if the opposing forces are those of a non-State entity, such as rebels.

[3] See below, p. 52.

(e) Civil war and insurgency[1]

International law is concerned not only with armed conflicts between States but also with hostilities occurring within a single State. Since such civil hostilities are essentially a matter internal to the State in which they take place, they are largely only the concern of international law in so far as they have side effects either outside the territory of that State or upon foreign rights or interests within it. The development of international law as to the nature of civil hostilities has reflected developments in the law concerning, for example, the creation and recognition of new governments (and even new international legal persons) as a result of civil wars,[2] and responsibility for damage caused by the rebels to the property of foreigners.[3] It is now usual to consider a situation involving civil disorders which go beyond mere ephemeral disorders as either one of insurgency or one of belligerency.[4]

Insurgency is a half-way house between essentially ephemeral, spasmodic or unorganized civil disorders and the conduct of an organized war between contending factions within a State. It is a shadowy condition, there being no well-defined conditions to be satisfied for its existence, and neither giving rise to any clearly recognizable consequences, nor conferring upon the insurgents any legal personality in international law. Insurgency is not a special status with special rights and duties of its own. About all that can be said is that a condition of insurgency will exist when there is within a State an armed conflict which has reached proportions necessitating outside

[1] In addition to the general bibliography at the beginning of this chapter, the Spanish Civil War (1936–9) occasioned a re-examination of a host of important questions on the legal nature and consequences of civil wars, and these were extensively written about: see Finch, 31 *A.J.* (1937), p. 74; Garner, *ibid.* p. 66 and 32 *A.J.* (1938), p. 106; Genet, *ibid.* p. 253; H. Lauterpacht, 3 *Modern Law Review* (1939), p. 1, and 46 *Revue Générale de Droit International Public* (1939), p. 513; McNair, 53 *L.Q.R.* (1937), p. 471; O'Rourke, 31 *A.J.* (1937), p. 398; Padelford, *ibid.* pp. 226 and 578, and 32 *A.J.* (1938), p. 264; Scelle, 45 *Revue Générale de Droit International Public* (1938), p. 265, and 46 *ibid.* (1939), p. 197; Smith, 18 *B.Y.* (1937), p. 17; Walker, 23 *Transactions of the Grotius Society* (1937), p. 177; and other works cited by Wehberg, 63 *Receuil des Cours* (1938-1), pp. 124–6. Numerous decisions are reported in the Annual Digest, vol. 8 (1935–7) onwards.

[2] See H. Lauterpacht, *Recognition in International Law*, pp. 175–278; Chen, *The International Law of Recognition*, pp. 303–407.

[3] See Briggs, *Law of Nations* (2nd ed.), p. 713, and H. Lauterpacht, *op. cit.* pp. 247–50 and 256–65.

[4] The distinction between belligerency and insurgency in civil wars is of relatively recent development. Up to the middle of the nineteenth century all rebellions were treated as much alike, and as mostly calling for the observance of neutrality and a policy of non-intervention by third States. Consequently, some care must be exercised in relying upon the older authorities, and in particular words such as 'insurrection' and 'insurgents' were used to denote both rebellions which had not attained to a state of belligerency and those in which belligerent rights were being exercised.

States taking cognizance of it, but not yet fulfilling the conditions calling for the recognition of a state of belligerency.

The acknowledgment of a situation of insurgency does not entitle either the insurgents or the parent State to exercise belligerent rights against foreign States, nor does it impose on such States the rights and duties of neutrals.[1] While outside States ought not to furnish aid to the insurgents (for to do so would constitute unlawful intervention in the affairs of the State), their right to meet requests for aid from, and have other dealings with, the Government against which the insurgents are fighting would seem unimpaired: that Government is still the only lawful Government of the State, and no obligations of neutrality yet prohibit any transactions with it. Nevertheless, by acknowledging the insurgency, a foreign State indicates that it will not treat any insurgents conducting hostilities at sea against the parent State as pirates,[2] and it may furthermore concede to the contestants certain rights or forbearances in so far as the conduct of hostilities affects its interests. It is probable, but not entirely clear, that insurgents may be regarded as a 'Party to the conflict' for purposes of the application of Article 3 of each of the four 1949 Geneva Conventions relating to certain humanitarian aspects of the conduct of hostilities.[3] That Article applies to an 'armed conflict not of an international character occurring in the territory of one of the High Contracting Parties' and binds 'each Party to the conflict' to apply certain provisions concerning the conduct of the conflict. It is expressly stated that the application of the provisions of the Article shall not affect the legal status of the Parties to the conflict.

The purported institution of a blockade, either by the parent State against the insurgents or by the insurgents against the parent State, has often given rise to problems. We shall see that the imposition of a blockade would transform the insurgency into a state of belli-

---

[1] Other States may, of course, decide to stand aloof from the conflict and to display an attitude of impartiality; this may in particular circumstances amount to a statement of neutrality so as to elevate the situation into one of belligerency, but need not necessarily do so (see n. 6, at p. 33 below). On the Rights and Duties of Third Powers and their Nationals in the event of Rebellions, see the *Règlement* adopted by the Institut de Droit International in 1900 (18 *Annuaire* (1900), p. 227).

[2] Oppenheim, I, p. 610; McNair, *Opinions*, I, pp. 267–80; H. Lauterpacht, *Recognition in International Law*, pp. 295–310, and 46 *Revue Générale de Droit International Public* (1939), p. 513; Chen, *The International Law of Recognition*, pp. 402–6. Compare the views of the British Government in 1873 concerning Spanish insurgent vessels in so far as they were not threatening British lives or property (Westlake, *International Law*, I, p. 186), with their attitude in 1877 in the case of the Peruvian insurgent vessel *The Huascar* which interfered with British shipping (Pitt Cobbett, I, p. 299). Note now the definition of piracy in Article 15 of the Geneva Convention on the High Seas, 1958. See also p. 54, n.1 below.

[3] See Draper, *The Red Cross Conventions*, pp. 13–17; Oppenheim, II, § 126.

gerency.[1] If the conflict is to remain an insurgency, the parent State may only impose such restrictions on shipping as do not involve the exercise of rights only available to belligerents: consequently, they must be seen as municipal regulations, effective only in its territorial and national waters and enforceable against the shipping of other States only in a manner compatible with the absence of belligerent rights.[2] Furthermore, it seems probable that ports occupied by the insurgents may not be closed by the parent State by mere proclamation but only by that State taking effective steps to ensure closure, as by instituting a blockade.[3] Blockades declared by the insurgents are not regarded as valid:[4] if the blockade were to be effectively maintained, it might have to be recognized as a valid blockade, but thereby the rebels would cease to be mere insurgents and would become belligerents. In so far as the rebels, while not being recognized as belligerents, are recognized as the *de facto* authority of the territory which they control, it would seem that they are probably to be acknowledged as having the same powers as the lawful government of closing by decree the ports in their possession and of enforcing such closure within territorial waters in any manner compatible with the non-possession of belligerent rights.

Belligerency. The hostilities within a State may reach such proportions that the situation can no longer be regarded as one of mere insurgency. Where there exists within a State an armed conflict of a general (as distinguished from purely local) character, where the insurgents occupy and administer a substantial portion of national territory, and where they conduct the hostilities in accordance with the rules of war and through organized armed forces acting under a responsible authority, it can be said that the situation has grown beyond one of insurgency and deserves to be considered one of belligerency. Where this occurs, the relationship between the parent State and the rebels, and between them and outside States, is for the purposes of the conflict the same as when there is a state of war between two independent States, and will be governed by the rights and duties of belligerency and neutrality. The rebels acquire an international legal status, and in general in the further conduct of the conflict they participate, from the point of view of international law, on the same legal footing as the parent State. As to the applica-

---

[1] See below, p. 33.

[2] See McNair, *Opinions*, II, pp. 379–80, 388.

[3] *Ibid.* pp. 379–93.

[4] This follows from the right to institute a blockade being a right possessed only by a belligerent. On 'blockades' by insurgents, see McNair, 53 *L.Q.R.* (1937), pp. 487–90; Dickinson, 24 *A.J.* (1930), p. 69.

tion of the 1949 Geneva Conventions, a civil conflict in which the rebels have achieved belligerent status is at least within Article 3 of the Conventions,[1] and it has further been argued authoritatively[2] that such a conflict may come within the more rigorous provisions of Article 2 as being a conflict having an international character.

The status of belligerents is not one which the rebels may confer upon themselves, nor probably is it one to which they have a legal right upon certain conditions being fulfilled;[3] rather it is a status which they possess only in so far as States recognize them to possess it. It may happen that the parent State will itself admit to a state of belligerency, either *expressis verbis*—this would be most unusual—or by taking some action (such as the institution of a blockade)[4] only justifiable as an exercise of belligerent rights. It has been said that where the parent State recognizes the belligerency of the rebels 'it is proper—and probably obligatory—upon other States to recognize a state of war as existing and to assume the duties of neutrality'[5]—and also, of course, to claim its rights. Certainly, if the parent State recognizes the rebels as belligerents, it cannot complain if other States do so too. The absence of any express or clearly implicit recognition of belligerency by the parent State in no way prevents other States which find it necessary to define their attitude to the conflict from recognizing, either expressly or by some unequivocal action,[6] the

---

[1] See p. 31, above.   [2] Oppenheim, II, § 126.

[3] McNair, 53 *L.Q.R.* (1937), pp. 477–83; Green, 3 *University of Malaya Law Review* (1961).

[4] As in the case of the American civil war: see 51 *B.F.S.P.* p. 185; see also many Opinions of the Law Officers of the Crown in McNair, *Opinions*, II, pp. 375 ff.

[5] Oppenheim, II, p. 209. See also the Opinion of the Law Officers of the Crown in 1895, in respect of the rebellion in Madagascar against the French authorities to which the United Kingdom had not accorded any recognition of belligerency, that there was a state of war which of itself, and independently of any action of other States, gave rise to the duties imposed upon belligerents by international law (McNair, *Opinions*, II, p. 371). But in Oppenheim, II, p. 660, a different view seems to be expressed: see also H. Lauterpacht, *Recognition in International Law*, p. 247, to the effect that recognition of belligerency by the parent State, while a 'weighty factor in the situation' and not to be brushed aside without good reason, does not impose an obligation upon other States to recognize the insurgents as belligerents (similarly, McNair, 53 *L.Q.R.* (1937), p. 477). Much of the uncertainty in this matter is due to the question of the belligerency of the insurgents being of effect not only upon the existence of the rights and duties of war and neutrality, but also upon the acquisition by the insurgents of some degree of international legal personality. A further complicating factor is that the attitude of the rebels to the state of hostilities is largely ignored because they lack sufficient international personality prior to the recognition of belligerency for their views to be legally relevant, while in the eyes of the parent State the rebels are violators of municipal law.

[6] A declaration of neutrality would be sufficient, as in the case of the British proclamation of neutrality at the time of the American civil war: 51 *B.F.S.P.* p. 165. But a statement that the Foreign Enlistment Act, 1870, applies is not sufficient as an acknowledgment of a state of belligerency: see below, p. 452. It is thought that a formal proclamation of neutrality is not necessary, so long as in some way a clear intention to act as a neutral

state of belligerency, thereby accepting the right of the parties to the civil war to exercise belligerent rights and at the same time claiming for itself the rights and obligations of neutrality.

Other States may, while not recognizing the belligerency of the revolutionary authorities, accord to them recognition as either the *de facto* or *de jure* government of the State, or of that part of it at least as is under their control. The considerations relating to recognition of Governments are beyond our present scope,[1] and we need only here emphasize that recognition of belligerency and recognition as a Government are quite distinct. Thus recognition as a Government does not itself involve any admission of the right of the newly recognized Government to exercise belligerent rights in the course of its conduct of hostilities against the former Government. Where the rebel authorities are granted recognition as a Government and at the same time recognition is withdrawn completely from the former Government, the roles of the two contending factions will be reversed and it will be the former Government which will now be the insurgents. It is thus the former rebels who may now properly be assisted, a significant difference from the situation which would have obtained had only a state of belligerency been recognized, with its concomitant duty of neutrality towards *both sides*.

B. ENGLISH LAW

We shall now consider whether, and if so to what extent, the various kinds of hostilities known to international law are in English law the subject of any technical legal rules affecting their meaning. We shall do so under five headings: (*a*) the United Kingdom at war; (*b*) the United Kingdom as a third party to a war between other States; (*c*) armed conflicts not amounting to war; (*d*) armed conflicts conducted under the authority of the United Nations; (*e*) civil disturbances in a foreign country.

(*a*) *The United Kingdom at war*[2]

English law, like international law, acknowledges that war has a technical meaning and recognizes only a state of war and a state of peace with no intermediate state.

State in a legal sense is made manifest: see the *Terceira Affair* in 1828–9 (McNair, *Opinions*, II, pp. 340–9; 16 *B.F.S.P.* pp. 417–69; Pitt Cobbett, II, pp. 367–8).

[1] See H. Lauterpacht, *Recognition in International Law*, and 3 *Modern Law Review* (1939), p. 1; Chen, *The International Law of Recognition*.

[2] As to the effect upon Commonwealth countries of a declaration of war by the United Kingdom, see Hood Phillips, *Constitutional Law* (3rd ed.), pp. 772 and 798. For a pro-

In 1811, in *Muller* v. *Thompson*,[1] Lord Ellenborough C.J., in answering a plea that a policy of insurance was illegal because it gave the ship liberty to proceed to Königsberg, said:

Königsberg belongs to Prussia. We are placed in a strange anomalous situation with regard to that country and others on the continent; but it is not that of war. We have published no declaration of war against Prussia; we have not issued letters of marque and reprisals; we have not done any act of hostility. Therefore, though the relations of amity are not very strong between us, yet we are not at war with Prussia, and a voyage from England to a Prussian Port is not illegal.

He thus recognized that war has a technical meaning which was not satisfied by the facts in the case before him.

Lord Macnaghten, in his speech in the House of Lords in *Janson* v. *Driefontein Consolidated Mines*,[2] said:

The law recognizes a state of peace and a state of war, but...it knows nothing of an intermediate state which is neither the one thing nor the other—neither peace nor war...However critical may be the state of affairs, however imminent war may be, if and so long as the Government of the State abstains from declaring or making war or accepting a hostile challenge there is peace—peace with all attendant consequences—for all its subjects.

This statement so far as concerns the meaning of 'war' in its strict legal sense was followed in *In re Cooper*, while in *In re Grotian*[3] arguments that Lord Macnaghten's statement was no longer applicable and that an intermediate stage between peace and war was now recognized in law were rejected. In the latter case Danckwerts J. said:[4]

[I]n my view it is still true to say, in a situation of this kind, that the termination of war and the declaration of peace are coincident events, and that the declaration, therefore, which declared the determination of the war, by inference, necessarily declared a state of peace to arise again between the two countries concerned.

Quite apart from the fact that 'the recent events in the world have introduced new methods and a new technique'[5] which have blurred even further the line between peace and war, much of the confusion on this subject has been due to the Courts, when faced with words such as 'war' and 'peace', having not always held that those words

tectorate being neutral while the protector is at war, see *Katrantsios* v. *Bulgaria* (Greek-Bulgarian M.A.T.); *The Ionian Ships*.

[1] 2 Camp. at p. 611.
[2] [1902] A.C. 484, at p. 497.   [3] [1955] 1 Ch. 501.   [4] At p. 507.
[5] *Per* Sir Wilfred Greene M.R. in *Kawasaki Kisen Kabushiki Kaisha of Kobe* v. *Bantham Steamship Co.* [1939] 2 K.B. 544, 556.

should be interpreted as referring to the strict legal states of war or peace but having given them some other meaning. Consequently there are not a few cases in which, for the purposes of the particular proceedings before it, the Courts have held that there was no state of war although it was clear that a formal state of war existed, and vice versa. This tendency is particularly evident in cases involving commercial contracts and wills in which Courts have been concerned not to apply any technical definition of war (unless that is clearly required) but to give the terms used the ordinary commonsense meaning which the parties intended to assign to them.[1] The Court of Appeal, in *Kawasaki Kisen Kabushiki Kaisha of Kobe* v. *Bantham Steamship Co.*, was even careful not to accept that in such cases involving commercial documents a statement by the Executive that a state of war existed would necessarily be binding on the Court for the purposes of interpreting the term 'war' in a commercial document.[2]

Since English law knows no technical definition of a state of war,[3] it would seem that an English court faced with the decision whether or not a state of war existed to which the United Kingdom was a party would have to approach the question by ascertaining, first, whether a state of war had broken out, and, if so, whether it had yet been terminated. As we shall see, both these issues are essentially in the last resort for the Executive to pronounce upon. Furthermore, an English court will not speculate on the likelihood of a war breaking out,[4] nor, once it has broken out, upon its duration.[5]

---

[1] See, e.g.: *Ruffy-Arnell, etc., Co. Ltd* v. *The King* [1922] 1 K.B. 599, 611–13; *In re Cooper; Tester* v. *Bisley; Pesquerias Y Secaderos de Bacalao de Espana, S.A.* v. *Beer; Martin* v. *Scottish Transport and General Workers Union* [1952] 1 All E.R. 691, 694. For similar cases decided by foreign courts, see *Girdler Corporation* v. *Charles Eneu Johnson & Co.* (U.S.A.); *Ex parte Kannegieser, N.O.* (S. Africa); *Rembrandt Painting Case* (Holland). There are numerous decisions upon the interpretation of such terms as 'war', 'warlike operations', 'restraint of princes', 'civil war', 'insurrection', 'rebellion' and 'revolt' occurring in documents such as policies of insurance, charterparties, and bills of lading, which will be found in the relevant books, such as Arnould, *Marine Insurance*; Carver, *Carriage by Sea*; Scrutton, *Charterparties and Bills of Lading*.

[2] In the *Kawasaki* case a letter from the Foreign Office pointed out that 'the question of the meaning to be attached to the term war as used in a charterparty may simply be one of interpreting the relevant clause, and that the attitude of H.M.G. may not necessarily be conclusive on the question whether a state of war exists within the meaning of the term 'war' as used in particular documents or statutes'. In *Luigi Monta of Genoa* v. *Cechofracht Co. Ltd*, a Foreign Office certificate as to the existence of a 'government' in a foreign territory was held not to be conclusive in interpreting a charterparty.

[3] In the *Kawasaki* case, *supra*, Sir Wilfred Greene M.R. observed: 'to say that English law recognises some technical and ascertainable description of what is meant by "war" appears to me to be a quite impossible proposition.'

[4] *Avery* v. *Bowden* (1855) 5 E. & B. 714, 724. [5] *Geipel* v. *Smith*.

Outbreak of war. War being waged by the Crown in the exercise of its prerogative,[1] we are entitled to look to the Executive branch of Government to inform us—either by proclamation or by some other express and overt act—when a state of war exists.[2] That is obviously the best evidence, and in modern times is generally available. Thus, at the beginning of the 1939–45 war,[3] the *London Gazette* of 3 September 1939, being the Third Supplement to the *Gazette* of 1 September 1939, contained the following statement:

It is notified that a state of war exists between His Majesty and Germany as from 11 o'clock A.M., to-day, the 3rd of September, 1939.

Our own legal authority is remarkably consistent on this point.

In the year 1480 we find Brian C.J., in an action of debt on an obligation to which a plea of alien enemy was raised,[4] saying:

It seems to me you ought to show how the league was broken, for that is matter of record; for if at one time there was a league between the King of this country and the King of Denmark, notwithstanding that all persons in England wanted to make war with those in Denmark, if our Lord the King would not assent to it, it would not be called war; but if there be no hostilities in fact, but the peace is broken between the King of Denmark and our Lord the King, as by ambassadors or otherwise, in that case where the peace and the league are broken [there is war].

In 1709, in *The Hoop*,[5] we find Lord Stowell saying that 'by the law and constitution of this country the sovereign alone has the power of declaring war and peace'.

In 1809, in *The Pelican*, upon the question arising whether a particular part of a certain island had been emancipated from French dominion so as to cease to be enemy territory,[6] Sir William Grant, in delivering the judgment of the Court of Appeal in Prize, said:

It always belongs to the Government of the country to determine in what relation any other country stands towards it; that is a point upon which Courts of Justice cannot decide.

[1] Section 3 of the Act of Settlement, 1700, requires the consent of Parliament in a particular (and remote) eventuality.

[2] On the general question of the practice of the courts in seeking and following the opinion of the Executive branch of Government in matters containing a foreign or international element, see Mann, 29 *Transactions of the Grotius Society* (1943), p. 143; Lyons, 23 *B.Y.* (1946), p. 240, and 33 *B.Y.* (1957), p. 302. A Foreign Office certificate is conclusive even in the face of contradictory evidence: *Carl-Zeiss-Stiftung* v. *Rayner* [1965] 1 All E.R. 300, 324.

[3] At the beginning of the 1914–18 war similar notifications were made.

[4] Y.B. Hil. 19 Edw. IV, f. 6.

[5] 1 C. Rob. 196, 199; 1 English Prize Cases, p. 106. *De facto* hostilities between two foreign States are discussed in *The Two Friends*.

[6] For an instance of the Court inquiring of the Foreign Office of the status of foreign territory, see *The Bolletta* (1809).

In 1812, in *Blackburne* v. *Thompson*,[1] Lord Ellenborough C.J. accepted the statement by Sir William Grant, quoted above, that

it belongs to the Government of the country to determine in what relation of peace or war any other country stands towards it; and that it would be unsafe for Courts of Justice to take upon them without that authority to decide upon those relations. [Lord Ellenborough added:] But when the Crown has decided upon the relation of peace or war in which another country stands to this, there is an end of the question; and in the absence of any express promulgation of the will of the Sovereign in that respect, it may be collected from other acts of the State.

In 1903, in *Janson* v. *Driefontein Consolidated Mines*,[2] a case involving the right to recover upon an insurance policy the value of gold seized by a foreign Government before and in immediate contemplation of war, Lord Macnaghten said:[3]

In every community it must be for the supreme power, whatever it is, to determine the policy of the community in regard to peace and war.

The realities of modern constitutional monarchy were taken into account by Scott L.J. in *R.* v. *Bottrill, ex parte Kuechenmeister*[4] in saying:

In the British constitution, which is binding on all British courts, the King makes both war and peace, and none the less so, in the eyes of the law, that he does so as a constitutional monarch upon the advice of his democratic cabinet.

But while it is usual for the commencement of a state of war to be determined expressly by an Executive pronouncement, it would not seem that this is always necessary. We have already referred to *Blackburne* v. *Thompson*[5] in which Lord Ellenborough C.J. said that in the absence of any express promulgation of the will of the Sovereign as to the existence of a state of war 'it may be collected from other acts of the State'.

That a formal proclamation of a state of war is not necessary is evident from *The Maria Magdalena*, decided in 1779. In that case a cargo belonging to London merchants consigned by a Swedish ship

---

[1] 15 East 81, 90. The Crown can also conclusively determine whether a particular piece of territory is hostile or not, for instance, places formerly but no longer in the possession of the enemy. For the power to determine the enemy status of territory for purposes of the Trading with the Enemy Act, 1939, see below, p. 49.

[2] [1902] A.C. 484.

[3] At p. 497.

[4] [1947] 1 K.B. 41, at p. 50.

[5] 15 East 81, 90.

to France was condemned on the ground of trading with the enemy. It appears that there had been a 'declaration of general reprisals' by the Crown against France, but no actual declaration of war by the British Crown, though something of this sort had been issued by the French Crown. Sir James Marriott, as Judge of the Prize Court, condemned the cargo, holding as 'Bynkershoek has a whole chapter to prove, from the history of Europe, that a lawful and perfect state of war may exist without proclamation'.

Similarly in 1813, in *The Eliza Ann*,[1] Lord Stowell said:

After this a declaration of war was issued by the Government of Sweden; but it is said that the two countries were not in reality in a state of war, because the declaration was *unilateral* only. I am, however, perfectly clear that it was not the less a war on that account, for war may exist without a declaration on either side.[2] It is so laid down by the best writers on the law of nations. A declaration of war by one country only is not, as has been represented, a mere challenge, to be accepted or refused at pleasure by the other. It proves the existence of actual hostilities on one side at least, and puts the other party also into a state of war, though he may, perhaps, think proper to act on the defensive only.

In 1814, in *R. v. De Berenger*,[3] when it was objected upon an indictment that it alleged a war to be in existence, which fact was not proved at the trial, Lord Ellenborough C.J. said that 'there were so many statutes which spoke of a war with France, that it was impossible for the Judges not to take judicial notice of it'.

An essential limitation, however, on the power of the Courts to look elsewhere in the absence of a proclamation by the Executive was expressed in two of the speeches in the House of Lords in *Janson* v. *Driefontein Consolidated Mines*.[4] Lord Halsbury L.C. said:[5]

The earlier writers on international law used to contend that some public declaration of war was essential, and Valin, writing in 1770, does not hesitate to describe Admiral Boscawen's operations in the Mediterranean in 1754 as acts of piracy, because no actual declaration of war had been made; but though it cannot be said that that view is now the existing

---

[1] 1 Dods. 244, 246; 2 English Prize Cases, 162, 164.

[2] But apparently only if there has been an actual commencement of hostilities: *The Teutonia*. As to a declaration of war by one side only, see also *The Nayade* (with reference to the Franco-Portuguese war), and Pearce Higgins, *War and the Private Citizen*, p. 27.

[3] 3 M. & S. 67, 69. In *Hagedorn* v. *Bell* the Court concluded that the plaintiffs were not 'enemies' by examining various relevant Orders in Council and concluding that they did not make trade with the plaintiffs' home town (Hamburg) totally illegal but that 'the Orders breathe something pacific'.

[4] [1902] A.C. 484.

[5] At p. 493.

international understanding,[1] it is essential that the hostility must be the act of the nation which makes the war, and no amount of 'strained relations' can affect the subjects of either country in their commercial or other transactions.[2]

Lord Macnaghten made the same point in a slightly different form, in saying:[3]

It is not, I think, for private individuals to pronounce upon the foreign relations of their Sovereign or their country and to measure their own responsibilities arising out of civil contracts with foreigners by a standard of public policy which they set up for themselves...However critical may be the state of affairs, however imminent war may be, if and so long as the Government of the State abstains from declaring or making war or accepting a hostile challenge there is peace—peace with its attendant consequences—for all its subjects.

Where there has not been any formal proclamation of war by the Executive, it would be usual in proceedings before the English Courts for the Executive to be asked to certify the precise moment of the commencement of the war. Thus in *Janson* v. *Driefontein Consolidated Mines* the Secretary of State for the Colonies signed a certificate to the effect that war broke out at 5 p.m. on 12 October 1899.[4]

End of war.[5] Just as the beginning of a state of war is primarily a matter for the Executive, so too is its end. 'In the British constitution, which is binding on all British Courts, the King makes both war and peace...When the King makes peace with an enemy State, that war comes to an end, but it does not come to an end before that peace is made' (*per* Scott L.J. in *R.* v. *Bottrill, ex parte Kuechenmeister*).

It is important to know definitely when a state of war comes to an end, so that normal commercial and other relations with the late enemy may be resumed.[6] An unconditional surrender does not produce this result.[7] Nor does an armistice: during the period of the armistice which concluded hostilities between the Allies and Germany in 1918 a Norwegian ship and her contraband cargo captured on a

---

[1] The correctness of the Lord Chancellor's opinion was illustrated two years later when Japan began hostilities against Russia without prior declaration of war, and the general conclusion was, we believe, that she was legally justified in doing so: see Pearce Higgins, *War and the Private Citizen*, p. 22. The controversy is discussed in Pitt Cobbett, II, p. 12.

[2] The Lord Chancellor went on to cite Vattel, *Droit Des Gens*, LIV. 3, c. 5, para 70.

[3] At p. 497. Note also Lord Davey, at p. 500.   [4] [1901] 2 K.B. at p. 427.

[5] While a war is in progress the courts will not speculate how long it will last: *Geipel* v. *Smith*.

[6] Commercial and other relations may be resumed earlier if special permission is given: see 29 *B.Y.* (1952), p. 439.

[7] *In re Cooper* [1946] 1 Ch. 109, 113; *R.* v. *Bottrill, ex parte Kuechenmeister*; *Tester* v. *Bisley*. But an unconditional surrender may amount to an armistice: *Re Orchard*. Upon the effect of an unconditional surrender on rights of prize, see *Schiffahrt-Treuhand G.m.b.H.* v. *H.M. Procurator-General* (Privy Council).

voyage to a German port were condemned as prize.[1] Nor does the signature of a treaty of peace have that effect so long as the treaty remains unratified.[2] It is likely that circumstances which would show that a state of war had in international law ceased to exist would normally be accepted by an English Court as having such an effect. However, in a situation which admitted of doubt as to the precise moment at which a state of war ceased, an English Court would look to the Crown for guidance,[3] and there is little doubt that such guidance would be forthcoming. If a certificate from the Executive were before the Court stating clearly that a state of war had not come to an end, then, whether or not in international law such state of war might be considered to have terminated, the Court would nevertheless regard the certificate as binding on it.[4]

Towards the end of the war of 1914–18 Parliament, by the Termination of the Present War (Definition) Act, 1918, conferred upon the Crown in Council power to declare the date of the termination of the war as regards any provision in any Act of Parliament, Order in Council or Proclamation, or in any contract, deed or other instrument referring to the existing war or hostilities:[5] such date was to be as nearly as might be the date of the exchange or deposit of ratifications of the treaty or treaties of peace, and might differ in the case of the different enemy States.[6]

In a number of cases wars have come to an end by the belligerents drifting into a state of peace after the cessation of hostilities. The situation as between the United Kingdom and Germany[7] at the end

[1] *The Rannveig* (the Armistice Agreement itself authorized the continuation of the Allied naval blockade). See also *Re Orchard*; *The Bellaman*. The circumstances of a cessation of hostilities may amount to an abrogation of rights of prize: *The Hermes and Four Hulls.*

[2] *The Eliza Ann*; *Rattray* v. *Holden*; *Kotzias* v. *Tyser*; *Lloyd* v. *Bowring*; *Fasbender* v. *Attorney-General.* Many foreign decisions will be found in the volumes of the Annual Digest and International Law Reports. See also, in general, Beckett, 39 *L.Q.R.* (1923), pp. 89–97. As to whether legislation is necessary to give effect to a treaty of peace, see the 3rd edition of this book, pp. 397–9, and three Canadian decisions, *Secretary of State for Canada* v. *Alien Property Custodian for the United States* (1931) 1 D.L.R. 890, 913; *Ritcher* v. *The King*; and *Bitter* v. *Secretary of State for Canada.*

[3] In *Hawtrey* v. *Beaufront*, and *Tester* v. *Bisley*, a public statement by the Prime Minister was considered sufficient.   [4] *R.* v. *Bottrill, ex parte Kuechenmeister.*

[5] For a consideration of the possible application of the Act to a contract referring to 'the duration of the war', see *Ruffy-Arnell, etc., Co. Ltd* v. *The King* [1922] 1 K.B. 599, 611–13.

[6] As a result of the non-ratification of the Treaty of Sèvres with Turkey, the precise state of our relations with Turkey remained in doubt for several years, until peace was definitely concluded by the ratification of the Treaty of Lausanne in 1924; but so far as we are aware it was never judicially considered in this country.

[7] The war with the other enemy States was terminated by peace treaties in the normal way: see the Treaties of Peace (Italy, Roumania, Bulgaria, Hungary and Finland) Act, 1947, the Japanese Peace Treaty Act, 1951, and the Austrian State Treaty Act, 1955. As to Siam, see above, p. 11, n. 1.

of the 1939–45 war affords an example of a long drawn out period of transition from war to peace. Briefly put,[1] the various stages were: (i) on 9 May 1945 Germany signed an instrument of unconditional surrender to the Allied forces;[2] (ii) on 7 June 1945 the United Kingdom, France, the United States and Russia made a joint Declaration—the Berlin Declaration—by which the Four Powers assumed 'supreme authority' with respect to Germany, but without annexing her territory;[3] (iii) the resumption of commercial and financial relations between Germany and the United Kingdom was authorized on 23 March 1949; (iv) the abrogation by Germany, as from 8 May 1945, by a law passed on 14 June 1951, of all provisions of law treating the opposing belligerents and their nationals as enemies; (v) notification of the termination of the 'formal state of war with Germany' was made on 9 July 1951. A peace treaty with Germany has not yet been signed.[4] Although for certain limited purposes and in the interpretation of certain documents,[5] the war was held by English courts to have ended earlier, the formal state of war between the United Kingdom and Germany subsisted until 9 July 1951:[6] the notice in the *London Gazette* of 9 July 1951 gave the terms of the Note communicated on that date by the United Kingdom High Commissioner in Germany to the Federal Government of Germany in which it was stated that 'the formal state of war with Germany has continued to subsist so far as the municipal law of the United Kingdom is concerned, and will so continue until appropriate

---

[1] For further details see Ottensooser, *B.Y.* (1952), p. 439; Kunz, 46 *A.J.* (1952), p. 114; and above, p. 12, n. 4. Not all the Allied countries followed the same practice as the United Kingdom. In the United States the President declared 'the cessation of hostilities' on 31 December 1946 (at the same time permitting the resumption of commercial intercourse with Germany), nearly 20 months after the unconditional surrender of Germany; the formal termination of the state of war was not declared until 24 October 1951, with effect from five days previously. As to the status of Germany in the years following June 1945, see the certificate given by the Secretary of State for Foreign Affairs in 1964 in *Carl-Zeiss-Stiftung* v. *Rayner* [1964] 1 All E.R. 300, 307 (C.A.).

[2] As to whether this constituted an 'armistice', see *Re Orchard*. See also *Martin* v. *Scottish Transport and General Workers Union* [1952] 1 All E.R. 691, 694, and *Schiffahrt-Treuhand G.m.b.H.* v. *H.M. Procurator-General*.

[3] In *The Hermes and Four Hulls* (Privy Council), this Declaration was held to constitute an abrogation by the Allies of their rights of prize.

[4] The Paris and Bonn Agreements of 1954 and 1952 contain much of the substance of a peace treaty. See above, p. 13, n. 5.

[5] Upon the effect of leases made 'for the duration of the war' or in similar terms, see the Validation of War-time Leases Act, 1944, and the Tenancy Agreements (End of the War in Europe) Order, 1945 (S.R. & O. 1945, no. 703) and the Tenancy Agreements (End of the War with Japan) Order, 1945 (S.R. & O. 1945, no. 1006). See also *Hawtrey* v. *Beaufront Ltd*; *Eker* v. *Becker*; *In re Grotian*; and in, general, Halsbury, *Laws of England* (3rd ed., Simonds), vol. 23, pp. 533–4.

[6] Germany did not, however, cease for all purposes of the Trading with the Enemy Act, 1939, to be treated as if it were enemy territory until 6 October 1952: S.R. & O. 1952, no. 1760.

action is taken by His Majesty's Government to terminate it'. That the state of war still existed even after the unconditional surrender and the Berlin Declaration was affirmed by a certificate from the Foreign Secretary in *R. v. Bottrill, ex parte Kuechenmeister.*

(b) The United Kingdom as a third party to a war between other States[1]

In this situation too we should expect the same rule to apply, whereby we are entitled to look to the Executive branch of Government to inform us when a state of war between two other countries exists, for this is a matter upon which the organs of a State should speak with a single voice. It could be embarrassing if the Executive held one view and the Courts propounded another.[2]

In *Thelluson v. Cosling*[3] the question arising on a policy of insurance was whether or not war had been declared by Spain against France on a particular date. A document (presumably a copy) consisting of a declaration of war by Spain had been transmitted by the British Ambassador in Madrid to the British Foreign Office and was produced in Court from the custody of the Foreign Office. Lord Ellenborough C.J. admitted it as evidence, not only as the only evidence but as proper evidence upon the particular matter of fact as to the date when war was declared. As MacKinnon L.J. remarked, in discussing this case later:[4] 'it was a Spanish document and would have been just as good evidence if it had been produced by the Spanish Ambassador'.

In *United States of America v. Pelly* Bigham J. had to decide, in an action for damages for breach of contract to sell two colliers, whether for the purposes of a clause in the contract and of the Foreign Enlistment Act, 1870, the United States of America were 'at war' with Spain on 23 April 1898. On 22 April an American warship had captured a Spanish merchant ship. On the same day the American President declared a general blockade of the coast of Cuba, and on 26 April the American Congress passed a resolution to the effect 'that war be and the same is hereby declared to exist, and that war has existed since 21 April 1898...between the United States of America and Spain'. Upon these facts the learned Judge gave an affirmative answer to the question stated above. He also referred to

---

[1] Certain consequences which follow upon the United Kingdom being a neutral are mentioned in chapter 19.

[2] However, as to embarrassing the Executive, Sir Wilfred Greene M.R. has said: 'I do not myself find the fear of the embarrassment of the Executive a very attractive basis upon which to build a rule of English law' (*Kawasaki Kisen Kabushiki Kaisha of Kobe v. Bantham Steamship Co.* [1939] 2 K.B. 544, at p. 552).

[3] (1803) 4 Esp. 266. This case was discussed in the *Kawasaki* case, *supra.*

[4] [1939] 2 K.B. at p. 550; see also at p. 555.

the British Proclamation of Neutrality dated 23 April and published in the *London Gazette,* and is reported to have described it as 'not evidence' but 'not without weight in his mind'. Having regard to the more recent attitude of the Courts to pronouncements of the Executive upon international affairs,[1] there is little doubt that today the Proclamation of Neutrality would be treated as conclusive.

Sir Wilfred Greene in *Kawasaki Kisen Kabushiki Kaisha of Kobe* v. *Bantham Steamship Co.*[2] expressed a clear, though *obiter,* opinion that if the Court of Appeal had been concerned

with the question whether His Majesty's Government recognizes a state of war as existing between China and Japan...the Court would be bound to take judicial notice of the fact of such recognition, and if the Court were unable to answer that question they would ascertain from the appropriate department of Government whether or not His Majesty's Government had recognised the existence of that state of war.

However, in many cases the view of the Executive is not sought[3] or, if sought, is temporizing. The Courts must then proceed as best they can to determine whether or not a state of war exists between two foreign States, and it may be assumed that they will not be unmindful of the rules of international law in this matter.

In *The Nayade* Sir W. Scott had to consider a situation where there had been a declaration of war by one side only. He said:

In cases of this kind, it is by no means necessary that both countries should declare war. Whatever might be the prostration and submissive demeanour of one side, if France was unwilling to accept that submission, and persisted in attacking Portugal, it was sufficient.

With reference to the Franco-Prussian war, Mellish L.J., delivering the opinion of the Privy Council in *The Teutonia,*[4] said:

And though it is true...that a War may exist *de facto* without a declaration of war, yet it appears to their Lordships that this can only be effected by an actual commencement of hostilities which, in this case, is not alleged.

Just as may happen in relation to a war to which the United Kingdom is a party, so too, in connection with a war between two other States, terms connoting war and peace and used in various legal documents may be interpreted in their context as not referring to their technical legal meaning but rather to some perhaps more

---

[1] See above, p. 37.   [2] [1939] 2 K.B. 544, 554.

[3] As for example in *Arab Bank Ltd* v. *Barclays Bank (D.C.O.),* where the House of Lords accepted that a state of war existed at the material time between Israel and the Arab States (e.g. by Lord Morton of Henryton, at p. 229). The caution with which Sir W. Scott, in *The Two Friends,* below, p. 46, dealt with the question of a possible state of war between two foreign States should be noted.

[4] (1872) L.R. 4 P.C. 171, 179.

commonsense meaning which the parties concerned may be taken to have intended.[1]

When the United Kingdom recognizes the existence of a state of war between two other States, it is usual for her to define her own position by deciding whether to become a co-belligerent with one of the parties or to remain neutral.[2] It is not uncommon for a State to announce its attitude to the world by means of a proclamation or declaration of neutrality.[3]

Neutrality is, strictly speaking, a matter of public international law, being a matter of rights and duties *between States* and not between belligerent States and the nationals of neutral States: we have therefore little concern with it in this volume. However, when the United Kingdom is neutral, three matters affecting rights and duties of private persons require mention: assistance by British nationals to the belligerents (particularly by enlisting in their armed forces); the rights and duties of British nationals in regard to breach of blockade, carriage of contraband, and similar activities; and the fate of their property in a belligerent's territory. These subjects are discussed in chapter 19.

(c) Armed conflicts not amounting to war

As we have seen,[4] English Courts do not recognize any intermediate state between peace and war. Therefore in the event of there being an armed conflict which does not give rise to a state of war, a state of peace would still be considered to subsist: and thus, for example, those rules of law requiring for their application the existence of a state of war would not come into operation.

In *Blomart* v. *Roxburgh*[5]—a Scottish case decided in 1664, in which

---

[1] See above, p. 36. In the *Kawasaki* case (*supra*) the Court of Appeal held that the Sino-Japanese conflict constituted a war within the meaning of that term used in a commercial document, although it probably did not constitute a war in the strict legal sense of the term.

[2] We need hardly say that the terms 'non-belligerent' and 'pre-belligerent' which have become fashionable recently to describe the neutral State which is waiting for a favourable moment to jump into the contest are political and have no legal meaning. When war exists between *A* and *B*, all other States are either belligerent or neutral.

[3] See for example the declaration of neutrality by the United Kingdom in the war between Spain and the United States of America in 1898 (90 *B.F.S.P.* 344): this declaration was considered in *United States of America* v. *Pelly* (1899) 15 T.L.R. 166. Other proclamations of neutrality have been made by the United Kingdom in connection with, for example, the wars between Greece and the Ottoman Empire in 1825 (12 *B.F.S.P.* 525), Russia and Turkey in 1877 (68 *B.F.S.P.* 857), Greece and Turkey in 1897 (89 *B.F.S.P* 451), Russia and Japan in 1904 (97 *B.F.S.P.* 476), Turkey and Italy in 1911 (104 *B.F.S.P.* 207), and in the Balkan war of 1912 (105 *B.F.S.P.* 163).

[4] See above, pp. 34–5.

[5] Mor. Dict. 16, 091, quoted in the *Sovfracht* case [1943] A.C. 203, 214.

the decision was the same as we conceive it would be in English law
—the question arose whether a Dutch alien was barred from suing
because he was an alien enemy. There had been no 'denunciation
of war by His Majesty as King of Scotland, nor any proclamation in
Scotland to that purpose', although 'there was a warrant by the
King and Council to seize upon all the Dutch vessels in Scotland'.
It was held that 'this was but an embargo, and no denunciation of
war in Scotland' and that therefore the Dutch alien was not an
enemy and could bring proceedings in Court. A somewhat similar
situation arose in *The Eastern Carrying Insurance Co.* v. *The National
Benefit Life and Property Assurance Co. Ltd.* In 1918 British troops were
fighting against the troops of the unrecognized Bolshevist Government in Russia. The plaintiff company was a company with its
registered office in Russia, and in an action by that company to
recover from the defendants certain money due to the plaintiffs, the
defendants contended, *inter alia*, that the plaintiff company was an
alien enemy and therefore unable to sue. Bailhache J. held that
notwithstanding the fighting, this country was not at war with
Russia and the plaintiffs were thus not alien enemies so as to be
prevented from instituting proceedings.[1]

The Courts would not, however, ignore the armed conflict and
always continue to apply the law as if the conflict did not exist.
Simply because it gives rise to a certain situation of fact, the conflict
could give rise to legal consequences—for example, in connection
with the application to contracts of the doctrine of frustration.[2] It
could also, to take another example, affect rights of salvage, as where
a vessel of one party to the conflict is rescued after having been seized
by the armed forces of the other. Thus in *The Two Friends* an
American vessel was, during hostilities between France (then at war
with the United Kingdom) and the United States of America, captured by a French ship. Later she was recaptured by the crew, who
then brought proceedings in the English courts for salvage; the
owners contested the propriety of their doing so. Sir W. Scott, after
observing that 'it is not for me to say whether America is at war with
France or not', found that nonetheless the conduct of France towards
America had been such *de facto* that, whatever the actual situation

---

[1] The learned judge went on to observe, *obiter*, that had the plaintiff company been
a supporter of the Bolshevist Government, or adhered to them, 'the position would be
different'. It is not clear just how the difference would have been material, since there
would still have been no state of war between this country and Russia.

[2] As to frustration in general, see below, chapter 5; with particular reference to the
application of the doctrine of frustration to the Suez incident of 1956, see below, pp. 192 ff.

of affairs between America and France might be, American ship-owners, by themselves acting in this connection in a manner only supportable on the assumption of there being subsisting hostilities, had recognized the legality of and necessity for salvage.

Perhaps a more usual way in which the conflict would come within the purview of the law would be as the result of the interpretation, in relation to the conflict, of terms used in rules of law or in legal documents. Thus, if a contract or statute uses a term such as 'war' or 'hostilities', it will be necessary to see whether it may be interpreted so as to apply to the particular armed conflict in question: if the facts about the conflict are in doubt the Court may well seek assistance from the Executive in ascertaining them. As we have already remarked,[1] in cases involving commercial documents and wills there is a tendency not to restrict a term such as 'war' to its technical legal meaning.

In *Kawasaki Kisen Kabushiki Kaisha of Kobe* v. *Bantham Steamship Co.*[2] the Court was faced with the conflict between Japan and China and in particular with the question whether on 18 September 1937 there was a war between these two States for the purposes of a contract which contained a clause allowing for cancellation 'if war breaks out involving Japan'. A letter from the Foreign Office to one of the parties dated 11 September 1937 stated 'that the current situation in China is indeterminate and anomalous and H.M.G. are not at present prepared to say that in their view a state of war exists'; with reference to the particular date of 18 September 1937, the Foreign Office repeated some four months later that H.M.G. were still not prepared to say that in their view a state of war existed.[3] Sir Wilfred Greene M.R. observed that the fact that H.M.G. did not recognize the outbreak of war between two third countries did not necessarily mean that war had not broken out.[4] In all the circumstances the Court of Appeal agreed that, for the purposes of the construction of the charterparty before the Court, it could be said that a war involving Japan had broken out.

---

[1] See above, p. 36.

[2] Another case arising out of the Sino-Japanese hostilities was *Court Line Ltd* v. *Dant & Russel, Inc.*, concerning the frustration of a contract.

[3] A letter from the Foreign Office in May 1938 said that H.M.G. were still not 'prepared to say that in their view a state of war exists': (1939) 55 T.L.R. 520.

[4] Similarly, where a charterparty contained the expression 'orders or directions... given by the Government of the Nation under whose flag the vessel sails...or by any other Government...' it was held that, there being a controversy between two rival Governments in a foreign State, China, the meaning to be given to the term 'Government' was not conclusively determined by the views of Her Majesty's Government, and an umpire was justified in finding that the Formosan Government possessed the qualities and character of 'any other Government' notwithstanding that that Government was not recognized as a Government by H.M.G.: *Luigi Monta* v. *Cechofracht Co. Ltd.*

The Suez incident of 1956 affords a recent example of a conflict in which the United Kingdom was engaged in hostilities against another State in circumstances not giving rise to a state of war. No case has so far come before the English courts which raises directly the status of the conflict,[1] but in five cases[2] the matter has been touched upon in passing. All five raised the question of the frustration of contracts by reason of the closure of the Suez Canal at the time of or as a result of the incident: in one case it was 'rightly' conceded before the Court that that closure was an act of hostilities within the meaning of a clause in the contract referring to 'hostilities',[3] and in another the Court repeated without dissent the finding of the commercial tribunal (which had stated a case for the Court) that 'there were hostilities but not war in Egypt at the material time',[4] while in the Court of Appeal Sellers L.J. said that 'although there were hostilities in Egypt and in the region of the Suez Canal at the material time, there has been no finding of war'.[5] Bearing in mind that the Courts have been known to look to public statements made by a Minister of the Crown,[6] it is useful to recall that the Prime Minister stated categorically in Parliament at the time that the United Kingdom was not at war with Egypt.[7]

Apart from situations involving fighting between opposing armed forces, measures may be taken by a State which may fairly be seen as establishing a situation of conflict or quasi-hostility between that State and another; the institution of a pacific blockade would be an example. In *Janson* v. *Driefontein Consolidated Mines Ltd*[8] the House

---

[1] In *Navios Corporation* v. *The Ulysses II*, a United States Court held that there was a 'declared war' for purposes of a contract using that term.

[2] *Carapanayotti & Co. Ltd* v. *E. T. Green Ltd*; *Tsakiroglou & Co. Ltd* v. *Noblee & Thorl G.m.b.H.*; *Albert D. Gaon & Co.* v. *Société Interprofessionelle des Oleagineux Fluides Alimentaires* (the last two cases were heard together in the Court of Appeal, and the *Tsakiroglou* case was heard in the House of Lords); *Société Franco Tunisienne d'Armement* v. *Sidermar S.P.A.*; *Ocean Tramp Tankers Corporation* v. *V/O Sovfracht*. For the application of the doctrine of frustration to these 'Suez' cases, see below, pp. 192 ff. See also *Union-Castle Mail Steamship Co. Ltd.* v. *United Kingdom Mutual War Risks Association Ltd.*

[3] [1959] 1 Q.B. 131, 142.   [4] [1959] 1 All E.R. 45, 52.

[5] [1960] 2 All E.R. 160, 163.   [6] *Supra*, p. 41, n. 3.

[7] 6 *I. and C.L.Q.* (1957), 333. The Lord Privy Seal, in a fuller statement of the position, expressed the view in Parliament that 'Her Majesty's Government do not regard their present action as constituting a war...There is no state of war, but there is a state of conflict' (*ibid.* pp. 332–3). The reference to a 'state of conflict' would not seem to refer to separate *legal* state. Some six months after the conflict was over, a Minister of the Crown said in Parliament: 'Whatever may have vitiated, or may vitiate still, relations between Britain and Egypt, neither Government, so far as I know, maintains that a state of war exists at all' (*ibid.* pp. 521–2). The statement by the Lord Privy Seal, later in the speech of his of which a part has already been quoted, that he was 'perfectly satisfied that a state of war exists' was probably a slip of the tongue or an error in reporting.

[8] In *Aubert* v. *Gray* (1861, 1862) 3 B. & S. 163, 169, the Spanish owners of a ship's cargo brought an action against the insurers of the cargo in respect of damage caused to it as

of Lords was concerned with a seizure of gold owned by the respondent company by the South African Government nine days before, and in immediate contemplation of, the outbreak of war between South Africa and the United Kingdom. In an action to recover from the appellant sums due under an insurance policy, the House of Lords held that the respondents were entitled to recover since notwithstanding the imminence of war and the very strained relations between the two countries the loss had in fact occurred in time of peace.

We shall add to appropriate chapters some notes on the effects of non-war conflicts upon the particular subject-matter of the chapter,[1] but here we shall mention certain general points.

Public policy. When the United Kingdom becomes a party to an armed conflict not amounting to the technical state of war, the automatic consequences of war such as enemy status, abrogation of most contracts, prohibition of intercourse, etc., are absent. Nevertheless, there are many acts, particularly within the sphere of contract or transfer of property, which, while normally free from objection, would become illegal on the ground that their performance during the armed conflict would be contrary to public policy as recognized by the common law. As Lord Alvanley said in *Furtado* v. *Rogers*,[2] 'it is not competent to any subject to enter into a contract to do anything which may be detrimental to the interests of his own country; and [that] such a contract is as much prohibited as if it had been expressly prohibited by Act of Parliament'.

Quasi-enemy territory and persons. Sub-section 1 A of Section 15 of the Trading with the Enemy Act, 1939, is as follows:

(1 A) The Board of Trade may by order[3] direct that the provisions of this Act shall apply in relation to any area specified in the order as they apply in relation to enemy territory and the said provisions shall apply accordingly.

a result of an embargo placed upon the ship by Spain for purposes of carrying on Spain's war with Morocco. It was held that the owners could recover under the policy. A distinction was drawn between an embargo imposed when peace prevailed between the countries of which the assured and the insurer were nationals, the embargo being wholly unconnected with existing or anticipated hostilities (sc. between those countries), and an embargo connected with such hostilities: the judgment expressly disclaims any concern with the latter situation.

[1] See chapters 5 (Frustration of Contract); 16 (Trading with the Enemy); 6 (Affreightment); 11 (Insurance); 13 (Sale of Goods); 17 (Belligerent Occupation).

[2] (1802) 3 B. & P. 191, 198; according to *Bell* v. *Reid* this rule does not apply to British subjects domiciled abroad, *sed quaere* today; and see Pollock on *Contracts* (13th ed.), p. 297. Note also the remarks of Lord Merriman P. in *The Glenearn* [1941] P. 51, at pp. 60–1.

[3] The words 'by order' were added by the Emergency Laws (Miscellaneous Provisions) Act, 1953.

This Act deals with both persons and property, and the exercise of the power[1] conferred by this subsection would enable the United Kingdom Government to sever all intercourse and relations between the United Kingdom and the area specified, with the same kind of effect upon contracts and other matters as applies to enemy persons and territory. Moreover, subsection 2 of section 2 of the same Act provides that

The Board of Trade may by order direct that any person specified in the order shall, for the purposes of this Act, be deemed to be, while so specified, an enemy.

Ad hoc legislation. If the existing powers of the Crown under the Defence Regulations, the Trading with the Enemy Act, 1939, and similar legislation are inadequate, they can readily be supplemented. For instance, the performance of a contract might fall within the prohibition of an Order in Council or other Order which the United Kingdom Government has power to make. The Export of Goods (North Korea) Order, 1950,[2] and the measures taken under the Southern Rhodesia Act, 1965, in connection with the Rhodesian rebellion, indicate the wide range of possible *ad hoc* legislative measures.

(d) Armed conflicts conducted under the authority of the United Nations

United Nations forces have so far only been established on four occasions,[3] and only in those which have operated in Korea and in Cyprus have United Kingdom armed forces been directly involved (although, of course, in a broader sense all United Nations actions may be said to involve the United Kingdom by virtue of its membership of the Organization). The only case concerning a conflict involving United Nations forces to come before an English court is a patent case: *Re Harshaw Chemical Co's Patent*.[4]

It has been suggested that it would be inappropriate to consider armed conflicts involving United Nations forces as constituting a war.[5] Statements in Parliament have made it clear that the British Government do not consider that the Korean conflict ever amounted to a state of war. On 11 June 1952 the Foreign Secretary stated in Parliament:[6]

We are not engaged in a war with the Republic of North Korea because we do not admit that there is such a State...What we are engaged on is

---

[1] As to whether this power is exercisable in the absence of a state of war, see below, pp. 363 ff.   [2] See below, p. 52.   [3] See above, p. 25.

[4] See below, p. 296, n. 5. Several foreign cases are referred to in nn. 3–5 on p. 51 below.

[5] See above, p. 28.   [6] 1 *I. and C.L.Q.* (1952), 578.

an action of the United Nations forces in lawfully resisting aggression under the United Nations Charter.[1]

In November 1956, in a debate on the Suez conflict, the Prime Minister said:[2]

It was never admitted that there was a state of war [in Korea], and Korea was never at war in any technical or legal sense...

There has been no occasion for any statements as to the view of the British Government in relation to the status of the other conflicts in which United Nations forces have been included.

Even if a conflict does not constitute a war in any strict legal sense, it may nevertheless be held to fall within the interpretation given to that term in a particular document or statute. Thus a number of foreign courts have held that the Korean conflict constituted a war for purposes of insurance policies,[3] and for purposes of military discipline,[4] as well as for other purposes.[5]

We should also mention section 1 of the United Nations Act, 1946, which empowers the Government to take certain measures not involving the use of armed force in support of decisions of the Security Council,[6] and also section 1 of the Defence Contracts Act, 1958,

---

[1] This statement would seem to leave open the question whether action by United Nations forces in which the United Kingdom participated could give rise to a state of war if the opposing party were a State recognized by the United Kingdom; nor does the statement shed light on the position which would ensue if the party opposing the United Nations forces were to be rebels to whom has been accorded recognition of belligerency.

[2] 6 *I and C.L.Q.* (1957), 333.

[3] *Western Reserve Life Insurance Co.* v. *Meadows* (U.S.A.); *Christensen* v. *Sterling Insurance Co.* (U.S.A.); *Langlas* v. *Iowa Life Insurance Co.* (U.S.A.); *Weissman* v. *Metropolitan Life Insurance Co.* (U.S.A.), 2 *I. and C.L.Q.* (1953), p. 650. Cf. *Beley* v. *Pennsylvania Mutual Life Insurance Co.* (U.S.A.), ibid., p. 316.

[4] *United States* v. *Bancroft* (U.S.A.). Cf. *War in Korea (Self-Mutilation) Case* (France); and see also *United States* v. *Sanders* (U.S.A.), holding that there was no war for disciplinary purposes after the conclusion of the armistice in Korea.

[5] *Burns* v. *The King* (Australia). Cf. *Australian Communist Party* v. *The Commonwealth* (Australia); and see also *In re Berry* (New Zealand).

[6] Subsection (1) of section 1 of this Act is as follows: 'If, under Article 41 of the Charter of the United Nations signed at San Francisco the twenty-sixth day of June, nineteen hundred and forty-five, (being the Article which relates to measures not involving the use of armed force) the Security Council of the United Nations call upon His Majesty's Government in the United Kingdom to apply any measures to give effect to any decision of that Council, His Majesty may by Order in Council make such provision as appears to Him necessary or expedient for enabling those measures to be effectively applied, including (without prejudice to the generality of the preceding words) provision for the apprehension, trial and punishment of persons offending against the Order.'

Article 41 of the Charter is as follows: 'The Security Council may decide what measures not involving the use of armed force are to be employed to give effect to its decisions, and it may call upon the Members of the United Nations to apply such measures. These may include complete or partial interruption of economic relations and of rail, sea, air, postal, telegraphic, radio, and other means of communication, and the severance of diplomatic relations.'

whereby the right of any Government department to use patented inventions for the services of the Crown is extended to cover the supply of articles required for any armed forces operating in pursuance of any resolution of the United Nations or an organ thereof. At the time of the Korean conflict the Export of Goods (North Korea) Order, 1950,[1] was made, prohibiting the export of goods to North Korea as from 6 July 1950. There was no war between the United Kingdom and North Korea: if there had been, the export of goods to North Korea would have amounted to trading with the enemy.

While the British Government did not consider there to have been a state of war in Korea, it was the opinion of the Attorney-General that the law of treason was applicable in connection with the conflict.[2] The Government also agreed that the usual wartime schemes for compensation would apply in the case of crews of British ships engaged in carrying troops or their supplies to Korea, and also that, if the insurance cover of a British ship chartered on the Government's behalf ceased to apply because of employment in Korean waters, the Government would pay the sum that would otherwise have been payable by the insurers.[3] The possible application of the Foreign Enlistment Act, 1870, both to the Korean conflict and to the United Nations later action in the Congo, is considered in chapter 19.

(e) *Civil disturbances in a foreign country*

It often becomes necessary for the private citizen, particularly the shipowner or merchant, to know how he ought to regard 'disturbances' (to use the equivocal term), or 'troubles' as they are called across the St George's Channel, when occurring in a foreign country.

The surest test for determining whether the disturbances have become of international significance and thus attract certain legal

---

[1] S.R. & O. 1950, no. 1117; revoked by S.R. & O. 1957, no. 246. North Korea is also included in the Strategic Goods (Control) Order, S.I. 1959, no. 190.

[2] Parliamentary Debates (5th Series) (Commons), vol. 478 (1950), col. *203*; see also cols. *278–9* and *299*. See also Green, 4 *I.L.Q.* (1951), p. 462. In connection with the involvement of China in the Korean conflict and the consequent state of the relations between the United Kingdom and China, the Minister of Defence, in a letter (written after discussion with the Attorney-General) to a Member of Parliament about the possibly treasonable nature of a journalist's conduct, said that the question 'does of course turn to some extent on the question whether or not we are at war with China. On this it seems likely that from a legal point of view the state of hostilities between China and ourselves is sufficient to bring the act of "giving aid and comfort" to the Chinese within the definition of treason': *The Times*, 13 April 1951.

[3] Parliamentary Debates (5th Series) (Commons), vol. 478 (1950), col. *172*.

consequences is whether the British Government have either granted recognition of belligerency, or, if the disturbances amount to something less than that, recognized the existence of a condition of insurgency.[1] Where there has been such formal recognition by the Government, a British Court will be bound to take notice of it.[2] Where the situation is in doubt, it is always open to the Court to consult the appropriate branch of the Executive, usually the Foreign Office.

Recognition of *belligerency* brings into operation as between this country and each of the belligerents the law of neutrality and all the rights and duties arising therefrom, and the subjects of this country are affected in the same way as if there were in progress a regular war in which the United Kingdom was neutral. On the other hand, recognition of a state of *insurgency* does not bring the laws of war and neutrality into operation: at the same time, the situation is not in all respects the same as in a normal state of peace. For example, the provisions of the Foreign Enlistment Act, 1870, become effective,[3] 'war risks' clauses in insurance contracts will usually apply,[4] and the insurgents or the parent Government may attempt to interfere with foreign shipping as by purporting to institute a blockade. Thus in *Tatem* v. *Gamboa* the Court was called upon to consider the interference with foreign shipping by the insurgents in the Spanish civil war. It was held that such interference had not been in pursuance of a lawful blockade, that the illegal seizure of a ship in those circumstances was not a risk which was contemplated by the parties when they entered into a charterparty in respect of the ship, and that the charterparty was frustrated. Similarly, in *Spanish Government* v. *The North of England Steamship Company* it was held that the purported blockade by the insurgents was not a blockade in its strict legal sense and that consequently the owners of a vessel which was on charter

[1] For the distinction between belligerency and insurgency, see above, pp. 30–33.

[2] See above, p. 37. But see *Luigi Monta of Genoa* v. *Cechofracht Co. Ltd*, where a certificate from the Foreign Office that one of the two rival Governments in China was not recognized as a Government by the United Kingdom was held not binding for the purposes of giving meaning to the word 'government' in a charterparty (and see note 4 below). It may be noted that no state of belligerency between the two rival Governments was recognized by the United Kingdom, at least in March 1956: 5 *I. and C.L.Q.* (1956), p. 437.

[3] See below, chapter 19.

[4] See *Pesquerias Y Secaderos de Bacalao de Espana, S.A.* v. *Beer*, and the definition of 'war risks' in section 10 of the Marine and Aviation Insurance (War Risks) Act, 1952. For the application of an insurance policy covering damage by 'war, bombardment, military or usurped power' to the rebellion in Ireland in 1916, see *Curtis & Sons* v. *Mathews*. But as already pointed out (above, p. 36) the meaning of such words as 'war' in an insurance contract, charterparty, bill of lading, etc., is a question of the interpretation of that document and does not turn solely on any pronouncement by the Government or on the absence of one.

did not enjoy the rights given to them in the charterparty in the event of certain ports being 'blockaded'.[1]

In *Eastern Carrying Insurance Company* v. *National Benefit Life and Property Insurance Company*[2] it was held that the fact that a British expeditionary force was fighting against the troops of an unrecognized (Bolshevist) Government in Russia in July 1918 during the civil war prevailing in Russia did not mean that the United Kingdom was at war with Russia, so as to make a Russian insurance company, registered and carrying on business in Petrograd, an alien enemy.

---

[1] The maritime activities of insurgents may give rise to questions of piracy under the Piracy Act, 1850, or at common law. It would seem that insurgent vessels committing acts of violence on the high seas against vessels of States other than that against which the insurrection is directed may properly be considered as pirates in English law, especially if the acts of violence are in no way connected with the insurrection: see *The Magellan Pirates*; *The Three Friends* (1897) (U.S.A., Supreme Court); and the statement of the Attorney-General in Parliament, H.C. Debates, 3rd Series, vol. 236, pp. 787 ff. (quoted in Oppenheim, I, § 273, n.). So long as the insurgent vessel refrains from molesting foreign shipping it is probably not to be considered piratical: but the American decision in *The Ambrose Light* (Moore, *Digest of International Law*, II, p. 1098) goes very close to holding otherwise. See above, p. 31, n. 2.

[2] Citing *Muller* v. *Thompson*.

2

BRITISH NATIONALITY AND ALIEN STATUS[1]

BIBLIOGRAPHY

Mervyn Jones, *British Nationality Law and Practice* (1947), cited as 'Mervyn Jones, 1947'.
Mervyn Jones, *British Nationality Law* (revised ed.) (1956), cited as 'Mervyn Jones, 1956'.
Clive Parry, *British Nationality and the History of Naturalisation* (1954), Communicazioni e Studi dell'Istituto di Diritto internazionale e straniere (University of Milan).
Clive Parry, *British Nationality* (1951), cited as 'Parry, *Nationality*'.
Clive Parry, *Nationality and Citizenship Laws of the Commonwealth and Republic of Ireland* (1957), and Supplements.
Oppenheim, I, §§ 293–326—published in 1955.
Dicey, ch. 6 (Domicile).
Halsbury, *Laws of England* (3rd ed. Simonds), I, Aliens and Nationality.

For the earlier law see:
Piggott, *Nationality, including Naturalization* (1907).
McNair, *Opinions*, II, pp. 14–30.
Van Pittius, *Nationality within the British Commonwealth of Nations* (1930).

In this chapter we are primarily attempting to state the law as it applies to citizens of the United Kingdom of Great Britain and Northern Ireland and the Colonies, and we shall describe them as British subjects or as United Kingdom citizens. But we must remind our readers, and particularly our foreign readers, that each self-governing Commonwealth country has a separate legal system and an entirely independent power of legislation, and that many of the surviving British colonies have a varying degree of subordinate legislative capacity. Accordingly, it is necessary for the reader in a given case to bear in mind the existence and relevance of legislation which cannot be described as United Kingdom legislation.

This chapter makes no attempt to summarize the law of British nationality, which has become very technical as the result of recent legislation by all the Commonwealth countries, including the United Kingdom, for which we must refer the reader to the books of Dr Clive Parry[2] listed at the beginning of this chapter.

---

[1] This chapter has derived great benefit from the comments of Dr Clive Parry.
[2] In particular his *Nationality and Citizenship Laws*, pp. 110–12 (and Supplements).

NATIONALITY, CITIZENSHIP, DOMICILE AND RESIDENCE

These are four terms which must be used in this book from time to time, and it will be useful at the outset to define or, if that is not possible, at least to describe them.

Nationality is the status of a natural person[1] who is attached to a State by the tie of permanent allegiance.[2]

Citizenship. This term is a comparative newcomer in British law and is highly technical. Thus in the British Nationality Act, 1948, now the principal Act, Part I is entitled 'British Nationality' and Part II 'Citizenship of the United Kingdom and Colonies'. The term 'Commonwealth' has now replaced 'British Commonwealth' and all or nearly all the countries of the Commonwealth have their own individual citizenship.

Section 1 of the Act of 1948, usually referred to as 'the common clause', is as follows:

(1) Every person who under this Act is a citizen of the United Kingdom and Colonies or who under any enactment for the time being in force in any country mentioned in subsection (3) of this section is a citizen of that country shall by virtue of that citizenship have the status of a British subject.

(2) Any person having the status aforesaid may be known either as a British subject or as a Commonwealth citizen; and accordingly in this Act and in any other enactment or instrument whatever, whether passed or made before or after the commencement of this Act, the expression 'British subject' and the expression 'Commonwealth citizen' shall have the same meaning.

(3) The following are the countries hereinbefore referred to, that is to say, Canada, Australia, New Zealand, the Union of South Africa, Newfoundland, India, Pakistan, Southern Rhodesia and Ceylon.

The list of countries contained in the foregoing subsection (3) has been modified by later events and legislation, and, at the time when this book goes to press, is as follows:

Canada, Australia, New Zealand, India, Pakistan, Southern Rhodesia, Ceylon, Ghana, Malaysia, Cyprus, Sierra Leone, Nigeria, Tanganyika, Jamaica, Trinidad and Tobago, Uganda, Kenya, Zanzibar, Malawi, Zambia, Malta and Gambia (Tanganyika and Zanzibar have now combined to form Tanzania).

---

[1] As to corporations, see p. 102 and Oppenheim, I, § 293, n. 3.

[2] Harvard Research Draft Convention, Article I (modified). 'Permanent' does not mean that it can never be changed, but is opposed to the temporary local allegiance owed to the Crown by an alien, at least so long as he remains on British territory; the decision in *Joyce* v. *Director of Public Prosecutions* shows that this temporary allegiance is based not on residence but on protection and can continue even after the alien has left this country; and see 62 *L.Q.R.* (1946), pp. 105–6.

The Act also contains special provisions enabling certain citizens of Eire, being on a certain date also British subjects, to continue as such on certain grounds.[1]

Domicile. Dicey's[2] Rule 2 is as follows:

(1) A person is, in general, domiciled in the country in which he is considered by English law to have his permanent home.

(2) A person may sometimes be domiciled in a country although he does not have his permanent home in it.

In an earlier edition he pointed out[3] that 'the word "home" is usually employed without technical precision', and that it usually combines both a physical and a mental element—the physical being the person's 'habitual physical presence', and the mental being his 'present intention to reside permanently, or for an indefinite period'.

Residence is not a term of art; it is an element in domicile but not the same thing. There are thousands of persons resident in the United Kingdom at any given moment, for the purpose of employment, education, medical treatment, etc., who are not in any sense domiciled there. It often means 'very little more than physical presence'.[4]

'Domicile' and 'residence' are important for most of the matters dealt with in this book, and we shall see that sometimes 'residence' touches vanishing point and means nothing more than presence at a particular spot at a particular time.[5]

ACQUISITION AND LOSS OF BRITISH NATIONALITY

To attempt a summary of the British law governing these matters would take us beyond the scope of this book, and our aim will be to refer only to those points which might become relevant to the question of enemy status.

Until the First World War British policy was to make it easy for the alien to become one of ourselves, and, even when he had not chosen to take that step, there were until recent years so few disabilities attaching to the alien who had no desire to take part in public life as to make him almost indistinguishable from the native citizen. But when the clouds were gathering for the War of 1914 to 1918 both Germany and the British Empire were found to be overhauling their nationality laws, and since 1914 there has been a definite tendency both to make it more difficult than formerly to become a naturalized British subject and also to stiffen the difference in the status of the British subject and the alien. In the United Kingdom

---

[1] Section 2. [2] P. 85. [3] 6th ed., pp. 77, 78.
[4] Dicey, p. 96. [5] See later in this book, p. 90.

the growing interest in nationality found expression in what was then called the British Nationality and Status of Aliens Act, 1914, which, though not a war measure, received the Royal Assent on 7 August 1914, and has been repeatedly amended since.[1] This legislation has now been greatly modified by the British Nationality Act, 1948, which came into force on 1 January 1949.

It may be stated in summary form that British nationality may now be acquired by

(a) birth;
(b) descent;
(c) registration;
(d) naturalization;
(e) annexation or incorporation of territory;
(f) adoption and legitimation.

We must consider the effect of the outbreak of a war in which the United Kingdom is involved upon certain of these modes.

(a) Birth

This factor can become relevant either by virtue of the *jus soli*—locality of birth, or by virtue of the *jus sanguinis*[2]—nationality of the father, or, in the case of an illegitimate child, in certain circumstances the nationality of the mother.[3]

While the normal rule was that a child born of whatever parentage in British territory became a natural-born British subject, the existence, at the time of the birth, of a war to which the United Kingdom was a party, could involve some modification of this rule.[4]

The normal rule, which was embodied in the now repealed section 1 (1) *a* of the British Nationality and Status of Aliens Act, 1914, was as follows:

The following persons shall be deemed to be natural-born British subjects, namely:

(a) Any person born within His Majesty's dominions and allegiance; [Note the words 'and allegiance'.]

It is now contained, so far as concerns persons born on or after 1 January 1949, in section 4 of the British Nationality Act, 1948, and is as follows:

4. Subject to the provisions of this section, every person born within the United Kingdom and Colonies after the commencement of this Act shall be a citizen of the United Kingdom and Colonies by birth:

---

[1] Its correct title since the Act of 1948 entered into force is the 'Status of Aliens Act, 1914'.   [2] See below, p. 61, 'Descent'.   [3] See n. 2 on p. 61.
[4] See Mervyn Jones (1947), pp. 123–32.

Provided that a person shall not be such a citizen by virtue of this section if at the time of his birth—

(*a*) his father possesses such immunity from suit and legal process as is accorded to an envoy of a foreign sovereign power accredited to His Majesty, and is not a citizen of the United Kingdom and Colonies; or

(*b*) his father is an enemy alien and the birth occurs in a place then under occupation by the enemy.[1]

[Note the absence of the word 'allegiance'.]

It is necessary also to note the transitional provisions made by section 12 regarding persons who were British subjects immediately before 1 January 1949, when the Act of 1948 came into force. The principal provision is contained in section 12 (1) as follows:

A person who was a British subject immediately before the date of the commencement of this Act shall on that date become a citizen of the United Kingdom and Colonies if he possesses any of the following qualifications, that is to say—

(*a*) that he was born within the territories comprised at the commencement of this Act in the United Kingdom and Colonies, and would have been such citizen if Section four of this Act had been in force at the time of his birth;

(*b*) that he is a person naturalized in the United Kingdom and Colonies;

(*c*) that he became a British subject by reason of the annexation of any territory included at the commencement of this Act in the United Kingdom and Colonies.

The effect of section 12 (8) is to assimilate persons within this provision to the category of citizens by birth.

Birth on British territory (not under enemy occupation)[2] *of an enemy father who is at the time of the birth interned as a matter of precaution on British territory.* Later we shall submit the opinion that both interned enemy civilians (at any rate when not interned by reason of action hostile to this country) and prisoners of war *stricto sensu* are within the King's protection and enjoy, except the right to sue out a writ of *habeas corpus*, full procedural status and as much personal and proprietary status as the enemy who is at large. The enemy civilian when he came to this country voluntarily placed himself within the King's protection and voluntarily undertook local allegiance to him. Why should later internment destroy his local allegiance to the Crown? If during internment he conspired against the Crown, say, by corrupting his guards, or aided the Crown's enemies by showing lights to guide enemy aircraft, would he not be guilty of

---

[1] See chapter 17 ('Belligerent Occupation').

[2] As to birth on territory under belligerent occupation, see later, chapter 17.

treason?[1] The children born on British territory of a father who is an interned enemy civilian are natural-born British subjects, for they are not excluded from British citizenship by the proviso contained in section 4 of the Act of 1948. We are inclined to add that for this purpose it makes no difference whether the internment was a matter of precaution or resulted from his hostile action.

Birth on British territory (not under enemy occupation)[2] *of an enemy father who at the time of the birth is a prisoner of war on British territory.* The case of the children of the prisoner of war *stricto sensu* was formerly not so clear. The father is certainly within the King's protection for procedural purposes. We are told in *Calvin's* case[3] that 'if an alien enemy come to invade this realm, and be taken in war, he cannot be indicted of treason; for the indictment cannot conclude *contra ligeant' suae debitum,* for he never was in the protection of the King, nor ever owed any manner of ligeance unto him...'. But our question is whether an enemy member of enemy forces taken in action against this country (whether within this country or outside it) and imprisoned in this country can be said to owe local allegiance to the Crown *from the moment of his imprisonment* on British territory. If taken within this country, he was sent here by order of his Government; if taken without this country, he was brought here against his will, unless it can be said that one who surrenders or is surrendered by his superior officer is thereby deemed to enter this country voluntarily and undertake local allegiance to the Crown. It is true that in *Sparenburgh* v. *Bannatyne*[4] Heath J. said of a prisoner of war:[5] 'If he conspires against the life of the King, it is high treason'; but this was not essential to the judgment of the Court, which rested on the King's protection, and moreover the prisoner of war in question was not an enemy subject but a neutral subject, of whom Eyre C.J. said:[6] 'But a neutral, whether in or out of prison, cannot, for that reason, be an alien enemy; he can be alien enemy only with respect to what he is doing under a local or temporary allegiance to a power at war with us. When the allegiance determines, the character determines.' We incline to the view that the child born at any time before 1949 in this country of a father of enemy nationality who is a prisoner of war is not a natural-born British subject, but that, if he is so born after 1948, it is arguable on two grounds that he is a natural-born British subject: (i) because proviso (*b*) in section 4 of the Act of 1948 only

---

[1] It is worth noting that 'treachery' under the Treachery Act, 1940, does not depend upon allegiance, whereas treason does: see Turner's 18th ed. of Kenny's *Outline of Criminal Law*, pp. 387 and 396.   [2] See later, ch. 17.   [3] (1608) 7 Co. Rep. 1*a*, 6*b*.   [4] (1797) 1 Bos. & P. 163.   [5] At p. 171.   [6] At p. 168.

excludes from British nationality a person whose father is an enemy alien and who is born 'in a place then under occupation by the enemy', and (ii) unlike section 1 of the Act of 1914, does not speak of birth within Her Majesty's 'allegiance'.[1] It is arguable that a prisoner of war of neutral nationality is deemed to be an enemy national by reason of his adherence to the enemy.

Birth on British territory of a father of enemy nationality who is at the time of the birth on enemy territory. Such a child is not born within the allegiance of the Crown, for to be born within the allegiance he must be born of a father owing allegiance, and we submit that, if born at any time before 1949, he is not a natural-born British subject; if born after 1948, the argument submitted above upon section 4 may make him also a natural-born British subject in addition to any other nationality that he may acquire.

Birth on British territory under enemy occupation. We shall deal with this and section 4, proviso (*b*), of the Act of 1948 in chapter 17 ('Belligerent Occupation').

(*b*) Descent

Section 5 of the Act of 1948 so far applies the principle of the *jus sanguinis* as to permit the automatic descent of citizenship of the United Kingdom and Colonies for one generation in the male line. That is to say, a child born outside the United Kingdom and Colonies always becomes a citizen at his birth if at that time his father is himself such a citizen by some means other than descent (i.e. by birth, registration, naturalization, adoption, etc.). The operation of this rule is not affected by the existence of a state of war at the time of the birth between the United Kingdom and the country in which the birth occurs. Nor is citizenship acquired in virtue of this rule affected by the subsequent outbreak of war even if the person concerned is still an infant.

It seems that a child born on enemy territory of a British father who satisfied the conditions of section 1 (*b*) of the Act of 1914, or, after 1948, satisfies the conditions of section 5 of the Act of 1948, is a British subject or citizen by descent.

Descent through the mother is not recognized by the law of the United Kingdom and Colonies,[2] but is admitted in some Common-

---

[1] Mervyn Jones (1947), p. 130; Parry, *Nationality*, p. 127.

[2] There is one case in which the law of the United Kingdom attaches consequences to female descent; for the British Nationality (No. 2) Act, 1964, provides in s. 2 (1) that a person who would otherwise be stateless shall be a United Kingdom citizen if born in the United Kingdom of a mother being then such a citizen.

wealth countries, e.g. Ghana, under the Ghana, Nationality and Citizenship Act, 1957, s. 8.

(c) *Registration*

Registration, under the British Nationality Acts, 1948–64, is the counterpart, in relation to citizens of the other countries of the Commonwealth (and of the Republic of Ireland), of the naturalization of aliens. But it is also the method whereby women who have married citizens of the United Kingdom and Colonies and minors, as well as certain transitional classes of British subjects or former British subjects, may acquire United Kingdom citizenship.

Registration is available as of right in the United Kingdom and Colonies to (1) citizens of other countries of the Commonwealth or of Ireland ordinarily resident in the United Kingdom and Colonies or in Crown service under the United Kingdom and Colonies,[1] and (2) women who have been married to citizens.[2] It may be granted by the Secretary of State at discretion to (3) minors,[3] and (4) the transitional classes of British subjects referred to.[4] And it should be noted that, where a person has once renounced or been deprived of citizenship of the United Kingdom and Colonies, he can usually only reacquire it by registration with the approval of the Secretary of State.[5]

(d) *Naturalization*

This means of acquiring British citizenship is now regulated by the Act of 1948 and particularly by section 10 and the Second Schedule to the Act. The Secretary of State has a discretion either to grant or refuse a certificate of naturalization. There is now no rule of law which precludes the naturalization of an alien enemy in time of war. It should be noticed that registration has, under the Act of 1948, replaced naturalization as the method whereby minors may be granted British nationality at discretion.[6] But naturalization,

---

[1] British Nationality Act, 1948, s. 6 (1). The provisions of this section have been seriously modified by the Commonwealth Immigrants Act, 1962, s. 12 (2) so that an aggregate period of five years residence and/or Crown service is now requisite before the right to registration can be exercised, though this period may be shortened at discretion.

[2] British Nationality Act, 1948, s. 6 (2); and see British Nationality Act, 1965.

[3] *Ibid.* s. 7. The British Nationality (No. 2) Act, 1964, passed to enable the United Kingdom to implement the United Nations Convention for the Reduction of Statelessness, adds another but inconsiderable class of persons entitled to registration as of right.

[4] British Nationality Act, 1948, s. 12 (4); British Nationality Act, 1958, s. 3; British Nationality Act, 1964, s. 1; British Nationality (No. 2) Act, 1964, s. 1.

[5] British Nationality Act, 1948, s. 6 (3), upon which a slight qualification has been made by the British Nationality Act, 1964, s. 1.

[6] S. 7.

and not registration, is the method available to British protected persons, though these are no longer aliens in terms of the law of the United Kingdom and Colonies.[1]

Territorial scope of naturalization. It must not be assumed that British naturalization produces effects throughout all the countries belonging to the Commonwealth. In each case it is necessary to examine the certificate of naturalization and the legislative enactment under which it was granted. Since 1948 a certificate of naturalization granted by the United Kingdom makes the grantee (section 10 of the Act of 1948) 'a citizen of the United Kingdom and Colonies'. The other countries of the Commonwealth have their own provisions for naturalization.[2]

(e) Annexation or incorporation[3] of territory

This does not appear to call for comment beyond saying that if the annexation has followed upon a war in which the United Kingdom was a party, the inhabitants of the territory annexed by the United Kingdom would normally have ceased to be enemies before a valid annexation could take place.

(f) Adoption and legitimation

These modes of acquiring British nationality or the citizenship of the United Kingdom and Colonies are described in the following passage in Mervyn Jones (1956):[4]

Adoption, legitimation, and recognition of paternity[5] are titles by which nationality is acquired under the laws of many states. Adoption is now a source of British nationality under the law of the United Kingdom,[6] but the same result may be achieved under the laws of other countries by treating an adopted child, for the purposes of the *jus sanguinis*, as a legitimate child.[7] Legitimation and recognition of paternity are formal processes by

---

[1] S. 10. During the War of 1939–45 there were many persons of enemy nationality living in this country who were technically known as 'victims of Nazi oppression', and a number of them received certificates of naturalization during the war. This practice was suspended; and a Press Notice was issued on 11 November 1940: see pp. 18, 19 of the 3rd edition of this book.

[2] Upon the local character of naturalization granted by Australia in 1908, see *Markwald's* case; and see Van Pittius, particularly chapters VI and XVIII.

[3] Section 11 of the Act of 1948 empowers the Crown to specify by Order in Council the persons who shall become citizens of the United Kingdom and Colonies.

[4] Pp. 11, 12.

[5] Recognition of paternity does not have this effect in the United Kingdom.

[6] Section 16 (1) Adoption Act, 1950, now section 19 (1) of Adoption Act, 1958.

[7] See section 5 (1) of the Nationality and Citizenship Act, 1948, of Australia, and Article 2 (4) of the Chinese Nationality Law, 1929, Flournoy and Hudson, *A Collection of Nationality Laws* (1929), p. 175. A third possibility is to treat adoption as a connection constituting a basis for naturalization: section 11 (2) of the Canadian Citizenship Act, 1946, as re-enacted in 1950.

which, under some systems of law, a child acquires, for nationality purposes, the same status as a legitimate child. Apart from these cases which are, in reality, merely other forms of adoption, there is quasi-adoption into a family, as where an alien, by marrying a Japanese woman, became head of her family, and *ipso facto* a Japanese national.[1]

The connection between these modes and the effect of war will be mentioned later[2] under 'Minor children'.

COMPULSORY LOSS OF BRITISH CITIZENSHIP

If war breaks out between the United Kingdom and a State whose nationality was held by a British naturalized citizen immediately prior to his naturalization, his British citizenship is not *ipso facto* affected. There are, however, circumstances in which he, like other naturalized citizens, may be deprived of his British citizenship, by an order of the appropriate Secretary of State.

During the last few decades before the war of 1914–18 national feeling in England was becoming intensified, and the traditional welcome extended to foreigners who for one reason or another, not necessarily political, did not wish to remain in their native countries, was being abandoned. The Aliens Act, 1905, may be mentioned, and the gradually increasing precariousness of British nationality acquired by naturalization points to the same conclusion. The Naturalization Act, 1870, repealed by the Status of Aliens Act of 1914, contained no provision for the revocation of a certificate of naturalization, and was content to assume that the Home Secretary would only grant certificates after adequate consideration. By the Act of 1914, section 7, the Secretary of State could revoke a certificate which appeared to him to have been obtained by 'false representation or fraud'. The Act of 1918, now repealed, added further grounds, and now section 20 ('Deprivation of Citizenship') of the Act of 1948 empowers the Secretary of State to deprive a naturalized person of his British citizenship if he is satisfied that (*inter alia*) he '(*a*) has shown himself by act or speech to be disloyal or disaffected towards His Majesty; or (*b*) has, during any war in which His Majesty was engaged, unlawfully traded or communicated with an enemy or been engaged in or associated with any business that was to his knowledge carried on in such a manner as to assist an enemy in that war...'.

The Secretary of State must also be 'satisfied that it is not conducive to the public good that that person should continue to be a citizen of the United Kingdom and Colonies' (subsection 5).

Flournoy and Hudson, *op. cit.* p. 382.   [2] Below, p. 68.

VOLUNTARY LOSS OF NATIONALITY

In addition to the compulsory loss of nationality by revocation of naturalization or deprivation of citizenship, provision now exists for voluntary loss. The common law rule *nemo potest exuere patriam* was abrogated by the Naturalization Act, 1870, which was repealed by the Status of Aliens Act of 1914. Sections 13–16 of the Act of 1914 contained provisions for the voluntary loss of British nationality and were repealed by the Act of 1948.

Section 19 of the Act of 1948, read with section 2 of the British Nationality Act, 1964, enables a citizen of the United Kingdom, if of full age and capacity, who is either already in addition a citizen of some other country within or without the Commonwealth, or who satisfies the Secretary of State that he is about to become such, to divest himself of his United Kingdom citizenship by declaration. A declaration to this end becomes ineffective unless within six months the person making it actually does become a citizen of another country. And no declaration is effective until registered, a point which may be seen to be important in the present context since during any war in which the Crown is engaged registration may be withheld by the Secretary of State in the case of any person who is a national of a foreign country.

Power of a British citizen to acquire the nationality of an enemy State

From *R. v. Lynch*[1] it appears that a British subject who in 1900 in time of war with traitorous intentions attempted to acquire the nationality of an enemy State by naturalization therein did not lose his British nationality, whether or not he succeeded in obtaining enemy nationality under the law of the enemy country. Lynch's attempt to become naturalized was itself an act of treason and was ineffective to bring into operation section 6 of the Naturalization Act, 1870, whereby British nationality would then have been lost automatically and he would thereafter be 'deemed to have ceased to be a British subject and be regarded as an alien'. The King's Bench Division in Lynch's trial at bar held that there was nothing in the Naturalization Act, 1870, 'to justify the contention that an act of treason can give any rights to any person whatever'; but the court did not expressly decide (and it was unnecessary to decide)

---

[1] [1903] 1 K.B. 444, 458; Mervyn Jones (1947), pp. 68, n. 1, 129, 200, 203; (1956), p. 207; Parry, *Nationality*, pp. 42, 161, 162; and see later p. 69 for *Freyberger's* case and *Gschwind* v. *Huntington*.

that a British subject could not become naturalized in an enemy State in time of war so far as English law was concerned, at least when (as now) the act of foreign naturalization did not automatically divest the subject of British nationality.[1] The British Nationality Act, 1948, contains no provision equivalent to section 6 of the Act of 1870. Under section 19 of the Act of 1948 a citizen of the United Kingdom and Colonies of full age and capacity who is also a national of a foreign country can make a declaration in the prescribed manner of renunciation of that citizenship; upon registration of this declaration by the Secretary of State, the declarant ceases to be a citizen of the United Kingdom and Colonies, but the Secretary of State may withhold registration during a war if the declarant is a national of a foreign country. Thus now the naturalization of a British citizen in a foreign country does not automatically involve loss of his British citizenship. Accordingly, it would seem that now, while it would still be an act of treason for a British citizen during war to acquire enemy nationality, whether or not he attempted to renounce his British citizenship, his declaration of renunciation would not be effective unless and until the Secretary of State has registered it. If we may invoke an expression used by Mr Justice Holmes in 1920 with regard to a judgment in favour of an alien enemy, there is nothing 'mysteriously noxious',[2] and nothing illegal, in a change of nationality involving a crossing of the line of war when it takes place under the control, or by the direct act, of the United Kingdom Government.[3] During the war of 1939–45, and even during hostilities, there were many cases of enemy refugees acquiring British nationality by naturalization.

Fasbender v. *Attorney-General*[4] in 1922 showed that a female British subject could during war contract a marriage in good faith with an enemy subject and thereby lose her British, and acquire enemy, nationality. In the case of *In re Chamberlain's Settlement* it was contended upon the authority of *R.* v. *Lynch* that an attempt by a British subject to become naturalized in Germany in 1916 was of no effect, but it became unnecessary to decide this question because it was held that, whether or not he thereby ceased to be a British subject, he

---

[1] In the judgment it was not held that Lynch did in fact become naturalized in the South African Republic; Lord Alverstone C.J. spoke of 'the alleged naturalization', and Wills J. referred to 'the letters of naturalization, if they were valid'.

[2] *Birge-Forbes Co.* v. *Heye*: A.D. [1919–1922] at p. 404.

[3] In *R.* v. *Home Secretary, ex parte L.*, there was no act of the British Government recognizing that the applicant for a writ of *habeas corpus* had ceased to be an enemy subject.

[4] See later, p. 340.

66

certainly became a 'German national' according to German law and was a German national for the purposes of the Treaty of Peace and Orders in Council made under the Treaty of Peace Act, 1919, to give effect to it, so that his property in England was liable to forfeiture thereunder.

Naturalization in a non-enemy State[1]

We are not aware that an English Court has ever found it necessary to pronounce upon the effect of an attempt by a British subject to become naturalized in a non-enemy State in time of war. In *Johnstone* v. *Pedlar* the plaintiff, a natural-born British subject, had become an American citizen by naturalization in January 1916, that is, during a war in which the United States were then neutral. The validity of this naturalization was not questioned either in the House of Lords or in the two Irish Courts. It was a very material point because the defence of 'Act of State' could not have been pleaded against a British subject in respect of an act done on British territory. In the light of section 19 of the Act of 1948 referred to above it seems that today the plaintiff in *Johnstone* v. *Pedlar* would not have ceased to be British unless and until the Secretary of State had registered his declaration of renunciation of British citizenship.

MARRIED WOMEN AND MINOR CHILDREN

Between the date of the Naturalization Act, 1870, and 1 January 1949, when the British Nationality Act, 1948, came into force, the general principle, subject to some exceptions, was that a married woman was deemed to be a subject of the State of which her husband was for the time being a subject. Since 1 January 1949 an alien woman who marries a United Kingdom citizen acquires that citizenship only if she makes an application therefor to the Secretary of State and takes the oath of allegiance, whereupon she becomes a United Kingdom citizen by registration. Conversely, before 1 January 1949, a British woman who married an alien husband automatically lost her British nationality provided that by her marriage she acquired his nationality. The British Nationality Act, 1948, also contains certain transitional provisions which need not be discussed here.

By reason of the Act of 1948 the United Kingdom Government

---

[1] For a claim by a British subject that he had ceased to be British because Eire had, by the Constitution of Ireland, 1937, seceded from the British Commonwealth of Nations, see *Murray* v. *Parkes*.

5-2

has been able to ratify the Convention on the Nationality of Married Women, of 20 February 1957.[1]

As a result of the Act of 1948 the nationality of a married woman, so far as concerns British law, is independent of that of her husband, and this is so whether she was married before or after the end of the year 1948. Accordingly, the question whether upon the outbreak of war or during war he is or becomes an alien enemy is irrelevant to the question of her national status, though of course she might be affected by emergency regulations concerned with association with an alien enemy.

Minor children, before 1 January 1949, followed their father's nationality in the event of it being changed, and so, if he became an alien enemy they also became alien enemies. Now, as Mervyn Jones says, 'minors cannot... be naturalized, and the action of their parents cannot cause them to lose their citizenship'.[2] So if the effect of the outbreak of war is to make their father or mother an alien enemy their national status is unaffected, whether they were born before or after the end of 1948.

DUAL NATIONALITY[3]

Our law recognizes the fact of dual (and even plural) nationality, which can arise in several ways, for instance (*jure soli*) by the birth on British territory of the child of a foreign father whose State adopts the *jus sanguinis* and attaches its nationality to the children of its nationals born abroad. War may introduce serious complications into the life of a dual national.

(1) Either of the States whose national he is can call upon him

---

[1] The principal articles are as follows:

'Article 1. Each Contracting State agrees that neither the celebration nor the dissolution of a marriage between one of its nationals and an alien, nor the change of nationality by the husband during marriage, shall automatically affect the nationality of the wife.

'Article 2. Each Contracting State agrees that neither the voluntary acquisition of the nationality of another State nor the renunciation of its nationality by one of its nationals shall prevent the retention of its nationality by the wife of such national.

'Article 3. 1. Each Contracting State agrees that the alien wife of one of its nationals may, at her request, acquire the nationality of her husband through specially privileged naturalization procedures; the grant of such nationality may be subject to such limitations as may be imposed in the interests of national security or public policy.

'2. Each Contracting State agrees that the present Convention shall not be construed as affecting any legislation or judicial practice by which the alien wife of one of its nationals may, at her request, acquire her husband's nationality as a matter of right.'

[2] (1956), p. 84; British Nationality Act, 1948, s. 7.

[3] Oppenheim, I, §§ 308–310*a*; Bar-Yaacov, *Dual Nationality* (1961), in particular pp. 210–38. Third States in dealing with a dual national must have regard to the provisions of the Hague Convention of 1930 on Certain Questions Relating to the Conflict of Nationality Laws if they have ratified it (as the United Kingdom has), and in particular the provisions of Article 5.

to perform military or other service, even against the other, though in practice we have sometimes mercifully assigned non-combatant duties to a person holding both British and enemy nationality; if such a person is taken in arms against Her Majesty, his enemy nationality will not protect him on a prosecution for treason.[1]

(2) A state of war places certain limitations upon the right of the person having dual nationality, British and another, to divest himself of the former. The Court of Appeal in *Freyberger's* case[2] construing section 14 of the Act of 1914 (which provided that the person making a declaration of alienage 'shall cease to be a British subject') stated that such a person 'cannot during a state of war divest himself of his allegiance to the British Crown in order to become solely the subject of an enemy State'. So a man who was born in the United Kingdom (and so became a British subject by English law) of parents who were Austrian subjects (so that, as was assumed by the Court, he became and remained an Austrian subject) was held to be not entitled to make a valid declaration of alienage on attaining the age of twenty-one years. He had been compulsorily enlisted in the British Army when twenty years of age, and on reaching his twenty-first birthday purported to make a declaration of alienage and claimed his discharge. The Court of Appeal was of opinion that section 14 of what was then the British Nationality and Status of Aliens Act of 1914 must be construed subject to general principles of law, amongst which they included that illustrated by *R. v. Lynch* to the effect that a British subject (in *Lynch's* case there was no question of dual nationality) cannot, when the British Empire is at war, become a subject of an enemy State and divest himself of his British nationality.[3] *Freyberger's* case was followed in *Gschwind v. Huntington*,[4]

---

[1] A Protocol of 1930 (T.S. No. 22 (1937)) which has been ratified or acceded to by a considerable number of States, including the United Kingdom and the United States of America, and described as 'Relating to Military Obligations in Certain Cases of Double Nationality', contains provisions which mitigate the lot of a dual national subject to military obligations in one or more States.

It is believed that this Protocol would not be abrogated by the outbreak of war in which one or both of the countries referred to in Article 1 were involved; if in spite of it such a British subject was taken in arms against Her Majesty, the Protocol would not protect him on a prosecution for treason. The object of the Protocol is to protect a person against the burden of double obligations of military service and does not affect his allegiance.

There is also a Convention of 6 May 1963, entitled a Convention on Reduction of Cases of Multiple Nationality and Military Obligations in Cases of Multiple Nationality, which has so far been signed by the United Kingdom, Austria, France, Germany, Italy, the Netherlands, Norway, and Belgium.

[2] [1917] 2 K.B. at p. 139. Article 278 of the Treaty of Versailles of 1919 deserves note. See comment in Parry, *Nationality*, pp. 161–2.

[3] [1917] 2 K.B. at p. 132; see also *Sawyer v. Kropp*.

[4] See also *Vecht v. Taylor* and *Dawson v. Meuli*.

where the dual national was British and Swiss, that is, the citizen of a neutral State, and the latter is a stronger case in the respect that the dual national, though subject to the operation of the Military Service Acts, had not actually become a member of the armed forces. In both these cases the dual national had already become subject to the operation of the Military Service Acts. Now, as we have seen,[1] the Secretary of State may withhold registration of a declaration made by any dual national, who is the national of a foreign country, whether enemy or not, while the United Kingdom is involved in war.

Summing up the present position of the dual national during a war in which the United Kingdom is involved,

(*a*) if he is both a citizen of the United Kingdom and Colonies and an enemy national, he is, as a matter of law, liable in his former capacity to the military and other obligations of such citizens and in his latter capacity to internment and similar measures;

(*b*) if he is both a citizen of the United Kingdom and Colonies and the national of a non-enemy foreign State (be it neutral or allied or merely associated with us in the war) he is liable to the military and other obligations of a United Kingdom citizen;

(*c*) if he is both a United Kingdom citizen and the national of a foreign country, whether enemy or not, registration of a renunciation of United Kingdom citizenship by him may be withheld during the war;

(*d*) if he possesses the nationalities of an enemy State and a non-enemy foreign State, we can treat him either as an enemy national and apply to him internment and similar measures or as an alien friend and apply to him the milder measures appropriate to that condition.

(*e*) if he is both a United Kingdom citizen and a citizen of another Commonwealth country or of Ireland and also a foreign national, registration of renunciation of United Kingdom citizenship may again be withheld during war;

(*f*) if, though not a United Kingdom citizen, he is still a British subject or is to be treated as such because he is a citizen of another Commonwealth country or of Ireland, and if he is also a national of a foreign country, he will also fall under head (*a*) or (*b*) above, according to whether that foreign country is enemy or non-enemy.

Dual nationality is not half one nationality and half another, but two complete nationalities and in time of war verily a *damnosa hereditas*. As Ridley J. said in *Ex parte Freyberger*,[2] 'such a person "is not half a subject of one State and half of another State...he is completely a subject of each State"'.

---

[1] P. 65 above.   [2] [1917] 2 K.B. 129, 135.

ALIEN STATUS

Section 27 (1) (still in force) of the Status of Aliens Act, 1914, provides that in this Act, unless the context otherwise requires, '"alien" means a person who is not a British subject', and the interpretation section (32) of the Act of 1948, provides that '"Alien" means a person who is not a British subject, a British protected person or a citizen of Eire'.[1]

In what respect does an alien differ in status from a British subject? It is natural to regard the latter's status as complete[2] and to describe the former's by way of deduction from it. The alien has full proprietary capacity, full contractual, testamentary, and procedural[3] capacity, but no parliamentary or municipal franchise, and no qualification for any public office. He owes local allegiance while within the realm, even when the United Kingdom is at war with his own country, and thus may be convicted of treason for assisting his own country while he is within the United Kingdom.[4] He has no right at common law or by statute to be admitted into the United Kingdom,[5] and the Aliens Restriction Acts, 1914 and 1919,[6] authorize the making of provision for the exclusion and expulsion of undesirable aliens. These provisions are, however, it is believed, purely declaratory, and the Crown can exclude or expel[7] an alien at will. A British subject can neither be excluded nor expelled;[8] and statutory

[1] The three principal Acts regulating the status of aliens are: (i) the Status of Aliens Act, 1914, which is the present title of the British Nationality and Status of Aliens Act, 1914 (see the Fourth Schedule, Part II, of the British Nationality Act, 1948); (ii) the Aliens Restriction Act, 1914, and (iii) the Aliens Restriction (Amendment) Act, 1919. The principal Order is now the Aliens Order, 1953 (1953, no. 1671). On the history, see McNair, *Opinions*, II, pp. 99–137.

[2] A denizen is only partially a British subject. By denization the Crown used in former times to confer by grant of letters patent a certain measure of nationality (see Holdsworth, *History of English Law*, IX, p. 77) and the royal prerogative was preserved by section 25 of the Act of 1914; that section has been repealed by the Act of 1948, which does not repeat the reservation. But is a reservation necessary? See Craies, *Statute Law*, 6th ed., ch. 16 and 17.

[3] Including, at any rate when in England, the remedy of *habeas corpus* (see the *Amand* cases discussed later at pp. 436–8), unless he is an enemy prisoner of war (see later, pp. 94–5).

[4] And see *Joyce* v. *Director of Public Prosecutions*; see also, on an alien's local allegiance, *In re P. an Infant*, and note in *Law Journal*, 12 February 1965, p. 104.

[5] *Musgrove* v. *Chung Teeong Toy*; *Attorney-General of Canada* v. *Cain*.

[6] There were some cases during and after the First World War in which the courts had to consider whether certain persons who had formerly had an enemy nationality should be treated as alien enemies on the ground that they might have certain vestigial rights of resuming their former nationality: *Ex parte Weber*; *Ex parte Liebmann*; *Stoeck* v. *Public Trustee*; and see pp. 29, 32, of 3rd ed. of this book.

[7] See Oppenheim, I, §§ 323, 324; *Netz* v. *Ede*. As to the effect of liability to deportation upon the acquisition of a domicile of choice: see *Boldrini* v. *Boldrini* and *May* v. *May and Lehmann*.

[8] Blackstone's *Commentaries*, I, 137. Under Defence Regulations, however, the entry of

authority was required for the compulsory transportation of convicted criminals from the United Kingdom, although their destination was within the British Empire.

Lord Atkinson in a Canadian appeal[1] to the Privy Council stated that

one of the rights possessed by the supreme power in every State is the right to refuse to permit an alien to enter that State, to annex what conditions it pleases to the permission to enter it, and to expel or deport from the State, at pleasure, even a friendly alien, especially if it considers his presence in the State opposed to its peace, order, and good government, or to its social or material interests.

The Aliens Restriction (Amendment) Act, 1919, regulates (*inter alia*) both the exclusion and the expulsion of aliens. With regard to expulsion or deportation—the latter term is said to connote some control over the destination—questions have sometimes arisen upon the claim, amounting almost to a necessity, of the Crown in the exercise of this right to impose a certain measure of extra-territorial restraint upon the alien. Blackstone[2] says that aliens are 'liable to be sent home whenever the king sees occasion', and both in *A.-G. for Canada* v. *Cain* and *R.* v. *Home Secretary, ex parte Duke of Chateau Thierry*,[3] arising upon statutes and regulations thereunder, the Privy Council in the former case, and the Court of Appeal in the latter, in effect justified extra-territorial constraint. The constraint was direct in the former case and indirect in the latter, where the Home Secretary was permitted to select the ship (and incidentally control the alien's destination) and to place the alien on board so that

when on board he remains in legal custody until the ship finally leaves the United Kingdom, and then the custody of and right to detain the alien ceases. It is quite possible that the result of action under this provision may be that the deportee from the force of circumstances may be compelled to disembark in the country to which the Government wish him to go.[4]

The right of the United Kingdom Government to select the ship or aircraft and thus indirectly control the destination of the alien being expelled or deported was again considered, and was affirmed, in *Ex parte Sacksteder* [1918] 1 K.B. 598, 591 and (at any rate by

certain British subjects may be controlled; and see also the significant restrictions on entry imposed by the Commonwealth Immigrants Act, 1962.

[1] *A.G. for Canada* v. *Cain* [1906] A.C. 542, 546.
[2] *Commentaries*, 1. 260.   [3] [1917] 1 K.B. 922 (C.A.).
[4] *Ibid.* at p. 934.

implication) *Ex parte Soblen*. See letters in *The Times*, 11 September 1962, and neighbouring dates; Fawcett in *The Listener*, 14 February 1963; Thornberry, 12 *I.C.L.Q.* (1963), pp. 414–74 (particularly on the nineteenth century); A.L.G. in 79 *L.Q.R* (1963), pp. 41, 44–8. The tendency to confuse deportation with extradition should be noted.

The Aliens Restriction (Amendment) Act 1919,[1] imposed a number of disabilities upon aliens, some of which were removed by the now repealed Former Enemy Aliens (Disabilities Removal) Act, 1925, but many still remain, for instance, in connection with shipping.[2]

Act of State.[3] The friendly alien resident in the United Kingdom is entitled to the benefit of the rule that the defence known as 'act of State' cannot be pleaded against him by the Crown or by a Government official,[4] though that is a valid defence against an alien resident abroad,[5] who is thereupon referred to any remedy there may be through the diplomatic channel. Thus, as Holdsworth pointed out,[6] the common law, having recognized by the end of the sixteenth century the right of the friendly alien in our midst to sue in tort, permitted him to participate in one of the logical consequences of the subsequently developed doctrine of ministerial responsibility— a remarkable instance of the liberality of our legal institutions.

Human Rights. Moreover, the States parties to the European Convention for the Protection of Human Rights and Fundamental Freedoms[7] of 1950, which include the United Kingdom, have undertaken by Article 1 that

The High Contracting Parties shall secure to *everyone* [italics ours] within their jurisdiction the rights and freedoms defined in Section 1 of this Convention.

Section 1 is in effect an extensive code of human rights and freedoms.

---

[1] As amended or supplemented by Defence Regulations.

[2] Temperley, *Merchant Shipping Acts* (6th ed. 1965), index.

[3] McNair, *Opinions*, I, pp. 111–17; distinguish the American meaning of this term and the doctrine associated with it: see American Law Institute's Restatement of 'Foreign Relations Law', § 41.

[4] *Johnstone* v. *Pedlar*.

[5] *Buron* v. *Denman*; *Johnstone* v. *Pedlar*, in the Irish Court of Appeal. Whether the defence is only available against the alien resident abroad in the case of an act done abroad is not yet clear—*Commercial and Estates Co. of Egypt* v. *Board of Trade* [1925] 1 K.B. at pp. 290, 297; and Oppenheim, I, § 148 (*n*).

[6] *History of English Law*, IX, pp. 97, 98; including resort to the historic writ of *habeas corpus*; *Ex parte Soblen*.

[7] T.S. no. 71 (1953); Cmd 8969.

STATELESSNESS

It was not until 1921 that an English Court was squarely faced with the question whether English law recognized the condition of statelessness, though English international lawyers such as Hall[1] and Oppenheim[2] had asserted that condition to be recognized by international law without throwing any doubt upon its recognition by English law. Then Russell J. in *Stoeck* v. *Public Trustee*, after mentioning an *obiter* statement to the contrary by Phillimore L.J. in *Ex parte Weber*,[3] unhesitatingly pronounced in favour of its recognition, and this view is now generally accepted. Stateless persons are aliens, because, as we have seen, section 27 (1) of the consolidated Act provides that 'In this Act, unless the context otherwise requires... the expression "alien" means a person who is not a British subject'; and the interpretation Section (32) of the British Nationality Act, 1948, provides that '"Alien" means a person who is not a British subject, a British protected person or a citizen of Eire'.[4]

In recent decades the manufacture of stateless persons has been speeded up, for instance, by wholesale measures[5] of denationalization upon political, racial and religious grounds.[6] At the same time something has been done for the protection of these persons—now increasingly also 'refugees'—for instance, by means of certain Conventions and Protocols emanating from the Hague Codification Conference of 1930 upon Nationality (amongst other matters); the Convention of 28 October 1933, relating to the International Status of Refugees, under which Nansen passports were issued;[7] and by the Convention of 25 July 1951, on the Status of Refugees. Thus the stateless person's original disadvantage of having no State to look to for protection has to some extent been mitigated, and the status has become less of an abnormality. Moreover, the European Convention on Human Rights referred to above embraces him within its scope.

---

[1] (7th ed.), § 74.　　　　　　　　　[2] (8th ed.), I, §§ 311–313*a*.

[3] [1916] I K.B. 280, 283.

[4] 'For the criterion of alienage is lack of the status of a British national' (Parry, *Nationality*, p. 9). For a Belgian decision in which a stateless person was regarded as coming within the expression 'Belgian, Allied or neutral persons', see *Marquet* v. *Office des Séquestres*.

[5] See Fischer Williams in 8 *B.Y.* (1927), pp. 45–61, and Abel in 6 *Modern Law Review* (1942), pp. 57–68.

[6] An enemy decree made during war and purporting to make enemy nationals stateless will not be recognized by British Courts—at any rate during the war: *R.* v. *Home Secretary, Ex parte L.*, and note in 61 *L.Q.R.* (1945), p. 126, and *Lowenthal* v. *Attorney-General*.

[7] See Oppenheim, I, § 313, for some description of these Conventions.

EFFECT OF OUTBREAK OF WAR UPON ALIENS

We have already discussed the meaning of 'war', and we must now consider how the outbreak of war affects the status of aliens, including stateless persons.

First of all, it divides aliens into (1) *Alien Enemies*, and (2) *Alien Friends*, with sometimes, as in the First and Second World Wars, a further subdivision of alien friends into (*a*) allies and (*b*) neutrals.[1] With alien friends, whether neutrals or allies,[2] when resident in their own countries, our law has little concern except—as the decisions of our Prize Court show—in so far as war affects them in their trading relations. As residents in our midst and litigants in our courts, war does not—apart from special statutes and administrative regulations —affect them except in the same way that it affects our own citizens. Among these special statutes are the Aliens Restriction Acts, 1914 and 1919. They arm the Executive with wide powers, in the event of war or 'an occasion of imminent national danger or great emergency', to regulate aliens—enemies or friends—as to landing, embarking, deportation, residence in certain districts, registration, change of abode, travelling, etc.; and such regulations may be made in relation to any particular class of aliens. Section 1 (4) of the Aliens Restriction Act of 1914 provides that a man is deemed to be an alien or an alien of a particular class until and unless he disproves it, so that if the police arrest any one and charge him with being an unregistered alien, the burden of proof lies upon him to show that he is not an alien.

[1] During the Second World War there were some political hybrids who described themselves as 'non-belligerents' or 'pre-belligerents'. 'Allies' means 'belligerent allies'. In the War of 1914 to 1918 the United States of America was not an Allied Power but an Associated Power. No doubt our Courts would treat the subject of a co-belligerent Associated Power as the subject of an Allied Power. The Allied Forces Act, 1940, now repealed, drew a distinction between allied and associated forces (section 1 (2)).

[2] The Allied Powers (War Service) Act, 1942, now repealed, empowered His Majesty to apply to the nationals of Allied Powers who were in Great Britain or subsequently entered it, the provisions of the National Service Acts, 1939 to 1941, as if they were British subjects and thus render them liable to service with the British Forces. 'Co-belligerent' can hardly be described as a technical term, but is used when the word 'ally' would for one reason or another be inappropriate. Thus in 1917 the Polish National Army, and in 1918 the Czechs and the Slovaks before they were recognized as a State, were called 'co-belligerents', and in 1943 the word was applied to Italy under the Badoglio Government fighting in association with the United Nations; see Oppenheim, II, § 76a, and *Re Scarpato*; and Parry, 31 B.Y. (1954), p. 437.

75

POSITION OF ALIEN ENEMIES

Let us now consider the position of alien enemies who happen to be in this country at the date of the outbreak of war. In ancient times the rule was that their persons could be seized and their goods confiscated by any one; they had no rights. The practice of making treaties stipulating for a right of exit to their own country led to what became almost a rule of international law permitting the departure within a reasonable time of all alien enemies who are not combatants, either active or reservists, in the enemy forces. There is no rule which requires a belligerent to allow enemy subjects to remain in his territory, and he is entitled to expel them if he chooses. If he allows them to remain, he is entitled to place restrictions upon their freedom such as are made under the Aliens Restriction Acts, 1914 and 1919, as amended by a number of Defence Regulations made in and after 1939. Numerous restrictions were made, partly as to all aliens, and partly as to alien enemies only, particularly as to registration and residence, notification of movements, and change of name, and as to the possession by alien enemies of certain articles, ranging from fire-arms to pigeons and cipher codes.

Having regard to the Aliens Restriction Acts, 1914 and 1919, and such of the Defence Regulations as have survived, and the comprehensive powers which they confer on the Executive or would confer on the Executive in the event of war, it is perhaps somewhat academic to consider what is the common law position. It is, however, interesting to notice an enlightened anticipation of subsequent practice contained in cap. 41 of Magna Carta,[1] dating from days before the idea of international law in the present sense had been conceived:

Merchant strangers in this realm...And if they be of a land making war against us and be found in our realms at the beginning of wars, they shall be attached without harm of body or goods until it be known to us or our Chief Justice how our merchants be intreated there in the land making war against us, and if our merchants be well intreated then theirs shall be likewise with us.[2]

---

[1] See Hague Convention VI (Status of Enemy Merchant Ships on the Outbreak of War), no longer binding on Great Britain, for a similar idea. Reciprocity is in practice a more valuable sanction in international relations than is commonly realized, particularly in the protection by Governments of their nationals in foreign countries. A minor illustration is afforded by S. 3 of the Diplomatic Privileges Act, 1964.

[2] Upon this Blackstone quotes the remark of Montesquieu that 'the English have made the protection of *foreign* merchants one of the articles of their *national* liberty' (*Commentaries*, 1, 260).

Definitions of alien enemy. Any definition of an 'alien enemy', if it is to be of any use at all, should state clearly the point of view from which the matter is approached. Broadly speaking, there are two main tests (the national and the territorial), and two main points of view from which, or purposes for which, a test is necessary. If we desire to ascertain a man's personal rights and liabilities, for instance, whether he is liable to be interned, whether he may live in a special area, or whether he comes under some particular clause of the Aliens Restriction Acts or Orders thereunder, then nationality is the main test. Of which State is he a national? To which State does he owe permanent allegiance? But if our object is to ascertain his position as a party to a contract, as a trader, as a litigant, as one with whom it is desired to have intercourse, personal or commercial, then our main test becomes his locality in some form or another. Sometimes this test takes the form of 'voluntary residence', sometimes 'the place where he carries on business', sometimes merely the place where he happens to be. If he is voluntarily present or resident or carrying on business in enemy or enemy-occupied territory, then, whatever his nationality may be, enemy, neutral, allied or British, or if he is stateless, he is an alien enemy for purposes of litigation and intercourse in the widest sense.

To put the matter shortly, it is lawful for a London tradesman to continue to supply goods to a customer of enemy nationality living in London. It is unlawful for a resident of London (without the permission of the United Kingdom Government) to continue to hold intercourse, personal or commercial, with a correspondent, even of British nationality, carrying on business or voluntarily present or resident or carrying on business in enemy or enemy-occupied territory.

These are very general statements. In the next chapter we shall examine in detail both the common law, and the statutory, definitions of 'enemy'.

3

PROCEDURAL STATUS OF
ALIEN ENEMIES

BIBLIOGRAPHY

Oppenheim, II, §§ 97–102.
Baty and Morgan, *War: its Conduct and Legal Results* (1915).
Page, *War and Alien Enemies* (1915).
Domke, *Trading with the Enemy in World War II* (1943).
Annual Practice (1965) *sub. tit.* Enemy.
Webber, *Effect of War on Contracts* (2nd ed. 1946), ch. IV.
Parry, 4 *Modern Law Review* (1941), pp. 161–82.
Fridman, 4 *I. and C.L.Q.* (1955), pp. 613–28.
Harris, 14 *I. and C.L.Q.* (1965), pp. 1360–70.

For the early history, see Appendix to second and third editions, and Holdsworth, *History of English Law*, Index volume, *sub. tit.* alien enemies, enemies, enemy character.

The main test of enemy character for the purpose of procedural status is a territorial one, not a national one. A person of any or no nationality voluntarily resident or present or carrying on business in territory owned or occupied by an enemy State is an enemy for procedural purposes.[1] An enemy national in British territory, who has complied with any requirements and restrictions imposed upon him as a matter of general policy, is deemed to have the permission of the Crown to be in this country and is said to be within the protection of the Crown; he is not an enemy for procedural purposes. We shall call him an enemy 'in protection'.

We shall now formulate and substantiate three general rules[2] and call attention to qualifications upon them later:

---

[1] For the position of Corporations, see below, pp. 102–4.

[2] The law of Scotland is substantially the same. A number of Scottish cases are reviewed by Lord Thankerton in *V/O Sovfracht* v. *N.V. Gebr. Van Udens Scheepvaart en Agentuur Maatschappij* [1943] A.C. 203, 214–17.

American practice. It is believed to be true to say that the rules governing the procedural status of alien enemies in the United States are, speaking broadly, similar to ours. But there are a number of cases where an action brought by an alien enemy plaintiff in the territorial sense has been allowed to proceed subject to the requirement that any sum recovered by him shall be paid to the Alien Enemy Custodian, whereas in similar circumstances in the United Kingdom the right of action would have been suspended until after the termination of the war. Thus in *Birge-Forbes Company* v. *Heye*, where war broke out after the beginning of an action to recover money, brought by a plaintiff who became an enemy, the United States Supreme Court affirmed a decision to allow the action to proceed on condition that the sum recovered from the American defendant should be paid to the clerk of the lower Court and by him turned over to the Alien Property Custodian. Mr

A. An enemy national in this country who is not 'in protection', and a person of any or no nationality who is an enemy in the territorial sense,[1] has no right of access to an English Court during the war as a plaintiff or other *actor* in any proceedings, except by licence of the Crown.[2]

B. The above-mentioned persons, and the enemy 'in protection', may be sued in an English Court during the war in the same way as a British subject, though with some of them difficulties of service may arise.

C. An enemy 'in protection' has, with one exception,[3] the same procedural capacity as a British subject.[4]

The leading authority for these three rules is the group of three cases, *Porter* v. *Freudenberg, Kreglinger* v. *S. Samuel and Rosenfeld*, and

Justice Holmes in delivering the Opinion of the Supreme Court (248 Fed. 636; 251 U.S. 317, 323; A.D. (1919–22) No. 284) said: 'There is nothing "mysteriously noxious" ...in a judgment for an alien enemy. Objection to it in these days goes only so far as it would give aid and comfort to the other side...Such aid and comfort were prevented by the provision that the sum recovered should be paid over to the Alien Property Custodian, and the judgment in this respect was correct'; and see Garner, *International Law and the World War*, vol. I, chap. v; and Hyde, §§ 606–14.

[1] Which, of course, includes an enemy Government; *Ex parte Colonna*, a decision of the United States Supreme Court in 1942 in which the 'enemy' was Italy; the American Trading with the Enemy Act (40 Stat. 411) expressly included an enemy Government as an 'enemy', and see American literature cited 10 A.D. (1941–2) at p. 455; the British Trading with the Enemy Act of 1939 includes 'any State, or Sovereign of a State, at war with His majesty'. On the effect of 'unfriendliness' or severance of diplomatic relations as a bar, see the *Sabbatino* decision of the U.S. Supreme Court, 14 *I. and C.L.Q.* pp. 474–5.

[2] For the procedure in obtaining a licence, see p. 108. In examining many of the cases to which it will be necessary to refer, it is useful to bear in mind a distinction which is apt to be obscured—particularly when an action by an enemy plaintiff fails. A successful defence may result from the procedural disability of the plaintiff, in which event it may be cured by the cessation of a state of war or its equivalent, or from a substantial defect in his cause of action such as original or supervening illegality, which would not be cured by the cessation of a state of war, or from both defects. Probably the older and stricter system of pleading would make this distinction more easily perceptible. Rowlatt J. in *Schmitz* v. *Van der Veen & Co.* (1915) 84 L.J.K.B. 861, 864, has stated the point as follows: 'It is essential to distinguish carefully between these two cases—that is to say, that where the cause of action is unexceptionable, but the plaintiff as an alien enemy is temporarily and personally incapable of being received as a plaintiff, and that where the cause of action, whoever puts it forward, fails in itself, and fails finally.' He then quoted Lord Ellenborough C.J. in *Flindt* v. *Waters* (1812) 15 East 260, 265: 'the defence of alien enemy...may go to the contract itself on which the plaintiff sues, and operate as a perpetual bar; or the objection may, as in a case of this sort, be merely personal, in respect to the capacity of the party to sue upon it.' See Bullen and Leake, *Principles of Pleading*, 3rd ed. (1865) (the most important edition because it immediately preceded the big changes in pleading which resulted from the Judicature Acts), pp. 435, 440–1, 468 and 475 and later in this book, p. 84, upon pleas in abatement and pleas in bar and the differences between them. As Maitland said of the forms of action, 'we have buried [them], but they still rule us from their graves': *Equity: The Forms of Action at Common Law*, p. 296.   [3] *Liebmann's* case. See later, p. 98.

[4] The analogy of procedural capacity has been applied in Southern Rhodesia so as to enable an enemy 'in protection' to apply for and receive a general dealer's licence. *Adler* v. *Salisbury City Council.*

In re Merten's Patents, which were decided by a full Court of Appeal in January 1915, and are usually referred to by the title of the first of them.[1] To these we must add the general approval given by the House of Lords in *V/O Sovfracht* v. *N.V. Gebr. Van Udens Scheepvaart en Agentuur Maatschappij*[2] (which we propose to refer to in future as 'the *Sovfracht* case') to the leading propositions contained in *Porter* v. *Freudenberg.*

In *Porter* v. *Freudenberg,* after quoting Lord Lindley's statement in *Janson* v. *Driefontein Consolidated Mines*[3] that 'the subject of a State at war with this country, but who is carrying on business here or in a foreign neutral country, is not treated as an alien enemy', the Court proceeded to elaborate the other side of the definition by stating[4] that

For the purpose of determining civil rights a British subject or the subject of a neutral state, who is voluntarily resident or who is carrying on business in hostile territory, is to be regarded and treated as an alien enemy and is in the same position as a subject of hostile nationality resident[5] in hostile territory.

The distinction is between, on the one hand, the enemy in the territorial sense together with such enemies in this country as may not be 'in protection', against whom the plea of alien enemy is valid, and, on the other hand, the enemy 'in protection', against whom it is not, that is, the alien enemy who in the older language is within the realm by licence of the King, or, as it is also put, 'has continued here by the King's leave and protection',[6] or has come here 'under a flag of truce, a cartel, a pass, or some other act of public authority that puts him in the King's peace *pro hac vice*'.[7] What exactly does this mean?

The enemy 'in protection'. The Aliens Restriction Act, 1914, passed immediately after the outbreak of the War of 1914 to 1918, and the Aliens Restriction Orders made thereunder (*inter alia*), required alien enemies to register themselves by supplying to a registration officer certain particulars concerning themselves.[8] It fell to the lot of Sargant J. in *Princess Thurn and Taxis* v. *Moffitt*[9] to give the first High Court

---

[1] See also *Princess Thurn and Taxis* v. *Moffitt* (plaintiff enemy 'in protection'); *Robinson & Co.* v. *Continental Insurance Co. of Mannheim* (defendant enemy in territorial sense); *Kraus* v. *Kraus and Orbach* (petitioner enemy 'in protection' and interned).

[2] [1943] A.C. 203.   [3] [1902] A.C. 484, 505.   [4] At p. 869.

[5] 'Resident in' in this connection has not a technical meaning and probably means no more than 'living or being in'; and see Fridman, on 'presence' and 'residence'. For the position of Corporations, see below, pp. 102–4.

[6] In *Wells* v. *Williams* (1697) 1 Ld. Raym. 282, 283; 1 Salk. 46; 1 Lutw. 34; *Ex parte Kawato* is an important decision of the Supreme Court of the United States to the same effect; as to Kawato's internment, see later p. 96 of this book.

[7] In *The Hoop* (1799) 1 C. Rob. 196, 201.

[8] For an earlier instance, see 43 Geo. III, c. 155, s. 22.

[9] [1915] 1 Ch. 58 (pre-war tort); see also *Volkl* v. *Rotunda Hospital* (1914) (pre-war tort).

decision upon the procedural effect of compliance with this Order, and his judgment received the approval of the full Court of Appeal in *Porter* v. *Freudenberg*. In the *Princess Thurn and Taxis* case the action was pending at the outbreak of war, and the plaintiff is stated[1] to have resided in the United Kingdom. She had complied with the Order in Council, and the defendant's application to stay all proceedings on the ground that she was an alien enemy was refused. Her husband, a national of Austria-Hungary, and thus an enemy, was 'abroad and probably engaged in fighting against this country'. Lord Reading C.J.,[2] in approving the decision, observed that 'such an alien [i.e. as the plaintiff] is resident here by tacit permission of the Crown. He has by registration informed the Executive of his presence in this country, and has been allowed thereafter to remain here. He is "sub protectione domini regis".' That seems to be the essential point. An enemy cannot be said to have the licence or be under the protection of the Crown unless he has taken the prescribed steps—be it registration or be it something else[3]—to make the Crown aware of his presence and to imply the Crown's consent. Many of the decisions given during the War of 1914 to 1918 in which enemy plaintiffs were allowed to sue expressly state that they had complied with the obligation to register themselves. That obligation existed also during the War of 1939 to 1945,[4] and it is unlikely that any enemy plaintiff would be allowed to sue unless he had complied with it or could show that in some other lawful manner he had made the Crown aware of his presence and had been allowed to remain.[5]

Comment upon and qualifications of these rules

After these rather general statements it will be convenient to consider the matter under the following headings:

---

[1] At pp. 59 and 61.

[2] [1915] 1 K.B. 857, 874. So also in Scotland, *Schulze* v. *Bank of Scotland*, and *Weiss* v. *Weiss*.

[3] See *Von Petersdorff* v. *Insurance Co. of N. America* (1944), for an enemy under order of deportation being allowed to sue.

[4] Under the Aliens Restriction Acts, 1914 and 1919, and the Aliens Order, 1920, as amended from time to time; the Order of 1920 has now been revoked and the principal Order is now the Aliens Order, 1953, and there are later Orders.

[5] *Boulton* v. *Dobree* (1808) 2 Camp. 163, 165: 'Although he went at large, it did not appear that government knew he was in the kingdom'—per Lord Ellenborough C.J.; *Alciator* v. *Smith* (1812) 3 Camp. 245, 246: 'There is no evidence that government knew of her being in this kingdom at the time when the action was commenced'—per Lord Ellenborough C.J.

On the effect of subsequent internment, see below, pp. 96–8.

We apprehend that if a person who has never done what is necessary to obtain the licence of the Crown is interned, he would nevertheless acquire the status of an internee: see pp. 96–8.

1. *Enemy plaintiffs*:[1]
    (*a*) the legal character of the plea;
    (*b*) in action pending at the outbreak of war;
    (*c*) co-plaintiff;
    (*d*) suing in representative capacity;
    (*e*) non-enemy suing on behalf of enemy;
    (*f*) enemy in foreign non-enemy territory;
    (*g*) non-enemy in enemy territory;
    (*h*) non-enemy in enemy-occupied territory;
    (*i*) non-enemy in territory formerly occupied by, and later recovered from, the enemy;
    (*j*) enemy prisoners of war, and enemies interned in British territory or repatriated;
    (*k*) enemy, wherever he may be, by reason of identification with the enemy Power, either by adherence to it or by control from enemy sources;
    (*l*) corporations;
    (*m*) in interpleader issue;
    (*n*) in Prize Court proceedings;
    (*o*) the statutory enemy;
    (*p*) suing by licence.
    (*q*) enemy holding licence to trade.
2. *Enemy defendants.*
3. *Enemy appellants.*
4. *Bankruptcy.*

We shall then consider the effect of
5. *The Statutes of Limitation.*

I. ENEMY PLAINTIFFS

(*a*) *The legal character of the plea of alien enemy*

Does the validity of the plea result from a strict rule of law or does it depend upon the discretion of the Court in applying a flexible rule of public policy?[2] This is not a purely theoretical question, as the

---

[1] In the extensive sense denoting an *actor* in any proceedings. The following cases show what is meant by 'actor': *The Charlotte* (1813) (claimant in prize) and see later, p. 105; *Porter* v. *Freudenberg* (defendant appellant not an *actor*) (as to bankruptcy, see later, p. 114); *Halsey* v. *Lowenfeld* (*Leigh and Curzon, Third Parties*) (defendant taking third party proceedings); *Geiringer* v. *Swiss Bank Corporation*; the *Sovfracht* case (summons for appointment of umpire).

[2] In *Driefontein Consolidated Mines* v. *Janson* Mathew J. allowed the defendant to waive the plea of alien enemy, but this practice was adversely criticized in the House of Lords by Lord Davey [1902] A.C. 484, 499, and is not likely to occur again.

decision in *Rodriguez* v. *Speyer Brothers* shows. Upon the theory there hangs a practical result. The House of Lords in that case had to consider whether the fact that one only of the plaintiffs, six persons who until the outbreak of war carried on business in partnership in London, was an alien enemy in the territorial sense (he was also an alien enemy in the national sense), was fatal to their recovery during the war of a debt due to the late firm. By a majority, Lord Finlay L.C., Lord Haldane and Lord Parmoor (Lord Atkinson and Lord Sumner dissenting), the House of Lords held that the action was maintainable. Lord Haldane, who was rather fond of 'a broad issue of principle', stated the issue as follows:[1]

Is the rule which prevents an enemy alien from suing in the King's Courts a crystallised proposition which forms part of the ordinary common law, and is so definite that it must be applied without reference to whether a particular case involves the real mischief to guard against which the rule was originally introduced? Or is the rule one of what is called public policy, which does not apply to a particular instance if that instance discloses no mischief from the point of view of public policy?

The majority preferred the latter explanation of the rule. Surely the best way to ascertain the true character of a rule of the common law is to examine its history, and in this case, unless the historical examination contained in Professor Holdsworth's ninth volume[2] and in the Appendix of the last edition of this book is wrong, we can find no warrant for saying that Coke and his predecessors who established the rule of the disability of the alien enemy plaintiff regarded the rule as anything but an unqualified rule.[3]

The fact that at a date subsequent to its establishment a rule of the common law should be found to be in accord with public policy does not entitle us to say that it can be applied or not be applied according to discretion as in the case of the rule which discourages unreasonable restraints of trade.

However, the law is now settled (or unsettled) by *Rodriguez* v. *Speyer Brothers*,[4] though we think there will be many *qui malunt errare cum* Lord Sumner in one of his most penetrating and characteristic speeches. Professor Holdsworth says:

---

[1] [1919] A.C. at p. 77.

[2] *History of English Law*, IX, pp. 98, 99 and note 1 on p. 99.

[3] Note Eyre C.J. in *Sparenburgh* v. *Bannatyne* (1797) 1 Bos. & P. 163, 170: 'I take the true ground upon which the plea of alien enemy has been allowed is, that a man, professing himself hostile to this country, and in a state of war with it, cannot be heard if he sue for the benefit and protection of our laws in the courts of this country.'

[4] The House of Lords have in the *Sovfracht* case substantially repaired the damage done by the majority speeches in *Rodriguez* v. *Speyer Brothers*.

The only doubtful question which was never quite settled, was whether an alien enemy, who was an executor or administrator to a subject, could sue in his representative capacity.[1]

But, as Lord Sumner points out,[2]

it is only possible to say that Herr von Speyer is on the record here, suing en autre droit, by assuming that, as against the defendant, he sues as trustee for certain beneficiaries, the other partners in Speyer Brothers of 1914 to wit. A trustee he is not, nor is he so described on the writ; and if he was, he would still sue for his own benefit as well, and not purely en autre droit.

(b) Plaintiff in action pending at the date of the outbreak of war[3]

Is such a plaintiff in any better position than one who issues his writ during time of war? Oppenheim stated in earlier editions[4] that 'if during time of peace a defendant obtains an opportunity to plead, and if subsequently war breaks out with the country of the plaintiff, the defendant may not plead that the plaintiff is prevented from suing', citing Shepeler v. Durant;[5] but it is submitted that this statement is not borne out by the cases. In Le Bret v. Papillon, an action in assumpsit on a French judgment, the plaintiff had exhibited his bill against the defendant, when subsequently war broke out between their respective countries. The defendant pleaded (inter alia) that the plaintiff was now an alien enemy, to which the latter replied that that did not matter, as he was not an alien enemy when he exhibited his bill. The Court held that the plaintiff was 'barred from further having or maintaining his action'. Lord Sumner pointed out in Rodriguez v. Speyer Brothers[6] that in Le Bret v. Papillon 'the objection of enemy character was wrongly pleaded in bar and not in abatement', and that 'the Court held that notice must be taken of the plaintiff's incapacity, although it was not properly pleaded'. In Vanbrynen v. Wilson a motion to stay judgment and execution, on the ground that the plaintiffs had become enemies since the verdict, was refused summarily, but the defendant was left to move formally, so that the case does not decide the point of substance.

---

[1] See below, p. 86, n. 2.   [2] [1919] A.C. at p. 119.

[3] For our present purpose enemy-occupied territory is in the same position as enemy territory, so that the act of occupation by the enemy would have the same effect upon pending proceedings instituted by a plaintiff resident there as the outbreak of war would have in the case of pending proceedings instituted by a plaintiff resident in enemy territory: the Sovfracht case.

[4] International Law, e.g. the second, II, p. 133.

[5] (1854). It does not appear from the report whether or not the plaintiff was resident in Russia, but it seems likely that he was as the contract was made there. There are three other reports, but they throw no further light on the case.

[6] [1919] A.C. 59, 109.

In *Shepeler* v. *Durant* the plaintiff, a Russian subject, suing in the Court of Common Pleas upon a pre-war contract for the sale of timber, delivered his declaration on 15 March, and on the 23rd the defendant obtained an order for time to plead on the usual terms. On the 28th war was declared against Russia, and the defendant took out a summons to stay proceedings on the ground that the plaintiff had become an alien enemy, or, in the alternative, for leave to plead such a plea in abatement. In April the summons was refused on the ground that the defendant by the terms on which he had obtained on 23 March an order for time to plead, namely, to plead issuably,[1] was by the rules of pleading then in force precluded from entering such a plea as that of alien enemy. No authorities are cited in the report, and it is submitted that the case turns purely on an obsolete rule of pleading, and is of no authority at the present day.

In November 1854, in the Queen's Bench, the defendant in the case of *Alcinous* v. *Nigreu* pleaded that the plaintiff, a Russian, was an alien enemy, was residing in the kingdom without the licence, safe-conduct, or permission of the Queen, and 'has become such enemy as aforesaid since the last pleading in this action'. On demurrer the Court (Lord Campbell C.J., Coleridge, Wightman and Erle JJ.) upheld the sufficiency of the plea. No cases are cited, and the plaintiff's counsel is not reported to have argued the point taken successfully in the earlier case, *Shepeler* v. *Durant*.

Alcinous v. *Nigreu* may not be very clear as to the circumstances of the plaintiff's residence here, but it certainly follows *Le Bret* v. *Papillon* and casts doubts upon *Shepeler* v. *Durant*. In *Von Hellfeld* v. *Rechnitzer*,[2] where the pleadings were closed on 31 July 1914, i.e. before the outbreak of war, the plaintiff, an alien enemy, was not allowed to proceed with his action. There can be no doubt today that the fact that the writ was issued or the pleadings closed before the outbreak of war does not enable an alien enemy to continue his action

---

[1] 'An issuable plea is one which puts the merits of the case in issue, either on the facts or on the law, and upon which a decision on demurrer or by a jury would determine the action upon the merits': Bullen and Leake, *Precedents of Pleadings* (3rd ed. 1868), p. 440. The authors add (on p. 441) that a plea of alien enemy is not an issuable plea, citing *Shepeler* v. *Durant*, where it was described as a dilatory plea, as it was in that case which was an action upon the breach of a pre-war contract which would be enforceable after the war. If, to use the words of Lord Ellenborough C.J. in *Flindt* v. *Waters* (see above, p. 79, n. 2), the plea of alien enemy had gone 'to the contract itself', e.g. asserted the abrogation by the outbreak of war of a pre-war executory contract, would not this have been an issuable plea?

[2] *The Times*, 11 December 1914; on 30 September 1914 the plaintiff left England under British permit and went to Amsterdam.

See also the Scottish decision *Gebr. van Uden* v. *Burrell* (1916), and an American decision cited by Baty and Morgan, p. 284, *Hutchinson* v. *Brock*.

during the war. The outbreak of war after verdict and before judgment must also, it is submitted, put a stop to further proceedings during the war.

But the fact that upon the outbreak of war a plaintiff in a pending action becomes an alien enemy need not in a proper case—at any rate when it is possible to serve notice of motion upon his solicitor—prevent the Court from striking out his statement of claim on the ground that it discloses no cause of action, for it is not fair to the defendant that such an action should be left hanging over him until after the war merely because the plaintiff is an alien enemy.[1]

(c) Enemy co-plaintiff

As has already been seen, it was decided by the House of Lords in *Rodriguez* v. *Speyer Brothers* that the fact that it is necessary to join an enemy as co-plaintiff with British and neutral subjects whose partner he formerly was does not enable the action to be defeated by the plea of alien enemy. This decision is considered to have approved *Mercedes Daimler Motor Co.* v. *Maudslay Motor Co.*, where of two joint owners of a patent the British owners had the sole right of bringing actions for infringement and the right to join a German co-owner as a co-plaintiff, and the action was allowed, and *J. B. Rombach Baden Clock Co.* v. *Gent*, where of three partners in a firm dissolved by the outbreak of war one was British, a second an enemy 'in protection' and the third an enemy in both the national and territorial senses, and the firm was allowed to sue because the action was in substance the receiver's action for the collection of a debt, the receiver being the British ex-partner.[2]

(d) Enemy suing as executor or administrator or in some other representative capacity on behalf of one who is not an alien enemy

This question must be regarded as still open,[3] but in the speeches of the majority in *Rodriguez* v. *Speyer Brothers* there is much *obiter* authority in favour of the view that the action would lie.[4]

---

[1] *Eichengruen* v. *Mond*; and see *Geiringer* v. *Swiss Bank Corporation* (a case of interpleader), below, at p. 104.   [2] See later, chapter 9.

[3] See, in addition to the majority speeches in *Rodriguez* v. *Speyer Brothers*, Holdsworth, *op. cit.* IX, pp. 98, 99 and n. 1 on p. 99. A number of old decisions will be found in the *English and Empire Digest*, Replacement volume 2, nos. 259–521.

[4] For a case in which the alien enemy administrator of the estate of an alien enemy was not allowed to sue, see *H.C. van Hoogstraten* v. *Low Lum Seng*. In *Azazh Kebbeda Tesema* v. *Italian Government* the Palestine Supreme Court dismissed upon the outbreak of war with Italy a pending action in which that State was plaintiff. In *Compagnie française de l'Afrique occidentale* v. *The Otho* a United States District Court permitted a British insurance company to sue for damage done to a cargo, by subrogation from an assured domiciled in enemy-occupied territory.

(e) *Non-enemy plaintiff suing on behalf of enemy*

Formerly there existed a fairly rigid rule to the effect that a non-enemy could not bring an action which was in substance for the benefit or in favour of an enemy.[1] There has, however, been a tendency to modify the rigour of this rule, and this relaxation is perhaps traceable to the appointment, in both the World Wars, of a Custodian of Enemy Property. In the absence of such machinery it was clearly dangerous to allow a plaintiff to sue if he was in effect suing for the benefit of an enemy. Now, if money is due to an enemy, it is more reasonable—from the British as well as the enemy's point of view—that it should go to the Custodian than that it should be retained by a debtor who has no right to it and might later on be unable to pay it. Accordingly in *Schmitz* v. *Van der Veen & Co.*,[2] Rowlatt J., after holding that Schmitz, a naturalized British subject, who had sold goods to the defendants, had sold them as a principal and not as the agent of an enemy, rejected the defence that he was suing for the benefit of an enemy and allowed him to recover judgment for the price of the goods, subject to a stay of execution pending the making of an order for vesting the proceeds in the Custodian. Nor did the learned judge overlook the fact that this form of judgment benefited the enemy by improving his prospect of ultimately recovering the money. This decision was followed in *Weiner* v. *Central Fund for German Jewry*, where the plaintiff had deposited with the defendants in June 1939, that is, before the outbreak of war, the sum of money required by them before they could sponsor the application (for permission to enter this country) of two persons in Vienna, now enemies, and was suing for the return of the money on the ground of breach of contract or failure of consideration; he admitted that any sum recovered by him ought to be handed over to the Custodian, and Singleton J., rejecting the defence that the action was one for the benefit of an enemy, gave judgment in a form similar to that given in *Schmitz* v. *Van der Veen & Co.* We suggest, however, that the value of these two decisions will require reconsideration in the light of the speeches in the House of Lords in the *Sovfracht* case, and particularly of the Lord Chancellor's fifth and sixth propositions.[3]

[1] E.g. *Brandon* v. *Nesbitt* (1794); *Bristow* v. *Towers*; as explained in *Flindt* v. *Waters* (1812) 15 East 260, 265.

[2] See *Stockholms Enskilda Bank* v. *Schering, Ltd* [1941] 1 K.B. 424 (C.A.).

[3] [1943] A.C. 203, 212.

(f) Enemy in foreign non-enemy territory

In *Janson's*[1] case Lord Lindley stated *obiter* that 'the subject of a State at war with this country, but who is carrying on business here or in a foreign neutral country, is not treated as an alien enemy', and this *dictum* was followed in the case of *Re Mary, Duchess of Sutherland, Bechoff, David & Co.* v. *Bubna*.[2] The plaintiff firm consisted of three partners carrying on business in Paris, that is, in allied territory (not in enemy occupation), and, at the time of the issue of the writ, all resident in Paris. One of them was a German subject who, after the issue of the writ and two days before war between this country and Germany broke out, left Paris for Spain, where he had since resided. Warrington J. refused an application to stay the proceedings based on the ground that one of the plaintiffs was an alien enemy, and the Court of Appeal, although the case does not appear to have been argued to a conclusion, were evidently in sympathy with the judgment of the Court of first instance. This inclination to allow an enemy subject resident in a neutral country to sue in an English Court receives some support from the judgment of Eve J. in the cases of *Re Grimthorpe's Settlement, Lord Islington* v. *Countess Czernin* and *Beckett* v. *Countess Czernin*, where the learned judge directed certain income to be paid to the Countess, an enemy subject, then resident in Rome (that is, in allied territory), so long as she resided in allied, neutral or British territory. Her husband was apparently still resident in Austria, and in October 1914 they had obtained from a Vienna Court upon their joint petition a decree of separation *a mensa et thoro*.

Will the position of the enemy plaintiff who is resident or carrying on business in a neutral country be adversely affected by being associated with, or interested in, a firm carrying on business in an enemy country?

The Scottish case of *Gebr. van Uden* v. *Burrell*[3] raises this somewhat curious point, and the decision must be of considerable persuasive authority. The pursuers (plaintiffs) were J. and C. van t'Hoff, residing and carrying on business in Rotterdam, and presumably Dutch subjects. The defender was a Glasgow shipowner, and the dispute arose out of a chartering transaction of 1907. J. and C. van t'Hoff were also individually interested in two firms carrying on business re-

---

[1] See also *J. G. White Engineering Corporation* v. *Canadian Car and Foundry Co.* (Canadian) (enemy domiciled in neutral country and temporarily resident in allied country), and '*Parfums Tosca*' v. *Peschaud* (French).

[2] See also Younger J. in *Schaffenius* v. *Goldberg* [1916] 1 K.B. 284, 291, 293, where he took the same view; and see later p. 150.

[3] [1916] S.C. 391, from which it appears that the plea of alien enemy was recognized in Scotland as long ago as 1664.

spectively at Duisberg, registered under German law, and at Antwerp registered under Belgian law. These two firms were independent of the Rotterdam firm, and were in no way concerned with the subject-matter of the action. J. and C. van t'Hoff were individually interested in each of the firms as partners, but in each case there were other partners. In these circumstances it was held that the pursuers, by reason of their individual interests in the Duisberg firm, were alien enemies in the sense of the Trading with the Enemy Act, 1914, and relative Proclamations, and their action—instituted before the war—was stayed until after the termination of the war.[1]

A defendant enemy national, resident in enemy territory at the time of action brought and when last heard of, is unable to take third-party proceedings, for in so doing he is an *actor*, and comes under the procedural disability of the alien enemy plaintiff.[2]

(g) *Non-enemy in enemy territory*

Prima facie the fact of a non-enemy person being voluntarily present, or carrying on business, in enemy territory will invest him with enemy character and prevent him from suing in an English Court.[3] Thus in *McConnell* v. *Hector*,[4] where the Court of Common Pleas declined to support a commission of bankruptcy granted at the suit of three partners, all British subjects, of whom two resided and traded at an enemy port,[5] Lord Alvanley C.J. said of them

there is an hostile adherence and a commercial adherence; and I do not wish to hear it argued that a person who lives and carries on trade under the protection and for the benefit of an hostile State, and who is so far a merchant settled in that State that his goods would be liable to confiscation in a court of prize,[6] is yet to be considered as entitled to sue as an English subject in an English court of justice.

This decision was approved by members both of the majority and the minority of the House of Lords in *Rodriguez* v. *Speyer Brothers*,[7]

---

[1] See also below, p. 107.   [2] *Halsey* v. *Lowenfeld (Leigh and Curzon, Third Parties).*

[3] For a curious case (which went to the Supreme Court) under the American Trading with the Enemy legislation of an enemy national normally resident in Hawaii who happened to be in Germany on a trip at the outbreak of war with Germany and was thereafter prevented from returning to Hawaii, see *Guessefeldt* v. *McGrath*, and see also two other American decisions: *Ecker* v. *Atlantic Refining Co.* and *Willenbrock* v. *Rogers*.

[4] (1802) 3 Bos. & P. 113, 114. And see *Roberts* v. *Hardy* and Lord Atkinson's comment upon it, [1919] A.C. at p. 97, and *O'Mealey* v. *Wilson* (1808) 1 Camp. 482, 483, where Lord Ellenborough C.J. said: 'If a British subject resides in an enemy's country without being detained as a prisoner of war, he is precluded from suing here.'

[5] Flushing, described as 'a port belonging to the enemies of this country'; the relevant date is not given but was probably during the period when Holland under a Francophile puppet Government was at war with Great Britain.

[6] For instance, *The Harmony*; *The Citto.*   [7] [1919] A.C. 59, 73.

and Lord Finlay L.C. said of it: 'All that was decided by the Court was that enemy character results from residence in the enemy country, and there is no doubt as to the correctness of this proposition.'

Moreover, it is reasonable to add that the fact that the enemy territory in question is occupied by British or allied forces does not remove the character of enemy territory.[1]

If, however, the presence of the British subject in the enemy country has been authorized by the Crown, either expressly or by implication as an incident to the carrying on there of a trade licensed by the Crown, the disability to sue does not attach to him.[2]

The same principles apply to the nationals of foreign States voluntarily present or resident or carrying on business in enemy territory.[3]

In *Porter* v. *Freudenberg*[4] we are told by the Court of Appeal that

For the purpose of determining civil rights a British subject or the subject of a neutral State, who is voluntarily[5] resident or who is carrying on business in hostile territory, is to be regarded and treated as an alien enemy and is in the same position as a subject of hostile nationality resident in hostile territory.

What amounts to voluntary residence?[6] Clearly internment as a civilian or detention as a prisoner of war[7] in an enemy country does not. But in the case of *Scotland* v. *South African Territories, Ltd* (1917), Darling J. regarded as 'voluntary residence' a certain measure of detention in enemy territory not amounting to complete captivity. The plaintiff was the defendant company's manager in German South-west Africa upon the outbreak of war, and, though subject to a measure of internment, and presumably unable to leave the country, he was able to protect the defendant company's interests and preserve their business.

---

[1] So held by the Court of Appeals of the District of Columbia, rightly it is submitted: *Feyerabend* v. *McGrath, Attorney-General of the United States.*

[2] *Ex p. Baglehole.*

[3] *Albretcht* v. *Sussmann.*

[4] [1915] 1 K.B. 857, 869.

[5] But even if he is present in enemy territory against his will, he is exposed to enemy pressure, and a judgment obtained by him might work a benefit to the enemy; see the *Sovfracht* case.

[6] *Vamvakas* v. *Custodian of Enemy Property & Another* in which Ormerod J., following Roxburgh J. in *In re Hatch*, referred to the difference in the test of enemy character arising from residence or presence in enemy territory applied by the common law and the Trading with the Enemy legislation respectively; in the former case residence or presence must be voluntary; in the latter '*de facto* residence irrespective of circumstances' sufficed.

[7] *Vandyke* v. *Adams*, where it was held that a British prisoner of war in Germany is not an 'individual resident in enemy territory' and thus an 'enemy' under section 2 (1) (*b*) of the Trading with the Enemy Act, 1939. In the case of *In re Hatch*, Roxburgh J. declined to extend the reasoning of *Vandyke* v. *Adams* so as to cover a British national temporarily resident in Jersey during its enemy occupation.

Darling J. held that the plaintiff was an alien enemy during his residence in German South-west Africa and could not recover his salary in respect of that period. In *Baumfelder* v. *Secretary of State for Canada*[1] the Exchequer Court of Canada held that a German national who, after being permanently resident in England, was interned and in 1919 was deported to Germany, and through poverty remained there until 1922 when he went to Canada, had not 'resided' in Germany within the meaning of the Canadian Treaty of Peace (Germany) Order, 1920, section 32 (*a*), because the conception of 'residence' implies voluntary presence within the territory of the State in question. But it must be noted that the question was not one of procedural status but one of the divesting of property under the Peace Treaty.

(*h*) *Non-enemy in enemy-occupied territory*[2]

The position of a non-enemy national, whether British or the subject of an allied or a neutral State, who is present in or carrying on business in non-enemy territory which is invaded and occupied[3] by the enemy requires particular consideration.[4] The occupied territory may be British, e.g. the Channel Islands, or allied, e.g. Dutch (though when invaded in 1940, Holland was neutral). The common law position did not call for much consideration during the War of 1914 to 1918,[5] and until the second World War the available authority was slender. The House of Lords, however, held in 1942 in the *Sovfracht* case[6] that a company incorporated under the laws of Holland, having its principal place of business at Rotterdam, and carrying on business in Holland before and after its occupation by Germany, was an alien enemy at common law so as to become incapable of suing

[1] And see *In re Otto Cloos and Chota Nagpur Co-operative Society*.

[2] See also Schmitthoff, 64 *L.Q.R.* (1948), pp. 485–91, and chapter 17.

[3] But not annexed in such circumstances that international law would regard the annexation as valid.

[4] Upon the application of British Defence (Finance) Regulations to British nationals involuntarily resident in enemy-occupied territory, see *Boissevain* v. *Weil*.

[5] See Younger J. and Lord Cozens Hardy M.R. in *Soc. Anon. Belge des Mines d'Aljustrel (Portugal)* v. *Anglo-Belgian Agency* [1915] 2 Ch. 409, 414, 419, and Russell J. in *Re Deutsche Bank (London Agency)* [1921] 2 Ch. 291, 295.

[6] See also later, ch. 14 (solicitor's retainer) and ch. 17 (the conditions and general effects of belligerent occupation). The House of Lords reversed the Court of Appeal [1942] 1 K.B. 222 on the common law point; as to the position of the Dutch company under the Trading with the Enemy Act, 1939, see below, p. 107. See also *H. P. Drewry S.A.R.L.* v. *Onassis* (1942) arising out of the occupation of France, which must now be read in the light of the *Sovfracht* decision, and its American sequel between the same parties in 10 A.D. (1941–2) no. 149, and *Owners of M.V. Lubrafol* v. *Owners of S.S. Pamia*; and see *Chemacid, S.A.* v. *Ferrotar* (1943) in a U.S. District Court. For a criticism of the *Sovfracht* decision, see Fridman, 4 *I. and C.L.Q.* pp. 613–28.

as a plaintiff or other *actor* in an English Court except by licence from the Crown.

The importance of this decision in view of the then prevailing war condition of Europe was very great. Its *ratio* covered the nationals of the country occupied and the nationals, caught therein, of the other countries which were enemy to Germany, including Great Britain; for instance, Dutch in Holland, British and Poles in France. It must not be assumed that it would have covered a Swedish national in Holland or a citizen of the United States of America who remained in France from June 1940 until his country became enemy to Germany in December 1941; it might be necessary in such cases to inquire whether the plaintiff could have left the occupied territory, and, if so, why he did not.[1] It is believed that in practice British and neutral nationals in enemy-occupied territory, who had interests to protect in the United Kingdom, were often helped by the grant from the Crown of licences to sue.[2]

(i) Non-enemy in territory formerly occupied by, and later recovered from, the enemy

In principle, a British citizen or the national or an allied or neutral country who is resident or present or carrying on business in enemy-territory would, upon the ejection of the enemy and the restoration of the territory to its former Government, lose his enemy character; but the question whether during the occupation he had assisted or adhered to the enemy might require consideration.

(j) Enemy prisoners of war, and enemies interned in British territory or repatriated

During the War of 1939 to 1945 there were large numbers of persons of enemy nationality in the United Kingdom who were, to use a non-committal term, 'in custody' and not at large. Some of them were prisoners of war, and the word 'internment' is not appropriate to their condition. This word is ambiguous. It may refer to the condition of members of British armed forces who, having sought refuge in or been driven by the exigencies of battle into the territory of a neutral country, have been 'interned' there by the neutral Government in accordance with international law. With these we are not concerned. The term 'internment' in the present context more appropriately describes the condition of those persons, of whatever na-

---

[1] See *The Anglo-Mexican*.
[2] As to persons detained in enemy territory, see the Limitations (Enemies and War Prisoners) Act, 1945, below, p. 115.

tionality, who, being found in this country in time of war or upon the eve of war, are placed under arrest in the interest of public safety, or, sometimes, of their own safety. With such of these persons as are of enemy nationality we are concerned.

Accordingly we shall deal with

(i) Enemy prisoners of war *stricto sensu*: that is to say, members of enemy forces who have been captured;[1]

(ii) Enemy civilians detained in custody by the Crown, or, to use a more popular word, interned;[2]

(iii) Repatriation.

We are primarily concerned with procedural status, but we shall find it convenient at the same time to consider their substantive rights and liabilities. It is true that persons in class (ii) were, at the time when they were detained, for the most part residing or present in this country with the implied licence of the Crown, and were thus here *per licentiam et sub protectione regis*, whereas persons in class (i) were taken in arms against the Crown, but that difference is not reflected in their status.

(i) *Enemy prisoners of war* stricto sensu.[3] Such a person has full civil capacity, i.e. as to contracting, marrying, acquiring and disposing of real and personal property *inter vivos* and by will, full procedural capacity (except as to the writ of *habeas corpus* to be mentioned later), and full liability to be sued in a civil action or prosecuted for a crime. He may bring an action for libel to defend himself against a charge of having committed a war atrocity; if he is allowed by the British Government to enter into a contract of service with a farmer, he may recover wages and he may sue for damages for an injury resulting from the negligence of his employer.

At first sight this statement may seem surprising, but its content seems to us to follow logically from the fact that a prisoner of war is

---

[1] Upon the meaning of the expression 'any person who has at any time since the beginning of the war been a prisoner of war, captured or interned by the enemy' in the Military Service Act, 1916 (Session 2), s. 8, see *Robinson* v. *Metcalf*.

[2] On the more general and political aspects of the internment of alien enemies during the war of 1939 to 1945, see Cohn in 4 *Modern Law Review* (1941), pp. 200–9. On the meaning of the expression 'captured or interned by the enemy' occurring in the Military Service Act, 1916, section 8, see *King* v. *Burnham*.

[3] It is necessary to bear in mind the Geneva Conventions Act, 1957, the Geneva Convention of 12 August 1949, Relative to the Treatment of Prisoners of War (scheduled to that Act), and any other relevant Convention to which the United Kingdom and the enemy State may be parties. Article 14 of that Convention provides that 'Prisoners of war shall retain the full civil capacity which they enjoyed at the time of their capture. The detaining Power may not restrict the exercise, either within or without its own territory, of the rights such capacity confers except in so far as the captivity requires.' See Joyce Gutteridge, 26 *B.Y.* (1949), pp. 294–326.

not *exlex*; he is 'in the peace'; he is living 'in protection' just as any ordinary resident is. The cases are not numerous, but it is suggested that they are adequate.

In *Sparenburgh* v. *Bannatyne*[1] the plaintiff—the subject of a neutral State, captured on board an enemy ship of war—entered into a contract with the defendant at St Helena, with the consent of the officer commanding that island, to serve as a seaman on a voyage to London. On arrival in London he was taken into custody as a prisoner of war, brought an action to recover his wages, and was met by the plea of alien enemy. The Court of Common Pleas (Eyre C.J., Heath and Rooke JJ.) gave judgment in his favour, the first mainly on the ground that, being originally a neutral subject, his hostile character was temporary and ceased when he was captured, but the last two have a good deal to say about the status of a prisoner of war. Heath J. says (p. 171): 'Officers on their parole must subsist like other men of their own rank; but according to such doctrine' (urged by the defendant) 'they must starve; for they could gain no credit if deprived of the power of suing for their own debts.' Later he says: 'If a prisoner of war is in confinement, he is protected as to his person; if he is on his parole, he requires further protection than what relates merely to his person.' He then cites a case of one Mississippi Law 'to show that a prisoner at (*sic*) war may sue and be sued', and later says: 'If a prisoner of war can be sued, there is no reason why he should not sue.' Rooke J. prefers to take his stand upon the reasons given by Eyre C.J., but adds (at p. 171): 'An enemy under the King's protection may sue and be sued: that cannot be doubted. A prisoner at war is, to certain purposes, under the King's protection, and there are many cases where he can maintain an action.' He then puts the case of an officer on parole who raises money by pledging a jewel and is then defrauded by the pledgee.[2]

In *Schaffenius* v. *Goldberg* in 1916 Younger J., Lord Cozens-Hardy M.R., and Warrington L.J. all accepted the decision in *Sparenburgh* v. *Bannatyne*.

The exception to his procedural capacity is that he is not entitled

---

[1] Note also the remarks of Heath J. (at 1 Bos. & P., p. 170) upon crimes: 'a prisoner of war is not adhering to the King's enemies, for he is here under the protection of the King. If he conspires against the life of the King, it is high treason' (an instance of the conviction of a French prisoner for larceny is given); 'if he is killed, it is murder; he does not therefore stand in the same position as when in a state of actual hostility'.

[2] See also *Maria* v. *Hall*. A better report of the case is to be found attached to the report of *R.* v. *Depardo* (1807) 1 Taunt. 26, 28, from which it appears that in *Maria* v. *Hall* the Court of Common Pleas was divided on the question whether the plaintiff, a prisoner of war, who worked a ship home to this country, could recover on a contract for wages.

to a writ of *habeas corpus*. In *R.* v. *Schiever* in 1759 the writ was denied to the subject of a neutral State captured upon an enemy ship and then held as a prisoner of war, though he contended that he had been forced to serve on the enemy ship. To the same effect is the case of the *Three Spanish Sailors*, who in 1779 moved for a writ against the commander of a sloop of war on the ground that they were unlawfully detained as prisoners of war. The Court of Common Pleas (Gould, Blackstone and Nares JJ.) in refusing the writ said:

these men, upon their own showing, are alien enemies and prisoners of war, and therefore not entitled to any of the privileges of Englishmen; much less to be set at liberty on a *habeas corpus*.

The reason given is too wide, and, as *Sparenburgh* v. *Bannatyne* shows, is incorrect. In *R.* v. *Vine Street Police Station Superintendent, ex parte Liebmann*,[1] these three decisions were accepted as 'settled law' by a Divisional Court consisting of Bailhache and Low JJ. Probably the true explanation is that the Crown in making a man a prisoner of war is acting under the royal prerogative (under which it wages war) and that its act, like certain other acts as a belligerent, is not examinable by the Courts; in other words, that this act by the Crown belongs to the group of acts sometimes referred to as 'acts of State'.[2] We can see no reason why a prisoner of war should not be entitled to a *habeas corpus* in respect of the detention of some person in whom he had an interest, such as a wife or child, in the same circumstances as anyone else would be,[3] or in respect of his own detention by a private person acting without the authority of the Crown.[4]

---

[1] See below, p. 98.   [2] *Cook* v. *Sprigg*; *West Rand Central Gold Mining Co.* v. *The King*.

[3] In *Furly* v. *Newnham* (1780) the Court of King's Bench declined to grant a writ of *habeas corpus ad testificandum* in the case of a prisoner of war, Lord Mansfield saying that the proper course in such a case was to obtain 'an order from the Secretary of State'. The prisoner of war was not the applicant but one whom the applicant wished to call as a witness in an insurance case. This suggests that the reason why the writ of *habeas corpus* is not available in the case of prisoners of war has nothing to do with the demerits of the prisoner of war but is to be found in some peculiar character of the function being exercised by the Crown when waging war and incidentally capturing enemy persons and holding them in captivity; see *R.* v. *Bottrill, ex parte Kuechenmeister*, and later p. 98, and McNair, *Law of Treaties* (1961), p. 89. It may be mentioned that a declaration of war by the Crown is an act of State: see Willes J. in *Esposito* v. *Bowden* (1857) 7 El. & Bl. 763, 781: 'The force of a declaration of war is equal to that of an Act of Parliament prohibiting intercourse with the enemy except by the Queen's licence. As an Act of State, done by virtue of the Prerogative exclusively belonging to the Crown, such a declaration carries with it all the force of law...' In *R.* v. *De Manneville* (1804) an alien enemy domiciled in England, answering to a writ of *habeas corpus*, was allowed to retain custody of his child of tender age as against the mother; but there is no indication that he was a prisoner of war or interned. On the question—which troubled the lawyers—whether Napoleon after his surrender would cease to be a prisoner of war upon the official end of the war and become entitled to a writ of *habeas corpus*, see McNair, *Opinions*, I, 106.

[4] See [1946] 1 K.B. at p. 54.

(ii) *Internment.* We now come to enemy civilians.[1] They are residing here permanently or temporarily *per licentiam et sub protectione regis*, and *prima facie* they are entitled to the benefit of the rule laid down in *Wells* v. *Williams*. Does their internment disentitle them? In that case Chief Justice Treby said: 'Though the plaintiff came here since the war, yet if he has continued here by the King's leave and protection ever since, *without molesting the Government or being molested by it*,[2] he may be allowed to sue, for that is consequent to his being in protection.' The expression in italics was considered by Younger J. and by the Court of Appeal in *Schaffenius* v. *Goldberg*,[3] and it was held that at any rate internment 'as a mere measure of police' did not amount to the molestation which would destroy the right to sue.

The plaintiff in *Schaffenius* v. *Goldberg*, an enemy national resident and carrying on business in England and duly registered under the Aliens Restriction Order, 1914, but not interned, entered into a contract with the defendant in March 1915, for the manufacture of goods, and advanced money to him. In July 1915, the plaintiff was interned, and the defendant refused to have any further dealings with him on the ground that he was an enemy. It was contended for the defendant that internment operated as a revocation of the licence to remain in this country, which, as appears from the *Princess Thurn and Taxis* case and the old cases on which it rests, is essential to the right of the enemy to sue. Younger J., however, refused to hold that internment made the plaintiff *exlex*,[4] and decided that the contract was not affected by the plaintiff's internment, and that he was entitled to maintain any action competent to him in respect thereof. This decision was upheld by the Court of Appeal. This seems to follow logically from the fact that the plaintiff was for some months allowed to remain at large and to continue his business. As Coke said:[5] 'for an alien (i.e. that is in league)[6] may trade and traffique, buy and sell, and therefore of necessity he must be of ability to have personal actions.' In *Nordman* v. *Rayner*, where the contract was entered into before the war, the internment of the plaintiff, who was registered as an alien enemy, lasted only a month, whereupon he

---

[1] Parry, 10 *Modern Law Review* (1947), pp. 403–10.

[2] The expression which is put into italics does not occur in the report in 1 Salk. 46.

[3] Cited with approval by the Supreme Court of the United States in *Ex parte Kawato* (1942) (Kawato was interned before the case reached the Supreme Court): *Robinson* v. *Metcalf, supra*. For other instances of an internee as *actor* in proceedings, see *Kraus* v. *Kraus and Orbach*, (probably) *Uhlig* v. *Uhlig*, and *Matthiesen* v. *Glas*.

[4] See Sir Frederick Pollock's note on this word [1916] 1 K.B. at p. 289.

[5] Co. Litt. 129*b*.   [6] That is to say, not enemy.

was released, being found to be an Alsatian of French extraction and anti-German sympathies. The case is interesting upon the effect of the internment in rendering it difficult, if not impossible (as was alleged), to perform the contract, but adds nothing to *Schaffenius* v. *Goldberg* from the procedural point of view.

These are, however, both cases of 'innocent' internment. As Younger J. said in *Schaffenius's* case,[1] 'it is common knowledge amongst us that the internment of a civilian enemy does not necessarily connote any overt hostile attitude on his part'. Supposing, however, that he was imprisoned on account of some overt hostile act or some serious offence against the Defence Regulations, or interned upon some definite suspicion of a 'hostile attitude', might it not be said that he has forfeited the King's protection, which, as is stated in *Wells* v. *Williams*,[2] lasts only while 'he has continued here ...without molesting the Government or being molested by it'? 'Innocent' internment, as we have seen, does not amount to molestation by the Government, but it may fairly be argued that 'criminal' internment both constitutes molestation by, and results from molestation of, the Government. This point appears to be still open,[3] and it will be noted that both in *Schaffenius's* and in *Nordman's* cases the innocent or colourless character of the internment as a mere act of general policy is insisted on. It is also probable that an alien enemy who assists the enemy and is either interned in consequence, or convicted of an offence and imprisoned, would lose his right to sue on the ground of adherence to the King's enemies.[4] Provided, however, that the internment is 'innocent', an interned alien enemy retains his procedural status, and, we submit, the right of entering into contracts during internment. And there appears to be no reason why he should not sue in respect of a tort of which he may be the victim before or during internment. It may be mentioned incidentally that the enemy shipowner who was allowed to be a claimant in the Prize Court in *The Möwe*, was then interned.

Interned enemy civilians do not fall within the Hague Conventions of 1899 and 1907 on the Laws and Customs of Warfare on Land, nor the Convention of 1929 relating to the Treatment of

---

[1] [1916] 1 K.B. at p. 295.

[2] (1697) 1 Ld. Raym. 282, 283; 1 Salk. 46; 1 Lutw. 34.

[3] See Lord Atkinson in *Johnstone* v. *Pedlar* [1921] 2 A.C. 262, 285.

[4] See *Netherlands South Africa Railway Co.* v. *Fisher*, where the plaintiff company, incorporated in Holland, a neutral State, and its directors, were trading with and obtaining money from the enemy Government during the war, and were found by the jury to be adhering to the King's enemies at the date of the issue of the writ.

Prisoners of War, nor the Geneva Convention of 1949 on the same matter (see Article 4 of the last-named Convention). They are, however, 'protected persons' within the Geneva Convention of 12 August 1949 relating to the Protection of Civilian Persons in Time of War;[1] it is submitted that (subject to the paragraph which follows) their procedural and their contractual status are not affected by their internment.

Although internment, or at any rate 'innocent' internment, does not destroy the alien enemy's normal procedural capacity, there is one remedy previously referred to which is denied to an alien enemy when interned, namely, the writ of *habeas corpus*. In *Weber's* case,[2] an interned alien enemy applied for a writ of *habeas corpus*, and the argument turned on the question of nationality. The Divisional Court, the Court of Appeal, and the House of Lords held that Weber had not completely ceased to be of German nationality, and the writ was refused. The point that he was a prisoner of war, and for that reason not entitled to a writ of *habeas corpus*, was not taken. Meanwhile, in the course of *Weber's* litigation *Liebmann's* case was decided by a Divisional Court consisting of Bailhache and Low JJ.[3] Liebmann was served with a document entitled 'notice of intended internment of an alien enemy', informing him 'that it is intended to intern you as a prisoner of war'. He applied without success to the Home Office Advisory Committee, was interned, and now applied for a writ of *habeas corpus* on the ground (not material for present purposes) that by reason of his discharge from German nationality he was not an alien enemy, though admittedly not a British subject. The Crown took the preliminary objection that Liebmann was a prisoner of war, and therefore the Court had no jurisdiction to grant a writ of *habeas corpus* to him, and upon the authority of the case of the *Three Spanish Sailors*, previously discussed, and two other cases, the objection was upheld. There can be little doubt that the true explanation[4] is that the Crown in imprisoning an alien enemy for reasons of security, whether he becomes a prisoner of war or not, is acting under the royal prerogative, and that its act, like certain other acts done as a belligerent, is not examinable in the Courts.[5]

[1] See Joyce Gutteridge, 26 *B.Y.* (1949), pp. 294–326.

[2] See also *R. v. Commandant of Knockaloe Camp, ex parte Forman*, and *R. v. Home Secretary, ex parte L.*, and note in 61 *L.Q.R.* (1945), p. 126.

[3] Approved by a strong C.A. in *R. v. Bottrill, ex parte Kuechenmeister*. See in particular the six propositions of Asquith L.J. in *R. v. Bottrill*.

[4] Above, p. 95.

[5] *R. v. Bottrill*. Deportation is a similar act: *Netz v. Ede*.

(iii) *Repatriation.* What is the effect of repatriation upon procedural capacity?[1]

In *Tingley* v. *Müller*[2] the defendant Müller, an alien enemy resident in London, not interned, but not allowed to move beyond a certain radius without a permit, gave to his solicitor on 20 May 1915[3] a power of attorney to sell certain leasehold premises. On 26 May, having obtained a police permit to travel to Tilbury with the object of embarking for Germany by way of Flushing, he started upon that journey. On 2 June the leasehold premises were sold by public auction to the plaintiff, and an agreement was signed. From letters from the defendant to his solicitor it was inferred that on 11 June he had reached Hamburg. The case was argued before a full Court of Appeal, which, reversing Eve J. on this point, held that the proper inference was that on 2 June (the material date) the defendant had reached and was resident in Germany (although many Germans in course of repatriation are believed to have found more pressing business in Holland), and was therefore an alien enemy. The Court further held that the power of attorney, being expressed to be irrevocable for twelve months, and having been given at a time when the donor was not an alien enemy, was not avoided by his subsequent change of status; and that the agreement of sale did not involve any intercourse with the defendant, and could therefore be legally carried out by the attorney, so that the plaintiff's qualms of conscience were ill-founded, and his claim for a declaration that the agreement was void *ab initio* or dissolved by the defendant's change of status was refused. Scrutton L.J., however, delivered a strong dissenting judgment, holding that the agreement of 2 June was one which purported to be made with an alien enemy and was therefore void, and the interposition of an English agent did not cure the defect. He expressed the opinion that Müller became an alien enemy the moment he left England, as at that time he lost his acquired English commercial domicile, and thereupon reverted to his national character,

---

[1] In *Brownell* v. *Oehmichen* a United States Court of Appeals held that a German national repatriated during war from the United States to Germany became an enemy.

[2] [1917] 2 Ch. 144 (C.A.). It should be noted that in this case, as in other cases of so-called 'repatriation', the enemy national could have stayed in the neutral country through which he had to pass, so far as Great Britain was concerned, though he might not have been allowed by the Government of that country to do so. Another consequence of repatriation is illustrated by *Stoeck* v. *Public Trustee* [1921] 2 Ch. 67, 71. It is evident from some of the speeches delivered in the *Sovfracht* case and from the Opinion of the Privy Council in *Hangkam Kwingtong Woo* v. *Liu Lan Fong* that the majority decision of the C.A. in *Tingley* v. *Müller* was not popular, and its authority is now open to question. *Pritzker* v. *Custodian of Enemy Property* is a Palestinian decision upon a power of attorney.

[3] It was common ground that he was then within the protection of the King.

determined by allegiance. *Uhlig* v. *Uhlig* is a case of a summons by a petitioner of German nationality who in 1916 had obtained a decree absolute of divorce, asking for the custody and education of his children. He had already been repatriated to Germany. Neither on this ground nor on the ground that his repatriation had revoked his solicitor's retainer did the Court of Appeal decline to entertain the summons, but it must be noted that in proceedings of this character the primary concern of the Court is to secure the welfare of the children and not to protect the interests of the parties. The Court declined to allow the children, who were British subjects, to be sent to an enemy country.

(k) Enemy (wherever he may be) by reason of identification with the enemy Power, either by adherence to it or rendering assistance to it or by control from enemy sources

This is a miscellaneous category, but the authority for its existence, though scattered and piecemeal, is, it is submitted, adequate.

(i) Thus it is believed that persons, of whatever nationality and wherever they may be, who are in the military or civilian employment of the enemy would be debarred from suing in an English Court. In *Sparenburgh* v. *Bannatyne*,[1] the plaintiff, who was a neutral (German) subject and was captured as a seaman on board a Dutch enemy ship of war, was regarded as an enemy until he had ceased to be in the service of the enemy, and was thereafter allowed to sue, though a prisoner of war. In *The Benjamin Franklin*,[2] the plaintiff was a British pilot suing to recover wages for navigating a neutral ship to an enemy port. Lord Stowell dismissed the action, observing:

I should first wish to hear how any suit can be maintained, on behalf of a British subject, for services performed in aiding the commerce and importation of the enemy. Is it not a contribution of his skill and experience to assist and promote the navigation of the enemy's ports?

It is not clear whether this should be regarded as a case of adherence to the enemy causing a procedural disability, or a case of trading with the enemy resulting in an illegal agreement.

(ii) In *Netherlands South African Railway Co.* v. *Fisher*[3] (which is not adequately reported) Lawrance J. left it to the jury to find that the plaintiff company, incorporated in a neutral country (Holland), and

---

[1] (1797). [2] (1806).

[3] (1901) 18 T.L.R. 116. For some account of the activities of this company, see Pitt Cobbett, II, p. 306, and Report of the Transvaal Concessions Commission (Cd. 623), pp. 17 *et seq.*

its directors, also plaintiffs but apparently not enemy subjects,[1] had 'adhered to the King's enemies' by trading with and obtaining money from the enemy Government, with the result that they were debarred from suing for libel in an English Court. The first Lord Parker of Waddington in the *Daimler* case[2] refers to this decision with approval. The acquisition of enemy character by a natural person by virtue of aiding the enemy or voluntarily residing in enemy territory is one of his main arguments for investing artificial persons with analogous enemy character, and when he says[3] that a company incorporated in the United Kingdom may 'assume an enemy character...if its agents or the persons in de facto control of its affairs, whether authorized or not, are resident in an enemy country or, wherever resident, are adhering to the enemy or taking instructions from or acting under the control of enemies', the statement applies *a fortiori* to a plaintiff, a natural person, who is adhering to the enemy Power or is under the control of alien enemies in the territorial sense. Thus if an enemy spy or agent in this country is injured owing to negligence in driving a car, he cannot, it is submitted, sue the driver for damages during the war. The Trading with the Enemy Act, 1939, adopted (subsection 1 of section 2)[4] the test of control in the case of 'any body of persons (whether corporate or unincorporate)', but we submit that this in no way excludes the common law test as applied to an individual.

(iii) In the *Daimler* case[5] the Lord Parker said:

A natural person, though an English-born subject of His Majesty, may bear an enemy character and be under liability and disability as such by adhering to His Majesty's enemies. If he gives them active aid, he is a traitor; but he may fall far short of that and still be invested with enemy character...Not only actively, but passively, he may bring himself under the same disability. Voluntary residence among the enemy, however passive or pacific he may be, identifies an English subject with His Majesty's foes...

Lord Parker does not confine this statement to British subjects in enemy territory, and we can see no reason why any person in this country, of whatever or no nationality, who adheres to His Majesty's enemies by overt acts[6] should not thereby invest himself with enemy

---

[1] It seems that one of them was at the material time resident in enemy territory.

[2] [1916] 2 A.C. 307, 339.   [3] At p. 345.

[4] See later, p. 106.

[5] [1916] 2 A.C. 307, 338. Note the different case of the alien in this country in time of peace who is guilty of active hostility to the Crown, discussed *obiter* in *Johnstone* v. *Pedlar* [1921] 2 A.C. 262, 273–5, 277, 285, 297.

[6] Such as rendering assistance to the enemy by means of propaganda activities: *Hansen* v. *Brownell*.

character and come under the disabilities appropriate to the enemy in the territorial sense.

(*l*) *Enemy corporations*[1]

A corporation is regarded as enemy for the purpose of being defeated as a plaintiff by the plea of alien enemy in the following circumstances:

(i) *When it owes its legal existence and incorporation to the laws of an enemy State.* It is believed that there was, strictly speaking, only *obiter* English judicial authority for this proposition. Of American law Beale[2] asserts the proposition on the strength of *Society for the Propagation of the Gospel* v. *Wheeler*.[3] In what was the leading English decision before the War of 1914 to 1918—*Janson* v. *Driefontein Consolidated Mines*[4]—five law lords (Lord Halsbury L.C. at p. 490, Lord Macnaghten at p. 497, Lord Davey at p. 498, Lord Brampton at p. 501, and Lord Lindley at p. 505) were of the same opinion. But it was not essential to the decision.[5] The Trading with the Enemy Amendment Act, 1916, section 15, provided express statutory authority for the proposition, and we shall cite later the provisions of the Trading with the Enemy Act, 1939. A corporation incorporated in a foreign State may *in addition* acquire for other reasons some other and additional national character, but at any rate the nationality of the State which brought it into being must be attributed to it.

(ii) *When, wherever incorporated, it has acquired enemy character by reason of the hostile residence or activities of its agents or other persons in* de facto *control of its activities.* This proposition rests upon the speech of Lord Parker in the *Daimler* case—*obiter*,[6] but surely no *obiter* judgment more deliberate and more closely approximating to binding law has ever been delivered. This speech, delivered with the concurrence of

---

[1] McNair, 4 *B.Y.* (1923–4), pp. 44–59; Baty, *International Law in South Africa*, ch. VI; Al-Shawi, *Role of the Corporate Entity in International Law*, pp. 77–117; and Mann, 11 *I. and C.L.Q* (1962), pp. 471–502.   [2] *Conflict of Laws*, § 153. 3.

[3] (1814); see also for English authority *Daniel* v. *Commissioners for Claims on France* (1825), and *Long* v. *The Same* (1832), which, however, involve other points. In a Belgian case *Huileries du Congo belge*, etc. v. *Office des Séquestres*, it was held by the Court of Cassation that a company incorporated in an enemy country is an enemy, even though the entire share capital was in allied hands; and see *The Roumanian*, where a company registered and carrying on business in Germany was treated as an enemy, although 90 per cent of its shares were held by allied or neutral subjects.

[4] [1902] A.C. 484.

[5] *Per* Lord Parker in *Daimler Co.* v. *Continental Tyre and Rubber Co.* [1916] 2 A.C. 307 (foot of p. 342).

[6] It sufficed for the purposes of the decision to hold, as their lordships unanimously did, that the secretary in England held no authority from the directors, who were German nationals resident in Germany, to institute the action and that there was no way in which after the outbreak of war he could acquire such authority.

Viscount Mersey, Lord Kinnear and Lord Sumner, shows that a test based on the country in which and under whose laws a company is incorporated is only a *prima facie* test and will give way[1] to the test of the national status and character of its agents or the persons who are in *de facto* control of its affairs; and that the national status and character of the individual shareholders, while not in themselves affecting the character of the company, are relevant to

the question whether the company's agents, or the persons in de facto control of its affairs, are in fact adhering to, taking instructions from, or acting under the control of enemies.[2]

So in a case (such as that under consideration) where the secretary held one share out of 25,000, and was the only shareholder and the only officer of the company who was not an enemy, the burden of proving that it was not an enemy as tested in the manner above indicated might well be thrown upon the company, and an investigation by the Court of first instance would be required. One of the strongest points in Lord Parker's reasoning is made, it is submitted, when he shows that the nationality of a natural person is by no means conclusive in determining his character, enemy or otherwise, and that just as voluntary residence or a commercial domicile in enemy territory or adhering to the enemy will invest a natural person with enemy character though he be not of enemy nationality,[3] so

in transferring the application of the rule against trading with the enemy from natural to artificial persons, something more than the mere place or country of registration or incorporation must be looked at.[4]

Lord Parker summarized his speech in six propositions[5] of which we shall quote the third and the sixth. The third is:

Such a company may...assume an enemy character. This will be the case if its agents or the persons in de facto control of its affairs, whether authorized or not, are resident in an enemy country, or, wherever resident, are adhering to the enemy[6] or taking instructions from or acting under the control of enemies. A person knowingly dealing with the company in such a case is trading with the enemy.

---

[1] To the detriment, not to the benefit, of the company.

[2] [1916] 2 A.C. at p. 345. For a decision of the American Supreme Court, rejecting on the ground of predominant enemy control and influence, a claim by a Swiss Corporation against the Alien Property Custodian to be entitled to certain shares of stock in American corporations, see *Uebersee Finanz-Korporation* v. *McGrath*, I.L.R. [1952] No. 126; and see note on p. 596 of this volume of the Reports. For some French decisions on enemy control, see 9 *A.D.* (1938–40), No. 213.

[3] See above, p. 89.   [4] [1916] 2 A.C. at p. 339.

[5] [1916] 2 A.C. at pp. 344–6.

[6] E.g. *Netherlands South Africa Railway Co.* v. *Fisher* discussed above on pp. 100-1. For a South African decision, see *Overseas Trust Corporation* v. *Godfrey*.

This proposition has been adopted in a number of cases, and it may now safely be regarded as part of the law of England.[1]

(iii) In the words of Lord Parker's sixth proposition: 'A company registered in the United Kingdom but carrying on business in an enemy country is to be regarded as an enemy.'[2]

The Trading with the Enemy Act, 1939, section 2 (1), as amended, includes 'for the purposes of this Act'[3] within its definition of 'enemy':

(c) any body of persons (whether corporate or unincorporate) carrying on business in any place, if and so long as the body is controlled by a person who, under this section, is an enemy.

(d) any body of persons constituted or incorporated in, or under the laws of, a State at war with His Majesty, and

(e) as respects any business carried on in enemy territory, any individual or body of persons (whether corporate or unincorporate) carrying on that business.

It must be noted that the fact that a company registered in the United Kingdom has acquired enemy character by reason of the *Daimler* rules does not convert it into an enemy corporation. It does not cease to be a United Kingdom company—with at least two consequences: (a) the authority of its directors and other agents in enemy territory to bind it by contract or otherwise is terminated, and (b) it is subject to the common law and statutory provisions prohibiting trading or other intercourse with the enemy.[4]

(m) *Plaintiff in interpleader issue*

In *Geiringer* v. *Swiss Bank Corporation*, it was held by Bennett J. that the claimant in an interpleader issue directed to be tried before the outbreak of war, who becomes an alien enemy in the territorial sense, cannot proceed with his claim after war has broken out, though, if

---

[1] McNair, 4 *B.Y.* (1923–4), pp. 44–59. In *Part Cargo ex M.V. Glenroy* the *Daimler* doctrine operated to make a German enemy company controlled by a (then neutral) Japanese company an enemy house of business of the Japanese company. In *The Unitas* an unsuccessful attempt was made to invoke the application of the *Daimler* doctrine in reverse, in order to displace the enemy character of a whaling-ship carrying the enemy flag, though substantially owned by non-enemies; on appeal, in the Privy Council, the enemy flag was regarded in the circumstances of this case as conclusive: see 3 *I. and C.L.Q.* (1950), pp. 562–4; and see below, *Kuenigl* v. *Donnersmarck*.

[2] At p. 346. But the mere fact that a British company had a rubber estate in enemy territory and was carrying on business there through a properly constituted agent up to the time of the outbreak of war does not make it an enemy company: *Re Hilckes, ex parte Muhesa Rubber Plantations*.

[3] Upon the effect of this expression, see below, p. 107.

[4] *Kuenigl* v. *Donnersmarck* also an unsuccessful attempt to apply the *Daimler* doctrine in reverse.

the issue had been framed so as to make him the defendant, the proceedings could have continued; but an order made during the war directing the plaintiff in the issue to give security for costs (which clearly he could not do) or, alternatively, to be for ever barred from prosecuting his claim, while leaving the defendant in the issue free to recover the sum claimed from the party who interpleaded, would be manifestly unjust because the alien enemy plaintiff in the issue might be the party lawfully entitled to payment of the sum in dispute. Accordingly, the learned judge declined to make such an order.

(n) *Claimant in Prize Court proceedings*

The practice governing enemy claimants in Prize Courts has been stated by Dr Colombos in his *Law of Prize*[1] (§§ 330–2 inclusive). Although it is the Crown which institutes proceedings for the condemnation of the property, there is no doubt that a party who enters appearance and claims the property is regarded as an *actor* in the proceedings.[2] At any rate, from *The Père Adam*[3] in 1778 until the outbreak of the War of 1914 to 1918, the enemy was not allowed to appear and claim his property unless he could point to some suspension of his hostile character. However, in *The Möwe* in November 1914, Sir Samuel Evans P., regarding the matter as one of practice and not of international law, directed that 'the practice of the Court shall be, that whenever an alien enemy conceives that he is entitled to any protection, privilege, or relief under any of the Hague Conventions of 1907, he shall be entitled to appear as a claimant and to argue his claim before this Court'. This practice was approved by the Privy Council in *The Vesta*[4] and generalized so as to apply to any international instrument.[5] In *The Glenroy*[6] Lord Merriman P. declined to extend the practice to cover the case of the enemy claimant who can point to no convention or Royal authority

---

[1] (3rd ed. 1949). See also *The Rebecca*; *The Charlotte*; *The Eliza Ann*; *The Frederick*; *The Maria Theresa*.

[2] *The Charlotte*.

[3] And see *The Hoop*.

[4] [1921] 1 A.C. 744, 786. There are other cases cited by Colombos, *op. cit.*, and see Hyde, II, § 612, and Garner, *International Law and the World War*, § 90.

[5] It is difficult to see how a Prize Court can properly discharge its functions unless the enemy claimant is regarded as having *persona standi in judicio* in all cases. Consider the statement by Lord Reading C.J. in *Porter* v. *Freudenberg* (a decision of the Court of Appeal) cited later on p. 112. The Prize Court is a British court, having absorbed as the result of a statute of 1825 the prize jurisdiction of the Scottish courts (Colombos, *op. cit.* § 1); but it administers international law.

[6] See Lord Parker in *The Hakan* [1918] A.C. 148, 150, and *The Dirigo, The Hallingdal and Other Ships* [1919] P. 204, 217, 219.

enabling him to sustain a *persona standi in judicio* and held that a Royal licence to sue was necessary.[1]

(o) The statutory enemy

The Trading with the Enemy Act, 1939,[2] does not specifically deal with procedural status, but 'enemy' is defined by section 2 of the Act as follows:

2 (1) Subject to the provisions of this section, the expression 'enemy' for the purposes of this Act means—

(a) any State, or Sovereign of a State, at war with His Majesty,

(b) any individual resident[3] in enemy territory,

(c) any body of persons (whether corporate or unincorporate) carrying on business in any place, if and so long as the body is controlled by a person who, under this section, is an enemy,

(d) any body of persons constituted or incorporated in, or under the laws of, a State at war with His Majesty, and

(e) as respects any business carried on in enemy territory, any individual or body of persons (whether corporate or unincorporate) carrying on that business;

but does not include any individual by reason only that he is an enemy subject.

(2) The Board of Trade may by order direct that any person specified in the order shall, for the purposes of this Act, be deemed to be, while so specified, an enemy.

To which it is necessary to add subsection (1) of section 15:[4]

(1) In this Act the following expressions have the meanings hereby respectively assigned to them:

'enemy subject'[5] means

(a) an individual who, not being either a British subject or a British protected person, possesses the nationality of a State at war with His Majesty, or

(b) a body of persons constituted or incorporated in, or under the laws of, any such State; and

---

[1] See below, p. 108, for the conditions affecting enemy plaintiffs generally. But it would seem that in prize, although the executive discretion is equally unfettered, the conditions are not so strict as in the case of enemy plaintiffs generally; the Prize Court exists, for the purpose, amongst others, of dealing with enemy property, and accordingly licences are granted more freely for prize than for other proceedings.

[2] In its present amended form.

[3] See *Stadtmuller* v. *Miller*; and *Vowinckel* v. *First Federal Trust Co.*

[4] For subsection (1 A) added in 1953, see below, p. 352, n. 4.

[5] The Treachery Act, 1940, section 5 (1), defines an 'enemy alien' for the purposes of that Act as 'a person who possesses the nationality of a State at war with His Majesty, not being either a British subject or a person certified by a Secretary of State to be a British protected person'.

'enemy territory' means any area which is under the sovereignty of, or in the occupation of, a Power with whom His Majesty is at war, not being an area in the occupation of His Majesty or of a Power allied with His Majesty.

It was under subsection (2) of section 2 of this Act that the Board of Trade issued during the War of 1939 to 1945 the 'Black Lists' containing hundreds of names of persons and firms and corporations carrying on business in neutral countries deemed to be enemies. The Board of Trade has power to specify 'any person' as an enemy.

The Court of Appeal in the *Sovfracht* case[1] held that this Act 'does not purport to impose or define enemy status otherwise than for the purposes of the Act, which are (so far as relevant) the prohibition of dealings with persons who, for the purposes of the Act, are to be regarded as enemies', and that 'a person, therefore, who is not an enemy at common law is not by the Act made an enemy', that is to say, for procedural purposes, so as to be prevented from suing by the plea of alien enemy. The House of Lords held the Dutch company to be an enemy at common law and therefore found it unnecessary to give an express ruling upon the meaning of such expressions as 'for the purposes of this Act' and 'in this Act', but Lord Wright[2] approved the view of the Court of Appeal referred to above and added that the statutory and the common law definitions were substantially the same. (*Gebr. van Uden* v. *Burrell*, already discussed,[3] was a decision upon the Trading with the Enemy Act, 1914, which resembles in many respects the Act of 1939 and contains the expression 'for the purposes of this Act'; there the purposes appear to have included the question of the plea of alien enemy.)[4]

In most cases a person who is an enemy in the territorial sense at common law is also a statutory enemy by reason of the Trading with the Enemy Act, 1939. The reverse is not true. As Ormerod J. pointed out in *Vamvakas* v. *Custodian of Enemy Property and Another*, the object of the Trading with the Enemy legislation is the control and administration of enemy property, while the common law rule of voluntary residence or presence is concerned more with *persona standi in judicio* and the effect of war upon contracts and is narrower than the statutory test which is substantially '*de facto* residence irrespective of circumstances'.

---

[1] [1942] 1 K.B. 222, 229; [1943] A.C. 203; see above, p. 91.
[2] [1943] A.C. at p. 219.   [3] P. 88.
[4] For a Canadian illustration of an enemy national who was an enemy for the purpose of certain legislation but not an enemy at common law or for the purpose of other legislation so as to be defeated by the plea of alien enemy, see *J. G. White Engineering Corporation* v. *Canadian Car & Foundry Co.*

When the Board of Trade, acting under subsection 2 of section 2 of the Act of 1939, specifies a person as an enemy, for instance, during the War of 1939 to 1945, a Spaniard in Barcelona who had some commercial connection with Germany, then it becomes criminal and illegal for any person in this country to have any intercourse or dealings with him, including the payment of money to him. Suppose that he becomes entitled to a legacy payable under a will proved in England out of assets situate in England, or is libelled by a person in England. Can he be defeated by the plea of alien enemy if he sues in England? Although procedural status may not be one of 'the purposes of the Act', it is difficult to believe that the 'Black-Listed' statutory enemy could recover in an English Court money which it would be illegal for the defendant to pay him before action brought.

It is worth mentioning that in *The Hoop* Lord Stowell attached so much importance to lack of *persona standi in iudicio* that he was prepared to infer from its absence 'a legal inability to contract'.

(p) Suing by licence

The ancient disability of the alien enemy to sue can be removed for a particular case or group of cases by the grant of a Royal licence. During, and later, for the purposes of, the War of 1939 to 1945, the practice was to apply to the Home Office for the licence (in actions in Scottish courts to the Secretary of State for Scotland). It was, however, considered desirable that the solicitor should first ascertain that he was in a position to accept a retainer from a client who was an alien enemy, and his application to the Trading with the Enemy Department for the grant of a licence to himself to accept the retainer ordinarily preceded his application to the Home Office for the grant of a Royal licence to his client to sue. That the distinction between these two licences was not always realized is evident from the observations of Viscount Simon L.C. in the *Sovfracht* case.[1] The issue of a licence being a matter of unfettered executive discretion, it was not possible to lay down any specific rules which govern the grant or refusal of a licence. No doubt an application from a person who by reason of enemy occupation had become an enemy in the technical territorial sense would receive more favourable consideration than an application from an enemy in the strict sense of the word. Even so, it would seem that a licence to an alien enemy to commence proceedings in the courts of this country would be granted only

[1] [1943] A.C. 203, 208.

rarely.[1] A judgment in the applicant's favour would in many cases confer a benefit on the enemy,[2] e.g. by enabling foreign exchange credit to be raised in a neutral country on the security of the contingent asset, and in such cases the application for a Royal licence would presumably be refused. Whilst these stringent conditions applied as long as actual hostilities continued, it is clear that a more favourable view of such applications was taken during the interval, sometimes long, between the 'cease fire' and the official end of the war with a particular enemy country. Indeed, official action was taken to dispense with the necessity of a Royal licence in certain cases during the waiting period. Soon after the cessation of hostilities the Government took steps to encourage trade with certain of the ex-enemy countries (though still technically at war with His Majesty), and for this purpose the Board of Trade from time to time made orders which were, in effect, general authorizations under paragraph (i) of the proviso to section 1 (2) of the Trading with the Enemy Act, 1939, permitting trade with these countries.[3] It was thought, moreover, that enemy traders would not be encouraged to take advantage of this opportunity if they had to obtain a Royal licence to sue in the English courts upon any question which arose out of the subsequent trading. A regulation[4] was therefore made providing that an alien enemy might, without a Royal licence, maintain legal proceedings arising out of any transaction entered into after the date of the regulation by virtue of such an authority. It will be noted that the regulation had no application to prize cases, and that until the war ended by the conclusion of the treaties of peace or otherwise, an alien enemy still required a Royal licence to commence proceedings in cases which did not fall within the limited terms of this regulation.

The issue of a license to a person to sue being an Executive act, the court is not competent to question its validity or to inquire into the circumstances in which it is given.[5]

[1] See p. 105 above as to permitting enemy claimants to appear in the Prize Court.

[2] *Sovfracht* case [1943] A.C. 203 at pp. 236, 252.

[3] E.g. the Trading with the Enemy (Authorization) (Italy) Order, 1945, S.R. & O. 1945 (no. 1098), I, p. 1210. Orders were also made authorizing trade with other countries.

[4] Regulation 9 of the Defence (Trading with the Enemy) Regulations, 1940 (added to the Regulations by Article 2 of an Order in Council of 7 December 1945), S.R. & O. 1945 (no. 1534), II, p. 100.

[5] *Bugsier Reederei-und-Bergungs Aktiengesellschaft* v. *Owners of S.S. Brighton*, applying *Usparicha* v. *Noble*.

(q) *Enemy holder of licence to trade*

In *Schering A.G.* v. *Pharmedica Proprietary Ltd* the Supreme Court of New South Wales held that the grant of a licence to trade to an enemy in the territorial sense carried with it 'the right to sue for the purpose of protecting the trade which is licensed'.

2. ENEMY DEFENDANTS

It is now clear that an enemy, wherever he may be and, if in this country, whether 'in protection' or not, can be made a defendant and served with a writ if service or substituted service can be effected, and is in the same position as any other defendant. Until the War of 1914 to 1918 English authority was scarce, and the Attorney-General's argument in *Porter* v. *Freudenberg* turned largely on the position of felons, outlaws, and attainted persons as declared in a series of decisions which he cited. *Bacon's Abridgement* (7th ed.), vol. 1, at p. 183, and *Albretcht* v. *Sussmann*, give some authority for saying that an alien enemy could bring a bill of discovery to assist him in his defence, and therefore that he could not repel an action by pleading that he was an alien enemy. A decision of the Supreme Court of the United States of America in 1870, *McVeigh* v. *United States*, afforded authority for the view that the alien enemy can be sued and can resort to the usual means of defence. Bailhache J. in *Robinson & Co.* v. *Continental Insurance Co. of Mannheim*[1] pointed out that to allow an alien enemy defendant to plead as a defence that he is an alien enemy was 'to injure a British subject and to favour an alien enemy, and to defeat the object and reason of the suspensory rule. It is to turn a disability into a relief.' He refused the defendant's application to stay all proceedings, fortifying his judgment by the passage from *Bacon's Abridgement* referred to above and by certain American decisions, and his judgment received the approval of the full Court of Appeal in *Porter* v. *Freudenberg*. Lord Reading C.J. in delivering the judgment of the Court said:

As was said by Bailhache J. in *Robinson & Co.* v. *Continental Insurance Co. of Mannheim*, 'to hold that a subject's right of suit is suspended against an alien enemy is to injure a British subject and to favour an alien enemy and to defeat the object and reason of the suspensory rule'. In our judgment the effect would be to convert that which during war is a disability,

---

[1] [1915] 1 K.B. 155, 159. On the effect of war upon the jurisdictional immunity of an enemy Government, see *Telkes* v. *Hungarian National Museum*.

imposed upon the alien enemy because of his hostile character, into a relief to him during the war from the discharge of his liabilities to British subjects.

He then referred to certain old cases in which it had been held that persons attainted or outlawed could be sued, and pointed out (p. 883) that 'the real difficulty that arises in seeking to enforce a right against an alien enemy is that of fixing him with proper notice of the suit and the proceedings in the action'.

Substituted service. The usual way in which a plaintiff attempts to meet this difficulty is by some form of substituted service either of the writ or of notice of the writ, and the matter was discussed at some length by the Court of Appeal in *Porter* v. *Freudenberg*.[1] The Court has at all times a wide discretion as to the form of substituted service, if any, which it will authorize, within the limits of the principle stated in that decision to be that the Court must satisfy itself that[2]

the method of substituted service asked for by the plaintiff is one which will in all reasonable probability, if not certainty, be effective to bring knowledge of the writ or the notice of the writ (as the case may be) to the defendant.

In that decision the Court authorized substituted service in one case upon the London agent of an enemy and in another case upon the London manager of the enemy's business, both enemies being in the enemy country.[3]

On 17 December 1940 the following notice was issued by the Lord Chief Justice:[4]

As the Government of Germany has refused to serve and has returned notice of writs forwarded by the United States Embassy, recourse must be had to the ordinary practice of substituted service—which may be by advertisement. Subject to the discretion of the Court or a Judge, proof of inability to effect personal service will be satisfied if the affidavit states

---

[1] [1915] 1 K.B. 857, 886. For an instance of service on the London branch of a Berlin bank, see *Leader, Plunkett and Leader* v. *Direction der Disconto Gesellschaft*. Later, the Legal Proceedings against Enemies Act, 1915, now repealed, facilitated service of proceedings instituted against enemies out of the jurisdiction in certain cases. There was no similar legislation during the 1939 to 1945 war until the making of the rule of the Supreme Court, mentioned on the next page, and now repealed.

[2] At p. 889.

[3] For an instance of the effective service of a writ of summons upon the manager in London of a partnership carrying on business in enemy-occupied territory, see *Meyer* v. *Louis Dreyfus et Cie*, and comment upon that decision, below, at p. 360; and see for another instance *Yokomuttu* v. *Saminathan*.

[4] See *Weekly Notes* of 21 December 1940, p. 456.

that the proposed defendant is resident in Germany or in a country occupied by Germany, and gives the grounds on which the deponent bases his statement.

This notice was referred to by the Court of Appeal in the case described as *Re An Intended Action between V. L. Churchill & Co. and Johan Lomberg*,[1] where it was pointed out that the notice referred to above did not purport to modify the law as laid down in *Porter* v. *Freudenberg*, that service by advertisement was only one variety of substituted service, and that the notice did not mean that advertisement in, say, *The Times* of London must, in all circumstances, be regarded as sufficient to bring a writ of summons to the notice of a person in enemy or enemy-occupied territory.[2]

A rule of the Supreme Court, Order IX, r. 14B, which came into force on 31 October 1941, and has since been revoked and not replaced,[3] enabled the Court to 'dispense with service of a writ of summons or a notice of a writ of summons[4] on any defendant who was an enemy within the meaning of the Trading with the Enemy Act, 1939, as amended by or under any enactment',[5] in the circumstances and subject to the safeguards specified in the rule.

Enemy's right of effective defence. Having dealt with substituted service, Lord Reading, C. J., in *Porter* v. *Freudenberg*, continued as follows:[6]

> Once the conclusion is reached that the alien can be sued, it follows that he can appear and be heard in his defence and may take all such steps as may be deemed necessary for the proper presentment of his defence... To deny him that right would be to deny him justice and would be quite contrary to the basic principles guiding the King's Courts in the administration of justice.

Thus, the enemy defendant, whether the proceedings are instituted before or after the outbreak of war, is entitled to be represented by solicitor and counsel and to exercise all the ordinary privileges,[7] and be subject to all the ordinary liabilities, of a defendant, except that

[1] Referred to by Uthwatt J. in *Re de Barbe*.

[2] And see *Vandyke* v. *Adams*, and *Luccioni* v. *Luccioni*.

[3] Halsbury (Hailsham) Cumulative Supplement, 1964, vol. 30, p. 24.

[4] Not a petition in divorce proceedings: *Read* v. *Read*.

[5] Which does not include a British officer captured by the enemy and a prisoner of war in enemy territory: *Vandyke* v. *Adams*.

[6] [1915] 1 K.B. at p. 883. For a case of adjournment until such time as an interned defendant could attend in Court, see *Munim* v. *Benz*.

[7] Including the right to move for a stay of proceedings: *Owners of M.V. Lubrafol* v. *Owners of S.S. Pamia*.

(i) he cannot counterclaim, but may plead his claim *pro tanto* as a set-off;[1]

(ii) he cannot take third party proceedings, because in doing so he would become an *actor*;[2] and

(iii) (probably) he cannot execute a judgment for costs during the war;[3]

(iv) it is unlikely that an application by him for a commission to examine witnesses in enemy territory will be granted, because that would involve the sanctioning of 'an unlawful communication with the Queen's enemies'.[4] (This defect would seem to be equally fatal in the case of such an application by a British litigant.)

It follows from the alien enemy defendant's right to defend proceedings that his solicitor and counsel may by obtaining a licence hold the intercourse with him required for obtaining instructions, and cases occurred in the War of 1914 to 1918 where consultation with him in a neutral country was permitted.[5]

3. ENEMY APPELLANTS

Their position was considered by the Court of Appeal in *Porter* v. *Freudenberg*, where it was laid down[6] that the appellate Courts are as much open to the enemy defendant as to any other defendant; he may be said to initiate the appeal but he was not the *actor* in the original proceedings. 'Once he is cited to appear he is entitled to the same opportunities of challenging the correctness of the decision of the judge of first instance or other tribunal as any other defendant.' The decision of the Supreme Court of the United States in *McVeigh* v. *United States* was followed. On the other hand, the position of the enemy plaintiff is different. We have seen that he cannot (except by licence of the Crown) during the war commence proceedings or con-

---

[1] *Re Stahlwerk Becker A.-G.'s Patent*, where it is made clear that an enemy patentee who is respondent to a petition for revocation of a patent (being in the position of a defendant —*Re Merten's Patents* [1915] 1 K.B. 857) may apply for leave to amend his specification by way of disclaimer, for in doing so he is not an *actor* in the proceedings but is resorting to a defensive procedure.

In *The Kaiser Wilhelm II* (damage by collision) it is not stated which shipowner initiated the proceedings and which was left to counterclaim or institute a cross action; at any rate in one of these proceedings an alien enemy was an *actor*; the ships being held to be equally to blame for the collision, it was ordered that no payment should be made under the judgment until the end of the war or the further order of the Court.

[2] *Halsey and Another* v. *Lowenfeld* (*Leigh and Curzon, Third Parties*).

[3] *Robinson & Co.* v. *Continental Insurance Co. of Mannheim*.

[4] *Barrick* v. *Buba* (1855).

[5] See Scrutton in 34 *L.Q.R.* (1918) at p. 124.

[6] [1915] 1 K.B. 857, 883, 884, 890; *A.-G. für Anilin Fabrikation and Another* v. *Levinstein*. See also *The Charlotte* and *Buxbaum* v. *Assicurazioni General*.

tinue proceedings initiated before the war. He is the *actor* throughout. Whether judgment has been pronounced against him before or during the war, he has no right of appeal during the war.

4. BANKRUPTCY

An enemy, whether 'in protection' or not, may be made bankrupt and may apply for and obtain his discharge.[1] But he cannot petition, for then he would be an *actor*. Can he prove for a debt in a bankruptcy resulting from a petition filed by one who is not under such disability? There is some authority[2] for saying that his proof ought to be considered during the war and that, if it is admitted, the sum due should be retained for him until after the war or paid during the war to a custodian of enemy property if one has been appointed. To proceed to distribute the bankrupt's assets without considering the enemy's proof would amount to distributing amongst the other creditors a sum which belongs to the enemy (unless and until it is confiscated by the Crown by the appropriate procedure).

5. STATUTES OF LIMITATION

The rules governing the limitation of actions—at any rate where no question of real property is involved—being part of the law of procedure, it is right that they should be considered here. It is useful to remind ourselves of the distinction between a secondary, remedial right such as a right of action and a primary right, the breach of which gives rise to a right of action; for instance, in the case of a pre-war contract, the distinction between a right of action which accrued before a war broke out and a right to performance which had not then become due. We are only concerned with rights of action; there are no statutes for the limitation of primary rights. The effect of the outbreak of war upon rights of performance raises questions which are considered elsewhere; that is not procedural but substantive law; at any rate statutes for the limitation of actions cannot touch them.

---

[1] *Re Levy, The Times* newspaper, 30 January 1915, where the enemy was probably in this country, and it was held by Mr Registrar Brougham that 'a bankrupt, although an alien enemy, was entitled to defend himself against the pursuit of creditors and to apply for his discharge'.

[2] *Ex parte Boussmaker*; per Scrutton L.J. in *Re Hilckes, ex parte Muhesa Rubber Plantations* [1917] 1 K.B. 48, 60. But if the trustee in bankruptcy rejects or reduces his claim, he cannot take proceedings to challenge the trustee's decision, because in doing so he is an *actor*: *Re Wilson and Wilson, ex parte Marum*. See Williams' *Bankruptcy* (17th ed.) (1958), pp. 167, 187, 573.

The present law

There is not a great deal of judicial authority available, but, contrary to some of the views expressed in previous editions of this book, we believe that the combined effect of the meagre judicial authority, of the Limitation Act, 1939, and of the Limitation (Enemies and War Prisoners) Act, 1945, can be summarized as follows:[1]

(1) The issue of a writ of summons or other initiation of legal proceedings stops the running of time, so that if an alien enemy *actor* has initiated proceedings before the outbreak of war, his action is not barred, however long the war may last; he has no complete assurance that his action may not be dismissed for want of prosecution, but the general treatment by English courts of enemy or ex-enemy litigants ought to suffice to give him some degree of confidence that he is not likely to meet with injustice. Likewise, an enemy defendant to an action instituted before the outbreak of war or during a war gains no protection by the lapse of time.

(2) At common law, the existence of a state of war does not *ipso facto* suspend the operation of a statute for the limitation of actions, whether the cause of action arose before the outbreak of war or during the war.[2]

(3) Now the Limitation (Enemies and Prisoners of War) Act, 1945,[3] which is not confined to the War of 1939 to 1945, provides in section 1 (1) that

If at any time before the expiration of the period of limitation prescribed by any statute of limitation for the bringing of any action any person who would have been a necessary party to that action if it had then been brought was an enemy or detained in enemy territory, the said period shall be deemed not to have run while the said person was an enemy or was so detained, and shall in no case expire before the end of twelve months from the date when he ceased to be an enemy or to be so detained, or from the passing of this Act, whichever is the later.[4]

[1] Proceedings in Prize Courts are not governed by any statute of limitation: see Colombos, *Law of Prize* (3rd ed. 1949), § 343.

[2] This conclusion arises from certain decisions given after the English civil war: *Prideaux* v. *Webber*; *Lee* v. *Rogers*; and receives support from later decisions: *Hall* v. *Wybourn*; *Aubry* v. *Fortescue*; and particularly *Bowring-Hanbury's Trustee* v. *Bowring-Hanbury*. See also Preston and Newsom, *Limitation of Actions* (3rd ed. 1953), p. 7; *Halsbury, Laws of England* (3rd ed. Simonds), vol. 24, §§ 353, 579, where (§ 353, note (q)), a remark by Bramwell B. in *De Wahl* v. *Braune* (1856) 25 L.J. Ex. 343, 345 was distinguished; and Webber, pp. 177–85. There are still some proceedings in equity which lie outside the Limitation Acts, for which see Preston and Newsom, *op. cit.*, in particular, chs. v and x.

[3] Still in force; passed after the Report of the Committee on Limitation of Actions and Bills of Exchange (Chairman, W. L. McNair, K.C.), Cmd. 6591; the text of the Act is printed in the Appendix of the 3rd ed. of this book; and see Preston and Newsom, ch. XIII.

[4] See Preston and Newsom, pp. 290–4, and *The Atlantic Scout*.

The expressions 'action', 'enemy', and 'enemy territory' are defined in section 2 (1).

The Act is (section 6 (2)) 'deemed to have had effect as from the third day of September, nineteen hundred and thirty-nine', and received the Royal Assent on 28 March 1945.

It should be noted (a) that both plaintiffs and defendants, or persons in their position, can benefit by this Act, and that the suspension of a period of limitation operates not only when a plaintiff or a defendant is an enemy or is detained in enemy territory, including enemy-occupied territory, but also when any other 'necessary party' is an enemy or is so detained; and (b) that persons detained include prisoners of war and civilian internees, and that the Act does not say 'detained *by the enemy*'; and (c) that the Act is permanent and, unless repealed, would apply in a future war.

Peace Treaties

After both World Wars the question of the effect of the war upon the limitation of actions was dealt with in some of the treaties of peace.[1] As in the case of war, so also in other armed conflicts the need of express provision concerning the limitation of actions can arise; for instance, Article III (h) of the Anglo-United Arab Republic Financial Agreement of 1959[2] in the course of the post-Suez settlement, which obliged the Republic to ensure that the running of time limits which had not expired at the time measures of sequestration were lifted should be suspended for three months in favour of British owners of property.

---

[1] *American law*. In the previous edition of this book an attempt was made to state the manner in which these matters are dealt with in the United States. Since then there have been many decisions, some of which will be found in the *Annual Digest* and the *International Law Reports*, for instance, *Frabutt* v. *N.T., Chicago and St Louis Railway Co.*, *Standard-Vacuum Oil Co.* v. *United States*; *Marcos* v. *United States*; *Sese* v. *United States*; *Drews* v. *Eastern Sausage & Provision Co.*, where the cause of action seems to have arisen before the outbreak of war. See also Hackworth's *Digest of International Law*, vol. VI, pp. 379–84.
[2] *T.S.* no. 35 (1919).

4

CONTRACTS: GENERAL PRINCIPLES (EXCLUDING FRUSTRATION)[1]

BIBLIOGRAPHY

Coleman Phillipson, *Effect of War on Contracts* (1909).
Baty and Morgan, *War: its Conduct and Legal Results* (1915).
Page, *War and Alien Enemies*, ch. VI (1915).
Nathan, *Influence of War on Contracts* (1916).
MacKinnon, F. D., *Effect of War on Contract* (1917) (though primarily concerned with Frustration).
Campbell, *Law of War and Contract* (1918).
Ghosh, *Effects of War on Contracts* (1920) (Calcutta).
Domke, *Trading with the Enemy in World War II* (1943).
Wolff, Ernest, *The Problem of Pre-war Contracts in Peace Treaties* (1946).
Webber, *Effect of War on Contracts* (2nd ed. 1946).
Baty, 31 *L.Q.R.* (1915), pp. 30–55.
Kronstein, 35 *Georgetown Law Journal*, no. 4 (1947).

We shall classify this matter under the following headings:

A. Contracts made before the outbreak of war in so far as not completely performed,

    (1) Where one of the parties becomes upon the outbreak of war an enemy in the territorial sense[2] and the other is in this country;

    (2) Where, whoever and wherever the parties may be, the effect of the outbreak of war is to make further performance illegal.

B. Contracts made before the outbreak of war, so far as concerns breaches which have already occurred: debts and rights of action which have already accrued.

C. Contracts made before the outbreak of war between the British Crown and persons who have become enemies in the territorial sense.

D. Contracts which are made, or which it is attempted to make, during war.

E. Contracts between persons in foreign non-enemy countries and enemies in the territorial sense.

F. Contracts between persons in this country and enemy nationals in foreign territory neither owned nor occupied by the enemy Power.

---

[1] The Peace Treaties at the end of the War of 1939 to 1945 and the arrangements made with the German Federal Republic contain many provisions relating to contracts.

[2] That is to say, a person of any or no nationality who is voluntarily resident or present or carrying on business in enemy or enemy-occupied territory.

G. Contracts made between persons in enemy territory during war.
H. Contracts which concern a status, see 'Marriage'.[1]
I. Contracts which are 'concomitants of rights of property'.[2]

A FEW PRELIMINARY REMARKS

(i) A good deal of confusion was introduced into the question of the effect of war upon contracts by premature attempts to generalize before enough cases had arisen to enable a general outline of the relevant principles to be worked out. The Napoleonic Wars made a small contribution, the Crimean[3] and the South African wars each another, though still a small one, and in the few years during which the mercantile community was contemplating the possibility of the War of 1914 to 1918 the strangest notions existed in the minds of business men and their legal advisers.[4] It was not until 1914 and 1915 that the actual effect of the full blast of war upon highly commercialized communities was perceived and the Courts became busy in working out the legal effects. We must avoid generalizations and over-simplifications. As Lord Dunedin said in the *Ertel Bieber* case:[5] 'There is indeed no such general proposition as that a state of war avoids all contracts between subjects and enemies', and in *Ottoman Bank* v. *Jebara*:[6] 'it is not every contract that is abrogated by war; it is only a contract which is still executory and which for its execution requires intercourse between the English subject and the enemy'.

(ii) It is of the first importance to distinguish between a right to the performance of a contract, which is a primary right, and a right of action to enforce it specifically (which is rare) or to recover damages for its breach, both of which are secondary or remedial rights.

As regards the right to performance of a pre-war contract, theoretically one of several events might happen: (*a*) abrogation, that is, complete dissolution of the contract from the moment of the outbreak of war; (*b*) suspension of performance until the end of the war, when the obligation revives; (*c*) no effect. We shall find that (*a*) is the normal event, while (*b*) and (*c*) are rare.

---

[1] See pp. 340–1.
[2] In the *Ertel Bieber* case [1918] A.C. 260, 269 Lord Dunedin said: 'there are certain contracts, particularly those which are really the concomitants of rights of property, which even so far as executory are not abrogated'; and see index *sub. tit.*: 'Concomitants of rights of property'.
[3] For the views prevailing in 1855, see a useful note appended to *Clemontson* v. *Blessig*.
[4] See for instance the undertaking given by the Chairman of Lloyd's in 1913 printed on p. 163 of the first edition (1920) of this book.
[5] [1918] A.C. 260, 269.   [6] [1928] A.C. 269, 276.

As regards the right of action for breach of the contract occurring before the outbreak of war, we shall find that when it has accrued *against* an enemy in the territorial sense it is enforceable if service or substituted service can be effected, and when it has accrued *to* an enemy in the territorial sense, the usual result is that it is preserved for him, though he will not be able to enforce it during the war.

(iii) Another preliminary and rather theoretical point. When an English Court holds a contract to be illegal, what exactly does illegality mean? Not, we submit, necessarily that, if the particular contract were performed, mischief of the kind aimed at by the law must result, but that the contract belongs to a category which the Courts in the process of centuries have found to be mischievous and have therefore stigmatized as illegal and declined to enforce either specifically or by imposing damages for their breach.

(*a*) In consideration of one hundred guineas promised by *A*, I procure a marriage between *A* and *B*. They really wanted to marry one another but each party lacked the courage to approach the other, and the marriage turns out to be a marriage 'made in heaven'. No damage has been done. Quite the contrary. But the contract is a marriage brokage contract and my reward is only recoverable in heaven.

(*b*) Upon the outbreak of war with Germany in 1939 I communicate with the manager of my factory in Germany, without obtaining a licence and through a pre-arranged secret channel, and I instruct him to send to England some blue-prints, my own property, which enable me to manufacture here a valuable engine. My motives are patriotic. Nevertheless my act is illegal because it belongs to the category of acts, namely, those involving intercourse with the enemy territory, which in the light of long experience have been found to be very dangerous to the State. As Lord Dunedin said of *The Hoop* in the *Ertel Beiber* case:[1]

The ground of judgment was that all trading with the enemy is unlawful at common law as against public policy. Why? Not because of the terms of the particular contract, but because such contracts in general might enhance the resources of the enemy or cripple those of the subjects of the King.

And as Lord Porter said in the *Sonfracht* case[2] in criticizing *Rodriguez* v. *Speyer Brothers*:

the question, however, whether a given act is against public policy must, I think, be decided on general principles. It is not permissible to say that

---

[1] [1918] A.C. 260, 273; and see Lord Atkinson at p. 277. For another illustration, see *The Rapid*. See also Bailhache J. in *Mitsui* v. *Mumford* [1915] 2 K.B. 27, 33.
[2] [1943] A.C. 203, 251.

a particular act will not in fact assist the enemy. The proper enquiry is whether that act is of a class which is likely to assist him, and it is immaterial whether in the individual case he may or may not be found to profit from it.[1]

There is nothing peculiar about this point. Whenever the law stigmatizes an act as illegal or criminal, it is because the act is within a category of acts which the experience of the law has found it to be necessary in the public interest to stigmatize as illegal or criminal. A rule of law is not made for particular individuals, though it is applied to them. It is general and is made for the community as a whole.

(iv) A few words must be said upon the different kinds of enemies.

(*a*) By *enemy in the territorial sense* is meant a person of any or no nationality who is voluntarily resident or present or carrying on business in enemy or enemy-occupied territory.

(*b*) *Enemy in British territory and 'in protection'*. Where an enemy party to a contract is in British territory and has complied with any requirements such as registration he is considered to be within the protection of the Queen and there is no reason why the existence of a state of war should in itself have any effect upon his pre-war contract[2] or a contract made by him during the war. The enemy living 'in protection' retains his full contractual rights except in so far as specific legislation may affect them; for instance, a prohibition against buying a wireless transmitter. So the butcher or baker may lawfully continue to supply his enemy customers and make binding contracts with them. Suppose, however, that the enemy is a prisoner of war *stricto sensu*. We have already examined cases[3] which tend to show that he also is 'in protection' and has contractual capacity. Suppose that he has been interned in pursuance of general policy and not by reason of an offence. We have already seen[4] that at any rate his internment does not prevent him from enforcing a contract made by him before internment and after compliance with any personal requirements such as registration, and there is no reason why he cannot validly enter into contracts during his internment, for he is 'in protection'.

---

[1] And see Lord Greene M.R. in *In re Anglo-International Bank* [1933] Ch. 233, 239, and Sellers J. in *Bevan* v. *Bevan*.

[2] *Schostall* v. *Johnson* (pre-war contract).   [3] Pp. 93–5.

[4] *Schaffenius* v. *Goldberg* (post-outbreak of war contract); see *supra*, p. 96; *Norman* v. *Rayner* (pre-war contract), where the plaintiff was registered as an alien enemy. But internment may have other consequences if it renders performance impossible.

(*c*) *Enemy in British territory but not 'in protection'.* An enemy in this country, whether he was here when the war broke out or came here subsequently, who has failed to register himself and comply with the requirements of any Aliens Restriction Acts, Aliens Orders, or similar legislation, and thus notify the Crown of his presence here, is not 'in protection'.[1] If he is furthering the cause of the enemy, *cadit quaestio*; apart from other unpleasant consequences, he is 'adhering to the enemy' and can be defeated by the plea of alien enemy.

(*d*) So much for the common law. As we have seen,[2] the Trading with the Enemy Act, 1939, contains an elaborate definition of 'enemy' 'for the purposes of this Act'. One of the main 'purposes of this Act' is to prevent the making or the performance of contracts with the enemy, and there can be no doubt that the statutory enemy as therein defined is in the same position in point of contractual disability as the enemy in the territorial sense is in at common law.

(v) In using the expression 'outbreak of war' in relation to contracts and trading with the enemy, it must be borne in mind that certain other and subsequent events may have the same effect; for instance:

(*a*) When non-enemy territory is occupied by the enemy;[3]

(*b*) When non-enemy territory is ceded to the enemy during the war;

(*c*) When a person in this country transfers himself, or is transferred, during the war to enemy territory; thus in *Tingley* v. *Müller* the Court of Appeal held that Müller, an enemy national, who left this country in May 1915, must be assumed to have arrived in Germany on a certain date and then became an enemy in the territorial sense, which event would, had it not been for the peculiar character of the irrevocable power of attorney previously granted by him, and of the agency thereby created, have avoided the agency, just as the outbreak of war would have done.[4]

---

[1] It is submitted that if an enemy has not disclosed to the Crown his presence here and the fact of his being an enemy, he cannot be said to have received the implied licence of the Crown to remain here 'in protection' (see above, p. 81).

[2] P. 106.

[3] P. 91; the *Fibrosa* case.

[4] See also a South African decision, *Treasury* v. *Gundelfinger and Kaumheimer.*

A. CONTRACTS MADE BEFORE THE OUTBREAK OF WAR[1] IN SO
FAR AS NOT COMPLETELY PERFORMED: ABROGATION
THE COMMONEST EFFECT

In this section we shall examine three possible results of the out-break of war upon a pre-war contract between a party in this country and a party in the enemy country; they are:

I. abrogation; II. suspension; III. no effect.

I. *Abrogation*

The commonest effect is abrogation as from the outbreak of war. This effect may result either (1) because one of the parties is in this country and the other becomes on the outbreak of war an enemy in the territorial sense, or (2) because, whoever and wherever the parties may be, the outbreak of war makes performance or further performance illegal. It may therefore be said that contracts in class (1) are abrogated *ratione personae* and those in class (2) *ratione materiae*.

(1) *Where one of the parties is in this country and the other becomes an enemy in the territorial sense.* In this case, however innocuous the actual performance required by the contract might be, the normal effect of the outbreak of war is that any performance or further performance of it is prohibited, and the contract is abrogated or dissolved as from the date of the outbreak of war, subject to the preservation of accrued rights of action which will be discussed later; for instance, the engagement by a British operatic company of an enemy singer to sing in London. This effect may be based on one of two grounds—either (*a*) that it is a consequence of the disability of the enemy party to sustain a *persona standi in judicio*,[2] or (*b*) the illegality of any kind of intercourse with an enemy in the territorial sense.

Ground (*a*) was stated by Lord Stowell in *The Hoop*[3] as follows:

In the law of almost every country, the character of alien enemy [i.e. in the territorial sense] carried with it a disability to sue, or to sustain, in the language of the civilians a *persona standi in judicio*. The peculiar law of our

---

[1] On the accord between the British and American cases on this point, see *Strauss* v. *Schweizerische Kreditanstalt*, and many other American decisions in the *Annual Digest*. For a case where a letter treated by the Franco-German Mixed Arbitral Tribunal as concluding the contract was in the post when war broke out, see *French and Italian Bank* v. *Warburg & Co.* For a comparison of the Anglo-American and the Continental doctrines as to the effect of war upon executory contracts, see *Binon* v. *German State and the Silesian Fire Insurance Co.*, and Garner, *International Law and the World War*, i, chap. ix. On the proper attitude of the courts of a neutral State towards a pre-war contract between two parties resident respectively in two States engaged in war with one another, see *Telefunken Co.* v. *N. V. Philips.*

[2] See Swinfen Eady L.J. in *Zinc Corporation* v. *Hirsch* [1916] 1 K.B. 541, 558.

[3] (1799) 1 C. Rob. 196, 200, though the actual trading there took place during war.

own country applies this principle with great rigour...A state in which contracts cannot be enforced, cannot be a state of legal commerce. If the parties who are to contract have no right to compel the performance of the contract, nor even to appear in a court of justice for that purpose, can there be a stronger proof that the law imposes a legal inability to contract? To such transactions it gives no sanction; they have no legal existence, and the whole of such commerce is attempted without its protection and against its authority.

This is nullity rather than illegality.

Ground (b) is the surer and the more modern ground, and indeed there is not much difference between them. The illegality of any intercourse with the enemy was barely recognized as a ground of abrogation of contract until Lord Stowell's judgment in *The Hoop* in 1799 and Lord Alvanley's judgment in *Furtado* v. *Rogers* in 1802; indeed we think it is fair to say that for an exhaustive consideration and an unequivocal establishment it had to await the judgment of Willes J. in the Exchequer Chamber in *Esposito* v. *Bowden* in 1857. It is therefore not surprising to find Lord Stowell stating the matter rather differently—the more so as he was not being asked to enforce a contract but to condemn a cargo as prize on the ground of trading with the enemy.[1]

(2) *Where the outbreak of war makes performance or further performance illegal, whoever and wherever the parties may be.* One of the simplest statements of the effect of war upon the kind of contract most commonly involved is Lord Lindley's in *Janson* v. *Driefontein Consolidated Mines*:[2]

War produces a state of things giving rise to well-known special rules. It prohibits all trading with the enemy except with the Royal licence, and dissolves all contracts which involve such trading: see *Esposito* v. *Bowden*.

For instance, a British charterer before the outbreak of war has chartered a British or allied or neutral ship to load a cargo at a port which becomes an enemy port, and the contract is still executory, i.e. the ship has not yet cleared from the enemy port. The contract is dissolved because further performance of it would involve illegal intercourse with enemy territory or persons. If she has loaded her

---

[1] In *Bayer Co.* v. *Farbenfabriken Vorm. Friedr. Bayer & Co. et al.*, it was held that a long-term pre-war contract between a German company and a Canadian company was rescued from abrogation by the fact that eight days before the outbreak of war 'property in such a contract' had vested in the Canadian Custodian of Alien Property, so that there was thereafter no 'contract with an alien enemy of a kind on which a state of war would operate to bring about a dissolution'. We believe that an English court would have held the contract to be abrogated.

[2] [1902] A.C. 484, 509.

cargo and cleared, and no further intercourse with enemy territory or persons is involved, the contract must be performed. The result is the same if the charterer is an allied or neutral national who is resident or carrying on business within British territory. (Contracts between persons resident or carrying on business in foreign non-enemy countries and enemies are considered later in this chapter.)

Logically, these two categories (1) and (2) are distinct, but the series of decisions in which the rules have been developed does not preserve the distinction, and it would, we think, be pedantic and would present a false picture of the development of the law if we attempted to separate the two classes in our review of the cases. Today the ground of abrogation in both classes is supervening illegality, though we must not forget that, as we have already seen, Lord Stowell in *The Hoop* in 1799 (speaking, it is true, by way of illustration, of a hypothetical contract which it was attempted to make during war) laid stress upon the inability of an enemy to sustain a *persona standi in judicio* as the ground of the non-existence of a contract made with an enemy.

What then is it that makes performance illegal? What are the acts performance of which is illegal? What is the mischief latent in the contract, or in the tendency of the contract, that makes it illegal?

There are two bases of illegality. The first is the extreme danger of permitting any kind of intercourse with enemy territory or any persons therein; the second is the necessity of repressing and prohibiting any contract which is injurious to the interests of this country, at any rate while the country is at war. The first is the more orthodox basis and the one most frequently invoked in the decisions; the second, though old, has again become prominent.

Lord Dunedin has described as 'landmarks in the law on the subject' *The Hoop* (1799), *Furtado* v. *Rogers* (1802), and *Esposito* v. *Bowden* (1857), and all these cases are reviewed by him in his judgment in the *Ertel Bieber* case about to be discussed.[1] *Furtado* v. *Rogers* contains what may, we think, be called the classic statement of the second and wider basis of illegality, occurring in the judgment of the Court of Common Pleas delivered by Lord Alvanley C.J.:[2]

We are all of opinion that on the principles of the English law it is not competent to any subject to enter into a contract to do anything which may be detrimental to the interests of his own country; and that such a

---

[1] *Ertel Bieber & Co.* v. *Rio Tinto Co.* [1918] A.C. 260, 273, 274.
[2] 3 Bos. & P. 191, 195, 198, cited by (*inter alios*) Swinfen Eady L.J. in *Zinc Corporation* v. *Hirsch* [1916] 1 K.B. 541, 558.

contract is as much prohibited as if it had been expressly forbidden by act of parliament.

From these cases [says Lord Dunedin in the *Ertel Bieber* case][1] I draw the conclusion that upon the ground of public policy the continued existence of contractual relation between subjects and alien enemies or persons voluntarily residing in the enemy country which (1) gives opportunities for the conveyance of information which may hurt the conduct of the war, or (2) may tend to increase the resources of the enemy or cripple the resources of the King's subjects, is obnoxious and prohibited by our law.

This statement relates to contracts to which one of the parties is an enemy in the territorial sense. But the mischiefs referred to by Lord Dunedin also exist in the case of a contract to which there is no party who is an enemy in the territorial sense but the performance of which involves a person who is in, or is carrying on business in, British territory, in intercourse with the enemy, as in *Esposito* v. *Bowden*. In that case a charterparty had been entered into before the outbreak of the Crimean War between a British charterer and a (neutral) Neapolitan shipowner, whereby the latter undertook to send a ship to Odessa to load a cargo of wheat and the former undertook to load it there. Upon the outbreak of war, before the ship arrived at Odessa, the British charterer declined to load her on the ground that it was impossible for him to do so without trading with the Queen's enemies. (The Kingdom of the Two Sicilies was neutral.) In an action brought by the Neapolitan shipowner the Court of Exchequer Chamber upheld the plea of the British charterer.

It is now fully established (said Willes J.)[2] that, the presumed object of war being as much to cripple the enemy's commerce as to capture his property, a declaration of war imports a prohibition of commercial intercourse and correspondence with the inhabitants of the enemy's country, and that such intercourse, except with the licence of the Crown, is illegal.

[1] [1918] A.C. 260, 274. According to Schuster in 1 *B.Y.* (1920–1), p. 183, Mendelssohn-Bartholdy maintained in the *Deutsche Juristenzeitung* (xx, pp. 662–7) that the 'acceptance by English authorities as rules of international law' of the general principles governing pre-war contracts with enemies illustrated in the *Ertel Bieber* case is 'due to a falsified quotation from Bynkershoek (*Quaestionum Juris Publici Libri Duo*, 1, chap. III— towards the end) in the course of Lord Stowell's well-known judgment in *The Hoop*'. We do not understand this statement. Lord Stowell's quotation from Bynkershoek, 1 C. Rob. at p. 199, is an accurate reproduction of the passage as it occurs in the text of 1737 adopted by the Carnegie Endowment for its reprint of the Classics of International Law, except that one word, *autem*, after *quamvis*, is omitted, and he appears to have correctly apprehended and applied it.

[2] 7 El. & Bl. 763, 779. And see Lord Reading C.J. in *Porter* v. *Freudenberg* [1915] 1 K.B. 857, 867, 868 as to the foundation of this rule, which includes 'public policy, which forbids the doing of acts that will be or may be to the advantage of the enemy State by increasing its capacity for prolonging hostilities in adding to the credit, money or goods, or other resources available to individuals in the enemy State'.

Later he said:[1]

The force of a declaration of war is equal to an Act of Parliament pro-hibiting intercourse with the enemy except by the Queen's licence. As an Act of State, done by virtue of the Prerogative exclusively belonging to the Crown, such a declaration carries with it all the force of law...As to the mode of operation of war upon contracts of affreightment, made before, but which remain unexecuted at, the time it is declared...the authorities establish that the effect is to dissolve the contract, and to absolve both parties from further performance of it.

This decision makes it clear that the abrogating effect of war upon contracts involving intercourse with the enemy is not due, or at any rate not solely due, to any intrinsic legal impossibility of the continued existence of a contractual relationship between parties 'separated by the line of war'.[2] It is due to the mischief which can result from intercourse between a person in this country and a person in the enemy country.

Let us now apply Lord Dunedin's statement quoted above to some common transactions entered into before the outbreak of war.

(*a*) Upon the outbreak of war one of the parties to a contract of agency becomes an enemy in the territorial sense, while the other is in this country. The contract is thereupon *ipso facto* dissolved.[3]

(*b*) Upon the outbreak of war one of the members of a partnership becomes an enemy in the territorial sense, while the other is in this country. The contract is thereupon *ipso facto* dissolved.[4] What hap-pens to the assets is a different matter.

(*c*) A contract for the sale of goods provided for the shipment of goods to or from what becomes an enemy country from or to this country. It is *ipso facto* dissolved upon the outbreak of war.

(*d*) In a similar contract of sale the date of delivery of the goods is such that the war may be over, or is in fact over,[5] before the date arrives. The contract is nevertheless dissolved upon the outbreak of war. The Court will not speculate upon the duration of a war. As Lush J. said in *Geipel* v. *Smith*:[6] 'A state of war must be presumed to be likely to continue so long, and so disturb the commerce of mer-

---

[1] At pp. 781–3.
[2] See note 2 on p. 150.   [3] *Maxwell* v. *Grunhut.*
[4] *Hugh Stevenson & Sons* v. *Aktiengesellschaft für Cartonnagen Industrie.*
[5] The first Lord Parker of Waddington speculated upon this point in the *Ertel Bieber* case [1918] A.C. 260, 283: 'It may be that a contract for the sale of goods to be delivered at a future date is abrogated by a war which begins and is brought to a conclusion between the date of the contract and the date fixed for delivery, but I prefer not to express an opinion upon this on the present occasion.' It is submitted that there can be no doubt that the contract is abrogated.
[6] (1872) L.R. 7 Q.B. at p. 414.

chants, as to defeat and destroy the object of a commercial adventure like this.'

The meaning of 'executed' and 'executory contracts'. In the *Ertel Bieber* case Lord Dunedin (at p. 267) refers to the proposition of law that

a state of war between this kingdom and another country abrogates and puts an end to all executory contracts which for their further performance require...commercial intercourse between the one contracting party, subject of the King, and the other contracting party, an alien enemy [*scilicet*, an enemy in the territorial sense], or anyone voluntarily residing in the enemy country.

He added that 'intercourse' is enough without the epithet 'commercial'. The expression 'executory contracts' requires examination. The terms 'executed' and 'executory consideration' are well established and have well-recognized meanings. The terms 'executed' and 'executory contracts' are not so well defined and are beginning to disappear from textbooks and judgments. Halsbury's *Laws of England*[1] tells us that 'An executed contract is one which has been wholly performed by one of the parties but remains to be performed by the other party. A contract is executory so long as something remains to be done under it by both parties.' If this is the right meaning of 'executed contract', it would not be correct to say that the outbreak of war never abrogates an 'executed contract'; for instance, in August 1939, that is, before the outbreak of war with Germany on 3 September 1939, *A* in England agreed with *B* in Germany that in consideration of £100 then received *A* would manufacture certain articles and send them to Germany in the course of December 1939; the outbreak of war on 3 September 1939 would free *A* from this obligation and destroy it, whether or not after the war *B* might be able to recover from *A* any part of the sum of £100. Suppose, however, a pre-war contract for the manufacture and sale of certain articles by *A* for delivery to *B* in Germany in consideration of £100 payable by *B* on 31 December 1939; before the outbreak of war *A* has delivered the articles to *B*; the right to the payment of £100 is a debt, though not presently payable, and is not destroyed by the outbreak of war; everything had happened that is needed to make the payment due except the lapse of time. Nor, it is submitted, is it correct to say that the outbreak of war abrogates all 'executory contracts', unless we exclude that part of an executory contract which consists of the payment of a liquidated sum of money; thus, *A* in London is the manager of a German company, *B & Co.*,

---

[1] 3rd ed. (Simonds), vol. 8, p. 55.

operating in England; he is employed by the calendar year at a salary of £1200 payable monthly; on the outbreak of war on 3 September 1939 he has not received his salary in respect of August 1939; the contract is executory and is certainly abrogated, but *A*'s right to recover £100 for his August salary survives the outbreak of war,[1] unless it has been possible to enforce it in a British court during the war.

It is suggested, therefore, that the distinction between 'executed' and 'executory contracts' may not be very helpful in this connection and that it may be found safer to say that (apart from the special cases of 'suspension' and 'no effect' considered later)[2] the effect of the outbreak of war upon contracts legally affected by it is to abrogate or destroy any subsisting[3] right to further performance other than the right to the payment of a liquidated sum of money, which will be treated as a debt and will survive the outbreak of war.[4] (We have not complicated the argument by dealing with severable contracts, but in that case each part for this purpose would be treated as a separate contract.[5])

Suspension clauses. Suppose that the parties to the contract in their anxiety to preserve it from the dissolving effect of war have introduced into it a clause whereby all performance shall be suspended during war and only resumed when the war is over. This point was the subject of much litigation during the War of 1914 to 1918.[6] For instance, there were in existence upon the outbreak of that war a number of long-term contracts for the delivery of ores of various kinds to German firms in which the parties had been astute enough to insert clauses purporting to suspend the delivery of instalments in the event of war, which presumably meant or included war between the British and German Empires. The effect of these clauses was considered by the House of Lords in three appeals heard together,[7] and it is now possible to summarize the various grounds on which

---

[1] See *Distington Hematite Iron Co.* v. *Possehl & Co.* [1916] 1 K.B. 811, 813, where Rowlatt J. came near this point but refrained from deciding it.   [2] See later, pp. 132–5.

[3] If a breach has already occurred, the right of action survives the outbreak of war: see later, p. 135.

[4] In *Schering Ltd* v. *Stockholms Enskilda Bank* [1946] A.C. 219, 240, Lord Thankerton was inclined to agree with the suggestion made in the text. (This case must not be confused with *Stockholms Enskilda Bank A/B* v. *Schering Ltd* [1941] 1 K.B. 424.) See also *Arab Bank Ltd* v. *Barclays Bank Ltd*, and Upjohn J. in *In re Helbert Wagg & Co.* [1956] 1 Ch. 323 at pp. 354, 355.

[5] See McNair, J. in *Kuenigl* v. *Donnersmarck* [1955], 1q. B at p. 537 (bottom).

[6] *Zinc Corporation* v. *Hirsch*; *Clapham Steamship Co.'s Case*; *Naylor, Benzon & Co.* v. *Krainische Industrie Gesellschaft*.

[7] *Ertel Bieber & Co.* v. *Rio Tinto Co.*, and two other cases; followed in *Fried. Krupp Aktien-Fesellschaft* v. *Orconera Iron Ore Co.*, and by the High Court of Southern Rhodesia in *Garbenfabriken Bayer Aktiengesellschaft* v. *Bayer Pharma (Proprietary) Ltd*.

the law will hold such contracts dissolved and not merely suspended.[1] The principal grounds are

(i) The abrogation by the outbreak of war of all (or most) executory contracts requiring for their further performance intercourse with the enemy—as explained by Lord Dunedin in the passage quoted above.[2]

(ii) That even if the suspension clauses are adequate to suspend deliveries, there are other obligations in the contracts not covered by the suspension, for instance, arbitration, declaration of quantities and character, which must or might involve intercourse during the war.

(iii) That, while deliveries during the war are illegal on ground (i) above mentioned, to hold that the British subject remained liable to make 'the deliveries, if any, which, according to the contract, fall to be made after the war is over'[3] would impose upon the parties a new contract and would be contrary to the decisions of the House of Lords in *Horlock* v. *Beal* and *Metropolitan Water Board* v. *Dick, Kerr & Co.* (This ground rests on Frustration.)[4]

(iv) That even if the interpretation of the suspension clauses is such as to suspend the entire operation of the contract during the war, the clauses would be contrary to public policy on the ground that they cripple the trading resources and operations of this country and enhance those of the enemy by ensuring to him a supply of raw materials upon the conclusion of peace. (This ground rests on our second basis of illegality, namely, that the clause is detrimental to the interests of this country.)

The effect of the immediate certainty of a future event is, or may well be, itself immediate and not merely future. As Lord Dunedin said in the *Ertel Bieber* case:[5]

It increases the resources of the enemy, for if the enemy knows that he is contractually sure of getting the supply as soon as war is over, that not only allows him to denude himself of present stocks, but it represents a present value which may be realized by means of assignation to neutral countries.

---

[1] The initial difficulty of bringing such a matter before the Courts at all during war was obviated by the Legal Proceedings Against Enemies Act, 1915, enabling a British subject to obtain a declaration upon such a contract. This statute has expired and no similar legislation was passed during the War of 1939 to 1945, though the rule of the Supreme Court referred to above at p. 112 to some extent met the need.

[2] P. 127.

[3] Per Lord Parker [1918] A.C. at p. 283.

[4] See later, chapter 5.

[5] [1918] A.C. at p. 275. See also Viscount Simon L.C. in the *Sovfracht* case [1943] A.C. 203, 212.

It is clearly a benefit to the enemy to tie up British resources during the war so that they may become available to the ex-enemy as soon as the war is over. Lord Alvanley pointed out in *Furtado v. Rogers*[1] that if the enemy is to receive his insurance indemnity after the war, he 'is very little injured by captures for which he is sure at some period or other to be repaid by the underwriter'.

This doctrine of the present value to the enemy of some post-war benefit is now well established, but it should be noted that its logic has not been ruthlessly applied. If everything which might benefit the enemy during or after the war is to be illegal, and forbidden on grounds of public policy, then it should follow that all private enemy property in this country should be confiscated (which is not done, though the Crown has power to do it);[2] that rights of action already accrued to enemies on the outbreak of war should be destroyed and not suspended; and that section 7 of the Trading with the Enemy Act, 1939, which empowers the Board of Trade to vest enemy property in custodians 'with a view...of preserving [it] in contemplation of arrangements to be made at the conclusion of peace' is a grim joke. Lord Parker made some remarks in the case of *Daimler Co. v. Continental Tyre and Rubber Co.*[3] upon the heresy of arguing that 'acts, otherwise lawful, might be rendered unlawful by the fact that they might tend to the enrichment of the enemy when the war was over', but he explained their limited application at a later date.[4]

A good illustration of the long-term contract type of case and of the method of handling it, which received the approval of the House of Lords, will be found in *Naylor, Benzon & Co. v. Krainische Industrie Gesellschaft*. The facts raised most of the points common in these cases, and the judgment of McCardie J. reviewed all the relevant authorities; it appears to have been delivered two days before the House of Lords gave judgment in the *Ertel Bieber* case, but the conclusions are the same.

The *Ertel Bieber* case formed a precedent for numerous similar judicial declarations that contracts of this nature were dissolved on the outbreak of war.

In one of these cases[5] an ingenious but unsuccessful attempt was made to avoid the consequences of the *Ertel Bieber* precedent by

---

[1] Cited [1918] A.C. at p. 274.
[2] By inquisition of office; see *In re Ferdinand, Ex-Tsar of Bulgaria*, and later, p. 331.
[3] [1916] 2 A.C. 307, 347.
[4] [1918] A.C. at p. 284. Note, however, the effect they produced upon the Court of Appeal in *Tingley v. Müller*.
[5] *Fried. Krupp A.-G. v. Orconera Iron Ore Co.*

suggesting that a contract for the supply of iron ore over a period of 99 years was analogous to a lease and should be treated as a 'concomitant of the rights of property',[1] and so not dissolved.

The disability of the enemy to sue can in effect be removed by the appointment by the Board of Trade of a controller under the Trading with the Enemy Act, 1939, who thereupon is able to collect the assets of the enemy person, firm, or company and to sell them, and for those purposes to sue (for instance, for the price of goods sold) without being defeated by the plea of alien enemy.[2] But the effect of such an appointment is not to revive dissolved contracts.[3]

Restrictive covenant in favour of an enemy. Closely akin to the suspensory clause is the restrictive covenant which requires a party to a contract not to sell a particular commodity during a certain number of years to any person other than the other party who has become an enemy in the territorial sense. Such a covenant is discharged by the outbreak of war, because it is detrimental to the interests of this country.[4]

The operation of dissolution. Having thus ascertained that the general rule is dissolution, we may inquire how it takes effect. It seems safe to say[5] that the effect is the same as that which occurs when a contract is discharged by supervening impossibility of performance or by frustration, and the reader is referred to chapter 5 on Frustration of Contract.

Lord Atkin has described it as an 'elementary proposition that if further performance of a contract becomes impossible by legislation having that effect the contract is discharged'.[6] It is submitted that this statement is also true when further performance becomes illegal owing to the outbreak of war, and the statement by Willes J. in *Esposito* v. *Bowden*, cited above,[7] is express authority for this proposition.

Dissolution is not the same thing as avoidance *ab initio*. Dissolution operates upon *subsisting* rights of performance, and we shall consider in the next section[8] the position of the right to recover a debt or liquidated sum of money and other rights of action which had already accrued before the war broke out.

---

[1] Lord Dunedin's expression [1918] A.C. at p. 269.

[2] *Continho Caro & Co.* v. *Vermont & Co.*

[3] Per Younger J. *In re Coutinho Caro & Co.* [1918] 2 Ch. 384, 389. (*Continho* and *Coutinho* denote the same firm.)

[4] *Zinc Corporation* v. *Hirsch* [1916] 1 K.B. 541, 558, 562, 564.

[5] In several of the frustration cases the cause of frustration is supervening illegality.

[6] *Reilly* v. *The King* [1934] A.C. 176, 180.

[7] P. 126. [8] P. 135.

Conflict of Laws. The second and third of the *Rio Tinto* cases[1] raised a point on the Conflict of Laws which, as it has no necessary connection with the effects of war and is thus not strictly germane to the content of this chapter, may be very shortly stated: even if it were true that the German contracts involved in those two cases and the circumstances of their making attracted German law for their interpretation, and even if a German Court would hold that they were not contrary to rules of English public policy, they could not be enforced by an English Court because to do so would be contrary to rules of English public policy. 'It is illegal for a British subject to become bound in a manner which sins against the public policy of the King's realm.'[2] The importance of this point lies in the fact that some contracts—particularly of sale of goods and of insurance—between British and foreign parties contain a clause whereby the parties accept the law of a foreign country as the law governing the contract. This decision enables us to say that, so far at any rate as illegality is concerned, the position of a contract which an English Court would refuse to enforce because it offends the principles which we have been discussing, cannot be improved by resort to an agreed system of foreign law.[3]

Redintegration of dissolved contract. In *Esposito* v. *Bowden*,[4] arising out of the Crimean War, it was urged that, notwithstanding the declaration of war which dissolved a charterparty by making performance of it illegal, it was *ipso facto* revived by a British Order in Council made seventeen days later which permitted British charterers to load cargoes at unblockaded enemy ports. Lord Campbell C.J. rejected this plea, saying that the Order in Council 'if contemporaneous with the declaration of war might have been material: but it could have no operation to prevent the alleged dissolution of the contract; and the contract, once dissolved, could not be redintegrated by it'.

II. *Suspension*

In the early days of the War of 1914 to 1918, before the rules governing the effect of war upon contracts had passed through the forensic and judicial furnace and been purified and refined, there

---

[1] Those brought against *Dynamit Actien-Gesellschaft* and *Vereinigte Koenigs and Laurahuette Actien-Gesellschaft* [1918] A.C. 260, 292, 303. See also an American decision *Rossie* v. *Garvan*.

[2] Per Lord Dunedin in [1918] A.C. at p. 294.

[3] See Dicey, Rule 149, and p. 809.

[4] (1855) 4 El. & Bl. 963, 975. The same point was argued in the Exchequer Chamber and Lord Campbell's opinion was expressly upheld, though on other grounds the judgment of the Court of Queen's Bench was reversed; (1857) 7 El. & Bl. 763, 778.

was but little authority to guide the legal advisers of parties to pre-war contracts who found themselves separated by the line of war, and much doubt prevailed as to the effect of the outbreak of war upon such contracts. In particular, there was doubt on the question whether the normal effect upon such a contract was to 'suspend' it, that is to say, performance of it, or to dissolve it. Moreover, the word 'suspend' was used somewhat loosely and ambiguously.[1] These doubts were due in part to a lack of appreciation of the distinction already referred to, in relation to a pre-war contract, between a right of action,[2] which is suspended until after the war when the action may be brought, and a right to performance,[3] which in the vast majority of cases is destroyed by reason of the dissolution of the contract. It is suggested that much of this uncertainty was due to an unfortunate passage occurring in the speech of Lord Halsbury L.C. in *Janson* v. *Driefontein Consolidated Mines*,[4] when he said:

No contract or other transaction with a native of the country which afterwards goes to war is affected by the war. The remedy is indeed suspended: an alien enemy cannot sue in the Courts of either country while the war lasts; but the rights on the contract [that is, we suggest, rights of action which had accrued before the outbreak of war] are unaffected, and when the war is over the remedy in the Courts of either is restored.[5]

Rowlatt J. in *Distington Hematite Iron Co.* v. *Possehl & Co.*[6] took an important step towards the elucidation of the meaning of 'suspension' when he said, dealing with a pre-war contract of sale for an indefinite number of years between a British vendor of pig-iron and an enemy purchaser (carrying on business in enemy territory):

the question is whether this contract is dissolved. The defendants have cited dicta[7] to the effect that contracts are not dissolved but are suspended by war. This is a loose expression which gives rise to confusion. The words themselves really mean that during war there is an interval in which the parties are not in contractual relations. But that is not the sense in which the phrase is used. It is used to convey the meaning that performance of the obligations of the contract is either postponed during war or that obligations falling due during war are cancelled, leaving a number of others to be performed in the ordinary way at the end of the war. That is the sense which the defendants wish to convey. The plaintiffs contended that all contracts were dissolved by war except executed contracts where

---

[1] See Lord Justice MacKinnon's *Effect of War on Contract* (1917), pp. 17, 18. The same ambiguity existed in the case of contracts between parties not separated by the line of war of the kind which became familiar in the 'frustration' cases.

[2] Which is a secondary or remedial right; see p. 118.

[3] Which is a primary right.   [4] [1902] A.C. 484, 493.

[5] See Lord Dunedin [1918] A.C. at p. 269.   [6] [1916] 1 K.B. 811, 813.

[7] E.g. from *Janson* v. *Driefontein Consolidated Mines*.

payment is the only obligation remaining to be performed, in which case, they suggest, payment may be postponed until after the war. I am not going to lay down that proposition in the present case.

He then proceeded to hold that the contract was dissolved by the outbreak of war on the ground that to hold that the parties were bound by the contract for an indefinite time, while being unable to act upon it, would be to 'substitute a different contract for it'. This is, in effect, to hold that the contract was dissolved by frustration. With great respect, it is believed that at a later stage in the war the learned judge would, having regard to the development of the decisions, have been content to hold that the contract was dissolved upon the outbreak of war by reason of supervening illegality, which is a simpler solution.

Are there then any true cases of suspension—that is to say, cases where the effect of war is merely to suspend performance or further performance of the contract, and not to abrogate the contract?

The shareholder's contract of membership of the company can properly be described as an instance of suspension.[1] During the war a shareholder in a British company who becomes an enemy in the territorial sense cannot exercise any of a shareholder's rights, such as the right of voting, nor can he receive dividends, but his share is not extinguished (unless the Crown chooses to confiscate it by 'inquisition of office' or legislation takes place having the same effect) and after the war he will resume his rights and perhaps recover any accumulation of dividends. This contract may be regarded both as a contract and as a piece of property, and we are reminded of Lord Dunedin's expression: 'concomitants of rights of property'.[2]

III. *No effect*

In rare cases, not easy to classify, the effect of the outbreak of war upon a contract between a person in this country and an enemy in the territorial sense may be *nil* or almost *nil*. In *Halsey* v. *Lowenfeld* (*Leigh and Curzon Third Parties*)[3] it was held that rent falling due *during*

---

[1] *Robson* v. *Premier Oil and Pipe Line Co.*; see later, p. 242.

[2] [1918] A.C. at p. 269, an expression discussed in *Schering Ltd* v. *Stockholms Enskilda Bank*. Note the word 'suspended' in clause 2 of Article 296 of the Treaty of Versailles, and its application to the contract of banker and customer in *Le Rossignol* v. *Deutsche Bank*. English law would regard the credit balance as a pre-war debt, the right of action to which, if it had accrued, was suspended like other rights of action. See *Arab Bank* v. *Barclay's Bank*. In the *Le Rossignol* case the customer's credit account received additions during the war.

[3] See below, chapter 12. *Porter* v. *Freudenberg* also arose upon a pre-war lease and the plaintiff sued for rent falling due after the outbreak of war, but the point that the lease was terminated by the outbreak of war was not taken, the defendant not being represented.

the war under a pre-war lease could be recovered by a lessor in this country, in respect of premises in this country, from a lessee who was resident in enemy territory, which shows that the outbreak of war did not dissolve the contract. As we shall see later,[1] a lease is something more than a contract; it creates an estate by demise for a term of years and vests it in the lessee.

In *Tingley* v. *Müller*[2] an irrevocable power of attorney for the sale of land was held to be not revoked by the fact of the donor becoming an enemy in the territorial sense (which for our present purpose is equivalent to the outbreak of war). These two decisions relate to property as well as contract, and therein probably lies their explanation. We are again reminded of Lord Dunedin's expression[3] 'concomitants of rights of property'. The effect of war upon marriage and other domestic relations will be discussed later.[4]

B. CONTRACTS MADE BEFORE THE OUTBREAK OF WAR,[5] SO
FAR AS CONCERNS BREACHES[6] WHICH HAVE ALREADY
OCCURRED: DEBTS AND RIGHTS OF ACTION WHICH
HAVE ALREADY ACCRUED

We have seen that the majority of pre-war contracts between a party in this country and a party in an enemy country are dissolved or abrogated by the outbreak of war. We must now state the meaning and effect of abrogation, which seems to be the more usual term in this connection. We shall find that the law is focused more on the contract itself than on the parties. If the effect is abrogation, it is abrogated for both parties. If anything is saved from abrogation, the parties during the war will be in a different position, for one of them—the enemy—will be defeated by the plea of alien enemy if he attempts to salvage anything from the wreck during the war, whereas the other—the party in this country—is entitled to sue and might be able to recover something if the enemy party had assets in this country.

---

[1] Chapter 12.   [2] See above, p. 99.
[3] [1918] A.C. at p. 269.   [4] Chapter 15.
[5] See above, p. 121.

[6] It may be that the breach was of such a character that it gave rise not only to a right of action but also to a right in the other party to treat the contract as discharged from that moment. If he has already exercised the latter right, well and good; the contract is at an end except for the right of action, and it is unnecessary to discuss any further effect of the outbreak of war upon the contract. If he has not already exercised that right, he has delayed at his peril and can no longer exercise it when the contract has been dissolved by the outbreak of war: *Reid* v. *Hoskins*, and *Avery* v. *Bowden*; there both the parties in each case were British, but the result would be the same if one party to each contract had become an enemy in the territorial sense.

Upon the occurrence of abrogation, it is necessary to consider its effect upon four kinds of rights:

(1) right to performance subsisting on the outbreak of war;
(2) right of action to recover a chattel, which will be discussed more conveniently later;[1]
(3) right of action to recover a debt or other liquidated sum of money;
(4) right of action for damages for pre-war breach.

(1) *Right to performance subsisting at the outbreak of war*

Consider the case of a right to performance which had not been broken before the war broke out, for instance, under a contract of employment, agency, carriage, sale of goods, etc. This is the true sphere of operation of abrogation. Apart from contracts which are 'concomitants of rights of property', and contracts concerned with status such as marriage, these rights to performance or further performance are completely destroyed. We have already cited a number of decisions illustrating this effect.

(3) *Right of action to recover a debt or other liquidated sum of money*[2]

What is the position of a debt, and what exactly is meant by a debt? Does it mean only an accrued right of action to sue at once for a liquidated sum of money? Or does it also include an obligation to pay in the future a liquidated sum of money (*debitum in praesenti solvendum in futuro*), e.g. after a demand or at a date which has not yet arrived, so that the right of action is not yet complete?

Before the outbreak of war between the United Kingdom and Germany in September 1939 *A* in Germany had borrowed £100 from *B* in England and was already in default as to £50, while the remaining £50 was due on 31 December 1939; *C* in England had sold and delivered goods to *D* in Germany at the price of £1000, of which £500 was already overdue, while the balance was due on 31 December 1939. Principle and judicial authority both point to the conclusion that the right to payment of the sums due on the outbreak of war and those due on 31 December 1939 is not discharged by the outbreak of war and that the money can be recovered when the war is over, apart from any provision to the contrary that may be made by a peace treaty or by legislation.

By English law the outbreak of war does not automatically involve

---

[1] P. 143 and chapter 15.

[2] On 12 November 1914 the Law Officers advised that, if after the outbreak of war an enemy creditor of a debtor in this country assigns the debt to a neutral, the assignee is in no better position than his assignor for enforcing payment in this country.

the confiscation of private enemy property in this country, though the Crown may by inquisition of office bring about a forfeiture, or Parliament may produce this effect by legislation. A debt is essentially a piece of property, and it is worth remembering that the action of debt was in origin a recuperatory action, the theory being that the defendant was wrongfully detaining the plaintiff's property.[1]

Ex parte Boussmaker[2] appears to be one of the first cases in which the effect of the outbreak of war upon an already accrued right of action, in that case a debt, was considered. An alien enemy (almost certainly in the territorial sense) was a petitioning creditor, and there was an appeal to the Lord Chancellor from the refusal of the Commissioners in Bankruptcy to admit the petition. Lord Erskine L.C. admitted the petition, saying:

If this had been a debt, arising from a contract with an alien enemy [i.e. an enemy at the date of the contract], it could not possibly stand; for the contract would be void. But, if the two nations were at peace at the date of the contract, from the time of war taking place the creditor could not sue: but, the contract being originally good, upon the return of peace the right would survive. It would be contrary to justice to confiscate this dividend. Though the right to recover is suspended, that is no reason, why the fund should be divided among the other creditors...Let a claim be entered; and the dividend be reserved.

He pointed out the importance of the matter 'from the analogy to the case of an action'.

In *Alcinous* v. *Nigreu*[3] an action for work and labour brought by a person who became an enemy 'since the last pleading in the action', Lord Campbell C.J. said: 'The contract, having been entered into before the commencement of hostilities, is valid; and, when peace is restored, the plaintiff may enforce it in our Courts.' It must be assumed that Lord Campbell meant that the accrued right of action for breach of the contract, e.g. non-payment of wages due, would survive the war; the plaintiff was in this country but had obtained no licence or permission from the Crown. It is probable that this action sounded in damages rather than in debt, but the point did not arise.

We had to wait a long time before we got an authoritative and unequivocal decision on the effect of the outbreak of war upon a pre-war right to recover a debt or other liquidated sum of money.

[1] Maitland, *Forms of Action* (1954), p. 63.
[2] The debt is described as a 'debt under a Commission of Bankruptcy'. Lord Reading C.J. in *Porter* v. *Freudenberg* [1915] 1 K.B. 857, 873, regarded this as a special case, justified so as to prevent the fund in bankruptcy from being distributed regardless of the alien enemy's claim. [3] (1854) 4 El. & Bl. 217, 219.

In *Schering Ltd* v. *Enskilda Bank Aktienbolaget*,[1] which was later described by Parker J. (as the present Lord Parker of Waddington C.J. then was) in *Arab Bank* v. *Barclays Bank (D.C. and O.) Ltd*,[2] 'as a case of a debt payable by future instalments in which it was held that the obligation to pay was only suspended', Lord Thankerton said: 'It is important to make clear that the principle of abrogation does not involve the destruction of the contract so far as already performed. That which is abrogated is the further performance of the contract, as from the outbreak of war; or as Lord Dunedin expresses it' in *Ertel Bieber & Co.* v. *Rio Tinto Co.*[3] 'the continued existence of the contractual relationship is prohibited'. Lord Thankerton's next sentence seems to explain and justify this distinction: 'As Lord Finlay L.C. states in *Hugh Stevenson & Sons* v. *Aktien-Gesellschaft für Cartonagen Industrie*:[4] "It is not the law of this country that the property of enemy subjects is confiscated."'

Accordingly, when Parker J. had to consider in the case mentioned above the effect of the outbreak of war upon a current account of the Arab Bank with the Jerusalem branch of Barclays Bank on 14–15 May when war broke out between certain Arab States and the State of Israel, he found no difficulty in holding that the sum due on current account to the Arab Bank would be recoverable as a 'liquidated sum of money', though the right to recover it was suspended during the war. This decision was affirmed by the Court of Appeal in 1953 and the House of Lords in 1954, the state of war still continuing.

(4) *Right of action for damages*

The survival of a pre-war right of action for damages was recognized in several cases upon marine insurance policies[5] but is in no way confined to them. In *Flindt* v. *Waters*[6], where the assured were alien friends when the policy was effected and the loss took place, Lord Ellenborough C.J., in delivering the judgment of the King's Bench in an action brought by an agent of the assured against an underwriter (apparently British), said:

[1] [1946] A.C. 219, 241. See further as to the two *Schering* cases, pp. 257–8.
[2] [1952] 2 T.L.R. 920, 921; [1953] 2 Q.B. 527; [1954] A.C. 495; and see chapter 15.
[3] [1918] A.C. 260, 274.
[4] [1918] A.C. 239, 269.
[5] Which are contracts of indemnity and sound in damages, not in debt. Marine Insurance Act, 1906, s. 1; Bullen and Leake, *Precedents of Pleading* (11th ed.), p. 244.
[6] (1812) 15 East 260, 266. He went on to say that this suspension could not, having regard to the form of the pleading, prevent the plaintiff, a British subject, the agent of the assured, from recovering, but we suggest that we must regard that statement as due to the form of pleading in which the plea of alien enemy had been raised.

The insurance, the loss, and cause of action had arisen before the assured had become alien enemies: when therefore they became such, it was only temporary suspence (*sic*) of their own right of suit in the Courts here, as alien enemies. . .

Substantially the same point arose in *Janson* v. *Driefontein Consolidated Mines*, where however the plaintiffs themselves were alien enemies, being a company incorporated in an enemy country, and the defendant, a British underwriter, had been allowed to waive the plea of alien enemy so as to enable the action to be tried during the war; permission to do this ought not to have been granted and a repetition of this practice is not likely to occur.[1] The plaintiffs sued to recover a loss occurring shortly before the outbreak of war upon a policy of insurance, which insured the plaintiffs' gold *inter alia* against 'arrests, restraints, and detainments of all kings, princes, and peoples'. Seven days before a state of war between Her Majesty and the South African Republic began, the gold was seized by the Government of the Republic on the frontier during transit; it must be noted that the loss occurred before the outbreak of war. The House of Lords affirmed the judgment of the Court of Appeal in favour of the plaintiffs. Lord Lindley, whose speech we find the most helpful of those made in the House of Lords, approved *Flindt* v. *Waters*, together with the statement based upon it contained in Arnould on *Marine Insurance*:[2] 'Where the party intended to be insured by the policy does not become an alien enemy until after the loss and cause of action have arisen, his right to sue on the policy is only suspended during the continuance of hostilities and revives on the restoration of peace.' Upon this point we do not think there was serious doubt. The main controversy turned on the questions when a state of war can be said to arise and how war can be distinguished from the strained relations and preliminary acts of violence which frequently precede its actual outbreak.[3]

For an instance occurring during the War of 1914 to 1918 we may turn to *Zinc Corporation* v. *Hirsch*,[4] where the Court of Appeal had to consider the position of a long-term pre-war contract for the supply of zinc concentrates by a British company to a firm carrying on

---

[1] See above, p. 82.   [2] (6th ed.), I, p. 135.

[3] The following dates should be noted: policy 1 August 1899; loss 2 October 1899; outbreak of war 12 October 1899; judgment in H.L. 5 August 1902; and official end of war probably 31 May 1902; the date of the issue of the writ is not mentioned; and see Lord Davey's remarks [1902] A.C. at p. 499 upon the agreement of the parties that 'this case should be treated as if the war were over' (per Mathew J. [1900] 2 Q.B. at p. 236); the date of his judgment is 1 June 1900.

[4] [1916] 1 K.B. 541, 556.

business in Germany. While holding that the effect of the outbreak of war was to dissolve the contract 'so far as regards the future performance after 4 August 1914', Swinfen Eady L.J. said: 'The remedy of either side[1] for what had previously been carried out remains in abeyance until the termination of the war: see *Esposito* v. *Bowden*; *Janson* v. *Driefontein Consolidated Mines*, per Lord Lindley.' It is only the fact that the English Courts are not open during the war to the enemy which makes his pre-war right of action unenforceable during the war; and the plea of alien enemy is then a plea in abatement and not in bar.[2] Accordingly, it is submitted that if anything should happen during the war to extinguish his enemy status, or if he should receive from the Crown a licence to sue,[3] he could at once sue. As Lord Stowell said in *The Hoop*,[4] speaking of the plea of alien enemy:

The same principle is received in our courts of the law of nations;[5] they are so far British courts, that no man can sue therein who is a subject of the enemy, unless under particular circumstances that *pro hac vice* discharge him from the character of an enemy; such as his coming under a flag of truce, a cartel, a pass, or some other act of public authority that puts him in the King's peace *pro hac vice*...

Some highly significant expressions were used in the House of Lords in the group of cases known as *Ertel Bieber & Co.* v. *Rio Tinto Co.*,[6] though that was an action brought during the war and our present point did not directly arise. Lord Dunedin said: 'Accrued rights [i.e. before the outbreak of war] are not affected though the right of suing in respect thereof is suspended';[7] and Lord Sumner said:[8] 'the suspension of the right of suit in the case of enemy nationals, for causes of action already accrued, until the conclusion of peace is not an argument in favour of substituting suspension by agreement for discharge by operation of law.[9] Whether it sounds in debt or in damages such a cause of action [that is, a cause of action already accrued] implies a present obligation to pay simultaneous with its coming into existence. Suspension of the remedy implies no continuance of the contract during the war, but only a recognition of its existence before the war as the basis or origin of a right, which, when it has accrued, is a chose in

---

[1] See, however, above, p. 110, as regards an enemy defendant.
[2] Bullen and Leake, *Precedents of Pleadings*, 3rd ed. (1868), p. 475 (n.); 11th ed. (1959), p. 913.
[3] See p. 108.   [4] (1799) 1 C. Rob. 196, 201.
[5] An interesting description of the Prize Court.
[6] [1918] A.C. 260.   [7] P. 269.   [8] P. 289.
[9] The contracts in this group of cases contained suspension clauses which purported to suspend their operation in the event (*inter alia*) of war, but that does not affect the question of the effect of accrued rights.

action, a form of property.' The dearth of recent express post-war authority on this point is probably due to the fact that after the Wars of 1914 to 1918 and 1939 to 1945 many matters which might have formed the subject-matter of litigation between persons in, or carrying on business in, the respective countries which had been at war, were disposed of by mixed arbitral tribunals or peace treaties and administrative measures and did not come before the courts.

The question whether an action in pursuance of the rights numbered (3) and (4) can be brought by a plaintiff in the United Kingdom against an alien enemy during the war depends on such matters as service or substituted service of the writ, availability of witnesses, documents, etc. The status of alien enemy does not protect an enemy defendant from being sued during the war.[1] If no writ had been issued before the war, some means of substituted service must be found; the facilities afforded for this purpose in the War of 1914 to 1918 by the now repealed Legal Proceedings against Enemies Act, 1915, were not renewed, and Order IX, r. 14B, which came into force on 31 October 1941, has been revoked.[2] The injured party is not compelled to sue the enemy during the war; that would be unfair because in many cases it might be more difficult to procure the evidence required to substantiate his claim than in time of peace.

A plaintiff who is in the enemy country would be defeated by the plea of alien enemy, unless for some reason that disability was removed, for instance, by receiving a licence to sue or (possibly) by reason of the occupation of the territory on which he is by British or allied forces. After the war if the Crown has not already confiscated the right of action by the appropriate process,[3] and if legislation does not deprive the enemy of it, and if by the treaty of peace it is not surrendered by the enemy State, the ex-enemy will be able to enforce it after the war.

Cessation of interest

In the case of a debt or other liquidated sum of money, will interest run during the war and be recoverable upon its conclusion?

This subject was very fully considered in the year 1909 in an article in the *Law Quarterly Review*[4] by C. N. Gregory, entitled 'Interest

---

[1] *Robinson and Co.* v. *Continental Insurance Co., of Mannheim,* approved by C.A. in *Porter* v. *Freudenberg* [1915] 1 K.B. 857, 880.

[2] See above, p. 112, and Webber, pp. 164–8.

[3] 'Inquisition of office' applies to choses in action: *Attorney-General* v. *Weeden and Shales*; *Re Ferdinand, Ex-Tsar of Bulgaria.*

[4] Vol. 25, pp. 297–316. See also Chadwick in 20 *L.Q.R.* (1904), pp. 167–85, and Webber, pp. 174–7.

on Debts during War', wherein, after an examination of both English and American decisions, the conclusion arrived at was that where debtor and creditor are separated by the line of war, interest ceases to run during the war whether the obligation to pay interest is express or is implied by law. The Trading with the Enemy Amendment Act, 1914, section 2 (now repealed), provided that any interest which would have been paid to an enemy but for the state of war should be paid to the Custodian to be preserved—a provision which appears to be comprised within the comprehensive terms of paragraph (a) of subsection 1 of section 7 of the Trading with the Enemy Act, 1939.[1]

The question was discussed indirectly in two cases during the War of 1914 to 1918. In the first,[2] Younger J. directed that the Custodian of the British assets of an enemy company should pay interest upon debts upon which by contract interest should be allowed, and, the contract falling to be interpreted by German law and being certainly one which apart from war would carry interest, he declined to recognize and give effect to a German war ordinance purporting to cancel interest during the war on debts to enemies of the German Empire. He based his refusal both on the ground that the ordinance was 'no part of the general German law, by which the parties to this contract alone agreed to be bound', and on the ground that at any rate this one-sided cancellation of interest was 'not conformable to the usage of nations'.[3] In the second[4]—a partnership case—it was not necessary to give a direct answer to the question of interest under discussion, but the decision that an enemy partner is entitled to some allowance (which presumably may take the form either of interest or a share of the profits) in respect of the use by the non-enemy partner of the assets of the firm during the war, would seem to show that there is nothing in English law repugnant to the idea of an enemy creditor receiving interest when he ultimately receives his debt. Several of their lordships appeared to take the view that no difference in prin-

---

[1] Section 3 of the Law Reform (Miscellaneous Provisions) Act, 1934, may require consideration. See also the Limitation (Enemies and War Prisoners) Act, 1945. The treatment of interest accruing during a war between persons separated by the line of war is a matter which can usefully be regulated by a Peace Treaty, e.g. Article 296 of the Treaty of Versailles, 1919.

[2] *In re Fried. Krupp Actien-Gesellschaft* [1917] 2 Ch. 188, 193, 194.

[3] Citing *Wolff* v. *Oxholm* (1817).

[4] *Hugh Stevenson & Sons* v. *A.-G. für Cartonnagen Industrie* [1918] A.C. at p. 245, which is not a clear authority on the point as it was a case between partners; Lord Finlay L.C. said: 'It is difficult to see on what principle the interest is to be forfeited if private property is to be respected.' But 'the question here is not of contract, but of property, and what is equitable as between two partners in respect of the property of the firm'.

ciple exists between the payment of interest and the payment of a capital sum. The two earlier English cases, *Wolff* v. *Oxholm*[1] and *Du Belloix* v. *Lord Waterpark*,[2] are not of much help, although in the latter case there are some remarks by Lord Tenterden C.J. which, though not necessary to the decision, are worth quoting:

> But there is another objection to the plaintiff's recovering interest on the debt, for during the greatest part of that time he was an alien enemy,[3] and could not have recovered even the principal in this country, and at all events during that portion of the time the interest could not have run, and it would even have been illegal to pay the bill whilst the plaintiff was an alien enemy.[4]

English Courts have not yet been called upon to pronounce definitely on the question of principle, and there is little that can be said with confidence. But, where interest runs from a particular time, such as the date of the failure to pay a bill of exchange upon presentation for payment or upon maturity, and the war makes it impossible or illegal at that date to pay the bill, interest will not run until the war is at an end, for during the war there was no breach of duty in not paying the amount of the bill.[5] Probably the demand of a customer upon his banker for the payment to him of money in the hands of the banker is governed by this rule.[6]

Summary. Remembering that there are certain contracts between a party in this country and a party in what becomes an enemy country which are not abrogated on the outbreak of war, the effect of abrogation is as follows:

(*a*) it destroys the contractual relationship;

(*b*) it precludes and prohibits any further performance of the contract;

(*c*) it does not destroy any accrued right of either party, such as the right to recover a chattel or a debt or other liquidated sum of money;

(*d*) it does not destroy any accrued right of either party to bring

---

[1] (1817).

[2] (1832) 1 Dow. & Ry. 16, 19 (italics ours).

[3] Apparently in the territorial sense, whatever his nationality may have been.

[4] There is also a Bombay case, cited in Campbell, *Law of War and Contract* (1918), *Padgett* v. *Jamshedji Hormusji Chothia*, 18 Bom. L.R. 190, but it does not throw much light on our problem.

[5] *Biedermann* v. *Allhausen & Co.* (1921) (bills of exchange accepted before the outbreak of war and falling due during the war—holder in Germany, acceptor in England); followed in *N. V. Ledeboter, etc.* v. *Hibbert* (1947) (pre-war bill drawn by Dutch company, acceptor in England). See below, p. 328. It is significant that in *Arab Bank* v. *Barclays Bank* no interest upon the credit balance appears to have been claimed.

[6] On the position of interest in the United States, see Hyde, § 614, *Hoare* v. *Allen*; *Foxcraft* v. *Nagle*; *Conn.* v. *Penn*; *Brown* v. *Hiatts*; *Hicks* v. *Guinness*.

an action for damages for a breach of contract which occurred before the war broke out.[1]

(*c*) and (*d*) are subject to the effect of the plea of alien enemy against an enemy plaintiff during the war.

C. CONTRACTS MADE BEFORE THE WAR BETWEEN THE BRITISH CROWN AND PERSONS WHO HAVE BECOME ENEMIES IN THE TERRITORIAL SENSE

There are many contracts which the British Crown might before the outbreak of war have entered into with foreign individuals and corporations who by reason of the outbreak of war (or the subsequent occupation by the enemy of non-enemy territory) become enemies in the territorial sense; for instance, contracts with a foreign whaling company to buy its output for a period of years, with a foreign cotton-growing company to buy its crop for a period of years, with a foreign shipping company to take up its tonnage on charter for thirty-six months, with a foreign insurance company to re-insure all risks accepted by it in regard to ships operating or cargoes carried to or from parts of the British Empire, with a foreign manufacturing company to supply to it all the bauxite required by it in return for a percentage of the aluminium manufactured from it, a concession to a foreign company to work minerals on Crown land, etc. When the effect of the outbreak of war (or a subsequent occupation of non-enemy territory by the enemy) is to convert the foreign individual or corporation into an enemy in the territorial sense, what is the position of such a contract?

Three preliminary points must be cleared out of the way.

(i) A petition of right is available to a foreign individual or corporation,[2] though not of course during a war in which the suppliant is an enemy in the territorial sense.

(ii) The answer to our problem in some cases may be found by ascertaining what is the proper law of the contract; for if the proper

---

[1] For an action brought during a war by a person in enemy territory to recover damage caused during the war by a maritime collision, see p. 328.

[2] For some decisions before the Crown Proceedings Act, 1947, see *Commercial and Estates Co. of Egypt* v. *Board of Trade* [1925] 1 K.B. 271, 297, and as illustrations see *Rederiaktiebolaget Amphitrite* v. *The King*; *Rex.* v. *International Trustee for the Protection of Bondholders Aktien-Gesellschaft*. It is now open to a foreign individual or corporation, not being an enemy in the territorial sense, to sue the Crown either in contract or in tort in the circumstances specified by the Crown Proceedings Act, 1947, but the generality of this liability of the Crown to be sued is strictly controlled by the terms of the Act, and, in particular, by section 11, which excludes from the scope of the Act certain prerogative and statutory powers connected with the defence of the realm.

law of the contract dissolves the contract the inquiry is answered. In determining what that law is, the Court will follow the general principles of the English rules upon the conflict of laws, namely, that 'it depends upon the intention of the parties either expressed in the contract or to be inferred from the terms of the contract and the surrounding circumstances'.[1] The House of Lords has rejected the contention (based upon a dictum of Lord Romilly M.R. in *Smith* v. *Weguelin*)[2] that when the British Government makes a contract which involves performance in a foreign country it must be presumed that the law of England is intended by the parties to be the proper law of the contract because only in England can the British Government be sued unless it submits to the jurisdiction. In the words of Lord Atkin,[3] 'in every case whether a Government be a party or not the general principle which determines the proper law of a contract is the same'.

(iii) But when the application of the proper law of a contract would involve a judgment against a party for not doing something which is contrary to the rules of English law based upon public policy[4] (of which the prohibition of intercourse with the enemy is typical), the proper law must give way to the positive rule of English law.

Clearly it would be beyond the scope of this work to consider the numerous proper laws which might govern a contract with the British Crown of the kind suggested. We shall accordingly confine our inquiry to considering the questions (1) whether, assuming the proper law of the contract to be English law, the contract is dissolved, and (2) whether, assuming that the proper law of the contract (being other than English law) does not dissolve the contract, English law precludes the success of a petition of right against the Crown. If the British party were a private individual or a corporation, the contracts instanced[5] would be dissolved under English law upon the other party becoming an enemy in the territorial sense, whether the proper law is English law or some other system of law which does not dissolve such a contract.[6] But it does not follow that the effect is the same when the British party is the Crown.

Let us look at three grounds upon which war can operate to dissolve a contract.

---

[1] Per Lord Atkin in *R.* v. *International Trustee, etc.* [1937] A.C. 500, 531.
[2] (1869) L.R. 8 Eq. 198, 213. [3] See note 1 above.
[4] *Dynamit Actien-Gesellschaft* v. *Rio Tinto Co.*; Dicey, Rule 149.
[5] With the possible exception of the concession.
[6] *Dynamit Actien-Gesellschaft* v. *Rio Tinto Co.*

(a) *Intercourse with the enemy.* It is not unlawful for the Crown to contract, or hold other intercourse, with persons who are enemies in the territorial sense or indeed with enemy Governments.[1] The Crown may license intercourse with the enemy, and what the Crown may license others to do it can do itself.[2] Whatever may be the underlying basis of the English rule which prohibits intercourse with the enemy —be it the danger of leakage of information or the procedural disability of the enemy—we are aware of no rule of law which prohibits the Crown from having intercourse with the enemy, and, that being so, we find it difficult to say that a contract involving intercourse between the Crown and an enemy in the territorial sense is *ipso facto* dissolved *for that reason* upon the outbreak of war or upon the other party becoming such an enemy. All the contracts instanced above, if a British subject or other private person in this country were a party instead of the Crown, would belong to the category of contracts dissolved by the outbreak of war, either because their performance involves intercourse with the enemy during the war, or because the suspension of performance until after the war would confer the present value of a post-war benefit upon the enemy within the *ratio decidendi* of the *Ertel Bieber* case; though it is arguable that a concession to work minerals is a 'concomitant of the rights of property' and survives the war unless confiscated by the Crown by the appropriate procedure during or after the war.

(b) *Increasing the enemy's resources or diminishing our own.* Can it be said that, 'the presumed object of war being as much to cripple the enemy's commerce as to capture his property',[3] the Crown may lawfully treat a contract as abrogated on the ground that its performance would tend to enrich the resources of the enemy and facilitate his prosecution of the war against us? It is submitted that the answer is in the affirmative. It seems fantastic to suppose that after a war an English Court would award damages against the Crown on a petition of right for doing during the war the very thing which the law enjoins upon the subjects of the Crown, namely, to treat as abro-

---

[1] In the sphere of International Law opposing belligerent States can enter into binding agreements during war, and there are certain pre-war treaties which continue to be binding upon them: McNair, *Law of Treaties* (1961), ch. XLIII, p. 696: 'There is no inherent juridical impossibility either (a) in the formation of treaty obligations between two opposing belligerents during war, or (b) in the continuance during war of obligations formed before the war.' There are many instances.

[2] The Trading with the Enemy Act, 1939, does not apply to the Crown (see section 16), but in practice the Crown has in general followed the provisions of the Act in regard to dealings with enemies, except in accordance with arrangements made with Allied Governments concerning allied nationals in enemy-occupied territory.

[3] Per Willes J. in *Esposito* v. *Bowden* (1857) 7 El. & Bl. 763, 779.

gated a contract tending to enrich the resources of the enemy or diminish our own. Having regard to the development, at any rate since *Esposito* v. *Bowden,* of the factor of the increase of the enemy's resources and the crippling of our own as a dominant ground for the invalidity of contracts, as illustrated by the *Ertel Bieber* and many other decisions, we cannot believe that a contract with the Crown the performance of which would have this tendency, would survive the fact of the other party becoming an enemy in the territorial sense.[1]

(*c*) *Frustration* is the third ground requiring consideration. It applies to a Crown contract with the same force as to a contract with a subject. Frustration will be discussed in chapter 5.

D. CONTRACTS WHICH ARE MADE, OR WHICH IT IS ATTEMPTED TO MAKE, DURING WAR

At common law any contract of the two following kinds which it is attempted to make during a war would (in the absence of licence from the proper authority) be void for illegality (quite apart from the criminal aspect): (*a*) contracts between any person, of whatever nationality or of no nationality, who is in, or is carrying on business in, British or allied territory, and an enemy in the territorial sense; (*b*) contracts between any persons, wherever they may be and whatever their national status may be, which involve any person who is in, or is carrying on business in, British or allied territory, in intercourse with an enemy in the territorial sense. By the Trading with the Enemy Act, 1939, any contract which involves 'trading with the enemy' in the wide sense thereby defined, would be void for illegality and would involve criminal liability.[2] Moreover, in time of war certain contracts which involve no trading with the enemy and which would be innocuous in time of peace can be illegal and void on the ground of public policy; for instance, a contract for the supply of raw materials to an enemy manufacturer as soon as the war comes to an end. Again, a contract which could not have lawfully been made during a war cannot be ratified or adopted after the war.[3]

Lord Stowell's observations in *The Hoop* have already been quoted.[4]

---

[1] Moreover, the Crown has power by 'inquisition of office' to confiscate the property of enemies, including their contractual rights, so that it could discharge the contract by vesting the other party's rights in itself. In the case of *In re Ferdinand, Ex-Tsar of Bulgaria,* it was held that the Trading with the Enemy Acts had temporarily put this right into abeyance; but section 16 of the Trading with the Enemy Act, 1939, states that 'This Act shall be without prejudice to the exercise of any right or prerogative of the Crown'.

[2] See chapter 16.　　　[3] *Kuenigl* v. *Donnersmarck.*　　　[4] P. 122.

To them we may add the statement of Burrough J. in *Willison* v. *Patteson*:[1] 'No contract can be enforced in a court of British judicature, which is made during the war, and which is made by an alien enemy'. That this rule is not confined to commercial transactions is clear from the judgment of the Court of Appeal in *Robson* v. *Premier Oil and Pipe Line Co.*[2]

E. CONTRACTS BETWEEN PERSONS IN FOREIGN NON-ENEMY COUNTRIES AND ENEMIES IN THE TERRITORIAL SENSE

In the nature of things these contracts are less likely to come before an English Court than those to which one party is in this country, but this can happen and the case must be discussed.

(*a*) *Where the non-enemy country is a co-belligerent ally*[3] *of Her Majesty*, our Courts will visit allied nationals with the consequences of intercourse with the enemy in the same way as persons in this country.[4] Thus in *The Panariellos* the Judge of the Prize Court (Sir Samuel Evans P.), in condemning the property of a French company which (though in good faith) had had commercial intercourse with the enemy immediately after the outbreak of war in connection with a pre-war contract of sale of the cargo seized as prize, stated the rule to be that where the

illegal intercourse is proved between allied citizens and the enemy, their property engaged in such intercourse, whether ship or cargo, is subject to capture by any allied belligerent, and is subject to condemnation in that belligerent's own Prize Courts.

Again, in an action brought by a Belgian firm carrying on business in Antwerp and London upon a pre-war contract with a German carrying on business at Hamburg and, before the war, in London, Bray J. held that the contract became illegal and was dissolved by the outbreak of war, after which there could be no breach of contract. It was just as illegal for the nationals of an ally to have intercourse with the enemy as it was for British subjects.[5]

---

[1] (1817) 7 Taunt. 439, 450 (bill of exchange).

[2] [1915] 2 Ch. 124, 136, adopted by Lord Dunedin [1918] A.C. at p. 268.

[3] It should be noted that co-belligerents are not always allies, and that an ally is not necessarily belligerent. In the course of the War of 1914 to 1918 the United States of America became 'associated' with us in the war, and in the Treaty of Versailles are described as an 'Associated Power'. In the War of 1939 to 1945 Soviet Russia was our ally at any rate as from 15 July 1941; see *The Times* newspaper, 16 July 1941.

[4] Except that the position of an allied national resident outside British territory would be different in so far as British criminal law is concerned.

[5] *Kreglinger & Co.* v. *Cohen, Trading as Samuel and Rosenfeld* (1915).

(*b*) *Where the non-enemy country is neutral*, a distinction must be made between (i) a contract which involves conduct inimical to the interests of this country and assistance to our enemy of a kind which international law entitles a belligerent to prevent and punish, though by the law of his own country the neutral national may lawfully render it,[1] that is, the carriage of contraband to our enemy, the breach of a blockade declared by us (including, presumably, the analogue of a blockade imposed by Retaliatory Orders in Council), or the rendering of unneutral service, and (ii) a contract which is devoid of such offence.

(i) During the War of 1940 to 1943 against Italy a Barcelona merchant (Spain being neutral) sold and shipped a contraband cargo to an importer in Genoa. After the war one of the contracts pertaining to this transaction—sale, affreightment, or insurance—might come before an English Court if the importer established a branch within the jurisdiction of the English Courts. It is inconceivable that they would enforce that contract, though it was perfectly lawful by the laws of Spain and Italy.

(ii) But suppose a war between Great Britain and Italy in which the port of Genoa is neither blockaded by us nor within the ban of a Retaliatory Order in Council, and suppose a non-contraband consignment of Spanish guitars shipped from Barcelona to Italy. Would an English Court treat the contract as illegal? Not on the ground of trading with the enemy, because that is only prohibited to persons in this country, to allied nationals and (probably) to any person in an allied country. On the ground that it enriches the enemy's resources? Probably not, because it does not enrich his war potential and it takes money or credit away from the enemy country. An enemy party could not enforce it in an English Court during the war because he would be defeated by the plea of alien enemy, but it is difficult to see why his former enemy status should defeat him after the war.

(iii) Again, suppose that during the same war against Italy a Barcelona merchant enters into a contract with an Italian shipowner which involves performance in England *after* the war—for instance, the charter of Italian ships to carry a series of cargoes to England after the war. Would an English Court, after the war, treat this contract as void because at the time of its making Great Britain was

---

[1] The law administered by the Prize Court permits the neutral national whom the outbreak of war finds with a commercial domicile in an enemy country a reasonable *locus poenitentiae* in which to dissociate himself from the enemy: see *The Anglo-Mexican* and *Part Cargo ex M.V. Glenroy*.

at war with Italy? Possibly, on the ground of the doctrine enunciated in the *Clapham Steamship* case and the *Ertel Bieber* case to the effect that it enhances the resources of the enemy prospectively, that is, by ensuring to him the post-war employment of his mercantile marine, which has a present value for him, amongst other reasons, because it gives him confidence to maintain or increase his fleet.

F. CONTRACTS BETWEEN PERSONS IN THIS COUNTRY AND ENEMY NATIONALS IN FOREIGN TERRITORY NEITHER OWNED NOR OCCUPIED BY THE ENEMY STATE

Where one of the parties to a contract is an enemy national living in foreign non-enemy territory, and the other is a person resident or carrying on business in this country, there is some authority[1] for saying that, though the enemy national is not living 'in protection', he can enforce the contract, whether made before or during the war, in an English Court. If an enemy national so situated has a right to sue in an English Court, it is a reasonable deduction that he has contractual capacity.[2] But an enemy in foreign non-enemy territory who is 'black-listed' by the Board of Trade under subsection 2 of section 2 of the Trading with the Enemy Act, 1939, would not have contractual capacity under our law.

G. CONTRACTS MADE BETWEEN PERSONS IN ENEMY OR ENEMY-OCCUPIED TERRITORY DURING WAR

(A) Where neither party is a prisoner of war or interned or detained by the enemy:
  (i)   between two British nationals;
  (ii) between a British national and the national of a neutral State;
  (iii) between a British national and an enemy national;
  (iv) between two enemy nationals;
  (v)   between an enemy national and a national of a neutral State;
  (vi) between two nationals of a neutral State or States.

---

[1] *In re Mary, Duchess of Sutherland, Bechoff, David & Co.* v. *Bubna*; see above, p. 88, and Webber, pp. 152–3.

[2] There is an American expression 'separated by the line of war', which supposes an imaginary cordon to be drawn round enemy and enemy-occupied territory and is used to distinguish contracts to which both the parties are outside such territory from contracts to which one party is within such territory and the other outside it. There is good reason to think that the 'line of war' runs round enemy and enemy-occupied territory and not round British and British-occupied territory, so that foreign non-enemy territory would lie on our side of the line. The idea is implicit in many of the English decisions, and occasionally the expression 'line of war' is found. Lord Wright used it in the *Sovfracht* case [1943] A.C. 203, 230.

(B) Where one or both parties are prisoners of war or interned or detained by the enemy.

We must rid our minds of the idea that a contract made in enemy territory during war is by reason of that mere fact one that can never be enforced in an English Court;[1] its enforceability depends also on the status of the parties and the content of the contract.

The mischiefs aimed at by the rule of law that renders void a contract which it is attempted to make with a person in enemy territory, namely, communication across the line of war, and (less certainly) the increase of the enemy's resources, do not exist when both parties are in enemy territory.

(A) *Where neither party is a prisoner of war or interned or detained by the enemy*

We shall leave to the next section (B) cases in which one or both of the parties are prisoners of war in the strict sense or interned by the enemy or merely prevented from leaving enemy territory. Few British nationals in enemy territory would fall outside those categories, but in many wars British nationals, particularly women and elderly men, have voluntarily remained in enemy countries after having the opportunity to leave.

(i) *Between two British nationals.* Two British nationals, voluntarily resident in enemy or enemy-occupied territory, during the war enter into a contract which is innocent in itself and in no way prejudicial to British interests, e.g. for instruction in playing the piano, for the loan of money. We can see no reason why an English Court if asked to adjudicate upon the contract after the war, or after both parties have departed from enemy territory, should not do so subject to the normal rules of conflict of laws.[2]

(ii) *Between a British national and the national of a neutral State.* We suggest that the view expressed in the preceding paragraph also applies to a contract between these persons. In *Houriet* v. *Morris* Swiss (neutral) subjects were allowed to sue a British subject during the war with France as the payees of a promissory note given to them by the defendant in France during the war in payment for goods bought there. Lord Ellenborough said:

[1] *Houriet* v. *Morris*; see also Dallas J. in *Antoine* v. *Morshead* ('this is a contract between two subjects [*scilicet*, British subjects] in an enemy's country, which is perfectly legal').

[2] For a case in which a Dutch (allied) subject temporarily resident in Monaco (probably enemy-occupied territory) during the War of 1939 to 1945 lent there a sum of money in French francs to a British subject also temporarily resident there, the loan to be repayable in sterling after the war, and failed to recover because the transaction was illegal by reason of certain British Defence (Finance) Regulations, 1939, see *Boissevain* v. *Weil*. See also *Seethalakshmi Achi* v. *V. T. Veerappa Chettiar*.

The contracting parties were not alien enemies; and it does not follow that the contract was void, though made in an enemy's country. The plaintiffs, who are domiciled in Swisserland [*sic*], might lawfully sell their goods in Paris; and it is not proved that the defendant, who is a British subject, purchased them there for any illegal purpose.

(iii) *Between a British and an enemy national.* Is such a contract, if it is innocent in itself and in no way strengthens the resources of the enemy or injures British interests, a trading with the enemy, and therefore criminal? At common law? No, unless it involves treasonable activities; because apart from a few exceptional crimes, such as treason, murder, manslaughter, bigamy, piracy, etc., our conception of crime is territorial.[1] Under the Trading with the Enemy Act, 1939? No; because that Act applies not to British nationals as such but to any 'person' in the United Kingdom, or, if extended by Order in Council, to certain other territories which are British or under British protection or mandate or jurisdiction.[2] We suggest, therefore, that it is neither criminal nor illegal for a British national in enemy territory to contract with an enemy national for such purposes as the giving of music lessons or the purchase of food or books, and that such contracts would be enforced in English Courts after the war subject to the normal rules of conflict of laws. But a contract involving treasonable activities would be both criminal and illegal, and one can imagine many contracts which, while not amounting to treason, would by reason of their tendency to maintain the enemy's trade and resources be treated after the war by an English Court as contrary to English rules of public policy and unenforceable.

In these cases, (i), (ii) and (iii), it would be injurious to British nationals present in enemy territory if they were precluded from making valid contracts for the borrowing or earning of money or for supplying themselves with food and clothing.

(iv) *Between two enemy nationals.* Two enemy nationals during the War of 1939 to 1945 enter into a contract in Berlin which has no connection with the war and neither injures Great Britain or her allies or assists the enemy—a qualification which would probably exclude most commercial transactions; for instance, Herr *X* and Herr *Y* agree that the former shall publish the next novel written by the latter; after the war Herr *X* establishes his residence in London and Herr *Y*

---

[1] Kenny, *Outlines of Criminal Law* (17th ed. Turner), p. 510.

[2] See n. 4 on p. 350 below. On the other hand, the Treachery Act, 1940, applies to anything done by a British subject 'elsewhere than in a Dominion, India, Burma or Southern Rhodesia', or 'by any person subject to the Naval Discipline Act, to military law or to the Air Force Act, in any place whatsoever...'.

sues him in an English Court for breach of contract. The contract does not offend against rules of English public policy, and we can see no reason why it should not be enforced in England, subject to the normal rules of conflict of laws. In *Ottoman Bank* v. *Jebara*,[1] the House of Lords after the war upheld a transaction, the delivery of goods in return for payment of bills of exchange, which took place between enemy nationals in enemy territory during the war. Lord Shaw,[2] speaking of Syria, being at the relevant time a part of Turkish (enemy) territory, said: 'Both bank and customer were Turkish subjects there; and the legitimacy of the payment to the bank in Beyrout is, therefore, beyond question, there being no international quality about that part of the transaction.'

(v) *Between an enemy national and a national of a neutral State.* The view expressed in the preceding paragraph would normally apply to a contract between an enemy national and a national of a neutral State; but a consideration of the observations made by Morris J. in *Wasa (O/Y) S.S. Co.* v. *Newspaper Pulp etc. Co.*[3] indicates that in proceedings after the end of the war an English court might refuse to enforce a contract the performance of which during the war would have been injurious to the United Kingdom; for instance, a contract the performance of which would have the effect of breaking a blockade instituted by the United Kingdom.

(vi) *Between two nationals of a neutral State or States.* Again, we suggest that the view expressed in paragraph (iv) applies to such a contract. Moreover, the question could arise during the war. In 1940, that is, before the United States entered the War of 1939 to 1945, two American citizens resident in Berlin entered into a contract of an unobjectionable character. In 1941 they left Germany and established their residence in London. Can they sue one another for breach of contract, e.g. a loan of money? We suggest that, subject to the conditions described in paragraph (iv), the contract is enforceable during the war. Any contract which tended to strengthen the trade and resources of the enemy would be unenforceable in England both during and after the war.

---

[1] [1928]. [A.C.] 269.

[2] At p. 280; see also Lord Dunedin at p. 276. In *Evans* v. *Richardson*, which arose upon a contract made in the United States of America during war with Great Britain, the parties are described as 'citizens of the United States of America', the plaintiff as 'a native of America usually resident there', the defendant as 'a Scotchman usually resident in England' (probably a double national, British and American). No objection was based on the fact that the contract was made in the enemy country, but the Court declined on other grounds to grant the relief sought.

[3] (1949) 82 Ll. Rep. 936, 958–60; Carver, *Carriage by Sea* (11th ed. 1963), § 491.

(B) *Where one or both parties are prisoners of war[1] or interned or detained by the enemy[2]*

We have already considered[3] the converse case of enemy prisoners of war, and enemy persons interned, in this country, and we noticed that they appear to possess full contractual and (apart from the writ of *habeas corpus*) procedural capacity; in *Sparenburgh* v. *Bannatyne* there is a suggestion that they must be allowed the degree of legal status necessary to enable them to subsist. Judicial authority upon the position of contracts made by British prisoners of war and persons interned or detained in enemy territory is not clear. It is submitted that the position of their contracts is at least as favourable as that of the contracts of other British nationals, which we have already attempted to describe, and in one respect much more favourable. There is considerable authority for the view that a contract connected with the object of supplyng such a person with the necessaries of life may be enforced in English Courts after the war even though it involved intercourse during the war between a person in enemy territory and a person in this country. In *Antoine* v. *Morshead*[4] one who was 'detained a prisoner...' in France drew a bill of exchange in 1806 (during the war with France) upon a British subject in this country in favour of another British prisoner in France, who thereupon indorsed it during the war to a French banker in France, as the only, or the obvious, way of making use of it; it was accepted by the defendant (described as 'resident here') and almost certainly during the war. After the war the French banker (Antoine) sued the defendant (Morshead)[5] upon the bill and succeeded in spite of the plea that what he sued upon was a contract made between a British prisoner of war and one who was then an alien enemy. In *Duhamel* v. *Pickering* a bill drawn by a British prisoner of war in France in favour of an enemy was regarded as void, but apparently by reason of a statute of 1794 which expired in 1800. In *Daubuz* v.

---

[1] In *Vandyke* v. *Adams* it was held that a British prisoner of war held by the enemy in enemy territory is not an 'individual resident in enemy territory' within the meaning of section 2 (1) (*b*) of the Trading with the Enemy Act, 1939.

[2] As to limitation of actions, see Limitation (Enemies and War Prisoners) Act, 1945.

[3] Above, pp. 92–8.

[4] It is clear that the Court was influenced by the humanitarian object of supplying the needs of a British prisoner, and later in *Willison* v. *Patteson* (1817) 7 Taunt. 439 Gibbs C.J., who presided in *Antoine* v. *Morshead*, said (p. 447) that 'the case was an excepted case, and did not come within the general rule'.

[5] Sir John Morshead, Bart., is described in *Duhamel* v. *Pickering* as a *detenu* and in *Daubuz* v. *Morshead* as being 'detained by the French Government'.

Morshead a bill of exchange was drawn during the war by a British subject detained as a prisoner in France, accepted by his son (almost certainly during the war and probably in this country), in favour of an enemy payee, who indorsed it to the plaintiff, who was allowed to recover upon it from the acceptor after the war, without prejudice to the question 'whether the Crown might or might not lay hands on it'.

In 1819 in *Crawford & McLean* v. *The William Penn*, a Washington Circuit Court, after a war, allowed an ex-enemy to enforce a bottomry bond entered into during a war by the master of an American cartel ship in an enemy port in order to enable him to refit and victual his ship for the purpose of bringing home American citizens who were prisoners of war. The judgment was based on *Antoine* v. *Morshead* and other English decisions mitigating the strict rigour of the law in the interests of prisoners of war. In an earlier stage of the case[1] it was said that a cartel amounts to a licence by both belligerents 'to perform the service in which [the ship] is employed, and sanctifies all the means necessary to that end'.[2]

APPLICATION TO OTHER ARMED CONFLICTS

It will have been noted in this chapter that the dominant factor is 'war' in the sense given to that word by the common law or by statute. It is the occurrence of 'war' in that sense which produces certain well-defined effects upon pre-war contracts, and precludes the making of new contracts, between a party in the United Kingdom and a party in enemy territory. It becomes *ipso facto* illegal to perform a pre-war contract or to attempt to make a new contract. Those effects are automatic. When, however, we turn to other armed conflicts we shall find that, though the conflict may affect existing contracts and hamper the making of new ones, the legal effects are not automatic as upon the occurrence of war but depend upon questions of public policy and other factors.

[1] 1 Peters C.C. 106.

[2] As to the giving of powers of attorney by British prisoners of war during the emergency period of the War of 1939 to 1945, see the Execution of Trusts (Emergency Provisions) Act, 1939.

5

CONTRACTS: FRUSTRATION

BIBLIOGRAPHY

Webber, *Effect of War on Contracts*, 2nd ed. (1940), parts III and IV on Frustration.
McElroy, *Impossibility of Performance*, edited by Glanville Williams (1941).
Glanville Williams, *Law Reform (Frustrated Contracts) Act, 1943* (1944).
Gottschalk, *Impossibility of Performance in Contract* (1945).
MacKinnon, *Effect of War on Contract* (1917).
Benjamin on *Sale* (8th ed., 1950) (Finnemore and James), pp. 565–80 (see summary on pp. 579–80).
Pollock on *Contracts*, 13th ed. 1950 (Winfield), ch. 7.
Scrutton, *Charterparties and Bills of Lading* (17th ed. 1955, W. L. McNair and Mocatta), Art. 31 and index.
Anson, *Law of Contracts* (22nd ed. 1964, Guest), ch. xv.
Cheshire and Fifoot, *Law of Contract* (5th ed. 1960), pp. 463–92.
Chitty on *Contracts* (22nd ed. 1961), paras 1171–1229.
Carver, *Carriage by Sea* (Colinvaux, 1963), §§ 436–71.
Campbell, *Law of War and Contract* (1918), pp. 263–304.
McElroy and Glanville Williams, *Modern Law Review*, IV (1941), pp. 241–60 and V (1941), pp. 1–20.
Gow, 3 *I. and C.L.Q.* (1954), pp. 291–318.
H. W. R. Wade, 56 *L.Q.R.* (1960), pp. 519–66.
Aubrey, 12 *I. and C.L.Q.* (1963), pp. 1165–88.

As we have already seen[1], the outbreak of war may discharge a pre-war contract by making its performance *ipso facto* illegal, even when neither party becomes an enemy in the territorial sense,[2] the sense in which we shall use the word 'enemy' in this chapter in the absence of contrary indication; and the mere fact that the outbreak of war makes one party to a contract an enemy does not necessarily mean that it is abrogated.[3]

In this chapter we are concerned with some other circumstances in which the outbreak of war or the consequences of war or warlike acts can have the effect of discharging a contract, either entirely or as to any further performance due in respect of it, even when no illegality is involved. In these circumstances the contract is usually said to be frustrated.[4] We shall now discuss the doctrine of frustration of contract and mention later some other but less important consequences of the effect of war in interfering with the performance of contracts.

[1] Chapter 4.
[2] *Esposito* v. *Bowden.*   [3] *Halsey* v. *Lowenfeld.*
[4] Decisions involving frustration are also dealt with in other chapters, particularly 6, Affreightment, and 13, Sale of Goods.

Frustration by reason of war is an elliptical expression. War does not itself frustrate a contract and is, of course, not in any way an essential ingredient in frustration. But war and its concomitants generally involve a violent interruption of commercial and other relations and thus provide the commonest causes of frustration. For the purposes of the effect of illegality and of a party to a contract being or becoming an enemy, 'war' has a technical meaning, and the question whether Great Britain is at war or not depends in case of doubt upon the statement of the appropriate department of the Executive.[1] For the purposes of frustration unconnected with illegality the term 'war' is not used in a technical sense; it is the actual facts and consequences which matter.[2]

It is submitted that the sense in which the word 'frustration' is used,[3] judicially and by text-writers, is not uniform and is changing, and it may be useful to examine its meaning at the outset. Historically, it is used to denote the operation of the law in discharging a contract by reason of the occurrence of events or circumstances which were not within the contemplation of the parties when making it, and which are of such a character that to hold the parties to their contract would be to impose a new contract upon them; the legal device underlying this legal operation is, as will later be submitted, that of the implied term. The effect of supervening illegality is, historically, quite different; the ensuing discharge operates simply and directly, and there is, strictly speaking, no need to speculate upon the expectations of the parties or to invoke the doctrine of frustration; a plain rule of law suffices to discharge the contract, just as if (to employ Lord Alvanley's illustration)[4] an Act of Parliament had been passed invalidating the contract thenceforward.

This distinction between supervening illegality and frustration in the strict, historical sense is recognized, for instance, by Viscount Simon L.C. in *Fibrosa Spolka Akcyjna* v. *Fairbairn Lawson Combe Barbour Ltd*[5] (hereinafter referred to in this chapter as 'the *Fibrosa* case');

---

[1] See chapter 1.

[2] See Branson J. in *Court Line* v. *Dant.*

[3] For a modern statement, see Viscount Simon L.C. in *Cricklewood Property and Investment Trust Ltd* v. *Leighton's Investment Trust Ltd* [1945] A.C. 221, 228 (which will be referred to as 'the *Cricklewood* case').

[4] In *Furtado* v. *Rogers* (1802) 3 Bos. & P. 191, 198. See above, p. 124.

[5] [1943] A.C. 32, 41: 'There is a further reason for saying that this subsidiary contention of the appellants must fail, namely...and, therefore, the contract could not be further performed because of supervening illegality', citing the *Ertel Bieber* case [1918] A.C. 260, which has usually been regarded as a straight case of supervening illegality.

by Simonds J. in *Schering Ltd* v. *Stockholms Enskilda Bank Aktiebolag*,[1] where he held the contract to be discharged upon the outbreak of war by reason of illegality and so found it unnecessary to deal with the plea of frustration; and by the Court of Appeal in[2] the latter case, which, while reversing Simonds J. on grounds not here relevant, dealt with supervening illegality and frustration as two separate points. Nevertheless, there is a growing tendency (which we venture to deplore) to include impossibility arising from supervening illegality within the conception and terminology of frustration,[3] and there can be little doubt that this kind of impossibility is covered by the following words occurring in subsection 1 of section 1 of the Law Reform (Frustrated Contracts) Act, 1943:[4]

Where a contract governed by English law has become impossible of performance or been otherwise frustrated, and the parties thereto have for that reason been discharged from the further performance of the contract...

We shall discuss the matter under the following headings:

A. The history up to the War of 1914 to 1918 (1) of the common law rule as to supervening difficulty and impossibility; (2) of the commercial doctrine of the frustration of the adventure; (3) of their coalescence.

B. The theory underlying frustration in its present sphere.

C. The present law.

A. HISTORY, INCLUDING THE TWO WORLD WARS

(1) *The common law as to supervening difficulty and impossibility*

In 1647, in *Paradine* v. *Jane*[5] in the King's Bench, a tenant of land pleaded in an action brought by his landlord to recover rent reserved by the lease (the reservation of rent being regarded as equivalent to a covenant to pay it) that

a certain German prince, by name Prince Rupert, an alien born, enemy to the King and kingdom, had invaded the realm with an hostile army of men; and with the same force did enter upon the defendant's possession, and him expelled...

[1] [1944] Ch. 13; see also [1946] A.C. 219.

[2] [1944] Ch. at p. 22.

[3] This is implicit throughout the speeches delivered in the House of Lords in the *Fibrosa* case. See also *The Steaua Romana*.

[4] See Glanville Williams, p. 23.

[5] Aleyn 26, and Style 47. See also *Harrison* v. *North* (1667), an inconclusive case also arising out of the Civil War.

This plea was held insufficient on the ground that

> when the party by his own contract creates a duty or charge upon himself, he is bound to make it good, if he may,[1] notwithstanding any accident by inevitable necessity, because he might have provided against it by his contract. And therefore if the lessee covenant to repair a house, though it be burnt by lightning or thrown down by enemies, yet he ought to repair it.

The passage last cited above has been accepted for more than three centuries as authority for the absolute character of a promise which the promisor had not the foresight or the desire to qualify; the law says to him, 'You have only got yourself to blame'. From time to time attempts were made to modify the rigidity of this rule by inviting the Court to imply a term excusing in certain events the performance of a promise in terms absolute. Instances are *Brecknock and Abergavenny Canal Navigation* v. *Pritchard* in 1796 and *Atkinson* v. *Ritchie*[2] in 1809, in both of which the attempt to imply a mitigating term was rejected in reliance upon *Paradine* v. *Jane*. In *Atkinson* v. *Ritchie*, Lord Ellenborough C.J. said: 'No exception (of a private nature at least) which is not contained in the contract itself, can be engrafted upon it by implication, as an excuse for its non-performance.' The rule received a somewhat severe shaking in *Hall* v. *Wright* (action for breach of promise of marriage against a man suffering from what appears to have been pulmonary tuberculosis), and in *Taylor* v. *Caldwell*,[3] a master of the common law, Blackburn J., made the first serious breach in it by implying a condition excusing a performance which can only be effected if a given thing continues to exist. In that case, the Surrey Music Hall, Newington, which the defendants had agreed to let to the plaintiffs for a series of concerts to be given by the latter, was destroyed by an accidental fire before the date of the first concert, and thus the defendants were unable to carry out their agreement. The agreement, which was in writing, contained no express reference to the destruction of the premises, though expressed to be made 'God's will permitting'. The plaintiffs claimed damages for breach of the agreement. Blackburn J. after admitting that

> where there is a positive contract to do a thing, not in itself unlawful, the contractor must perform it or pay damages for not doing it, although in consequence of unforeseen accidents the performance of his contract has become unexpectedly burthensome or even impossible,

drew from the English authorities the conclusion that

---

[1] Probably in the former sense of 'can'.   [2] 10 East 530, 533.
[3] (1863) 3 B. & S. 826, 833. For another case arising from a fire, see *New System Private Telephones (London) Ltd* v. *Edward Hughes & Co.*

this rule is only applicable when the contract is positive and absolute, and not subject to any condition express or implied: and there are authorities, which, as we think, establish the principle that, where, from the nature of the contract, it appears that the parties must from the beginning have known that it could not be fulfilled unless when the time for the fulfilment of the contract arrived some particular specified thing continued to exist, so that, when entering into the contract, they must have contemplated such continued existence as the foundation of what was to be done; there, in the absence of any express or implied warranty that the thing shall exist, the contract is not to be construed as a positive contract, but as subject to an implied condition that the parties shall be excused in case, before breach, performance becomes impossible from the perishing of the thing without the default of the contractor.

Note that Blackburn J. resorted to an implied condition for the purpose of doing what justice seemed to him to require.

Four years later *Taylor* v. *Caldwell* was followed in another case of a contract *de certo corpore, Appleby* v. *Myers* (1867), where *A* contracted to erect machinery in buildings belonging to *B*, payment to be made on completion, and, the buildings being burnt down before the work was completed, the contract was held to be discharged, and *A* was unable to recover payment for the work already done. Lord Parker of Waddington, the Lord of Appeal in Ordinary, pointed out[1] the difference between these two cases, namely that in *Taylor* v. *Caldwell* a condition precedent was implied, whereas in *Appleby* v. *Myers* the Court implied a condition subsequent.

Some years elapsed before any further extension of the *Taylor* v. *Caldwell* principle was made. *Howell* v. *Coupland* (1874) is a case of the actual perishing of the thing, a potato crop, which was not in existence at the time of the contract. In *Robinson* v. *Davison* (1871) (a case of a contract to play the piano), Mrs Davison did not perish before her concert, but became incapacitated by illness from performing. *Taylor* v. *Caldwell* was prayed in aid—unnecessarily, it is submitted, because contracts for personal services are governed by a rule which was laid down long before *Taylor* v. *Caldwell*, and was relied upon by Blackburn J. in that case. Still, *Robinson* v. *Davison* is interesting as showing a readiness to extend the legal effect of the perishing of a person or thing to cover the case of a person or thing ceasing to exist in the state contemplated by the contract. Mrs Davison continued as a woman, but was no longer a piano-playing woman. *Nickoll* v. *Ashton*[2] illustrates

---

[1] [1916] 2 A.C. at p. 423.

[2] [1901] 2 K.B. 126 (C.A.). It is interesting to note that the judgments of A. L. Smith M.R. and Romer L.J. are based on *Taylor* v. *Caldwell* and show no trace of connection with or influence by the commercial doctrine of the frustration of the adventure, while

this extension in the case of a thing. The defendants had sold to the plaintiffs a cargo of Egyptian cotton-seed 'to be shipped by the steamship *Orlando* at Alexandria...during the month of January 1900'. The *Orlando* was stranded in December 1899, and, although she existed in January 1900, she was not available as a cargo-carrying ship when and where required. The Court of Appeal held by a majority that the contract was subject to the 'implied condition' that the parties should be excused if before breach the *Orlando* should cease to exist as a cargo-carrying[1] ship without the defendants' default (or, more precisely, cease to be available as a cargo-carrying ship at the stipulated time and place), and so the plaintiffs failed in their action for damages for failure to ship the cargo under the contract.

So far then we find the discharging effect of supervening impossibility of performance confined to the perishing of a person who is a party to the contract, or of a thing which is the subject-matter of the contract or stands in essential relationship to it, or to the cessation of the essential condition of that person or thing. It remained for King Edward VII to afford the occasion for the next extension of the doctrine. Amongst the group of Coronation Seat cases to which the illness of that monarch in June 1902 gave rise, *Krell* v. *Henry*[2] is perhaps the most important. The defendant had agreed to hire a flat in Pall Mall for two days, the 26th and 27th of June, and had paid a deposit. The letters exchanged between the parties contained no reference to the Coronation procession, but it was obvious from all the surrounding circumstances (including previous conversation with the plaintiff's house-keeper) that the flat was hired for the purpose of viewing the procession. When the King's illness made it impossible for the procession to take place on those days, the defendant declined to pay the balance of the rent, and made a counter-claim (abandoned in the Court of Appeal) for the deposit already paid. That Court held that the Coronation procession was the foundation of the contract, just as the continued existence of the Surrey Music Hall was the foundation of the contract in *Taylor* v. *Caldwell*, and that its

the dissentient judgment of Vaughan Williams L.J. (at p. 137) contains a direct reference to that doctrine; he uses the expression 'unless indeed the anticipated circumstance which has failed to occur or continue is of such a character as to put an end in a commercial sense to the commercial speculation entered upon by the parties to the contract'.

[1] For which may be cited *D/S A/S Gulnes* v. *Imperial Chemical Industries Ltd.*

[2] This decision takes us a long way from *Taylor* v. *Caldwell*, for the destruction of the music hall made it impossible to carry out that contract, whereas the payment of money is never objectively impossible. The decision was regarded by the Court of Appeal as an extension of *Taylor* v. *Caldwell*, but they also derived support from the doctrine of frustration.

non-happening without the defendant's default excused him from the performance of the contract. But this doctrine must not be thought to cover the case where the event which failed to happen, e.g. the Royal Naval Review at Spithead on 28 June 1902, was not the foundation of the contract. The Review was merely the motive which induced the defendant to charter the plaintiff's vessel 'for the purpose of viewing the naval review' (which was cancelled) 'and for a day's cruise round the fleet' (which remained anchored at Spithead).[1]

In *Krell* v. *Henry*[2] Vaughan Williams L.J. said of *Nickoll* v. *Ashton*:

Whatever may have been the limits of the Roman law, [this case] makes it plain that the English law applies the principle not only to cases where the performance of the contract becomes impossible by the cessation of the existence of the thing which is the subject-matter of the contract, but also to cases where the event which renders the contract incapable of performance is the cessation or non-existence of an express condition or state of things, going to the root of the contract, and essential to its performance.[3]

(2) *The commercial doctrine of the frustration of the adventure*

We must now turn to the other source of the present rules as to frustration of contract, namely, cases of maritime ventures, and we shall find later that the two distinct streams of authority have merged. It is submitted that the source of the commercial doctrine of frustration is the test which prudent business men faced with a casualty would apply; if it is physically impossible to proceed with the venture, because, for instance, the ship is at the bottom of the sea, *cadit quaestio*; if, on the other hand, it is physically possible but commercially impracticable, then prudent business men would regard the venture as at an end. This is the conception which underlies constructive total loss; as Maule J. said in *Moss* v. *Smith*:[4]

it may be that it may be physically possible to repair the ship, but at an enormous cost: and there also the loss would be total;[5] for, in matters of business, a thing is said to be impossible when it is not practicable; and a thing is impracticable when it can only be done at an excessive or unreasonable cost.

---

[1] *Herne Bay Steamboat Co.* v. *Hutton*.   [2] [1903] 2 K.B. 740, 748.

[3] The effect of discharge by frustration upon the rights and duties of the parties was discussed in some of the Coronation Seat cases, but, having regard to the decision of the House of Lords in the *Fibrosa* case, we can defer that question until later.

[4] (1850) 9 C.B. 94, 103. The point of contact between the doctrine of frustration and insurance is also shown by cases such as *Carras* v. *London & Scottish Assurance Corporation* and *Kulukundis* v. *Norwich Union Fire Insurance Society*.

[5] That is, a constructive total loss.

In 1831, in *Freeman* v. *Taylor*[1] we find an instance of the frustration of a charterparty by reason of delay and deviation on the part of the shipowner. Tindal C.J. left it to the jury to say 'whether the delay was so great as entirely to frustrate the freighter's whole object in chartering the ship', and the Court of Common Pleas upheld the direction.[2] In the next case we find the doctrine connected with the effects of war. In *Geipel* v. *Smith*, in 1872, where a shipowner had before the outbreak of war contracted to carry a cargo of coal from Newcastle to Hamburg, the Court held that he was justified in refusing to load under a charterparty containing an exception of 'restraints of princes and rulers' when the French blockade of the port of Hamburg prevented its performance. This exception not merely protected the shipowner from an action for damages, but operated to release him from the charter.

The object of each of them [said Blackburn J.][3] was the carrying out of a commercial speculation within a reasonable time; and if restraint of princes intervened and lasted so long as to make this impossible, each had a right to say, 'Our contract cannot be carried out'; and therefore the shipowner had a right to sail away, and the charterer to sell his cargo or refrain from procuring one, and treat the contract as at an end.

Again, Lush J. said:[4] 'a state of war must be presumed to be likely to continue so long, and so to disturb the commerce of merchants, as to defeat and destroy the object of a commercial adventure like this'. *Taylor* v. *Caldwell* is not mentioned, though *Paradine* v. *Jane* is. *Geipel* v. *Smith* may well be the first case in which the outbreak of war or its consequences brought the doctrine into play, but it has no essential connection with the outbreak of war and other warlike operations.

Two years later, in *Jackson* v. *Union Marine Insurance Co.*,[5] the Exchequer Chamber had to decide in an action upon a policy of

---

[1] 10 L.J.C.P. 26, 28. No doubt earlier express references to frustration can be found; we are merely concerned to show that the doctrine was well established before *Taylor* v. *Caldwell* and has a different origin. From the cases cited in *Freeman* v. *Taylor* it is clear that it owes much to decisions upon the questions whether a particular term in a contract is or is not a condition precedent, whether a non-performance goes to the whole root and consideration of the contract, etc. In *Hongkong Fir Shipping Co. Ltd* v. *Kawasaki Kisen Kaisha, Ltd* [1962] 2 Q.B. 26, at p. 70, Diplock L.J. speaks of the doctrine of frustration as 'being foaled [in 1874] by "impossibility of performance" out of "conditions precedent".' And see McElroy, pp. 121 *et seq.*, where the following references to the use of the term 'frustration' are given: *Spence* v. *Chodwick* (1847) 10 Q.B. 517, 530 (charterparty), including a reference to *Paradine* v. *Jane* (*supra*), and *Atkinson* v. *Ritchie* (*supra*); *Tarrabochia* v. *Hickie* (1856) 1 H. & N. 183, 185 (charterparty); *MacAndrew* v. *Chapple* (1866) L.R. 1 C.P. 643, 648 (charterparty).

[2] (1872) L.R. 7 Q.B. 404.   [3] At p. 413   [4] At p. 414.

[5] A decision much discussed in the C.A. in *Parkinson* (*Sir Lindsay*) *& Co. Ltd* v. *Commissioners of H.M.'s Works and Public Buildings*.

insurance whether there had been a loss of chartered freight by perils of the seas. The shipowner undertook by charterparty dated in November 1871 to proceed from Liverpool to Newport (Mon.) with all possible despatch (dangers and accidents of navigation excepted), and there load a cargo of iron rails and carry them to San Francisco. On the voyage round from Liverpool the vessel went aground on 4 January 1872, and was got off on 18 February in such a condition that her repairs would not be completed until the end of August. Meanwhile, on 15 February, the charterer threw up the charter and chartered another ship. The effect of the delay would have been to substitute an autumn for a spring voyage, which meant a different adventure. The Court held that the shipowner could not have maintained an action against the charterer for not loading, and therefore had sustained a loss of chartered freight by perils of the seas. The finding of the jury upon which the majority judgment of Baron Bramwell is based was that the time necessary to get the ship off the rocks and repair 'her so as to be a cargo-carrying ship was so long... as to put an end in a commercial sense to the commercial speculation entered into by the shipowner and charterers', and so far from being deterred by the severer principles laid down in *Taylor* v. *Caldwell*, the learned judge said that it (*Taylor* v. *Caldwell*) 'is a strong authority in the same direction'. Mr Justice Blackburn, who delivered the judgment of the Court of Queen's Bench in *Taylor* v. *Caldwell*, concurred in Baron Bramwell's judgment in *Jackson* v. *Union Marine Insurance Co*. The fact that these cases of maritime ventures involve the construction of special clauses in charterparties and similar documents is apt at first sight to obscure their bearing upon the general principles of the discharge of contracts, but a few words from Baron Bramwell's judgment in *Jackson's* case put these special clauses in their proper light. At p. 143 he said:

The shipowner, in the case put, expressly agrees to use all possible despatch: that is not a condition precedent; the sole remedy for and right consequent on the breach of it is an action. He also impliedly agrees that the ship shall arrive in time for the voyage: that *is* a condition precedent as well as an agreement; and its non-performance not only gives the charterer a cause of action, but also releases him. Of course, if these stipulations, owing to excepted perils [as actually happened in this case] are not performed, there is no cause of action, but there is the same release of the charterer.

Here lies the point in *Jackson's* case for us. The excepted perils ('dangers and accidents of navigation') protect the shipowner from an action, but if the contract is such that the Court will imply a term that the vessel will arrive to load at a certain time, then they will not protect him from the right of the charterer to a discharge of the contract if that term is not fulfilled. It is the implied term that is of interest for our present purpose. Again, on p. 144, speaking of the excepted perils, he said:

> The words are there. What is their effect? I think this: they excuse the shipowner but give him no right. The charterer has no cause of action, but is released from the charter. When I say *he* is, I think *both* are. The condition precedent has not been performed, but by default of neither. It is as though the charter were conditional on peace being made between countries *A* and *B*, and it was not...

In 1881 in *Dahl* v. *Nelson, Donkin & Co.*[1] the House of Lords held that a shipowner who had undertaken to take his vessel and her cargo to the *X* Docks, 'or so near thereunto as she may safely get', and found when she arrived outside the docks that she must wait at least five weeks, was entitled to call upon the charterer to take delivery outside the *X* Docks at the charterer's expense. Five weeks would have been an unreasonable period to wait, and in the words of Lord Blackburn,[2] after referring to *Moss* v. *Smith*, *Geipel* v. *Smith* and *Jackson* v. *Union Marine Insurance Co.*: 'a delay in carrying out a charterparty, caused by something for which neither party was responsible, if so great and long as to make it unreasonable to require the parties to go on with the adventure, entitled either of them, at least while the contract was executory, to consider it at an end'.[3] He did not consider it necessary to refer to *Taylor* v. *Caldwell*, and indeed any reference would have been out of place.

In all these cases of maritime ventures the judgments, in so far as they rest upon precedent and not merely upon a business-like construction of a written contract, rely upon an entirely different line of authority from that under consideration in *Taylor* v. *Caldwell*. The arguments have a definitely maritime flavour, and any references to the ordinary principles of the common law affecting discharge of contract are subsidiary.

---

[1] (1881) 6 App. Cas. 38. See also *Assicurazioni Generali* v. *s.s. Bessie Morris Co.*
[2] At p. 53.
[3] On the question of what degree of delay or unseaworthiness suffices to produce frustration, see *Freeman* v. *Taylor*; *Universal Carriers Corporation* v. *Citati*; and *Hongkong Fir Shipping Co. Ltd* v. *Kawasaki Kishen Kaisha Ltd*.

(3) Their coalescence

We now come to the coalescence of these two streams of authority.[1] Although we find them making earlier contact (as in *Jackson* v. *Union Marine Insurance Co.* and *Krell* v. *Henry*), it was not until the War of 1914 to 1918 that the real fusion took place. Lord Loreburn in the passage about to be quoted asserted that the principles applicable in cases of maritime ventures are the same as in others, but it is believed that, historically speaking, it would be more correct to say that if the principles are the same now, it is mainly due to the maritime venture cases that this is so.

When this question [the discharge of a contract by the operation of an implied condition, says Lord Loreburn][2] arises in regard to commercial contracts, as happened in *Dahl* v. *Nelson, Donkin & Co., Geipel* v. *Smith* and *Jackson* v. *Union Marine Insurance Co.*, the principle is the same and the language used as to 'frustration of the adventure' merely adapts it to the class of cases in hand. In all these three cases it was held, to use the language of Lord Blackburn, 'that a delay in carrying out a charterparty, caused by something for which neither party was responsible, if so great and long as to make it unreasonable to require the parties to go on with the adventure, entitled either of them, at least while the contract was executory, to consider it at an end'.

B. THE THEORY UNDERLYING FRUSTRATION

Without attempting an exhaustive examination of the theory underlying frustration, we shall enumerate what seem to us to be the principal theories or explanations which are or have been prevalent in England,[3] and say something about each of them. They are as follows:

[1] A good instance of the coalescence will be found in a remark by Lord Wright in a maritime case, *Joseph Constantine Steamship Line Ltd* v. *Imperial Smelting Corporation* [1942] A.C. 154, 182: 'I must briefly explain my conception of what is meant in this context by impossibility of performance, which is the phrase used by Blackburn J. [in *Taylor* v. *Caldwell*]. In more recent days the phrase more commonly used is "frustration of the contract" or more more shortly "frustration". But "frustration of the contract" is an elliptical expression. The fuller and more accurate phrase is "frustration of the adventure or of the commercial or practical purpose of the contract". This change in language corresponds to a wider conception of impossibility, which has extended the rule beyond contracts which depend on the existence, at the relevant time, of a specified object, as in the instances given by Blackburn J., to cases where the essential object does indeed exist, but its condition has by some casualty been so changed as to be not available for the purposes of the contract either at the contract date, or, if no date is fixed, within any time consistent with the commercial or practical adventure. For the purposes of the contract the object is as good as lost.'

[2] *F. A. Tamplin Steamship Co.* v. *Anglo-Mexican Petroleum Products Co.* [1916] 2 A.C. at p. 404.

[3] See Webber, Parts III and IV; Anson, pp. 437–43; Carver, § 441. For foreign (including Scottish) solutions of similar problems, see *Journal of Comparative Legislation*, 1946 and 1947 (including Zepos on 'The New Greek Civil Code').

(*a*) the theory of an implied term which the law imputes to the parties, in order to regulate a situation which in the eye of the law the parties themselves would have regulated by agreement if the necessity had occurred to them; this we venture to call the classic theory;

(*b*) the theory of the disappearance of the basis or foundation of the contract: *non haec in foedera veni*;[1]

(*c*) Lord Wright's theory to the effect that, the parties not having dealt with the matter, the Courts must determine what is just, must find a reasonable solution for them, a theory which, we suggest, involves the importation of another implied term;

(*d*) the theory of common mistake;

(*e*) the theory of supervening impossibility.

The judicial output on the theory of frustration is copious and far from uniform.

(*a*) *The theory of the implied term*[2]

We shall cite five statements of this theory. The first is by Lord Loreburn in *F. A. Tamplin Steamship Co.* v. *Anglo-Mexican Petroleum Products Co.*:[3]

In the recent case of *Horlock* v. *Beal* this House considered the law upon this subject, and previous decisions were fully reviewed, especially in the opinion delivered by Lord Atkinson. An examination of those decisions confirms me in the view that, when our Courts have held innocent contracting parties absolved from further performance of their promises, it has been upon the ground that there was an implied term in the contract which entitled them to be absolved. Sometimes it is put that performance has become impossible and that the party concerned did not promise to perform an impossibility. Sometimes it is put that the parties contemplated a certain state of things which fell out otherwise. In most of the cases it is said that there was an implied condition in the contract which operated to release the parties from performing it, and in all of them I think that was at bottom the principle upon which the Court proceeded. It is in my opinion the true principle, for no Court has an absolving power, but it can infer from the nature of the contract and the surrounding circumstances that a condition which is not expressed was a foundation on

---

[1] Per Lord Finlay L.C. in *Bank Line* v. *Arthur Capel & Co.* [1919] A.C. at p. 442; see later p. 172, as to the source of this expression.

[2] See Scrutton, Art. 31: 'The contract in such a case comes to an end not by reason of any absolving power in the court but by virtue of an implied term in the contract itself. It is for the court to find the existence of the full term as a matter of construction. If an event makes the implied term operative, the contract is automatically terminated thereby and not by reason of the election of either party' (citing decisions).

[3] [1916] 2 A.C. at p. 403; adopted by Lords Dunedin and Atkinson in the *Metropolitan Water Board* v. *Dick, Kerr & Co.* [1918] A.C. at p. 127 and p. 131.

which the parties contracted...Were the altered conditions such that, had they thought of them, they would have taken their chance of them, or such that as sensible men they would have said 'if that happens, of course, it is all over between us'?

Secondly, in the *Bank Line* case Lord Sumner said:[1]

The theory of dissolution of a contract by the frustration of its commercial object rests on an implication, which arises from the presumed common intention of the parties.

The third is to be found in the opinion of the Privy Council delivered by Lord Sumner in *Hirji Mulji* v. *Cheong Yue Steamship Co.*[2]

Frustration...is explained in theory as a condition or term of the contract, implied by the law ab initio, in order to supply what the parties would have inserted had the matter occurred to them,[3] on the basis of what is fair and reasonable, having regard to the mutual interests concerned, and of the main objects of the contract...It is irrespective of the individuals concerned, their temperaments and failings, their interests and circumstances. It is really a device, by which the rules as to absolute contracts are reconciled with a special exception which justice demands.

And on p. 507 he said:

An event occurs, not contemplated by the parties and therefore not expressly dealt with in their contract, which, when it happens, frustrates their [common] object.

Fourthly, Russell J. in the case of *In re Badische Co.*:[4]

The doctrine of dissolution of a contract by the frustration of its commercial object rests on an implication arising from the presumed common intention of the parties. If the supervening events or circumstances are such that it is impossible to hold that reasonable men could have contemplated that event or those circumstances and yet have entered into the bargain expressed in the document, a term should be implied dissolving the contract upon the happening of the event or circumstances. The dissolution lies not in the choice of one or other of the parties, but results automatically from a term of the contract. The term to be implied must not be inconsistent with any express term of the contract.

To catalogue all the judicial opinions expressed in cases involving frustration would be to overburden a chapter which is bound in any case to be long. To mention only a few, Swinfen Eady and

---

[1] [1919] A.C. at p. 455.   [2] [1926] A.C. 497, 510.

[3] Or had been brought to their attention by Mackinnon L.J.'s 'officious bystander': *Shirlaw* v. *Southern Foundries (1926) Ld.* [1939] 2 K.B. 206, 227. For a disinterment of the officious bystander, see Viscount Simonds in *A. V. Pound & Co. Ltd* v. *M. W. Hardy & Co. Inc.* [1956] A.C. 588, 606.

[4] [1921] 2 Ch. 331, 379.

Bankes L. JJ. in *Scottish Navigation Co.* v. *W. A. Souter & Co.* both accepted the theory of the implied term. So did Pickford L.J. in *Countess of Warwick Steamship Co.* v. *Le Nickel Société Anonyme*,[1] and it is interesting to note that he cited as one of his authorities the passage from Lord Haldane's speech in the *Tamplin* case, which we shall presently quote as a statement of the basis of the contract theory.

In the *Hirji Mulji* case Lord Sumner in 1926 was able to look back at the leading frustration decisions of the War of 1914 to 1918, and he adopted the theory of the implied term without hesitation and without discussing any alternative. Yet in those cases evidence can be found both for the implied term theory and for the basis of the contract theory next to be mentioned. In the *Tamplin* case the theory of the implied term commended itself to Lord Loreburn[2] and to Lord Parker,[3] while the basis of the contract theory was espoused by Lord Haldane.[4] In the *Metropolitan Water Board* case, the implied term theory was adopted by Lord Dunedin,[5] Lord Atkinson[6] and Lord Parmoor,[7] while Lord Finlay L.C.[8] might be claimed as an adherent of the other theory. In the *Bank Line* case Lord Sumner[9] adopted an earlier statement of the implied term theory by Lord Watson, and Lord Wrenbury[10] took the same view; whereas Lord Finlay L.C.[11] preferred the basis of the contract theory. In *Kursell* v. *Timber Operators and Contractors*[12] (not a war case) Scrutton L.J. based the doctrine upon an implied term.

Fifthly, in 1941 members of the House of Lords gave their adhesion to the implied term theory in *Joseph Constantine Steamship Line* v. *Imperial Smelting Corporation*[13] (not a war case). Viscount Simon L.C. regarded it as 'the most satisfactory basis'.[14] He pointed out that it had history on its side, having been adopted by Blackburn J. 'in *Taylor* v. *Caldwell*, which is practically the first case of the modern line of authorities'. Moreover, 'it has the advantage of bringing out the distinction that there can be no discharge by supervening impossibility if the express terms of the contract bind the parties to performance notwithstanding that the supervening event may occur'. He added:[15] 'Every case in this branch of the law can be stated as

---

[1] [1918] 1 K.B. 372, 376.
[2] [1916] 2 A.C. at p. 404.　　　　　　　　　　　[3] At p. 422.
[4] At pp. 407 and 411. Lord Atkinson at p. 422 referred to the 'foundation of the contract', but we think that his speech in the *Metropolitan Water Board* case [1918] A.C. at p. 135, places him among the angels.
[5] [1918] A.C. at p. 127.　　　　[6] At p. 135.　　　　[7] At p. 137.　　　[8] At p. 127.
[9] [1919] A.C. at p. 459.　　　[10] At p. 461.　　　[11] At pp. 442 and 444.
[12] See also *Russkoe, etc.* v. *John Stirk & Sons.*
[13] [1942] A.C. 154.　　　　　[14] At p. 163.　　　　　[15] At p. 164.

turning on the question whether from the express terms of the particular contract a further term should be implied which, when its conditions are fulfilled, puts an end to the contract.'

Viscount Maugham[1] based the doctrine 'on the presumed common intention of the parties', either by the implication of a term or in some other way, 'e.g. by a legal presumption', and, it seems, on the whole inclined to the implied term. Lord Russell of Killowen, who was already deeply committed to the implied term, by inference affirmed his opinion[2] in relying upon the statement by Blackburn J. already quoted from *Taylor* v. *Caldwell*. Lord Wright,[3] without again examining the question, was of the opinion that 'the explanation which has generally been accepted in English law is that impossibility or frustration depends on the court implying a term or exception and treating that as part of the contract'.[4] Lord Porter expressed no decided opinion but, it seems, inclined to the view that the matter is one of the construction of the contract. Is it absolute in its nature, or is it one 'where the promisor is only obliged to perform if he can?'[5]

In *Ocean Tramp Tankers Association* v. *V/O Sovfracht*[6] (which will be discussed later as one of the Suez cases),[7] the learned Master of the Rolls said, at p. 238, 'the theory of an implied term has now been discarded by everyone, or nearly everyone, for the simple reason that it does not represent the truth'. We assume that he does not mean merely that a party seeking to invoke frustration sometimes alleges an implied term which is unrealistic, but rather that the assertion that an implied term is the basis of frustration is unsound and contrary to legal principle. In the words of Lord Sumner[8] 'it is really a device, by which the rules as to absolute contracts are reconciled with a special exception which justice demands'; indeed Lord Wright has described it as a 'fiction';[9] and we submit, with respect, that there are many legal devices and fictions which serve a useful purpose in enabling the courts to reconcile the strict rules of law with justice.

Turning from judicial authority, we find two Reports by legal committees in which the theory of the implied term is adopted. In the Report[10] of the Committee on the position of British Manu-

---

[1] At p. 169.   [2] At p. 177.   [3] At p. 186.

[4] In *Port Line Ltd* v. *Ben Line Steamers Ltd* [1958] 2 Q.B. 146, 162, Diplock J. described himself as 'an unrepentant adherent of the "implied term" theory of frustration'.

[5] At pp. 203, 204. See Blackburn J.'s expression in *Taylor* v. *Caldwell* quoted above at p. 159: 'where there is a positive contract to do a thing, not in itself unlawful', etc.

[6] [1964] 2 Q.B. 226. Reported also as *The Eugenia*.

[7] P. 196 below.   [8] P. 168 above.   [9] *Legal Essays and Addresses*, p. 255.

[10] Cd. 8975 of 1918, a statement adopted by the Andrewes-Uthwatt Committee on Liability for War Damage to the Subject-matter of Contracts: Cmd. 6100 of 1939.

facturers and Merchants in respect to Pre-war Contracts (Chairman, Viscount Buckmaster) it is stated that

If relief from the burden of a contract because performance proves to be impossible is given, it is because the court holds that it was an implied term of the contract that it should be dissolved in the event which has arisen and created the impossibility. Impossibility for this purpose means commercial impossibility...

The Law Revision Committee, Chairman, Lord Wright, in its Seventh Interim Report[1] on the Rule in *Chandler* v. *Webster*, was not called upon to report on the theory underlying frustration, but it is clear from the reasoning contained in the Report that they regarded the doctrine of frustration as being based on an implied term:

There is no doubt that a Court will hesitate to construct a contract for the parties, but, under certain circumstances, it is necessary in the interests of justice to imply a term which was not in the contemplation of the parties. An illustration of this is the doctrine of impossibility of performance itself, because the doctrine is applicable only in those cases in which it is clear that the parties did not themselves have the event in contemplation... (p. 6).

(*b*) *The theory of the disappearance of the basis or foundation of the contract*

In the *Tamplin* case this theory was stated by Lord Haldane as follows:[2]

When people enter into a contract which is dependent for the possibility of its performance on the continued availability of a specific thing [in that case a ship on charter], and that availability comes to an end by reason of circumstances beyond the control of the parties, the contract is prima facie regarded as dissolved. The contingency which has arisen is treated, in the absence of a contrary intention made plain, as being one about which no bargain at all was made.

He then discussed the case of a suspensory stipulation providing for a partial or temporary suspension of certain obligations of the contract in certain events, and continued:

Although the words of the stipulation may be such that the mere letter would describe what has occurred, the occurrence itself may yet be of a character and extent so sweeping that the foundation of what the parties are deemed to have had in contemplation has disappeared, and the contract itself has vanished with that foundation.

We suggest that the word 'deemed' is significant; it usually indicates in the mouth of a lawyer that the speaker is resorting to a legal fiction or is implying something which is not express.

[1] Cmd. 6009 of 1939.   [2] [1916] 2 A.C. at p. 406.

Lord Finlay L.C. in the *Bank Line* case uses an expression some-times employed in stating the basis of the contract theory,[1] 'the doctrine that a contract may be put an end to by a vital change of circumstances. . .'. And after describing the events which interrupted the performance of the charterparty he said:[2]

In such a case the adventure contemplated by the charter is entirely frustrated, and the owner, when required to enter into a charter so dif-ferent[3] from that for which he had contracted, is entitled to say 'non haec in foedera veni'.[4] In other words the owner is entitled to say that the contract is at an end on the doctrine of the frustration of the adventure as explained in [the *Tamplin* case].

In effect this means that as the result of some event the performance which the parties are, or one party is, called upon to give is so different from what was contracted for that it could not have been in the contemplation of the parties. As he said in *Larrinaga & Co.* v. *Société Franco-Américaine des Phosphates de Medulla*:[5]

If, in consequence of war, there is a compulsory cessation of the execution of a contract for construction of works of such a character and duration that it fundamentally changes the conditions of the contract and could not have been in the contemplation of the parties when it was made, to hold that the contract still subsists would be 'not to maintain the original contract but to substitute a different contract for it' (*Metropolitan Water Board's* case; *Distington Hematite Iron Co.* v. *Possehl & Co.*).

Here, it seems to us, the two theories under discussion come very close together, for Lord Finlay, an advocate of the disappearance of the foundation of the contract theory, couples with it the test that the change of circumstances 'could not have been in the contempla-tion of the parties'. The basis of the contract theory was found attractive by Goddard J., in *W. J. Tatem Ltd* v. *Gamboa*,[6] arising

---

[1] [1919] A.C. at p. 441.   [2] At p. 442.

[3] A *different* contract; see also Goddard J. in *W. J. Tatem Ltd* v. *Gamboa (infra)*, 'the performance is really in effect that of a different contract'. This seems to us to be the root of the matter. It follows inevitably that in such circumstances failure to perform the original contract is no breach of contract.

[4] We are indebted to one of Her Majesty's Judges learned both in the classics and the law for the source of this expression: *Aeneid*, IV, lines 338, 339, where Aeneas says to the infuriated Dido when leaving her: 'nec conjugis umquam / praetendi taedas aut haec in foedera veni', I never promised to *marry* you; see 15 *Classical Journal* (1920), pp. 304–6 for the use of this expression in American legal decisions.

[5] (1923) 29 Com. Cas. 1, at p. 7.

[6] [1939] 1 K.B. 132. But in *Court Line* v. *Dant* Branson J. said he thought that Goddard J. must have considered himself to be bound by what Bankes L.J. said in *Comptoir Commercial Anversois* v. *Power, Son & Co.* [1920] 1 K.B. at p. 886, if it had been brought to his atten-tion. In justice to Goddard J. it should be pointed out that in the *Court Line* case the parties could not reasonably have foreseen the frustrating event, whereas in Goddard J.'s case both parties, if they did not envisage the precise cause of the frustration, knew very well that the ship was going into the lion's mouth.

out of the Spanish civil war, in order to meet the case in which the parties have foreseen the possibility of the occurrence of the frustrating event and yet have not provided what effect it should have. In that case the learned judge felt unable to hold that the parties had failed to contemplate the risk that a British ship, chartered for the purpose of evacuating civilian refugees from North Spanish ports, might be seized and detained beyond the period of the charter by the insurgent Government. Accordingly, when the shipowners sued the charterer for charter hire in respect of the days exceeding the period of the charter and were met with the plea of frustration, he upheld that plea but rested it upon the ground that the seizure and detention had destroyed the foundation of the charter.

If the foundation of the contract goes, either by the destruction of the subject-matter or by reason of such long interruption or delay that the performance is really in effect that of a different contract, and the parties have not provided what in that event is to happen, the performance of the contract [i.e. to pay the daily hire until re-delivery] is to be regarded as frustrated.[1]

This short citation does not do justice to the learned judge's judgment, but, with great respect, may it not be asked whether this explanation of the doctrine of frustration does not also rest upon an implied term? Whether the parties are unlikely to have foreseen the frustrating event, as in the case of King Edward VII's illness on the eve of his Coronation, and so did not provide for it, or did foresee it, as in the case of the requisition of the ship in the *Bank Line* case, and yet failed to provide for all its consequences, is it unreasonable for the law to impute to them, and to imply in the contract, a term to the effect that upon the occurrence, and as a result, of these events and their consequences they would have regarded the contract as being at an end? If the continuance of a state of affairs or the non-happening of a certain event clearly underlies the whole contract— whether the parties say so or not—and if that state of affairs comes to an end or that event happens, then we suggest that it is reasonable for the Courts to imply a condition that the contract comes to an end. That is what Blackburn J. did in *Taylor* v. *Caldwell*, where it is very unlikely that the parties contemplated the destruction of the Surrey Music Hall. When Lord Haldane, in the passage which Goddard J. cites from his speech in the *Tamplin* case, says that 'the foundation of what the parties are *deemed* to have had in contemplation has disappeared, and the contract itself has vanished with that

---

[1] At p. 139.

foundation', we suggest that this also happens as the result of an implied condition—a condition that the foundation shall continue. We cannot see that it matters whether or not the frustrating event was foreseen by the parties, provided (*a*) (positively) that the event and its consequences are such that performance under the contract would be performance of a different contract, and (*b*) (negatively) that the parties have not expressly or by implication agreed that in spite of the event and its consequences performance should take place; if (*a*) is present and (*b*) is not, we suggest that the contract is dissolved by an implied term.

We submit that the antithesis between these two theories is an unreal one, and that they can be reconciled.[1] The second, the theory of the disappearance of the foundation of the contract, is a statement that in the opinion of the Court what has happened would make performance in the altered circumstances so different from what was agreed upon as to amount to performance of a new contract. The first, the implied term theory, is a statement of the legal theory or device by means of which justice is done—a device, as Lord Sumner said,[2] 'by which the rules as to absolute contracts are reconciled with a special exception which justice demands'. Perhaps the dissentient Baron Cleasby in *Jackson* v. *Union Marine Insurance Co.*[3] put his finger upon the true explanation when he said:

No doubt, when the existence of a particular person or thing, or state of things, can be regarded as the very foundation of a particular transaction, it may be implied that, if the foundation fails, the transaction which is founded upon it ceases to be effectual. But, upon this subject I would beg to refer to the clear and comprehensive judgment of my Brother Blackburn in *Taylor* v. *Caldwell*.

Is not the disappearance of the basis of the contract really an inference of fact which is drawn by the Court and upon which the Court bases the implication of a term to the effect that the parties should thereupon be discharged?

(*c*) Lord Wright's theory[4]

Lord Wright, in an address entitled 'Some Developments of Commercial Law in the Present Century', preferred to regard the doctrine of frustration as an instance of the practice and duty of the judge to

---

[1] The respective merits of the two explanations was much discussed in *Davis Contractors Ld.* v. *Fareham U.D.C.*

[2] Above, p. 168. [3] (1874) L.R. 10 C.P. at p. 141.

[4] *Legal Essays and Addresses*, pp. 252–86.

make sense of a contract to which the parties have given incomplete expression, to do for the parties what, if they had been more enlightened, they would have done for themselves, to interpret the contract *ut res magis valeat quam pereat*. This is presumably our old and much respected friend *The Moorcock*.[1] It is certainly true that Lord Mansfield has impressed our commercial law with a strong sense of the duty to make it work for commercial men and to supply them with a serviceable instrument for the conduct of their business—to do for them often what they ought to have done for themselves, instead of telling them that they must suffer for their own neglect or stupidity. But has not this mainly been done, as it was in *The Moorcock*, by legitimate resort to the doctrine or fiction of the implied term?

Lord Wright's view of the doctrine of frustration will be found at p. 258 of the address quoted above,[2] and reference should also be made to what he said in the *Fibrosa* case[3] of the theory of the implied term: 'I do not see any objection to this mode of expression so long as it is understood that what is implied is what the court thinks the parties ought to have agreed on the basis of what is fair and reasonable, not what as individuals they would or might have agreed.' But in *Denny, Mott & Dickson Ltd* v. *James B. Fraser & Co. Ltd*[4] he repeated his repugnance to the implied term: 'To my mind the theory of the implied condition is not really consistent with the true theory of frustration.'

(d) The theory of common mistake

This was referred to by Viscount Haldane in the *Bank Line* case[5] as one available theory and the one which was 'the real ground of the judgments in *Baily* v. *De Crespigny*'; but, as Lord Wright pointed out in the *Joseph Constantine* case,[6] while that may do for 'cases where the parties intend to contract on the basis of something which, though

---

[1] (1888), upon which see MacKinnon L.J. in *Shirlaw* v. *Southern Foundries (1926) Ld.* [1939] 2 K.B. 206, 227, and an article in *Law Times*, vol. 209, 27 January 1950, on the implication of business terms; see also p. 311 of this book.

[2] He cited four decisions, which are examined in 56 *L.Q.R.* (1940), pp. 180, 181: *Acebal* v. *Levy*; *Ford* v. *Cotesworth*; *Hillas & Co.* v. *Arcos Ltd*; *Hick* v. *Raymond*.

[3] [1943] A.C. at p. 70.   [4] A.C. [1944] 265, 275.

[5] [1919] A.C. 435, 445.

[6] At p. 186. Williston, *Law of Contracts* (Revised edition, 1938), § 1937, considers that the foundation of the defence of impossibility based upon an implied or constructive condition' is fundamentally the same as the basis of the defence of mistake. 'As the basis for the defense of mistake is the presumed assumption by the parties of some vital supposed fact, so the basis of the defense of impossibility is the presumed mutual assumption when the contract is made that some fact essential to performance then exists, or that it will exist when the time for performance comes.' He prefers 'constructive' to 'implied'. Another edition is in progress.

they do not know it, has [already] perished by causes beyond their control', it is difficult to regard it as an adequate explanation of the effect of 'supervening impossibility or frustration'.

(e) *The theory of supervening impossibility*

It cannot be denied, as has already been shown, that the rule established by Blackburn J. in *Taylor* v. *Caldwell* upon the effect of supervening (physical) impossibility is one of the two historical sources of the doctrine of frustration. But it is submitted that the impetus derived from this source has led to the creation of a *nova species*. Blackburn J. was speaking of physical impossibility; the Surrey Music Hall had been destroyed by fire, and the defendant, as its proprietor or lessee, was unable to give the plaintiff the use of it for a series of concerts. But the doctrine of frustration embraces many cases where there is no physical impossibility; in the Coronation Seat cases it was still possible for the letter to enable the hirer to spend a pleasant afternoon sitting at the window, and the payment of money can never be impossible, for 'there is plenty of money in the world', to quote Pollock's citation from Savigny.[1] As Viscount Simon L.C. said in the *Joseph Constantine* case:[2] 'the explanation of supervening impossibility is at once too broad and too narrow. Some kinds of impossibility may in some circumstances not discharge the contract at all. On the other hand, impossibility is too stiff a test in other cases—for example', *Krell* v. *Henry*.

Conclusion

Our submission is that the balance of judicial authority[3] is in favour of the implied term as the basis of the doctrine of frustration, and history appears to be on that side.[4] If you regard the doctrine as a development of the rule as to supervening impossibility, then you find Blackburn J., who may fairly be called the pioneer in this field, resting his judgment in *Taylor* v. *Caldwell* upon the view that[4] 'in contracts in which the performance depends on the continued existence of a given person or thing, a condition is implied that the impossibility of performance arising from the perishing of the person or thing shall excuse the performance'. If, on the other hand, you prefer to trace a different and more distinctively mercantile pedigree for the doctrine—*Geipel* v. *Smith*, *Jackson* v. *Union Marine Insurance*

---

[1] *Contracts* (13th ed.), p. 223.   [2] [1942] A.C. 154, 164.
[3] And see Exchange Control Act, 1947, s. 33 (below, p. 202).
[4] [1863] 3 B. & S. 826, 839.

Co., and *Dahl* v. *Nelson, Donkin & Co.*—we suggest that you will be led to the same conclusion.

In *Jackson* v. *Union Marine Insurance Co.*, where again we find the familiar mercantile refrain ('put an end in a commercial sense to the commercial speculation'), the Exchequer Chamber implied a term (that the ship shall arrive 'in time for that adventure' or 'in a reasonable time') and held (per Bramwell B., at p. 148) that 'not arriving in time for the voyage contemplated, but at such a time that it is frustrated, is not only a breach of contract, but discharges the charterer'; again, at p. 144: 'When I say *he* is [released], I think *both* are. The condition precedent has not been performed, but by default of neither.' Both the majority and the minority judgments cite with approval *Taylor* v. *Caldwell*, and Cleasby B. accepted the doctrine of the implied term in the passage already cited,[1] though the doctrine did not lead him to the conclusion of the majority. Again, in *Dahl* v. *Nelson, Donkin & Co.*,[2] Lord Watson expressly affirmed the doctrine as a characteristic of a mercantile contract, and based it upon an implied term.

C. THE PRESENT LAW[3]

In attempting to state the present position of the doctrine of frustration, it will be convenient to illustrate its operation and effect in the case of particular kinds of contract in the chapters which follow, but there are some general observations which may be made at this stage.

We shall deal with: (1) the circumstances in which the doctrine can apply; (2) the character of its operation; (3) the consequences of its operation; (4) suspension clauses; and (5) the behaviour of a party about to allege frustration.

(1) *The circumstances in which the doctrine applies*

(*a*) There must have supervened since the formation of the contract certain events or circumstances of such a character that the

---

[1] Above, p. 174.

[2] (1881) 6 App. Cas. 38, 59. Pollock (*The Pollock-Holmes Letters*, II, p. 38), writing to Holmes in 1920, said of the Frustration cases: 'After all, is not the implied condition in those cases something of a fiction to screen rules of policy imposed on the parties and becoming, like equity of redemption, a real part of the contract only after the pressure has been applied?' Perhaps Williston (see above, p. 175) has something like this in mind when he uses the words 'constructive condition'.

[3] A summary of the law as it stood in January 1918 will be found in the Report of the Pre-War Contracts Committee (the Buckmaster Committee) (Cd. 8975 of 1918) and is reproduced in paragraph 4 of the Report of the Committee on Liability for War Damage to the Subject-matter of Contracts (Cmd. 6100 of 1939).

Court will form the view that reasonable men in the position of the parties would not have made that contract, or would not have made it without inserting another term, if they had known what was going to happen,[1] or likely to happen; that is to say, events or circumstances of such a character that to hold the parties to their contract would be to impose upon them a new and different contract.[2]

(b) The following are some of the supervening events or circumstances which can raise the question whether the doctrine applies:

(i) The cessation of a particular state of affairs.[3]

(ii) The non-happening of an expected event, e.g. the Coronation of Edward VII.[4]

(iii) The occurrence of an unexpected event, e.g. the outbreak of the Franco-Prussian War and the French blockade of Hamburg,[5] or the physical blocking of the Suez Canal in 1956.[6]

(iv) The requisition by the Government of something which is the subject-matter of the contract or otherwise essential to its performance, for instance, a ship under charter,[7] something contracted to be sold,[8] etc.

(v) A prohibition against beginning or continuing performance as a result of legislation[9] or the lawful action of the Executive in the exercise of its common law powers. For instance, in *Metropolitan Water Board* v. *Dick, Kerr & Co.*[10] the Minister of Munitions in the exercise of statutory powers directed a contractor in 1916 'to cease work upon your contract for the Metropolitan Water Board' and to comply with instructions as to the dispersal of labour and plant; the

---

[1] Compare an old opinion expressed in *Doctor and Student*, Dialogue II, chap. XXIV: 'And, after some doctors, a man may be excused of such a promise in conscience by casualty that cometh after the promise, if it be so, that if he had known of the casualty at the making of the promise he would not have made it.'

[2] See Morris J. in *O/Y Wasa S.S. Co.* v. *Newspaper Pulp and Wood Export Ltd.* For an unsuccessful attempt to dissect a contract and save part of it from frustration, see *Denny, Mott & Dickson Ltd* v. *James B. Fraser & Co. Ltd.*

[3] *Nicholl* v. *Ashton.*   [4] *Krell* v. *Henry.*

[5] *Geipel* v. *Smith*; *White & Carter* v. *Carbis Bay Garage* (display of advertisement rendered impossible by a Defence Regulation); the express provision in the contract was probably adequate to ensure a *pro rata* recovery of the sum due for displaying the advertisement, but the Court of Appeal went further and held that the contract was frustrated. *Jennings & Chapman Ltd* v. *Woodman, Matthews & Co.*, may be mentioned, though it is not a case on frustration; it appears from it that the doctrine of frustration can apply to an event which the parties realized might happen, though they did not expect it to happen.

[6] See later, pp. 192–8.

[7] See below, chapter 6.   [8] See below, chapter 13.

[9] See later, p. 202, *Hillingdon Estates Co.* v. *Stonefield Estates Ltd* (a compulsory purchase order), and *Oxford Realty Ltd* v. *Annette* (an Ontario case, expropriation of land by a municipality).

[10] See also *White & Carter* v. *Carbis Bay Garage* (*supra*); *Egham & Staines Electricity Co.* v. *Egham U.D.C.* and *Leiston Gas Co.* v. *Leiston-cum-Sizewell U.D.C.* The last case was doubted in *Denny, Mott & Dickson Ltd* v. *James B. Fraser & Co. Ltd.*

contract was dated 24 July 1914 (modified by a supplemental contract of 10 May 1915) and contemplated the completion of a reservoir within six years. The House of Lords held that the contract was dissolved by frustration; to have kept the contract alive and to compel the parties to resume performance when the prohibition expired would be 'not to maintain the original contract but to substitute a different contract for it'.[1]

(vi) Many governmental acts during a war done in pursuance of statutory or of common law powers may produce frustration, e.g. the demolition of houses as impeding the operations of a battery of guns, the billeting of soldiers whereby a householder is unable to fulfil a contract with a lodger, the calling up of a man or woman who is under contract of employment.[2]

Many cases of governmental action are, in effect, equivalent to a change of the law of our own country which, when producing impossibility, amounts to a defence as in *Baily* v. *De Crespigny*, where a railway company acting under compulsory statutory powers purchased the defendant's land and built a railway station upon it contrary to the provisions of a restrictive covenant as to building which the defendant had given to the plaintiff. This was held to excuse the defendant, on the ground that Parliament has 'repealed the covenant'.[3]

(vii) The occurrence of an unexpected event, such as the outbreak of a war, or the occupation of territory by the enemy,[4] which, without any change in the law, makes performance or further performance of the contract illegal.

(viii) The occurrence of a cause of delay of such probable duration that the object of the contract is defeated[5] or that its performance at the end of the delay would involve the parties in the performance of a new and different contract.

For instance, we may refer to the remarks of Blackburn and Lush JJ. in *Geipel* v. *Smith*, a charterparty case, quoted above,[6] and later

---

[1] In the words of Rowlatt J. in *Distington Hematite Iron Co.* v. *Possehl & Co.* [1916] 1 K.B. 811, 814.

[2] See below, chapter 10.

[3] *Brewster* v. *Kitchell* (1697) 1 Ld. Raym. at p. 321; 1 Salk. 198. And see *Eyre* v. *Johnson* for the case of a tenant unsuccessfully alleging prevention by a Defence (General) Regulation from performing a repairing covenant.

[4] The *Fibrosa* case.

[5] A delay 'so great and long as to make it unreasonable to require the parties to go on with the adventure'—per Lord Blackburn in *Dahl* v. *Nelson, Donkin & Co.* (1881) 6 App. Cas. 38, 53, in reference to *Geipel* v. *Smith* and *Jackson* v. *Union Marine Insurance Co.*; and see *Baxter Fell & Co.* v. *Galbraith and Grant*.

[6] At p. 163.

adopted and elaborated by Lord Wright.[1] And in *Jackson* v. *Union Marine Insurance Co.*,[2] an action upon a policy of insurance on chartered freight, where the ship went aground, the Court of Exchequer Chamber held that the shipowner could not have maintained an action against the charterer for not loading because the jury had found that 'the time necessary to get the ship off and repairing [*sic*] her so as to be a cargo-carrying ship was[3] so long as to put an end in a commercial sense to the commercial speculation entered into by the shipowner and charterers', so that the charterer was justified in throwing up the charter and hiring another ship. In effect, a voyage carried out after the ship had been repaired would have been 'a different voyage'—'different as a different adventure'.[4]

(*c*) The question whether or not there has supervened an event or circumstance of such a character as to produce frustration is an objective one; that is to say, 'it does not depend on ['the parties'] intention or their opinions or even knowledge as to the event'.[5] 'It is irrespective of the individuals concerned, their temperaments and failings, their interest and circumstances'.[6]

(*d*) The event or circumstance which produces frustration must not be attributable to the fault of the party alleging frustration. As Lord Sumner said in the *Bank Line* case:[7] 'the principle of frustration of an adventure assumes that the frustration arises without blame or fault on either side. Reliance cannot be placed on a self-induced frustration...'. And Lord Wright in delivering the opinion of the Privy Council in *Maritime National Fish Ltd* v. *Ocean Trawlers Ltd*[8] dealt fully and expressly with this point. But the question of the burden of proof has given some difficulty, and it was held in the House of Lords in the *Joseph Constantine* case that the party alleging frustration is under no duty to approve affirmatively that there was no default (which is wider than negligence) on his part. If the facts

---

[1] *Denny, Mott & Dickson Ltd* v. *James B. Fraser & Co. Ltd* [1944] A.C. 265, 278. In the *Cricklewood* case [1945] A.C. 221, 231, 232, Viscount Simon L.C., in very different circumstances, considered that the unexpired period of a building lease was relevant in assessing the effect of a dislocation resulting from war.

[2] (1874) L.R. 10 C.P. 125, 141; and see Bailhache J. in *Admiral Shipping Co.* v. *Weidner, Hopkins & Co.* [1916] 1 K.B. 429, 436; [1917] 1 K.B. 222, 242.

[3] That is 'would be', for it appears that at the time of the trial she had not been repaired (8 C.P. 572, 573).

[4] 10 C.P. at p. 141.

[5] Per Viscount Maugham in the *Joseph Constantine* case [1942] A.C. 154, 170. Note his 'four propositions' formulated in this case.

[6] Per Lord Sumner in *Hirji Mulji* v. *Cheong Yue Steamship Co.* [1926] A.C. 497, 510.

[7] [1919] A.C. 435, 452.

[8] And see *Equitable Steam Fishing Co.* v. *Cochrane; Mertens* v. *Home Freeholds Co.*; and *Monarch Steamship Co. Ltd* v. *Karlshamns Olgefabricker (A.B.)* [1949] A.C. 196, 229.

proved raise a presumption of default on his part, then he must rebut that presumption; but if the facts raise no presumption either way, then the party who alleges that the frustration was due to the other party's default must prove it.[1]

A fortiori, a party who deliberately does something which produces the frustration, e.g. a shipowner who scuttles a ship, cannot rely upon frustration.

(*e*) The operation of the doctrine of frustration is not excluded merely by the presence in the contract of a clause in which the parties envisage and even make certain provision for the supervening event or circumstance; the presence of the clause shows that the parties had in mind the possibility of the particular event or circumstance supervening, whereupon the question for decision shifts and it becomes necessary to consider (i) whether the words of the clause are apt to cover what has happened, and, if they are, (ii) whether the consequences of the supervening event or circumstance are nevertheless so drastic and disruptive that reasonable men in the position of the parties would not have made the contract they did make if they could have foreseen how disruptive the consequences of the event or circumstance would prove to be. In the words of Lord Haldane in the *Tamplin* case:[2]

Although the words of the stipulation may be such that the mere letter would describe what has occurred, the occurrence of itself may yet be of a character and extent so sweeping that the foundation of what the parties are deemed to have had in contemplation has disappeared, and the contract itself has vanished with that foundation.

(*f*) The operation of frustration by circumstances arising out of a war is not confined to pre-war contracts, though it is clearly more difficult to substantiate a plea of frustration in the case of a contract made after the outbreak of war.[3] For instance, frustration of a contract by requisition or other governmental act, such as calling up, can easily arise upon a contract made during the war. The Pre-war Contracts Committee's Report of 1918 pointed out 'that the war did not create its more serious effect on trade, especially in regard

---

[1] It is submitted that the rule is the same whether the party alleging frustration is plaintiff or defendant.

[2] [1916] 2 A.C. 397, 406. See also *Jackson* v. *Union Marine Insurance Co.*; *Bank Line* case; *W. J. Tatem Ltd* v. *Gamboa*; the *Fibrosa* case. *Banck* v. *Bromley & Son* appears to be a case where the ice clause in the charterparty 'exactly applied to the events which occurred' and accordingly, those events being within the ambit of the parties' contemplation, the allegation of frustration was rejected.

[3] The following are some instances of the frustration of contracts made during a war: *Marshall* v. *Glanvill*; *Federal Steam Navigation Co.* v. *Sir Raylton Dixon & Co.*; *Woodfield Steam Shipping Co.* v. *J. L. Thompson & Co.*; *Bank Line* v. *Arthur Capel & Co.*

to freights, until the Spring of 1915, while no general deficiency of labour was experienced till later in that year'. It remains to be seen whether any bold litigant will be able to establish the frustration of a contract made during the war on the ground that the parties would not have made it if they had foreseen that the war would come to an end so soon.

(2) *The character of its operation*

The operation is automatic; no question arises of either party electing whether or not to maintain the contract, as occurs when a right of rescission occurs. In the words of Viscount Simon L.C. in the *Joseph Constantine* case:[1] 'when "frustration" in the legal sense occurs, it does not merely provide one party with a defence in an action brought by the other. It kills the contract itself and discharges both parties automatically.' At the same time, it is not the duty of the Court to raise the question of frustration if the parties refrain from doing so, so long as no question of illegality or public policy is involved.[2]

(3) *The consequences of its operation*

As we have just seen, when frustration operates, it 'kills the contract and discharges both parties automatically'.[3] It discharges them from liability for acts of performance not yet due, but how does it affect acts of performance, e.g. the payment of money, which have already taken place, or defaults in acts of performance already due? Until 1942 the leading authority was the decision of the Court of Appeal in *Chandler* v. *Webster*, which may be summarized by saying that the loss must lie where it falls[4] at the moment of the operation of frustration, in the sense that money already paid cannot be recovered back,[5] and that rights already accrued according to the

---

[1] [1942] A.C. 154, 163, and see Lord Sumner in the *Hirji Mulji* case [1926] A.C. 497, 510.

[2] Just as it is not the duty of the Court to raise a question of fundamental mistake of kind which vitiates a contract.

[3] In *Heyman* v. *Darwins* [1942] A.C. 356 the House of Lords questioned Lord Sumner's somewhat incautiously wide statement, in delivering the opinion of the Privy Council in the *Hirji Mulji* case upon the effect of frustration, when operating upon a contract containing an arbitration clause, in bringing that clause 'to an end too' [1926] A.C. 497, 505. It is a matter on which it is difficult to make a general statement, as it must depend to some extent upon the precise wording of the arbitration clause.

[4] Note Lord Roche [1943] A.C. at p. 74: 'The true rule, I think, is that in cases of frustration the loss does lie where it falls, but that this means where it falls having regard to the terms of the contract between the parties.'

[5] Contrast the law of Scotland which applies the rule of restitution: *Cantiare San Rocco, S.A.* v. *Clyde Shipbuilding and Engineering Co*, and *Penney* v. *Clyde Shipbuilding and Engineering Co*. Both are war cases.

terms of the contract will not be disturbed, so that money already due but not paid must be paid.[1] This state of the law was the subject of much adverse criticism, and in May 1937 the Lord Chancellor, Lord Maugham, referred to the Law Revision Committee the following question:

Whether, and, if so, in what respect the rule laid down or applied in *Chandler* v. *Webster* [1904] 1 K.B. 493 requires modification, and in particular to consider the observations made thereon in *Cantiare San Rocco, S.A.* v. *Clyde Shipbuilding and Engineering Co. Ltd* [1924] A.C. 226 by Lords Dunedin and Shaw at pp. 247, 248 and 259.

After discussing the relevant decisions the Committee gave the following reply to the question:[2]

We therefore recommend that, when performance of a contract has been frustrated in whole or in part and any money has been paid, or has been agreed to be paid, at a time prior to the frustration of the contract, the following rules shall apply unless a contrary intention appears from the terms of the contract:

(1) Money paid by the one party to the other in pursuance of the contract shall be recoverable, but subject to a deduction of such sum as represents a fair allowance for expenditure incurred by the payee in the performance of or for the purpose of performing the contract. In fixing the amount of such deduction the Court shall include an allowance for overhead expenses but shall also take into account any benefits accruing to the payee by reason of such expenditure, and the amount recovered shall not exceed the total of any money so paid or agreed to be paid under the contract. Loss of profit shall in no case be taken into consideration.

(2) When at the moment of frustration the contract has been performed in part and the part so performed is severable, these rules shall apply only to that part of the contract which remains unperformed, and shall not affect or vary the price or other pecuniary consideration paid or payable in respect of that part of the contract which has been so performed.

(3) For the purpose of these recommendations no regard shall be had to amounts receivable under any contracts of insurance.

We do not recommend any alteration in the law relating to freight *pro rata itineris*, since the rule relating thereto, although frequently criticized, has become so firmly fixed that it would be undesirable to alter it. For the same reason we do not recommend any alteration in the law relating to advance freight except in the case of hire paid in advance under a time charter which, as explained in Appendix B, we think should be recoverable in the event of frustration of the adventure in the same manner and to the same extent as other payments in advance made under a contract.

[1] See Lord Russell of Killowen [1942] A.C. at p. 55.

[2] Seventh Interim Report: Cmd. 6009 of 1939. Reference should also be made to the Report of the Committee on Liability for War Damage to the subject-matter of contracts: Cmd. 6100 of 1939.

Appendix B to the Report consisted of a note upon Advance Freight and Freight Payable *pro rata itineris*.

Two members of the Committee, Lord Justice Goddard and the late Mr W. E. Mortimer, a solicitor of great experience, added the following note to the Report:

We have signed the Report because we think that the suggested alterations in the rule in *Chandler* v. *Webster* would make the law fairer than it is at present. The Report contains no recommendation regarding the converse case where the promisee has paid nothing; in this case it appears the loss is still to 'lie where it falls'. Presumably owing to the limited terms of reference it is not in the Committee's power to deal with either this question or the other questions which arise on frustration.

The Report received consideration in the proper quarters, but no legislative action had been taken when in 1942 the House of Lords by their decision in the *Fibrosa* case,[1] received, and took, the opportunity of overruling *Chandler* v. *Webster*, in so far as was necessary in order to hold that where money has already been paid under a contract which in the event is frustrated, and there has been a total failure of consideration for that payment, the sum may be recovered upon the ground of a failure of consideration. Accordingly, where a pre-war contract for the supply of machinery from England to Gdynia in Poland was frustrated by the enemy occupation of Poland, the purchaser was allowed to recover the sum of £1000 paid by him to the supplier in pursuance of the contract at the time when the contract was made.[2] The justness of the effect of the decision was universally admitted, though there were some who questioned the wisdom of overruling a decision of the Court of Appeal which had formed part of our law for more than forty years, and would have preferred the method of legislation.

It was at once recognized that legislation had now become necessary in order to permit a wider adjustment of the rights and liabilities of all the parties to a frustrated contract, and on 5 August 1943 the Law Reform (Frustrated Contracts) Act, 1943, received the Royal Assent.[3]

---

[1] Thus bringing the English law into line with the Scots law illustrated by *Cantiare San Rocco, S.A.* v. *Clyde Shipbuilding and Engineering Co.*

[2] Sections 56 and 65 of the Indian Contract Act, 1872, provide for the restoration by a party of any advantage received by him under a frustrated contract.

[3] The Appendix to the 3rd edition of this book contains the text of the Act and a commentary upon it by Lord McNair, reprinted from 60 *L.Q.R.* (1944).

(4) *In relation to suspension clauses*

A clause in a contract which in certain events automatically suspends, or enables a party to suspend, its further performance, is a particular illustration of the clauses already discussed in chapter 4. Sometimes the effect of these clauses is to suspend during the period of the dominance of a certain event any obligation to perform the contract and to cancel any instalments or performance due during that period; sometimes it is both to suspend and to postpone until the cessation of the inhibiting cause any instalments of performance, e.g. the delivery of ore, or the supply of tonnage, which would otherwise have fallen due during the period of its dominance.[1] Whenever the effect of such a clause is either to 'suspend' or to 'suspend and postpone' performance, then the question can arise whether—quite apart from the clause—performance at a later date would be so different from performance at the time stipulated for and contemplated by the parties as to amount to the performance of a new contract; if so, the Court may hold the original contract to be frustrated. The variety of suspension clauses is infinite. It is perhaps unnecessary to add that the existence of a suspension clause does not preclude the operation of the doctrine of frustration, which may be described as possessing a sort of paramount dissolving power. Indeed, often it is the presence of a suspension clause that attracts the doctrine, namely, when a purely mechanical application of the clause would have, in the light of what has happened, the effect of imposing a new contract upon the parties.

Thus it will be seen that suspension clauses give rise, so far as concerns us, to three problems: (*a*) whether the clause is apt to cover the war consequences which are present in the case in question; (*b*) whether, that being so, it would be illegal to give effect to the clause; and (*c*) whether, in spite of the clause being adequate to cover the events which have happened so as *prima facie* to suspend the operation of the contract and in some cases *pro tanto* prolong its duration, the events which have happened transcend in their effects the disturbing factors which the parties had contemplated in agreeing upon the clause and are such as to attract the doctrine of frustration.

Problem (*a*) depends upon the circumstances of each case. Problem (*b*) has already been discussed[2] and may here be dismissed shortly as follows: even when the clause provides for complete cessation of

---

[1] E.g. *Pacific Phosphate Co.* v. *Empire Transport Co.*
[2] Above, pp. 128–30.

intercourse with the enemy and does not stop short of that, e.g. by merely suspending deliveries, it is illegal and void on the ground of public policy if to give effect to it is to cause a detriment to this country or an advantage to the enemy, even in the future, as for instance by enhancing the post-war resources of the enemy or crippling our own.[1]

Problem (c) requires comment. Whereas an exceptions clause contains a list of events or 'excepted perils' the occurrence of which excuses one party or sometimes both parties from further performance of the contract at any time, however remote, the object of a suspension clause is either merely to cancel the instalments of performance due during the operation of the inhibiting cause, or to preserve the right to performance until such time as it may be possible. Where, therefore, the words of a suspension clause are apt to cover an event causing delay or dislocation, the right to performance (apart from questions of illegality as in the *Ertel Bieber* case) goes into temporary abeyance until the cause ceases to operate. The parties have foreseen both the event and the character and dimensions of its consequences and have stipulated that it shall not dissolve the contract or excuse all further performance but shall either cancel certain instalments of performance or postpone them until they become possible, as the case may be. Accordingly, the law will give effect to their stipulation. When, however, the event and its consequences, though falling within the letter of the clause, are so sweeping and destructive in character and extent that the parties cannot be said to have stipulated for what should happen, the presence of the clause will not prevent the doctrine of frustration from applying.

Lord Haldane in the *Tamplin* case put the matter thus:[2]

There may be included in the terms of the contract itself a stipulation which provides for the merely partial or temporary suspension of certain of its obligations, should some event (such, for instance, as in the case of the charterparty under consideration, restraint of princes) so happen as to impede performance. In that case the question arises whether the event which has actually made the specific thing no longer available for performance is such that it can be regarded as being of a nature sufficiently limited to fall within the suspensory stipulation, and to admit of the con-

---

[1] *Ertel Bieber & Co.* v. *Rio Tinto Co.*

[2] [1916] 2 A.C. 397, 406. The relevant clause in the charterparty (which was for a period of sixty months) did not contain any provision for prolonging the charterparty to the extent that its performance might be suspended. 'The time [of the Admiralty requisition] might extend until after the period of the charterparty had run out' (at p. 411).

tract being deemed to have provided for it and to have been intended to continue for other purposes. Although the words of the stipulation may be such that the mere letter would describe what has occurred, the occurrence itself may yet be of a character and extent so sweeping that the foundation of what the parties are deemed to have had in contemplation has disappeared, and the contract itself has vanished with that foundation.

A good instance of this proposition is to be found in *Pacific Phosphate Co.* v. *Empire Transport Co.* In *Naylor, Benzon & Co.* v. *Krainische Industrie Gesellschaft*,[1] McCardie J. discussed a suspension clause, but his remarks were *obiter*—very *obiter*, for there were several other and better points upon which the case had been decided. His judgment, however, should be noted, both for his analysis of the word 'suspend'[2] and as an instance of his willingness to apply the doctrine of frustration in the events which had happened, even on the assumption that the suspension clause was apt to cover the war between Great Britain and Austria. 'A clause,' he said, 'though broad in its meaning, may not cover a set of facts so fundamental and far-reaching in extent and operation and so prolonged in duration as to change the whole circumstances of the contract and the character of its performance.'[3]

(5) *Behaviour of a party about to allege frustration*

In the *Taylor* v. *Caldwell* type of case, when the destruction occurs, the fact of the physical impossibility of performing the contract is patent, and there is nothing more to be said about it. There is no occasion for either of the parties to calculate probabilities, to wonder how long an interruption or difficulty will last; there is no need for a weighing up and determination upon the matter. But frustration is not a physical fact but an intellectual conception. When it operates, it does so automatically, and for both parties, and not by reason of the election of either.[4] Nevertheless, before a party to a contract claims that it is frustrated, he must do some thinking and come to a decision. If both parties agree, *cadit quaestio*. If they do not agree, or if they cannot or do not get into touch with one another, one of them will have to decide whether or not he considers the contract to be frustrated, and he will be answerable to a court of law subsequently for the results of his decision.

Several questions thus arise.

(*a*) Will it suffice that the decision is subjective, that is, his own

---

[1] [1918] 1 K.B. 331; affirmed [1918] 2 K.B. 486.   [2] And see above, pp. 132–4.
[3] [1918] 1 K.B. at p. 339.
[4] See Lord Sumner [1926] A.C. at pp. 509, 510.

bona fide opinion, or must it be objective, such as an impartial third party might properly have arrived at?

(*b*) How long must a party wait before claiming that the contract is frustrated?

(*c*) Does the validity of the decision depend upon the facts so far as they could be ascertained by the party who made the decision at the time when he made it?

As to (*a*), clearly the decision, though the decision of one party, must be an objective one. As Bailhache J. once put it:[1]

The question will then be what estimate would a reasonable man of business [Lord Bowen's shipowner or charterer travelling up to the City on the top of the Clapham omnibus] take of the probable length of the withdrawal of the vessel from service with such materials as are before him, including, of course, the cause of the withdrawal, and it will be immaterial whether his anticipation is justified or falsified by the event.

Questions (*b*) and (*c*) can arise whatever the frustrating cause may be, but frustrating causes produced by war raise some special problems of their own, to which we must devote a few remarks.

(*b*) In the eye of the law the essence of war is the uncertainty of its duration. This rule has been laid down time after time. Lord Shaw once called it a 'presumption'.[2] In *Esposito* v. *Bowden*[3] occurs the expression 'a war, the end of which cannot be foreseen'. Lush J. in *Geipel* v. *Smith* said:[4] 'A state of war must be presumed to be likely to continue so long, and so disturb the commerce of merchants, as to defeat and destroy the object of a commercial adventure like this.' The Court will not speculate upon the duration of a war.

In some cases the frustrating cause is inseparably connected with the war and must, humanly speaking, last as long as the war; for instance, where the named source of supply of goods is an enemy country, in which case the mere outbreak of war discharges the contract on the ground both of illegality and of frustration,[5] or where a ship is detained in an enemy port, subject to the bare possibility of days of grace, which did not materialize in the War of 1914 to 1918, and could hardly materialize in the War of 1939 to 1945 as Great Britain denounced Hague Convention VI in 1925.[6] But where the frustrating cause is not something inseparably connected with the

---

[1] In *Anglo-Northern Trading Co.* v. *Emlyn Jones and Williams* [1917] 2 K.B. 78, 85.

[2] [1916] 1 A.C. at p. 510. See also at p. 507. Contrast the attitude of the law towards strikes in relation to frustration, *Reardon Smith Line Ltd* v. *Ministry of Agriculture* [1960] 1 Q.B. 439, 479.

[3] (1857) 7 El. & Bl. 763, 791. [4] (1872) L.R. 7 Q.B. at p. 414.

[5] *In re Badische Co.* [6] *Embiricos* v. *Reid*; *Horlock* v. *Beal*.

war though produced by it, is not something which inherently must last as long as the war, but is only something which would not have happened but for the war, for instance, the action of the Legislature or the Executive, it is necessary for a party who wishes to allege frustration to walk more warily and not to do anything which indicates indecent haste.

We say nothing of *Hadley* v. *Clarke*, for that decision—upon the temporary character of an embargo removed after two years—has been seriously discredited.[1] In *Geipel* v. *Smith*,[2] where the cause of the frustration was the blockade of Hamburg by the French fleet, Cockburn C.J. said: 'At all events it must be taken that the restraint must cease within a reasonable time, and that the duty of the defendants was to wait only a reasonable time prepared to carry out their contract should the restraint be removed';[3] and Blackburn J. said[4] that the effect of a blockade of the port of discharge is 'that, after a reasonable time it relieves the parties, the contract being altogether executory, from the performance of it'.

In *Andrew Millar & Co.* v. *Taylor & Co.*[5] there were pre-war contracts between English purchasers and Irish vendors for the supply and export of confectionery to what became a neutral port, Mogador. The alleged frustrating cause was the issue of general Proclamations under the Customs and Inland Revenue Act, 1879, on 5 and 10 August 1914 prohibiting the export of (*inter alia*) confectionery. On 20 August the prohibition upon the export of confectionery was removed. No specific date for export had been stipulated, and in the ordinary course of events shipment would have taken place within a reasonable time, probably in August or September. On 14 August the vendors purported to 'cancel' the contracts—in effect repudiated them. The Court of Appeal held that the vendors had been too precipitate, that they should have waited for a reasonable time before treating the contracts as impossible of performance, and that the contracts were not in the event frustrated. Warrington L.J. in a short and illuminating judgment points out the distinction between illegality which 'arises *ipso facto* from a state of war' and impossibility which may or may not be the result of an act of the Executive. The same necessity of waiting a reasonable time appears from *Geipel* v. *Smith*.[6] This rule does not touch the case where the operative cause

---

[1] E.g. in *Horlock* v. *Beal* and the *Metropolitan Water Board's* case.
[2] (1872) L.R. 7 Q.B. 404.   [3] At p. 410.
[4] At p. 412.   [5] [1916] 1 K.B. 402 (C.A.).
[6] L.R. 7 Q.B. at p. 410 (a blockade). *Austin, Baldwin & Co.* v. *Wilfred Turner & Co.* (1920) 36 T.L.R. 769 is also a warning against assuming too hastily that, once a licence

is so conclusive as to discharge the contract at once, for in such a case it would be unreasonable to demand delay.[1]

A remark by Lord Dunedin in the *Metropolitan Water Board's* case[2] is suggestive: 'But to make what I may call a clean case of illegality the illegality must be permanent', as it was held to be in that case. 'Permanent', in the mouths of lawyers as of laymen, does not mean eternal. It means rather that at present the end of the duration cannot be foreseen. The remark is described as suggestive because it helps to explain why pre-war contracts which involve intercourse with the enemy (whether an enemy is a party or not) are completely destroyed and not merely suspended. The reason is that in the eye of the law the duration of a war is 'permanent'. The law will not permit the Courts to speculate upon the duration of a war, 'the end of which cannot be foreseen'.[3] An illegality not arising from the fact that performance would involve intercourse with the enemy may be 'temporary' in the eye of the law and may not result in the discharge of the contract; for instance, *Andrew Millar & Co.* v. *Taylor & Co.* But it will be noted that in *Esposito* v. *Bowden* the effect of the illegality (arising from the prosecution of a voyage to an enemy port, Odessa) was not undone by the fact that within nineteen days of the outbreak of war a British Order in Council was issued permitting a British subject to trade by means of a neutral ship (as the ship in this case was) with non-blockaded Russian ports, of which Odessa was one.[4]

We think we can safely say that before a party to a contract can claim that it has been frustrated he must do what is in his power to avoid that fate.[5] For instance, if a charterer has power to direct a ship either to a United Kingdom port or to a Danish port and, owing to a system of rationing of nitrate soda imposed by Great Britain upon Danish imports during a war, no Danish port is available because the year's ration has already been imported, it is useless for the charterer (or his assignee) to nominate a Danish port and then to claim damages for the shipowner's failure to go there, and the

to import is refused, that is an end of the contract and frustration is established; in that case a restriction upon importation was removed after a few weeks and within the period during which delivery would have been in compliance with the contractual obligation to deliver within a reasonable time. Avory J.'s remark (at p. 771) should be noted: 'I think it was the defendants' duty to wait a reasonable time to see if permission could (?would) have been granted later.'

[1] See *Atlantic Maritime Co. Inc.* v. *Gibbon* [1954] 1 Q.B. 88, 115, 132.

[2] [1918] A.C. 119, 128.

[3] See *Denny, Mott & Dickson Ltd* v. *James B. Fraser & Co. Ltd* [1944] A.C. 265, 278.

[4] The doctrine of the *Ertel Bieber* case, that the suspension of obligations towards an enemy until after the war confers a benefit upon him and imposes an injury upon this country affords another, and historically later, reason.

[5] *Bakubhai and Ambahal Ltd* v. *South Australian Farmers Co-operative Union Ltd.*

captain was justified in discharging his cargo at a United Kingdom port.[1]

Similarly, if a Government prohibition takes the form of making some act illegal unless a licence to do it is obtained, it is the duty of the party whose act is thus made illegal without a licence to bestir himself and apply for a licence promptly; if he fails to do so, he cannot plead that the contract has been frustrated.[2]

(c) A party is entitled to base his determination upon the facts available within a reasonable time and does not take the risk of an early and unexpected removal of the cause of disappearance. Scrutton J. made some valuable observations on this point in *Embiricos* v. *Reid*:[3]

If there is such a likelihood and probability [defeat and destruction of the object of a commercial venture by the detention of a ship in an enemy port] the fact that unexpectedly the restraint is removed for a short time does not involve that the parties should have foreseen this unexpected event, and proceeded in the performance of an adventure which at the time seemed hopelessly destroyed.

He then quoted Lord Gorell in *The Savona*[4] and continued:

Commercial men must not be asked to wait till the end of a long delay to find out from what in fact happens whether they are bound by a contract or not;[5] they must be entitled to act on reasonable commercial probabilities at the time when they are called upon to make up their minds.[6]

Lord Sumner in the *Bank Line* case made some remarks to the same effect:[7]

The probabilities as to the length of the deprivation and not the certainty arrived at after the event are also material. The question must be considered at the trial as it had to be considered by the parties, when they came to know of the cause and the probabilities of the delay and had to decide what to do...Rights ought not to be left in suspense or to hang on the chances of subsequent events.

---

[1] *Aktieselskabet Olivebank* v. *Dansk Svovlsyre Fabrik.*

[2] *In re Arbitration between Anglo-Russian Merchant Traders and John Batt & Co.; J. W. Taylor & Co.* v. *Landauer & Co.*

[3] [1914] 3 K.B. 45, at p. 54. The fact that the detention was an excepted peril, 'restraint of princes', must not obscure the fact that this is a frustration case.

[4] [1900] P. 252, at p. 259.

[5] Approved by Lord Sumner in *Watts, Watts & Co.* v. *Mitsui & Co.* [1917] A.C. 227, 246; but when to an action on a charterparty the exception of 'restraint of princes' is pleaded, there must be an actual 'restraint of princes': 'Restraint of princes, to fall within the words of the exception, must be an existing fact and not a mere apprehension' (per Lord Dunedin at p. 238).

[6] Here again (see p. 162 (n. 4), above) there is a certain resemblance to constructive total loss: see section 60 of the Marine Insurance Act, 1906, and *Marstrand Shipping Co.* v. *Beer* (1936) 56 Ll. L. Rep. 163, 173.

[7] [1919] A.C. at p. 454.

It is submitted that the test[1] can be stated as follows: Would a reasonable man in the position of the party alleging frustration, after taking all reasonable steps to ascertain the facts then available, and without snapping at the opportunity of extricating himself from the contract, come to the conclusion that the interruption was of such a character and was likely to last so long that the subsequent performance or further performance of the contract would really amount to the performance of a new contract? If so, there is frustration. And in considering the probability of the duration, he is entitled to assume that, in so far as the outbreak or the existence of a war is the cause of the interruption, that cause is of uncertain duration. Moreover, the Court will not let him suffer for a determination thus reached if subsequent unexpected events shew that he was unduly pessimistic in his forecast.[2]

OTHER ARMED CONFLICTS

We have seen that, although war is not the sole seed-bed of questions of frustration, it is a very fertile one. This is equally true of other armed conflicts. Thus during and after the Suez crisis of 1956[3] the question of the applicability of the doctrine arose again when, in the course of military operations in Egypt in 1956, the Suez Canal was physically blocked on 31 October by the sinking of block-ships and was closed to navigation from 2 November 1956 to 9 April 1957. At first sight this event might reasonably have been regarded as a classic cause of frustration. But the harvest is disappointing and it is probably true to say that the application of the doctrine of frustration is now less clear than it was before.

Carapanayoti & Co. Ltd v. *E. T. Green, Ltd*[4] arose on a c.i.f. contract

---

[1] Adopted by Evershed M.R. and Jenkins L.J. in *Atlantic Maritime Co. Inc.* v. *Gibbon* [1954] 1 Q.B. 88, 113, 133; see chapter 6, 'Affreightment'.

[2] Compare cases of constructive total loss, e.g. *Polurrian Steamship Co.* v. *Young*.

[3] The following are other cases arising out of the Suez crisis: *Union-Castle Mail Steamship Co. Ltd* v. *United Kingdom Mutual War Risks Association Ltd* [1958] Q.B. 380 (frustration not involved); *Tsakiroglou & Co. Ltd* v. *Transgrains S.A.* (frustration alleged but case decided on condition precedent).

[4] [1959] 1 Q.B. 131, 149. In this case, having regard to the obligation upon the seller under a c.i.f. contract to place the goods on board in a condition fitting them to stand up to the normal circumstances of the contemplated voyage, if there had been evidence that cotton-seed cake, while fit for a voyage northward from Port Sudan through the canal to Belfast, was not fit as to degree of moisture, etc., to pass round the Cape, there could have been no doubt, *pace* Pearson J., that the contract was frustrated. McNair J. expressed the opinion at p. 145 that 'where a contract, expressly, or by necessary implication, provides that performance, or a particular part of the performance, is to be carried out in the customary manner, the performance must be carried out in a manner which is customary at the time when the performance is called for', and Lord Reid expressed the same opinion in the next case to be mentioned [1962] A.C. 93, at p. 118, and see Viscount Simonds at p. 114.

dated 6 September 1956 for the shipment of groundnuts from Port Sudan to Belfast. The contract did not specify a voyage through the Canal or refer to shipment by any usual or customary route. On a special case stated by the Appeal Arbitrators of the appropriate trade association, McNair J. held that the contract was frustrated on the ground that 'the continued availability of the Suez route was a fundamental assumption at the time when the contract was made [6 September 1956], that to impose upon the sellers the obligation to ship by an emergency route via the Cape would be to impose upon them a fundamentally different obligation which neither party could, at the time when the contract was made, have dreamed that the sellers would be required to perform and that, if the parties to the contract had thought of the matter at the time, both, as reasonable men, would have accepted at once that, if the canal was closed for an indefinite period at a time when the sellers were not in breach for failure to ship earlier, the contract would be off'. It should be noted that the Appeal Arbitrators in the special case in which the decision was given found as facts that 'at the time when the contract was made the usual and customary route for the shipment of goods from Port Sudan to Belfast was via the Suez Canal and [at that time] shipment via the Cape was not a usual or customary route'. There was no appeal from his judgment but the Court of Appeal in the two later cases now to be discussed made it clear that they disapproved of it, and it was definitely overruled by the House of Lords in the *Tsakiroglou* case now to be mentioned.

Tsakiroglou & Co. Ltd v. *Noble and Thorl G.m.b.H.* arose out of a c.i.f. contract dated 4 October 1956. In it Diplock J. was confronted with a new factor, namely, certain 'mixed findings of law and fact' by the Appeal Arbitrators of the relevant trade association[1] (not the same association as in the *Carapanayoti* case) as follows:

(iv) It was not an implied term of the contract that shipment or transportation should be made via the Suez Canal. (v) The contract was not frustrated by the closure of the Suez Canal. (vi) The performance of the contract by shipping the goods on a vessel routed via the Cape of Good Hope was not commercially or fundamentally different from its being performed by shipping the goods on a vessel routed via the Suez Canal.

The learned judge regarded this finding as 'a conclusion of fact', by which he was bound, and which 'constitutes a crucial difference between the facts of this case and those of' the *Carapanayoti* case.

---

[1] The award is to be found in [1958] 2 Ll. L. Reports, at p. 519.

Accordingly, he held that 'the Appeal Board was right in law in deciding that the contract was not frustrated by the closing of the Suez Canal'. But for this conclusion on the facts he seems to have been inclined to follow McNair J.

Albert D. Gaon & Co. v. *Société Interprofessionelle des Oleagineux Fluides Alimentaires* came before Ashworth J. in the form of a case stated by the Appeal Arbitrators of the same trade association as in the *Tsakiroglou* case but unlike the award in the latter case the award[1] contained no express finding to the effect that the contracts were not frustrated. (The two contracts were dated respectively 12 and 31 October 1956. The date of the beginning of military operations by the Israeli forces against Egypt was 29 October.) Ashworth J., in holding that these two contracts were not frustrated, relied mainly on the test of frustration adopted by Lord Radcliffe in *Davis Contractors Ltd* v. *Fareham Urban District Council*,[2] namely, that 'there must be...such a change in the significance of the obligation that the thing undertaken would, if performed, be a different thing from that contracted for'. Applying that test, the learned judge, while recognizing that the sellers would be involved in greater expense in resorting to the alternative route, held 'that no such fundamental commercial difference has been established on the facts of this case' and 'that the alleged basis, namely, the continued availability of the Suez Canal, was not the basis on which the parties "must have made" their bargain'.

Thereupon the *Tsakiroglou* case and the *Gaon* case were heard by the Court of Appeal[3] together, and the Court, without deciding whether Diplock J. was conclusively bound by the findings quoted above in the *Tsakiroglou* case, refused to accept the view that there was any fundamental assumption underlying these contracts that it should continue to be possible to ship the groundnuts through the canal, and considered that the longer distance and the increased freight involved in a voyage round the Cape of Good Hope were not enough to bring about a fundamental change in the performance of the contract. From the point of view of an implied term, the Court declined to imply a term that the goods must either be shipped through the canal or by a customary or usual route. From the point of view of *non haec in foedera veni*, the Court held that the change of route was not fundamental.

The *Tsakiroglou* case then went to the House of Lords[4] and the judgment of the Court of Appeal was upheld. The following observa-

---

[1] [1959] 2 Ll. L. Reports, at p. 32.   [2] [1956] A.C. 696, 729.
[3] [1960] 2 Q.B. 318.   [4] [1962] A.C. 93.

tions by Viscount Simonds[1] should be noted: 'it does not automatically follow that because one term of a contract, for example, that the goods shall be carried by a particular route, becomes impossible of performance, the whole contract is thereby abrogated. Nor does it follow, because as a matter of construction a term cannot be implied, that the contract may not be frustrated by events. In the instant case, for example, the impossibility of the route via Suez, if that were assumed to be the implied contractual obligation, would not necessarily spell the frustration of the contract.'

In the *Massalia* case—*Société Franco-Tunisienne d'Armement* v. *Sidermar S.P.A.*[2]—the contract, a charterparty for the carriage of iron ore (that should be noted) from the east coast of India to Genoa, which was concluded on 18 October 1956, clearly contemplated passage through the canal by imposing a duty on the captain 'to telegraph Maritsider Genoa (the charterer's telegraphic address) on passing Suez Canal'. Pearson J., after an exhaustive examination of the authorities, distinguished the three cases referred to above on the ground that in the present case 'it was a term of the contract (whether express or implied) that the vessel was to go by the Suez Canal route' ('a term implied directly from an express term') (p. 306), and held that the route via the Cape of Good Hope was 'so circuitous, and so unnatural, and so different in a number of respects, from the route via the Suez Canal that it should be regarded as fundamentally different for the present purposes' (p. 307); that the shipowners' contention that the charterparty was frustrated was right, and that, having carried the cargo to its destination via the Cape with the consent of the charterers, they were entitled to recover a reasonable sum on the basis of a *quantum meruit*. The learned judge also referred to the decision of the Court of Appeal in the two cases previously mentioned and pointed out that there was a difference, from the point of view of frustration, between a contract for the sale of goods c.i.f., and a charterparty; in the case of the former 'the only differences would be that the seller would pay more than he expected for the freight and the buyer would have to wait longer than he expected for the goods' (p. 308), which were not considered by the Court of Appeal to be 'fundamental differences'.[3]

---

[1] [1962] A.C. at p. 112.

[2] [1961] 2 q.B. 278. Reference was made to an American decision—*The Glidden Company* v. *Hellenic Lines Ltd*, in which the frustration of a charterparty by the closing of the Suez Canal was alleged without success.

[3] On p. 305 the learned judge uses the words 'the different climatic conditions, which would not affect a cargo of iron ore, but might have some effect on the vessel's cargo'.

There was no appeal in the *Massalia* case, but in the case about to be discussed both Lord Denning M.R. and Donovan L.J. expressed the view that this decision of Pearson J. was wrong.

In *Ocean Tramp Tankers Corporation* v. *V/O Sovfracht*,[1] a vessel then at Genoa was let to the charterers for a 'trip out to India via Black Sea' on a charterparty concluded on 9 September 1956, when both parties must have realized that the Suez Canal might be closed before the contemplated voyage was completed but made no provision for that event. The principal facts were stated by Lord Denning M.R. in the Court of Appeal as follows:

On 26 July 1956 the Government of Egypt nationalized the Suez Canal. Soon afterwards the United Kingdom and France began to build up military forces in Cyprus. It was obvious to all mercantile men that English and French forces might be sent to seize the canal, and this might lead to it becoming impassable to traffic. It was in this atmosphere that negotiations took place for the chartering of the vessel *Eugenia*...On 25 October 1956 the *Eugenia* sailed from Odessa. The customary route at this time for India was still by the Suez Canal...The *Eugenia* arrived off Port Said at 11 a.m. on 30 October 1956 and entered port at 4.30 p.m. At that time Egyptian anti-aircraft guns were in action against hostile reconnaissance planes...

The *Eugenia* entered the canal on the morning of 31 October, and in the evening of the same day the Egyptian Government blocked the canal by sinking ships at Port Said and Suez, so that she was trapped. The charterers claimed that the contract was thereupon frustrated and was at an end. Two main points arose: (i) The arbitrator and the judge of first instance, Megaw J., held that the charterers by allowing the *Eugenia* to enter the canal at the time mentioned were in breach of a war clause which prohibited her entry into a dangerous zone of this character, and the Court of Appeal agreed. (ii) The arbitrator held that there was no frustration. Megaw J. held that there was. The Court of Appeal held (*a*) that the charterers could not invoke a self-induced frustration, for it was they who allowed or directed the *Eugenia* to enter the canal. But (*b*) the charterers argued that, even if she had not entered the canal at the crucial moment, she would still have had to go round the Cape, which would have brought about a frustration—a view which Megaw J. accepted, following Pearson J.,[2] in holding 'that the

---

[1] Reported as *The Eugenia* [1964] 2 Q.B. 226, 233, 234, 235. The Special Case will be found in [1963] 2 Lloyds' Reports 155; the position in the canal was such that the *Eugenia*, once released, would be able to go northward (as in fact happened) earlier than she could go southward.

[2] In *Société Franco-Tunisienne d'Armement* v. *Sidermar S.P.A.*

adventure, involving a voyage round the Cape is basically or funda-mentally different from the adventure involving a voyage via the Suez Canal'.[1] The Court of Appeal reversed Megaw J.'s decision.

Certain points in the judgment of Lord Denning M.R. should be noted. (a) He stressed[2] the arbitrator's finding that on September 9 when the charter-party was concluded 'it was obvious to all mercan-tile men that English and French forces might be sent to seize the canal, and this might lead to it becoming impassable to traffic'. (b) He stated the doctrine of frustration in this form:[3] 'It is simply this: if it should happen, in the course of carrying out a contract, that a fundamentally different situation arises for which the parties made no provision—so much so that it would not be just in the new situation to hold them bound to its terms—then the contract is at an end.' He then gave his reasons[4] for coming to the conclusion that the blockage of the canal did not bring about a 'fundamentally different con-clusion' such as to frustrate the venture—a conclusion in which Donovan L.J. concurred.

Whilst this decision, including its disapproval of the judgment of Pearson J. in the *Massalia*, effects a reconciliation between the c.i.f. contract cases and the affreightment cases in the context of the closure of the canal, it may also have the practical consequence of restricting the application of the doctrine of frustration in relation to the facts of future cases. Thus it may be said to have been a strong decision against frustration *on the facts*, and to have gone much further in this respect than the decisions in the c.i.f. contract cases, where the practical effect of the closure of the canal upon the contractural obligations of the parties was clearly much less important.

What estimate can be made of the contribution of the Suez crisis to the doctrine of frustration?

(i) The question whether the circumstances create a frustration is a question of legal appreciation of the facts, and accordingly the court is not bound by an arbitrator's conclusion that there has or has not been a frustration though it is bound by his findings of fact.

(ii) When a contract has provided that the shipment should take place by the customary route or in the customary manner, this means customary at the time when performance is due, not customary at the time when the contract is made.

(iii) The doctrine of frustration can apply in a proper case to a contract for the sale of unascertained goods.

(iv) The *non haec in foedera veni* aspect of the doctrine is emphasized.

[1] [1964] 2 Q.B. at p. 238. [2] At p. 233.
[3] At p. 238. [4] At p. 240.

(v) The element of unexpectedness must not be overlooked, in the sense that it is very difficult for a person to allege and prove frustration by an event which was, if not imminent, at least capable of being foreseen by persons of his profession or occupation and for which he made no provision in the contract alleged to be frustrated.[1]

In conclusion, after attempting to state what the operation of the doctrine of frustration is, and in what circumstances it applies, it may be useful to state what its operation is not. When a court has decided that the circumstances are such as to attract the operation of the doctrine, it holds the contract to be discharged as from the date of the occurrence of the supervening event or circumstances. Whether the court relies on the doctrine of an implied term or prefers to say that as the result of supervening events or circumstances the basis of the contract has disappeared, so that to enforce it would be to make for the parties and then enforce upon them a new contract (*non haec in foedera veni*), the effect is that the contract is declared to be at an end. The operation of the doctrine is destructive, not constructive. In a case, *British Movietone News Ld* v. *London and District Cinemas Ld*,[2] upon a contract between a company of film suppliers and a company of film exhibitors, in which the facts were greatly complicated by a series of war-time statutes and emergency regulations, the Court of Appeal, acting upon what the House of Lords regarded as an erroneous interpretation of the judgment in *Parkinson (Sir Lindsay) & Co.* v. *Commissioners of Works and Buildings*, exercised what was described by Denning L.J. in the leading judgment as 'a qualifying power'[3] and made a new contract for the parties— 'a power to qualify the absolute, literal or wide terms of the contract —in order to do what is just and reasonable in the new situation'... 'Until recently the court only exercised this power when there was a frustrating event, that is, a supervening event which struck away the foundations of the contract. But in the important decision of *Parkinson & Co. Ld* v. *Commissioners of Works*, this court exercised a like power when there was no frustrating event, but only an uncontemplated turn of events...' The House of Lords reacted vigorously against this view, reversed the decision and reaffirmed the rule that the effect of the doctrine of frustration when applicable, which it was not in this case, is to terminate the contract and not to enable the court to make for the parties what it might regard as a 'just and

---

[1] Nevertheless, even a foreseen event can produce frustration in certain cases: see *W. J. Tatem Ltd* v. *Gamboa* and Lord Denning [1964] 2 Q.B. at p. 239.

[2] [1951] 1 K.B. 190; [1952] A.C. 166.

[3] [1951] 1 K.B. at p. 200.

reasonable' modification of it. In the words of Viscount Simon L.C.,[1] 'what distinguishes "frustration" cases is that the interpretation involves the consequence that, in view of what has happened, further performance is automatically ended'.[2]

Frustration is also referred to in the following chapters: 6, 8, 11, 12, 13, and 15.

MISCELLANEOUS PROVISIONS CONCERNING PERFORMANCE OF CONTRACTS

(a) Bailees generally, and the defence of 'King's enemies' in particular

In broadest outline the position at common law is that the ordinary bailee (i.e. any person having in his possession goods of another for whatever purpose) is only liable for negligence and accordingly, subject to any express assumption of absolute liability contained in the contract out of which the bailment arises, he would not be liable for war damage occurring without his negligence...

So runs paragraph 20 of the Report of the Committee on Liability for War Damage to the Subject-Matter of Contracts.[3] The Committee then point out that common carriers and common innkeepers are 'entitled to rely upon the implied exception of act of God or King's enemies'. After quoting Blackburn J. in *Taylor* v. *Caldwell*[4] upon the liability of the ordinary bailee as follows:

It may, we think, be safely asserted to be now English law, that in all contracts of loan of chattels or bailments if the performance of the promise of the borrower or bailee to return the things lent or bailed becomes impossible because it has perished, this impossibility (if not arising from the fault of the borrower or bailee from some risk which he has taken upon himself) excuses the borrower or bailee from the performance of his promise to redeliver the chattel...

the Report continues:

The exceptions to this rule are (1) where the bailee keeps the goods after the bailment is properly determined, and (2) where the bailee departs from the terms of his bailment, e.g. keeps the goods in the wrong place or deviates. In these excepted cases the bailee is under an absolute liability for all loss, including loss by King's enemies.

---

[1] [1952] A.C. at p. 186. Note also, at p. 185, his expression: 'a fundamentally different situation has now unexpectedly emerged'.

[2] In *Arab Bank Ltd* v. *Barclays Bank (D.C. and O.) Ltd* frustration was one of the grounds on which the plaintiff bank sought to recover the balance standing to its credit on current account at the Jerusalem branch of the defendant bank (Barclays) when war broke out between Israel and the Arab States on 14 May 1948, and the two banks became separated by the line of war, but the judgment in favour of the plaintiff does not rest on that ground: see later, chapter 8.

[3] Cmd. 6100 of 1939.   [4] (1863) 3 B. & S. 826, 838.

'King's enemies'[1] means primarily enemies in the international sense, but probably includes persons engaged in a domestic rebellion supported by an army and amounting to more than a mere local disturbance.

(b) Express terms

The parties may have expressly provided in their contract that the fact of war or the consequences of war shall afford a defence.

An early recognition of the need of making special provision against the occurrence of war is found in the year 1340 in Y.B. Pasch. 14 Edw. III[2] where it appears that in a charter of the King granting to the Abbot of Ramsey and his successors the right of holding a fair at St Ives in return for a rent of £50 since assigned to the plaintiff in this case it was provided in the King's charter that

if the merchants should be disturbed by reason of war in his realm, so that they could not come there nor make their profit, the suit of the fair should cease for the time.

The report continues:

and we tell you that by reason of the war between the King and the French the merchants, etc., have been hindered from coming there; judgment whether for that time we shall, in opposition to the charter, be charged.

Ultimately it was held that there had been no war '*in* the realm', and the plaintiff recovered.

Again the parties may have expressly excluded war and its consequences from the ambit of their contract, for instance, in a policy of insurance, which is not the same thing as pleading war and its consequences as a defence. Thus, after the Agadir incident in 1911, it became almost universal for marine insurance policies to contain some form of F.C. and S. clause—'Warranted free of capture, seizure, arrest, restraint, or detainment and the consequences thereof, etc...' leaving the owner of the property free to effect a separate insurance against war risks, or to arrange with his underwriters to delete this clause upon payment of an extra premium.

---

[1] As to innkeepers, see the *Marshal of the Marshalsea's* case (1455) Y.B. Hil. 33 Hen. VI, fol. 1, pl. 3, discussed in Holmes *The Common Law*, pp. 177, 200. As to carriers, see the *Marshal of the Marshalsea's* case; Scrutton, Article 82; Carver, §§ 14, 172. *Curtis* v. *Mathews*; *Sec. of State for War* v. *Midland Great Western Railway of Ireland*. The expression when occurring in a bill of lading or a charterparty appears to include the public enemies of the shipowner's State: *Russell* v. *Nieman*.

In two American cases, *L. N. Jackson & Co.* v. *Seas Shipping Co.* and *The Same* v. *Lorentzen*, there was a discussion of frustration and the effect of directions given by an official Maritime Commission.

[2] Rolls Series, p. 128, and see note at p. xv of the Introduction.

It is important to recognize that when the parties to a contract use the expression 'war', 'warlike operations' or some similar expression, the problem before the Court is to decide not whether there exists what international law or English municipal law would regard as 'war',[1] but to assign to the expression the ordinary meaning which a person of common sense would assign to it in the relevant context.[2]

Again, expressions such as 'restraint of princes'[3] and 'restraint of peoples'[4] frequently cover the consequences of war and warlike operations, and the Courts are constantly being called upon to construe them.[5]

(c) *Supervening impossibility created by destruction of or injury to an essential person or thing may be such as to discharge a contract*

If the Surrey Music Hall had been destroyed by enemy action instead of a domestic fire, the effect upon the contract before Blackburn J. in *Taylor* v. *Caldwell* would have been the same. If Mrs Davison had been prevented by injury due to enemy action instead of illness from performing her contract to play the piano, the effect, illustrated by the decision in *Robinson* v. *Davison*, would have been the same.

(d) *Liability for War Damage (Miscellaneous Provisions) Act*, 1939

This Act which emanated from the Report of the Committee mentioned above, defines 'loss by war' and 'damage by war' for the purposes of the Act as meaning 'respectively loss (including destruction) and damage caused by, or in repelling, enemy action, or by measures taken to avoid the spreading of the consequences of damage caused by or in repelling enemy action', and provides, *in certain circumstances*, for relief or increased relief from liability in respect of such loss or damage for bailors and for bailees, for buyers and potential buyers of goods delivered 'on approval or on sale or return or other similar terms' or on condition of liability to pay the price of the goods in the event of their being lost or damaged before the property passes, for innkeepers and for pawnbrokers. It also contains provisions for the relief of hardship arising in certain cases from liability in respect of customs and excise duties.

[1] See chapter I.

[2] *Kawasaki Kisen Kabushiki Kaisha of Kobe* v. *Bantham Steamship Co.*

[3] *Watts, Watts & Co.* v. *Mitsui & Co.*

[4] For the application of such expressions to revolutionary disturbances, see *Soc. Belge des Betons S.A.* v. *London & Lancashire Insurance Co.*

[5] See, for instance, Scrutton, Articles 82 and 83; and Arnould, *Marine Insurance* (15th ed. 1961), §§ 823-32.

(*e*) An illustration of what may perhaps be called 'statutory frustration' will be found in section 33 of the Exchange Control Act, 1947, (which incidentally reflects the theory of the implied term as the basis of the doctrine) as follows:

33.—(1) It shall be an implied condition in any contract that, where, by virtue of this Act, the permission or consent of the Treasury is at the time of the contract required for the performance of any term thereof, that term shall not be performed except in so far as the permission or consent is given or is not required:

Provided that this subsection shall not apply in so far as it is shown to be inconsistent with the intention of the parties that it should apply, whether by reason of their having contemplated the performance of that term in despite of the provisions of this Act or for any other reason.

6

AFFREIGHTMENT: CHARTERPARTIES AND BILLS OF LADING

BIBLIOGRAPHY

Carver, *Carriage by Sea* (11th ed. 1963, Colinvaux).
Scrutton, *Charterparties* (17th ed. 1964, W. L. McNair, Mocatta and Mustill), Article 31 and index.
Webber, *Effect of War on Contracts* (2nd ed.) (1946), ch. 12.

(A) When the United Kingdom is a belligerent: (B) When the United Kingdom is a neutral.

A. WHEN THE UNITED KINGDOM IS A BELLIGERENT

We shall deal (1) with the effect of war in rendering contracts illegal, and (2) with their frustration by war.

1. *Illegality*

Scrutton L.J. has reminded us[1] that the offence of 'trading with the enemy was at first committed principally in relation to ships, their cargoes and the insurances thereon'.

Illegality can arise in two ways:

(*a*) when one party becomes an enemy in the territorial sense;[2]

(*b*) when, though neither party becomes an enemy in the territorial sense, the performance of the contract would involve intercourse with the enemy in that sense or with enemy or enemy-occupied territory.

Under the Trading with the Enemy Act, 1939 (subsection (2) of section 1), a person shall be deemed to have traded with the enemy '(*a*) if he has [*inter alia*]...carried, any goods consigned to or from an enemy or destined for or coming from enemy territory...'.

The contract may be embodied in a bill of lading, a time charter, a voyage charter, or a charter by demise.[3] The effect of the outbreak of war upon a pre-war contract is abrogation, dissolution, not suspension.

---

[1] In *Tingley* v. *Müller*.

[2] By reason of the outbreak of war or of the occupation of territory by the enemy or by transferring himself to enemy territory, see above, p. 121.

[3] Scrutton, p. 4, and notes, and Carver, § 451.

Proposition (*a*) was examined in *Arnhold Karberg & Co.* v. *Blythe, Green, Jourdain & Co.*, and *Theodor Schneider & Co.* v. *Burgett & Newsam*,[1] cases of pre-war c.i.f. contracts between two pairs of firms who were all British or were treated as being British. The question before the Court was not one of the legality of the main contract, the c.i.f. contract, in each case, but of the effect upon the main contract of the consequence of the outbreak of war upon the ancillary contracts of insurance and affreightment, because the performance of a c.i.f. contract by the buyer requires the tender of valid and effective documents embodying these two ancillary contracts. In both cases the cargoes were shipped before the outbreak of war by German steamers which upon the outbreak entered neutral ports of refuge and remained there. In due course the seller tendered to the buyer the shipping documents which included two bills of lading embodying contracts with shipowners who had become enemies in the territorial sense. It was held both by Scrutton J. and the Court of Appeal[2] that the buyer was entitled to refuse the tender, because the contracts of affreightment (and in one case the policy of insurance) had become void upon the outbreak of war. The following passage in the judgment of the Court of Exchequer Chamber in *Esposito* v. *Bowden*,[3] delivered by Willes J., was cited:

As to the mode of the operation of war upon contracts of affreightment, made before, but which remain unexecuted at, the time it is declared, and of which it makes the further execution unlawful or impossible, the authorities establish that the effect is to dissolve the contract, and to absolve both parties from further performance of it.

Esposito v. *Bowden* (British charterer and neutral shipowner) properly belongs to the class of case which we are next about to consider, but the effect, abrogation, is the same when the effect of the war is to make the two parties to the contract enemies to one another. In *Duncan, Fox & Co.* v. *Schrempft & Bonke* it was the British party who pleaded the effect of war. In *Barrick* v. *Buba*,[4] an action brought by a British shipowner against a Russian merchant, it was the defendant, an enemy in the national and territorial senses, who was allowed to

---

[1] Of the four parties three are described as 'English firms', and the fourth, Arnhold Karberg & Co., as 'a firm carrying on business in England'. Its exact composition is stated in *The Derfflinger*. Scrutton J. treated them as a British firm for the purpose of the decision—[1915] 2 K.B. at p. 385. See also *Duncan, Fox & Co.* v. *Schrempft & Bonke* (both parties British firms).

[2] We need not consider here the difference of opinion between Scrutton J. and the Court of Appeal as to the real nature of a c.i.f. contract.

[3] (1857) 7 El. & Bl. 763, 783.

[4] A unanimous judgment by four judges, including Cockburn C.J. and Willes J.

plead that the charter had been abrogated by the outbreak of the Crimean War, but whether he relied upon illegality by English or by Russian law does not appear. Even if neither party pleaded illegality arising from the outbreak of war, it would be the duty of the Court to take notice of it and give effect to it.[1]

(b) Circumstances occur in which, while neither party becomes an enemy in the territorial sense, the performance of the contract would involve intercourse with the enemy in that sense or with enemy or enemy-occupied territory.

In *Esposito* v. *Bowden* (British charterer and neutral shipowner) it became illegal upon the outbreak of the Crimean War for the British charterer to load a cargo of grain at Odessa, and it was held by the Court of Exchequer Chamber that the contract was abrogated as from that moment. The ship had not arrived at Odessa when the war broke out. The result would be the same if the shipowner was British.[2] It is not necessary that it should become illegal for both parties to perform the contract. The further question arises—who may plead that the contract is discharged by illegality? Certainly a British party as in *Esposito* v. *Bowden*. We suggest also that a neutral party can plead that the contract is discharged because *qua* the British party, though not *qua* himself, performance has become illegal. *Barrick* v. *Buba*, where an enemy defendant was allowed to plead illegality, gives some support to this view. Moreover, principle seems to point to the same conclusion, for when the illegality *qua* the British party arises, it does not give him an option either to perform the contract or not, either to plead illegality or not; he is absolutely prohibited from performance. The cause of dissolution does not lie in his hands; it operates by an external force. Nor can it be said against the neutral defendant that he is making use of his own wrong.

It might seem to be a praiseworthy act for a British shipowner or charterer to remove a cargo of grain from an enemy port; but, as Willes J. pointed out (at p. 789), 'the passing it through the custom

---

[1] Atkin J. in Duncan, *Fox & Co.* v. *Schrempft and Bonke* [1915] 1 K.B. 365, 370. Contrast with this case *In re Weis & Co. and Crédit Colonial et Commercial (Antwerp)* where, delivery of the goods at the agreed port (Antwerp) being impossible owing to risk of enemy action but not unlawful because Antwerp was not at that time in enemy hands, the tender of the documents was valid, although the ship (British) had been seized by the enemy before tender of the documents.

[2] 7 El. & Bl. at p. 786. In *Reid* v. *Hoskins* and *Avery* v. *Bowden* both parties were British. The main point argued in these cases was whether there had been a breach or a renunciation of the contract before it was dissolved by the outbreak of war. If a party to a contract acquires the right to treat the conduct of the other party as equivalent to a renunciation of the contract and omits so to treat it, he delays at his peril and can no longer so treat it when the contract has been dissolved by subsequently arising illegality. See Bullen and Leake, *Precedents of Pleadings*, 3rd ed. (1868), pp. 558–9 for some more decisions.

house and obtaining a Russian permit for its shipment might have been but a slight case; still it would have been a case of dealing with the enemy'. (The remedy would be to obtain a licence from the British Crown.)

The question remains—what ought to happen if a British ship, or a neutral ship under charter to a British subject, had already been loaded when the war breaks out and is lying in an enemy port ready to sail? We suggest that if any port dues and export duty have already been paid and if the ship can get clearance without involving any intercourse between the British shipowner or charterer or his agent and any enemy person, there is no obligation to unload the ship, but on the contrary she ought to sail, if she can, and it would be a breach of the charterparty (apart from any special exceptions clause) for her not to sail. So far as concerns a ship lying in a port of the enemy of her flag-State, it must be remembered that some States[1] follow the practice of granting days of grace during which enemy merchant ships may depart unmolested. It is hard to believe that a British shipowner or charterer who took advantage of these days of grace would be guilty of trading with the enemy and that the charterparty would thereby be dissolved; it is in fact the duty of a British ship to escape from the enemy port at once.[2]

On the other hand, if upon the outbreak of war a British shipowner or charterer has already loaded a ship at a non-enemy port for an enemy destination, then—in the opinion of Lord Tenterden[3]—

the contract for conveyance is at an end, the merchant must unlade his goods, and the owners find another employment for their ship. And probably the same principles would apply to the same events happening after the commencement and before the completion of the voyage, although a different rule is laid down in this case by the French ordinance...

Lord Tenterden's observations relate to the case of a ship bound *for* an enemy destination, and we do not think they are relevant to the case of a ship due to sail *from* an enemy destination.

We have dealt with the following cases: (i) British seller and buyer, enemy ship (*Arnhold Karberg & Co.* v. *Blythe, Green, Jourdain & Co.*); (ii) British charterer, neutral shipowner, enemy port of loading (*Esposito* v. *Bowden*); (iii) British shipowner and British charterer, enemy port of loading (*Reid* v. *Hoskins*; *Avery* v. *Bowden*);

---

[1] Including for a period Great Britain; see Oppenheim, II, § 102 *b*.

[2] 7 El. & Bl. at p. 786.

[3] Abbott's *Law of Merchant Ships and Seamen* (14th ed. 1901), p. 867, where it is pointed out that Lord Tenterden's opinion is fortified by *Avery* v. *Bowden*.

(iv) British shipowner and enemy charterer, enemy port of loading (*Barrick* v. *Buba*). So also (v) a charterparty between a British charterer and a foreign non-enemy but belligerent shipowner, the port of loading being within the territory of the latter's enemy, is dissolved by the outbreak of war.[1] There still remains the case where the outbreak of war does not make performance illegal but results in (vi) the shipowner becoming the subject of a non-enemy but belligerent State, so that the ship may become the legitimate object of attack by the opposite belligerent as private enemy property on the high seas. It is suggested that the character and the *termini* of the voyage may be such that the continuance of the non-belligerent status of the ship is a condition precedent of the charterparty, e.g. that she carries a non-belligerent flag, and that the change of her status from pacific to belligerent may fundamentally change the character of the voyage and dissolve the charterparty on the ground that to enforce it would impose a new contract upon the parties.[2] What is a fundamental change? The decisions upon seamen's employment to be discussed later give little help. There is a relativity in these matters, and the extension of sea warfare to new dimensions by means of the submarine and the air-bomber has greatly increased the danger to which merchant ships carrying the flag of a belligerent are exposed. We submit that, in the case of a pre-war contract of affreightment relating to a British ship, each case must be considered on its merits; while the outbreak of war would not *ipso facto* dissolve the contract, the voyage might be such that its peaceful character was fundamentally changed and the contract dissolved. Contrast, in September 1939, the voyage of a British ship from Newcastle-on-Tyne to Gothenburg and the coasting voyage of a British ship between two Australian ports.

'*Queen's enemies*' *as an excepted peril*. Apart, however, from dissolution of the contract, the question arises whether default by the shipowner resulting from enemy action renders him liable or not. A common carrier is protected by the common law from loss or damage resulting from the act of the 'Queen's enemies'. We shall not discuss the questions whether and, if so, in what circumstances, a shipowner can be a common carrier, because charterparties and bills of lading commonly include the 'Queen's enemies'[3] amongst

---

[1] 7 El. & Bl. at pp. 791, 792.

[2] *Behn* v. *Burness* (1863) 3 B. & S. 751, 757, cited in Scrutton, Art. 26, and *Hoyland* v. *Ralli*, *loc. cit.* note (q).

[3] Which means (Scrutton, Art. 82) the enemies of the sovereign of the shipowner, and see *Russell* v. *Niemann*.

the excepted perils, and the Carriage of Goods by Sea Act, 1924, Rule 2 of Article IV of the Schedule,[1] enumerates 'Act of War' and 'Act of Public Enemies' amongst the statutory exceptions from liability.[2]

Suspension clause. In discussing the *Ertel Bieber* case we noticed the view formed by the House of Lords upon the effect of a suspension clause in a long-term contract for the supply of goods. The same principle has been applied to a suspension clause in a time charter. In *Clapham Steamship Co.* v. *Handels-en-Transport Maatschappij Vulcaan of Rotterdam* a British ship was let in 1913 on a time charter for five years to a Dutch company so closely associated with the enemy that the effect of the charter was 'to oblige British subjects to render service for the benefit of enemies'. A clause provided that in the event of such a war as broke out in August 1914 'charterers and/or owners shall have the option of suspending this charter for the time during which hostilities are in progress'. The shipowners brought an action for a declaration that the charter, 'as being a contract with or on behalf of alien enemies, and as involving, if kept alive, an unlawful contractual relationship and trading with alien enemies', was dissolved on the outbreak of war. Both on the principle of *Tamplin Steamship Co.* v. *Anglo-Mexican Petroleum Products Co.*, and on the strength of the suspension clause in the charter, it was argued by the charterers that they were entitled to the use of the steamship after the war. This contention was, however, rejected, Rowlatt J. pointing out that the effect of maintaining the charter in a state of suspension secured shipping facilities to the enemy upon the conclusion of peace and thus fortified his commercial position during the war, while hampering the British shipowner in the disposal of his tonnage. These grounds were enough to avoid the contract *in toto*, and whether the fact that a contrary decision would benefit the enemy after the war as well as during its continuance also had the same vitiating effect upon the contract the learned judge did not consider it necessary to decide. We now know from the *Ertel Bieber* case that it would.

I do not base my decision [said Rowlatt J.][3] on the ground that the maintenance of the charterparty in a state of suspension during the war will benefit the enemy after the war. That may or may not of itself make it illegal. What I say is that it supports the enemy during the war.

---

[1] Which applies primarily to bills of lading.
[2] See Scrutton, ch. xiii for the text of this Act and the meaning of 'Act of War', 'Act of Public Enemies', etc., and see later, pp. 217–18.
[3] [1917] 2 K.B. at p. 646.

The ground of this conclusion is that

if at the moment when war breaks out the enemy is entitled to retain his assurance of tonnage to be available at the end of the war his commercial position is fortified even during the war. He is enabled, by the prospect of shipping facilities which he has, to keep together his connection with neutral or enemy merchants overseas, and even (if he likes to speculate on the war being short or if he can obtain contracts with conditions protecting him if it should be long) to enter de praesenti into new contracts to be performed when peace arrives.[1]

Incidentally, this passage is also valuable in that it points out clearly the reason why, at any rate in the case of a pre-war commercial contract which benefits the enemy, we must expect to find its fate to be abrogation and not merely suspension.

Recovery of freight. When a party to a contract is unable to perform it because it has become illegal to do so, he is unable to recover the reward which would have been due to him if he had performed the contract. So a British shipowner who has undertaken by a pre-war bill of lading to carry a cargo to a port, Hamburg, which upon the outbreak of war becomes an enemy port, so that the further prosecution of the voyage becomes illegal, may retain any advance freight[2] but is not entitled to recover other freight; nor in the absence of provision to the contrary in the bill of lading or of a new agreement will he be entitled to freight *pro rata itineris* for carrying it to a reasonable non-enemy port, Runcorn.[3] 'If a contract once made becomes legally impossible of performance, then in the absence of a new agreement the parties remain in the circumstances in which they find themselves.'[4]

2. *Frustration*

We have already seen that the charterparty cases are the primary source of the doctrine of frustration of the adventure, and nowhere is the conception of an 'adventure' more appropriate.[5] Consequently, we have already had occasion to examine a number of decisions upon charters in chapter 5 in tracing the history of the doctrine and examining the theory which underlies it.[6] We must

---

[1] [1917] 2 K.B. at p. 645.

[2] By a peculiar rule of the law merchant which is preserved in the Law Reform (Frustrated Contracts) Act, 1943; upon which Act see Appendix, II and III, of 3rd ed. of this book.   [3] *St Enoch Shipping Co.* v. *Phosphate Mining Co.* [1916] 2 K.B. 624.

[4] *Ibid.* per Rowlatt J. at p. 628.

[5] Upon the applicability of the doctrine of frustration to bills of lading, see Carver, § 462.

[6] For a valuable summary of the application of the doctrine to charterparties, see Scrutton, Article 31, and Carver, ch. 7.

refer the reader to these earlier pages. Frustration in time of war is more likely to arise when the United Kingdom is a belligerent but can also occur when it is a neutral.[1]

Lord Sumner said in the *Bank Line* case:[2] 'The principle of frustration was originally decided on a voyage charter', doubtless referring to *Geipel* v. *Smith* and *Jackson* v. *Union Marine Insurance Co.*, and it was so applied in a number of cases before[3] and during the War of 1914 to 1918. A charter for a single voyage lends itself more easily to the notion of an 'adventure' than a charter for a period of time, and it was with some difficulty that the doctrine was applied to time charters. In *Tamplin Steamship Co.* v. *Anglo-Mexican Petroleum Products Co.* there was a conflict of opinion in the House of Lords on this point, and in fact the doctrine was not applied to the time charter under consideration. In *Scottish Navigation Co.* v. *W. A. Souter & Co.* and *Admiral Shipping Co.* v. *Weidner, Hopkins & Co.* the charters entered into before the war ('one Baltic round' in the former and 'two Baltic rounds' in the latter) were ambiguous in character and were both held by the Court of Appeal to have been frustrated when the two ships were detained in Russian ports upon the outbreak of war between Germany and Russia and there remained up to the date of the trial. But in the *Bank Line* case we get a clear decision from the House of Lords applying the doctrine to a time charter entered into after the outbreak of war which was frustrated upon requisition by the British Government.[4] Lord Sumner's speech is of particular value. He adopts from Lord Dunedin[5] one of the best definitions of the circumstances which cause the doctrine to apply: 'an interruption ...so long as to destroy the identity of the work or service, when resumed, with the work or service when interrupted'. Other instances of a time charter to which the doctrine was applied are to be found in the *Hirji Mulji* case and in *W. J. Tatem Ltd* v. *Gamboa*,[6] which we have already discussed from a wider point of view and *Blane Steamships Ld.* v. *Minister of Transport*.[7]

[1] For instance, *Geipel* v. *Smith* (1872) during the Franco-Prussian War; *Embiricos* v. *Reid* (1914) (war between Greece and Turkey).

[2] [1919] A.C. at p. 452; and see *Monarch Steamship Co.* v. *Karlshamns Oljefabriker* (A/B).

[3] *Embiricos* v. *Reid*.

[4] In *Port Line Ltd* v. *Ben Line Steamers Ltd* Diplock J. held that a requisition of a ship which was expected to and did, last for 3 months, leaving 10 months of a time charter unexpired did not produce a frustration.

[5] *Metropolitan Water Board* v. *Dick, Kerr & Co.* [1918] A.C. at p. 128.

[6] See also *Banck* v. *Bromley & Son* discussed above, p. 181, n. 2.

[7] See also *Hongkong Fir Shipping Co. Ltd* v. *Kawasaki Kisen Kaisha Ltd*, where it was held by the C.A. on a time charter that there was no frustration but it was not doubted that frustration could arise on a time charter.

In *Associated Portland Cement Manufacturers* v. *William Cory and Son*[1] Rowlatt J. had to consider the effect of dislocating circumstances produced by war upon a pre-war contract for the carriage of cement from the Thames to the Forth during a period of six years at agreed rates of freight. (It is unnecessary to deal with the argument based upon the exceptions clause, and, in particular, 'restraint of princes'.) The shipowner, having refused to carry at the agreed rates, while willing to carry at a higher rate, was sued for damages for breach of contract and pleaded *inter alia* that the contract had been frustrated. Among the circumstances alleged to have produced this result were the following: Government requisitioning of a considerable portion of the shipowner's fleet; interruption with the shipowner's regular return trade in carrying to London coal from Forth ports which had been closed owing to the war; numerous restrictions upon navigation causing excessive delay. Rowlatt J. declined to hold that the contract had been frustrated either on the plea that the parties had contracted on the basis of the continuance of peace or on the plea that 'the return coal trade lay at the root of the contract'. On the other hand, the same learned judge was faced in *Pacific Phosphate Co.* v. *Empire Transport Co.* with circumstances in which he applied the doctrine of frustration. A contract was made in August 1913, whereby the shipowners agreed to supply to the charterers twelve steamers of a certain class in each of the years 1914 to 1918 inclusive to load phosphate from the Pacific to Europe. It contained a clause which (*inter alia*) contained the following provision:

In the event of a war in which Great Britain is engaged and which is likely to affect the safety of the steamers or their cargoes, shipments may at the option of either party be suspended until the termination of the war, and the period of such suspension shall be added on to the end of the contract period.

But he held that the war and its dislocating consequences transcended in magnitude and character what the parties had contemplated:

The parties had contemplated a state of affairs in which there would be some risk but they never contemplated such a war as actually happened or its consequences. The whole shipping industry had been dislocated; the Government had taken control and shipowners were *de facto* not free. Increase in cost was not in itself a cause of frustration, but it could be looked on as an indication of the change in conditions generally.

Here the change was so great that the doctrine of frustration applied,

[1] See also *Bolckow, Vaughan & Co.* v. *Compania Minera de Sierra Minera*, and Carver, § 461.

and the charterers were not entitled to a declaration that the contract of August 1913 was still valid and subsisting. Rowlatt J.'s test of frustration is that 'the change in circumstances must be so great that no reasonable man would have entered into the contract in the new circumstances'.

Larrinaga & Co. v. *Société Franco-Américaine des Phosphates de Medulla*[1] requires notice for Viscount Finlay's statement of the theory of frustration in which he refers both to the basis of the continued existence of a certain state of facts and to an implied condition, and for Lord Sumner's remark[2] that 'if a contract is really a speculative contract, as this plainly is, the doctrine of frustration can rarely, if ever, apply to it for the basis of a speculative contract is to distribute all the risks on one side or on the other and to eliminate any chance of the contract falling to the ground, unless, indeed, the law has put an end to it'.

Presumably its speculative character negatives any presumption of the parties' implied agreement to terminate the contract in the event of some unforeseen event on its consequences. But it is also important upon the bearing of the doctrine of frustration upon a charter involving six successive shipments of six substantially identical cargoes between the same ports at the same rate of freight. The parties agreed to waive their rights as regards the first three shipments, which would have taken place during the War of 1914 to 1918, and when towards the end of the war the charterers intimated to the shipowners that they would expect to carry out the remaining three shipments as soon as the war was over, the latter pleaded that the contract had been discharged by frustration. It was, however, held upon the construction of the charter that it provided for distinct and separate, though almost identical, commercial adventures, and that the mere fact that the parties had agreed to waive the first three did not amount to a frustration of the contract. There was no question of illegality or of prohibition by legal authority.

It seems reasonable to suppose that the unexpected destruction of a specific cargo for the shipment of which a ship has been chartered could in proper circumstances produce a frustration of the charter-party, though this effect would be very unlikely where the cargo is not specific.[3]

Abandonment of the venture. It is perhaps worth mentioning, in order to distinguish it from frustration, the abandonment of a maritime

---

[1] (1923) 29 Com. Cas. 1.
[2] At p. 18.
[3] See below, p. 314: *E. B. Aaby's Reveri A/S.* v. *Lep. Transport Ltd.*

venture by the party in a position to do so, namely, the shipowner being (normally) the person in control of the ship and, by consequence, of the cargo. The case may arise in which the master, who is the shipowner's agent for this purpose, may decide that owing to pressure of circumstances, for instance, stress of weather, the agreed voyage cannot be completed and must be abandoned. It is abandoned—voluntarily and without hope or intention of resuming it— and the owner of the cargo is notified by the shipowner or the master. Later the cargo comes into the possession of its owner, and the question arises whether the stipulated freight or any part of it is due. The decisions[1] apply a general principle of the law of contract, namely that 'if one party to a contract repudiates it and declines to perform it, the other party may accept the repudiation',[2] and the contract is at an end, so that no freight is due. Abandonment usually occurs as the result of extreme stress of weather, and the vessel then becomes derelict. During the War of 1914 to 1918 the question arose, in *Bradley* v. *H. Newsom, Sons & Co.*,[3] of the effect of an abandonment following enemy action. A ship, apparently British, was attacked while on a voyage from Archangel to Hull by an enemy submarine, and the master and crew were ordered to abandon her. They did so and believed (erroneously as it turned out) that she was later sunk by the submarine. In fact she was towed into a British port in a waterlogged condition by naval patrols. After much conflict in the Courts below the House of Lords held (*dissentiente*, however, Lord Sumner) that the cargo-owner was not entitled to the cargo free of freight (by arrangement and without prejudice the shipowner had completed the voyage and delivered the cargo), because there had been no abandonment. The master and crew had not '*abandoned* her without any intention of returning to her, and without hope of recovery'. They 'simply yielded to force. There was no voluntary act on their part, and the case stands exactly as it would have done if they had been carried off the vessel by physical violence on the part of the crew of the German submarine'.[4]

We do not think that this decision means that in no circumstances can there be a voluntary abandonment of a ship so as to constitute her a derelict when the cause of the abandonment is enemy action. It is conceivable that a timorous neutral master, on learning that his

---

[1] *The Kathleen*; *The Cito*; *The Arno*.

[2] Per Bankes L.J. in *H. Newsom, Sons & Co.* v. *Bradley* [1918] 1 K.B. 271, 277.

[3] Scrutton himself had doubts about this decision, p. 344 n. (h) and p. 346, n. (a); and see Carver, 1963, § 773.

[4] Per Lord Finlay L.C. [1919] A.C. at p. 27. See also *The San Dimitrio* and *The Albionic*.

ship was about to enter a zone infested by submarines and bombers, might be unwilling to risk the lives of himself and his crew and might elect to abandon a ship, and we see no reason why his abandonment should not be voluntary and *sine animo revertendi vel spe recuperandi*, so as to amount to a renunciation of the contract.

B. WHEN THE UNITED KINGDOM IS A NEUTRAL[1]

In a war to which Great Britain is not a party different questions arise. We can treat the matter under two headings.

(i) *When the carriage of contraband, the breach of blockade or the rendering of other unneutral service is not involved*

A British subject who has entered into a contract of affreightment with a person whose country is, or becomes, a belligerent, may find that his contractual rights are affected by the fact of war. Just as it is illegal for a British subject or person resident or carrying on business in this country to have intercourse with Great Britain's enemy, so it is usually *ipso facto* illegal, or made illegal by legislation, for the nationals of most other countries to have intercourse with the enemies of their countries. In *Esposito* v. *Bowden* it was lawful for the neutral Neapolitan shipowner to load a cargo at Odessa on his ship but unlawful for the British charterer to do so, and therefore the contract was discharged. But, as Willes J. said:[2] 'this is not an unequal law, because, if war had broken out between the Czar and the King of the Two Sicilies, instead of Her Majesty, the vessel would, according to the principles stated above, have been absolved from going to Odessa, and might forthwith have proceeded upon another voyage'. A British charterer cannot compel a foreign shipowner to engage in illegal trade with the latter's enemy.

But when no question of illegality arises[3]—when neither the owner of the ship nor the owner of the cargo becomes the subject of a belligerent State, when neither the port of loading nor the port of destination is in the territory of a belligerent State—what effect, if any, does its outbreak apart from special provision have upon the contract of affreightment? War undoubtedly aggravates the perils of maritime transport to an increasing extent, as insurance rates bear

---

[1] See chapter 19.

[2] 7 El. & Bl. at p. 791; see above, p. 125. See *Furness, Withy & Co.* v. *Rederieaktiebolaget Banco*.

[3] For a case in which the charter provided for different rates of hire in the case of trading to neutral and to belligerent ports respectively, see *Halcyon Steamship Co.* v. *Continental Grain Co.*, where the expressions 'trading neutral' and 'trading belligerent' occur.

witness; but it is submitted that, apart from special provision in the contract, the mere outbreak of war will not affect the contractual obligations. The outbreak of the War of 1939 to 1945 made employment in London, Liverpool and many other places more dangerous than it was in 1938, but that fact could not be said to affect the obligations of a pre-war contract of employment in such a place. The observations of Lord Campbell C.J. in *Avery* v. *Bowden*[1] upon the effect of a war between Russia and Turkey point *a fortiori* to this conclusion, as does the following extra-judicial remark by Lord Tenterden:[2]

But if war or hostilities break out between the place, to which the ship or cargo belongs, and any other nation, to which they are not destined: although the performance of the contract is thereby rendered more hazardous, yet is not the contract itself dissolved, and each of the parties must submit to the extraordinary peril, unless they mutually agree to abandon the adventure.

Surely in the case of a war to which neither the State of the shipowner or of the cargo-owner becomes a party, this statement is even more true. It cannot be said that there has been a fundamental change in the character of the contract, such as occurs when the outbreak of war converts a peaceful voyage into a blockade-running trip. On the other hand, if it is shown that one of the belligerents, whether after declaring a particular area to be a war zone or not, is sinking, at sight and regardless of the flag and the character of the voyage, all ships proceeding upon the agreed voyage, then it might be maintained that the character of the voyage has been changed and the contract dissolved.

(ii) *When performance of the contract involves carriage of contraband, breach of blockade, or the rendering of other unneutral service*

Our municipal law does not treat the carriage of contraband or blockade-running or other unneutral service as illegal,[3] and our Government recognizes the right of belligerents to check these practices by the infliction of the customary penalties. When therefore a contract for such a purpose is entered into either before or during the war, then, at any rate where the party against whom it is sought to enforce it knew or ought to have known of the peculiar nature

---

[1] (1855) 5 El. & Bl. 714, 724, 725.

[2] Abbott's *Law of Shipping and Merchant Seamen* (14th ed.), p. 867. It is fair to say that sea warfare is now a much more ruthless and indiscriminate affair than it was, say, at the time of the Crimean War.

[3] See below, p. 453.

of the venture,[1] the law will enforce it. But where the contract is made, for instance, before and not in contemplation of war, or before and not in contemplation of the blockade of the agreed destination, the circumstances could be such that the contract must be treated as discharged on the ground that a totally new state of affairs has arisen, and the contract has ceased to involve an ordinary commercial adventure.[2]

Some countenance is lent to this view by the case of *The Teutonia*[3] in 1871, although the ship was Prussian and Prussia became a belligerent, so that it is not a simple case of a neutral ship bound for a blockaded port. There a British merchant had shipped goods at a South American port on board a Prussian vessel to be discharged at any port in Great Britain or on the Continent between Havre and Hamburg, and the cargo-owner had ordered the goods to be delivered at Dunkirk. The ship arrived off Dunkirk on 16 July 1870 and lay to about fourteen miles away, the master having heard rumours of war between Prussia and France. Presently a regular pilot, in official uniform, came aboard and told the master that war had been declared two days ago. Accordingly the master took his ship over to the Downs, and on the 19th took her into Dover. As a matter of fact, a state of war did not begin until the 19th, so that the master could have entered Dunkirk on the 16th without committing what for him would be the offence of trading with the enemy. The master then demanded freight before releasing his cargo at Dover. The Privy Council, affirming the decision of the Court of Admiralty (Sir Robert Phillimore), held that the master was justified in making further inquiries before entering Dunkirk and that the British cargo-owner could not complain of his taking reasonable and prudent steps for the preservation of his ship; also, that since the charterparty had originally contemplated delivery at Dover as possible and had named a freight for that port, the master was entitled to his freight before releasing the cargo.

Geipel v. *Smith*, where a British ship[4] was under a pre-war charter to carry coal to Hamburg when the Franco-Prussian War broke out and that port was blockaded by the French, shows that the outbreak of war by converting what was purely a commercial venture into an

---

[1] See *Palace Shipping Co.* v. *Caine*, and other cases cited below in chapter 10 upon Employment; and see Carver, § 499.

[2] See above, pp. 209–12.

[3] A decision much discussed in *Reardon Smith Line Ltd* v. *Ministry of Agriculture*, see Scrutton, pp. 112–13.

[4] The nationality of the charterer is not stated.

attempt to run a blockade discharges both shipowner and charterer from performance. The fact that, as the Court held, a blockade came within the 'restraint of princes' clause in the charterparty would have been enough to protect the shipowner from an action for damages for refusing to attempt to run the blockade or even send his ship to the loading port, but for the reasons discussed above in chapter 5 the drastic change in the character of the voyage produced by the blockade dissolved the contract entirely.

The effect of the decisions upon a seaman's contract of service[1] also points in the same direction.

APPLICATION TO OTHER ARMED CONFLICTS

For a maritime country nothing is more sensitive to the outbreak of war, or any other armed conflict, than its shipping. This fact is reflected by the extent to which charterparties and bills of lading[2] make express provision for dealing with the event of war and other armed conflicts, and numerous decisions have been given upon the terms used for this purpose, usually known as the 'excepted perils', liability for which the shipowner wishes to exclude. This matter is amply dealt with in the books listed at the beginning of this chapter —particularly Scrutton's—and we shall do no more than draw attention to them, because they may be relevant to 'other armed conflicts'.

'*War.*' In *Kawasaki Kisen Kabushiki Kaisha of Kobe* v. *Bantham Steamship Co.* in 1939 the Court of Appeal had to consider the meaning of the word 'war' occurring in a term in a time charterparty to the effect that: 'Charterers and owners to have the liberty of cancelling the charterparty if war breaks out involving Japan.' The Charterers were a Japanese company. At the relevant time there was intense fighting between Chinese and Japanese armed forces in North China, and many battles were taking place, though there had been no declaration of war. The British Foreign Office, when appealed to by one of the parties for information, stated 'that the current situation in China is indeterminate and anomalous and His Majesty's Government are not at present prepared to say that in their view a state of war exists'. The arbitrator found that 'the said military operations

---

[1] Chapter 10. In *Crawford & Rowat* v. *Wilson, Sons & Co.* (1896) 1 Com. Cas. 154 and 277 the expression 'unavoidable accident or hindrance in discharging the cargo' protected the charterer from a claim for demurrage when a rebellion at the port of discharge dislocated arrangements for unloading.

[2] And marine insurance policies—see chapter 11.

constituted a war in the ordinary and popular meaning of that word between Japan and China', and this practical finding was upheld by Goddard J.[1] who remarked that he had to determine

what the parties meant by this clause. I think that they were using the word 'war' in this clause, and must be taken as intending it to be construed as war in the sense in which an ordinary commercial man would use it...

The Court of Appeal affirmed this view.[2]

'*Arrests or restraints of princes*,[3] *rulers and peoples*' is much wider and, in the words of Scrutton,[4] 'applies to forcible interference by a state or the government of a country taking possession of the goods by a strong hand, such as arrest, embargoes, or blockades' and many other forms of government action and even 'the operation of the common law as to trading with the enemy on the outbreak of war...'.

Articles contained in the Schedule to the Carriage of Goods by Sea Act, 1924, which are incorporated by statute in many bills of lading though not (except by agreement) in charterparties, enunciate certain perils in regard to which neither the ship nor the carrier shall be responsible for loss or damage resulting therefrom:

(i) *Act of War*, which is described in Scrutton[5] as wider in scope than the Queen's Enemies '(e.g. it certainly includes acts of war where the carrying ship is a neutral)' and as probably covering 'acts done in civil war and in the course of hostilities between governments still in diplomatic relations'.

(ii) *Act of Public Enemies*.[6]

(iii) *Arrest or restraint of princes, rulers or people, or seizure under legal process*.[7]

(iv) *Pacific blockade*.[8] In the nineteenth century, and even later, many instances occurred of blockades being instituted without any declaration of war, and, though the matter was controversial, it was widely recognized that such blockades did not create a state of war

---

[1] [1938] 3 All E.R. at p. 83.

[2] [1939] 2 K.B. 544. On the meaning of 'blockade' in a charterparty when a foreign Government involved in a civil war purported to blockade all its coasts, see *Spanish Government* v. *North of England Steamship Co.*

[3] For instance, a French blockade of the port of Hamburg in the Franco-Prussian War, Great Britain being neutral and the ship in question being a British merchant ship: *Geipel* v. *Smith.*

[4] At p. 221. A note in Scrutton, p. 224, describes the difference between 'The King's Enemies', 'Restraint of princes or rulers', and 'Capture and Seizure'.

[5] At p. 423.   [6] At p. 421.   [7] *Ibid.*

[8] See on the whole question Hogan, *Pacific Blockade* (1908), and his bibliography, and p. 20 above.

unless the State whose coasts or ports were blockaded elected to treat the blockade as an act of war. Pacific blockades were usually instituted by powerful States, singly or in groups, against weak States. The notification of a pacific blockade generally contained threats of capture and other coercive action against the ships of the State blockaded and of third States, but we are not aware of any satisfactory judicial or arbitral examination of the problems arising. Closely akin are certain forms of embargo and reprisals.

7

AGENCY

BIBLIOGRAPHY

Das, *Japanese Occupation and Ex Post Facto Legislation in Malaya*, chap. VI.
Webber, *Effect of War on Contracts* (2nd ed.) (1946), chap. VI.

A. BY COMMON LAW

(i) *As between principal and agent*

If we look at the matter from the point of view of principle, agency is certainly a contract which we should expect to be abrogated by reason of the prohibition of intercourse with enemies in the territorial sense, and moreover incapable of being created during the war.[1] Apart from cases in which there is an element of accountability for property or profits, the normal effect of war must be abrogation. In *Tingley* v. *Müller*[2] (which we shall discuss later) Lord Cozens-Hardy M.R. said: 'it is true that most agencies, involving as they do continuous intercourse with an alien enemy, are revoked, or at least suspended.' (The suspension theory was then at its last gasp.) And in *Hugh Stevenson & Sons Ltd* v. *Aktiengesellschaft für Cartonnagen-Industrie* (a partnership case) it was held by Atkin J. and by the Court of Appeal that both the partnership and the contract of agency between the partners were *ipso facto* abrogated by the outbreak of a war which made one of them an enemy in the territorial sense. In the words of Swinfen Eady L.J.[3] 'the contract of agency was terminated by the war. It was a trading contract, and war dissolves all contracts which involve trading with the enemy.'[4] There was little serious controversy on this point, the real question being: What happens to the enemy partner's share of the assets? But although the contract of agency is abrogated, rights of action already accrued and rights which are 'the concomitant of rights of property' are preserved. There can be no doubt that an agent must account to his

---

[1] The *Sovfracht* case [1943] A.C. 203, 253, 254; *Kuenigl* v. *Donnersmarck* [1955] 1 Q.B. 515, 536. On the effect of belligerent occupation, see the *Sovfracht* case, *supra*; *Loh K'hing Woon* v. *Lai Kong Jin* (fluctuating occupation); *Krishna Chettiar* v. *Subbiya Chettiar*; *Seethalakshmi Achi et al.* v. *V. T. Veerappa Chettiar*.

[2] [1917] 2 Ch. 144, 156.   [3] [1917] 1 K.B. at p. 845.

[4] And an enemy principal cannot after the war ratify any activities on the part of the British agent *bona fide* purporting to act for his former principal: *Boston Deep Sea Fishing Co. Ltd* v. *Farnham*.

principal after the war for the principal's property in his possession or for money due to the principal. This decision also makes it probable that, if he made use of the principal's property during the war, he would be made to account to his principal after the war for the profits he has made. As Lord Atkinson said in this decision: 'This is not a case of mere debtor and creditor. It is a case...between a principal and an agent who has got possession of his principal's property and traded with it for profit.'[1]

We shall discuss later[2] the effect of the grant by the Crown of a licence to an agent in this country of an enemy principal to continue his agency, and shall submit the view that we are not constrained by the decision of the Court of Appeal in *Meyer* v. *Louis Dreyfus et Cie.*[3] to hold that the grant of a licence renews an agency interrupted by the outbreak of war (or the enemy occupation of the territory in which the principal is located) *ipso facto* and without fresh authority from the principal.

(ii) *As regards third parties*

If the agency is abrogated as between principal and agent by the outbreak of war, the agent has no longer power to bind his principal, for the agent derives his power from the principal. In *Maxwell* v. *Grunhut*[4] the agent in this country of an enemy in both the national and the territorial senses brought an action against his principal in which he sought a declaration that he was entitled to collect debts due to his principal and pay debts due from his principal in pursuance of a power of attorney granted to him by his principal upon the eve of the outbreak of war. The declaration was refused to him by a full Court of Appeal, partly because the action was misconceived, but also because 'the agent could have no greater right than his principal who, being an alien enemy, could not sue'. (He also applied for the appointment of a receiver of the assets of the business, but the Court took the view that there was no jurisdiction to appoint one. This decision and *In re Gaudig and Blum*, which followed it, illustrated the necessity of the institution of a Custodian of Enemy

---

[1] [1918] A.C. at p. 256. But when the enemy principal's property is vested in the Custodian of Enemy Property there is no rule of law which prevents the British agent from buying the property from the Custodian, unless it can be shown that the circumstances placed the agent under a fiduciary duty to his principal which could survive the outbreak of war: *Nordisk Insulin* v. *Gorgate Products Ld.*

[2] Below, pp. 360–1.   [3] See also below, chapter 14 (Solicitor's Retainer).

[4] See also *Brandon* v. *Nesbitt*, with which *Maxwell* v. *Grunhut* is in accord. Baty and Morgan (p. 273) explain *Flindt* v. *Waters* by pointing out that there the defendants 'had failed to plead specially the defence of alien enemy' as was then required.

Property. But there were several cases of receivers being appointed in the case of partnerships dissolved by the outbreak of war in 1914.)

Not only has the agent in this country no power to sue on behalf of a principal who is in the enemy country, but (apart from the criminal aspect) he has no power to contract for or bind his principal in other respects, for he derives his power from his principal.[1] Both civilly and criminally, the interposition of an agent cannot cure what is in effect a transaction with the enemy.[2] Nor can a principal separated from his agent by the line of war ratify after the war an act which the agent purported to do during the war. As McNair J. said in *Kuenigl* v. *Donnersmarck*[3]

no one can ratify an agreement or adopt an act which could not lawfully have been made or done at the time when the agreement was purported to be made or the act to be done on behalf of the person ratifying.

Irrevocable power of sale. There is, however, one kind of agency which may almost be called a 'concomitant of the rights of property' and requires special consideration. In *Tingley* v. *Müller*,[4] the facts in which have already been stated,[5] five out of six members of a full Court of Appeal held that an irrevocable power of attorney to sell land in England granted in England by an enemy national was not revoked by his departure from England and arrival in Germany before the date of the sale. The grounds of the five majority judgments are not entirely uniform. The main ground is the special character of the agency in question arising from the nature of an irrevocable power of attorney to sell land—described by Lord Cozens-Hardy M.R. as an 'equitable conveyance'. Warrington L.J. spoke of a contract for the sale of land as being 'indeed in equity itself a conditional disposition'. Another important ground is that by reason of the

---

[1] In *Schmitz* v. *Van der Veen & Co.* the plaintiff, the correspondent in England of an enemy, was allowed by Rowlatt J. to recover the price of goods sold and delivered on the ground that he sold as a principal, though under a duty to account to the enemy for a percentage of the excess over a minimum price. The learned judge was of the opinion that the sale in England was between two principals; the plaintiff had in fact consented to the sum due from him to the enemy being vested in the Public Trustee. This decision may have to be reconsidered in the light of the *Sovfracht* case: see above, p. 87.

[2] For the position of the proxy in this country of an enemy shareholder, see below, p. 242.

[3] [1955] 1 Q.B. 515, 539

[4] Moore, *Digest of International Law*, vol. 7, § 1137, cites three American decisions pointing in the same direction; and see Hyde, III, § 609. Upon *Tingley* v. *Müller*, see the speeches of Lord Wright and Lord Porter in the *Sovfracht* case [1943] A.C. at pp. 236 and 255, and *Hangkam Kwingtong Woo* v. *Liu Lan Fong*.

[5] Above, p. 99. For American decisions on the effect of war on contracts of agency, see Hyde, III, § 609; Moore, *Digest of International Law*, vol. 7, §§ 1136, 1137; Baty and Morgan, *War: Its Conduct and Legal Results*, pp. 273–6.

nature of this power of attorney the agent was empowered to act without the need of any further communication with his principal. Scrutton L.J.'s vigorous dissent rests mainly on the view that at the date of the sale by the auctioneer Müller was an alien enemy, so that the transaction amounted to trading with the enemy and was void at common law.

Where the agent in this country of an enemy holds an authority coupled with an interest, for instance, for the purpose of protecting or securing his own interests, there is much to be said for the view that his authority is not abrogated by the outbreak of war.

B. BY STATUTE

The Trading with the Enemy Act, 1939, contains ample authority for the view that the interposition of an agent cannot, for the purposes of the Act, cure a transaction which is in substance one with an 'enemy' as extensively defined by the Act. For instance, section 1 (2) in defining the offence of trading with the enemy includes transactions 'for the benefit of an enemy'; section 1 (3) declares that 'Any reference in this section to an enemy shall be construed as including a reference to a person acting on behalf of an enemy'; and 'enemy property' is defined by section 7 (8) (relating to the custody of enemy property) as 'any property for the time being belonging to or held or managed on behalf of an enemy or an enemy subject'.

8

BILLS OF EXCHANGE AND PROMISSORY NOTES: BANKING: BUILDING CONTRACTS

BIBLIOGRAPHY

Building Contracts

Hudson, *Building and Engineering Contracts* (8th ed. 1959), pp. 168–76.
Chitty on *Contracts* (22nd ed. 1961), sections 1207–9, and 1216–26.
Halsbury, *Laws of England* (3rd ed. Simonds), vol. 3, sections 841–51.

BILLS OF EXCHANGE AND PROMISSORY NOTES[1]

We start with the common law prohibition of trading with the enemy (which includes non-commercial intercourse) and the provisions of the Trading with the Enemy Act, 1939. We shall use the word 'enemy' in the territorial sense and in the sense of the definition contained in the Act, as they are substantially identical.

The effect of the statutory provisions may be summarized by saying that when there is any dealing with a bill of exchange between a person in this country and an enemy or some person acting on behalf of an enemy—be it drawing, acceptance, indorsement or other transfer—that dealing at any rate is void and ineffective; that any dealing with a bill of exchange which is for the benefit of an enemy is void and ineffective; but that does not necessarily mean that a bill is avoided for all purposes by the fact that at some time before the outbreak of war a person who has become an enemy (or a person acting on his behalf) has been a party to a dealing with it.[2] Moreover, even if none of the original or subsequent parties to a bill is an enemy, its 'acceptance, issue or subsequent negotiation' may be 'affected with...illegality' arising from intercourse with the enemy, with the consequences described in section 30 of the Bills of Exchange Act, 1882; for instance, *A* and *B* being resident in this country, if *A* agrees

[1] See Report of Committee on Limitation of Actions and Bills of Exchange, 1945, Cmd. 6591, pp. 11, 12, dealing with 'Bills of Exchange to which Enemies are Parties'. This Committee recommended that no amendment in the Bills of Exchange Act, 1882, or other statutory enactments relating to negotiable instruments was required.

[2] See *Wilson* v. *Ragosine & Co.* (assignment for valuable consideration before the outbreak of war); *Haarbleicher and Schumann* v. *Baerselman*, and Webber, *Effect of War on Contracts* (2nd ed.) (1946), ch. x.

to lend *B* £100 for the purpose, known to *A*, of enabling *B* to trade with the enemy, and *A* then accepts a bill for £100 drawn by and payable to *B*.

In *Willison* v. *Patteson*,[1] which may probably be regarded as the leading case, the Court of Common Pleas treated bills of exchange as falling within the general rule that no contract can be made during war between a person in this country and a person in the enemy country, and declined to enforce after the war three bills of exchange drawn by an enemy national in enemy territory upon the defendants in London, accepted by them and indorsed by the drawer in favour of the plaintiff, an 'English-born subject' then resident in enemy territory. 'At the time of drawing, accepting and endorsing these bills of exchange, France and England were in an open state of war with each other, and [the drawer] was then an alien enemy.'[2] Gibbs C.J. said 'an alien enemy resident in France has no right to draw on this country for a fund due to him here'; that is 'the very sort of communication which the policy of the law meant to prevent'.[3]

The Trading with the Enemy Act of 1939, section 1 (2), after a general definition of trading with the enemy, provides that

a person shall be deemed to have traded with the enemy...(*a*) if he has
    (ii) paid or transmitted any money, negotiable instrument or security for money to or for the benefit of an enemy or to a place in enemy territory, or
    (iii) performed any obligation to, or discharged any obligation of, an enemy, whether the obligation was undertaken before or after the commencement of this Act...

The definition of 'enemy' has already been quoted[4] and section 1 (3) provides that 'any reference in this section to an enemy shall be construed as including a reference to a person acting on behalf of an enemy'.

Moreover, section 4 (1) provides that 'neither a transfer of a negotiable instrument by or on behalf of an enemy,[5] nor any subsequent transfer thereof, shall, except with the sanction of the Treasury, be effective so as to confer any rights or remedies against any parties to the instrument'; and subsection 4 of the same section enables any

---

[1] (1817) 7 Taunt. 439.   [2] At p. 440.
[3] The prisoner of war cases form an exceptional class and have already been dealt with above, chapter 4.
[4] Above, p. 106.
[5] And see *Weld* v. *Fruhling & Goschen*.

person in doubt as to the lawfulness of satisfying a claim made upon him in respect of a negotiable instrument to pay the money into Court and thus obtain a good discharge.

These provisions make many of the decisions of earlier wars[1] of secondary importance.

P, a person in this country, bought before the war goods from *V*, a person who became upon the outbreak of war an enemy. Before the war *P* had accepted a bill of exchange for the price which is payable after the outbreak. Can *P* lawfully pay the bill? Yes, if the holder of the bill is an enemy and the Board of Trade requires payment to the Custodian under section 7 (1) (*a*) of the Act, or vests the debt in the Custodian under section 7 (1) (*b*).[2] Likewise, if the holder is not an enemy, but, for instance, a neutral bank, and there has been no transfer which conflicts with section 4 of the Act, *P* can lawfully pay the bill and must pay it.

Effect of interference by war with presentment for acceptance or payment. Many cases of impossibility or impracticability of presentment will be adequately dealt with by ss. 41 and 46 of the Bills of Exchange Act, 1882.

Section 41 (2) (*b*) provides that presentment for acceptance is excused, so that the bill may be treated as dishonoured by non-acceptance, 'where, after the exercise of reasonable diligence, such presentment cannot be effected'.

Section 46 (1) provides that 'Delay in making presentment for payment is excused when the delay is caused by circumstances beyond the control of the holder,[3] and not imputable to his default, misconduct, or negligence. When the case of delay ceases to operate, presentment must be made with reasonable diligence.'

Section 46 (2) provides that 'Presentment for payment is dispensed with, (*a*) where, after the exercise of reasonable diligence presentment, as required by this Act, cannot be effected...'.[4]

When this provision, which has no special reference to war conditions, operates to relieve a party from the necessity of a presentment in enemy or enemy-occupied territory which would involve illegal intercourse with the enemy, the effect is merely to expunge the obligation of presentment and not to render the obligation to pay the amount of the bill illegal; for such a construction, so far from relieving

---

[1] See Campbell, *Law of War and Contract*, pp. 184 *et seq.*

[2] And see the supplementary power given to the Custodian by section 7 (2), which is useful in cases of doubt, e.g. as to whether the creditor is in fact an enemy.

[3] *Patience* v. *Townley* (place of payment in a state of siege).

[4] *In re Francke & Rasch.*

the party under the obligation of presentment, would place him in a worse position by precluding him from recovering the amount of the bill.[1]

Where bills of exchange were accepted before the outbreak of war and fell due in this country or in the enemy country during the war, the drawer who was resident in enemy territory was not allowed after the war to recover interest on the bill from the acceptors in this country in respect of any period during the war, because there was no breach of the duty in not paying during the war, so that interest did not begin to run until the war came to an end.[2]

Section 72 (5) of the Act of 1882 provides that 'Where a bill is drawn in one country and payable in another, the due date thereof is determined according to the law of the place where it is payable'.

It is not infrequent in time of war to find belligerent countries postponing by statute or decree the due date of bills of exchange and promissory notes. Provided that the statute or decree is not penal or confiscatory, an English Court will give effect to it.[3]

BANKING[4]

In our earlier discussion of the general principles of the effect of war upon contracts we found it necessary to refer to the more important decisions upon the law of banking and it must suffice here to summarize the small though weighty amount of judicial authority.

In *Arab Bank Ltd* v. *Barclays Bank* the House of Lords in 1954 established the point that the amount standing to the credit of a customer with his banker is a debt or liquidated sum of money and the right to receive it is an 'accrued right' within the meaning of Lord Dunedin's language in *Ertel Bieber & Co.* v. *Rio Tinto Co. Ltd*;[5] and that this right is not destroyed when the outbreak of a war finds the customer on one side of the line of war and his banker on the other,

---

[1] *Cornelius* v. *Banque Franco-Serbe*. Note also that in the case of a bill governed as to presentment by English law an acceptance to pay at a particular specified place without the addition of a requirement to pay there *only and not elsewhere* is a general acceptance (Bills of Exchange Act, 1882, s. 19), so that an acceptance to pay in an enemy or enemy-occupied country is general and under section 52 of the Act presentment for payment may be dispensed with: *Banku Polskiego* v. *K. J. Mulder & Co.*

[2] *Biedermann* v. *Allhausen & Co.*; followed in *N. V. Ledeboter* v. *Hibbert*; and see *The Berwickshire*.

[3] *Rouquette* v. *Overmann*; *In re Francke & Rasch*.

[4] See Domke, *Trading with the Enemy in World War II* (1943) and *Control of Alien Property* (1947); and see below, p. 353, n. 2.

[5] [1918] A.C. 260, 269: 'There is indeed no such general proposition as that a state of war avoids all contracts between subjects and enemies. Accrued rights are not affected though the right of suing in respect thereof is suspended.'

but is only suspended until the war comes to an end.[1] Moreover, it is an accrued right in spite of the fact that a customer must make a demand for payment at the branch where his current account is kept before he acquires a right of action against his bank.[2] The decision of the House of Lords in the *Arab Bank* case was made easier by the decision in *Schering* v. *Stockholms Enskilda Bank* in 1945,[3] of which the particular relevance is the point therein established that an accrued right, namely, the right to receive payment of a debt, is none the less an accrued right because the parties have agreed that the debt shall be paid by instalments spread over a period of many years. In the *Arab Bank* case the amount standing to the credit of that bank's balance with Barclays Bank was on current account; it can hardly be doubted that the result would be the same in the case of a sum on deposit account; indeed, it is an *a fortiori* case.

Nevertheless, the executory side of the contract between banker and customer is destroyed when either of them becomes an enemy. A cheque drawn by a customer on a British bank and unpaid before the outbreak of war is void if the customer becomes an enemy, and *a fortiori* a cheque drawn by an enemy customer upon his British bank during the war is void.

BUILDING CONTRACTS

As we have already seen[4] in the case of a contract to do work and supply materials upon certain premises, 'where...the premises are destroyed [by fire] without fault on either side, it is a misfortune equally affecting both parties; excusing both from performance of the contract, but giving a cause of action to neither'. The general principles of frustration have already been discussed, and here it is only necessary to mention *Metropolitan Water Board* v. *Dick, Kerr & Co.*[5] In that case there was a pre-war measure and value contract (supplemented by a contract made after the outbreak of war) for the construction of a reservoir over a period of six years. Work began, apparently, on 16 August 1914, just after the outbreak of war, and

---

[1] For an American decision as to the effect of war on deposits in Japanese banks see 58 *A.J.* (1964) p. 194—*Aratani* v. *Kennedy*.

[2] *Joachimson* v. *Swiss Bank Corporation*.

[3] Discussed above, p. 138; see also *Bevan* v. *Bevan* (periodical payments of maintenance due under a separation agreement).

[4] Above, p. 160, *per* Blackburn J. in *Appleby* v. *Myers* (1867) L.R. 2 C.P. 651, 659. As to the effect of the Law Reform (Frustrated Contracts) Act, 1943, upon this decision, see Chitty, sections 1216–26.

[5] [1918] A.C. 119.

continued until the contractors (the defendants) received from the Ministry of Munitions in February 1916 a notice requiring them in pursuance of certain statutory powers 'to cease work on your contract for the Metropolitan Water Board' and 'to comply with such instructions with regard to your plant and the labour at your disposal as may be conveyed to you' on behalf of the Minister of Munitions. Here we get the element of illegality. It was clearly illegal to proceed with the contract; there was no dispute about that. But the illegality would not last for ever, and, in the Metropolitan Water Board's action for a declaration that the contracts were still binding on the parties, the question at issue was whether the effect of the prohibition, coupled with the compulsory sale and dispersal of the plant, was such as to frustrate and discharge the contracts. The Court of Appeal and the House of Lords, with the experience of *Horlock* v. *Beal* and *Tamplin's* case behind them, had little difficulty in holding that the contracts were discharged. To hold that they were still binding would be, said Viscount Finlay L.C.[1] adopting the words of Rowlatt J. in the *Distington* case,[2] 'not to maintain the original contract, but to substitute a different contract for it'. 'The whole character of such a contract for construction may be revolutionized by indefinite delay, such as that which has occurred in the present case, in consequence of the prohibition.'[3] And Lord Dunedin said:[4] 'The difference between the new contract and the old is quite as great as the difference between the two voyages in the case of *Jackson* v. *Union Marine Insurance Co.*'[5]

The doctrine of frustration has also been applied to contracts for the building of ships. In two similar cases, *Federal Steam Navigation Co.* v. *Sir Raylton Dixon & Co.*[6] and *Woodfield Steam Shipping Co.* v. *J. L. Thompson & Sons*, the contracts were entered into during the war (and in the former case supplemented by another contract made

---

[1] At p. 127.   [2] [1916] 1 K.B. 811, 814.

[3] Per Viscount Finlay L.C. at p. 126. It is unnecessary to discuss cases arising under the Courts (Emergency Powers) Act, 1917, which gave the Court power to suspend or annul certain contracts, e.g. *Charles Schofield & Co.* v. *Maple Mill.*

[4] At p. 129.

[5] The contract before Ridley J. in *Innholders' Co.* v. *Wainwright* would today probably be held to be dissolved by frustration, and not merely suspended. In *Mertens* v. *Home Freeholds Co.*, upon a building contract, the defendant (the builder) was not allowed to plead as an answer to an action for damages that the contract had been frustrated by reason of the refusal of a licence by the Minister of Munitions, because he had brought about the refusal by his own act. Many of the decisions upon frustration connected with war were discussed in *Davis Contractors Ltd* v. *Fareham Urban District Council* in 1956 (building contract).

[6] (1919) 1 Ll. L. Rep. 63; 64 S.J. 67. 'In all these cases one must examine first the degree of interference, and, secondly, its duration'—per Lord Birkenhead L.C. 1 Ll. L. Rep. at p. 65.

during the war) and were held to be frustrated by reason of Government intervention which took the form of suspending the building of ships of the kind contracted for, while permitting the building of ships of a different kind. The Government control was 'of such a character that it completely transformed the nature of the contract and the ambit of the obligation entered into'.[1]

It is also necessary to bear in mind that section 8 of the Foreign Enlistment Act, 1870,[2] makes it a criminal offence in certain circumstances to build or agree to build or cause to be built without the licence of the Crown any ship, 'with intent or knowledge, or having reasonable cause to believe that the same shall or will be employed in the military or naval service of any foreign state at war[3] with any friendly state'.

[1] 1 Ll. L. Rep. at p. 66. *In re an Arbitration between New Zealand Shipping Cp. and Soc. des Ateliers et Chantiers de France* turned upon the meaning of a clause in a contract for the building of a ship and contains a discussion of the rule that a party to a contract cannot take advantage of his own wrongful act.

[2] Chapter 19.

[3] See chapter 1 on the meaning of 'war', and also below, p. 451.

9

PARTNERSHIP: COMPANIES

BIBLIOGRAPHY

Partnership

Lindley on *Partnership* (12th ed.), pp. 106–10, 133, 303, 421 and 612.
Webber, *Effect of War on Contracts* (2nd ed.) (1946), ch. VII.
Yahuda, 21 *Modern Law Review* (1958), pp. 637–41.

Companies

Webber, *Effect of War on Contracts* (2nd ed.) (1946), ch. VIII.
Domke, 3 *I.L.Q.* (1950), p. 52.
Halsbury, *Laws of England* (3rd ed. Simonds), vol. 39, pp. 60–2.
McNair, 4 *B.T.* (1923–4), p. 44.
Palmer, *Company Law* (20th ed.), pp. 72–4.
Domke, *Trading with the Enemy in World War II* (1943) and *Control of Alien Property* (1947).

PARTNERSHIP

Partnership, where one partner is in this country and another in an enemy country[1] (whom we shall refer to as 'the enemy partner'), affords a clear case of abrogation or dissolution by the mere outbreak of war.[2] In this relationship continuous communication or the opportunity of it is essential, and communication during war, even if feasible, is illegal. It is perhaps unnecessary to add that the conclusion of the war does not effect an automatic resumption of the partnership.

We must consider[3] (*a*) the contract of partnership itself, (*b*) the agency thereby created, (*c*) the consequences of the dissolution, (*d*) the position of the firm as plaintiffs in an English Court, (*e*) the position in the Prize Court.

(*a*) *The contract itself.* A decision by Chief Justice Kent in 1818, *Griswold* v. *Waddington*,[4] upon a partnership between Henry Wad-

---

[1] It is clear that in the case of this contract as in the case of others it is not nationality but place of voluntary residence or of carrying on business that matters (*McConnell* v. *Hector* (three British partners, two in enemy territory); *In re Mary, Duchess of Sutherland, Bechoff, David & Co.* v. *Bubna and Others*).

[2] Or equivalent events, see above, p. 121, and *Treasury* v. *Gundelfinger and Kaumheimer*, where the partnership was treated as dissolved when one partner was repatriated to Germany on 31 December 1916.

[3] Clearly English law, not the law of the enemy country, must be applied to determine these matters: see an American decision *Rossie* v. *Garvan*.

[4] Cited by Chadwick, 20 *L.Q.R.* (1904) at p. 176. Hyde, III, p. 1709, n. 9, also cites *The William Bagaley* ('effect of the war was to dissolve the partnership'), *Hanger* v. *Abbott*, 6 Wallace 532, 535, and *Matthews* v. *McStea*. See also *Rossie* v. *Garvan*; *Sutherland* v. *Mayer*.

In *Evans* v. *Richardson* there was a contract made in the United States during the

dington, a British subject in London, and Joshua Waddington, an American citizen in New York, existing when the War of 1812 to 1814 between Great Britain and the United States of America broke out, gives a clear lead. Griswold sought to hold Henry liable upon a debt contracted during the war by Joshua. The learned Chief Justice held that the partnership was dissolved by the outbreak of war, giving two reasons: (1) that partnership involves the reciprocal control by partners of one another's activities, which is impossible during a war that makes them hostile to one another, and (2) the law cannot contemplate an association in which one partner may be engaged in business which is inimical to the interests of the other partner's country and from which the latter partner derives a profit, and 'it would be impossible for the one partner to be engaged in any commercial business which was not auxiliary to the resources and efforts of his country in a maritime war'. This decision was referred to with approval by Willes J. in delivering the judgment of the Court of Exchequer Chamber in *Esposito* v. *Bowden*.[1]

That, briefly, was the situation before the War of 1914 to 1918. Section 34 of the Partnership Act, 1890, whereby 'A partnership is in every case dissolved by the happening of any event which makes it unlawful for the business of the firm to be carried on or for the members of the firm to carry it on in partnership' also pointed towards dissolution. Then in 1915 in *R.* v. *Kupfer*,[2] where there was in question a partnership between a British subject in London and two British subjects in Frankfurt-am-Main, Lord Reading C.J. assumed

that the partnership came to an end by operation of law as soon as war was declared. There can be no partnership between enemies of this country [*scilicet*, in the territorial sense] and a subject of this country when once war has been declared. Commercial intercourse is prohibited, and immediately that prohibition comes into force it is impossible for the relationship of partners to subsist, at any rate during the war.

Anglo-American War of 1812–14, between an American citizen normally resident in his own country and a person who was both a British subject and an American citizen and was normally resident in England, for the exportation of goods from England to the United States 'on their joint account', with the condition: 'provided that a peace should not be likely to take place at the time of shipping the goods'. The case is not important beyond showing that in the opinion of Lord Eldon L.C. the contract was illegal being 'a contract to defeat the laws of the country' prohibiting trade with the enemy, though in fact the shipment was not made until after peace had been declared.

[1] (1857) 7 El. & Bl. 763, 784.
[2] [1915] 2 K.B. 321, 338. There are several cases in which upon the outbreak of war in 1914 a receiver was appointed in the case of a firm containing an enemy partner but it was not necessary for the court to decide whether or not the outbreak of war *ipso facto* dissolved the partnership, e.g. *Armitage* v. *Borgmann*.

And in 1916 in *Hugh Stevenson & Sons* v. *Aktiengesellschaft für Carton-nagen-Industrie*[1] we find Atkin J. holding that 'the agreement [of partnership] was one which it became illegal to perform after the outbreak of war. It necessarily involved commercial intercourse with an enemy, and could not be fulfilled without such intercourse'. The Court of Appeal[2] and the House of Lords[3] endorsed that view.

Where there is an enemy partner and more than one non-enemy partner, what is the effect? Is the partnership dissolved as regards all of them or only as between the enemy and the non-enemy partners? It is clear from *Rodriguez* v. *Speyer Brothers*[4] that the partnership is dissolved as regards all the partners. This is what principle would demand, as in the case of death or bankruptcy of any partner[5] unless the articles of partnership contain a contrary provision. It is believed also that it would be lawful to provide in partnership articles that if one partner should become an enemy and thus cease to be a partner, with the result that the partnership is dissolved, it should be renewed and continued between the non-enemy partners—that is, assuming that the effect of the outbreak of the war is merely to make some of the partners enemies in the territorial sense and not to render the object of the partnership or the means of its pursuit unlawful.

The following passage from Lindley on *Partnership*[6] describes one consequence of war as illustrated in the War of 1914 to 1918:

During the War of 1914–18 several cases came before the courts for the appointment of a receiver in connection with businesses carried on with enemy subjects or by firms with enemy partners in them;[7] but in cases of this description the ordinary procedure of the courts was practically superseded by the provisions of the various Trading with the Enemy Acts.

These Acts provided a practical remedy for most of the difficulties arising in the case of enemy, or mixed enemy and non-enemy, part-

---

[1] [1916] 1 K.B. 763, 767.   [2] [1917] 1 K.B. 842.

[3] [1918] A.C. 239. Where a country in which a partnership is established is occupied by the enemy and some of the partners remain in that country while others flee to an allied country, the law of the country in which the partnership is established will not regard the partners who have fled or the partners who have remained as having become enemies, and the partnership will not be dissolved: *Li Tsz Chiu and others* v. *Lo Kar Yam and others* (Hong Kong); *Hangkam Kwingtong Woo* v. *Liu Lan Fong*. See also Das, *Japanese Occupation and Ex post facto Legislation in Malaya*, pp. 52 and 66 ff.

[4] In *McConnell* v. *Hector* (1802) it was held that a firm consisting of three British partners, of whom two were resident and carrying on business in enemy territory, could not sue in an English Court, but the question of the dissolution of the partnership did not arise.

[5] Section 33 (1) of the Partnership Act, 1890.

[6] (12th ed.) 1961, p. 563, also referring to the 9th ed., pp. 655, 656.

[7] Citing *Rombach* v. *Rombach*; *Kupfer* v. *Kupfer*; *Armitage* v. *Borgmann*; *Re Bechstein*; *In re Gaudig and Blum*; and *Maxwell* v. *Grunhut*.

nerships, by setting up a system of supervision and control, which was applied to partnerships in substantially the same manner[1] as it was applied to companies.[2]

(b) *The agency created by the partnership.* We have already seen[3] that the reciprocal agency of the partners is terminated by the outbreak of war, so that according to English law neither can thereafter bind the other, which indeed would follow from the dissolution of the partnership. As Swinfen Eady L.J. said in *Hugh Stevenson's* case,[4] 'the contract of agency was terminated by the war. It was a trading contract, and war dissolves all contracts which involve trading with the enemy'.

(c) *The consequences of the dissolution.* When we turn to consider the consequences of the dissolution, we pass from contract to property,[5] and we find that—unless and until the Crown takes the appropriate steps[6] to bring about a confiscation of the enemy partner's share of the assets—it remains his property and he will be entitled to recover it at the end of the war, subject to any provisions such as those of section 7 of the Trading with the Enemy Act, 1939, whereby it can be vested in the Custodian of Enemy Property, and to any provisions of the Treaty of Peace whereby the enemy partner's Government may surrender his property.[7] The general principles governing the distribution of assets upon a dissolution of a partnership apply, save that the enemy partner cannot receive anything during the war. In *Hugh Stevenson's* case the right of the enemy partner to receive—after the war—at least his share of the assets as ascertained upon the outbreak of war was not in doubt. But the non-enemy partner continued to use the assets of the partnership, in particular certain machinery, for the purpose of making profits, and the Court of Appeal and the House of Lords held that after the war the enemy partner would be entitled not 'to any share of the profits attributable to the skill or industry of the English partner', but to 'some allowance...in lieu of interest on [the value of the machinery] in respect of the use by the English partner of the German share in the machinery'.[8] If the assets had not been used, or if in spite of their use no profits had been made, the enemy partner would have been entitled to the principal

---

[1] See *Re Koppers Coke Oven & Bye-Products Co.*

[2] See below, p. 239. There is no reason why section 3 A of the Trading with the Enemy Act, 1939, should not be applied to a partnership business.

[3] Above, p. 220.   [4] [1917] 1 K.B. 842, 845.

[5] See Lord Finlay L.C. in *Hugh Stevenson's* case [1918] A.C. 239, 245: 'The question here is not of contract, but of property.' The decision of the United States Supreme Court in *Sutherland* v. *Mayer*, though the facts are not identical, follows similar lines.

[6] Below, p. 330.   [7] Below, p. 335.   [8] At p. 245.

sum due to him upon the outbreak of war together 'with any interest or dividends which had accrued in the meantime'.[1] Where a partnership has been dissolved owing to a partner having become an enemy and the non-enemy partner has exchanged partnership assets for some other asset vested in his own name, the non-enemy partner may be considered to be a trustee for the partnership of the asset which in this manner has come into his hands.[2]

Conversely, the British partner can recover from the enemy partner after the war (or during the war if any recognized form of effective service is possible) the latter's share of liabilities incurred before the outbreak of war and discharged by the former.

(*d*) *The firm as plaintiffs in an English Court.* We have already seen[3] in *Rodriguez* v. *Speyer Brothers*[4] that, when the non-enemy partners are seeking to collect by action the assets of the late partnership, the fact that it is necessary to join their late enemy partner does not enable the action to be defeated by the plea of alien enemy.

(*e*) *The position in the Prize Court.* This matter lies somewhat outside our scope, and it will suffice to refer to three decisions—*The Clan Grant, The Eumaeus*[5] and *The Anglo-Mexican.*[6] When the Prize Court is asked to condemn as enemy property the property of a partnership, it is prepared to examine the national character of the partners and to condemn only the shares of the property which belong to persons possessing enemy character. In *The Clan Grant* the Crown, without asking for a decision, expressed its willingness to release the share of a partner who was an enemy national residing in a neutral country. In *The Eumaeus* the Court was prepared to allow the British partners in an enemy firm to give evidence as to the steps taken by them to sever their connection with the firm upon the outbreak of war. From the decision of the Privy Council in *The Anglo-Mexican* it is clear that the share of a neutral partner in an enemy firm who was resident, and managed a branch of the firm, in a neutral country, would have escaped condemnation if he had dissociated himself from the firm with sufficient promptitude; his property (in this case a pre-war shipment) was seized and condemned as enemy property taken on

---

[1] At p. 244.   [2] *Gordon* v. *Gonda.*   [3] Above, p. 86.

[4] It seems probable that this decision has overruled *Candilis & Sons* v. *Victor & Co.*, for it is difficult to see how the point could depend upon the question whether the enemy partners are in a majority or not. *Rodriguez* v. *Speyer Brothers* was far from finding favour in the *Sovfracht* case, and we may see judicial attempts to distinguish it when a similar question arises.

[5] See also *The Manningtry.*

[6] In *The Derfflinger* (no. 3), the proportionate shares of British partners who had severed all connection with their enemy partners within a reasonable time were released to them.

board a British ship and thus not protected by the Declaration of Paris.[1] On the other hand, the case of a British partner in an enemy firm is not so clear.

COMPANIES

Under this heading it is proposed to deal, firstly, with the effect of the outbreak of war upon companies registered under the Companies Acts, and other corporations, which by place of incorporation, place of carrying on business, national status of members[2] or otherwise, may become affected with enemy character; secondly, with the supervision, control, and winding up of certain businesses during war; and, thirdly, with the effect of war upon the position of enemy shareholders, debenture-holders and directors. Having regard to the comparatively recent development of joint-stock enterprise on a large scale, it is not surprising to find that on both these points the inquirer at the outbreak of the War of 1914 to 1918 found remarkably little authority to guide him. As the first Lord Parker said:[3] 'Joint-stock enterprise and English legislation and decisions about it have developed mainly since this country was last engaged in a great European war, and have taken little, if any, account of warlike conditions.'

(a) The position of the corporation itself

We have already had occasion[4] to refer to this matter for the limited purpose of determining the circumstances in which a corporation when suing can be defeated by the plea of alien enemy, and we saw that a corporation is regarded as enemy for that purpose

(i) when it owes its legal existence and incorporation to the laws of an enemy State;[5]

(ii) when, wherever incorporated, it has acquired enemy character

---

[1] There was also a British partner but he was in Germany when the war broke out and continued to reside there, thus acquiring enemy character, and made no claim to his share of the cargo seized.

[2] It should be remembered that, apart from war, aliens may be shareholders in a British company, and even subscribers to its Memorandum of Association; indeed, all the shareholders may be aliens.

[3] In the *Daimler* case [1916] 2 A.C. 307, 344.

[4] Above, pp. 102 ff., where the *Daimler* case is discussed. And see Farnsworth, *Residence and Domicil of Corporations*, pp. 125 et seq.; and his *Income Tax Case Law* (1947), pp. 118–23. The statement of Bailhache J. in *W. L. Ingle v. Mannheim Insurance Co.* [1915] 1 K.B. 227, 231 (top), to the effect that dealings with the branch office in England of a company having its head office in enemy territory in respect of the business carried on in England are lawful, must be regarded as overruled by Lord Parker's speech in the *Daimler* case and its subsequent acceptance (see above, pp. 102–4).

[5] As to the effect of enemy occupation of an allied country upon a company incorporated therein, see *Société Anonyme Belge Des Mines d'Aljustrel (Portugal) v. Anglo-Belgian Agency Ltd*; *Central India Mining Co. v. Société Coloniale Anversoise*; *Re Deutsche Bank (London Agency)*; the *Sovfracht* case; *Lubrafol Motor Vessel Owners v. Pamia SS. Owners, The Pamia*.

by reason of the hostile residence or activities of its agents or other persons in *de facto* control of its activities;

(iii) when, even though registered in the United Kingdom, it is carrying on business in enemy territory.

There are, however, other aspects of the matter, and, in particular, trading with the enemy and the position of contracts with an enemy corporation. There can be no doubt that a corporation which is an enemy under one of these rules for the purpose of the plea of alien enemy is also an enemy for the purposes of the prohibition against trading with an enemy and of the rules governing the effect of war upon contracts with an enemy in the territorial sense; though, as we shall see, the converse proposition is not true. Lord Parker, after defining in the paragraph already quoted[1] the circumstances which invest a British company with enemy character, added: 'A person knowingly dealing with the company in such a case is trading with the enemy'.[2]

We should also note again here that a company incorporated in this country is not regarded as an enemy company just because its shareholders or directors are enemy nationals or resident in enemy territory.[3] Nevertheless, the national status and character of the shareholders and directors does have a bearing upon the question whether the company's agents or the persons in *de facto* control of its affairs are in fact adhering to, taking instructions from, or acting under the control of, enemies, which in turn is relevant to a determination of the enemy character of the company itself.[4]

In *Elders and Fyffes, Ltd* v. *Hamburg-Amerikanische Packetfahrt A.-G.* it was unsuccessfully argued that the *Daimler* doctrine operated to convert a company registered in England into a foreign company on the ground that the majority of the shares were held in the United States of America (it seems probable that the writ was issued when that country was still neutral in the War of 1914 to 1918) and that the directors acted upon instructions from that country. The object of this argument, which was advanced by an enemy defendant, was to impute to the British company American character and so avoid the abrogation of certain long-term contracts, which must have happened if it took its character from its place of registration, i.e. England. A British company, even if foreign control be proved, does not cease to be a British company, nor would foreign control protect British

---

[1] P. 103. [2] [1916] 2 A.C. at p. 345.
[3] *Amorduct Manufacturing Co.* v. *Defries & Co.*; *The Poona*
[4] The *Daimler* case [1916] 2 A.C. 307, 345.

directors from liability for trading with the enemy. *In Kuenigl* v. *Donnersmarck*[1] a British registered company which was, under the *Daimler* doctrine, a company having enemy character by reason of enemy control, was held not for that reason to have ceased to be in the eye of English law an English company and as such subject to the prohibition imposed by the common law against trading with the enemy. 'Enemy character is not substituted for the original character, but is something added to it.'

In *Re Badische Co.* Russell J. applied the *Daimler* doctrine for the purpose of the abrogation upon the outbreak of war of executory contracts with a British registered company controlled in Germany.

Turning to the legislation of the 1939–45 War, which is simpler and more compact than that of the War of 1914 to 1918, we have seen[2] that by section 2 (1) of the Trading with the Enemy Act, 1939,[3] the expression 'enemy' for the purposes of this Act means...

(*c*) any body of persons (whether corporate or unincorporate) carrying on business in any place, if and so long as the body is controlled by a person who, under this section, is an enemy;

(*d*) any body of persons constituted or incorporated in, or under the laws of, a State at war with His Majesty; and

(*e*) as respects any business carried on in enemy territory,[4] any individual or body of persons (whether corporate or unincorporate) carrying on that business.

Upon this definition it must be noted that it is given 'for the purposes of this Act', and Lord Greene M.R. in the case of *In re an Arbitration between N. V. Gebr. van Udens Scheepvaart en Agentuur Maatschappij and Sovfracht*[5] said that the Act

does not purport to impose or define enemy status otherwise than for the purposes of the Act, which are (so far as relevant) the prohibition of dealings with persons who, for the purposes of the Act, are to be regarded as enemies.

But from the decision of the House of Lords[6] reversing the Court of Appeal in this case it appears that the effect of the definition quoted by Lord Greene M.R. is more limited than he found it to be.

There can be no doubt that the prohibition of trading with the

---

[1] [1955] 1 Q.B. 515, 535; see comment by Thomas, 4 *I. and C.L.Q.* (1955), p. 140.

[2] Above, p. 104.

[3] As amended by the Emergency Laws (Miscellaneous Provisions) Act, 1953, s. 2 and Second Schedule.

[4] Which is defined in section 15 (1) of the Act. The meaning of 'carrying on business in enemy territory' was considered in *Central India Mining Co.* v. *Société Coloniale Anversoise*. See also *Re Hilckes, ex. p. Muhesa Rubber Plantations*.

[5] [1942] 1 K.B. 222, 229.   [6] [1943] A.C. 202.

enemy comprises the carrying out of a contract with a company carrying on business in enemy-occupied territory as from the date of the occupation and abrogates a contract which is executory at that date and is of the type stated above[1] to be abrogated by the outbreak of war. If the effect is to inflict hardship upon a company which is a 'friendly' enemy as was the company in that case, the remedy is by legislation. It is difficult to see how a licence from the Crown can *ipso facto* redintegrate a contract once abrogated, though it may authorize the British party to contract with the 'friendly' enemy so as to produce that effect.[2]

(b) *Supervision, control and winding up of a 'business'*

Section 3 (1) of the Trading with the Enemy Act, 1939, enables the Board of Trade to authorize an inspector to inspect the books and documents of any person (which includes a corporation) and to require any person to give information in respect to any business carried on by him. Section 3 (2) enables the Board of Trade to appoint a 'supervisor' when that is necessary for ensuring compliance with section 1 of the Act which contains the prohibition of trading with the enemy.

Section 3 A (introduced into the Act by the Defence (Trading with the Enemy) Regulations, 1940)[3] empowers the Board of Trade 'where any business is being carried on in the United Kingdom by, or on behalf of, or under the direction of, persons all or any of whom are enemies or enemy subjects or appear to the Board of Trade to be associated with enemies' to make either

(a) a 'restriction order' prohibiting the carrying on of the business absolutely or *sub modo*, or

(b) a 'winding up order' requiring the business to be wound up.[4]

Having made either of these orders, the Board of Trade may appoint a 'controller to control and supervise the carrying out of the order, and, in the case of a winding up order, to conduct the winding up of the business, and may confer on the controller any such powers in relation to the business as are exercisable by a liquidator in the voluntary winding up of a company in relation to the company', and such other powers as may be necessary.

It will be noticed that these provisions do not expressly refer to the winding up of a *company*, but only to the winding up of a business, and

---

[1] P. 122 ff.   [2] Above, p. 132.

[3] S.R. & O. 1940, no. 1092; now permanently enacted in the Emergency Laws (Miscellaneous Provisions) Act, 1953, s. 2 and Second Schedule.

[4] The nature of such a winding up is fully considered in *In re Banca Commerciale Italiana*.

it is only in relation to the business that the Board of Trade may confer on the controller the powers of a liquidator in the voluntary winding up of a company (including power to convey or transfer any property). These powers are contained in the Companies Act, 1948, sections 278–310 (see in particular section 303), and they include the power to wind up the company's affairs and distribute its assets and then bring about the termination of its existence by dissolution. It is not clear whether a controller can, in the exercise of these powers, bring about the dissolution of a company whose ' business is being carried on in the United Kingdom by, or on behalf of, or under the direction of, persons all or any of whom are enemies or enemy subjects or appear to the Board of Trade to be associated with enemies'; at any rate the mere appointment of the controller does not put into liquidation the company of whose business he is in control.[1] If it is desired to put the company into liquidation, the Board of Trade can do so, for under subsection 8 of section 3 A 'where the business is carried on by a company the Board of Trade may present a petition for the winding up of *the company* [italics ours] by the Court, and the making of an order under this section shall be a ground on which the company may be wound up by the Court'.

The provisions of section 3 A just quoted follow closely those of subsection 7 of section 1 of the Trading with the Enemy Amendment Act, 1916,[2] under which it was held that if the Board of Trade conferred upon a controller power to sue in the name and on behalf of the 'person, firm or company' for pre-war debts, he could not be defeated by the plea of alien enemy.[3] But the appointment of a controller does not have the effect of reviving any pre-war contracts which were abrogated upon the outbreak of war by reason of the fact that one party was an enemy or that their performance would involve intercourse with the enemy.[4]

It seems probable that certain other decisions upon section 1 of the Trading with the Enemy (Amendment) Act, 1916, also apply to section 3 A. In *In re W. Hagelberg A.-G.*[5] it was held that when a business carried on by a company in the United Kingdom is being

---

[1] *In re Fr. Meyers Sohn* [1917] 2 Ch. 201, 203.

[2] The judgment of Younger L.J. in one of the later of the many decisions upon this Act, *Meyer & Co.* v. *Faber* (no. 2) [1923] 2 Ch. 421, 442, contains a useful commentary upon some of the leading decisions upon it. He said at p. 446: 'The fragmentary character of a winding up [i.e. of a business] under the Act, the essential difference between such a winding up and the liquidation of a company or the bankruptcy of a firm or individual is shown by *In re Dieckmann.*' See also *In re Vulcaan Coal Co.*

[3] *Continho Caro & Co.* v. *Vermont.* Continho and Coutinho denote the same firm.

[4] *In re Coutinho Caro & Co.*

[5] See also *In re Anglo-Austrian Bank.*

wound up, the assets of that business are not available for creditors whose debts arise out of transactions or dealings with the company in respect of business being carried on outside the United Kingdom. In *In re Kastner & Co.* it was held that the controller had power to deal with the whole of the assets of the company notwithstanding the existence of debentures secured by a floating charge and the appointment of a receiver on behalf of the debenture-holders; his appointment had been made by the Court after the appointment by the Board of Trade of a supervisor of the company's business, who later became the controller, and in ignorance of the pending proceedings before the Board of Trade for the winding up of the company. In *In re Th. Goldschmidt*[1] it was held that the expression 'assets of the business' contained in subsection 3 of section 1 of the Act of 1916, the wording of which closely resembles that of subsection 3 of section 3 A of the Act of 1939, does not include the company's uncalled capital. Younger J. said that a business with which the Board of Trade was empowered by the Act of 1916 to deal

is treated by the Act as an entity separate and distinct from any other property, whether in the United Kingdom or abroad, and from any other business not in the United Kingdom, of the person, firm, or company owning or controlling it; that, accordingly, it is only the debts of the business, as distinct from the debts of such person, firm, or company irrespective of the business, that under the Act are to be paid; and it is only the assets of the business, as distinct from the general assets of the person, firm, or company that are made, so far as the Act is concerned, available for their discharge.

Amongst other powers, the controller has power to discharge 'debts due to the creditors of the business', and some light is thrown upon the meaning of this expression in *In re Banca Commerciale Italiana*.

(c) The shareholder's contract of membership

If a shareholder of enemy nationality is in British or (probably) in allied[2] or neutral territory, then it seems to follow from the decisions already discussed[3] and, in particular, *Porter* v. *Freudenberg* and *Schaffenius* v. *Goldberg*, that, upon principle and apart from the emergency legislation to be discussed later, his contract of membership of a British company is unaffected by the outbreak of war and he continues to enjoy the rights and be subject to the liabilities of the normal British shareholder.

If, however, the shareholder is an enemy in the territorial sense—

[1] [1917] 2 Ch. 194, 197; see also *In re Fr. Meyers Sohn*.
[2] See *Lepage* v. *San Paulo Copper Estates*.   [3] Above, p. 150.

the sense in which the word 'enemy' is used in what follows—then a different situation arises. We may look upon his share in a British company both as a contract and as a piece of property.[1] Viewed as a contract, one of two things might, it seems, happen to it upon the outbreak of war. (i) The contract might be dissolved, in which event he would drop out entirely except that at the end of the war he would be entitled to come and claim from the company the value of his share at the outbreak of war. This is the partnership analogy.[2] What is to happen if by this process of dissolution of the contract of membership the number of shareholders is reduced below seven in a public, or two in a private, company, as would occur, for instance, in the case of the Continental Tyre and Rubber Company, the plaintiffs in the *Daimler* case previously discussed? (ii) Or we might regard the contract of membership as suspended[3] and not dissolved, so that during the war the right to dividends and perhaps the liability for calls made during the war are in suspense and revive upon the conclusion of the war, whereupon the enemy would once more become fully a shareholder. The argument that private enemy property on land is not forfeited to the Crown unless the Crown sets in motion the procedure of 'inquisition by office',[4] supports either view —dissolution or suspension—because neither involves confiscation.

It now seems clear that the suspension theory is the right one. In *R.* v. *London County Council*[5] Lord Reading C.J. intimated his opinion *obiter* that an alien enemy (apparently resident or carrying on business in enemy territory) could not vote by proxy in respect of his shares in an English company, but the question whether the rights of the enemy shareholders and directors resident in Germany were suspended or not, though argued, was not decided. Later in *Robson* v. *Premier Oil and Pipe Line Co.* the Court of Appeal definitely refused to allow an enemy corporation to vote by proxy[6] in respect of shares in an English company, resting their decision upon the general prohibition of intercourse, commercial or otherwise, with enemies across the line of war but in no way dissenting from the judgment of Sargant J., based both upon the incapacity of a proxy to act on behalf of an enemy principal and upon the suspension of the right of an enemy shareholder to vote during the war.

---

[1] That no shares can lawfully be allotted to an enemy is obvious, for it would involve the making of a contract with him: *Eichengruen* v. *Mond* [1940] 1 Ch. 785, 787.

[2] *Hugh Stevenson & Sons'* case.

[3] This is the view adopted by the editor of Lindley on *Companies* (6th ed. 1902), I, p. 53, citing *Ex parte Boussmaker*, and by Pitt Cobbett, II, p. 113.

[4] See below, p. 330.   [5] [1915] 2 K.B. 466, 478.

[6] It is probable, though not certain, that the proxies were granted during the war.

These two cases throw some weight into the scale of the suspension theory, because it does not seem to be doubted that the shares continue to exist as contracts and not merely as pieces of property, though the rights attached to them are in suspense during the war. Further, there are several passages[1] in the speeches in the House of Lords in the *Daimler* case which affirm with complete confidence that the rights of enemy shareholders are placed in suspense by the war. In the case of *In re Anglo-International Bank*, the Court of Appeal held that the right of shareholders having registered addresses in enemy-occupied territory to receive notices of meetings of the company was in suspense during the war and, accordingly, that the company could treat them as being not entitled to receive notices of meetings held during the war—a decision which involves the opinion that they remained shareholders whose rights are in suspense.

Moreover, the state of suspense is capable of being determined by the vesting of the shares in the Custodian of Enemy Property under section 7 of the Trading with the Enemy Act, 1939. Thus in a case[2] arising upon the Trading with the Enemy Amendment Act, 1914, now repealed, where a block of shares in an English company amounting to 16,250 out of a total of 16,501 belonged to a firm of alien enemies carrying on business in the Turkish Empire and were vested in the Custodian, the Court of Appeal held that he need not remain purely passive. He inherits the character and powers of a shareholder and may, without asking the Court for its sanction, exercise all the rights of a shareholder to which his voting power entitles him. He can receive dividends[3] and vote at general meetings, and (if he prefers cash to shares) he may take steps, by signing a requisition, to have an extraordinary general meeting convened for the purpose of submitting a resolution for the winding up of the company.

Some inference in favour of the continued existence of the share as a contract may be drawn from section 2 (1) of the Trading with the Enemy Amendment Act of 1914, though not specifically re-enacted during the War of 1939 to 1945 because it is covered by more general provisions. That subsection directed that 'any sum which, had a state of war not existed, would have been payable and paid to or for the

---

[1] See [1916] 2 A.C. 307; Lord Shaw twice at p. 330; Lord Parmoor twice at p. 352. (The fact that these two noble lords were largely dissentient does not impair their authority on this point.)

[2] *In re R. Pharaon et Fils.*

[3] A resolution directing that dividends due to shareholders resident in enemy countries should be paid out of assets in those countries is void: *Aramayo Francke Mines* v. *Public Trustee.*

benefit of an enemy, by way of dividends, interest or share of profits, shall be paid...to the Custodian...', a provision which clearly contemplated the accrual of dividends or interest to an enemy shareholder or debenture-holder, though not receivable by him until after the end of the war, and even then only if the treaty of peace should not otherwise provide.

Section 5 of the Trading with the Enemy Act, 1939, which applies to 'annuities, stocks, shares, bonds, debentures or debenture stock registered or inscribed in any register, branch register or other book kept in the United Kingdom', provides that if any securities of the kinds enumerated above are transferred by or on behalf of an enemy (as defined by the Act), or, being securities issued by a company within the meaning of the Companies Act, 1929, are allotted or transferred to or for the benefit of an enemy without the consent of the Board of Trade, the transferee shall not thereby acquire any rights or remedies in respect of those securities except with the sanction of the Board of Trade; and no body corporate by whom the securities are issued or managed may give effect to the transfer.

Section 7 of the Trading with the Enemy Act, 1939,[1] enables the Board of Trade to vest any 'enemy property' in the widest sense of the term in a Custodian of Enemy Property and requires the payment to him of money (including dividends) which but for the existence of a state of war would be payable to or for the benefit of an enemy.

Taking the Treaty of Versailles as a sample of the Peace Treaties of 1919–20, we find that by the terms of the Annex referred to in Article 297 (d) all the exceptional war measures, such as vesting orders and orders for the winding up of businesses or companies, were agreed to be considered as final and binding upon all persons subject to any reservations contained in the treaties. By paragraph 10 of the same Annex Germany undertook to

deliver to each Allied or Associated Power all securities, certificates, deeds or other documents of title held by its nationals and relating to property, rights or interests situated in the territory of that Allied or Associated Power, including any shares, stock, debentures, debenture stock, or other obligations of any company incorporated in accordance with the laws of that Power—

a provision which suggests the continued legal validity of the obligations evidenced by these instruments.

---

[1] As amended by paragraph 4 of the Defence (Trading with the Enemy) Regulations, 1940, now permanently enacted by the Emergency Laws (Miscellaneous Provisions) Act, 1953, s. 2, Second Schedule.

On the whole, the conclusion would appear to be that, subject to any contrary provisions in the Treaty of Peace, unless the company has been wound up during the war, the ex-enemy shareholder would resume the enjoyment of his shares at the end of the war. If this view is correct, the partnership analogy does not apply,[1] and the analogy is not a true one, because it is of the essence of a partnership that there should be intercourse between the partners, and it is difficult to see how a partnership can continue to function without it; a partnership is not a legal entity, though for purposes of suing and being sued it is convenient that the Rules of the Supreme Court[2] should treat it as such. On the other hand, a company is a legal person distinct from its shareholders and, provided that it has directors or other agents in this country who are free from enemy control, there is no reason why it should not continue its operations. Any other conclusion would produce chaos, for there must have been during the War of 1914 to 1918 or that of 1939 to 1945 thousands of British companies who have enemy shareholders on their registers.

If a share in a company is regarded as a piece of property, as it certainly is, there is nothing startling in the view that it survives the war and that the ex-enemy owner of it once more resumes the enjoyment of his ownership, together (possibly) with dividends which have accrued upon it,[3] unless it or the dividends have been confiscated by the Crown by the ancient and appropriate process or by legislation or have been surrendered by the treaty of peace.[4] Subject to similar events, the ex-enemy resumes the enjoyment of his ownership of a horse or a piano in this country, including the progeny of a mare.

Debentures. A debenture is an instrument which evidences a debt due to a company and usually mortgages or charges some or all of the assets of the company for the purpose of securing the debt. A debenture is both evidence of a contract and a piece of property. It differs from a share in that it does not normally give the holder any power of controlling the activities of the company except in certain specified events when his security is in danger. During the war the enemy holder cannot transfer it, and the interest must not be paid to him; but, subject to the causes of loss which we have

---

[1] See above, pp. 231 ff.   [2] Order 81.

[3] This must, in the absence of legislation or provision made by a treaty of peace, remain in doubt; and note the slender nature of the enemy's interest in shares which were vested in the Custodian during the War of 1914 to 1918, and in the dividends accruing upon them: *In re Münster.*

[4] On the *situs* of shares, see Dicey, pp. 506–7, two American cases reported in *Décisions des tribunaux arbitraux mixtes*, vol. v (1925), p. 255, and *Cities Services Co. and Chase National Bank* v. *Attorney-General* (U.S. Supreme Court), noted in 2 *I. and C.L.Q.* (1953), p. 152.

stated to be applicable to shares, he is entitled to resume the enjoyment of his ownership of it at the end of the war, or its proceeds if it has been paid off, together with accumulations of interest which have accrued upon it.[1]

Directors.[2] The editor of 'Pitt Cobbett'[3] expresses the view that upon the outbreak of war 'enemy directors would *ipso facto* vacate their seats, although retaining otherwise such rights as belong to enemy shareholders'. The *Daimler* case in the House of Lords contains a number of passages[4] which bear witness to the suspension of the rights of enemy directors during the War. What happens upon the conclusion of peace, supposing the company still to exist, is not stated, but in essence the relation of a director to his company is a contract of employment creating agency, and the general principles of the effect of war upon contracts of employment and agency discussed elsewhere in this volume[5] point towards the abrogation and not the mere suspension of this contract, so that their re-election would be necessary it if is desired that they should resume their office. In *Kuenigl* v. *Donnersmarck*[6] McNair J. had to consider an agreement purportedly concluded in 1940 in Germany on behalf of an English registered (but enemy controlled) company by directors or agents of the company. He held that 'as a company can only act through directors or other agents, the authority of the...company's directors and other agents in enemy territory was automatically determined on the outbreak of war...From this it results that in English law (1) no act purported to have been performed in Germany on behalf of the company can be taken to be the act of the company, and (2) no agreement made by persons in Germany purporting to act on behalf of the company can be taken to be the agreement of the company.'[7]

---

[1] Phillipson, *Effect of War on Contracts* (1909), p. 104 (*n*) says that after the South African War 'the British Government, as successor to the Transvaal Government, paid all arrears of debenture interest to British shareholders of an enemy company—the Pretoria-Pietersburg Railway Co. Ltd'. Reference, however, to the Report of the Transvaal Concessions Commission (Cd. 623), pp. 58, 59, shows that the company was incorporated in London, though operating in the Transvaal. The Government of the South African Republic had guaranteed the principal of and interest on the debentures, and the British Government took over that Government's interest in, and liabilities in respect of, the company. So the case is quite exceptional.

[2] Note the definition of 'director' for purposes of the Trading with the Enemy Act, 1939: Section 15 (4).   [3] II, p. 113.

[4] See Lord Atkinson [1916] 2 A.C. at pp. 325–6; Lord Shaw at p. 330; Lord Parmoor at p. 352.

[5] Chapter 10 and chapter 7. It was held that the effect of Article 299 (*a*) of the Treaty of Versailles and corresponding provisions of the other Peace Treaties of 1919–20, upon the directorship of an enemy in a British company, is abrogation: *Fr. Meyer's Sohn Ltd* v. *Meyer*.

[6] [1955] 1 Q.B. 515.   [7] At p. 536.

Shareholders, debenture-holders and directors in enemy-occupied territory.
It is clear that care is required on the part of British companies in
order to prevent these persons from suffering from British war
measures primarily directed against enemy shareholders, debenture-
holders and directors. For instance, it would be hard upon a director,
resident in Holland, of a British company that his directorship should
be allowed to lapse merely by reason of the occupation of his country
by the enemy, but it does not follow that all enemy-occupied territory
or all persons in enemy-occupied territory should be treated alike.
Some very pertinent remarks upon this point were made by Lord
Greene M.R. in the *Sovfracht* case.[1]

[1] [1942] 1 K.B. 222, 225–32; but see [1943] A.C. 203.

10

EMPLOYMENT: GUARANTEE

EMPLOYMENT

We have already dealt with Agency, which is a species of employment, and later we shall deal with the Solicitor's Retainer. This chapter is concerned with Employment generally, (1) with illegality and (2) with impossibility and frustration.

(1) *Illegality*

In accordance with general principle no contract of employment can, during war, be validly made (*a*) between a person within British territory and a person voluntarily resident or carrying on business within enemy territory, or (*b*) wherever the parties may be, if it involves a person within British territory in intercourse with enemy territory or any person therein during the war; and a pre-war contract of employment is dissolved by reason of supervening illegality (*a*) if one party is within British territory and the other is voluntarily resident or carrying on business in enemy territory, or (*b*) if the contract in any other way involves intercourse with enemy territory or any person therein.[1]

We have seen[2] that there is some evidence for the view that an

---

[1] Suppose that during a war in which the United Kingdom is involved a British trading corporation contracts with a person in this country that as soon as the war is legally at an end he shall proceed to the former enemy country and represent the corporation there. It is suggested that this is a valid contract.

[2] P. 94; and see *Sparenburgh* v. *Bannatyne*, there cited. The provisions of chapter II of the Regulations annexed to Hague Convention IV of 1899 and 1907 (Laws and Customs of War on Land), Section III of the International Convention of 27 July 1929, relative to the Treatment of Prisoners of War (Treaty Series no. 37 (1931)), and Section III of the Geneva Convention Relative to the Treatment of Prisoners of War, 1949 (Treaty Series no. 39 (1958)), governing the work of prisoners of war, should be consulted. Articles 134 and 135 of the last-mentioned Convention set out the relationship between its provisions and those of the earlier Conventions (see also Article 89 of the 1929 Convention). The United Kingdom has signed and ratified all these Conventions, but in order to ascertain whether they are binding upon the United Kingdom in any particular war other factors must be considered, such as the 'general participation clause' (Article 2 of Hague Convention IV of 1899 and 1907) and, in the case of the Convention of 1929, the question whether the enemy Power to whose forces the prisoner of war belongs is also a party. Note that Article 82 of the Convention of 1929 departs from the pernicious policy of the 'general participation clause', as does the Convention of 1949 (see Article 2); the latter may even bind a State which has ratified it *vis-à-vis* a State which has not but which accepts and applies its provisions. See Joyce Gutteridge, 26 *B.Y.* (1949), pp. 294–326. It is also necessary to consider whether the employment of a prisoner of war rests upon

enemy prisoner of war may enter into a valid contract of employment and enforce it.

It should also be noted that the engagement of a British subject or the national of a neutral State to serve an enemy State will usually result in his being affected with enemy character.[1]

(2) Impossibility and frustration

(a) The outbreak of war may produce a fundamental change in the character of the service: (b) the war may cause the servant or the subject-matter of his service to be no longer available.

(a) Before a war a seaman signs on for an ordinary commercial voyage. There breaks out a war of such a kind that changes the character of the voyage by exposing the ship, whether sailing under a belligerent flag or not, to a grave risk of capture or sinking by enemy action. Usually the contract thereupon comes to an end. It is no longer the contract made by the parties. The seaman would, or can reasonably assert that he would either have declined to sign on for a voyage of that character, or would only have done so for much increased remuneration. If responsibility for the change in the character of the voyage can be laid upon one of the parties, he has committed a breach of contract. If it cannot be, it is a case of frustration. The ship is there; the seaman is there; either the shipowner or the seaman may wish to abandon the voyage; there is no impossibility of fact. To insist upon performance is to create a new contract for the parties, and, as Rowlatt J. said in *Distington Hematite Iron Co.* v. *Possehl & Co.*[2] 'War does not create any contract'.

In *Burton* v. *Pinkerton*[3] the Court of Exchequer held that the outbreak of war between Spain and Peru, followed by the conduct of the captain (the defendant) in placing the ship (which was British) virtually under the orders of the Peruvian supercargo on board, and in sailing as a tender to or consort of Peruvian ships of war, terminated the pre-war contract of service of the plaintiff, a seaman, by converting what was intended by him to be a purely commercial voyage into a warlike one, which was a breach of contract. Illegality was discussed, but the decision rests on breach of contract. There is no reference to frustration. It is insisted that the seaman could not

administrative regulation or upon contract; for a case in which the Franco-German Mixed Arbitral Tribunal took the former view, see *Daniels* v. *Germany*, and Rosenberg in 36 *A.J.* (1942), pp. 294–8.

[1] *Sparenburgh* v. *Bannatyne*; *The Endraught*; *The Benjamin Franklin*. See also as to the nationals of a neutral State Article 17 of Hague Convention V (Neutral Powers and Persons in Land Warfare).   [2] [1916] 1 K.B. at p. 814.

[3] See also *The Justitia* and *Palace Shipping Co.* v. *Caine*.

be compelled to perform an engagement fundamentally different from the one contracted by him. In *O'Neil* v. *Armstrong, Mitchell & Co.*[1] the plaintiff, a seaman, undertook to serve on board a newly-built torpedo-boat on a voyage from Newcastle to Yokohama. He apparently did not know whether she then belonged to the Japanese Government or not. After sailing the captain (by consent treated as the defendant) hoisted the Japanese flag, and during the voyage war broke out between China and Japan. The plaintiff left the ship at Aden, and claimed wages for the whole voyage. The Court of Appeal held that the act of the defendant's principals, the Japanese Government, in declaring war against China, completely changed the character of the voyage by exposing the plaintiff to new and additional risks and terminated the contract. In the words of A. L. Smith, L.J.,[2] 'the peace adventure had become frustrated and put an end to'. Stress is laid upon the fact that the alteration has been brought about by the defendant's principals, but it is submitted that the contract would also have come to an end if China had declared war against Japan, though it was probably essential to the plaintiff's recovery of the whole amount of the wages agreed for the voyage for him to establish the fact that it was due to the fault of the defendant's principals that the original contract was not completed.[3] The Foreign Enlistment Act, 1870, was referred to, but the decision is not based on it.

In *Liston* v. *Owners of SS. Carpathian*[4] twelve members[5] of the crew of a British ship lying at Port Arthur and homeward bound refused on 16 August 1914 to proceed to sea without extra remuneration, on the ground that the outbreak of war between Great Britain and Germany and the ensuing danger of capture or injury from mines had terminated their pre-war engagements to serve upon an ordinary commercial voyage. The captain agreed to pay them extra remuneration, and the question of his authority to do so turned upon the effect of the outbreak of war and consequent risks upon the pre-war contracts of service. Lord Coleridge J. based his decision to the effect that the seamen were entitled to recover the extra remuneration, upon the fact that the war risks in existence on 16 August (the mere outbreak of war would not be enough) were not in the contemplation

---

[1] [1895] 2 Q.B. 70; *ibid.* 418.

[2] At p. 422. But we submit that the word 'frustrated' is not used *stricto sensu*.

[3] *Appleby* v. *Myers*.

[4] See also *Austin Friars Shipping Co.* v. *Strack* (pre-war contract); *Lloyd* v. *Sheen* (post-outbreak of war contract); *Sibery* v. *Connelly* (post-outbreak of war contract).

[5] Their nationality is not stated. It is doubtful whether this decision would be followed today in the case of a British seaman.

of the parties when the contract was made, so that that contract came to an end when the risks arose.

The authorities cited above are cases relating to the effect of the outbreak of war upon a pre-war contract of employment, but the principle involved has no necessary connection with the outbreak of war, and precisely the same principle must be applied to a contract entered into after the outbreak of war when the character of the service which the employee is asked to perform differs fundamentally from the character of the service he contracted to perform. In *Palace Shipping Co. v. Caine*,[1] the seamen during the Russo-Japanese War contracted to serve on a voyage from Cardiff to Hong Kong and/or any other ports within limits which included Japanese ports; upon arrival at Hong Kong they were told for the first time that the ship, carrying a cargo of coal (which had been declared by both belligerents to be contraband), would proceed to Sasebo, a Japanese naval base, within the geographical limits of the contract, and they declined to proceed upon that voyage. They were upheld by the House of Lords, on the ground that they had signed on 'for an ordinary commercial voyage to a neutral port' and were then asked to undertake a voyage to Sasebo which, in the words of Lord Macnaghten, 'would necessarily involve risks to life and property different from and in excess of those incident to the employment of seamen engaged in peaceful commerce'. This decision was applied in *Robson* v. *Sykes*,[2] where seamen engaged for a voyage of not more than two years' duration within very wide geographical limits were upheld by the King's Bench Division in their refusal to sail to a Spanish port which, though within the geographical limits of the articles, was situate in a part of Spain where a civil war (in existence when the articles were signed) was in progress, so that the voyage was likely to be attended with danger to themselves. Branson J. stated the principle to be that 'apart from special circumstances, a crew signing articles in the ordinary form must be taken to have engaged themselves to carry out an ordinary commercial voyage'.

(*b*) We now come to the cases where frustration is caused by the fact that one of the parties (usually the servant), or the subject-matter of the contract of service, is no longer available. In *Horlock* v. *Beal* the wife of a British seaman sued a British shipowner upon a pre-war allotment of part of her husband's wages. In May 1914 he signed on for a voyage not exceeding two years. On 2 August his ship arrived at Hamburg. On 4 August war broke out, and she was not allowed to leave. In November the officers and crew, including the plaintiff's

---

[1] [1907] A.C. 386, 393.   [2] [1938] 2 All E.R. 612, 616

husband, were removed from the ship and shortly afterwards interned. The House of Lords (with one dissentient) held that the contract of service was dissolved upon the outbreak of war by the impossibility of performance which supervened, one member of the majority preferring to fix that point of time in November. Many authorities relating to the special character of the seaman's contract were referred to, but a majority of their Lordships used the language of frustration and cited the familiar cases.

In *Marshall* v. *Glanvill*[1] the Divisional Court (Rowlatt and McCardie JJ.) held that a contract between a firm of drapers and a commercial traveller, made after the outbreak of war, was dissolved when the traveller was called up under the Military Service Act, 1916 (or, to be precise, anticipated his call by joining the Royal Flying Corps four days earlier). 'The effect of his enlistment or of the Military Service Act, 1916, was to sweep away the basis of the arrangement between the parties', said McCardie J., citing a typical frustration case, *Tamplin Steamship Co.* v. *Anglo-Mexican Petroleum Products Co.* It would, we suggest, have sufficed for him to say that the Military Service Act, 1916, made performance of the contract unlawful, but, under the influence of the frustration cases, the learned judge added that 'a state of war is assumed to be of such prolonged duration as *prima facie* to put an end to contracts which are conditional upon the continuance of a particular state of things which is only consistent with peace'.[2] He also pointed out that in *Nordman* v. *Rayner*,[3] where he held that a contract of agency was not dissolved by the internment of an agent who was registered as an alien enemy, the *ratio decidendi* was that 'it was doubtful from first to last whether it would last for any substantial period'; in fact it lasted one month. On the other hand, in *Unger* v. *Preston Corporation*,[4] where the internment of a 'friendly' refugee of enemy nationality, employed by the defendants as an assistant school medical officer, lasted for nine months, Cassels J. held that his contract of service was frustrated and dissolved by the fact, and at the date, of his internment, although it could not then be known that it would last for so long a period.

---

[1] [1917] 2 K.B. 87, 91, 92; and see *Morgan* v. *Manser*, which, it is submitted in spite of the criticism in 64 L.Q.R. 179, is right, because the essence of frustration, as of the kindred conception—constructive total loss, is that it depends on the facts available when the unexpected event occurs.

[2] The Act did not say that it was illegal to be a commercial traveller. By converting a commercial traveller into a soldier it made him no longer available as a commercial traveller, and presumably it would be illegal knowingly to employ a deserter.

[3] Followed in *Schostall* v. *Johnson*.

[4] See Glanville Williams in *Modern Law Review*, vol. 6 (1943), p. 160.

GUARANTEE

In addition to the common law prohibition of 'trading with the enemy',[1] we start with the general prohibition by the Trading with the Enemy Act, 1939 (section 1) of 'any commercial, financial or other intercourse or dealings with, or for the benefit of, an enemy', and we must consider the more particular prohibitions (section 1 (2) (*a*) (ii)) of paying money 'for the benefit of an enemy', and (section 1 (2) (*a*) (iii)) of performing 'any obligation to, or [discharging] any of, an enemy, whether the obligation was undertaken before or after the commencement of this Act'. So far as we are aware, guarantee or suretyship is nowhere prohibited *eo nomine*.

As a matter of principle, there are several ways in which war can affect the transaction: (i) when a relevant party becomes an enemy (which term we shall use in the territorial and substantially identical statutory[2] senses); (ii) when, no relevant party being or becoming an enemy, the transaction guaranteed involves illegal intercourse with the enemy; (iii) when, no relevant party being or becoming an enemy, the transaction is beneficial to the enemy or prejudicial to Great Britain by enhancing the resources of the enemy or diminishing those of this country; and (iv) when, no relevant party becoming an enemy, the outbreak of war frustrates a contract which is the subject of the guarantee.

The rights of a surety are in part the creation of equity, in part depend on quasi-contract, and are often supplemented by express contract, so that it may sometimes be more difficult to assess the impact of war upon them than in the ordinary case of contract, pure and simple. If we attempted to examine every aspect of guarantee, we should find that we were devoting to it an amount of space disproportionate to the actual incidence of the effect of war upon it.

Pre-war guarantee

Three parties require our attention—the creditor, the debtor[3] and the surety (be it noted in passing that a surety may, consideration

---

[1] Below, p. 347.   [2] Below, p. 351.

[3] The terms 'creditor' and 'debtor' are not confined to the case of a money debt and denote the two parties to an obligation in the wide sense, e.g. to deliver goods sold, to return a borrowed chattel, to serve a master faithfully, to perform faithfully the duties of an office, etc. It must be borne in mind that a guarantee is 'a collateral obligation, postulating the principal liability of another, the principal debtor' (Rowlatt, *Principal and Surety* (3rd ed. 1936), p. 1. References to this book do not mean that it deals with the effect of war).

being present when his promise is not given by deed, guarantee a debt whether already incurred or still to be incurred).

(i) *Right of action on the guarantee already accrued.* If upon the outbreak of war a right of action has already accrued to a non-enemy surety against an enemy creditor 'to have his remedies exercised and his securities enforced against the principal [debtor]', or 'against [an enemy] principal debtor...to be indemnified and to have the remedies and securities of the creditor kept alive for that purpose',[1] the general principle already stated must apply: the right of action may be enforced if it can be, having regard to difficulties of service and other obstacles.[2] If it is the surety who is enemy, then in accordance with the principle already stated his rights of action are not destroyed but suspended until after the war.[3]

If a right of action has already accrued against an enemy surety to a non-enemy creditor or against a non-enemy surety to an enemy creditor, the same principles are applicable.

(ii) *No right of action on the contract of guarantee already accrued.* If on the outbreak of war no default by the debtor has taken place so that no right of action against the surety has accrued, it becomes necessary to consider what is the effect of the outbreak of war upon the obligation guaranteed, for the fate of the principal obligation guaranteed will affect, and may decide, the fate of the collateral obligation. Let us consider some illustrations. (S = surety; D = principal debtor; C = principal creditor.)

(*a*) S guarantees the payment by D to C of the price of goods agreed to be sold and delivered to D. Upon the outbreak of a war which makes D an enemy the goods have not been delivered and the money is not due. The contract to sell the goods is abrogated, and the guarantee falls to the ground.

(*b*) S guarantees faithful service by D to C as C's resident agent in a foreign country. Upon the outbreak of a war which makes D an enemy, the contract of agency is abrogated, and the guarantee falls to the ground.

(*c*) S guarantees the manufacture of goods by D and the delivery of them by D to C for the agreed purpose of shipment to X in Germany. Upon the outbreak of war with Germany, neither D nor C becomes enemy, but the contract to manufacture and deliver is discharged by supervening illegality, and the guarantee falls to the ground.

---

[1] Rowlatt, *op. cit.* p. 172. The position of co-sureties must be borne in mind, but it is unnecessary to complicate the matter by examining it.

[2] Above, ch. 3.   [3] *Ibid.*

(*d*) *S* guarantees the performance by *D* of a contract with *C* for laying out a dog-racing track and building a stand. Upon the outbreak of war circumstances arise which have the effect of discharging this contract by the operation of the doctrine of frustration, and the guarantee falls to the ground.

(*e*) *S* is British, *C* is British or neutral, *D* is enemy. If the contract of guarantee cannot be carried out without involving *S* in intercourse with *D*, for instance, by inquiring as to the state of account between *C* and *D*, or without conferring a benefit upon *D*, it would appear that no action will lie upon the contract of guarantee until after the end of the war.[1]

Suppose, however, that the outbreak of war does not abrogate the transaction guaranteed, it may nevertheless affect the guarantee.

(*a*) *S* guarantees the performance by *D* in favour of *C* of the covenants contained in a lease, including the payment of rent. The outbreak of a war makes *D* an enemy. The lease continues to be valid,[2] and likewise the guarantee.

(*b*) *S* or *C* becomes an enemy. It is submitted that the general rule relating to executory contracts will apply and that the contract of guarantee is abrogated.

(*c*) *S* becomes an enemy. The British debtor must pay the debt guaranteed and cannot plead that he is prohibited from doing so by section 1 (2) of the Act of 1939 because payment by him discharges the obligation of an enemy; it is submitted that that obligation has already been discharged not by the payment of the debt but by operation of law.

Judicial authority

The war decisions are few.

In *Seligman* v. *Eagle Insurance Co.*[3] a British insurance company before the outbreak of war lent the sum of £2500 to a person who later became an enemy, upon the security of two life policies issued to him by the company and mortgaged to the company as security for the loan. At the same time, and as part of the same transaction, a surety guaranteed the payment of the loan and of the annual premiums; the enemy left the country and failed to pay the premiums due; the surety tendered them to the company which accepted them

---

[1] *Stockholms Enskilda Bank, A/B* v. *Schering Ltd.* [1941] 1 K.B. 424 (C.A.); this case must not be confused with the later case *Schering Ltd* v. *Stockholms Enskilda Bank A/B* [1944] 1 Ch. 13; [1946] A.C. 219.

[2] *Halsey* v. *Lowenfeld (Leigh and Curzon Third Parties)*.

[3] See below, chapter 11, where this case is discussed in connection with Life Insurance.

subject to a reservation, and later the surety tendered the whole of the amount due on the loan and claimed from the company an assignment of the policies held by it to secure the loan to the enemy. Neville J. held that the payment by the surety of the premium and of the whole amount of the loan was unobjectionable and that he was entitled to an assignment of the policies. To the argument that these payments were payments for the benefit of the enemy, the learned judge's reply was that, the enemy's rights under the policy being suspended during the war, the enemy could not *while an enemy* benefit from the receipt of the premiums (or, *semble*, of the amount of the loan); 'what will result (he said)[1] is that perhaps some day somebody who is not an enemy alien may have a right to sue the company for the amount assured'. It was assumed throughout that the loan by the insurance company was not abrogated by the outbreak of war, and it was held by the learned judge that the policies, which of course contained covenants to pay the premiums, did not become void by the mere fact of the assured becoming an enemy.

The learned judge having held that no illegal intercourse with the enemy was involved in the receipt of the premiums, there remained the more difficult plea by the insurance company that the payments by the surety were payments on behalf of or for the benefit of an enemy and were within the mischief of the Trading with the Enemy Act, 1914, section 1 (2), the Proclamation of September 9, 1914, section 5 (5, 6 and 7), and the Trading with the Enemy Amendment Act, 1914, sections 2, 6 (1) and 10. It should, however, be noted that none of these provisions expressly prohibited the discharge of any obligation of an enemy, as section 1 (2) (*a*) (iii) of the Act of 1939 does, and that is essentially what a surety does when he pays the creditor under his guarantee; it is true that the debtor's obligation to the surety remains but his obligation to his creditor is discharged.

In *R. & A. Kohnstamm Ltd* v. *Ludwig Krumm (London) Ltd.*[2] (principal debtor enemy, principal creditor and surety British), there was what Macnaghten J. described as 'a perfectly plain guarantee' (entered into before the outbreak of the war) by the defendants of any debt that a German company carrying on business in Germany might owe to the plaintiffs for goods supplied. The plaintiffs having sued the defendants shortly after the outbreak of war for the amount then due by the German company to the plaintiffs,

---

[1] At p. 526.
[2] This decision must now be regarded as questionable in view of the decision about to be discussed.

the defendants objected that by paying the debt which they had guaranteed they would commit an offence under section 1, subsection 2 (*a*) (iii) of the Trading with the Enemy Act, 1939. Macnaghten J., however, held that the words of the Act 'mean a complete discharge', and do not cover the case where the effect of the payment by a surety is merely to convert the enemy's obligation from an obligation to pay the principal creditor into an obligation to pay the surety.[1] He pointed out the absurdity which would arise in the case before him, namely, that the principal creditor was permitted by the provisions of proviso (ii) to section 1 (2) of the Act to receive payment of the debt directly from the enemy and yet would not be permitted to receive payment from the surety. Note that in this case both surety and principal creditor were British, so that the effect of payment under the guarantee was to convert the enemy debtor's obligation from a debt owed to one British corporation into a debt owed to another—neither of them likely to be recoverable during the war.

We then come to the decision of the Court of Appeal in *Stockholms Enskilda Bank A/B* v. *Schering Ltd*[2] (principal debtor enemy, principal creditor neutral, surety British). This is anything but a case of 'a perfectly plain guarantee' and relates to a highly complicated financial transaction, described as a 'contract of debt' whereby the British surety was both a guarantor of the debt and a purchaser of it by instalments. The principal matter for decision was whether or not a payment by the British surety was a payment 'for the benefit of an enemy' under the Trading with the Enemy Act, 1939, section 1 (2). The Court of Appeal held that a payment by the British surety to the neutral creditor which had the effect of preserving to the enemy debtor a substantial discount and of substituting for an obligation from it to a neutral company a more problematical obligation to a British company, which was unlikely to be able to enforce it during the war, was a payment 'for the benefit of an enemy' and also discharged the obligation of an enemy, and therefore could not be enforced. It is not stated that the 'contract of debt' and of guarantee was regarded as abrogated upon the outbreak of war or the enactment of the Trading with the Enemy Act, 1939, and the Court was not called upon to decide that question.[3] There were special circumstances which enabled the Court of Appeal to distinguish the *Kohnstamm* decision.

---

[1] And see comment in 56 *L.Q.R.* (1940) at p. 436.

[2] [1941] 1 K.B. 424 (C.A.), not to be confused with the action referred to in n. 3 on this page. See also *Weiner* v. *Central Fund for German Jewry*.

[3] So held in *Schering Ltd* v. *Stockholms Enskilda Bank A/B* [1944] Ch. 13; [1946] A.C. 219.

In later proceedings[1] upon the same complicated transaction the British surety raised the issue referred to above as left open, namely, the effect of the outbreak of war upon the continued validity of the main contract, partly a guarantee and partly a purchase of a debt by instalments. The whole transaction received an exhaustive analysis from Simonds J., the Court of Appeal and the House of Lords, where it was held by a majority (Lord Thankerton, Lord Porter and Lord Goddard, with Lord Russell of Killowen and Lord Macmillan dissenting) that, as at the time of the outbreak of war the neutral principal creditor (the Stockholm bank) had wholly performed its obligations towards the enemy debtor and nothing remained to be done as between the British surety and the Stockholm bank but the payment by the former to the latter of certain instalments of money remaining due and the corresponding assignments of debt by the latter to the former, the British surety was not entitled to a declaration that the main contract was abrogated. Lord Porter and Lord Goddard further held that the outstanding obligations and the right to enforce them were merely suspended until such time as these things could be done without conferring a benefit upon the enemy, but it does not appear that this opinion was essential to the decision.[2]

Guarantee which it is attempted to make during the war

Principle demands that no valid contract of guarantee can be made during a war if any of the parties is an enemy or if it involves illegal intercourse with the enemy or if it is beneficial to the enemy or detrimental to Great Britain.

---

[1] *Schering Ltd* v. *Stockholms Enskilda Bank A/B* [1944] Ch. 13 and [1946] A.C. 219; much discussed in *Arab Bank Ld.* v. *Barclay's Bank* (*Dominion, Colonial and Overseas*).

[2] The transaction in question was a very special and a very complicated one, and the members of the House of Lords differed not so much as to the law but in its application to the exceptional circumstances of the transaction and more particularly on the question whether upon the outbreak of war the Stockholm bank held an accrued right to certain liquidated sums of money and was under no obligation to do anything further. That seems to turn on the question whether the main contract is construed *au pied de la lettre* or whether its substance only is looked at, so that the obligation of the Stockholm bank to assign to the British surety the instalments of the debt owed to the former by the German company may be ignored.

11

INSURANCE

BIBLIOGRAPHY

Arnould, *Marine Insurance* (15th ed. 1961), §§ 16, 31, 135–51, 751–7, 798, 897–909 b (this edition being referred to as 'Arnould', unless otherwise stated).[1]
MacGillivray, *Insurance Law* (5th ed. 1961, Denis Browne).
Halsbury, *Laws of England*, (3rd ed. Simonds) vol. 13, 'Insurance'.
Preston and Colinvaux, *Law of Insurance* (2nd ed. 1961), pp. 22, 296, 511, 318–19.
Pennant, 18 *L.Q.R* (1902), pp. 289–96.
Domke, *Control of Alien Property* (1947).
Webber, *Effect of War on Contracts* (2nd ed.) (1946), ch. XI (Life).

I. Marine and Non-Marine Insurance of Property; II. Life Insurance; III. Foreign Proceedings against British Insurance Companies.

I. MARINE AND NON-MARINE INSURANCE OF PROPERTY[2]

A. PRE-WAR MARINE INSURANCES WHERE ONE PARTY BECOMES AN ENEMY IN THE TERRITORIAL SENSE

(i) *Historical*

Before and during the Napoleonic Wars, that is, before the law relating to trading with the enemy had hardened and the effect of war upon contracts had crystallized out into certain principles, there existed in regard to contracts of insurance what appears to us today to be a certain confusion of thought. It may help us to understand the present law if we try to clear up this confusion.

The period before 1802–3. This period is under the influence of standards of opinion on the subject of trading with the enemy which today would be regarded as very lax. William Murray (later Lord Mansfield) was one of the foremost exponents of the essentially mercantilist point of view. 'If we don't trade with them, neutrals will. Why should not our merchants get the benefit?' Fifoot[3] quotes a speech made by him as Solicitor-General in 1747, when opposing a

---

[1] Some of the earlier editions, e.g. the 6th, 1887, contains a good deal on war and alien enemies.
[2] The Marine and Aviation Insurance (War Risks) Act, 1952, empowers 'the Minister of Transport to undertake the insurance of ships, aircraft and certain other goods against war risks', see article in *The Solicitor*, June 1953, pp. 150–4. See p. 52 above (lines 8–10), and see Hansard (Lords) 16 December 1965, cols. 838–44, and (Commons) same day, col. 1462–5.
[3] *Lord Mansfield* (1936), p. 83, quoting from Holliday's *Life of Lord Mansfield*, pp. 90–7.

Bill to 'prevent the insurance of French ships and their loading during the war with France'. He warned the House of Commons that the effect of the Bill would be 'to transfer to the French a branch of trade which we now enjoy without a rival...Not only the nations we are in amity with, but even our enemies, the French and Spaniards, transact most of their business here at London.' The French writer Valin pointed out[1] that the effect of allowing British underwriters to insure enemies against capture by British forces was that one part of the British nation restored to the French by the effect of insurances what the other part took from the French by the rights of war.

Lord Mansfield as a judge appears to have retained the view which he had previously advocated, and strongly discouraged the raising of the defence that such insurances were illegal,[2] and it was not until the judgment of the Court of Common Pleas in *Furtado* v. *Rogers* was delivered by Lord Alvanley C.J. in 1802 that it was established that a pre-war policy of insurance, whereby a British insurer undertook to indemnify a foreign shipowner against the loss of his ship by British capture, was abrogated upon the outbreak of a war which made the shipowner an enemy. This judgment was followed and adopted in the year 1803 by Lord Ellenborough C.J. in delivering the judgments of the Court of King's Bench in *Kellner* v. *Le Mesurier* (enemy shipowner—insurance effected during the war) and *Gamba* v. *Le Mesurier*[3] (enemy shipowner—pre-war insurance). In 1803 this rule was in effect extended, in *Brandon* v. *Curling*,[4] to insurance against capture by a co-belligerent with Great Britain, though, that circumstance not being stated in the case submitted to the King's Bench, it was apparently not considered to be open to the Court to rest their judgment specifically upon capture by a co-belligerent and it is based on more general grounds. Meanwhile substantially the same result had been reached by means of the operation of the plea of alien enemy in *Brandon* v. *Nesbitt* in 1794. There an insurance upon cargo was effected before the outbreak of war by a British agent on behalf of French owners who became enemies upon the outbreak of war. The ship (American) and cargo were captured as prize (apparently by

---

[1] Tit. vi, *Des Assurances*, art. 3, p. 215, cited by Arnould, § 135.

[2] See Lord Alvanley C.J. in *Furtado* v. *Rogers* (1802) 3 Bos. & P. 191, 197, 199, and the remarks of Buller J. in *Bell* v. *Gilson* (1798) 1 Bos. & P. 345, 354, upon Lord Mansfield's attitude, and of Lord Ellenborough C.J. in *Kellner* v. *Le Mesurier* (1803) 4 East 396, 403. A kind of gentleman's agreement appears to have existed in the insurance market that the fatal defence should not be raised, and no doubt the great weight of Lord Mansfield's opinion survived him for a time. For an Opinion by a King's Advocate, Jenner, in 1833 on what was called the 'Honour Clause', see McNair, *Opinions*, iii, p. 19.

[3] See also *Ex parte Lee*.

[4] (1803), 4 East 410.

Great Britain). When the British agent of the enemy cargo-owner sued the underwriters, his action was defeated, upon the ground, not that an insurance against British capture was illegal, but that 'an action will not lie either by or in favour of an alien enemy'. In *Flindt* v. *Waters*[1] Lord Ellenborough C.J. approved this decision and said, 'the point there decided was that the fact of the parties interested in the insurance having become alien enemies before the loss happened might be pleaded to an action brought in the name of the British agent who effected the insurance'. But in *Flindt* v. *Waters* 'the insurance, the loss, and cause of action had arisen before the assured had become alien enemies: when therefore they became such, it was only a temporary suspence [*sic*] of their own right of suit in the Courts here, as alien enemies; but that objection cannot be carried further, nor applied to the plaintiff as their trustee, who is a subject of the King: otherwise, if it could avail upon this plea, it would be making a perpetual which in its nature is only a temporary bar'.[2] The remarks of Rowlatt J. in *Schmitz* v. *Van der Veen & Co.*,[3] in commenting upon the last two cases cited, require notice; he points out the necessity of distinguishing two cases, the first, 'that where the cause of action is unexceptionable, but the plaintiff as an alien enemy is temporarily and personally incapable of being received as a plaintiff' [action to recover pre-war loss], and the second, 'that where the cause of action, whoever puts it forward, fails in itself, and fails finally'.

The period since 1802–3. The second stage is reached when it is realized and enunciated, as it was *obiter* in 1803 in *Brandon* v. *Curling*,[4] that, quite apart from capture by Great Britain and her allies, every insurance of enemy property is contrary to the public interest and a loss occurring during the war cannot be recovered. There Lord Ellenborough C.J. said:

where the insurance is upon goods generally, a proviso to this effect shall in all cases be considered as engrafted therein, viz.: 'Provided that this insurance shall not extend to cover any loss happening during the existence of hostilities between the respective countries of the assured and assurer.' Because during the existence of such hostilities the subjects of the one country cannot allowably lend their assistance to protect by insurance the property and commerce of the subjects of the other.

[1] (1812) 15 East 260, 265, 266.
[2] The concluding remark of Lord Ellenborough C.J. in *Flindt* v. *Waters* is significant: 'I do not say that the Crown might not still interfere.'
[3] (1915) 84 L.J.K.B. 861, 864.
[4] (1803) 4 East 410, 417. Pre-war policy—French cargo—capture by Spain, an ally of, or co-belligerent with, Great Britain.

Thus the earlier distinction (if indeed it ever had a sound legal basis) between the insurance of enemy property against British (and allied) capture on the one hand and its insurance generally on the other, disappeared, and all pre-war insurances of enemy property by persons in this country were dissolved as from the outbreak of war. Accordingly, in *Ingle* v. *Mannheim Insurance Co.* where there was a loss during the war upon a pre-war policy of marine insurance, the defendant company, a German company having a branch office in London which had power to transact business and issue policies,[1] argued that 'a contract cannot be carried out if it involves inter-course with the enemy', and (unsuccessfully) that its London branch office which issued the policy was an enemy, whereas the plaintiffs contended (October 1914) with success that it was not.[2] Conversely (in 1915), in *Theodor Schneider & Co.* v. *Burgett and Newsam* Scrutton J., and the Court of Appeal, had no hesitation in holding that a pre-war contract of marine insurance whereby the goods of a British company were insured with a German insurer was abrogated upon the outbreak of war (no claim had accrued upon the policy). It is significant that Scrutton J. dealt with the two contracts involved —affreightment with a German shipowner and insurance with a German insurer—together and upon precisely the same lines and regarded the cause of abrogation in both cases to be the same, namely that they involved trading or further trading with the enemy and therefore fell within the principles laid down in *Potts* v. *Bell* and *Esposito* v. *Bowden.*

The strange thing is that it should have been considered necessary, at any time since 1802, to resort to arguments peculiar to insurance, namely, the folly of indemnifying the enemy against losses resulting from British and allied belligerent action, when there lay ready to hand a principle of general application, namely, that all com-mercial intercourse with the enemy is illegal. Lord Alvanley C.J. in *Furtado* v. *Rogers* in 1802 invoked this principle but seemed to regard it as less important than the reason based on indemnity against British capture.

Even in 1914 this ghost was not yet completely laid, and the first Trading with the Enemy Proclamation, dated 5 August, contained the following prohibition:

Not to make or enter into any new marine, life, fire, or other policy or contract of insurance with or for the benefit of any person resident, carrying

---

[1] The loss under the policy had accrued before a Proclamation of 8 October 1914. [2] See above, p. 236, n. 4.

on business, or being in the said [German] Empire, nor under any existing policy or contract of insurance to make any payment to or for the benefit of any such person *in respect of any loss due to the belligerent action of His Majesty's forces or those of any ally of His Majesty.* [Italics ours.]

This Proclamation was revoked by the Proclamation of 9 September, 1914, the corresponding clause in which—paragraph 5 (6) —omitted all reference to the consequences of belligerent action. *Requiescat in pace!*

It is submitted that the following conclusions are justified:

(*a*) A pre-war contract of marine insurance between a British subject and an enemy in the territorial sense is abrogated on the outbreak of war, whether the British subject or the other party is the insurer and whether the premium has already been paid or not[1] (we shall deal later with non-marine insurance), subject to what is said below (ii) as to pre-war losses and claims.

(*b*) This rule is not confined to insurance upon commercial property, e.g. merchant ships and cargoes, but extends to all property, and is not confined to insurances against the consequences of British or allied belligerent action.[2]

After these preliminary remarks we can address ourselves to:

(ii) *Losses happening and claims accruing before the outbreak of war*

Harman v. *Kingston*,[3] *Flindt* v. *Waters* and *Janson* v. *Driefontein Consolidated Mines*[4] show that where a loss has occurred and a right of action upon the policy has accrued to an enemy before the outbreak of war, his right of action is not destroyed but merely suspended until after the war.[5] In the last-named case Lord Lindley quoted with approval the following passage from Arnould:[6]

Where the party intended to be insured by the policy does not become an alien enemy until after the loss and cause of action have arisen, his

---

[1] The premium is presumably a debt: see above, p. 136.

[2] Pennant in 18 *L.Q.R.* (1902), pp. 289–96 would not accept this last sentence and held the view that a pre-war insurance by a British company of an enemy's property is only illegal and void in so far as it relates to property which it is the aim of the British Government to destroy by belligerent action, i.e. 'if it would indemnify the enemy against a loss which the British Government intended him to undergo' (p. 293). We do not see how he could reconcile this view with such cases as *Furtado* v. *Rogers* and *Esposito* v. *Bowden*, which enunciate quite general principles.

[3] Where Lord Ellenborough C.J. said, in a case upon a policy of marine insurance, 'the fact of the persons interested [on whose behalf, it seems, the plaintiffs were suing] having become alien enemies since the loss, only goes to suspend the remedy, and ought not to have been pleaded in abatement'. The cause of the loss does not appear.

[4] [1902] A.C. 484. See also *Robinson Gold Mining Co.* v. *Alliance Insurance Co.*

[5] In the Wars of 1914 to 1918 and 1939 to 1945 steps would probably have been taken to vest it in the Custodian of Enemy Property.

[6] *Marine Insurance* (6th ed.), I, p. 135.

right to sue on the policy is only suspended during the continuance of hostilities and revives on the restoration of peace.[1]

In the cases mentioned above it was the assured who became an enemy. In *Robinson & Co.* v. *Continental Insurance Co. of Mannheim* it was the insurance company which became the enemy,[2] and Bailhache J. held that the British assured could sue the company for a pre-war loss during the war.

Actions to recover premiums are rare, and in many policies the receipt of the premium is acknowledged whether it has been paid or not; but if a British assured owed a premium to a foreign insurer upon the outbreak of a war which made the latter an enemy, the right to sue for the premium would be suspended until after the war.

Harman v. *Kingston, Flindt* v. *Waters* and *Janson* v. *Driefontein Consolidated Mines* do not lay down a rule peculiar to insurance. We have already noticed authority for the same rule in *Ex parte Boussmaker, Ertel Bieber & Co.* v. *Rio Tinto Co.*,[3] and *Zinc Corporation* v. *Hirsch*.[4] *Janson* v. *Driefontein Consolidated Mines* deserves notice on two further points: (*a*) that a British underwriter is not likely in future to be allowed to waive the plea of alien enemy so as to enable an enemy assured to sue him during the war for a pre-war loss; and (*b*) that war is war and not merely strained relations and it is for the Executive to tell us (and the Courts) when Her Majesty is at war.[5] *Nigel Gold Mining Co.* v. *Hoade*[6] also requires consideration. The plaintiff company had been registered in Natal in 1888 and had subsequently received a 'supplemental incorporation' in the Transvaal. It was working a gold mine situated in the territory of the Transvaal Republic. Before the South African War it had effected an insurance with the defendant, a Lloyd's underwriter, upon the products of its mine against (*inter alia*) 'arrests, restraints, and detainments of all kings, princes and people'. A few days after the outbreak of war the enemy Government seized and carried away certain gold products

---

[1] Provided, of course, that the British underwriter is not released from payment by the Treaty of Peace and ensuing legislation. For a summary of the provisions of the Peace Treaties of 1919–20 upon contracts of marine insurance, see Arnould, § 136 (n. 11).

[2] Or at any rate was treated as an enemy, for it does not appear whether the policy was effected with the head office in Mannheim or with the London branch, which in *Ingle* v. *Mannheim Insurance Co.* (the same company) was regarded as not being an enemy at common law; in that case the claim accrued after the outbreak of war and the action was allowed to proceed. The Proclamation of 9 September 1914 merely confirmed the common law status of the London branch and the Proclamation of 8 October 1914 was not retrospective.

[3] [1918] A.C. 260, 269.   [4] [1916] 1 K.B. 541, 556.   [5] Above, chapter 1.

[6] See later, p. 277, n. 4.

from the plaintiff company's mine. The mine was closed upon the outbreak of war and there was no evidence of intention to carry on mining operations during the war. Mathew J. declined to invest the plaintiff company with enemy character or to treat their property as enemy property and allowed them to recover their loss on the policy.

We have stated that an underwriter may, apart from any provision to the contrary which may be embodied in the Treaty of Peace, pay to an enemy after the war losses which accrued before the war, though in most cases he will probably be found to have paid them during the war to the Custodian of Enemy Property.[1] It is, however, worth noting that before the War of 1914 to 1918 it was the public and avowed intention of Lloyd's underwriters, and also of most of the companies, to waive the plea of alien enemy and hold themselves subject to an honourable obligation to pay to enemies *during* the war losses which accrued *before or during* the war. The avowal, so far as Lloyd's is concerned, is contained in a statement made by the then Chairman of Lloyd's at the International Conference on maritime law at Copenhagen on 16 May 1913.[2] This honourable undertaking which was made in complete good faith was (it is submitted) based on a misconception in the minds of the underwriters' advisers as to the nature of the plea of alien enemy and the prohibition of intercourse with enemies. These rules, now at any rate, rest on public policy and not on the protection of the British subject so as to be waivable at his option, and it would be illegal, even apart from the express provisions of the Trading with the Enemy Act, 1939, to carry out such an undertaking. The blame for the prevalence of such views, which remind one of Lord Mansfield's comment above quoted,[3] must be laid at the door of the House of Lords, who in *Janson's* case ought not to have condoned the action of the underwriters sued by an enemy plaintiff during war in waiving the plea of alien enemy and permitting themselves to be sued. The fact that the war was over when the case reached the House of Lords should (it is submitted) have made no difference, and the case should have been stopped.

Even after the conclusion of peace, the underwriter cannot be compelled to pay to those who were enemies losses upon pre-war policies which accrued *during* the war.

---

[1] During the War of 1939 to 1945 in practice British debtors were bound merely to register with the Custodian debts owing to enemies who may be described as 'friendly' enemies, e.g. a Dutchman in enemy-occupied Holland, whereas they had to pay to the Custodian debts due to real enemies.

[2] Printed as an Appendix to the first edition of this book.

[3] Above, p. 259.

(iii) *Dissolution of the contract*

Apart from losses which have already happened and claims which have already accrued, the effect of the outbreak of war is to dissolve a contract of insurance with an enemy as from that time. The reason is that the contract belongs to the class of contracts which involve intercourse with the enemy. Any particular contract might not; the premium may have been paid before the war broke out, no loss may occur and no occasion for the assured to communicate with his underwriters. Those considerations are irrelevant. It is the class of contract that matters.[1] Moreover, it is safe to say, upon the analogy of the cases upon long-term contracts for the sale of goods and upon time charters,[2] that, although the duration of a policy upon enemy property may in terms extend beyond the period of a short war, yet it is dissolved and will not revive after the war.

It is difficult to see how the doctrine of frustration could operate so as to dissolve any contract of insurance, whether of property or of life; for insurance involves the payment of money and, to quote again Pollock's citation from Savigny: 'there is plenty of money in the world and it is a matter wholly personal to the debtor if he cannot get the money he has bound himself to pay.' But, as we shall see later, frustration of the voyage or adventure, which is a different matter, is an insurable risk.[3]

B. PRE-WAR MARINE INSURANCES WHERE NEITHER PARTY BECOMES AN ENEMY IN THE TERRITORIAL SENSE

This contract, like any other, is dissolved upon the outbreak of war by reason of illegality if in itself it involves intercourse with the enemy, or if it is ancillary to a transaction involving intercourse with the enemy or is otherwise detrimental to the interests of this country.

(i) *Involving intercourse with the enemy*

This factor is not likely to occur except in the case where the insurer or the assured is an enemy, and that case has already been considered. It is, however, possible to imagine circumstances in which it might occur; for instance, where the broker effecting the insurance becomes an enemy and further communication with him after the outbreak of war might be involved.

---

[1] Above, p. 119.

[2] E.g. *Ertel Bieber & Co.* v. *Rio Tinto Co.*; *Clapham Steamship Co.* v. *Handels-en-Transport Maatschappij Vulcaan.*   [3] Below, p. 270.

(ii) *Upon illegal trading with the enemy*

One of the commonest causes of dissolution occurs when the insurance covers property involved in unlicensed trading with the enemy. There is no doubt since *The Panariellos* that the contract is also dissolved when the property covered and involved in trading with the enemy belongs to the nationals of an allied Power which is co-belligerent with Great Britain.

(iii) *Upon licensed trading with the enemy*

The effect of a licence granted to a British or an enemy subject permitting trading with the enemy legalizes not only the trading transaction but ancillary contracts such as affreightment and insurance.[1]

(iv) *Indemnity against the consequences of carriage of contraband, blockade-running and other service*

The case of insurances upon the property of neutral subjects requires more detailed consideration. Aid rendered by neutral subjects to a belligerent in the form of carriage of contraband, blockade-running or other 'unneutral service' (as it is called in the unratified Declaration of London) is not regarded as illegal by the municipal law of England, though the British Government recognizes the right of a belligerent to protect himself against these practices by the capture and condemnation of ships and cargoes involved in them.

United Kingdom[2] *a neutral*. Thus, when the United Kingdom is a neutral, insurances (effected either before or during the war) by British insurers upon such ventures, whether undertaken by British subjects or others, are not illegal,[3] though the outbreak of war, or some development of the war, may, by converting a peaceful voyage into a blockade-running expedition or an innocent cargo into a contraband one, affect the continued validity of the policy; that is a question of its terms and of the circumstances which attended its making. The question of concealment may easily arise upon such policies.

United Kingdom a belligerent. When, however, Great Britain is a belligerent, a different attitude towards the activities of neutral subjects must be adopted. Their property involved in attempts to aid

---

[1] Below, pp. 269, 356.

[2] On a number of points relating to neutral ships and cargoes, the duties of neutrality, blockade, contraband, etc., see references in index of Arnould.

[3] *Hobbs* v. *Henning* (1864) (where the ship was the 'Peterhoff', which gave her name to one of the leading American prize decisions of the Civil War); *Seymour* v. *London & Provincial Marine* ('warranted no contraband of war').

or supply Great Britain is lawfully insurable by British insurers; if involved in attempts to aid or supply the enemy, it is not. On grounds of general principle it is inconceivable that a British under-writer should be allowed to pay in the latter case, whether the policy was issued before or during the war, and thus indemnify a neutral subject—whether the loss or damage arises from British capture or perils of the seas—in respect of property involved in succouring Great Britain's enemy. Such a contract would, in the words of Lord Alvanley C.J.,[1] be a 'contract to do [something] which may be detrimental to the interests of his own country'. It is just as absurd to indemnify a neutral subject as an enemy subject against the con-sequences of British capture.[2]

There is no objection to a policy of insurance issued before or during the war by a British subject to cover the property of a British subject against loss or damage resulting from enemy action or from action taken to avert or minimize enemy action, provided that the property is not involved in trading with the enemy. Nor is there any objection to such an insurance upon the property of the subject of a neutral State, provided that it is not involved in the carriage of contraband to Great Britain's enemy or the breach of a British blockade or in some other activity hostile to Great Britain.

C. CONTRACTS OF MARINE INSURANCE MADE OR WHICH IT IS ATTEMPTED TO MAKE DURING THE WAR

Except by licence of the Crown, express or implied, no valid contract of insurance can be made during the war between a person in this country and an enemy in the territorial sense, whichever of them may be insurer or assured.

This rule results from general principle but was only established on a firm foundation in the year 1800 by the judgment of the Court of King's Bench in *Potts* v. *Bell*, a decision of great importance, for Park J. in *Willison* v. *Patteson*[3] said of it: 'Before the case of *Potts* v. *Bell*, there was an opinion prevalent in Westminster Hall, that the commerce with an enemy was not illegal.' In *Potts* v. *Bell* the plaintiffs, who insured their interest in the goods, were British mer-

---

[1] In *Furtado* v. *Rogers* (1802) 3 Bos. & P. 191, 198.

[2] Arthur Cohen, K.C., a great authority on marine insurance, expressed the view in Halsbury, *Laws of England* (1911), xvii, § 844, that 'as a general rule, whenever any property is according to prize law as administered by the courts of this country liable to British capture, the insurance in this country on such property [query, against any risks] is illegal and void'.

[3] (1817) 7 Taunt. 439, 449.

chants carrying on business in London; the policy on ship and goods was subscribed in London by the defendant (apparently British) and was dated 7 December 1797; the ship was Prussian (neutral); but the voyage, which began on 18 December, was from Rotterdam, an enemy port, to Hull, and thus involved trading with the enemy, for Great Britain and Holland (under a puppet Francophile Government) were at war; the loss was due to capture by a French enemy ship. The plaintiff failed to recover on the policy, and the reason given in a regrettably terse judgment[1] is that 'it might now be taken that it was a principle of the common law that trading with an enemy without the King's licence, was illegal in British subjects'. Counsel for the successful defendant contended that the policy was 'void', that is, void *ab initio*.

Moreover, the premium paid in respect of an insurance which is void *ab initio* by reason of this kind of illegality cannot be recovered back from the underwriter.[2]

An express licence to insure enemy property or to effect an insurance with an enemy is rarely, if ever, granted. But when the Crown licenses a particular trading transaction or a particular kind of trade with the enemy, or trading generally with him, it thereby licenses by implication the contracts usually ancillary to the main contract, e.g. insurance and affreightment. Thus in *Usparicha* v. *Noble*,[3] a Spaniard resident in this country during war between Great Britain, on the one hand, and France and Spain, as co-belligerents on the other hand, was licensed by the Crown to ship goods by a (neutral) Prussian vessel from this country to Spain and insured the goods with the defendant, who was apparently a British underwriter; it was agreed at the time of the action that the plaintiff had shipped the goods on account of correspondents who were residing in enemy territory and not on his own account; the goods were lost owing to capture by a French privateer, a loss covered by the policy; the plaintiff recovered upon the policy, for 'The Crown, in licensing the end, impliedly licenses all the ordinary legitimate means of attaining that end'.[4]

We must now mention briefly three groups of cases which do not illustrate the impact of war upon the general principles of the law of marine insurance so much as the interpretation of certain expressions of frequent occurrence in policies.

---

[1] The arguments are valuable and are fully reported.
[2] *Vandyck* v. *Hewitt* (1800).
[3] (1811) 13 East. 332.   [4] At p. 341.

D. THE EFFECT OF WAR IN PRODUCING A FRUSTRATION OF THE VOYAGE OR ADVENTURE[1]

The decision of the judge of first instance, Bailhache J., in *British and Foreign Marine Insurance Co.* v. *Sanday*,[2] probably caused more consternation in the limited community which it affected than any other decision during the War of 1914 to 1918 in that or any other section of the mercantile community. The plaintiffs were the British owners of cargo laden on board two British vessels on the high seas upon the outbreak of the War of 1914 to 1918 and consigned to Hamburg. One vessel on 9 August was stopped by a French cruiser and told to go to Falmouth for security; the other, in response to a pre-war suggestion from the Admiralty, was on 7 August diverted by her owners to a British port. The plaintiffs warehoused the goods and on 7 September gave notice of abandonment and claimed for a constructive total loss. The usual F.C. and S. clause ('free from capture and seizure', meaning that the risks of capture and seizure are excluded) had been deleted in consideration of an extra premium, and the material perils insured against in the body of the policy were 'takings at sea, arrests, restraints, and detainments of all kings, princes and people of what nation, condition, or quality soever'. The first point taken by and decided against the underwriters was that the Marine Insurance Act, 1906, had not abrogated the old rule that: 'Upon an insurance on goods...the frustration of the adventure by an insured peril is a loss recoverable against underwriters, though the goods themselves are safe and sound.'[3]

There was nothing startling about that. The 'subject-matter' of

---

[1] Arnould, §§ 16, 829. For a case upon the effect of war in producing a constructive total loss, see *Polurrian Steamship Co.* v. *Young*. The suggestion made by Bailhache J. *obiter* in *Mitsui* v. *Mumford* (timber in Antwerp on the outbreak of war in August 1914) that the doctrine of constructive total loss is not confined to marine insurance and that an analogous principle (minus notice of abandonment) applies to an insurance upon goods on land, appears to have influenced Bray J. in *Campbell & Phillips* v. *Denman* (also goods in Antwerp in August 1914). This suggestion was disapproved by Lord Atkinson in delivering the judgment of the House of Lords in *Moore* v. *Evans* [1918] A.C. 185, where incidentally he pointed out (at p. 194) that the doctrine of constructive total loss based upon notice of abandonment had its origin in cases of capture. In *Moore* v. *Evans* it was held that a non-marine policy for twelve months issued in January 1914, to a firm of London jewellers on pearls in Brussels and Frankfort-on-Main against 'loss of and/or damage or misfortune to' the goods was a policy on goods and not on an adventure, so that the mere fact that as a result of the outbreak of war they were unable to recover possession of their pearls did not constitute a loss upon the policy, there being no evidence that the jewellery had not remained in the possession of the consignees in Brussels and Frankfort or their bankers.

[2] [1915] 2 K.B. 781 (decisions of Bailhache J. and Court of Appeal); affirmed [1916] 1 A.C. 650.

[3] [1916] 1 A.C. at p. 656.

an insurance of goods from *A* to *B* is not merely the physical existence of the goods but their transportation and safe arrival.

But upon the second question—whether the loss was by a peril insured against—it was contended by the underwriters (*a*) that the restraint clause in the policy must be taken not to include restraints, or at any rate proper and legal restraints, by the British Government, and (*b*) that even if the 'municipal law of this country and the authoritative acts of the British Government' were covered, restraint connoted the actual use of physical force and did not comprise mere voluntary compliance with the law of the country or the commands of the Government.[1]

Bailhache J., in a judgment which was affirmed by the Court of Appeal (Swinfen Eady L.J. dissenting) and by the House of Lords unanimously, held (*a*) that the proximate cause of the loss was a restraint of princes which 'took the form of the common law, which upon the outbreak of war sprang automatically into force, and of the commands issued by proclamation',[2] namely, not to navigate a ship or carry goods to a German port; and (*b*) that the restraints clause included restraints by the British Government. Upon (*a*) Earl Loreburn remarked that he was 'not pressed by the circumstance that force was neither exerted nor present, for force is in reserve behind every State command',[3] and in a later case[4] Lord Sumner pointed out that the ground of the decision in *Sanday's* case was 'the illegality of any further prosecution of the voyage, both ship and master being British'. Upon (*b*) the authority for including restraints by the British Government rested almost entirely upon the works of Marshall, Phillips and Arnould, but no authority was necessary, for the words of the clause clearly included the British Government, unless some more limited meaning could be given to it by custom or was demanded by some rule of public policy.[5]

The effect of the judgment in *Sanday's* case was to produce a considerable amount of surprise in the marine insurance community. It had never been decided, and it had probably never before entered

[1] The case of an illegal or *ultra vires* requisition by the British Government was considered by Bailhache J. in *Russian Bank for Foreign Trade* v. *Excess Insurance Co.*

[2] [1915] 2 K.B. at p. 789.

[3] [1916] 1 A.C. at p. 659; and see Lord Wright in *Rickards* v. *Forestal Land, Timber & Railways Co.* [1942] A.C. 50, 81.

[4] *Becker, Gray & Co.* v. *London Assurance Corporation* [1918] A.C. 101, 117. Note also Willes J. in *Esposito* v. *Bowden* (1857) 7 El. & Bl. 763, 781; 'The force of a declaration of war is equal to an Act of Parliament prohibiting intercourse with the enemy except by the Queen's licence.'

[5] The decision was followed by Atkin J. in *Associated Oil Carriers Ltd* v. *Union Insurance Society of Canton* (insurance on freight).

the head of a broker or an underwriter, that British restraints were included in the ordinary restraints clause in the body of the policy; such a decision upon so venerable a document was equivalent to laying hands upon the ark of the covenant of marine insurance. The ocean suddenly became dense with constructive total losses, and Lloyd's underwriters quickly devised the following 'British and Allies Capture Clause, 1916':

Warranted free of any claim arising from capture, seizure, arrest, restraint or detainment, except by the enemies of Great Britain or by the enemies of the country to which the assured or the ship belongs.

In 1919 this clause was superseded by one of a more permanent character as follows:

Warranted free of any claim based upon loss of, or frustration of, the insured voyage or adventure, caused by arrests, restraints, or detainments of kings, princes or peoples,

the words 'usurpers or persons attempting to usurp power' being sometimes added later.[1]

This clause was also used in the case of hulls and freights insured for the voyage.

A case in which *Sanday's* case was invoked and which followed it up to the House of Lords, is *Becker, Gray & Co.* v. *London Assurance Corporation*.[2] The plaintiffs were British merchants owning a cargo of jute laden on board a German steamship, the *Kattenturm*, which at the outbreak of war was on a voyage from Calcutta to Hamburg, the jute having been shipped under a c.i.f. contract. On 3 August she left Malta bound westwards, later heard of the declaration of war, and, voluntarily and without being chased, entered the then neutral port of Messina where she arrived on the 6th; after lying there for about a month she proceeded to Syracuse. A letter from the British Admiralty, which was treated as evidence, stated that: 'Any German

---

[1] The appropriate method of using the new clause was described in a statement appearing in *Lloyd's List* of 19 June 1919 and printed on pp. 143, 144 of the first edition of this book. The attitude of underwriters towards the risks disclosed by *Sanday's* case and thereafter intended to be excluded by the Frustration Clause and imposed upon shipowners and merchants raises a big question which is economic rather than legal. A view which is critical of the underwriters' attitude found expression in two letters from Charles Wright of Lloyd's to *The Times* newspaper published on 31 July and 5 August 1919. For the modern forms of the clause see Arnould, § 829 and his Appendix 2.

Upon restraints and seizures of people in civil war, see *Soc. Belge des Betons* v. *London & Lancashire Insurance Co.* [1938] 2 All E.R. 305, and *Pesquerias y Secaderos* v. *Beer* [1949] 1 All E.R. 845 (H.L.). 'People' seems to mean the body which is in control of a country or part of it, or at any rate the body striving for control, and not a mere mob of starving individuals who seize a ship and cargo: *Nesbitt* v. *Lushington* (1792) 4 T.R. 783.

[2] [1915] 3 K.B. 410; [1916] 2 K.B. 156; [1918] A.C. 101.

steamer proceeding on or after 5 August last through the Mediterranean on a voyage to Hamburg would, in their Lordships' opinion, have been in peril of capture by British or allied warships when outside neutral waters.'

On 1 September the plaintiffs gave notice of abandonment to the underwriters. As in *Sanday's* case, the F.C. and S. clause had been deleted upon payment of an extra premium, and the perils insured against included 'men-of-war...enemies...takings at sea, arrests, restraints and detainments of all kings, princes and people of what nation, condition or quality soever'.

All three Courts had no difficulty in distinguishing the case from *Sanday's* case, and in giving judgment for the defendant insurer. The adventure was frustrated when the master prudently put into Messina with no thought of resuming his voyage until after the war. 'It was self-restraint, not restraint of princes, that hindered the captain from putting to sea' (per Lord Sumner).[1] It was not illegal, as in *Sanday's* case, for him to continue his voyage. To the plaintiffs' other main point, that there was a constructive loss due to the peril of capture, the answer was that the loss was due not to the peril of capture but to the fear of it, and the peril had not yet begun to operate. Moreover, the voluntary act of the master intervened between the occurrence of any peril insured against and the loss, so that it could not be said that any peril was the proximate cause of the loss.

There the question remained until the outbreak of the War of 1939 to 1945 gave rise to three test cases of great importance—*Rickards* v. *Forestal Land, Timber and Railways Co.*; *Robertson* v. *Middows*; and *Kahn* v. *W. H. Howard*,[2] which were tried together by Hilbery J. and went to the Court of Appeal and the House of Lords. The policies, though not identical, were similar enough to raise the same main point of law. They all covered cargoes against both marine and war risks, and they were all subject to the diminution of war risks resulting from the inclusion of the so-called 'Frustration Clause', which was in one of the forms introduced after *Sanday's* case and quoted above,[3] with the irrelevant exception that the concluding words were 'kings princes peoples usurpers or persons attempting to usurp power'. The main question was whether in the circumstances the loss fell within the risks *included* in the war risks clause or within the risks *excluded* by the Frustration Clause.

The cargoes were all on board German steamers which were pursuing their voyages when the war broke out. The masters of the

---

[1] [1918] A.C. at p. 111.   [2] [1942] A.C. 50.   [3] P. 272.

steamers had been instructed that in the event of war between Germany and Great Britain they must either enter a German port or, rather than be captured, scuttle their ships. One reached a German port, the other two were scuttled to avoid capture.

In all three cases the owners of cargo lost their cargo, and in the absence of the Frustration Clause could have recovered under their policies on the ground that there was a constructive total loss due to one or more of the war risks enumerated therein, such as 'men-of-war ...enemies...surprisals, takings at sea, arrests, restraints, and detainments of all kings, princes and people...', when the masters acted upon the instructions of their Government so that the cargoes were converted to the use of that Government, with the consequences described above. It was, however, argued that the loss in these cases was due to the frustration of the adventure arising from a restraint of princes, namely, the orders of the German Government and the execution of those orders by the masters of the ships, and that this was a risk excluded by the Frustration Clause. The answer to this contention given by the Court of Appeal (reversing Hilbery J.) and upheld by the House of Lords was that loss of goods and 'loss of, or frustration of, the insured voyage or adventure' are not identical or co-terminous. The risk to the goods and the risk to the voyage or adventure are different risks. The latter risk, unless excluded by the Frustration Clause, is an additional risk, not an essential part of the former risk. In the words of Lord Wright:[1]

The primary subject of the insurance is the goods as physical things, but there is superimposed an interest in the safe arrival of the goods....a policy on goods is in truth one covering a composite interest, the physical things or chattels, and also the expected benefit from their arrival. The subject-matter may be described as chattels-cum-adventure...the adventure may be lost even though the goods are neither damaged nor lost nor taken from the assured's possession or control[2]...To cases of that type the frustration clause has a clear and precise application, but in my opinion it cannot be applied to a case where the assured is claiming for loss of or damage to the actual physical things or chattels. He is entitled to resist the application of the clause on the ground that the primary subject-matter is the goods, and that the adventure is merely ancillary or accessory...

Accordingly, the Frustration Clause did not protect the underwriters, and the cargo-owners recovered. The foregoing summary is a simplification, but, perhaps, not an over-simplification of facts and points of law that were not identical in all three cases. It does not

---

[1] [1942] A.C. at pp. 90, 91.   [2] E.g. *Sanday's* case, above, p. 270.

do justice to a controversy which evoked arguments of great acuity and a series of impressive judgments, but it will be pardoned on grounds of space if it has made clear the main question which was raised and answered—a question extending far beyond the impact of war upon the traditional Lloyd's form of marine and war risks policy.

The meaning which should be given to the word 'frustration' occurring in a policy of insurance is not necessarily the same as its meaning in judicial decisions involving the doctrine of frustration or in the Law Reform (Frustrated Contracts) Act, 1943. The primary consideration in interpreting a contract must be what the parties meant when they used the words.

E. WAR OR MARINE RISKS

There are two other questions which arise frequently during war and form the subject of numerous decisions. They also do not illustrate the effect of the impact of war upon principles of law, and we shall do little more than call attention to their existence.

The first question owes its prominence to the German policy of 'spurlos versenkt'[1] adopted during the War of 1914 to 1918. It arises when it is not clearly apparent whether a missing ship was lost by perils of the seas or by war risks, and she was insured with one set of underwriters against marine risks and with another set of underwriters against war risks, or is only insured against one or the other of these classes of risks. Who is to pay? The decisions given during the last war are numerous and will be found in Arnould.[2] The law was carefully examined by Bailhache J. in *Munro, Brice & Co.* v. *War Risks Association*, though the Court of Appeal held that his inference of fact was wrong.

F. CONSEQUENCES OF HOSTILITIES OR WARLIKE OPERATIONS

The second question is purely a matter of interpretation. It has been productive of a very large number of decisions, which, not unlike the innumerable decisions upon testamentary expressions, are of great importance to the parties litigating, but make little contribution to

---

[1] The expression occurred in an intercepted despatch from the German *chargé d'affaires* in Argentina to his Government in 1917, in which he recommended the application of this policy to Argentinian ships: Garner, *International Law and the World War*, § 490.

[2] §§ 902, 903.

18-2

the development of the law. In its commonest form, the question is: What is the meaning of such expressions as 'war risks', 'warlike operations', 'hostilities', and the 'consequences' of such things, either occurring in a policy amongst the risks specifically insured or in a clause specifically excluding them from the scope of the policy. The principal decisions are given by Arnould[1] and some of them are referred to below. The intended effect of using expressions such as those mentioned above is to cover risks arising from various events and acts resembling, though not amounting in law, to war *stricto sensu*.

G. FIRE AND OTHER NON-MARINE INSURANCES ON PROPERTY[2]

Attempts to make such insurances during war

Any attempt by a person in this country (except by licence) to make such a contract during war with a person on enemy territory would be illegal and void of effect, and probably criminal as amounting to the offence of trading with the enemy, which is not confined to commercial transactions. There is no ground for exempting these contracts from the general principle.[3]

Pre-war insurance contracts

We can see no reason why these contracts should not be governed by the general principle, stated in chapter 4, that pre-war contracts between a party in this country and a party in enemy territory are dissolved upon the outbreak of war, while any right of action which has already accrued to either party upon such a contract will survive the outbreak of war but cannot be enforced by an enemy claimant during the war.[4]

[1] §§ 820, 843, 849, 897–909b; *J. Wharton Shipping Co.* v. *Mortleman*; *Yorkshire Dale Steamship Co.* v. *Minister of War Transport*; *Clan Line Steamers* v. *Liverpool & London War Risks Insurance Association Ltd*; *Larrinaga Steamship Co.* v. *The King*; *Athel Line Ltd* v. *Liverpool & London War Risks Association Ltd*; *Liverpool & London War Risks Association Ltd* v. *Ocean Steamship Co. Ltd*, and see *Western Reserve Life Insurance Co.* v. *Meadows*, (the Korean conflict), on 'war' in insurance policies. On the similar Dutch 'molest' clause, see two Dutch decisions, *Amstel Insurance Co. Ltd.* v. *Van der Wal* (1950) and *American Business Machines* v. *Onderlinge Dorlogsschade-Versekering Maatschappij* (1951). On the question when the term 'war' includes civil war, see *Curtis & Son* v. *Mathews*; *Pesquerias y Secadero, etc. S.A.* v. *Beer*; Arnould, § 823; *Atlantic Maritime Co. Inc.* v. *Gibbon*; and an American case, *Republic of China and others* v. *National Union Fire Insurance Co.*
[2] For Life Insurance, see pp. 278–284.
[3] Halsbury, *Laws of England* (3rd ed. Simonds), vol. 22, 5, 50; Bunyon, *Fire Insurance* (7th ed. 1923), p. 415; and see chapter 4 of this book.
[4] For a summary of the provisions of the Peace Treaties of 1919–20 upon contracts of fire insurance, see Bunyon, *op. cit.* pp. 422–6.

Macgillivray[1] and his editors have examined the effect of war on policies of insurance in great detail; in § 557 it is stated that:

> Any contract which operates to indemnify an alien enemy against a commercial loss which is caused by the action of Her Majesty's armed forces is, *pro tanto*, illegal and void, there being an implied exception from the general terms of the contract of any promise the performance of which would be illegal either by the common law or by any emergency or other legislation.

Let us take the case of a policy issued in July 1939, whereby a British underwriter insured a house and contents belonging to a German householder in Germany against loss by ordinary fire or burglary for a period of twelve months. No loss has occurred before the outbreak of war on 3 September 1939. Surely the authorities already cited must drive us to the conclusion that upon the outbreak of war this policy was abrogated,[2] for the reason that it is an executory contract involving intercourse with the enemy.[3] Even if that view is wrong and the contract is not abrogated, we find it difficult to see why a distinction should be drawn between a commercial loss and a non-commercial loss.

In *Janson* v. *Driefontein Consolidated Mines* and in *Robinson Gold Mining Co.* v. *Alliance Assurance Co.*, the policies were both marine policies and the losses occurred on land through seizure by a foreign Government *before* and in anticipation of war with Great Britain. In the former case the plaintiff company was enemy in the territorial sense when the writ was issued; in the latter case the plaintiff company had been enemy, but the war was officially at an end before the writ was issued. It was not suggested that the fact that the losses occurred on land attracted rules of law different from those that governed marine insurance.[4]

From the point of view of the general principle that all[5] pre-war contracts which involve intercourse with the enemy are abrogated

---

[1] § 557.   [2] See, however, Macgillivray, § 557.

[3] *Furtado* v. *Rogers*, *supra*; *Esposito* v. *Bowden*, *supra*. It might be said that once the policy has been issued and the premium paid there may be no further need for intercourse with the enemy; but the point is that if the policy is maintained as a valid contract it might at any time involve intercourse with the enemy.

[4] In *Nigel Gold Mining Co.* v. *Hoade*, the policy was not a marine one. It merely insured the plaintiff company's property while on the premises at its mine in the Transvaal and would normally have been followed by another policy to cover transit to England. The seizure by the Government of the South African Republic took place at the mine *during* the war. The national character of the plaintiff company was ambiguous, but the learned judge preferred to regard it as British, and the war was at an end before the writ was issued. Not a satisfactory case. See also *The Venus* (1814), and Arnould, § 146.

[5] See pp. 134–5 for certain exceptions.

upon the outbreak of war (with a saving for rights of action already accrued), we can see no difference whatever between marine insurance and any other kind of insurance upon property. If the premium has already been paid, there need be no intercourse with the enemy unless a loss occurs; but that is quite immaterial, because the parties, in making the contract, contemplate that, if a loss occurs during its currency, intercourse between them must take place for the purposes of its settlement and payment. It is, therefore, not surprising that in *Excess Insurance Co.* v. *Mathews* it was assumed that a pre-war policy issued by a British insurance company to a Hungarian company against loss by fire upon the profits of a mill in Hungary would have been abrogated by the outbreak of war between Great Britain and Hungary if the Treaty of Peace between those countries had not preserved or restored its validity. By reason of the provisions of the Treaty the British insurance company paid under the Clearing Office procedure a loss incurred by the Hungarian company, and thereupon succeeded in this action in recovering the proportionate amount due from one of their reinsurers, the defendant.

II. LIFE INSURANCE

PRELIMINARY

Here indeed we are upon a still more or less uncharted sea. So far as we are aware, there was no English judicial authority before the War of 1914 to 1918, and the American authorities, though numerous, emit no very helpful ray of light.

The typical contract of life insurance differs fundamentally from typical contracts of insurance on property, both marine and non-marine. (*a*) The former is usually a contract intended to last for many years, and is sometimes only terminated by death. A marine policy is usually a contract for the voyage or for 12 months, while a non-marine policy is often capable of annual renewal by agreement between the parties. (*b*) In the former the assured may at any time terminate the contract by not paying the annual premium, but if he pays it the insurer is bound to accept it. In the latter the insurer is not bound to renew the contract. (*c*) The former is usually a piece of property which increases in value year by year and the assured usually has the right to surrender it in return for a lump sum. No such right is appropriate to the latter. Both types are technically choses in action, but the former is more in the nature of a piece of property than the latter. Thus it is frequently the subject of a mortgage and can be bought and sold on the open market.

If our Courts had formed a clear view as to the nature of a policy of life insurance, our problems would be easier to solve. But unfortunately it cannot be said that they have. Macgillivray[1] says that:

There has... been considerable difference of judicial opinion as to whether the contract of life insurance made in consideration of an annual premium is an insurance for a year with an irrevocable offer to renew upon payment of the renewal premium, or whether it is an insurance for the entire life subject to defeasance or forfeiture upon non-payment of the renewal premium at the times stated.

And later[2]

in America, where the subject has been more carefully considered, it has been held that a life policy is not an insurance for a single year with a privilege of renewal from year to year by paying the annual premium, but is an entire contract of insurance for life, subject to discontinuance of forfeiture for non-payment of any of the stipulated premiums.[3]

Although there is no express English judicial authority on the point, this is the opinion which seems to have the largest support in England today, and the policies of some companies seek to emphasize this construction by avoiding the use of the term 'renewal premiums' and speaking of 'first premium' and 'subsequent premium'. In Halsbury, *Laws of England*,[4] we are told that 'a contract of life assurance in its strict form may be defined as a contract under which the insurers undertake, in consideration of specified premiums being continuously paid throughout the life of a particular person, to pay a specified sum of money upon the death of that person....'.

In *Seligman* v. *Eagle Insurance Co.*, which is believed to be the only English decision upon the effect of war upon a life insurance policy, Neville J. expressed no opinion upon this question of principle but held that 'there was nothing in the nature of the contract to put an end to it upon the outbreak of war'.[5]

---

[1] Para 765, citing Willes J. in *Pritchard* v. *The Merchants' Life* (1858) 3 C.B. (N.S.) 622, 643, Lord Chelmsford in *Phoenix Life* v. *Sheridan* (1860) 8 H.L.C. 745, 750, *Stuart* v. *Freeman* (1903) and (a Canadian Case) *Frank* v. *Sun Life* (1893).

[2] *Ibid.*, citing *New York Life Insurance Co.* v. *Statham* (1876).

[3] A number of conflicting American decisions are examined by Campbell, *Law of War and Contract* (1918), pp. 198–217; they all appear to be decisions given in cases arising out of the Civil War, and it is not always safe to argue from these cases to cases arising out of international war.

[4] (3rd ed. Simonds), vol. 22, § 538.

[5] [1917] 1 Ch. 519, where counsel cited in favour of the United States view *Fryer* v. *Morland* (1876) 3 Ch.D. 675, 685; *In re Anchor Assurance Co.* (1870) L.R. 5 Ch. 632, 638; and *In re Harrison & Ingram* [1900] 2 Q.B. 710, 717; and see comment in *Lai Ah Heng* v. *China Underwriters Ltd* [1948] Singapore Law Reports, at p. 93.

CONTRACTS ATTEMPTED TO BE MADE DURING THE WAR

Let us begin by disposing of what is almost the only aspect of life insurance which is not controversial. It is clear that during the war no contract of life insurance can be effectively made between any person resident, being or carrying on business in this country (including a corporation registered under the law of or carrying on business in this country) and an enemy in the territorial sense, which is the sense in which the term 'enemy' is used in this chapter. Any attempt to make such a contract is both criminal and nugatory, as a trading with the enemy, unless licensed by the Crown, and it is immaterial whether the 'life' insured is British, neutral, or enemy.

In theory, the fact that the 'life' insured is an enemy would not vitiate an insurance otherwise lawful, provided that no enemy is a party to the contract or takes any benefit from it and the effecting of the insurance involves no intercourse with an enemy; in practice, it would in many cases be almost impossible to effect such an insurance without some intercourse with the 'life' such as procuring evidence of age, arranging for medical examination, etc., though it must be remembered that for certain purposes insurances are frequently effected upon the lives of prominent persons, such as members of a Royal family, without medical examination. When, however, the enemy 'life' assured dies as a result of action by British forces or of service in enemy forces opposing British forces, Macgillivray states— rightly, it is believed—'the risk is illegal and the policy-holder cannot recover'.[1]

PRE-WAR CONTRACTS

We now turn to the difficult and highly controversial question of the effect of the outbreak of war upon pre-war contracts, and we shall begin by confining our attention to the case which arouses most interest in a country like the United Kingdom which is an 'exporter' of life insurance, that is, a contract between a British insurance company and an enemy. Let us first attempt to make certain statements of principle.

Consideration of principles. (1) A distinction is necessary between rights of performance under a contract and property rights connected with a contract, for there is no automatic confiscation of private enemy property by our law; that can only be done by the Crown,

---

[1] § 560.

using the appropriate procedure, or by the legislature, of which the Crown is a part.[1]

(2) There seem to be three possible effects which the mere outbreak of war might have upon a pre-war contract of life insurance between a British insurance company and an enemy. First, it might be automatic abrogation, which is the commonest, though not the universal, effect upon contracts still executory upon the outbreak of war. Secondly, it might be suspension (a rare case, of which the shareholder's contract of membership is probably the only clear instance), that is, suspension for the duration of the war of performance of some or all of the obligations of the contract, which is different from the suspension during the war of an enemy's right of action arising upon a default in performance occurring before the war, or, in the case of a contract which survives the outbreak of war, upon a default occurring during the war.[2] Thirdly, it might be *nil*, as in the case of a lease,[3] that is to say, all the obligations might remain unaffected by the mere outbreak of war, though their performance may be hampered by the rule against intercourse with the enemy.

(3) If the third possible solution is the correct one, then the contract has survived the first critical point of time, that is, the outbreak of war, and attention must be focused upon its second crisis, namely, the first or any subsequent date after the outbreak of war upon which a premium falls due. If there is a default in payment, either voluntarily or because the law of the enemy country prohibits payment or English law prohibits receipt of the payment, further questions arise. By the terms of the policy, does non-payment of the premium *ipso facto* terminate the contract, or does it merely give the insurance company the option to terminate it? Is there any other source from which payment may lawfully be made for instance, by a surety or by the insurance company out of its own funds, and, if so, is the insurance company obliged to resort to that source or has it an option in the matter? In short, whereas in the case of an executory contract of sale of goods or of affreightment, the critical question is the effect of the outbreak of war, in the case of a contract of life insurance the critical question may be not only that but also the effect of default in payment of the first premium due after the outbreak of war or of any subsequent premium.

---

[1] See ch. 15.
[2] See Lord Reading C.J. in *Halsey* v. *Lowenfeld* [1916] 2 K.B. 707, 714 (top).
[3] See above p. 134, n. 3 and below pp. 289–293.

(4) If a contract between a person in this country and a person in the enemy country is by operation of law abrogated upon the outbreak of war, nothing that the Crown acting through a Trading with the Enemy Branch may do can redintegrate that contract;[1] redintegration can only be effected by the agreement of both parties; the Crown may license intercourse with the enemy party but it must be shown that both parties have agreed to redintegrate the contract.

(5) The Crown, acting through a Trading with the Enemy Branch or some other appropriate organ of government, has a common law power of licensing intercourse with the enemy and a statutory power under subsection 2 of section 1 of the Trading with the Enemy Act, 1939, of rendering innocent an act which would otherwise amount to statutory trading with the enemy; but it has no power to make new rules of law or to revive a contract abrogated by operation of law.

Judicial authority. What light can be obtained from this source? If it may be said with great respect, the judgment of Neville J. in *Seligman* v. *Eagle Insurance Co.*[2] is not entirely free from obscurity. All that it decides is (i) that two policies of insurance which had been issued before the war by a British company to, and upon the life of, an enemy national who shortly after the outbreak of war left this country and went to the enemy country, and which had been mortgaged to the company by him in order to secure a loan, were not abrogated by the fact of the policy-holder becoming an enemy in the territorial sense; (ii) that the company could, as the law then stood, lawfully and without committing the offence of trading with the enemy, accept from a surety in this country the premiums due upon the policies in October 1914 and October 1915, that is, after the outbreak of war; and (iii) that the surety was entitled, upon paying to the company the amount due under the mortgage, to an assignment of the policies. The learned judge said:[3]

The right of the policy-holder is clearly suspended during the war, and were he to die tomorrow his executors would recover nothing from the company; but whenever peace is restored between the countries normal relations in this regard will be resumed, and, although the right of the policy-holder is undoubtedly suspended, if the policy itself is not made void either at the time when war was declared or at the time when the current year of the policy ran out, I can see nothing illegal in the accept-

---

[1] *Esposito* v. *Bowden* (1855) 4 El. & Bl. 963, 975; (1857) 7 El. & Bl. 763, 778; and see above, p. 132.
[2] [1917] 1 Ch. 519. [3] At p. 526.

ance of the premiums by the company because no benefit can accrue to the enemy alien at all as the result of the payment of his premium; but what will result is that perhaps some day somebody who is not an enemy alien may have a right to sue the company for the amount assured. It seems to me this is one of those cases where the right is suspended.

The learned judge's view is clearly against abrogation; he said[1] 'there is nothing in the nature of the contract [scilicet, of life insurance] to put an end to it on the outbreak of war...the insurance company could have sued the assured under his contract for the amount of the premiums due under the covenant contained in the policy...', provided that in so doing they would not be guilty of unlawful intercourse with the enemy, which in his opinion would not be the case. It is pertinent to remark that upon the outbreak of war the assured by going to the enemy country, the law of which prohibited him from remitting a payment to this country, put it out of his power to perform his contracts with the company and with the surety, whose security was thus jeopardized and who took appropriate action to safeguard it by tendering the premiums when they became due.

It should also be noted, on the subject of accepting payments from an enemy, that in 1917 there was in force a Trading with the Enemy Proclamation of 9 September 1914, which contained a proviso to the effect that 'Nothing in this Proclamation shall be deemed to prohibit payments by or on account of enemies to persons resident, carrying on business or being in Our Dominions, if such payments arise out of transactions entered into before the outbreak of War or otherwise permitted'; whereas now the proviso in section 1 (2) of the Trading with the Enemy Act, 1939, is to the effect that 'a person shall not be deemed to have traded with the enemy by reason only that he has...(ii) received payment from an enemy of a sum of money due in respect of a transaction under which all obligations on the part of the person receiving payment had already been performed when the payment was received, and had been performed at a time when the person from whom the payment was received was not an enemy'. The same proviso protects acts authorized by the appropriate organ of the British Government.[2]

[1] At p. 525.
[2] Here a number of American decisions were referred to in the third edition of this book.

Conclusions from principle and judicial authority

An attempt must now be made to draw certain conclusions from what seem to be the relevant general principles and from the slender judicial authority available. In the present lack of clear guidance we may be pardoned if we state our conclusions tentatively, and what follows must be so regarded by the reader.

It is submitted that the clue lies in the proprietary character of the ordinary policy of life insurance. It is true that a right under any contract is a chose in action and falls within the category of property. But, as has already been suggested, a policy of life insurance is in a peculiar sense a piece of property. It is frequently sold and mortgaged, and it may provide for the acquisition of a surrender value.[1] It may not strictly fall within Lord Dunedin's category of contracts which are 'concomitants of rights of property',[2] an expression which is more appropriate to the covenants contained in a lease or a restrictive covenant attached to land,[3] but it can be said not unfairly to fall within the general intention of that expression. It is submitted that, amongst the contracts upon which there exists a clear English pronouncement as to the effect of a war, the nearest analogy is the lease in *Halsey* v. *Lowenfeld*, and that, apart from certain special cases to be mentioned, the mere outbreak of war does not abrogate a contract between a British insurance company and an enemy,[4] whatever its later fate may be, bearing in mind that the word 'enemy' is used in the territorial sense.

DEATH BY BRITISH BELLIGERENT ACTION

Quite apart from the previous submissions, the question arises whether a contract of insurance, otherwise valid so far as concerns the effect of war thereon, and not lapsed by reason of non-payment of premiums, may become void, either wholly or only in respect of certain risks, by reason of its tendency regarded from the point of view of public policy.[5] Let us consider the following cases.

[1] A statutory right to a surrender value exists in the case of policies of industrial assurance in the circumstances described in the Industrial Assurance Act, 1923: see Macgillivray, § 339.   [2] In the *Ertel Bieber* case [1918] A.C. 260, at p. 269. See above, p. 118.

[3] See Lord Reading C.J. in *Halsey* v. *Lowenfeld* [1916] 2 K.B. 707, 713.

[4] In pp. 266–73 of the third edition of this book some attempt was made to apply these conclusions.

[5] In the case of a policy upon the life of, say, Hitler or Mussolini it would have been interesting to refer to the well-known case of the wager upon the life of Napoleon Bonaparte: *Gilbert* v. *Sykes* (1812). As to the legality of a clause in a policy issued by a British company to a British subject which makes it void if he engages in military service outside the United Kingdom, see *Duckworth* v. *Scottish Widows Fund* (1917).

(a) Before the outbreak of the War of 1939 to 1945 a British insurance company issued to a German national a policy upon his life which covered the risk of death as a combatant. Upon the outbreak of war he is embodied in the German armed forces and, before the next premium has become due, he is killed in action by British forces. Do the marine insurance cases already discussed afford any support for the view that the policy is not enforceable, either during or after the war, on the ground that it would be absurd to allow a British company to pay an indemnity against the consequences of British belligerent action?[1] We suggest that, while there was good reason in the old cases for applying this doctrine to a marine policy, the case for its application to a life policy is not so strong.[2] An enemy shipowner or merchant would be encouraged to expose his ship or cargo to the risks of British capture if he knew that he would be indemnified after the war by a British insurance company. The German combatant is compelled by law to expose himself to the risk of death by enemy action and is unlikely to be affected by the knowledge that a British insurance company will pay the sum insured to

[1] Macgillivray, § 562.
[2] The effect of death resulting from the hostile action of a co-belligerent with Great Britain is probably the same as in the case of death by British belligerent action: see above, p. 260.

Note on Administrative Arrangements made during and after the War of 1939 to 1945.

The United Kingdom being a world market for insurance and re-insurance contracts it is not surprising that the War of 1939 to 1945 gave rise to a mass of complicated problems which could more conveniently be dealt with by administration, particularly by the Custodian of Enemy Property, and by the Peace Treaties and similar agreements rather than be left to the courts to deal with as and when litigation might arise.

We are not aware of any publication which describes the administrative machinery established to deal with this problem, and we can only say that British insurance interests were in close contact with the Board of Trade and the Custodian of Enemy Property and that one of the operating factors was the conservation of the goodwill of British underwriters and companies in their relations with foreign policy-holders, in so far as that was consistent with the prevention of any benefit accruing to enemies during the war.

The Insurance Contracts (War Settlement) Act, 1952, section 1, empowered the Crown to do all things necessary for carrying into effect (a) a certain agreement with Finland (T.S. no. 9, 1950) relating to contracts of insurance and re-insurance, and (b) 'any future Agreements between Her Majesty's Government in the United Kingdom and any foreign Government relating to contracts of insurance and reinsurance made by any persons who subsequently become enemies as the result of any war in which His late Majesty was engaged'.

An Order in Council made under this section could transfer to any specified person any rights and liabilities vested in a custodian of enemy property arising out of such contracts of insurance and re-insurance.

The following Orders in Council were made under this Act:

Finland	Statutory Instrument 1954 no. 1464.
Italy	Statutory Instrument 1954 no. 1463.
Germany	Statutory Instrument 1961 no. 1497.

The following may also be mentioned:

Trading with the Enemy (Custodian) (Amendment) (Insurance), no. 2 Order, 1945.
Distribution of German Enemy Property, no. 2 Order, 1951 no. 1899 and (Amendment) Order 1951, no. 1943.

his personal representatives. If the German national is a non-combatant and is merely exposed to the risk of incidental and unintentional killing as the result of British aerial bombardment, the case again is not so strong as that of the combatant, as it is not the aim of British belligerent action to kill non-combatants.

(*b*) Suppose that the policy referred to in (*a*) was issued not to the German national but to his creditor, a British national in this country. We see no reason why the risk of death by British belligerent action, intentional or unintentional, should become illegal upon the outbreak of war.[1] The same is probably true where the creditor policy-holder is an enemy national in this country.

(*c*) When before the outbreak of war a British insurance company has issued to a person who becomes an enemy a policy upon the life of a person who becomes an enemy, and the latter dies during the war, there appears to be no reason why the enemy policy-holder should not recover the sum insured after the war (if it has not been vested in the Custodian of Enemy Property or otherwise disposed of), unless the death was due to the belligerent action of the United Kingdom or its allies.[2]

III. FOREIGN PROCEEDINGS AGAINST BRITISH INSURANCE COMPANIES[3]

It will be convenient to deal here with a contingency which, though not peculiar to British insurance companies, is one to which they are exposed in an unusual degree by reason of the amount of foreign business transacted by them, namely, the possibility of being sued in a foreign country. Their operations in foreign countries may take a variety of forms. Amongst others,

(*a*) they may cause to be incorporated in a foreign country a company which is, legally speaking, an entirely independent corporation or entity owing its existence to the laws of the foreign country, though its operations may be controlled from the head office in Great Britain;

(*b*) they may establish in a foreign country a branch office or an agency which is not a separate legal entity but complies with any local law as to registration of particulars and establishment of a place for service of local proceedings, etc.;

---

[1] See Macgillivray, § 562.   [2] See, however, Macgillivray, § 560.

[3] See an Opinion given in 1917 by John Bassett Moore on the 'Legal Position of the United States Branches of Foreign Insurance Companies, their Lawful Continuance in Business during War and the Interests of their Policy Holders', in his *Collected Papers*, IV pp. 176–87; and Vance on *Insurance* (1951), pp. 148, 632–40, upon American law.

(*c*) they may issue from the head office policies containing a clause which gives jurisdiction to a foreign court and authorizes the service of process upon its agents in a foreign country or accepts the law of a foreign country.[1]

In any of these cases (*a*), (*b*) and (*c*) a number of questions can arise. What is to happen if the proper law of the contract as applied by the foreign court does not coincide with the law applied by an English Court as to the effect of war upon contracts of insurance, be it abrogation or some other effect? How far can the British company safely act in reliance upon English law?

These and similar questions can arise in English Courts (and probably also in Scottish Courts, but we cannot profess to speak of them) in two main ways:

(1) directly in an English action;

(2) indirectly in an English action brought upon a foreign judgment.[2]

(1) In most of these cases the judgment of the House of Lords in *Dynamit Actien-Gesellschaft* v. *Rio Tinto Co.*[3] will afford an answer. There their lordships had to consider what they called a 'German contract', a contract made in Germany in the German language by a German agent of the British principal, and containing an arbitration clause, which provided for the appointment of an umpire by the Chamber of Commerce of Frankfort-on-the-Main, and they were prepared to assume for the purposes of the argument, without deciding the point, that the contract must be construed according to German law. They had already held in the *Ertel Bieber* case[4] that a similar pre-war contract made between a British company and an enemy company, which they regarded as an 'English contract', became illegal and void upon the outbreak of war as involving intercourse with the enemy and was not saved by its suspension clause, which was contrary to English public policy as tending to benefit the enemy and injure Great Britain, and they now had to consider whether, if the 'German contract' was to be construed by German

---

[1] For an instance of a policy of a foreign company containing a clause stipulating that it should be construed according to English law, see *New York Life Insurance Co.* v. *Public Trustee* [1924] 2 Ch. 101, 106. See also *Prudential Assurance Co.* v. *Al Goumhouria Insurance Co. A.S.E. and Another* (*The Times*, 12 March 1960), which is not a war case but an 'other armed conflict' case arising out of the Suez crisis of the autumn of 1956, and illustrates the practice, required by some countries of foreign insurance companies carrying on business there, whereby the foreign company must deposit securities, together with blank transfers, for the purpose of covering their liabilities on policies; an interim injunction was granted at the instance of the Prudential Assurance Co. for the purpose of preventing the transfer to an Egyptian company of certain British Savings Bonds, but the action was later settled.

[2] See Cheshire, *Private International Law* (6th ed. 1961), ch. xvii (Foreign Judgments).

[3] [1918] A.C. 260, 292; Dicey, pp. 752, 762.   [4] [1918] A.C. 260, 267

law and if German law differed from English law and would uphold the contract, an English Court would follow suit. In particular, it appears to have been suggested, though no evidence was taken, that by German law the suspension clause would save the contract from abrogation. The House of Lords held that, whatever the relevant foreign law might say, an English Court could not uphold and enforce a contract which was contrary to English public policy.[1] There can be no doubt that the rules relating to contracts of insurance with persons who are or become enemies in the territorial sense fall within the scope of public policy, and that an insurance policy which is unenforceable, by reason of a state of war, when regarded as governed by English law is equally unenforceable in this country whatever the relevant rules of its proper law may be.

(2) But the enemy or ex-enemy may sue the British company in his own country or in a neutral country, either during or after the war, and obtain judgment. If the company has sufficient assets there, *cadit quaestio*. If not, the ex-enemy comes here after the war and seeks to enforce his judgment. In what circumstances, if any, will he succeed?

There seems to be no doubt that an ex-enemy would not be able to enforce in an English court a judgment obtained in such circumstances that the cause of action upon which it was obtained would be unenforceable in England for reasons of illegality or public policy.[2] In the case of contracts which English law treats as abrogated by the outbreak of war, the ground in some cases, i.e. those contracts whose performance would involve intercourse with the enemy, is sheer illegality, equivalent, as Willes J. has pointed out,[3] to a crime by statute (and probably also by common law); in other cases, for instance, the invalidity of a suspension clause as in the *Rio Tinto* cases, or of a restrictive clause as in *Zinc Corporation* v. *Hirsch*, the effect can more truly be ascribed to public policy.

In conclusion, it is necessary to bear in mind the possibility of an enemy policy-holder seeking to improve his position by assigning his policy to some person in a foreign country in which the British company has assets.

---

[1] See p. 302, where Lord Parker of Waddington cited Westlake, *Private International Law* (4th ed.), § 215: 'Where a contract conflicts with what are deemed in England to be essential public or moral interests, it cannot be enforced here notwithstanding that it may have been valid by its proper law'; and see the same in 7th ed. 1925, by Bentwich. Note also once more Willes J. in *Esposito* v. *Bowden* (1857) 7 El. & Bl. 763, 781: 'The force of a declaration of war is equal to that of an Act of Parliament prohibiting intercourse with the enemy except by the Queen's licence', and Lord Alvanley C.J. in *Furtado* v. *Rogers* (1802) 3 Bos. & P. 191, 198: 'if a man contract to do a thing which is afterwards prohibited by Act of Parliament, he is not bound by his contract....'.

[2] Dicey, Rule 185.   [3] Above, n. 1.

12

LEASES AND TENANCIES: PATENTS, DESIGNS, TRADE MARKS AND COPYRIGHTS

BIBLIOGRAPHY

Leases: Woodfall, *Landlord and Tenant* (26th ed.), §§ 323, 1275, 2207–8.

LEASES AND TENANCIES[1]

The operation of supervening impossibility in the case of leases, conveyances and mortgages was examined by Walford in an article entitled 'Impossibility and Property Law';[2] and it is proposed here to say very little upon the matter. The doctrine of frustration is predominantly a commercial doctrine and the Courts have so far declined to apply it to covenants in leases and tenancies.[3] When immovable property is involved, the fact that land is indestructible —unlike the buildings which rest upon it—appears to prevent a lessee, when called upon to pay rent or to repair a building in pursuance of his covenants, from pleading the destruction of the building as a defence; much less from pleading that the whole contract has thereby been frustrated.[4]

As regards leases, the following statement of the law may be quoted from paragraph 3 of the Report of the Committee on the Responsibility for the Repair of Premises Damaged by Hostilities:[5]

*Law in England relating to repairing leasehold property
suffering war damage*

3. The law in England as regards the rights and liabilities of landlord and tenant in the event of the demised premises being destroyed or damaged by or in consequence of hostilities is reasonably clear from the decisions in *Paradine* v. *Jane* (Aleyn 26), *Surplice* v. *Farnsworth* (7 Man. &

---

[1] As to leases made 'for the duration of the war' or in similar terms, see note 5 on p. 42 above.

[2] 57 *L.Q.R.* (1941), pp. 339–72.

[3] This principle is not yet settled: see below, p. 291, n. 4.

[4] See Walford, *op. cit.* at pp. 340, 341; at p. 345 he suggests that the reason why the doctrine of frustration does not apply to leases is that lessees are regarded as purchasers of an estate or interest in land and therefore exposed to 'the risk of any calamity which befalls the land or anything upon it'. And see *Eyre* v. *Johnson.*

[5] Cmd. 5934 of 1939.

G. 576), *Redmond* v. *Dainton* [1922] 2 K.B. 256 and *Matthey* v. *Curling* [1922] 2 A.C. 180 (see especially per Lord Atkinson at pp. 233 ff.)[1]...

The result of these cases is as follows:

(i) Damage to or destruction of leasehold property by the King's enemies or by the armed forces of the Crown does not relieve the lessee from his obligation to pay rent nor does it relieve either party from his obligation to perform a covenant to repair which will, if the damage is extensive enough to require it, extend to the complete rebuilding of the premises.

(ii) A lessee cannot compel his landlord who has entered into a covenant to repair specifically to perform his covenant nor does failure to repair by a landlord in accordance with his covenant absolve the tenant from liability for rent or entitle him to quit; the tenant, of course, has his action for damages.

(iii) In the absence of a covenant in the lease to repair, there is no obligation on either party to repair or rebuild in the case of damage or destruction by enemy action. This follows from the general rule that in the absence of a covenant the lessor has no obligation to repair and that the tenant's liability with regard to repairs is measured by the doctrine of waste. In no case does waste extend to repairing damage resulting from any cause such as fire or enemy action which is beyond the control of the tenant.

The matter is now regulated by the Landlord and Tenant (War Damage) Acts, 1939 and 1941.[2] Section 1 of the Act of 1939 relieved persons who are liable under any instrument or oral transaction for doing any repairs in relation to land (which includes buildings or work situated on, over or under land) from any liability to make good any 'war damage', an expression which has since been defined in section 80 of the War Damage Act, 1941. Section 11 of the Landlord and Tenant (War Damage) Amendment Act, 1941, provides (*inter alia*) that 'any express obligation to insure land against war damage shall be void and be deemed always to have been void' and that 'any obligation to insure land against fire or other risks shall be construed[3] as not including, and as never having included, an obligation to insure against war damage'.[4]

The indestructibility of land, coupled with the theoretical identification of buildings upon it with the land itself, might be an adequate

---

[1] But see the *Cricklewood* case, *infra*, in which *Matthey* v. *Curling* is discussed.

[2] Nothing in the Acts expressly limits their application to the 1939–45 war, and they would now appear to be permanent statutes. See Halsbury, *Laws of England* (3rd ed. Simonds), vol. 23, p. 692, n. (*s*).

[3] For the meaning, before this Act, of the expression 'loss or damage by fire' occurring in a covenant to insure, when fire is caused by enemy incendiary bombs, see *Enlayde Ltd* v. *Roberts*.

[4] This section is retrospective: *In re Moorgate Estates Ltd.*

reason for not discharging a lease when subsequently it becomes physically impossible to enjoy the buildings because they are destroyed or rendered uninhabitable. But something more is required to explain the refusal of the Courts to apply the doctrine of frustration to leases. That 'something more' consists of the fact that the legal character of a lease, including even a tenancy agreement, is twofold: it is both a contract and a conveyance: it creates both rights *in personam* and rights *in rem*. In the words of Lush J. in *London and Northern Estates Co.* v. *Schlesinger*:[1]

It is not correct to speak of this tenancy agreement as a contract and nothing more. A term of years was created by it and vested in the appellant, and I can see no reason for saying that because this Order disqualified him from personally residing in this flat, it affected the chattel interest which was vested in him by virtue of the agreement.

The tenancy began before the outbreak of war and was for three years; the event alleged to frustrate the contract was that the premises were situate in a prohibited area, in which the tenant, on becoming an alien enemy, was unable to reside. This decision was followed by Lord Reading C.J. in *Whitehall Court Ltd* v. *Ettlinger*, where two residential flats (apparently unfurnished) were let after the outbreak of war for a term of three years and were later requisitioned by the War Department. *Matthey* v. *Curling*[2] concerned a pre-war lease for twenty-one years of a house and land of which a Competent Military Authority took possession in January 1918; a year later the house was destroyed by fire. Among the many grounds upon which the Court of Appeal and the House of Lords held that the lessee was not excused from performance of his covenants to pay rent and to repair, approval was expressed of the two earlier decisions. In *Swift* v. *Macbean*[3] Birkett J. declined to apply the doctrine of frustration to a pre-war tenancy of a furnished house which was stipulated not to begin unless and until Great Britain became involved in war and to terminate with the cessation of hostilities; the house was requisitioned by the Ministry of Health in March 1941.[4] Tucker J. in *Pelepah*

---

[1] [1916] 1 K.B. 20, 24.

[2] See also *Walton Harvey Ltd* v. *Walker and Homfrays Ltd*.

[3] See Landlord and Tenant (Requisitioned Land) Act, 1942.

[4] In *Cricklewood Property and Investment Trust Ltd* v. *Leighton's Investment Trust Ltd*, the House of Lords was invited to apply the doctrine of frustration to a building lease for 99 years. It became unnecessary to settle the principle thus raised, and the House of Lords was divided upon it. See also the discussion of this case by the Privy Council in *Hangkam Kwingtong Woo* v. *Liu Lan Fong*; and for another case on a lease where the doctrine was evoked, see *Jennings and Chapman Ltd* v. *Woodman, Matthews & Co.* In the absence of a decision by the House of Lords the decisions of the Court of Appeal, holding

Valley (Johore) Rubber Estates Ltd v. *Sungei Besi Mines Ltd*[1] declined to apply the doctrine to a mining lease the lessee's enjoyment of which had been affected by enemy occupation.

The line of distinction between a true demise or letting, as in the cases discussed, and a licence to occupy premises for a brief period, as in *Taylor* v. *Caldwell* and *Krell* v. *Henry*, is not always easy to draw.

If the doctrine of frustration which is in principle applicable to contracts is in fact not applicable to contracts for leases largely because of the proprietary interest created by a lease, it may be that other rules normally applicable to contracts are similarly subject to some modification in their application to contracts for leases. Where a lease is entered into in time of peace and, upon the outbreak of war, the lessee becomes an enemy in the territorial sense, abrogation —the effect of the outbreak of war on most contracts when one party becomes an enemy[2]—seemed inappropriate. Accordingly, the Court of Appeal, in *Halsey* v. *Lowenfeld*, held that where the further performance of the contract involved no unlawful intercourse with the enemy (namely, where the only substantive obligations under the lease which remain to be performed are those to be performed by the enemy alien lessee and the performance of those obligations requires no unlawful concurrence by the lessor—the mere receipt of rent not constituting unlawful concurrence) the contract is not determined and the lessee remains liable to pay rent during the war under the covenants in the lease. This does not mean that the lessee could have sued the lessor during the war, for he would have been defeated by the plea of alien enemy; but it does show that the outbreak of war did not dissolve the contract. It was manifestly to the benefit of this country that the lessor should receive the rent, which the Trading with the Enemy Proclamation of September 9, 1914 (probably declaratory in this respect), allowed. Lord Reading C.J. upheld[3] 'the continued validity of the lease at [*scilicet* after] the outbreak of war', and rejected the contention 'that a lessee who has become an alien enemy is released from all obligations undertaken before the war' —provided, of course, that the Crown does not deprive him of his property. It would seem to follow that after the end of the war the

that the doctrine of frustration cannot apply to a lease, still stand: *Denman* v. *Brise* [1949] 1 K.B. 22, 26–28 (C.A.); *Cusack-Smith* v. *London Corporation* [1956] 1 W.L.R. 1368, 1373 (both cases involving destruction of leased premises by enemy action).

[1] For an account of the treatment of leases in Malaya as a result of the 1939–45 war, see Das, *Japanese Occupation and Ex Post Facto Legislation in Malaya*, pp. 119–23.

[2] See above, p. 122.

[3] [1916] 2 K.B. 707, 713.

lease (if the term had not expired and the lease had not been for-feited) would continue.

Is the position any different if the further performance of the contract involves unlawful intercourse between the lessor and the enemy lessee? Warrington L.J., in *Halsey* v. *Lowenfeld*, seems to have been of the view that unlawful intercourse would render the contract illegal and discharge both parties from their obligations. Lord Reading C.J., on the other hand, considered[1] that the lessee retains his liability to perform his obligations under the contract: 'it would be manifestly absurd that he should derive the advantage of holding the property[2] without liability to perform the obligations incident to his right of ownership. For example, if a freehold is held by him subject to a restrictive covenant not to build within a period of years, can it be said that the consequences of war are that the alien enemy is allowed to remain the owner of the estate but is freed from the obligations of the covenant? If the contract is dissolved as contended, the estate would be freed for ever from the burden of the covenant.'[3] In *Edward H. Lewis & Son Ltd* v. *Morelli*[4] the question was whether a lease granted in 1926 remained in existence after the outbreak of war when the lessee became an enemy alien. Denning J. held that the lessee could not fulfil the covenants in the lease without committing the illegality involved in having intercourse with the enemy, with the result that the lessor, after the outbreak of war, became in a position to forfeit the lease (which in the circumstances he was held to have done). This too would imply that the contract was not automatically dissolved on the outbreak of war. If the lessor had chosen not to forfeit the lease it would seem that, notwithstanding that the contract was one performance of which during the war would have involved unlawful intercourse with the enemy, at the end of the war that contract would still be in existence and the lease would continue on the basis of its terms.[5]

PATENTS, DESIGNS, TRADE MARKS,
AND COPYRIGHT

The law relating to patents, designs, trade marks and copyright is a very specialized study, and the reader will wish to consult authoritative

---

[1] At p. 713. [2] Because, in principle, the property is not confiscated.

[3] In the case of a lease, there would be total obscurity as to the terms on which the alien after the war held his lease.

[4] [1948] 1 All E.R. 433 (reversed on different facts, [1948] 2 All E.R. 1021).

[5] In *Porter* v. *Freudenberg* the defendant, a tenant, became an alien enemy on the outbreak of war; see above, p. 134, n. 3.

works on these subjects on points of detail. We shall here only draw attention to a few salient points.

Patents, designs, trade marks and copyrights are items of property, and an enemy owner of such property is no more automatically divested of his title to it by the outbreak of war than is the enemy owner of any other property.[1] At the end of the war the property will in principle still belong to him.[2] However, to ensure the continued validity of a patent, trade mark or design, renewal fees have to be paid, and the procedure for the payment of such fees by an enemy during a war would involve unlawful intercourse with the enemy: during the 1939–45 war the Board of Trade licensed the payment in certain circumstances of renewal fees in respect of a patent, design or trade mark owned by an enemy, and also their payment on behalf of British subjects or allied nationals (or a body of persons controlled by such persons) who were enemies merely through being resident in enemy-occupied territory.[3] Under section 4 of the Patents, Designs, Copyright and Trade Marks (Emergency) Act, 1939,[4] it is even lawful for a patent to be granted and for a trade mark or design to be registered on the application of an enemy (i.e. during a war), although in that event the patent or the rights conferred by the registration are forthwith subject to the statutory provisions relating to enemy property. Rules were made laying down, *inter alia*, procedures whereby such applications might be made,[5] and by a General Licence[6] the Board of Trade permitted such communications with enemies and such acts for or on behalf of or in relation to enemies as may have been necessary to enable those procedures to be carried out. The Patents, Designs, Copyright and Trade Marks (Emergency) Act, 1939, furthermore permits the Comptroller-General of Patents, Designs and Trade Marks to extend various time limits having regard to circumstances arising from the existence of a state of war, even though this might benefit the enemy.[7]

---

[1] See below, pp. 329 ff. For comment on the seizure of enemy patents in the United States of America during the 1914–18 and 1939–45 wars, see Holtzoff, 26 *A.J.* (1932), p. 272 and Borchard, 37 *A.J.* (1943), p. 92.

[2] Subject, of course, to any provisions of the peace settlement. After the 1939–45 war, the Treaties of Peace with Italy, Roumania, Bulgaria, Hungary and Finland (T.S. nos. 50, 52–5 (1948)), and with Japan (T.S. no. 33 (1952)), and the Austrian State Treaty (T.S. no. 58 (1957)) contained provisions relating to Industrial, Literary and Artistic Property. See also the Enemy Property Act, 1953, Part II. *In re Hicklin* is an example of an enemy-owned patent still belonging to the enemy even during the war.

[3] S.R. & O. 1942, no. 2104.

[4] The Act is a permanent statute, although its operation depends (see section 10 (1)) upon there being persons who fulfil the definition of 'enemy' and 'enemy subject' in the Trading with the Enemy Act, 1939.   [5] S.R. & O. 1939, no. 1375.

[6] S.R. & O. 1940, no. 181.   [7] Section 6. See also the Patents Act, 1957, section 3.

During the war the enemy owner's enjoyment of his patent, design, copyright or trade mark is of course considerably affected, principally by his property being subject to the Trading with the Enemy Act, 1939.[1] Thus in *R. J. Reuter Co. Ltd* v. *Mulhens* the Court of Appeal held that under section 7 of that Act an enemy-owned trade mark could properly be vested in the Custodian of Enemy Property and could subsequently be assigned by him. Furthermore, the Comptroller-General of Patents, Designs and Trade Marks has power to grant licences under enemy-owned patents, designs and copyrights to persons who are not enemies or enemy subjects,[2] and to suspend the trade mark rights of an enemy or enemy subject.[3]

An enemy owner of a patent, design or copyright may, before the outbreak of war, have granted in favour of a person resident in the United Kingdom or Isle of Man a licence under a patent or for the application of a registered design or granting an interest in a copyright. To prevent any such licence being rendered invalid on the outbreak of war, section 1 of the Patents, Designs, Copyright and Trade Marks (Emergency) Act, 1939, provides that such licence, notwithstanding the Trading with the Enemy Act, 1939, or any rule of law relating to dealings with or for the benefit of enemies, is not invalidated by reason only of the enemy ownership of the patent, design or copyright, nor is any contract in so far as it relates to such a licence invalidated just because a party to it is an enemy.[4]

The converse situation might also arise, where an owner in the United Kingdom of a patent has before the outbreak of a war granted to a person who becomes an enemy permission to use the patented invention in consideration of the periodic payment of a fee. While the continued receipt by the owner of the patent of fees from an enemy might not in itself be unlawful,[5] the contract between them would seem to be of a kind to which the outbreak of the war would put an end.[6]

The Crown has certain rights to make use of patented inventions and registered designs in connection with hostilities. Government departments may make use of any patented invention or registered design for 'the services of the Crown'. This phrase includes the

---

[1] See also the Patents and Designs Act, 1946, section 4.

[2] Patents, Designs, Copyright and Trade Marks (Emergency) Act, 1939, section 2. See *Novello & Co.* v. *Hinrichsen Edition Ltd*; *In re Farbenindustrie A.G.'s Agreement*.

[3] Section 3.

[4] But any grant or assignment of such a licence or contract is not validated if it was made during the war and is unlawful under the normal laws relating to trading with the enemy, nor may the contract be performed in a manner contrary to those laws.

[5] See below, p. 353. [6] See above, p. 122.

supply to the government of any country outside the United Kingdom, in pursuance of an agreement or arrangement between the governments of this country and that other country, of articles required for the defence of that country or of any other country whose government is party to any agreement or arrangement with Her Majesty's Government in respect of defence matters; it also includes the supply to the United Nations or to the government of a member state, in pursuance of an agreement or arrangement between Her Majesty's Government and the United Nations or that other government, of articles required for any armed forces operating in pursuance of a resolution of the United Nations.[1] The Crown may also during any period of emergency make use of a patented invention or registered design as may be necessary, *inter alia*, for the efficient prosecution of any war in which Her Majesty may be engaged, and for assisting the relief of suffering and the restoration and distribution of essential supplies and services in any part of Her Majesty's dominions or any foreign countries that are in grave distress as a result of war.[2]

Lastly we may mention that while the term of a patent is normally sixteen years from the date of the patent,[3] the term may upon the application of the patentee be extended for any period not exceeding ten years if the patentee[4] has as such suffered loss or damage (including loss of opportunity of dealing in or developing the invention) 'by reason of hostilities between His Majesty and any foreign state'.[5] No such extension may be made on the application of a person who is a subject of that foreign state[6] or of a company or business managed or controlled by such persons or carried on wholly or mainly for the benefit of or on behalf of such persons,[7] even if the company is registered within Her Majesty's dominions.[8]

---

[1] Patents Act, 1949, section 46, and paragraph 1 of the First Schedule to the Registered Designs Act, 1949, both as amended by the Defence Contracts Act, 1958, section 1.

[2] Patents Act, 1949, section 49, and paragraph 4 of the First Schedule to the Registered Designs Act, 1949.

[3] Patents Act, 1949, section 22.

[4] Or an exclusive licensee: section 25.

[5] Section 24 (1). In *Re Harshaw Chemical Co's Patent* this provision was held not to be applicable to the Korean conflict, since North Korea was not a 'foreign State' at any relevant time.

[6] See *In re Mangold's Patent* (and note in 28 *B.Y.* (1951), p. 406) for the application of this provision to a former Austrian national resident in England, who was held to have acquired German nationality upon the German annexation of Austria in 1938; and also *Lowenthal* v. *A.G.* for the case of German Jews in England who had allegedly been divested by Germany of their German nationality during the war.

[7] See *In re Rice Springs Letters Patent*; *Re Ezio Giacchino's Patent*; *In re La Précision Mécanique's Application.*   [8] Section 24 (8).

13

SALE OF GOODS

BIBLIOGRAPHY

Campbell, *Law of War and Contract* (1918), index, 'Sale of Goods'.
Webber, *Effect of War on Contracts* (2nd ed. 1946), ch. IX.
Benjamin on *Sale*, 8th ed. 1950 (Finnemore and James), pp. 565–80.

We shall discuss this contract under the following headings:

(1) Illegality;
(2) Special position of c.i.f. contracts;
(3) Effect of governmental action;
(4) Frustration; and
(5) Cancellation clauses;

though we shall find that it is not always possible to disentangle (1) and (3), or (1) and (4), when present in the same case.

Some cases arising out of the Suez crisis in 1956 have been discussed in chapter 5.

(1) ILLEGALITY

At common law it is both criminal and illegal to sell goods to or buy them from an enemy, and under the Trading with the Enemy Act, 1939 (subsection 2 of section 1) 'a person shall be deemed to have traded with the enemy (*a*) if [*inter alia*] he has (i) supplied any goods to or for the benefit of an enemy,[1] or obtained any goods from an enemy, or traded in, or carried, any goods consigned to or from an enemy or destined for or coming from enemy territory...';[2] but 'a person shall not be deemed to have traded with the enemy by reason only that he has...(ii) received payment from an enemy of a sum of money due in respect of a transaction under which all obligations on the part of the person receiving payment had already been performed when the payment was received, and had been performed at a time when the person from whom the payment was received was not an enemy'.

---

[1] As defined in section 2 of the Act as amended (see below, p. 351). 'Enemy' included the many hundreds of persons whose names appeared on the Statutory Lists issued by the Board of Trade in pursuance of subsection 2 of section 2 of the Act. See also the definition of 'German enemy' in section 12 of the Enemy Property Act, 1953.

[2] As defined in section 15 of the Act as amended (see below, p. 352).

A person who is 'deemed to have traded with the enemy' for the purposes of the Act is liable to the penalties prescribed by the Act, and the provisions quoted apply to acts committed during a war in pursuance of a contract made either before or during the war.

A contract which is made during the war and offends either the common law or any statutory provision is illegal and void *ab initio*. A pre-war contract the performance, or further performance, of which would offend either the common law or any statutory provision is dissolved upon the outbreak of war, with a reservation of any right of action which may already have accrued from a breach of any of its terms.[1]

Sale of goods being the commonest commercial transaction, the Wars of 1914 to 1918 and 1939 to 1945 furnished a multitude of decisions. Any doubt which may have existed in 1914 as to the effect of the outbreak of war upon the simple case of an executory contract[2] for the sale of goods wherein one party became an enemy in the territorial sense or some other intercourse with the enemy was involved in its performance, was soon dispelled by early Trading with the Enemy Proclamations. Accordingly most of the reported decisions contain some further element which could be plausibly advanced as a ground for excluding this effect. In April 1915 in *W. Wolf & Sons* v. *Carr, Parker & Co.*[3] the Court of Appeal had no difficulty in holding that pre-war contracts between British vendors (the defendants) and German purchasers (the plaintiffs) resident and having their principal place of business in Germany were abrogated by the outbreak of war;[4] the only question seriously argued before the Court of Appeal being whether paragraph 6 of the Trading with the Enemy Proclamation No. 2 of 9 September 1914 saved the transaction and enabled the plaintiffs in virtue of their branch in Manchester to sue.[5]

Suspension clauses

One of the commonest elements which are invoked to avert the dissolution of a contract of sale is a suspension clause. To these clauses we have already referred in the discussion of general principles,[6] for

---

[1] Above, ch. 4. [2] Upon the meaning of this term, see above, pp. 118, 127.

[3] Nor does the appointment by the Board of Trade of a controller to wind up the enemy business revive a dissolved contract: *In re Coutinho Caro & Co.*

[4] It was unnecessary to discuss the effect of war upon certain pre-war breaches of the contracts. In *Jager* v. *Tolme and Runge,* the illegality was due to the fact that upon the outbreak of war the subject-matter of the sale was in an enemy port.

[5] On this point see *Schering A.G.* v. *Pharmedica Property Ld.* (licence to trade).

[6] P. 128.

they also occur in other contracts. During the years preceding 1914 the shadow of war cast a deepening shade upon the commercial community of Europe, and business men sought to diminish the dislocating effects of war by inserting in their contracts clauses providing for the suspension of acts of performance, or at any rate the main acts of performance such as delivery and payment, during war or a war between named countries until the war was concluded, hoping thereby to preserve their contracts until better days should come. As we have already seen,[1] a group of these cases was reviewed by the House of Lords in three decisions in which the respondents were the *Rio Tinto Co.*, a British company, and the appellants were three German companies, *Ertel Bieber & Co.*, *Dynamit Actien-Gesellschaft*, and *Vereinigte Koenigs and Laurahuette Actien-Gesellschaft fuer Bergbau and Huettenbetrieb*, the two last being distinguished from the first by the fact that in them the contract was made in Germany in the German language by a German agent of the British company, a distinction which, so it was unsuccessfully argued, made it necessary to apply German law to the contracts with a result differing from that which governed the *Ertel Bieber* case.[2]

In all three cases there were long-term contracts for the supply of ore by the British company to the German companies over a period of years, such as from February 1911 to November 1914, from February 1915 to November 1919, and from 1912 to 1918, and the contracts contained clauses (similar but not identical) which provided that if, in the event of strikes, war or any other cause over which the sellers had no control, or in all cases of *force majeure* including war, the sellers were prevented from shipping or delivering the ore, the obligation to ship and/or deliver and the corresponding obligation to take delivery should be suspended during the continuance of the impediment and for a reasonable time thereafter or for the duration of the effects of the impediment. The intention was that upon the cessation of the impediment and its effects the obligations should once more attach and performance should be resumed. The House of Lords, considering that the war which broke out between Great Britain and Germany on 4 August 1914 was one of the contemplated impediments, held (briefly) (1) that, even if the suspension clauses were adequate to suspend deliveries, they did not suspend certain other obligations such as arbitration, declaration of quantities and

---

[1] Pp. 128 ff.

[2] Another distinction turned upon the interpretation of the Legal Proceedings against Enemies Act, 1915, which we need not pursue.

character, which must or might involve the mischief of intercourse with the enemy during the war, and (2) that, even if the suspension clauses were apt to suspend the entire operation of the contracts during the war, and thus exclude all intercourse, they were contrary to public policy and void on the ground that they crippled the trading resources and operations of Great Britain by tying the hands of British traders and enhanced the resources of the enemy by ensuring to him after the war the resumption of his supply of raw materials. 'It increases the resources of the enemy, for if the enemy knows that he is contractually sure of getting the supply as soon as the war is over, that not only allows him to denude himself of present stocks, but it represents a present value which may be realized by means of assignation to neutral countries.'[1]

The second and third cases raised a point on the conflict of laws,[2] which has already been referred to but may be stated again: even if it were true that the German contracts and the circumstances of their making attracted German law for their interpretation, and even if a German Court would hold that they were not contrary to German public policy, they could not be enforced by an English Court because to do so would be contrary to English rules of public policy. 'It is illegal for a British subject to become bound in a manner which sins against the public policy of the King's realm.'[3]

Two further questions arise on suspension clauses. (1) The effect of a suspension clause of this kind often arises in the case of contracts one party to which becomes an enemy in the territorial sense upon the outbreak of war. Suppose, however, the case of such a clause in a contract between two British subjects or between a British subject and a friendly alien involving the delivery of goods to an enemy. The mischief is the same, and it is submitted with confidence that the answer is the same. The contract is dissolved.

(2) The effect of a suspension clause of this kind in a contract for the sale of goods has often arisen where the goods are to be supplied *to* the enemy.[4] Suppose, however, a contract for goods to be supplied *by* the enemy. It is submitted that the mischief is the same and the answer is the same. To secure to the enemy a post-war market for his goods confers a present benefit upon him and, where the goods

---

[1] Per Lord Dunedin [1918] A.C. at p. 275. For comment upon this doctrine, see above, p. 129.

[2] Above, p. 132. See also *Rossie* v. *Garvan*, an American case on a partnership.

[3] Per Lord Dunedin [1918] A.C. at p. 294.

[4] Or, as in the *Clapham Steamship Co.'s* case, the use of a ship by enemy charterers after the war.

are to be delivered in this country, may impose a detriment upon the British trader by tying his hands and preventing him from obtaining the goods in question from another source or upon more advantageous terms during or after the war.[1]

Alternative to illegal performance

Although for the reason stated the Courts decline to give effect to an attempt to save an otherwise dissolved contract by means of a suspension clause, no objection is taken to a stipulation—in a contract neither party to which becomes an enemy—whereby upon the outbreak of war an offending term is cancelled and an innocent term substituted therefor. As Lord Cozens-Hardy M.R. said in *Smith, Coney & Barrett* v. *Becker, Gray & Co.*:[2] 'Putting it shortly it was this: "I sell you a lot of sugar at Hamburg to be delivered f.o.b. either on board ship or in warehouse, or if by reason of war that cannot be done, I will pay you a sum of cash." What is the difficulty? There is no illegality at all. It is a contract with two branches, two alternatives: "If I cannot deliver you the specific goods I will pay you a sum of cash." On the face of the contract that is its true construction and effect, and there is absolutely nothing in the contention of illegality.' Thus a pre-war contract between two wholly British firms for the delivery of sugar f.o.b. Hamburg, which contained a clause cancelling delivery 'in the event of Germany being involved in a war with either England [*sic*], France, Russia and/or Austria' and substituting a Clearing House arrangement whereby the contract was closed at an average quotation calculated in a certain manner, was held to be not illegal, and the substituted money equivalent could be awarded by an arbitrator if upon the true construction of the contract it was due.[3]

Somewhat similar are the cases of contracts which give to one party the right of choosing one of several modes of performance, e.g. the

---

[1] The following are also cases involving suspension clauses: *Ebbw Vale Steel, Iron & Coal Co.* v. *Macleod & Co.*; *Zinc Corporation Ltd* v. *Hirsch*; *Blythe & Co.* v. *Richards, Turpin & Co.*; *Bolckow, Vaughan & Co.* v. *Compania Minera de Sierra Minera*; *North-Eastern Steel C.* v. *Same*; *C. S. Wilson & Co.* v. *Tennants (Lancashire), Ltd*; *S. Instone & Co.* v. *Speeding, Marshall & Co.*; *Peter Dixon & Sons Ltd* v. *Henderson, Craig & Co.*; *Ertel Bieber & Co.* v. *Rio Tinto Co.*; *Fried. Krupp A.G.* v. *Orconera Iron Ore Co.*; *Naylor, Benzon & Co.* v. *Krainische Industrie Gesellschaft*.

[2] [1916] 2 Ch. 86, 92. *Jager* v. *Tolme and Runge* is another Clearing House case.

[3] *Ibid.* For the case of an unsuccessful attempt by one party *after the outbreak of war* to substitute a lawful place of performance for an unlawful one, namely, a non-enemy place of delivery of goods for one which had become unlawful by reason of enemy occupation, see *Fibrosa Spolka Akcyjna* v. *Fairbairn Lawson Combe Barbour, Ltd*, discussed later, p. 302. For an instance of a clause in a charterparty substituting in the event of a war breaking out, a lawful for an unlawful port, see *Avery* v. *Bowden*.

right, in a contract for the sale of goods, of naming one of several ports of delivery. In *Hindley & Co.* v. *General Fibre Co.*,[1] under a pre-war contract of sale of jute made between two British companies, the buyer had the right to name Hamburg, Bremen, Rotterdam or Antwerp as the port of delivery. The effect of the outbreak of war was to delete from the contract Hamburg and Bremen but not to destroy the contract, because it could still be performed in a lawful manner; the buyer (for some reason not apparent) named Bremen on 11 September 1939; the seller claimed that in consequence of that nomination the contract must be regarded as cancelled, but the Court treated the nomination as a nullity and allowed the buyer to substitute Antwerp and, the seller having declined to deliver at Antwerp, the buyer recovered damages for breach of contract. In *Fibrosa Spolka Akcyjna* v. *Fairbairn Lawson Combe Barbour Ltd*,[2] there was a contract, made in July 1939, that is, before the outbreak of war, between a British company and a Polish company for the supply by the British company of machinery to the Polish company to be delivered c.i.f. at the Polish port of Gdynia in or about October 1939. The Germans having occupied Gdynia on 23 September 1939, the buyers expressed their willingness to take delivery at either Riga or at Leeds. The sellers nevertheless threw up the contract on the ground that as from 23 September performance had become illegal, and an action was brought by the buyers for specific performance and/or damages and for the return of £1000 already paid. Tucker J. and the Court of Appeal held that the obligation to deliver at Gdynia was not a term inserted solely for the benefit of the buyers and capable of being waived by them; that the buyers' claim to be able to substitute another place of delivery had no foundation in law; and that the contract was frustrated, with the consequence, illustrated by *Chandler* v. *Webster*, that the loss must lie where it fell and the sum of £1000 could not be recovered. The House of Lords, however, while agreeing that the contract was frustrated, overruled *Chandler* v. *Webster* and held, for reasons that have already been discussed,[3] that the sum of £1000 could be recovered as money paid the consideration for which had wholly failed.[4]

---

[1] Much reliance being placed upon *The Teutonia*.
[2] See now Law Reform (Frustrated Contracts) Act, 1943, above, pp. 182–4.
[3] Pp. 182–4.
[4] Upon the unsuccessful argument in the Court of Appeal that there could be no frustration of a contract containing a clause expressly providing for the contingency which arose, see above, pp. 181 and 186.

Restrictive covenant in favour of the enemy

So far we have been considering executory contracts of sale which involve positive intercourse with the enemy. There is, however, another, a negative, aspect of the matter. A pre-war contract with the enemy may involve no intercourse with him at all, but may help Great Britain's enemy by placing a restriction upon the trading activities of a British subject. In *Zinc Corporation Ltd* v. *Hirsch* a long-term contract resembling those which were present in the *Rio Tinto* cases contained a clause which provided that 'The sellers shall not so long as this agreement shall be in force sell any zinc concentrates to any person or persons firm or firms or corporation or corporations other than the [German] buyers'. The Court of Appeal held that, quite apart from the suspension clause contained in the contract, this clause sufficed to vitiate the contract, because it tied the hands of a British subject and prevented him from using his resources for the benefit of his country and was therefore contrary to public policy. The decision of the Court of Appeal in this case was approved by the House of Lords in the *Rio Tinto* cases, but as the contracts in those cases did not contain a restrictive clause of the kind quoted above, it cannot be said that the decision was *specifically* approved on this point. There can, however, be no doubt that approval of it is carried by the general principle enunciated in the House of Lords in holding that a contract with an enemy which cripples the trading resources and operations of a British subject to the detriment of his country, is void.

Might not the same point arise in a case like the famous *Nordenfelt* case[1] if a British vendor of the goodwill of an armament or any other business to a firm which became an enemy had covenanted not to be engaged in a similar business for a period of twenty-five years?

(2) C.I.F. CONTRACTS

The classic definition of a C.I.F. contract is that of Hamilton J. (as Lord Sumner then was) in *Biddell Brothers* v. *E. Clemens Horst & Co.*[2] in a judgment which was supported by the minority judgment of Kennedy L.J. in the Court of Appeal and affirmed by the House of Lords. But a modern description of this type of contract may be

---

[1] Nordenfelt was a Swede.
[2] [1911] 1 K.B. 214, 220 cited by Warrington L.J. [1916] 1 K.B. at p. 513 (printed in previous editions).

more useful. In the current edition of Scrutton's *Charterparties and Bills of Lading*,[1] we are told that

In a contract for the sale of goods upon 'c.i.f.' terms, the contract, unless otherwise expressed, is for the sale of goods to be carried by sea, and the seller performs his part by shipping goods of the contractual description on board a ship to the contractual destination, or purchasing afloat goods so shipped, and tendering within a reasonable time after shipment, the shipping documents [a bill of lading, a policy of insurance and an invoice], to the purchaser the goods during the voyage being at the risk of the purchaser.

It will be noted that performance of a c.i.f. contract involves the bringing into existence by the seller of two subsidiary contracts, affreightment and insurance.

(*a*) A pre-war c.i.f. contract between British firms provided for the delivery of goods at Hamburg. The goods were shipped in Chile by a German vessel which was on the high seas when war with Germany broke out. At that moment further performance of the contract became illegal, and the contract was dissolved; the buyers could not call upon the sellers to tender the documents, nor could the sellers call upon the buyers to pay for the goods.[2] In two further cases[3] there were pre-war c.i.f. contracts between two pairs of firms who were British (or were treated as British) for the shipment of beans from neutral oriental ports to neutral European ports, Naples and Rotterdam. In both cases the beans were shipped before the war upon German vessels and insured against ordinary marine risks, in one case by an English policy, in the other case by a German policy. No question arose as to the ultimate destination of the goods in either case. Upon the outbreak of war both vessels made their way to ports of refuge. In both cases the sellers tendered the documents to their respective buyers at the appropriate date, namely, three months from dates of bills of lading, but those documents consisted in the one case of a German bill of lading and an English marine policy, in the other of a German bill of lading and a German marine policy. The point in which these cases go beyond *Duncan, Fox & Co.'s* case above discussed is that there the main contract itself, the contract of sale c.i.f., became illegal upon the outbreak of war because the destination was an enemy port; but in these cases it was one or both of the subsidiary contracts, whose existence is essential to performance of a c.i.f. contract, that became illegal. Shortly put,

---

[1] (17th ed. 1964, by W. L. McNair and Mocatta), Article 60, p. 173.

[2] *Duncan, Fox & Co.* v. *Schrempft & Bonke.*

[3] *Arnhold Karberg & Co.* v. *Blythe, Green, Jourdain & Co.*; *Theodor Schneider & Co.* v. *Burgett & Newsam.*

was their continued existence, their continued validity, up to the date of the tender of the documents embodying them essential? The Court of Appeal answered, Yes, and in consequence the buyer was entitled to refuse to accept the documents and to pay the price. They (or more strictly those relating to the contracts with enemy parties) had ceased to be valid and effective because the contracts embodied in them had been dissolved upon the outbreak of war as regards any future acts of performance. Moreover, the bills of lading were not merely invalid, but to carry out the obligations contained in them, the shipowner being an enemy, would be illegal.

The foregoing are cases where the c.i.f. contract, or one or both of the subsidiary contracts, became illegal upon the outbreak of war. We now come to the case where the effect of the outbreak of war upon the subsidiary contract of affreightment and by consequence upon the c.i.f. contract itself is to make them not illegal but impossible of performance. In the case of *In re Weis & Co. and Crédit Colonial et Commercial (Antwerp)*,[1] there was no question of the primary or the subsidiary contracts becoming illegal by reason of a party becoming an alien enemy, or of an illegal destination. A cargo on board a British ship, the subject of a c.i.f. contract, for delivery in Antwerp, was afloat when war broke out on 4 August 1914. On some date between the outbreak of war and 18 August the ship was captured on the high seas and taken to Hamburg. On 18 August the seller tendered to the buyer the shipping documents in London but he declined to take them up; at that date Antwerp had not fallen to the German forces and delivery there would have been lawful. Bailhache J. held that 'the fact that it became impossible to perform the contract did not prevent the tender of the documents from being valid', which, it is suggested, means that the seller's obligation under the contract was to tender valid documents, which he did, and the buyer's obligation to accept the documents was not rendered impossible by the capture of the ship.

(*b*) In the last case Bailhache J. pointed out that the real origin of the buyer's objection to accept the documents when tendered was that the policy of insurance merely covered marine risks and excluded war risks by means of the F.C. and S. clause. How does this question of insurance under a c.i.f. contract stand in relation to war? In a judgment already mentioned[2] Lord Sumner spoke of 'an insurance

---

[1] [1916] 1 K.B. 346, 350. No difficulty seems to have arisen from the facts that the sellers carried on business in London and Antwerp and the buyers were a Belgian company, and that Belgium was wholly occupied by Germany in December 1915 when the action was tried.　　　[2] P. 303: *Biddell Brothers* v. *E. Clemens Horst Co.*

upon the terms current in the trade' as an essential part of performance of a c.i.f. contract. Current at what point of time? At the date of shipment. In several cases it has been held or assumed that in the months preceding the outbreak of war insurance against war risks was not 'current in the trade', but this must always be a question of fact in each case. Moreover, it is always open to the buyer to supplement his protection against loss or damage by effecting a more comprehensive or different insurance himself.[1]

It can thus be said that decisions arising from the War of 1914 to 1918 helped to clarify the nature of the contract c.i.f. by showing that, while it is not true to say that it is a sale of documents rather than of goods,[2] it is a sale of goods to be performed by the tender of documents which are proper at the time of the making of the contract and valid and effective at the time when the tender is due—in spite of the fact, notorious when the tender is due, that as a result of enemy action the buyer will not be able to obtain the goods. We do not suggest that this was a new point because the result flows naturally from the nature of the contract, but the war decisions reinforced it.[3]

Finally, it must be noted that a contract is not necessarily a c.i.f. contract, thus attracting the legal consequences somewhat lightly indicated above, merely because the parties so describe it: 'the crucial question seems to me (Asquith L.J.) to be not what label can properly be attached to such a contract, but what the actual terms of these contracts were'.[4]

(3) EFFECT OF GOVERNMENTAL ACTION[5]

During war a Government is driven to take action of various kinds which may interfere with the performance of contracts for the sale of goods, notably requisition[6] and the prohibition or control of ex-

---

[1] C. Groom Ltd v. Barber [1915] 1 K.B. 310, which contains an interpretation of the expression 'War risk for buyer's account' occurring in a c.i.f. contract; there it was held to mean that 'war risk is the buyer's concern, and if he wants to cover war risk he must get it done' (p. 322).

[2] With regard to the dictum of Scrutton J. on this matter in [1915] 2 K.B. at p. 388, see the C.A. [1916] 1 K.B. 495 and p. 749 of Benjamin on Sale (8th ed.).

[3] On the Sale of Goods Act, 1893, section 32 (3) and Wimble Sons & Co. v. Rosenberg & Sons, see pp. 297–8 of the 3rd ed. of this book and Benjamin on Sale (8th ed.), pp. 736–40.

[4] In Comptoir d'Achat et de Vente v. Luis de Ridder Limitada, 177 L.T. 648, 653; approved [1949] A.C. 293, 321; the House of Lords held that there was a frustration of the adventure and that, as in the Fibrosa case, the buyers were entitled to recover the price upon a total failure of consideration.

[5] Whether legislative or executive, and whether under statutory or common law powers. There are numerous decisions on requisitioning and other war-time powers of Government: see vol. 39 of Halsbury's Laws of England (3rd ed. Simonds): 'War and Emergency'.

[6] E.g. Regulation 53 of the Defence (General) Regulations, 1939.

ports and imports. In some of the cases to be mentioned the goods forming the subject-matter of the contracts were specific, in some they were not. That does not form the basis of a useful distinction, though for obvious reasons it is easier to justify a breach of contract on the ground of governmental intervention when the goods are specific, but it is not impossible to do so when they are not.

There is no doubt that the intervention of Government has formed an element in a number of admittedly war 'frustration' cases. But it is submitted that McCardie J. was right when he surmised *obiter* in the *Blackburn Bobbin Co.'s* case[1] that we ought to place in a separate and independent category cases in which 'British legislation or Government intervention has removed the specific subject-matter of the construction [? contract] from the scope of private obligation', meaning, it is suggested, its permanent removal or its removal for such a time that it cannot become available again for the purposes of the contract. This class of case has a respectable ancestry, *Brewster* v. *Kitchell* in 1697 and *Baily* v. *De Crespigny* in 1869, and there is no reason why the more modern and more prolific 'frustration' stock should claim it as its own.[2] We must define the limits of the category. It cannot include all cases of governmental activity.

Re Shipton, Anderson & Co. and Harrison Brothers & Co.'s Arbitration may be regarded as typical. There was a sale (during a war) by one British firm to another, of a specific parcel of wheat. Six days later the British Government requisitioned the wheat, apparently under the Army (Supply of Food, Forage and Stores) Act, 1914, which was in force at the date of the sale. The wheat had not been delivered to the purchasers and the property had not passed. The Court, on a special case stated by the arbitrator, held that the seller was excused from performance of the contract. Nothing was said about frustration. Lord Reading C.J. uses the expression 'and bearing in mind also the principles laid down in *Krell* v. *Henry*', but *Baily* v. *De Crespigny* was relied upon and was clearly enough.

In *Lipton* v. *Ford*,[3] the seller was required by the Government in pursuance of a Defence of the Realm Regulation 'to place at the

---

[1] [1918] 1 K.B. at pp. 547, 548.

[2] In *Kursell* v. *Timber Operators and Contractors* (not a war case) Scrutton L.J. held that a contract for the sale of standing timber was frustrated by the nationalization of the forest by a foreign Government. On the question whether the doctrine of frustration can apply to a contract for the sale of land, see *Hillingdon Estates Co.* v. *Stonefield Estates Ltd*, where it should be noted that the equitable interest in the land with regard to which a compulsory order was made had already passed to the purchaser; Chitty on *Contracts* (22nd ed. 1961), para. 1213.

[3] See also *Brightman & Co. Ltd* v. *Tate*, and *Hudson's Bay Company* v. *Maclay*.

disposal of the Army Council 363 tons of raspberries', which was in effect the whole remainder of his growing crop of raspberries, and was thereby prevented from completing delivery under a contract made during the war to sell 'fifty tons Scotch raspberries (Blairgowrie)' to the plaintiff buyer, but they were not specific or required to be the produce of a particular farm and the contract would have been satisfied if the seller had been able to buy raspberries from other Blairgowrie growers, which he could not do. Atkin J., after dealing with a number of other points, including the validity of the requisition (which he construed as 'a notice of intention to take possession of the raspberries when gathered'), held that its effect was to prevent the seller from disposing of his crop when gathered except to the Government, that but for the requisition he 'would have distributed what raspberries he had after that date [i.e. the date of the requisition] in equal proportions [amongst a number of buyers] towards satisfaction of the amounts undelivered', and that therefore he was excused from delivering to the plaintiff buyer a certain proportion of the amount of raspberries which he was unable to deliver to him. A point which does not appear to have been argued is that the requisition was in fact induced by the buyer who intimated to the Government with whom he had contracted to sell a certain number of tons, that they would not get them unless they exercised their statutory power of requisitioning them.[1] In *Dale Steamship Co.* v. *Northern Steamship Co.*, it was held by the Court of Appeal that a contract for the sale by one shipowner to another of the skeleton of a steamer in the course of being built was discharged by reason of impossibility when the Admiralty, acting under the Royal prerogative, requisitioned the ship and directed that it should be completed for use in a different way.

Similarly, the *Baily* v. *De Crespigny* line of authority is adequate to cover not only cases in which the result of the governmental action actually deprives the vendor of his property but also cases in which it becomes illegal for him to 'buy, sell or deal in' the kind of commodity which he has contracted to sell.

Where, however, governmental action does not have the effect of making performance of the contract illegal or of removing its subject-matter from the sphere of private obligation (as in *Shipton, Anderson & Co.'s* case), it can only take effect, if at all, as a cause of difficulty amounting to frustration, and it forms an element in frustration in many of the cases to be discussed in the next section.[2] *Andrew Millar*

----

[1] At p. 649.   [2] P. 311.

& Co. v. *Taylor & Co.*, already referred to,[1] illustrates the importance of not being too precipitate in coming to the conclusion that State action has made it impossible to carry out a contract. A party to a contract before making this allegation and acting upon it must wait for a reasonable time in order to see whether the State interference is brief in its operation or likely to be for all practical purposes permanent.

Invalid governmental action

The effect of voluntary compliance with invalid action by Government is not entirely clear, but it will be noticed that the courts are prepared to examine closely the validity of the exercise of a power to requisition or other emergency power. Invalidity may arise: (*a*) where a regulation or order is *ultra vires* the statute under which it purports to have been made, or (*b*) where the action of Government is *ultra vires* the Royal prerogative upon which, if upon anything, it must rest, or (*c*) where, the regulation or order being valid, a purported exercise of the powers thereby conferred is *ultra vires* or otherwise invalid. In *Lipton* v. *Ford* the validity of the order of the Government with which the owner of goods complied, and which indeed he invited, was questioned on grounds (*a*) and (*c*), but its validity was upheld. In *Russian Bank for Foreign Trade* v. *Excess Insurance Co.*[2] ground (*c*) arose. In that case a Proclamation of 3 August 1914 (apparently made under the Royal prerogative) had given to the Admiralty power to requisition for His Majesty's service any British ship 'within the British Isles or the waters adjacent thereto'. In purported exercise of this power the Admiralty directed the owners of a British ship lying in a Russian port to place her at the disposal of the Russian Government. The shipowner complied with this purported requisition, and the owner of cargo which was to have been carried by her to England thereupon claimed against his underwriters, the defendant company, on the ground that there had been a constructive total loss by reason of a 'restraint of princes' within the meaning of his policy. Bailhache J. held that voluntary compliance with an *ultra vires* order of the Admiralty purporting to requisition a ship outside the British Isles and the waters adjacent thereto did not amount to a 'restraint of princes'; 'as disobedience to an *ultra vires* order is not illegal, obedience to such an order, unless compelled by force, or threats of force, is a voluntary act and not a restraint of princes'. This judgment was affirmed by the Court of

---

[1] Above, p. 189.   [2] [1918] 2 K.B. 123, 131; [1919] 1 K.B. 39 (C.A.).

Appeal on another ground, and Scrutton L.J. inclined to doubt Bailhache J.'s view.[1] It may also be necessary to decide what is the effect of invalid governmental action which is enforced by the use or threat of actual force.

Export and import licences

Many prohibitions of exportation or importation imposed during the war have merely been prohibitions in form and have in substance been the means of regulating exportation or importation by a system of licences or permits. Failure to obtain the necessary licence or permit has frequently given rise to disputes, as it may happen that a seller on a rising market will not display as much zeal in his attempts to obtain a licence from the appropriate Government department as his buyer considers to be due from him.[2] It is necessary to distinguish between an absolute promise to obtain an export licence and a mere promise to use one's best endeavours to obtain it. In the case of *In re Anglo-Russian Merchant Traders and John Batt & Co.'s Arbitration*[3] there was an agreement to sell and deliver abroad aluminium made at a time when *to the knowledge of both parties* aluminium could only be exported from the United Kingdom under licence from the British Government. The sellers duly applied for an export licence but their application was refused. Upon the assumption that both parties contemplated shipment from this country, were the sellers liable to pay damages for breach of the contract which was in terms absolute and contained no such expression as 'subject to permit being obtained'? The umpire and Bailhache J. held that the sellers, having entered into a positive contract to ship aluminium and not having stipulated for the event of being unable to obtain a permit, were liable in damages; they had (in the words of the umpire) 'assumed the obligation and risk of obtaining a permit equally with the obligation and risk of obtaining the goods or freight room'. There is a great deal to be said for this view of the obligations of one who enters into a positive contract with

---

[1] See *Evans* v. *Hutton* (1842) upon the validity of a prohibition issued by a governmental officer which interfered with the performance of a charterparty.

[2] Upon the duty to apply for a licence to exceed a quota, see *Leavey & Co.* v. *Hirst & Co.*

[3] Where the refusal of the Government to grant a licence to proceed with building work has been brought about by the action of a party to the contract, he cannot take advantage of the self-induced refusal in order to found upon it a claim that the contract has thereby been frustrated: *Mertens* v. *Home Freeholds Co.* For a case in which it was the seller's duty to apply for a licence, see *H. O. Brandt & Co.* v. *H. N. Morris & Co.*, distinguished in *A. V. Pound & Co. Ltd* v. *M. V. Hardy & Co. Ltd.*

his eyes open, but the Court of Appeal took an entirely different line and applied *The Moorcock*; to give 'business efficacy' to the contract it was necessary to imply an obligation that the sellers should use their best endeavours to obtain a permit; they had done so and failed, and therefore there was no breach of contract.[1] It is not easy to define the limits of *The Moorcock* doctrine, but unless it is applied with care, it may injure the interests of business, 'the essential basis of all trade' being 'the right to rely upon contracts'.[2]

In the case just discussed the contract could not be carried out unless the licence was obtained. That is different from a case like *McMaster & Co.* v. *Cox, McEuen & Co.*,[3] where there was a sale of unascertained jute f.o.b. Dundee, and the buyer intended to export it but was disappointed in his intention because a subsequent official regulation prohibited export without a licence which he applied for but did not receive.[4] There was no contract to sell the goods for export. 'The purchaser had a perfect right when he got them to export them, but that was a right which sprang from his ownership of them and not from any stipulation of the contract.' Therefore his plea of frustration failed. There could be no frustration unless it could be shown that continued liberty to export was an implied term of the contract.

It is necessary in cases of governmental intervention resting on statute or statutory order to see whether the statute or order contains any provision specifically enabling a contracting party affected thereby to plead the necessity arising from compliance with a direction from the Government or from other governmental action as a defence to any action brought against him for the non-fulfilment of his contract.[5]

(4) FRUSTRATION

Amongst other causes of frustration we shall find examples of governmental action which have not been so direct as to remove the subject-

---

[1] The seller must, however, do his best to obtain any necessary licence; he cannot just do nothing about it, unless he can show that an application would be futile: *J. W. Taylor & Co.* v. *Landauer & Co.*, and *Ross T. Smyth Ltd* v. *W. N. Lindsay Ltd*, where Devlin J. distinguished *In re Anglo-Russian Traders and John Batt & Co.*, *supra*. Contrast the case of a licence to communicate with an enemy shareholder: *In re Anglo-International Bank* [1943] Ch. 233, 244.

[2] In the words of a witness who gave evidence before the Pre-War Contracts Committee (Cd. 8975 of 1918).

[3] [1921] Session Cases (H.L.) 24; 58 *Scottish Law Reporter*, p. 70.

[4] On the circumstances determining the question whether it is the duty of the seller or the buyer to obtain a licence, see *A. V. Pound & Co. Ltd* v. *M. W. Hardy & Co. Inc.*

[5] For instance, above, p. 202.

matter of the contract from the scope of private obligation. If I agree to build a ship for you, and before it has been delivered the Lords Commissioners of the Admiralty requisition it and direct me to deliver it to them, there is no need to talk about frustration; the ship has been removed from the scope of private obligation, and I am excused. This was clear law long before the doctrine of frustration was even thought of.

In the cases that we are about to consider, sometimes the goods are specific and sometimes unascertained. We shall merely note the fact in passing and discuss the distinction later.

Distington Hematite Iron Co. v. *Possehl*[1] is an early case of a contract of sale in which both illegality and impossibility were present. The goods (pig iron) were unascertained. The duration of the contract was apparently not fixed. The vendors were a British company, the purchasers an enemy firm. The distinction between 'suspension' and dissolution was not at the time so clearly marked as it became later, and Rowlatt J. held, on the impossibility point, that, as the effect of 'suspension' would have been to impose upon the parties a different contract and 'war does not create any contract' the contract is dissolved, 'war having interfered with' its performance. 'To affirm such a contract as standing generally although at the present time and for an indefinite period it cannot be acted on is not to maintain the original contract but to substitute a different contract for it.'[2]

In *Andrew Millar & Co.* v. *Taylor & Co.*, which has already been referred to,[3] there was no question of trading with the enemy, and the interfering cause, a Proclamation prohibiting exportation, was temporary and not in the event adequate to create impossibility.

In *Naylor, Benzon & Co.* v. *Krainische Industrie Gesellschaft* there was a pre-war contract between a British company and an Austrian company for the shipment to Austrian ports of 40,000 tons of iron ore and pyrites during 1914 and 1915, and upon the outbreak of war between Great Britain and Austria in 1914 the contract had been only partly performed. There was enough illegality and to spare to discharge the contract on that ground alone, but McCardie J. observed[4] that, even if the suspension clause was adequate to postpone

---

[1] [1916] 1 K.B. 811.

[2] At p. 814. The decision in *Leiston Gas Co.* v. *Leiston-cum-Sizewell Urban District Council*, gravely doubted in the *Denny, Mott* case, is some authority for the undoubtedly correct view that, before frustration can take effect, it must be complete, that is to say, that performance of what still remains possible would amount to performance, not of the original contract, but of an entirely different one; and see *Egham and Staines Electricity Co.* v. *Egham U.D.C.*

[3] P. 308.

[4] [1918] 1 K.B. at pp. 339, 340.

performance until after the war, performance would then be so different that the contract must be regarded as dissolved.

In the case of *In re Badische Co.*[1] Russell J. had to deal (after the end of the war) with the effect of the outbreak of war upon contracts for the supply of dyestuffs made before the war between British firms and six British registered companies, of which controllers had been appointed under the Trading with the Enemy Acts. These contracts did not 'cross the line of war', but the dyestuffs, sold by sample, were identified by letters and numbers as being the manufactured products of certain concerns in Germany, so that Germany was clearly designated as the source of supply.[2] Among other grounds for holding the contracts to be dissolved, Russell J. had no difficulty in including frustration.

The event [he said (at p. 379)] which has happened here is the war between this country and Germany, of long duration, bringing in its train complete stoppage of supplies of dyestuffs from Germany, upheavals in prices, freights and values, dislocation of shipping and commerce, Government restrictions and embargoes, and culminating after the conclusion of hostilities in the passing by the Legislature of this country of an Act (the Dyestuffs (Import Regulation) Act, 1920) prohibiting until the year 1931 the importation into the United Kingdom of all synthetic dyestuffs and intermediate products.

After referring to Lord Loreburn's speech in *Tamplin's* case[3] he continued:

In my opinion, the parties contracted on the footing that peace would continue to exist between the country of the contracting parties and the country of the source of supply, and that the source of supply would remain open; and (subject to two other points) a term should be implied providing for the dissolution of the contract in the event of war breaking out between those two countries, whereby the source of supply became blocked for an indefinite period of time. That is a term which should be implied so as to give to the contracts the effect which the contracting parties must as business men be deemed to have intended.

The dyestuffs were unascertained goods.

In *Bolckow, Vaughan & Co.* v. *Compania Minera de Sierra Minera*[4] we find a useful instance of what does not amount to frustration. A con-

---

[1] [1921] 2 Ch. 331.
[2] Contrast *Twentsche Overseas Trading Co.* v. *Uganda Sugar Factory Ltd.*
[3] [1916] 2 A.C. 397.
[4] (1916) 85 L.J. (K.B.) 1776; affirmed (1917) 86 L.J. (K.B.) 439, 444. It would be quite a mistake to think that a contract made during a war can never be frustrated by circumstances arising out of a state of war; see, for instance, the *Bank Line* case, [1919] A.C. 435.

tract was made in November 1914, after the outbreak of the War of 1914 to 1918, whereby the sellers, a Spanish mining company, undertook to sell and deliver to the buyers at Middlesbrough, 50,000 tons of iron ore during 1915. In the contract there was a suspension clause containing the words 'in the case of war', which was held by Bailhache J. to mean, not 'in case war breaks out' because the War of 1914 to 1918 had already broken out, but in case of war preventing performance. After delivering part of the ore sold, the sellers, who had made a subsidiary contract with a Spanish shipping company for the shipment of the ore to England, found that the rise in freights and the dislocation of shipping conditions were such that they 'would incur a loss in carrying out their contract' and declined to deliver the remaining ore due, alleging 'commercial prevention'. Both the learned judge of first instance and the Court of Appeal declined to apply the doctrine of frustration and gave judgment for the buyers.

Application to unascertained goods

It is obvious that a sale of specific goods lends itself more readily to the doctrine of frustration than a sale of unascertained goods.[1] In the first place, in the case of specific goods the attention of both parties is already focused upon the actual subject-matter of the sale, and there is no occasion to speculate as to where the vendor intended to get the goods from and whether that intention was known to the purchaser and formed part of the basis of the contract. *Prima facie* a vendor is free to get the goods from whatever source he chooses, just as a purchaser is free to do what he chooses with them.[2] In the second place, the weight of the influence of the rules relating to the physical destruction of goods which are the subject of a contract of sale tells against the application of the doctrine to unascertained goods; for instance, section 7 of the Sale of Goods Act, 1893, and *genus nunquam perit*. It is therefore not surprising to find that it was with some reluctance that the doctrine was extended to cover a sale of unascertained goods, though it must not be thought that the doctrine can never apply in the case of unascertained goods.

The judgment of McCardie J. in *Blackburn Bobbin Co.* v. *T. W.*

---

[1] An analogy occurs in *E. B. Aaby's Reveri A/S* v. *Lep. Transport Ltd*, where Sellers J. declined to hold that a charterparty for the loading of about 65,000 cubic feet of wool was frustrated when the wool, which had not been agreed upon between charterer and shipowner as a specific cargo, was destroyed in a warehouse fire on the night before loading; a part cargo of the same wool was available and there was a possibility of obtaining more.

[2] *McMaster & Co.* v. *Cox, McEuen & Co.* See above, p. 311.

Allen & Sons,[1] like so many of his judgments, contains an admirable review of the authorities. There was no element of illegality. Both parties were British. The goods were unascertained. He had to deal with a pre-war, wholly executory, contract for the supply of Finland birch timber, free on rail at Hull, for the manufacture of bobbins. He found as facts that the purchasers (plaintiffs suing for damages for breach of contract) 'were unaware at the time of the contract of the circumstance that the timber from Finland was shipped direct from a Finnish port to Hull',[2] and that the vendors (defendants) held no stocks in this country. In 1916 it became possible to send Finnish timber by rail across Norway or Sweden, and the vendors offered to supply it at more than double the contract price, contending that 'all pre-war contracts were cancelled by the war'. McCardie J. declined to apply the doctrine of frustration in such a case. He did not say that in no circumstances could it apply to a sale of unascertained goods, but that[3] 'an ordinary and bare contract for the sale of unascertained goods gives no scope for the operation of the *Krell* v. *Henry* rule, unless the special facts show that the parties have clearly (though impliedly) agreed upon a set of circumstances as constituting the contractual basis'. The judgment was upheld by a strong Court of Appeal, Pickford, Bankes and Warrington L.JJ.[4] As the last-named said:[5] 'The normal mode of transport [sea transit from Finland to Hull] was not in fact in the mind and intention of the plaintiffs, and I see no reason for holding that that normal mode must be deemed to have been in their mind and intention.' Bankes L.J.'s brief enumeration[6] of the alternative tests is interesting.

In re Arbitration between Thornett & Fehr and Yuills Ltd[7] is not a war case, but illustrates the difficulty of invoking the doctrine of frustration in the case of unascertained goods. Difficulty having arisen in the performance of a contract for the sale of tallow, the sellers put forward by way of excuse the closing of one of their factories owing to the unprofitable state of trade, the effects of a strike and bad weather conditions interfering with the supply of their raw material. The Earl of Reading C.J. said:[8]

I am of opinion that there was no frustration or cancellation of the contract. This was a sale not of specific goods, but of goods of the particular

---

[1] [1918] 1 K.B. 540; and see *Ashmore* v. *Cox*; *Beves & Co.* v. *Farkas*, and *W. J. Sargant & Son* v. *Eric Paterson & Co.* (occupation of Smyrna by Turkish troops).
[2] [1918] 1 K.B. at p. 552.
[3] At p. 551.　　　　　　　　　　　　[4] [1918] 2 K.B. 467.
[5] At p. 471; and see *Twentsche Overseas Trading Co.* v. *Uganda Sugar Factory Ltd.*
[6] At p. 471.　　　　　[7] [1921] 1 K.B. 219.　　　　　[8] At p. 227.

description mentioned in the contract, but which were in fact unascertained under the contract. Once the conclusion is arrived at that the sale was not of specific goods then the mere fact that the company manufacturing the goods did not produce the full quantity of 200 tons is no answer to the claim made by the buyers in this case against the sellers.

Darling and Acton JJ. concurred.

In re Badische Co.[1] shows that Russell J. had no difficulty in applying the doctrine to unascertained goods; he said

I can see no reason why, given the necessary circumstances to exist, the doctrine should not apply equally to the case of unascertained goods. It is of course obvious from the nature of the contract that the necessary circumstances can only very rarely arise in the case of unascertained goods.[2]

Among the 'necessary circumstances' existing in this case may be mentioned: interruption in obtaining dyestuffs from the named country of supply which became an enemy country, government intervention on a large scale with the trade in dyestuffs in place of unrestricted trade, and the fact that the contracts provided for continuous performance within fixed times, comparatively short.[3]

The judgment of the Earl of Reading C.J. referred to above was mentioned by Russell J. in the *Badische* case. Having regard (amongst other matters) to the exhaustive manner in which the latter case was argued and considered, the views of Russell J. in so far as they are in conflict with those expressed in the *Thornett and Fehr* case are preferable. When we are considering whether we can imply that the parties would have assented to a particular term had it been brought to their attention at the time of the negotiation of the contract, there is no valid reason for restricting the character of the term. Clearly the burden of proof upon the party asserting such a term is greater when the goods are unascertained than when they are specific, because, when the goods are already specific and within the contemplation of the parties, the focus of their attention is smaller. The scope for the operation of uncertainty is less. But the difference is one of degree rather than of kind.[4]

---

[1] [1921] 2 Ch. 331.

[2] At p. 382. *Veithardt & Hall* v. *Rylands Brothers* is not unlike *In re Badische Co.* but rests on the ground that, the agreed source of supply of the unascertained goods being Germany, further performance of the contract between two companies both apparently incorporated and carrying on business in the United Kingdom became illegal as involving intercourse with the enemy.

[3] For an instance of the effect upon a contract for the supply of paper of a restriction of the importation of paper-making material, see *E. Hulton & Co.* v. *Chadwick & Taylor, Ltd.*

[4] Approved by Morris J. in *Soc. Co-op. Suisse des Cereales, etc.* v. *La Plata Cereal Co.* (1946 –47) 80 Ll. L. Rep. 530, 542.

In re Comptoir Commercial Anversois and Power, Son & Co.[1] illustrates the effect which the impossibility of making a secondary contract by one party has upon the primary contract to which he and another person are parties. In June and July 1914 *A* sells wheat to *B* f.o.b. including freight and insurance from the United States of America to Rotterdam and Antwerp, and it is well known to *B* that *A*, having shipped the wheat, obtained a bill of lading and an insurance policy, prepared an invoice and drawn a draft upon the buyer of the wheat, will then go to a 'buyer of exchange' and sell to him the draft with the bill of lading attached. The seller will thus get his money at once instead of waiting until the buyer of the goods receives them and honours the draft. When the sellers during the first few days of August 1914 found that they were unable to effect insurance against war risks and were therefore unable to 'sell the exchange', they asked the buyers to arrange payment in New York and upon their refusal to do so cancelled the contracts. In the buyers' action for damages for breach of contract it was pleaded by the sellers (*inter alia*) that the contracts were frustrated by reason of their inability to 'sell the exchange'. Upon a special case stated by the Appeal Committee of the appropriate trade association, Bailhache J. held that there was no frustration, and his judgment was affirmed by the Court of Appeal. It was true that the sellers' intention to 'sell the exchange' (an intention known to the buyers) was defeated, but 'it is necessary that there should be a frustration of the common purpose of the adventure'.[2] The sellers were under no obligation to 'sell the exchange'; the performance of the contract for the sale of the goods was unaffected by the sellers' inability to 'sell the exchange', and just because the parties were aware of the danger of war (as they were) and the sellers' intention to 'sell the exchange' was known to the buyers, the learned judge was not prepared to imply a term to the effect that, if war defeated this intention on the part of the sellers, the contract came to an end. The judgments in this case are valuable as negativing the suggestion that, merely because the parties are aware that a certain event will embarrass one of them in the performance of his obligations, the law will therefore impute to them an agreement that, if the event happens, the contract comes to an end.

Another illustration of this point is to be found in *Lewis Insurance & Son Ltd* v. *Sammut* where, on a contract c.i.f. London for the shipment of a cargo of unascertained new potatoes from Malta to London, Pearson J. declined to hold the contract to be frustrated when the

[1] [1920] 1 K.B. 868.   [2] At p. 881.

seller was unable to obtain shipping space; the 'officious bystander' would certainly have said that it was the seller's duty and responsibility to find shipping space and not the concern of the buyer.

(5) CANCELLATION CLAUSES

Whereas the object of a suspension clause is to preserve the operation of the contract until happier times arrive, the object of a cancellation clause is to enable one party or either party to put an end to the contract and free himself from all further obligation under it. Governmental action is one, but only one, of the many events upon the occurrence of which a cancellation clause may come into play. It is important to remember that when a clause enumerates specific impediments, such as governmental interference, upon the occurrence of which a party has the option of cancelling the contract, what the Court has to do is to construe the clause—not merely to decide what the effect of the impediment would be in the absence of the clause. For instance, if the effect of governmental action is to remove the specific subject-matter of the contract from the sphere of private obligation by requisition, then the contract comes to an end without the action of either party. If, however, the parties have provided in their contract for the effect of the impediment, then the first duty laid upon the Court is to construe the provisions which they have inserted. Clearly the parties cannot avert the consequences of impediments outside their control, but they can—within the limits set by rules of law and public policy—determine what the effect of an impediment upon their mutual rights and duties shall be. It would, however, be a mistake to think that the existence of a cancellation clause precludes the operation of the doctrine of frustration. The dislocation arising may be so great that, even if a party entitled under the clause to give notice of cancellation does not exercise that right, the Court may hold that performance or further performance of the contract is frustrated so that the contract is dissolved; and frustration operates independently of the election of a party.

An instance of a cancellation clause will be found in *Ford & Sons (Oldham) Ltd* v. *Henry Leetham & Sons Ltd*, where the seller had the option of cancelling a contract for the sale of unascertained flour 'in case of prohibition of export, blockade, or hostilities preventing shipment or delivery of wheat to this country'. Later, export was prohibited from twenty-one countries, but remained permissible in the case of three countries which were the principal sources of supply to this country. The price of wheat rose considerably as the result of the prohibition, and the seller made a short delivery, and claimed to cancel the contract. Bailhache J. held that the fact of one or more substantial sources of supply being closed by prohibition of export enabled him to exercise his right of cancellation.[1]

[1] See also *Scheepvaart Maatschappij Gylsen* v. *North African Coaling Co.*; *In re Arbitration between Thornett & Fehr and Yuills, Ltd.*

14

SOLICITOR'S RETAINER

We have seen in chapter 3 that an enemy in the territorial sense, which is the sense in which we are now using the word 'enemy', can be sued, provided that service or substituted service can be effected, and that there are certain circumstances in which he may obtain a licence permitting him to sue.[1] It follows that, either as plaintiff or as defendant, he must be able to obtain the services of a solicitor and counsel.

The retainer of a solicitor is a species of the contract of employment, and moreover involves an agency and an intimate and confidential relationship upon which the law in certain circumstances confers a privilege. We should therefore expect it to be governed in general by the principles relevant to agency and employment, upon which something has already been said.[2] It is also something more than a contract, for a solicitor is an officer of the Supreme Court and is subject to the disciplinary control of the Court.

We shall consider the matter under the following headings:

Pre-war retainer.

Position of a solicitor on the record as representing a party who becomes an enemy.

Creation of retainer during war.

PRE-WAR RETAINER

The contract belongs to the category of contracts which involve intercourse between the two parties and it cannot be described as a 'concomitant of the rights of property'. Principle seems to demand that such a contract between a solicitor in this country and an enemy is abrogated by the outbreak of a war which makes the client an enemy. This would be so, it is submitted,[3] even if the solicitor's instructions were complete and, so far as could be seen, no further

---

[1] See *Annual Practice* during War of 1939 to 1945, and for solicitor's licence to act for an enemy see above, p. 108; and see 21 *B.Y.* (1944) at pp. 225, 226, and the unreported *Virgilio* case; see also *Eichengruen* v. *Mond*.

[2] Chapters 7 and 10.

[3] In spite of the facts that the retainer of a solicitor to conduct litigation is an entire contract to conduct the case to an end and that as a matter of law he need not obtain instructions from his client for each step in the action: *Underwood Son, & Piper* v. *Lewis*.

communication with his client would be necessary. That is a mere incident in a particular case and does not alter the fact that the contract belongs to the category of those which involve, or may at any moment involve, communication between the parties, just as employment and agency do. As Lord Porter said in *V/O Sovfracht* v. *N.V. Gebr. Van Udens Scheepvaart en Agentuur Maatschappij*:[1] 'at any moment the necessity (of communication) may arise; the very relationship requires it even if it is desired only to terminate the mandate itself'.

The rule is the same, we submit, whether the solicitor is retained for the purpose of litigation or of non-litigious work. An apparent exception is illustrated by *Tingley* v. *Müller*, where a power of attorney, irrevocable for a period of twelve months, given to his solicitor by an enemy national resident in England who immediately thereafter left England and was assumed to have arrived a few days later in enemy territory, was held not to have been revoked upon the donor becoming an enemy in the territorial sense. But, as we have suggested,[2] that decision rests upon the peculiar character under the Conveyancing Acts of an irrevocable power to sell land; and, moreover, the decision would have been the same if the donee of the power had not been the donor's solicitor.

What authority is there—apart from the decisions upon agency and employment already cited—for the submission that the pre-war retainer held by a solicitor from a now enemy client is abrogated upon the outbreak of war?[3] We are aware of no positively direct authority.[4] In the *Sovfracht* case[5] it was argued in the Court of Appeal that the retainer of the party in the position of a plaintiff, a Dutch shipping company continuing to carry on business in Holland after

---

[1] [1943] A.C. 243, 251, 252, 254.

[2] Above, pp. 99, 100. And note the comments made upon *Tingley* v. *Müller* referred to below, on p. 323.

[3] The importance of this question to solicitors is obvious from a perusal of such cases as *Yonge* v. *Toynbee*; *Simmons* v. *Liberal Opinion Ltd*; *Fernée* v. *Gorlitz*; *D. Glanville & Co. Ltd* v. *Lyne*. See also *Continental Tyre and Rubber Co.* v. *Daimler Co.* [1915] 1 K.B. 892, 913; [1916] 2 A.C. 307, 337.

[4] For an instance of an English solicitor's pre-war retainer for the purpose of litigation being dissolved under Article 299 (a) of the Treaty of Versailles, see *Oppenheimer* v. *Heirs of Oscar Lewy*.

[5] See also *H. P. Drewry S.A.R.L.* v. *Onassis* [1941] 71 Ll. L. Rep. 179, where the Court of Appeal held that, assuming the claimants in an arbitration, a French company of which a British subject apparently in England was managing director and virtually 'owner', was an enemy within the definition of the Trading with the Enemy Act, 1939, two letters from the Trading with the Enemy Branch addressed to the solicitors of the British subject constituted an authority to continue the arbitration notwithstanding the occupation of France. Neither Atkinson J. nor the Court of Appeal dealt with the question whether or not the company became an enemy at common law. This decision may require consideration in the light of the decision of the House of Lords in the *Sovfracht* case.

its occupation by the enemy, and the respondents in these proceedings, was abrogated when that company became enemy within
the definition of, and 'for the purposes of', the Trading with the
Enemy Act, 1939. Lord Greene M.R., in delivering the judgment
of the Court, said:[1]

The result [of the occupation of Holland by the enemy] was that, thereafter, it was illegal for anyone to act for them in proceedings in the courts
of this country to recover a business debt or to enforce a business claim...

The learned Master of the Rolls then referred to

the proviso in section 1 (2) of the Act, which says that a person shall not
be deemed to have traded with the enemy by reason only that he has
done anything under an authority given 'by, or by any person authorized
in that behalf by, a Secretary of State, the Treasury or the Board of
Trade.'

He proceeded to point out that the authority contained in a letter
dated 22 May 1940, from the Custodian of Enemy Property to the
Dutch company's solicitors, purporting to enable them to continue
to act for the company, was an authority which the Custodian had
no power to give, so that they had no authority to take further steps
in the arbitration.

The result, in my opinion [he continued],[2] is that the respondents' application for the appointment of an umpire was one which ought not to have
been entertained. It was impossible for anyone to act on behalf of the
respondents in the matter of such an application without offending against
the Trading with the Enemy Act, 1939.

In the course, however, of the argument in the Court of Appeal,
the hearing was adjourned in order to give the respondents an opportunity of curing the defect in the authority which the Custodian had
purported to give to their solicitors, who thereupon obtained two
letters from the Trading with the Enemy Branch (Treasury and
Board of Trade) and from the Permanent Secretary to the Treasury,
apparently authorizing the respondents' solicitors to continue to act
for them. The authority therein contained was, in the opinion of the
Master of the Rolls,[3] 'irregular in one respect, in that it purports to
be retrospective so as to cover the action of the respondents' solicitors
since 22 May 1940 [the date of the Custodian's letter], a thing which
it obviously could not do'. Nevertheless, by the agreement of the
appellants' counsel and to avoid a waste of time and money, the
authority was accepted *nunc pro tunc* and the proceedings before the

---

[1] [1942] 1 K.B. 222, 229.   [2] At p. 230.   [3] At p. 231.

Master and Asquith J. were treated by the Court of Appeal as if the giving of the authority had preceded them, with the result that the defect was cured and the authority of the respondents' solicitors was upheld. In view of the fact that the House of Lords held that the respondents were enemies at common law and had therefore no *persona standi in judicio*,[1] it was unnecessary for their Lordships to express a direct opinion upon this ruling by the Court of Appeal, but it is clear from the statements of Lord Wright[2] and Lord Porter[3] that the ruling was not approved. The larger question of the effect of the outbreak of war (or an equivalent event such as the occupation by the enemy of territory in which a litigant is resident), whereby an English solicitor and his client become enemies, is dealt with by these two learned Lords and primarily by Lord Porter, in whose view Viscount Simon L.C. expressly concurred. After referring to the termination of the relation of principal and agent when the parties to it become enemies to one another, as in *Hugh Stevenson & Sons* v. *Aktiengesellschaft für Cartonnagen-Industrie*, Lord Porter said:[4]

It is true that in that instance the agency was a mercantile one, but the prohibition of intercourse with an enemy is not confined to trade, and would therefore apply to a solicitor, who, at any rate in this country, is the mandatory of his principal for the purposes of litigation. This view is in accordance with that expressed by Scrutton L.J. in *Tingley* v. *Müller*[5] and by Lord Sumner in *Rodriguez* v. *Speyer Brothers*.[6] If the majority of the Court of Appeal took a contrary view in the former case, with all due respect I am unable to accept their conclusions. Lord Sumner's opinion is not, I think, controverted in this respect by the views of the majority of their Lordships who sat to hear the appeal, nor is it contrary to the grounds upon which their decision was reached.

It also seems clear from the *Sovfracht* decision that while a solicitor can obtain a licence from the Trading with the Enemy Department under the Trading with the Enemy Act, 1939, to represent an enemy client in English litigation, such a licence cannot redintegrate a retainer once it has been abrogated by the outbreak of war or an equivalent event such as the occupation by the enemy of the territory in which the client is resident. *Esposito* v. *Bowden*[7] contains express

---

[1] This aspect of the decision has already been discussed above, at pp. 91, 92.
[2] [1943] A.C. at p. 236.   [3] At p. 253.
[4] [1943] A.C. at p. 254.   [5] [1917] 2 Ch. 144, 177.
[6] [1919] A.C. 59, 130.
[7] [1855] 4 El & Bl. 963, 975; the same point was argued in the Exchequer Chamber and Lord Campbell's opinion was expressly upheld, though on other grounds the judgment of the Court of Queen's Bench was reversed [1857] 7 El. & Bl. 763, 778. See above, p. 132.

authority to the effect that a contract, once dissolved by the outbreak of war on the ground that it involves intercourse with the enemy cannot be redintegrated, though the formation of a new and identical contract between the parties becomes lawful if licensed by the Crown. It may well be that a new contract may arise by implication from the facts, but that is not redintegration.

SOLICITOR ON THE RECORD AS REPRESENTING A PARTY WHO BECOMES AN ENEMY

There may, however, be another aspect of the matter. It appears that, though the outbreak of war determines the retainer of a solicitor by a person engaged in litigation who thereupon becomes an enemy, the solicitor remains on the record for certain purposes.[1] In *Eichengruen* v. *Mond*[2] the plaintiff had before the war begun what the Court of Appeal considered to be a frivolous and vexatious action; before the outbreak of war which made him an enemy in the territorial sense the statement of claim and the defences had been delivered and he had made certain admissions of fact. After the outbreak of war the defendants applied to have the statement of claim struck out as disclosing no cause of action and to have the action dismissed as frivolous and vexatious, and served their notice of motion upon the enemy plaintiff's solicitors who were still on the record. It appears to have been objected that as the result of the outbreak of war, presumably in revoking the retainer, this was not good and effective service. Lord Greene M.R. disposed of this objection in these words:[3]

The outbreak of war has not had the result of removing from the record the name of the solicitors who were acting for the plaintiff, and, indeed, according to the rules and practice of the Court, a solicitor who is once on the record remains on the record notwithstanding that his retainer may be revoked. The only way by which his name can be got off the record is by appointing another solicitor in his place and that solicitor being entered upon the record as the solicitor for the party in person [?'in question', or some words omitted]. Therefore, according to the rules, the service upon that firm of solicitors was perfectly good and effective service.

It may have to be considered how far this decision can stand after the speeches in the House of Lords in the *Sovfracht* case referred to above. It should be noted that in *Robinson & Co.* v. *Continental Insurance Co. of Mannheim* (continuance of a pre-war action against an

---

[1] See Order 67 in the *Annual Practice*. [2] [1940] 1 Ch. 785.
[3] At p. 790. As to the solicitor's duty in these circumstances, see bottom of p. 791.

enemy) it was not suggested that the defendants' solicitors had no power to act for them or that their retainer had been revoked. Whether or not the solicitors obtained a licence from the Crown does not appear. That the defendant enemy has a right to legal representation was expressly asserted by the Court.

CREATION OF RETAINER DURING WAR

It is abundantly clear, from the numerous cases[1] arising in the past in which an enemy was a defendant and the smaller number in which he was a plaintiff, that when he is allowed to sue or is sued he is entitled to 'all the means and appliances' including representation by solicitor and counsel, open to the ordinary litigant, and cases have occurred in which consultation with an enemy client in a neutral country was permitted.[2] It must, however, be realized that to accept a retainer from an enemy amounts to intercourse with the enemy and the contract between solicitor and client cannot be created without the licence of the Crown. The practice now would be for the solicitor to apply to the Trading with the Enemy Department for a licence to communicate with the enemy and to act on his behalf. Such an application would usually occur in the case of litigation but circumstances can be imagined when it might be necessary in non-litigious business, for instance, in regard to patents. It is not the practice for counsel to apply for a licence, and it appears to be assumed that they are covered by the solicitor's licence. The solicitor's licence must not be confused with the Royal licence to sue which must be obtained by an enemy and has already been discussed.[3]

[1] See chapter 3; *Robinson & Co.* v. *Continental Insurance Co. of Mannheim*; *Porter* v. *Freudenberg* [1915] 1 K.B. 857, 882, 883; and *The Glenroy* [1943] P. 109, 124.
[2] See Scrutton, 34 *L.Q.R.* (1918) at p. 124.   [3] See above, pp. 108–9.

15

TORTS: PROPERTY: WILLS AND INTESTACY: MARRIAGE

BIBLIOGRAPHY

Phillimore (3rd ed.), III, ch. VI.
Oppenheim, II, §§ 140–54.
Baty and Morgan, *War: Its Conduct and Legal Results* (1915), ch. IV.
Latifi, *Effects of War on Property* (1909).
Bentwich, *War and Private Property* (1907).
McNair, *Opinions*, vol. III, section XIX.
Scobell Armstrong, *War and Treaty Legislation 1914–1921*.
Fischer Williams, *Chapters on Current International Law* (1929), pp. 188–208.
Mann, *The Confiscation of Corporations, etc.*, 11, *I. and C.L.Q.* (1962), pp. 471–502.

We have dealt in preceding chapters with the *procedural* and the *con-tractual* status of enemies, both those who are within the Queen's protection and those who are not. It remains to consider the residue of their civil status.

The enemy 'in protection' (and, probably, the enemy in an allied or neutral country) would seem to have complete civil status.[1] He may make valid contracts; he can acquire rights of action in tort and become liable in tort; he can acquire and dispose of real and personal property, *inter vivos* or by will, and he can take property upon an intestacy. He does not lose this status by internment, at any rate if it be in pursuance of a general policy.[2]

The position of the enemy in the territorial sense (the sense in which we shall use the term throughout the remainder of this chapter unless another sense is indicated), that is, the person who is voluntarily in enemy territory, whether resident or not, or who is carrying on business there, is different. We shall discuss his status under the following headings:

   A. Torts.

   B. Proprietary Rights of the Enemy, Wills and Intestacy.

   C. Marriage and other Domestic Relations.

---

[1] Except that, when a prisoner of war or interned, a writ of *habeas corpus* is not available to try the issue of his liberty (see above, pp. 93, 98) and that he may become subject to restrictions as to his place of living, his freedom of movement, his possession of certain things, such as weapons, radio transmitters and receivers, etc.

[2] See above, pp. 96, 97.

A. TORTS

(i) *As the victim of a tort*

(a) *Pre-war torts.* We have already seen that rights of action which have already accrued to an enemy before the outbreak of war are suspended and unenforceable by him in the Courts of this country until after the war. We are not aware of a reported decision upon a pre-war right of action in tort[1] but see no reason why it should not be subject to the same rule as that which governs a pre-war right of action in contract, of which there are many illustrations.

It is true that the history of the development of the law of torts is a history of remedies rather than of rights: *ubi remedium, ibi jus.* But this undoubted historical fact must not be allowed to obscure the fact that a right of action for the redress of an injury recognized by English law as tortious is a chose in action, a piece of property. For instance, in 1938, *X*, a person resident in Germany, is libelled in a single issue of a newspaper published in London.[2] War breaks out between Great Britain and Germany on 3 September 1939, and *X* continues voluntarily to remain in Germany throughout the war. During that period his right of action exists but is in suspense, in the same way as pre-war debts and accrued rights of action for breach of contract. During that period he is capable of owning the right of action, and, when the period is past, we can see no reason why he should not be able to enforce it.[3] (We need not again discuss the question of the Limitation Act, 1939.)[4]

(b) *Post-outbreak of war torts.*[5] Suppose that an English newspaper during the war publishes the following false statement of an enemy: 'Mr *XY* while enjoying the hospitality of our country during the past few years prior to his hurried departure, systematically abused it by employing his time in taking photographs of vital objectives, and the enemy's air force are now finding these photographs very useful.' Can *XY* after the war bring an action for libel against the editor and the proprietors of the newspaper? Why not? No intercourse with enemy persons or territory is involved in the acquisition of the right of action such as would be involved in the making of a contract between a person in this country and an enemy. If the

---

[1] For the case of a registered enemy plaintiff in action of tort, see above, p. 81, and see *Maerkle* v. *British & Continental Fur Co.* [1954], 3 All E.R. 50 (conversion).

[2] The tort is thus complete, and no question of a continuing tort arises.

[3] Always assuming that the Crown has not confiscated it by due process.

[4] See above, pp. 114–16.

[5] Article 68 of the Geneva Convention of 12 August 1949, relative to the Treatment of Prisoners of War, makes some provision for compensation for 'injury or other disability arising out of work'.

enemy is capable of owning property during the war, including (as we submit to be the case) a pre-war right of action in tort, why is he not capable of acquiring a right of action in tort during the war? In *The Berwickshire*[1] proceedings were instituted after the war by the French owners and crew of a fishing vessel lost on 2 November 1940 as the result of a collision with a British steamship; at that time and until the liberation the whole of France had been declared to be enemy territory, so that the plaintiffs became technically enemies and so remained until 13 October 1944, when the French Provisional Government of General de Gaulle was recognized by the United Kingdom Government. In the action tried in 1947 the British ship was held to be solely to blame, and the French owners and crew recovered not only damages but interest thereon from the date of the collision until the award of the admiralty registrar fixing the amount of damages. The point that no action in tort could accrue to an enemy during a war does not appear to have been taken.

Let us see whether instances can be found of an enemy acquiring other rights of action during a war. If such can be found, it is some evidence in favour of the view that he is not incapable of acquiring a right of action in tort during the war.[2] In *Halsey* v. *Lowenfeld* (*Leigh and Curzon Third Parties*), where an enemy lessee of a London theatre residing in Austria was held liable during the war upon a covenant to pay rent which fell due during the war, it was not doubted that he thereupon acquired a right of indemnity against a pre-war assignee of the lease; but it was held that he could not recover from him during the war under a third party notice because in that proceeding the defendant would be an *actor*. In *Hugh Stevenson & Sons* v. *A.-G. für Cartonnagen Industrie*,[3] where the outbreak of war dissolved a partnership between an English company and a German company and the former carried on the business in England during the war with the aid of the latter's share of the assets, the House of Lords held that the latter, an enemy, became 'entitled to a share of the profits earned since the dissolution, so far as attributable to the use of their share of the capital,[4] though it could not be recovered during the war. Lord Atkinson said[5] that 'the error underlying the argument pre-

---

[1] See above, pp. 143, 227.

[2] In *Sylvester's Case* (1702) it was said by the Court of Queen's Bench: 'if an alien enemy come into England without the Queen's protection [and the alien enemy in the territorial sense is in much the same position in our Courts] he shall be seized and imprisoned by the law of England, and he shall have no advantage of the law of England, nor for any wrong done to him here; but if he has a general or a special protection, it ought to come of his side in pleading'.

[3] [1918] A.C. 239.   [4] At p. 240.   [5] At p. 253.

sented in support of this appeal…is this, that the temporary suspension of the remedy is confounded with the permanent loss of the right'.[1] It must not be assumed that, because an action can during the war be defeated by the plea of alien enemy, there can be no valid cause of action underlying it. Moreover, we shall find later in this chapter a number of instances of enemies holding during the war other kinds of property, and even acquiring property during the war —at any rate when the acquisition does not involve the forbidden intercourse across the line of war. For these reasons it is submitted that, subject to any question of the limitation of actions,[2] XY should be able to bring an action after the war against the English newspaper.[3]

(ii) *As a tort-feasor*

(*a*) and (*b*). Whether the tort is committed before or during the war, his enemy status affords no protection against an action brought against him during or after the war.

B. PROPRIETARY RIGHTS OF THE ENEMY[4]

(i) *Ownership and control of property in the United Kingdom: the custodian of enemy property*

Upon the outbreak of war between the United Kingdom and a foreign country there is likely to be much private property in this country owned by enemy nationals, such as houses, or land, or money deposited in banks, or goods purchased and awaiting shipment. We must now consider how the outbreak of war affects such property, and we shall consider the extent to which an enemy national may, during a war, acquire or dispose of property.

Ownership and control. It is not surprising that a mercantile nation should early have had to concern itself with these matters. As long ago as the thirteenth century it was provided, in a statutory pro-

---

[1] A recognition of the distinction between substantive and procedural liability will be found in *Dickinson* v. *Del Solar, Mobile and General Insurance Co., Third Party* [1930] 1 K.B. 376: 'Diplomatic agents', Lord Hewart C.J. said at p. 380, 'are not…immune from legal liability for any wrongful acts. The accurate statement is that they are not liable to be sued in the English Courts unless they submit to the jurisdiction.' That is to say, legal liability can coexist with temporary immunity from suit. If that is so, why cannot a legal right coexist with a temporary inability to enforce it?   [2] See above, pp. 114–16.

[3] For a libel action in a Chinese court brought by a German national held prisoner under suspicion of war crimes, see *The Times* newspaper, 18 September 1946. Whether he was resident in China or not, does not appear. And see, as to torts generally, P. H. W[infield] in *Cambridge Law Journal*, vol. 9 (1945), p. 129.

[4] As to proprietary rights of neutrals, see below, p. 455. Property of British subjects may also be affected by war-time action taken by the Crown, giving rise to claims for compensation against the Crown: see *Burmah Oil Co., Ltd.* v. *Lord Advocate* [1963] S.C. 410; [1965] A.C. 75, and the War Damage Act, 1965.

vision (which has not yet been repealed), that enemy merchants in this country at the beginning of the war shall be attached without harm of body *or goods* until it is known how British merchants in the enemy's country are being treated: if our merchants are being well treated the enemy merchants are similarly to be well treated.[1] It would seem from this that the enemy merchant's goods would only be seized by way of reprisals. But in general, and apart from such special statutory provisions, it was well established that the Crown by virtue of the prerogative had the right to seize the property in this country of enemy aliens. We must note that the outbreak of war did not *ipso facto* operate so as to vest the title to the enemy's property in the Crown:[2] the Crown possessed the right to claim title as forfeited to the Crown, and if it wanted to exercise that right it had to assert and establish its title by the procedure of 'inquisition of office'.[3]

However, the practice of seizing private enemy property in this way became less and less frequently resorted to.[4] In 1813 Sir W. Scott, in *The Charlotte*[5] remarked that 'it has not been much the practice in modern times' to confiscate the property of enemies in this country by way of inquisition of office, and a hundred years later Lord Parker, in the *Daimler* case, could say that the Crown's right of seizure 'has long fallen into disuse'.[6]

While the practice of States generally now seems to accept that private enemy property on land is not confiscated upon the outbreak of war, it is, as Oppenheim observes, 'controversial to what extent that practice has definitely crystallised into a customary rule of In-

---

[1] Statute *Confirmatio Cartarum*, 1297 (25 Ed. 1 c. 30).

[2] Among other authorities for this statement see Lord Stowell in *The Nostra Senora de Los Dolores* [1809] Edw. 60; Lord Parker in *The Roumanian* [1916] 1 A.C. 124, 135 and in the *Daimler* case [1916] 2 A.C. 307, 347; Lord Finlay and Lord Haldane in *Hugh Stevenson & Sons'* case [1918] 239, 244, 247; Lord Birkenhead in *Fried Krupp* v. *Orconera Iron Ore Co.* [1919] 88 L.J. (Ch.) 304, 309; and see generally the notes in Oppenheim, II, § 102. It is difficult to reconcile *In re Ferdinand* (*infra*) with the passages referred to above except on the basis that they mean that there is no automatic confiscation of enemy private property.

[3] As to this procedure, see Chitty, *Prerogatives of the Crown* (1820), pp. 246 ff.

[4] This followed the general tendency of international practice in the eighteenth century: see *The Roumanian* [1915] P. 26, 38 ff. and Bentwich, *War and Private Property* (1907), ch. I, for a review of historical developments in this matter.

[5] 1 Dods. 212, 214. See also the decision of the U.S. Supreme Court in *Brown* v. *The United States* (1814) (Pitt Cobbett, II, p. 55). For some early nineteenth-century opinions of the Law Officers of the Crown, see McNair, *Opinions*, III, pp. 8–13. See also Dr Lushington in *The Johanna Emilie* (1 Sp. Ecc. & Ad. 317, 319): 'I believe no such instance [of the seizure of the property on land of alien enemies] has occurred from the time of the American War to the present day.' In 1899 the Law Officers referred to the general right to seize an enemy's property in this country as 'in practice obsolete': McNair, *Opinions*, III, p. 239 (see also the remarks of Lord Halsbury, L.C., at p. 243). On 8 September 1914 the Attorney-General advised the Crown that land in England held by an alien enemy in this country is in the same position as any other property so held.

[6] [1916] 2 A.C. 307, 347. See also *The Roumanian*.

ternational Law'.[1] Furthermore, in order to avoid a confusion which contributed to the doubts attending this whole subject during the War of 1914 to 1918, we may observe that the question whether International Law wrought or permitted the confiscation of enemy private property upon the outbreak of war is quite distinct from the question whether English law contained any provision for that purpose, either upon a wholesale scale or in relation to particular persons. Even though, as we have seen, English authority in the nineteenth century recognized that the Crown's right to confiscate enemy property under the procedure of inquisition of office had been infrequently exercised of late, there was no doubt that the right still remained for exercise by the Crown if it saw fit. The Court of Appeal in 1920 confirmed that the Crown's rights had not been abandoned by desuetude.[2]

Subject, then, to any statutory provisions (and we shall see that this is an important qualification) the common law position may be summarized as being that

(i) the outbreak of war does not *ipso facto* bring about the confiscation to the Crown of the private property of enemies in the national or territorial sense;

(ii) the Crown may before the conclusion of peace[3] (which means the conclusion of peace in the legal sense and not the mere suspension of hostilities by an armistice) resort to the ancient procedure of inquisition of office and confiscate the property of an enemy (including almost certainly an enemy only in the national sense);

(iii) the property which may be so seized may comprise choses in action[4] or other personal property and, since aliens may now hold real property, it is difficult to see why the rule should not apply also to such property;[5]

(iv) as a necessary deduction from (i) and (ii) the enemy national

---

[1] Oppenheim, II, p. 326; see also Jessup, 49 A.J. (1955), p. 57. Lord Ellenborough in *Wolff* v. *Oxholm*, referred only to the practice of a State confiscating the private debts owed by its nationals to enemy subjects being not conformable to the *usages* of nations. For an Opinion of the Law Officers on the confiscatory decrees which were the subject of *Wolff* v. *Oxholm*, see McNair, *Opinions*, III, p. 7; and for comment upon the contemporary authority of that case, see *In re Ferdinand, Ex-Tsar of Bulgaria* [1921] I Ch. 107, 125 ff.

[2] *In re Ferdinand, Ex-Tsar of Bulgaria*. For the ultimate fate of the property of the Ex-Tsar, see Oppenheim, II, p. 326, n. 3.

[3] [1921] I Ch. at pp. 132, 139; citing *Attorney-General* v. *Weeden and Shales* (1699). See also *R.* v. *Williamson* and *The Charlotte* (1813).

[4] *Attorney-General* v. *Weeden and Shales*. This case is examined at some length by Farrer in 37 *L.Q.R* (1921) at pp. 234 *et seq.*, from which it appears that the chose in action, which would probably have been forfeitable by inquisition of office if the inquisition had been held before the conclusion of peace, was a legacy given by the will of a naturalized British subject dying during the war (apparently in England) to an enemy national resident in enemy territory.   [5] *Contra*, Farrer in 37 *L.Q.R* (1921), p. 347.

retains the capacity to hold the property which he owned at the outbreak of war.

In the absence of any resort to the right to confiscate enemy property, such property in this country during a war would, without more, be largely unmolested. This was of little significance in the wars of the nineteenth century and earlier. All the same, the wealth of a belligerent State which it may use in furtherance of its war effort comprises not only property and assets within its own territory but also the property and assets abroad of its nationals, since these too might be used, for example, to pay for purchases of war material from neutral countries or for financing propaganda or subversive activities. In modern conditions of war, it is imperative to deny to the enemy the possibility of any such benefit. The result has been the development of a practice recognized as valid in international law whereby private enemy property, while not being seized and the enemy owner deprived of title, is placed under the administrative control of the State so as to prevent its use for the benefit of the enemy.

In the United Kingdom this practice was introduced during the War of 1914 to 1918. It is now regulated by the Trading with the Enemy Act, 1939.[1] Section 7 of that Act provides that 'With a view to preventing the payment of money to enemies and of preserving enemy property in contemplation of arrangements to be made at the conclusion of peace,[2] the Board of Trade may appoint' a Custodian of Enemy Property; may by order require the payment to him (*inter alia*) of money which would, but for the existence of a state of war,[3] be payable to or for the benefit of an enemy; may vest[4] in the Custodian such enemy property as may be prescribed and the right to transfer such other enemy property as may be prescribed; and may confer and impose upon the Custodian a multitude of rights, powers,[5] duties and liabilities.[6] Subsection (8) of section 7

---

[1] See also the Emergency Laws (Miscellaneous Provisions) Act, 1953, section 2 and paragraphs 6 and 9 of the Second Schedule.

[2] The opening words of this section, 'with a view to...the conclusion of peace', were considered in *R. J. Reuter Co. Ltd.* v. *Mulhens*: see below, p. 333. As to the significance of the word 'arrangements' see the remarks of Lord Reid in *Bank voor Handel en Scheepvaart N.V.* v. *Administrator of Hungarian Property*. The arrangements actually made upon the conclusion of peace after the War of 1939 to 1945 are outlined below, pp. 335-6.

[3] On this expression, see S.R. & O. 1946, no. 1040.

[4] As to the meaning of 'vest' see *In re Pozot's Settlement Trusts*.

[5] The Custodian as such has no power to consent on behalf of an enemy party to a settlement to the exercise of a power of advancement, and it is at least doubtful whether the Board of Trade could confer that power upon him: *Re Forster's Settlement*.

[6] The Enemy Property Act, 1953, indemnifies persons who in good faith acted in relation to enemy property, or to property which they supposed to be enemy property, in excess of the powers conferred on them by the trading with the enemy legislation, and gives a good title to transferees of such property. See also the Indemnity Act, 1920.

of the Act defines 'enemy property' and 'property'.[1] Effect was given to these statutory provisions during the War of 1939 to 1945 by a vast and complex amount of subordinate legislation.

As the provisions of section 7, and also the term 'Custodian' itself, imply, the vesting of enemy property in the Custodian is primarily a matter of ensuring its conservation rather than its confiscation. Nevertheless, the Custodian may be given a power to sell property vested in him, the purchase price in such circumstances remaining in his hands under the same conditions as the property for which it has been transferred.[2] In *R. J. Reuter Co. Ltd* v. *Mulhens* the Court of Appeal rejected the argument that the words which introduce section 7 ('With a view to preventing the payment of money to enemies, and of preserving enemy property in contemplation of arrangements to be made at the conclusion of peace') limit the Board of Trade's powers to make orders to the achievement of the purposes expressed in those words. Evershed M.R. and Birkett L.J. considered that those words only indicated the purpose which Parliament had in mind in giving the Board of Trade the extensive and detailed powers set out in the Act, and that they did not limit the much wider powers expressly given by the Act which included, in the particular case, the power to authorize the Custodian to assign certain enemy-owned trade marks vested in him.

The effect of vesting enemy property in the Custodian is to deprive the enemy of all control over and beneficial interest in his property.[3] But the Custodian only acquires certain limited powers in respect of the property, and does not have the beneficial interest vested in him (or in the Crown): consequently the property is in the anomalous

---

[1] Upon statutory protective trusts, see *In re Gourju's Will Trusts*, and *In re Wittke*. As to the inclusion within the meaning of 'property' of rights of action in tort, see *Maerkle* v. *British and Continental Fur Co.*; of goodwill, see *Adrema Werke G.M.b.H.* v. *Custodian of Enemy Property and German Enemy Property Administrator*, and *R. J. Reuter Co. Ltd* v. *Mulhens* [1954] 1 Ch. 50, 96; of a charge upon an insurance policy, see *Re Ruben*; and of a trade mark, see *R. J. Reuter Co. Ltd* v. *Muthens* (and also a Dutch case and an Egyptian case reported in 26 I.L.R. (1958—II), pp. 656 and 657). As to whether the estate of a non-enemy deceased person, some beneficiaries being enemy, is held or managed on behalf of an enemy by the administrator so as to be 'enemy property', see *Custodian of Enemy Property* v. *Coulson* (Kenya).

[2] *Vamvakas* v. *Custodian of Enemy Property*. For a case in which a foreign equivalent of our Custodian of Enemy Property purported to sell property which was legally situated not in that foreign country but in the United Kingdom, see *Prudential Assurance Co. Ltd* v. *Al Goumhouria Insurance Co. S.A.E.*, *The Times*, 12 March 1960.

[3] See *Maerkle* v. *British and Continental Fur Co. Ltd* and cases cited in the immediately following note. It is not clear whether the enemy owner's bare legal title is extinguished, or whether it remains in existence but is temporarily submerged: see, e.g. the conflicting dicta in the *Bank voor Handel* case [1954] A.C. 584, 632, 639, *In re Ring Springs Ltd's Letters Patent* and *Fischler* v. *Administrator of Roumanian Property* [1960] 3 All E.R. 433, 438–9, 446.

situation of being without a beneficial owner.[1] However, on a transfer of property by the Custodian, the beneficial interest once again attaches to it, in the interest of the transferee.[2] The Custodian is not the agent or trustee of the enemy owner.[3]

The Custodian is a servant of the Crown, but in virtue of the peculiar circumstances in which he holds enemy property, he is a Crown servant of an unusual kind; for example, the property held by him as a Crown servant is not Crown property and income accruing to him upon it is not Crown income.[4]

The effect of these statutory provisions upon the Crown's right to confiscate an enemy national's property under the old procedure of inquisition of office is not altogether clear. In the case of *In re Ferdinand, Ex-Tsar of Bulgaria*,[5] the Court of Appeal held that the procedure was temporarily superseded and put in abeyance by the Trading with the Enemy legislation of the War of 1914 to 1918. Since that legislation contained provisions broadly the same as the equivalent provisions of the 1939 Act, it might be thought that the same conclusion would still be drawn in respect of that Act. However, section 16 of the 1939 Act provides that the Act 'shall be without prejudice to the exercise of any right or prerogative of the Crown', and it would seem that this provision (which had no counterpart in the Trading with the Enemy legislation of the 1914–18 war) has the effect of preserving the Crown's rights to confiscate an enemy national's property by inquisition of office.[6]

While it is perhaps now unlikely that enemy persons would, as the result of any general statutory measures of seizure, be deprived of title to their property during the course of a war, this may well happen as a result of the peace settlement. Section 7 of the Trading with the Enemy Act, 1939, expressly envisages the preservation of

---

[1] *In re Munster; Bank voor Handel en Scheepvaart N.V.* v. *Administrator of Hungarian Property.*

[2] *Vamvakas* v. *Custodian of Enemy Property.*

[3] See cases cited in note 1 *supra.* As to the nature in this respect of a foreign sequestrator of enemy property, see *Lepage* v. *San Paulo Copper Estates Ltd.*

[4] *Bank voor Handel en Scheepvaart N.V.* v. *Administrator of Hungarian Property*: but the Crown was nevertheless held to have a sufficient interest in the property under the Trading with the Enemy legislation to entitle it to invoke immunity from taxation on the income if it chose to do so. See also the Enemy Property Act, 1953, section 4.

[5] [1921] 1 Ch. 107 (C.A.); following a statement in *Porter* v. *Freudenberg* [1915] 1 K.B. 857, 869, 870; and see Farrer in 37 *L.Q.R.* (1921), pp. 218–41 and 337–62 for a criticism of the decision in *In re Ferdinand*. At the relevant dates in July and August 1919 the ex-Tsar was still an enemy; he was not 'within the protection of the King' and was probably living in Germany. It seems that the right of the Crown to confiscate the goods of enemies by means of inquisition of office applies whether the enemy is in this country, within or without the protection of the King, or abroad.

[6] See *Vamvakas* v. *Custodian of Enemy Property* [1952] 2 Q.B. 183, 190.

enemy property 'in contemplation of arrangements to be made at the conclusion of peace'. In connection with, and even prior to,[1] whatever arrangements may be made in the peace settlement (which need not be embodied in a formal treaty of peace)[2] statutory provision may be made whereby enemy persons are permanently deprived of their property.

The peace settlements at the end of the War of 1939 to 1945[3] took various forms. In respect of Italy, Bulgaria, Roumania, Hungary and Japan,[4] each of the Allied Powers was, subject to certain limitations, given the right to seize, retain, liquidate or otherwise deal with enemy property, rights and interests which on the entry into force of the treaty were within its territory, and to apply such property or the proceeds thereof to such purposes as it wished. The liquidation and disposition of enemy property was to be carried out in accordance with the law of the Allied Power concerned, and the enemy owner was to have no rights with respect to such property except those which may be given him by that law. German property had to be dealt with rather differently, since there was no peace treaty. Statutory provision was made for collecting and realizing German enemy property in this country and for distributing the proceeds,[5] and when the Bonn Conventions were signed subsequently to deal with many matters usually dealt with in a peace treaty it was provided simply that Germany would not object to any measures already taken, or to be taken in the future, with regard to German property outside Germany which was seized for purposes of reparation or restitution or as a result of the state of war.[6] Owing to the special circumstances attending Austrian and Finnish participation in the war, the property of their nationals on allied territory was, in general, to be restored.[7]

In respect of Italian, Bulgarian, Roumanian, Hungarian, Finnish, Japanese and Austrian property statutory power was taken to enable

[1] As with the Distribution of German Enemy Property Act, 1949, which was enacted in advance of the peace settlement with Germany.

[2] The peace settlement with Germany after the War of 1939 to 1945 was, in matters relating to German property, mainly embodied in the Bonn Convention on the Settlement Matters Arising out of the War and the Occupation, 1952 (T.S. no. 13 (1959)).

[3] A brief summary of the treatment of enemy private property by the peace treaties which concluded the War of 1914–18 will be found in Oppenheim, II, pp. 328–9; and see Scobell Armstrong, *War and Treaty Legislation, 1914–1922.*

[4] Treaties of Peace with Italy (Article 79), Roumania (Article 27), Bulgaria (Article 25), Hungary (Article 29) and Japan (Article 14).

[5] Distribution of German Enemy Property Act, 1949: see Cohn, 3 *I.L.Q.* (1950), pp. 391, 530, and 4 *ibid.* (1951), p. 60.

[6] Article 3 of chapter VI of the Convention referred to in n. 2 above.

[7] Article 27 of the Peace Treaty with Finland, 1947, and Article 27 of the Austrian State Treaty, 1955.

335

His Majesty to made such appointments, establish such offices, make such Orders in Council, and do such things as appear to Him to be necessary for giving effect to the peace arrangements.[1] As we have just remarked, statutory provisions in respect of German property were made before the conclusion of any peace arrangements with Germany.[2] In those cases where enemy property was to be seized, the practice was to appoint an Administrator of the enemy property, who could be given extensive powers to secure the declaration to him of enemy property and its subsequent realization, liquidation or distribution.[3] Like the Custodian of Enemy Property, the Administrator is also an agent of the Crown.[4]

(ii) *Acquisition of property* inter vivos

Can the enemy acquire during the war property situate in England? We suggest that the answer to this question is, Only when no illegal intercourse is involved in the acquisition. That would seem to rule out the modes of acquisition which involve contemporaneous agreement, e.g. purchase, or gift[5] involving present delivery, but a gift by deed is valid until it is declined, and might be in a different position.

(iii) *Acquisition of property under a will or trust or upon an intestacy*

An enemy can acquire a legacy under the will, or a share upon the intestacy, of a person dying in England during the war, though he could not receive the property during the war, and in those circumstances it could be vested in the Custodian.[6] In two cases[7] where testators died during the War of 1914 to 1918 having made English

[1] The Treaties of Peace (Italy, Roumania, Bulgaria, Hungary and Finland) Act, 1947; the Japanese Peace Treaty Act, 1951; and the Austrian State Treaty Act, 1955.
[2] The Distribution of German Enemy Property Act, 1949. See also the Enemy Property Act, 1953, Part II.
[3] See the Treaty of Peace (Bulgaria) Order, 1948; the Treaty of Peace (Hungary) Order, 1948; the Treaty of Peace (Italy) Order, 1948; the Treaty of Peace (Roumania) Order, 1948; the Treaty of Peace (Bulgaria) Vesting Order, 1948; the Treaty of Peace (Hungary) Vesting Order, 1948; the Treaty of Peace (Roumania) Vesting Order, 1948; the Distribution of German Enemy Property (no. 1) Order, 1950; the Distribution of German Enemy Property (no. 2) Order, 1951; the Japanese Treaty of Peace Order, 1952. For dealings in relation to Italian property in this country, see *Republic of Italy* v. *Hambros Bank Ltd.*
[4] *Hungarian Property Administrator* v. *Finegold*; *Austrian Property Administrator* v. *Russian Bank for Foreign Trade.*
[5] Which is a bilateral transaction involving agreement between donor and donee. The law relating to gifts is not as clear as might be expected in so simple a transaction: see Jenks, *English Civil Law* (4th ed.), §§ 1494, 6, 7; Halsbury, *Laws of England* (3rd ed. Simonds), vol. 18, §§ 728–9.
[6] *In re Jacob Schiff*; for exceptions to the general rule that a grant will be made to the Public Trustee, see *In re Grundt*; *In re Oetl*, and see Tristram and Coote, *Probate Practice* (20th ed. 1955), pp. 20, 268 and 344. *In re de Barbe*; and *In re Wittke.*
[7] *In re Schiff, Henderson* v. *Schiff*; *In re Levinstein, Levinstein* v. *Levinstein.*

wills, whereby they bequeathed the income of a trust fund in one case and annuities in the other to enemies, the intrinsic capacity of these enemies to take under the wills was not questioned; the argument turned upon the effect of the Trading with the Enemy Acts, the Peace Treaties, and the legislation passed to give effect to them. During the war, of course, they could not receive the sums which would otherwise have been due to them. What was the nationality of the testators and where they died does not appear.

In the case of *In re Neuburger's Settlement*,[1] certain children, enemies, became entitled in possession upon their mother's death (apparently in Germany) in July 1918 to a contingent interest in an annuity payable under their mother's marriage settlement and secured by the covenant of her parents with trustees—her parents and the trustees being all British subjects. Where the parents and the trustees were resident at the date of the mother's death does not appear, but it was probably in the United Kingdom. The children's interests were contingent upon attaining twenty-one years of age or marrying. It was held that upon their mother's death the children acquired 'a plain right and interest' in the trust fund fed by the covenant, but of course it passed to the Custodian and was later caught by the charge created by the Treaty of Versailles. Their enemy status did not prevent them from acquiring the same interest in the fund as they would have acquired if they had not been enemies.

In the case of *In re Sampietro*, where two enemies, both in the national and the territorial senses, had before the war become entitled to reversionary interests in an English trust fund upon the death of their mother before the war, the Public Trustee sought and received a grant of administration *ad colligenda bona*; and in the case of *In re van Tuyll van Serooskerken*, a similar grant was made to the Public Trustee where the testator died in England and the sole executor was resident in enemy-occupied territory.[2]

---

[1] In the case of *In re Schulze* (1917) it was held by the Second Division of the Scottish Court of Session that an enemy 'in protection', having complied with the requirements of the Aliens Restriction Act, 1914, could be appointed executor-dative to a British subject who died intestate.

[2] For the practice followed upon the administration of the estate of a person dying in England and owing debts to persons in enemy-occupied (and presumably enemy) territory, see *In re Gess*. For some American and other decisions, see *In re Kielsmark's Will*; Hudson's *Cases on International Law*, 3rd ed., p. 643; *In re Roeck's Estate*; *In re Bendit's Estate*; *In re Budwilowicz* (South Australia), *Custodian of Enemy Property* v. *Coulson* (Kenya) and many others in *Annual Digest* and I.L.R.

(iv) *Disposition of property* inter vivos

At common law the governing factor would seem to be whether the disposition by an enemy of property situated in this country could be effected without intercourse with the enemy.[1] It is not clear what is meant by intercourse with the enemy and what intercourse is illegal. Suppose an enemy to own shares in an English company or a motor car garaged in a London garage. A *sale* of the shares or the car would involve communication across the line of war, and even if the enemy, without previous communication, merely sent a duly signed transfer of the shares or an order to the garage-proprietor to deliver the car to the purchaser, without expecting the proceeds to be remitted to him during the war, the act of the transferee in signing the transfer and putting it forward to the company for registration, or the act of presenting to the garage-proprietor the order for delivery, would involve intercourse with the enemy, namely, an attempt to contract with him. Suppose, however, that the enemy desiring to *give* me the shares and the car sends to me in England a signed transfer of the shares and an order to the garage-proprietor to deliver the car to me, it is again submitted that my acceptance of either gift, though I address no communication to the enemy, involves intercourse with the enemy and is illegal and void; gift is a species of agreement, a bilateral transaction; a would-be donor cannot make me the owner of property without my assent, and even if my assent is tacit and involves the making of no overt communication to him, it is submitted that my assent is an 'act in the law' and creates a legal relationship.[2]

During the currency of legislation such as the Trading with the Enemy Act, 1939, these questions are not likely to arise, as the enemy's property in this country would almost certainly be taken out of his control and vested in the Custodian of Enemy Property.

Section 5 of the Trading with the Enemy Act, 1939, renders ineffective the transfer by an enemy (as defined by the Act as amended) of any 'securities' as therein defined.

There remains the question of the employment by the enemy of

---

[1] See below, pp. 348–9.

[2] See above, p. 336, n. 5. An Irish case, *Grundy* v. *Broadbent*, presents some difficulty. There the Irish Chancery Division upheld as valid an equitable assignment of a chose in action for valuable consideration made during the war by a firm in Austria to a firm in London, so that the latter was able to prove against the estate of a deceased debtor. The assignment involved the despatch from Austria to London of a letter which contained a notice of assignment addressed to the debtor. (See section 4 (1) of the Trading with the Enemy Act, 1939, as to assignments of choses in action.)

an agent in this country. Can the enemy effectively transfer property in this country when he has, before becoming an enemy, irrevocably empowered an agent to do so on his behalf in circumstances which involve no intercourse with him? The decision of a full Court of Appeal in *Tingley* v. *Müller*,[1] to which reference has already been made, might suggest that we can, in spite of the vigorous dissent of Scrutton L.J., who regarded buying or selling the land of an enemy as intercourse with an enemy and illegal, give an affirmative answer to this question, either by reason of the peculiar nature of an irrevocable power of attorney under section 9 of the Conveyancing Act, 1882, now re-enacted in the Law of Property Act, 1925, section 127, or on the ground that no further communication by the agent with his principal is necessary. There appears to be no reason to confine this proposition to real property.

(v) *Disposition by Will: Intestacy*

An enemy dies during a war, leaving property in England. The fact that he was an enemy will not (apart from the claims of the Custodian of Enemy Property or an inquisition of office or the provisions of the Peace Treaty) affect the distribution of his property either in accordance with his will or upon an intestacy, except that the persons entitled, if enemy, will not be able to receive what is due to them during the war.

The practice governing grants of probate and letters of administration upon the death of enemy nationals leaving property in this country was made clearer by the decision in *Re Fischer*[2] and a Practice Note issued by the Senior Registrar of the Principal Probate Registry.[3] In that case upon the death of an enemy national intestate in England during the war the family's adviser was informed by the Board of Trade that

if the deceased at the date of his death was resident in this country, there was no objection to his estate being administered in the usual way, provided that a return was made to the Custodian of Enemy Property of any part of the estate demised [? devised] to, or held for the benefit of, the members of his family resident in enemy territory, and that no part of his estate or the proceeds thereof was transmitted to such members of his family without the necessary government authority.

[1] See above, p. 99; but the authority of that decision was severely damaged by certain speeches delivered in the *Sovfracht* case.

[2] And see *Re Loewenstein* (deceased an allied national resident in enemy-occupied territory).

[3] [1940] 2 All E.R. p. 253. And see *In re Schiff*; *In re Grundt*; *Allen et al.* v. *Markham, Aliens Property Custodian*; *Clark A.G.* v. *Allen et al.*, where, however, a treaty was involved, and Halsbury *Laws of England* (3rd ed. Simonds), vol. 16, § 308.

The Court granted letters of administration to a son of the deceased resident in England and to his solicitor upon an undertaking to comply with the foregoing directions.

C. MARRIAGE AND OTHER DOMESTIC RELATIONS

We speak of the 'marriage contract', and marriage in the United Kingdom is based on consent. But it is something much more than a contract, both because it produces not only reciprocal obligations but also a status, and because it can only be terminated by the parties in a manner authorized by law. Accordingly, we must expect to find that the general principles concerning the effect of war upon contract do not apply to the contract of marriage.

Pre-war marriage

In *Bevan* v. *Bevan*,[1] Sellers J., in considering the effect of war upon a separation agreement between a wife voluntarily resident in enemy territory and a husband in England, remarked that 'Marriage is not affected [by the outbreak of war] because it is a contract creating a status and the status continued'. The wife claimed that payments under the agreement should continue during the war but should be made to the Custodian of Enemy Property, and the learned judge, after a very full examination of the effect of war upon executory contracts between parties separated by the line of war, gave judgment in favour of her claim; in coming to this conclusion he was influenced by the status aspect of the contract of marriage, by the analogy between a contract which is the concomitant of status and Lord Dunedin's contracts 'which are really the concomitants of rights of property',[2] and by the fact that public policy did not require the abrogation of the agreement in question.

Marriage during war

A valid marriage can be contracted in good faith during war between a British subject and an enemy in the national or the territorial sense. 'Marriage is not only a contract, it is a transaction involving and establishing status, and in the absence of authority I am of opinion that there is nothing in our law to render the marriage of a domiciled Englishwoman with an alien enemy an invalid mar-

---

[1] [1955] 2 Q.B. 227, 242, citing *Niboyet* v. *Niboyet* (1878) 4 P.D. 1, 11. On the suggestion that the doctrine of frustration can apply to marriage, see *Kenward* v. *Kenward*.
[2] See above, p. 134.

riage'—per Lord Sterndale M.R. in *Fasbender* v. *Attorney-General*,[1] where a British woman domiciled in England went from England to Germany lawfully between the dates of the signature and ratification of the Treaty of Peace and married a German national there.

Not only is such a marriage valid but the consequences upon nationality which resulted from the marriage of an Englishwoman to an alien before the year 1949 took effect. In the *Fasbender* case cited the woman effectively exchanged her nationality for German nationality, but stress was laid upon the complete good faith of the parties; it by no means follows that an enemy woman who went through a ceremony of marriage with a British subject in time of war merely in order to escape the inconvenience of being an enemy in this country or for some other fraudulent purpose would acquire British nationality.

Many marriages to which one party was British and the other an enemy national took place in England during each of the two World Wars. The automatic acquisition by a foreign woman of British nationality upon being married to a British national came to an end when the British Nationality Act, 1948, entered into force on 1 January 1949; but under subsection 2 of section 6 of that Act, upon making an application to the Secretary of State and upon taking the oath of allegiance in the specified form, she will be 'entitled... to be registered as a citizen of the United Kingdom and Colonies' (which in effect means a British national). There does not seem to be any reason why this national status should not be acquired in the same way as the status of married women, whether the woman is enemy in the personal or the territorial sense or in both.

A very limited amount of correspondence between the United Kingdom and enemy countries can take place under licence. Can a person in this country and a person in an enemy country exchange binding promises to marry? It is submitted that, so far as English law is concerned, the answer is in the negative.

An English Court can grant a decree of divorce against a respondent of enemy nationality.[2]

---

[1] [1922] 2 Ch. 850, 858. The woman had to contend that her marriage was invalid (in spite of the prohibition against bastardizing one's own issue—whether there was any or not does not appear). She also contended that by marrying an enemy she was guilty of treason! See also *Doe* v. *Jones* and comment thereon by Younger L.J. [1922] 2 Ch. at p. 869.

[2] On the question of service of petitions for dissolution of marriage upon persons in enemy or enemy-occupied territory, see *Read* v. *Read* and *Luccioni* v. *Luccioni*.

Guardianship

Hyde[1] cites a passage in *Lamar* v. *Micou*[2] to the effect that

A state of war does not put an end to pre-existing obligations or transfer the property of wards to their guardians, or release the latter from the duty to keep it safely, but suspends until the return of peace the right of any one residing in the enemy's country to sue in our courts.

NOTE ON WILLS OF SOLDIERS, SAILORS AND AIRMEN

A summary of the rules governing these wills, whether written or nuncupative, will be found in Halsbury, *Laws of England* (3rd ed. Simonds), vol. 39, §§ 1342–4. Section 11 of the Wills Act, 1837, is as follows:

Provided always, that any soldier being in actual military service, or any mariner or seaman being at sea, may dispose of his personal estate as he might have done before the making of this Act

which means that any words, clearly expressed, either in speech or in writing, will suffice. We need mention only two points. (*a*) The existence of a legal state of war is not essential: *In the Estate of Rippon*, where a testamentary document made by an officer in the Territorial Army on 25 August 1939, eight days before mobilization and nine days before a state of war came into existence was upheld. (*b*) It is not necessary that the testator should be in the service of the Crown. In 1840 Sir Herbert Jenner[3] said:

with respect to marines, the exemption is extended to merchant seamen, and by parity of reasoning persons in the military service of the East India Company would seem to be included in the term 'soldiers': there is nothing in the [11th] section of the [Wills] Act [1837] which restricts the exemption to the Queen's service. I am of opinion that a soldier in the East India Company's service comes within the exception.

This decision has a bearing upon persons serving in forces under the United Nations command, whether they are members of national forces placed at the disposal of the United Nations or are directly and individually recruited by the United Nations.

In the New Zealand decision, *In re Berry*, an infant soldier in the New Zealand forces who was killed in Korea in 1952 was held by the Supreme Court to have been 'in actual military service' within the meaning of the Wills Act, 1837, s. 11. No declaration of war had been made, and the Court considered it to be unnecessary to decide whether a *de jure* war was in progress or not.[4]

---

[1] III, § 609, p. 1708, n. 5.　　[2] 112 U.S. 452, 464.　　[3] *In the Goods of Donaldson*.
[4] And see *In the Will of Anderson* (1958), a New South Wales case arising upon the death of a soldier in Malaya.

16

TRADING WITH THE ENEMY

BIBLIOGRAPHY

Halsbury, *Laws of England* (3rd ed. Simonds), vol. 39, pp. 55–64.
Baty, 31 *L.Q.R.* (1915), pp. 30–49.
Baty and Morgan, *War: Its Conduct and Legal Results*, pp. 294 ff.
Bentwich, *War and Private Property*, ch. 5.
Hyde, III, pp. 1699 ff.
Huberich, *Trading with the Enemy.*
McNair, *Opinions*, III, pp. 14 ff.
Oppenheim, II, § 101.
Phillimore's *International Law*, III, pp. 165–224.
Pitt Cobbett, II, pp. 86 ff.
Scobell Armstrong, *War and Treaty Legislation, 1914–22.*
Domke, *Trading with the Enemy in World War II* (1943).
Parry, 4 *Modern Law Review* (1941), pp. 161–82.

Having endeavoured to state in chapters 4 and 5 the general principles relating to the effect of war upon contracts, and in later chapters to illustrate those principles by applying them to certain particular contracts, we shall now examine the general expression 'trading with the enemy', which is wider than 'contracting with the enemy' and, according to some authorities, is derived from a different source.

'Trading with the enemy' denotes a criminal offence, a cause of illegality and nullity in a contract or other transaction, and a ground of condemnation by the Prize Court. In due course we shall deal with its present scope and meaning and it will suffice for the present to say that it is, at any rate to-day, equivalent to 'intercourse or contact with the enemy'.

The prohibition of 'trading with the enemy' is of respectable antiquity.[1] Lord Mansfield in *Gist* v. *Mason* refers to 2 Rolle's Abridgement, 173, *Guerre*, where mention is made of a licence granted in the thirteenth year of the reign of Edward II by the keepers of the truce (*custodes treuge*) 'to certain men to go and sell and buy their merchandise in Scotland which was then an enemy of the King', a thing clearly illegal, if not criminal, without a licence, and also states that in the reign of William III the King's judges on being asked whether it was a crime to carry corn to the enemy in time of war

---

[1] See Holdsworth, *History of the English Law*, IX, pp. 99 ff.

replied that it was a misdemeanour. Valuable examinations of the historical aspect of the prohibition will be found in Lord Stowell's judgment in *The Hoop* in 1799, the arguments of counsel in *Potts* v. *Bell*[1] in 1800, and the judgment of Willes J. in *Esposito* v. *Bowden* in 1857.

BASIS OF THE RULE

Many sources or explanations of the prohibition have been put forward from time to time, of which we shall mention the following:

(i) Per Lord Stowell in *The Hoop*,[2] there is

a general rule in the maritime jurisprudence of this country, by which all trading with the public enemy, unless with the permission of the sovereign, is interdicted. It is not a principle peculiar to the maritime law of this country; it is laid down by Bynkershoek as an universal principle of law...

Upon this it is fair to say that it is controversial whether there is any such rule in international law, and that according to the law of many or most European countries there is no *ipso facto* prohibition of intercourse, though the Government of any belligerent State may lawfully prohibit it to its subjects.[3]

(ii) That war involves personal enmity between the nationals of the opposing States. Perhaps the judgment of the United States Supreme Court in *The Rapid*[4] contains the best exposition of this view. In that case an American citizen, upon the outbreak of the Anglo-American War of 1812 to 1814, prudently sent a ship to a British island near Nova Scotia in order to remove to the United States property belonging to him and deposited there 'a long time ago', and the ship and goods were captured by an American privateer on the voyage home. The voyage involved no commercial transaction with the enemy, and the purchase of the goods from England and their deposit on the British island had taken place before the war broke out, so that 'it was all pure gain to the Americans'.[5] The goods, being

---

[1] In *Willison* v. *Patteson* (1817) 7 Taunt. 439, 449, Park J. said: 'Before the case of *Potts* v. *Bell*, there was an opinion prevalent in Westminster Hall, that the commerce with an enemy was not illegal.'

[2] (1799) 1 C. Rob. 196, 198.

[3] See Schwarzenberger, *International Courts* (2nd ed.), pp. 273–6; Oppenheim, II, § 101; Hyde, III, p. 1701. See also *Robson* v. *Premier Oil and Pipe Line Co. Ltd* [1915] 2 Ch. 124, 136, where the Court of Appeal approved the proposition that 'the law of nations as judicially declared prohibits all intercourse between citizens of two belligerents which is inconsistent with the state of war between their countries'.

[4] (1814) 8 Cranch 155, 160. It is unnecessary to stress the relevance of these early decisions of the American Supreme Court in a sphere which great American judges expressly acknowledge to be a common inheritance with England.

[5] Baty and Morgan, p. 298.

libelled in prize by the captor, were condemned to him. Johnson J. based the opinion of the Court upon the personal enmity of the nationals of the opposing States.

In the state of war [he said] nation is known to nation only by their armed exterior; each threatening the other with conquest or annihilation. The individuals who compose the belligerent states exist, as to each other, in a state of utter occlusion. If they meet, it is only in combat...The whole nation are embarked in one common bottom, and must be reconciled to submit to one common fate. Every individual of the one nation must acknowledge every individual of the other nation as his own enemy— because the enemy of his country.

It is this doctrine of personal enmity against which Rousseau protested in his often quoted passage in the *Contrat Social*:[1]

La guerre n'est donc point une relation d'homme à homme, mais une relation d'Etat à Etat, dans laquelle les particuliers ne sont ennemis qu'accidentellement, non point comme hommes, ni même comme citoyens, mais comme soldats; non comme membres de la patrie, mais comme ses défenseurs—

a conception of war which, after being adopted by the French Prize Court at the beginning of the nineteenth century, has obtained a considerable hold upon the European Continent.

It must be noted that the reason given in *The Rapid* proves too much because it applies with almost equal force to enemies in our midst who are not enemies in the territorial sense.

(iii) Again, per Lord Stowell in *The Hoop*—the prohibition is based upon 'the total inability to sustain any contract by an appeal to the tribunals of the one country, on the part of the subjects of the other'.[2] As we have seen in chapter 3 the common law rule which imposes procedural disability upon enemies is not in any way associated with 'trading with the enemy' and was laid down at a time when the King's Courts did not deal with mercantile transactions, so that it cannot be said that the disability is a corollary of the prohibition. Moreover, in the early days the disability seems to have applied to enemies generally, and not merely to enemies in the territorial sense with whom 'trading' was prohibited.[3]

(iv) In the words of Willes J. in delivering the judgment of the King's Bench in *Esposito* v. *Bowden*[4] in 1857,

[1] 1 C. 4.
[2] At p. 200. See Lord Sumner's remarks in *Rodriguez* v. *Speyer Brothers* [1919] A.C. 59, 122, upon the different origins of the prohibition against trading with the enemy and the plea of alien enemy.
[3] See the *Sovfracht* case [1943] A.C. 203, 217, 232.   [4] (1857) 7 El. & Bl. 763, 779.

it is now fully established that the presumed object of war being as much to cripple the enemy's commerce as to capture his property, a declaration of war imports a prohibition of commercial intercourse and correspondence with the inhabitants of the enemy's country and that such intercourse, except with the licence of the Crown, is illegal.

In the *Clapham Steamship Co.'s* case,[1] Rowlatt J., in holding that a pre-war charterparty was abrogated because it benefited or supported the enemy during the war, said that in basing his decisions on this ground 'I am applying what I conceive to be the principle which lies at the very root of the rule which makes trading with the enemy illegal'. Lord Macmillan expressed much the same view in *Schering Ltd* v. *Stockholms Enskilda Bank Aktiebolag*,[2] saying:

The root of the matter is that a country at war cannot allow transactions to proceed which are calculated to aid the enemy in the prosecution of hostilities. A subject of this country must have no truck with the enemy. It is illegal for him to do anything which may tend to increase the war potential of the enemy in goods, money, credit or information.

It is clear that this modern explanation, of which there are traces earlier than 1857, does not explain a case like *The Rapid*, where there was no conceivable benefit to the enemy.

(v) The danger of the leakage of information if intercourse with the enemy, that is to say, across the line of war, were permitted. Lord Stowell said in *The Hoop*:[3]

Who can be insensible to the consequences that might follow, if every person in time of war had a right to carry on a commercial intercourse with the enemy, and under colour of that had the means of carrying on any other species of intercourse he might think fit?

In *Potts* v. *Bell* one of the grounds urged by counsel for the successful litigant was that 'the intercourse which [trading with the enemy] creates between subjects of hostile States necessarily tends to facilitate the conveyance of intelligence to the enemy'. And in the *Ertel Bieber* case[4] one of the grounds upon which Lord Dunedin and Lord Atkinson based the illegality of a contract with the enemy in the territorial sense was, in the words of the former,[5] that it 'gives

---

[1] [1917] 2 K.B. 639, 646.
[2] [1946] 1 A.C. 219, 253.
[3] At p. 200. It is on this ground that in the opinion of Dr Baty (31 *L.Q.R.* (1915), pp. 30–49) the prohibition of trading with the enemy rests. This article is of particular value from the historical point of view and examines both the English and the American cases.
[4] [1918] A.C. 260.
[5] At p. 274.

opportunities for the conveyance of information which may hurt the conduct of the war'.

(vi) The courts have on occasion—particularly in recent years—been content to take the general view that 'the prohibition of intercourse with alien enemies rests upon public policy'.[1]

COMMON LAW

Whatever the true explanation may be, it is clear that by the common law trading with the enemy is, unless performed under licence,[2] both criminal and illegal and that it vitiates both the actual contract,[3] if any, involved in it, and any ancillary contract, such as affreightment or insurance.[4] There is no precise definition of the common law meaning of trading with the enemy. 'Enemy' is here used in the sense of an enemy in the territorial sense (thus covering both enemy territory and enemy occupied territory),[5] for we are not aware that it has ever been criminal or illegal by the common law (or the law maritime) to hold intercourse, otherwise lawful, with an enemy national in England,[6] whether or not he is there within the protection of the Crown.[7] Similarly, it is suggested that a British subject who happens to be in enemy territory and is allowed by the enemy to remain there would not be violating the common law prohibition of trading with the enemy if he were there to enter into various innocent transactions with enemy subjects (as he would have to in order to purchase food and clothing).[8] The prohibition is concerned, in Lord Wright's phrase, with intercourse 'across the line of war'.[9] Furthermore, we must note that in each case the enemy with whom inter-

---

[1] *Robson* v. *Premier Oil and Pipe Line Co. Ltd* [1915] 2 Ch. 124, 136, approved by Lord Dunedin in *Ertel Bieber & Co.* v. *Rio Tinto Co.* [1918] A.C. 260, 268. See also *Porter* v. *Freudenberg* [1915] 1 K.B. 857, 868; *Bevan* v. *Bevan*; the *Sovfracht* case [1943] A.C. 203, 216; *Halsey* v. *Lowenfeld* [1916] 2 K.B. 707, 712, 713.

[2] See below, pp. 356–63. As to intercourse between the Crown and the enemy, see above, pp. 144–6.

[3] If neither of the parties raises this objection, it is the duty of the Court to do so: *Evans* v. *Richardson*. See also the *Sovfracht* case [1943] A.C. 203, 218.

[4] *Potts* v. *Bell*.

[5] As to what constitutes enemy occupied territory, see below, pp. 372–80.

[6] But if a company registered in England acquires enemy character by reason of being under the *de facto* control of enemies in the territorial sense, dealings with it amount to 'trading with the enemy', both at common law (see Lord Parker in the *Daimler* case [1916] 2 A.C. 307, 345) and by statute.

[7] See above, p. 120. *Sed quaere*, dealings with an individual in England who adheres to the enemy?

[8] See above, p. 152, and below, p. 350, n. 4.

[9] In the *Sovfracht* case [1943] A.C. 203, 230: the prohibition thus applies to a neutral alien in the United Kingdom—*The Indian Chief* (1801), 3 C.Rob. 12, 22.

course is illegal must be a person regarded as an enemy by the Court which has to determine the illegality: this is a consideration of particular significance in relation to the Courts of a territory which has been under enemy occupation when, after the end of the occupation, they have to deal with transactions taking place during the occupation. Thus the Privy Council held in *Hangkam Kwingtong Woo* v. *Liu Lan Fong*[1] that an inhabitant of an enemy-occupied country who remains there and such an inhabitant who has left the country prior to the occupation are not, from the point of view of the courts of that country and once the enemy occupation has come to an end, enemies so as to make applicable between them the principle upon which the common law prohibition against trading with the enemy is based.

'Trading with the enemy' covers, as well as trading in the sense of ordinary commercial transactions,[2] intercourse which may have nothing commercial about it.[3] Innocence or ignorance is no defence: in *The Hoop*[4] the claimants had been informed by the Commissioners of Customs at Glasgow that existing Orders in Council permitted the trade with Rotterdam, even though England was at war with Holland, but the property was nevertheless condemned. The prohibition against having intercourse with the enemy is usually expressed in all-embracing terms. Thus, for example, Warrington L.J. in *Halsey* v. *Lowenfeld* considered it 'clearly established' that it was in war time 'unlawful for a British subject to engage in any intercourse with an enemy, whether of a commercial nature or otherwise': intercourse with the enemy is probably unlawful irrespective of whether it may or may not tend to the advantage of the enemy or the detriment of this country.[5] Not only is actual intercourse with the enemy illegal as

---

[1] (1951). See also *Krishna Chettiar* v. *Subbiya Chettiar* (1948) (Burma), and *Li Tsz Chiu and others* v. *Lo Kar Yam and another* (Hong Kong). The Privy Council made further observations on the *Hangkam* case in *The Chartered Bank of India, Australia and China* v. *Wee Kheng Chiang* (1957). See also 28 *B.Y.* (1951), p. 402.

[2] For an instance of barter, see *Van Zijl* v. *Pienaar* (cited in *English and Empire Digest*, vol. 2)—a South African case.

[3] *The Panariellos*; *Robson* v. *Premier Oil and Pipe Line Co. Ltd*.

[4] (1799). See also *The Panariellos*.

[5] *Tingley* v. *Muller* [1917] 2 Ch. 144, 166 (*per* Warrington L.J.) and 171 (*per* Scrutton L.J.), thereby deciding the issue expressly left open by the Court of Appeal in *Robson* v. *Premier Oil and Pipe Line Co. Ltd* [1915] 2 Ch. 124, 136. See also *In re Anglo-International Bank* [1943] 1 Ch. 233, 239. The test of benefit to the enemy or detriment to this country is probably better regarded not as a necessary element in determining the unlawfulness of intercourse, but rather as an additional test by which to determine the illegality of situations in which no actual intercourse with the enemy is involved, as where a contractual relationship is with a neutral (see *Schering Ltd* v. *Stockholms Enskilda Bank Aktiebolag*; *R.* v. *Kupfer*) or in those situations referred to above where the enemy alien concerned is not an enemy in the territorial sense.

a violation of the prohibition on trading with the enemy but even a transaction which merely might involve such intercourse may come within the prohibition.[1] However, particularly where it is a matter of *possible* intercourse only, these considerations are not always to be pursued to their fullest logical extent:[2] the Court is likely to look at the situation with which it is faced in the light of the broad general principles of public policy underlying this part of the law.[3]

The prohibition on trading with the enemy applies equally to the subjects of an ally as to British subjects, and will be enforced by our courts against them.[4] This is more likely to happen in Prize Court proceedings[5] than in others, but in *Kreglinger & Co.* v. *Cohen, trading as Samuel and Rosenfeld* Bray J. held that it was equally illegal for the subject of an ally to trade with the enemy.

Criminally, it appears from *Gist* v. *Mason*[6] that, according to the opinion of all the Judges in King William's time therein referred to, trading with the enemy is a misdemeanour, and we are told[7] that Lord Mansfield, when Solicitor-General, admitted this *arguendo* in 1749. Sir John Marriott, in *The Maria Magdalena* said in 1779 that it was 'a misdemeanour of a very high order to carry on commerce with the enemies of the Crown and kingdom'. In 1900 the Law Officers were quite clear that trading with the enemy was a misdemeanour at common law.[8]

---

[1] Thus where there is a relationship of principal and agent, it is clear that the agent 'may require to have...intercourse with their principal...and I do not think it is an answer to say that in the event it may not be found necessary for the one to communicate with the other': *per* Lord Porter in the *Sovfracht* case [1943] A.C. 203, 254. Compare *Tingley* v. *Muller*, where an irrevocable power of attorney given by an enemy alien to a British agent was, in view of its irrevocability, held to require no intercourse (this decision was strongly criticized in the *Sovfracht* case; see also the comments, above, p. 99).

[2] See *Bevan* v. *Bevan*; *Seligman* v. *Eagle Insurance Company*.

[3] See *Arab Bank Ltd* v. *Barclays Bank* (*D.C.O.*) [1954] 2 All E.R. 226, 239 (*per* Lord Tucker) and *Bevan* v. *Bevan* [1955] 2 All E.R. 206, 212 (*per* Sellers J.).

[4] *The Panariellos*; *The Nayade*; *The Neptunus* (no. 5)—not a very clear case because the traders in the allied country were British subjects. See also *The San Spiridione* and McNair, *Opinions*, III, pp. 17–19, for the situation where the authorities of the ally have granted their subject a licence to trade.

[5] See later, p. 355.

[6] (1786). In *The Odin* (no. 1) (1799) 1 C. Rob. 248, 251, Lord Stowell refers to trading with the enemy as a 'criminal transaction'. In a more recent case Lord Porter seemed to accept that a person 'may be guilty of a crime, albeit only a misdemeanour, if he continues to have intercourse by trading with the enemy': the *Sovfracht* case, [1943] A.C. 203, 249.

[7] By Sir John Nicholl *arguendo* in *Potts* v. *Bell* (1800) 8 T.R. 548, 556.

[8] McNair, *Opinions*, III, p. 29.

BY STATUTE AND DEFENCE REGULATIONS

The common law relating to 'trading with the enemy' is now supplemented[1] by the Trading with the Enemy Act, 1939,[2] as amended by the Emergency Laws (Miscellaneous Provisions) Act, 1953.[3] The Act is still in force, It defines the offence of, and specifies the penalties for any person,[4] trading with the enemy; defines 'enemy';[5] provides for the inspection and supervision of businesses; and prohibits, except by licence, the transfer of negotiable instruments and choses in action[6] by enemies and the transfer of securities by or to enemies and the allotment of securities to them.

For the purposes of the Act[7] a person is deemed to have traded with the enemy[8]—

(a) if he has had any commercial, financial or other intercourse or dealings with, or for the benefit of, an enemy, and, in particular,

---

[1] *Robson* v. *Premier Oil and Pipe Line Co. Ltd* [1915] 2 Ch. 124, 130–1. See also *Bevan* v. *Bevan.*

[2] The Act was deemed to have come into operation on 3 September 1939: section 17 (2) and S.R. & O. 1939, no. 1195. For all purposes of the Act and Orders made thereunder, Germany ceased to be treated as if it were enemy territory on 6 October 1952 (S.R. & O. 1952, no. 1760): similar provision was made in respect of the other states against which the United Kingdom had been at war (S.R. & O. 1948, nos. 157–61, and S.R. & O. 1952, nos. 1923 and 1989). As to the application of the Act to the Isle of Man, Channel Islands, colonies, British protectorates, trust territories and foreign countries or territories in which the Crown has jurisdiction, see section 14 and Orders in Council made thereunder. The Act repealed all but a trifling part of the Trading with the Enemy legislation of the 1914–18 war. Other statutes may affect trade with the enemy, such as the Exportation of Arms Act, 1900, and the Customs (Exportation Restriction) Act, 1914. And see the Finance Act, 1944, 4th Schedule, Part II, in connection with estate duty.

[3] This Act puts on a permanent basis certain amendments to the Trading with the Enemy Act, 1939, which were made by Defence Regulations made under the Emergency Powers (Defence) Act, 1939.

[4] Not a British subject in enemy territory—see Attorney-General in Hansard, *Commons* (15 December 1944), col. 1583. But see *Kuenigl* v. *Donnersmarck* [1955] 1 Q.B. 515, 539, where McNair J. remarked (*obiter*) that he was by no means satisfied that a British subject voluntarily residing in enemy territory 'would be freed from the prohibitions imposed by the Trading with the Enemy Act. Many of the old decisions dating from a more liberal age which suggest that British subjects in enemy territory enjoy a measure of freedom of action in their dealings with the enemy are of doubtful authority today.'

[5] See Parry in 4 *Modern Law Review* (1941), pp. 161–82.

[6] Where an enemy's goods have been seized and ordered to be sold by the Prize Court, the proceeds being payable to the Custodian of Enemy Property, the enemy's rights in respect of the property are choses in action; and if he has insured the goods with a neutral insurer and, after the Prize Court's seizure and order, he has abandoned his rights to them in favour of the insurer who has accepted the abandonment and paid the money due under the policy of insurance, the transaction constitutes an assignment of the chose in action which will be ineffective unless it has been licensed: *Allgemeine Versicherungs-Gesellschaft Helvetia* v. *Administrator of German Property.*

[7] As to the meaning of the phrase in the Act 'for the purposes of this Act', see p. 107 above.

[8] Section 1 (2). References in the section to an enemy include a person acting on behalf of an enemy: section 1 (3).

but without prejudice to the generality of the foregoing provision, if he has—

    (i) supplied any goods to or for the benefit of an enemy, or obtained any goods from an enemy, or traded in, or carried, any goods consigned to or from an enemy or destined for or coming from enemy territory, or

    (ii) paid or transmitted any money, negotiable instrument or security for money to or for the benefit of an enemy or to a place in enemy territory, or

    (iii) performed any obligation to, or discharged any obligation of, an enemy, whether the obligation was undertaken before or after the commencement of this Act; or

(b) if he has done anything which, under the following provisions of this Act,[1] is to be treated as trading with the enemy....

However, a person is not deemed to have traded with the enemy by reason only that he has—

    (i) done anything under an authority given generally or specially by, or by any person authorized in that behalf by, a Secretary of State, the Treasury or the Board of Trade, or

    (ii) received payment from an enemy of a sum of money due in respect of a transaction under which all obligations on the part of the person receiving payment had already been performed when the payment was received, and had been performed at a time when the person from whom the payment was received was not an enemy.

The expression 'enemy' for the purposes of the Act means[2]—

(a) any State, or Sovereign of a State, at war with His Majesty,

(b) any individual resident[3] in enemy territory,

(c) any body of persons (whether corporate or unincorporate) carrying on business[4] in any place, if and so long as the body is controlled by a person who, under this section, is an enemy,

(d) any body of persons constituted or incorporated in, or under the laws of, a State at war with His Majesty,[5]

---

[1] See sections 3A (7), 4 (3) and 6 (1).

[2] Section 2 (1).

[3] Residence does not have to be voluntary, the mere fact of residence being sufficient: *Re Hatch, Public Trustee* v. *Hatch*; *Vamvakas* v. *Custodian of Enemy Property*. See also *Kuenigl* v. *Donnersmarck* [1955] 1 Q.B. 515, 539. But a British prisoner of war in enemy territory is not resident there so as to be an enemy: *Vandyke* v. *Adams*. Cf. *Scotland* v. *South African Territories Ltd.*

[4] For the meaning of carrying on business, see *Central India Mining Co.* v. *Société Coloniale Anversoise.*

[5] Thus mere constitution or incorporation of a company in or under the laws of an enemy-occupied State does not appear to make the company an enemy, although control by a person resident in enemy-occupied territory, or territory assimilated to enemy territory by the Board of Trade, does.

and

(*e*) as respects any business carried on in enemy territory, any individual or body of persons (whether corporate or unincorporate) carrying on that business;

but does not include any individual by reason only that he is an enemy subject.

Furthermore, the Board of Trade may by order direct that any person specified in the order shall, for the purposes of the Act, be deemed to be an enemy.[1]

Other terms whose meanings in the Act have been defined and which we should mention are 'enemy subject' and 'enemy territory'. 'Enemy subject' means[2]

(*a*) an individual who, not being either a British subject or a British protected person, possesses the nationality of a State at war with His Majesty, or

(*b*) a body of persons constituted or incorporated in, or under the laws of, any such State.

The expression 'enemy territory' means[3]

any area which is under the sovereignty of, or in the occupation of, a Power with whom His Majesty is at war, not being an area in the occupation of His Majesty or of a Power allied with His Majesty.

The Board of Trade also has power to direct[4]

that the provisions of this Act shall apply in relation to any area specified in the order as they apply in relation to enemy territory, and the said provisions shall apply accordingly.

A few comments are required.

(i) It should be noted how wide may be the scope of the definition of enemy in the territorial sense as a result of the power conferred upon the Board of Trade by section 15 (1 A).[5] In addition the certificate of a Secretary of State is made by subsection 2 of section 15

---

[1] Section 2 (2). In pursuance of this power the Board of Trade issued from time to time lists of persons who were for the purposes of the Act deemed to be enemies. The first of these Orders was S.R. & O. 1939, no. 1166. These Lists of Specified Persons have now been revoked: S.R. & O. 1946, no. 1041, and see nos. 1040, 1042 and 1044. Note also the United States of America's Proclaimed List of certain 'blocked' nationals which was promulgated in the United States in pursuance of the President's Proclamation of 17 July 1941, and embraced all the names contained in the United Kingdom lists of Specified Persons and others in addition.

[2] Section 15 (1).   [3] Section 15 (1).   [4] Section 15 (1 A).

[5] Orders were made under this power applying the Act to the formerly Unoccupied Zone of France, including Corsica and Algeria, the French Zone of Morocco and Tunisia, to other countries which were or had been under enemy occupation, and to some which without formal occupation had been dominated by enemy influence. And note section 2 and paragraph 9 of the Second Schedule to the Emergency Laws (Miscellaneous Provisions) Act, 1953 (replacing with permanent effect S.R. & O. 1943, no. 1034).

conclusive on the question of the fact of any area at any time becoming or ceasing to be under the sovereignty or occupation of any power.[1]

(ii) The generality of the offence as defined in subsection 2 (*a*) of section 1 should be noted—'any commercial, financial or other intercourse or dealings with, or for the benefit of, an enemy'.[2]

(iii) It is not forbidden to receive payment of money from an enemy[3] in respect of a transaction under which the recipient had performed all his obligations when the payment was received and while the payer was not an enemy.[4] Another instance of permitting an enemy to make payments in this country occurred in connection with Patents, Trade Marks and Designs under General Licences, referred to above,[5] so long as those General Licences were in force.

(iv) Quite apart from the saving of the rights of the Crown contained in section 16, the power of the Crown to grant general or special licences to trade is implicit in proviso (i) to subsection 2 of section 1 of the Act.

(v) The Act by subsection 1 (*c*) of section 2 adopts (extending it to unincorporate bodies) the famous *Daimler* test of the enemy character of corporations, which we have already discussed.[6]

Reference should be made to some of the decisions given upon the legislation of the Wars of 1914 to 1918 and 1939 to 1945. The expression 'for the benefit of an enemy' occurs both in the legislation of the War of 1914 to 1918 and in the Trading with the Enemy Act, 1939. The decision of the Court of Criminal Appeal in *R.* v. *Kupfer* shows that these words have a wide application. Lord Reading C.J. said of them that they

were deliberately introduced for the purpose of preventing devices, tactics, and various means by which mercantile houses might seek, but for these

---

[1] See chapters 17 and 18, Belligerent Occupation, and the cases there cited.

[2] On the subject of credit balances due to British subjects in enemy-occupied territory from local branches or subsidiaries of British banks, and their recoverability in England, see a debate in the House of Lords on 16 July 1940 (*Hansard*, vol. 116, no. 72), *Clare & Co.* v. *Dresdner Bank*, and *Richardson* v. *Richardson*. See also above, pp. 227–8.

[3] For instances from the War of 1914 to 1918 see *Halsey* v. *Lowenfeld* and *Seligman* v. *Eagle Insurance Co.*: while the judgments in the first case were clearly related to the terms of the Proclamation which permitted the receipt of payments from an enemy, Neville J.'s judgment in the latter appears (although it is far from clear) to consider the Proclamation as in this respect merely confirmatory of the position at common law.

[4] Since payment by the enemy himself is not forbidden, payment to a British creditor by a British surety for the enemy debtor has also been held to be not prohibited: *R. & A. Kohnstamm Ltd* v. *Ludwig Krumm (London) Ltd*, which was mentioned in *Stockholms Enskilda Bank Aktiebolaget* v. *Schering Ltd* discussed later; see also *Seligman* v. *Eagle Insurance Co.* for a payment by a British surety of a debt due by an enemy to a British creditor, where it was very much in the interest of the surety to make the payment.

[5] P. 294. [6] Above, p. 102.

words, to make payments indirectly, notwithstanding that there is an express prohibition of a direct payment. It was doubtless considered that it was necessary...to throw the net wide in order that there should not be this means of evading the law and therefore of assisting the enemy by adding to or protecting his resources.

Accordingly where the London partner of a firm which also comprised two partners at Frankfurt-am-Main (the firm being *ipso facto* dissolved by the outbreak of war) paid during the war to a person in a neutral State a pre-war debt which had become due from the firm as the result of a transaction between the neutral and the Frankfurt partners, thus extinguishing the obligations of the latter, it was held that the London partner was rightly convicted of having made a payment 'to or for the benefit of an enemy'.

In *Stockholms Enskilda Bank A/B* v. *Schering Ltd*[1] a British company successfully resisted a claim by a Swedish Bank upon a pre-war agreement to pay a debt by instalments upon receiving assignments of corresponding parts of the Bank's claim against a German company, the grounds being that payment under the agreement would be a financial dealing for the benefit of the enemy and would operate to discharge an obligation of the enemy, though substituting therefor an obligation to the British company. From the decision of the Master of the Rolls in this case it is clear that the expression 'for the benefit of an enemy' in section 1 (2) of the Trading with the Enemy Act, 1939, is 'of the widest possible character' and is 'wide enough to sweep in any transaction of which it can be truly said (and this is a question of fact in each case) that it is for the benefit of an enemy'.

On the other hand, benefit to the enemy is not an essential feature of the statutory offence. Thus in 1915, when a person in this country obtained after the outbreak of war from enemy territory property belonging to him and in the hands of persons thereon, though no payment was due from him therefor, he was held by the Court of Criminal Appeal[2] to have been rightly convicted under a clause in a Proclamation (having statutory force), which forbade persons to obtain 'from the [German] Empire any goods...'. No doubt this would also be a common law misdemeanour. The mischief and the danger lie in the communication.[3]

---

[1] It is important not to confuse this action brought by the Stockholm Bank against Schering [1941] 1 K.B. 424 (C.A.) with the later action brought by Schering against the Stockholm Bank [1944] Ch. 13; [1946] A.C. 219, on which see above, p. 138.

[2] *R. v. Oppenheimer and Colbeck.*

[3] As to the receipt of sums of money from an enemy, see the second proviso to section 1 (2) of the Trading with the Enemy Act, 1939, and p. 353, n. 4 above.

IN PRIZE[1]

'Trading with the Enemy' in the technical sense has nothing to do with the carriage of contraband, the breach of a blockade or the rendering of 'unneutral service'.[2] These are acts which cannot be described as unlawful but are acts which international law permits a belligerent to prevent if he can and to punish by means of the machinery of his Prize Court, by condemnation of the property involved. The reason why forfeiture of the property involved is the appropriate penalty appears to be, in the words of the Court (presumably Lord Stowell) in *The Nelly*, 'that it is taken adhering to the enemy, and therefore the proprietor is *pro hac vice* to be considered as an enemy'. It is in fact enemy property.

From early times the Prize Court has enforced the prohibition against 'trading with the enemy' by condemning ships and cargoes involved therein. Lord Stowell in *The Hoop*[3] gives many instances of condemnation from 1750 onwards. In *The Jonge Pieter* he applied the doctrine of continuous voyage, and condemned goods which were consigned from London to a neutral port 'with an ulterior purpose of sending them on to' an enemy port.

In view of the improbability of a continuance[4] of the practice of granting licences to carry out ordinary trading transactions with the enemy it is unnecessary to examine the numerous decisions given before and during the period of the Napoleonic Wars. Hall[5] gives a useful summary of some of the principal rules that were laid down, in the main, by the Prize Court. Lord Stowell's judgment in *The Hoop*[6] may be regarded as the leading exposition of the attitude of the Prize Court in the matter. Perhaps the most important decision in prize given upon this matter during the War of 1914 to 1918 is that of Sir Samuel Evans P., in *The Panariellos*,[7] in which he laid down certain general propositions which may be summarized as follows:

    (i) upon the outbreak of war all intercourse, commercial or

---

[1] See Colombos, *Law of Prize* (3rd ed. 1949), to which we are much indebted.

[2] One consequence of this distinction is illustrated by the opinion of the Privy Council in *The Panariellos* (1916) 32 T.L.R. 459, 462, namely, that a cargo involved in trading with the enemy does not cease to be confiscable because the actual *delictum* has come to en end.

[3] (1799) 1 C. Rob. 196, 198, and see Sir John Nicholl's argument in *Potts* v. *Bell*. For later cases see *The Cosmopolite* (no. 2).

[4] In the early part of the 1939–45 War it was necessary, for urgent industrial reasons, to grant a number of licences for the importation through neutral countries of small lots of enemy goods. Later there was a good deal of licensing of innocuous transactions with persons in unoccupied France.

[5] *International Law*, § 196.   [6] *Supra*, p. 344.

[7] (1915) 31 T.L.R. 326; affirmed by the Privy Council (1916) 32 T.L.R. 459.

otherwise,[1] with the enemy (*scilicet*, in the territorial sense) becomes illegal, unless licensed;

(ii) the prohibition applies equally to the subjects of allies;[2]

(iii) the property of the subjects of allies involved in such trading may be captured by any allied belligerent and condemned by his Prize Court;[3]

(iv) property may be condemned, whether the owner is acting with good faith or not.[3]

'Trading with the enemy', as the term implies, denotes an act which takes place during a war, and accordingly the Prize Court declined to regard as unlawful and contrary to public policy an ingenious transaction of barter—carried through before the war broke out—which had the effect of enabling a certain cargo *ex* a British ship to escape condemnation as enemy property.[4] (That was the ground on which condemnation was sought—not trading with the enemy.) 'The common law of England', said Lord Merriman P.,[5] 'and the legislation relating to trading with an enemy...forbids any form of commerce with the enemy, but, as the word implies, that assumes that the commerce is transacted after war has broken out.'

Old cases will be found in which a British subject, resident and trading in a neutral country, has been invested by our Courts with neutral character, and allowed to recover upon a claim involving trading with a country at war with Great Britain;[6] but we should not recommend a British subject to-day to test the continued validity of these decisions by a personal experiment.

TRADING WITH THE ENEMY UNDER LICENCE

Up to and including the early years of the nineteenth century the orthodox view upon trading with the enemy was not nearly so severe as it is now,[7] and it was customary frequently to relax the general

---

[1] *Obiter*, on this point; see also *Robson* v. *Premier Oil and Pipe Line Co.* [1915] 2 Ch. 124, 136, adopted by Lord Dunedin in the *Ertel Bieber* case [1918] A.C. 260, 268.

[2] In this respect following Lord Stowell in *The Nayade* and *The Neptunus*. It has been held that it is not competent to one ally, acting alone, to license trade with the enemy so as to bind his allies: *The San Spiridione*; see also, for the view of the Law Officers fifty years earlier, McNair, *Opinions*, III, pp. 17–19.

[3] On this point see also *The Hoop*. *The Madonna Delle Gracie* (1802) is a curious case of trading with the enemy for the purpose of supplying the British Navy with wine: property not condemned.

[4] *The Glenearn*; see note in 58 *L.Q.R* (1942), pp. 19–21. For another instance of a pre-war transaction, see *Wilson* v. *Ragosine & Co.*

[5] [1941] P. at p. 61.   [6] *The Danous*; *Bell* v. *Reid.*

[7] 'Thus in the year 1809 sixteen thousand licences were granted, and in the year 1811 eight thousand' (Butler and Maccoby, *Development of International Law*, p. 325). 'The

principle by granting to persons in this country, and in the enemy country 'licences to trade', either general or special, which had the effect of legalizing *pro tanto* intercourse with the enemy and of making enforceable in English Courts contracts directly or collaterally involved in the process.[1] The case law which grew up round this practice will be found in the text-books[2] and need not detain us, as, so far as the Wars of 1914 to 1918 and 1939 to 1945 were concerned, the practice of granting licences for general trading purposes was not revived and the law is mainly of historical interest. However, the Trading with the Enemy Act, 1939, preserves the possibility of licences being given, and under proviso (i) to section 1(2) a person is not deemed to have traded with the enemy by reason only that he has done something under an authority given generally or specially by a Secretary of State, the Treasury or the Board of Trade.

Licences to engage in trade which would otherwise involve the criminality and the nullity of the transaction may be granted (*a*) to or for the benefit of British subjects,[3] (*b*) to enemy subjects, resident either in this country[4] or in their own country[5] or (*c*) to neutral subjects.[6] Practice during the War of 1914 to 1918 showed a number of exceptional instances of permitting intercourse with the enemy under licence from the appropriate Department of the Government,[7] and during the War of 1939 to 1945 the extension of the area of

particular mode in which [the consent of the Crown] may be expressed is not material. It may be signified in a variety of ways—by a licence granted to the individual for the special occasion, by an order in council, by proclamation, or under the authority of an act of parliament, to which the Crown is necessarily a party' (per Lord Stowell in *The Charlotta* (1814) 1 Dod. 387, 390).

[1] Persons in neutral countries also sometimes received licences which protected them from the normal consequences of carriage of contraband or breach of blockade, but these were not licences to trade with the enemy in the strict sense. *The Rannveig* is a case in which a neutral shipowner unsuccessfully contended that his contraband trade with the enemy was by implication licensed by Great Britain; it turned upon the interpretation of the agreement alleged to confer such a licence, and it was not contended that such trade would not have been protected if the agreement had extended to it.

[2] For instance, Halleck, *International Law* (3rd ed. 1893, by Sherston Baker), chap. xxx; Oppenheim, II, p. 536 (n. i); *Usparicha v. Noble*, and comment in Pitt Cobbett, II, p. 93; Hall, § 196; Halsbury, *Laws of England* (3rd ed. Simonds), vol. 39, pp. 36–8. Numerous instances will be found in *English Prize Cases*, vols. I and II, and in the *English and Empire Digest* (1958), vol. 2, Aliens, Part VII, Section 6.

[3] *The Cousine Marianne*; *Flindt v. Scott*, where many cases upon licences are referred to.

[4] *Usparicha v. Noble.*

[5] *Kensington v. Inglis* (1807) 8 East 273, 290 (where Lord Ellenborough C.J. held that the enemy could not sue in his own name but that his British agent or trustee could sue on his behalf). He expressed the opinion that 'the King's licence cannot, in point of law, have the effect of removing the personal disability of the [enemy] trader, in respect of suit, so as to enable him to sue in his own name'. *Sed quaere.*

[6] *Anthony and Another v. Moline.*

[7] Scobell Armstrong, *War and Treaty Legislation, 1914–22* (2nd ed. (1922)), contains much information on this subject.

'enemy territory' by occupation and the misfortunes of some thousands of British and allied nationals detained therein involved fairly extensive licensing of transactions which, though for their benefit, did not involve profit to the enemy either in foreign exchange or in goods.[1] Moreover, it was the practice of the Trading with the Enemy Department to issue licences permitting actions to be instituted or carried on by or on behalf of enemies in the territorial sense subject to any objection that might be raised by defendants and to the order of the Court thereon.

(i) *Patents, trade marks and designs*

Licences were granted in respect of certain transactions concerning patents, trade marks and designs: the matter is discussed in more detail in chapter 12.

(ii) *Life insurance policies*

The effect of war upon this contract is discussed in chapter 11.

(iii) *Purchase of books*

During the earlier part of the War of 1914 to 1918 a number of booksellers in this country received licences to procure books published in enemy countries, and these licences were exercised by invoking the aid of a bookseller in a neutral country. Later this practice was modified and such books were obtained upon application to H.M. Stationery Office, which presumably procured them through our diplomatic or consular representatives in neutral countries. During the War of 1939 to 1945 until the invasion of Holland the Trading with the Enemy Branch in approved cases licensed English booksellers to procure books of a scientific or educational character from enemy countries. Thereafter the purchase of enemy books was much restricted, and the procedure was that H.M. Stationery Office bought them on request through safe channels in neutral countries, thus exercising a sort of censorship.

(iv) *Intercourse by solicitor and counsel*

The licensing of solicitors (and, apparently by implication, of counsel) acting on behalf of enemies is referred to above.[2]

---

[1] As to the possibility of a company having a duty to seek a licence to communicate with shareholders in enemy territory, see *In re Anglo-International Bank Ltd* [1943] 1 Ch. 233, 244.

[2] P. 325.

(v) *Release of cargoes*

Another instance of licensed transactions with the enemy occurred where, acting through the London Chamber of Commerce, British owners of cargo on vessels in non-enemy ports were permitted, in order to obtain possession of it, 'to pay freight and other necessary charges to or for the benefit of any enemy'.[1]

(vi) *Miscellaneous intercourse*

Circumstances arise in which a trader in this country may wish to communicate with an enemy correspondent, for instance, to ascertain whether goods shipped or commercial documents have reached their destination (information which may be of value in any post-war clearing of debts), or to learn whether the latter concurs in the view of the former that a particular contract between them has been dissolved by the outbreak of war, and the Trading with the Enemy Department had power to permit the necessary communication. Licences were also granted for the transmission of documents establishing or negativing the title to property or of documents required in Probate proceedings.

An official notice issued in July 1940 stated the conditions upon which persons in this country were authorized to communicate upon personal matters with friends in enemy and enemy-occupied territory.

(vii) *During an armistice*

A long interval elapsed between the cessation of hostilities between Great Britain and Turkey in 1918 and the coming into effect of the Peace Treaty of Lausanne by its ratification in 1924. A shorter interval occurred between the cessation of hostilities with Bulgaria in 1918 and the coming into effect of the Peace Treaty of Neuilly on 9 August 1920. Nevertheless, doubtless in order that British traders might not suffer from the competition of commercial rivals not handicapped by a state of war, the Board of Trade issued a general licence to trade with those countries dated 17 February 1919, and trading took place thereunder.[2] There is little doubt that as a matter of law (apart from any exercise of power by the Crown under the Termination of the Present War (Definition) Act, 1918) a state of war with

[1] S.R. & O. 1939, no. 1695; and see S.R. & O. 1940, no. 1567, as amended by S.R. & O. 1941, no. 244.

[2] See Beckett in 39 *L.Q.R.* (1923), p. 89; Scobell Armstrong, *op. cit.* Appendix x, prints a number of Post-Armistice Licences for the Resumption of Trade. See also *Fasbender* v. *Attorney-General* [1922] 2 Ch. 850, 864, for permission given to a British subject to go to Germany during the period of the armistice in order to marry a German national; above, p. 341.

those countries continued until the respective peace treaties came into force. Similarly, after the end of fighting in the War of 1939 to 1945 and in the absence of a peace treaty with Germany, a general licence to trade was issued in respect of Germany by the Board of Trade on 29 March 1949.[1]

(viii) *Collateral effects of licence*

Does a licence, general or special, merely protect the trader acting under it from a criminal prosecution, or does it do something more? We shall consider, first, the effect upon the contracts involved and, secondly, the right to sue.

(*a*) *Contracts.* It may be stated generally that the effect of the licence is to validate and render enforceable in English Courts both the contract directly authorized by it, for instance, a contract of sale, and any contract collateral or incidental thereto, for instance, affreightment and insurance.[2]

It is, however, difficult to see how it can *ipso facto* revive a contract upon which the effect of war has already operated and in regard to which the effect is dissolution. Suppose that *A* in London was at the time of the outbreak of war the agent of *B* in Berlin. The outbreak of war dissolved the agency. At a later stage *A* succeeds in persuading the Trading with the Enemy Branch that it is in the national interest that he should be licensed to act as *B*'s agent for a particular transaction or class of transactions. *A* may be the channel of importation into this country of a certain enemy product which we shall be glad to continue to receive until the enemy Government discovers the trade and stops it. *A* and *B* may thereupon create a new and valid contract of agency,[3] either expressly or by implication, but the grant of the licence does not *ipso facto* revive the agency sundered by the outbreak of war. There is express authority in *Esposito* v. *Bowden*[4] for the view that a contract once dissolved by the outbreak of war on the ground of illegality cannot be *ipso facto* redintegrated by a subsequent Order in Council permitting the otherwise illegal trading. There can be no doubt upon the legal principle involved, as has now been made clear by speeches in the House of Lords in the *Sovfracht* case.

The decision of the Court of Appeal in *Meyer* v. *Louis Dreyfus et Cie*[5]

---

[1] S.R. & O. 1949, no. 605.

[2] *Usparicha* v. *Noble* (the licensee was an enemy national resident in this country); *Morgan* v. *Oswald*.

[3] See *Duhammel, Administrator of La Tailleur* v. *Pickering*, for a promise, made after the end of a war, to pay on a void contract concluded during the war being held to be enforceable.

[4] (1855) 4 El. & Bl. 963, 975; (1857) 7 El. & Bl. 763, 778. See above, p. 132.

[5] The facts are not clear to us.

has given rise to misunderstanding and must be read in the light of the preceding paragraph. The question before the Court was whether, after the occupation of Paris by the Germans, service of a writ of summons upon one Gamburg, the London manager of a Paris firm carrying on business in England, was effective service upon the firm. Conditional appearance was entered on behalf of the four partners constituting the firm, and the action proceeded against the firm. Gamburg and his successors received a licence from the Trading with the Enemy Branch—its date and terms do not appear in the reports— to carry on the business of the then enemy firm on a basis of accountability to the Custodian, and the assets were treated as being held on the Custodian's account—not on the firm's account. There was no question, therefore, of any revival of Gamburg's previous agency for the firm and no evidence that he had ever sought to bring this about. The Court of Appeal held that as a result of the licence he was a 'person having at the time of service the control or management of the partnership business' in London, so that service upon him of a writ of summons satisfied the requirements of Order 48A, rule 3, of the Rules of the Supreme Court, relating to service upon a partnership. That is not equivalent to saying that Gamburg, without any renewal of his agency after the occupation of Paris and the issue of the licence, had power to bind Louis Dreyfus et Cie by contracts made by him on their behalf. As MacKinnon L.J. said, the objection to the validity of the service was a 'pure technicality...If the defendants here had been an individual and not a firm, the service of the concurrent writ on Mr Gamburg would have been perfectly proper; and on the authority of *Porter* v. *Freudenberg*[1] the initiation of these proceedings would have given to the plaintiff the right to come to the court...' In that case the Court of Appeal intimated that, upon the materials before it, service of the notice of the writ should be effected by substituted service on the person who at the outbreak of war was the agent in England of the enemy defendant, but there is no suggestion that the agent still had power to bind his enemy principal by contract. MacKinnon L.J., by invoking the analogy of substituted service, seems to indicate that what matters is that the person served should be so circumstanced in regard to the enemy defendant that 'in all reasonable probability, if not certainty' service upon him would 'be effective to bring knowledge of the writ or the notice of the writ (as the case may be) to the defendant'.[2] The fact that Gamburg had been licensed to continue to manage the defendant's business contri-

---

[1] [1915] 1 K.B. 857 (C.A.).   [2] At p. 889.

buted to the 'reasonable probability' if it did not create a 'certainty'. The Court of Appeal—whether rightly or wrongly does not matter for our purpose—considered that 'reasonable probability' existed and therefore upheld the service of the writ. It would be a profound mistake to draw from this decision the conclusion that the grant of the licence to Gamburg *ipso facto* redintegrated his pre-occupation authority to bind the Paris firm by contract or otherwise.[1]

(*b*) *The right to sue.* The person licensed, be he the grantee of a special licence or be he merely acting under a general licence, can certainly sue in connection with the trading in an English Court, except that according to the decision of the Court of King's Bench in *Kensington* v. *Inglis* a licensee who is an enemy national, resident in his own country, cannot sue in his own name but only through a British agent or trustee. *Usparicha* v. *Noble* shows that a licensee who is an enemy national, resident in this country, may sue in his own name.[2] The more difficult question is that of the right of the other party to the trading, the enemy (in the territorial sense) who is traded with, to sue in an English Court. We are not aware of any express decision upon this question in the affirmative or negative.[3] There are many dicta to the effect, in the words of Lord Stowell in *The Hoop*, that 'the legality of commerce and the mutual use of courts of justice are inseparable', and Sir Eric Beckett[4] contended that, more particularly since the House of Lords laid it down by a majority in *Rodriguez* v. *Speyer Brothers*[5] that the plea of alien enemy is based upon a flexible rule of public policy which must give way when to allow an alien enemy to sue would not involve mischief from the point of view of public policy, the enemy traded with under licence should be allowed

---

[1] In *Arnhold Karberg & Co.* v. *Blythe, Green, Jourdain & Co.*; *Theodor Schneider & Co.* v. *Burgett & Newsam* [1915] 2 K.B. 379, 383, 391, Scrutton J. had to consider the effect of a licence granted by the Board of Trade on 25 September 1914 to a British party to a contract of affreightment which was dissolved on 4 August 1914 on the ground that its performance involved intercourse with the enemy or that an enemy was a party to it or on both these grounds. He had no hesitation in holding that the licence authorized the British subject to perform with impunity the act specified in it, namely to pay freight and charges to the agent of an enemy shipowner for the purpose of obtaining possession of his cargo, but that it in no way validated the dissolved contract, either prospectively or retrospectively. This view was affirmed expressly by two members of the Court of Appeal and, by implication, by the third ([1916] 1 K.B. 495, 508, 515). Warrington L.J. expressed the opinion (at p. 515) that the point had already been decided in *Esposito* v. *Bowden*.

[2] There is some discussion of the right to sue in *Public Trustee* v. *Davidson*, a Scottish case.

[3] In the *Sovfracht* case [1943] A.C. 203, 218, Lord Wright considered a licence to trade with the enemy as adequate to avoid the prohibition on trading with the enemy but as 'not dealing' with the inability of the enemy to proceed in court.

[4] 39 *L.Q.R.* (1923), pp. 89–97.

[5] See, however, above, pp. 82–4.

to sue in an English Court. The question is far from being one of purely academic interest. The occasion of Sir Eric Beckett's examination of it was the position of Turkish residents with whom persons in this country were allowed to trade under a general licence issued by the Board of Trade in 1919, and we apprehend that the same question would arise if an English solicitor licensed to defend and receive instructions from a client who was an enemy in the territorial sense were negligent in the protection of his interests. We suggest that it would be repugnant to English justice that an enemy traded with under licence should have no recourse to an English Court during war for the enforcement of his contract.[1]

Licences to enemies to bring suit are granted in certain cases by the Home Office.[2]

ADMINISTRATION

On 3 September 1939, the Treasury and the Board of Trade as the Departments charged with the administration of the Trading with the Enemy Act set up a joint Branch (Trading with the Enemy Branch)[3] to act as a watchdog in matters of trading with the enemy, and in proper cases to issue licences or admonitions to banks, insurance companies, and traders generally. For convenience these functions were performed by the Patent Office in respect of patents, designs and trade marks, and matters involving the investigation and subsequent action upon the affairs of companies in the United Kingdom thought to be enemy-owned or possibly acting or capable of acting in enemy interests were dealt with by the Companies Department of the Board of Trade. A Notice to Traders was issued by the Board of Trade on the outbreak of war and widely distributed.

TRADING WITH THE 'ENEMY' IN CASES OF CONFLICTS NOT AMOUNTING TO WAR

It is uncertain to what extent the Trading with the Enemy Act, 1939, can apply if the United Kingdom is not in a state of war with another country. In a strict sense there are only 'enemies' and 'enemy ter-

---

[1] An alien enemy authorized to enter into a transaction under the first proviso to section 1 (2) of the Trading with the Enemy Act, 1939 (quoted above, p. 351), was authorized to institute legal proceedings arising out of such a transaction by the Defence (Trading with the Enemy) Regulations, 1940 (S.R. & O. 1940, no. 1092) regulation 9 (added by S.R. & O. 1945, no. 1534). In *Schering A.G.* v. *Pharmedica Property Ltd*, an Australian court held that a licence to trade carried with it the right to sue for the purpose of protecting the trade which is licensed.

[2] See pp. 108–9, but note n. 1 on p. 109; as to the enemy's solicitor, see p. 325.

[3] Later called the Trading with the Enemy Department.

ritory' during a state of war, and several provisions of the Act refer to there being a 'war' or 'state of war'.[1] But we should note that section 15 (1 A) empowers the Board of Trade by order to direct that the provisions of the Act shall apply to any area specified in the order as they apply in relation to enemy territory. This clearly allows the Act to be applied to territory which, during a state of war, is not strictly enemy territory because it is not under the sovereignty or occupation of the enemy. But may it also allow the Act to be applied to territory which is not enemy territory because there is no war: if the Act can be applied despite the former missing condition, may it not also be applied despite the latter? Taken by itself the power conferred by section 15 (1 A) would seem to enable the Act to be applied to the territory of a State against which the United Kingdom was engaged in an armed conflict not amounting to war; but it may be that, considering the scope of the Act as a whole, the power enables the notion of 'enemy territory' to have an extended meaning only during a state of war. Similar considerations apply to the Board of Trade's power under section 2 (2) by order to direct that any person specified in the order shall be deemed to be an enemy for purposes of the Act.

Apart from any such possible action under that Trading with the Enemy Act, 1939, and in the absence of any special enactments, it would seem that no prohibition on trading with the enemy would apply in an armed conflict. The common law rules would seem to be dependent upon there being a war *stricto sensu*. However, we must not underestimate the capacity of the common law to develop in such a way as to be able to deal appropriately with the various problems associated with armed conflicts. Many acts of the kind associated with trading with the enemy would be likely to become illegal on the ground that their performance during the armed conflict would be contrary to public policy. In *Furtado* v. *Rogers*[2] Lord Alvanley observed that 'it is not competent to any subject to enter into a contract to do anything which may be detrimental to the interests of his own country; and [that] such a contract is as much prohibited as if it had been expressly prohibited by Act of Parliament'. In *The Eastern Carrying Insurance Co.* v. *The National Benefit Life and Property Assurance*

---

[1] Lord Merriman P. in *The Glenearn* [1941] P. 51, at p. 61, remarked that 'the legislation relating to trading with the enemy...forbids any form of commerce with the enemy but, as the word implies, that assumes that the commerce is transacted after the war has broken out'.

[2] (1802) 3 B. & P. 191, 198; see above, p. 49, in chapter 1. But see *The Glenearn* [1941] P. 51, at pp. 60–61.

Co. Ltd, Bailhache J. seemed to be of the opinion, *obiter*, that where, without the United Kingdom being at war with Russia, British troops were fighting troops of the (unrecognized) Bolshevist Government of Russia, a Russian company which during this conflict adhered to the Bolshevist Government might be defeated by the plea of alien enemy if it instituted proceedings in the English courts; if that is so, might not such a company also be an enemy for trading purposes?[1]

Special *ad hoc* legislative or administrative measures may, of course, be taken in relation to any particular conflict in order to prevent, in whole or in part, dealings between this country and the other party to the conflict. In the case, for example, of a pacific blockade imposed by the United Kingdom it is self-evident that the British Government could, and probably would, prohibit British ships from entering the ports of the blockaded State. A recent example of *ad hoc* legislation is the Export of Goods (North Korea) Order, 1950,[2] which prohibited the export of goods to North Korea at the time of the Korean conflict in which British troops were involved. This Order was made under the powers conferred upon the Board of Trade by section 1 of the Import, Export and Customs Powers (Defence) Act, 1939—a temporary Act,[3] but still in force. Mention should also be made of the United Nations Act, 1946, which confers powers to take action that might be required by the Security Council of the United Nations, acting under Article 41 of the Charter. While that Article is expressly limited to measures not involving the use of armed force, it does contemplate measures such as the complete or partial interruption of economic relations and of means of communication.

---

[1] Particularly bearing in mind Viscount Simon's first proposition in the *Sovfracht* case, quoted at p. 375 below.

[2] S.R. & O. (1950), no. 1117; revoked by S.R. & O. (1957), no. 246.

[3] See section 9 (3); see also section 3 of the Emergency Laws (Re-enactment and Repeals) Act, 1964.

17

EFFECTS OF BELLIGERENT OCCUPATION OF TERRITORY[1]

BIBLIOGRAPHY

Das, *Japanese Occupation and Ex Post Facto Legislation in Malaya.*
Feilchenfeld, *The International Economic Law of Belligerent Occupation.*
Hackworth, *Digest of International Law,* I, § 29, and VI, § 587.
Harvey, 11 *Modern Law Review* (1948), p. 196.
Hyde, III, §§ 688–702 A.
H. Lauterpacht, *Recognition in International Law,* pp. 175–269 (especially Opinions of the Law Officers of the Crown).
McNair, *Opinions,* III, pp. 35–9.
Morgenstern, 28 *B.Y.* (1951), p. 291.
Moore, *Digest of International Law,* I, § 21, and VII, §§ 1143–55.
Oppenheim, II, §§ 133–48 and 166–72 b.
Pesmazoglou, 2 *Revue Hellénique de Droit International* (1949), p. 168.
Pitt Cobbett, II, pp. 165–74.
Sauser-Hall, 1 *Schweizerisches Jahrbuck für international Recht* (1944), p. 60.
Stodter, *Deutschlands Rechtslage.*
Stone, *Legal Control of International Conflict,* ch. 26.
Van Nispen tot Sevenaer, *L'occupation Allemande pendant la dernière guerre mondiale* (1946).
Domke, *Control of Enemy Property* (1947).
Bathurst and Simpson, *Germany and the North Atlantic Community* (1956).
Jennings, 23 *B.Y.* (1946), pp. 112–41.
Schwarzenberger, *International Courts* (2nd ed.), chap. 30.
Spaight, *War Rights on Land* (1911), ch. XI.

During a large part of the War of 1939 to 1945 many thousands of square miles of European and Asian territory were under enemy occupation, that is to say, under the occupation of a Power other than, and hostile to, the normal local sovereign. Large portions of British territory, including the Channel Islands,[2] were so occupied. This state of affairs gave rise to a crop of questions which have gradually been settled by British and other Courts, although we should here remark that the standpoint of the courts of countries which were not occupied was in some respects different from that of the courts of countries which were.[3] It is the object of this and the

[1] Dana in his edition of Wheaton's *International Law* (1866) uses this expression, which is clearly better than 'military occupation', which can occur in time of peace. This chapter is not concerned with the military occupation of foreign territory which may occur in time of peace or in pursuance of an agreement for an armistice.

[2] The position of the Channel Islands was considered in *In re Hatch,* and in *In re Anglo-International Bank Ltd.*

[3] See *Hangkam Kwingtong Woo v. Liu Lan Fong*; *Krishna Chettiar v. Subbiya Chettiar.*

next chapter to explore this piece of legal territory.[1] We are not here concerned with the public international law aspects of enemy occupation, but it is necessary to state—very briefly and rather dogmatically —some of the internationally recognized principles because they have some bearing upon questions that can come before national Courts.

The following are the topics we shall discuss:

A. Summary of public international law.

B. What amounts to belligerent occupation of territory by the enemy?

C. Birth in territory under belligerent occupation.

D. Marriage in territory under belligerent occupation.

E. Effects of acts of the authorities of an occupying belligerent, whether:

    (1) an enemy in an international war, or

    (2) a revolutionary authority in a civil war.

F. Post-war remedies of inhabitants of occupied territories for wrongful acts of an occupying belligerent.

G. Military occupation during an armed conflict not amounting to war.

A. SUMMARY OF PUBLIC INTERNATIONAL LAW

International law recognizes three stages which normally occur in the process of conquest: (*a*) invasion; (*b*) occupation; and (*c*) transfer of sovereignty by means of a treaty of cession, or as the result of subjugation without cession. It is believed to be true to say that English law makes the same distinction. We shall see later that, at any rate according to the view of the British Foreign Office and of English Courts, it may become necessary in some cases to interpose between (*b*) and (*c*) a stage during which the occupant is something more than a mere belligerent occupant and is exercising *de facto* administrative control, being virtually the sovereign though not yet *de iure*.[2]

Occupation is something more than invasion. Oppenheim[3] defines it as 'invasion *plus* taking possession of enemy country for the purpose of holding it, at any rate temporarily. The difference between mere

---

[1] The volumes of the *Annual Digest* and *International Law Reports*, particularly for the years immediately following the Wars of 1914 to 1918 and 1939 to 1945, contain many decisions upon all aspects of belligerent occupation only the more significant and representative of which are expressly mentioned in this chapter. See also a series of articles on the territories occupied in the War of 1939 to 1945, in the *Journal of Comparative Legislation* (3rd Ser.), vols. 29 (1947) (Netherlands and Belgium), 30 (1948) (Burma, the Philippines, Greece and France), 31 (1949) (Denmark, Norway and Jersey) and 33 (1951) (Malaya); and Schwenk, 54 *Yale Law Journal* (1945), pp. 393–416.

[2] See later, pp. 396–9 and 407–8.

[3] II, § 167. On the distinction between invasion and occupation see *Re Lepore* (Italy); *In re List and Others.*

invasion and occupation becomes apparent from the fact that an occupant sets up some kind of administration, whereas the mere invader does not.'[1]

The question whether the whole or a particular part of the territory of a State has been occupied or not is a question of fact,[2] but, once the fact of occupation is established, that fact gives rise to certain legal rights and duties. 'The occupant', says Professor Hyde,[3] 'enjoys the right and is burdened with the duty to take all the measures within his power to restore and insure public order and safety.'

The most important principle of law incident to belligerent occupation—one that was not established until the last century[4]—is that occupation does not displace or transfer sovereignty.[5] The occupant

---

[1] For the purposes discussed in this chapter, it does not matter whether the belligerent occupation follows an act of submission by the sovereign of the occupied territory (as in the case of France) or a mere laying down of arms by the military commanders (as in the case of Holland—see letter from the Netherlands Foreign Minister to *The Times* of 20 June 1940 and *In re Rauter* (Holland, Special Cour de Cassation)).

[2] See *Wandel-Hirschberg* v. *Jacobsfeld-Yakurska* (Israel). For a decision that on the entry of Allied forces into Austria at the end of the War of 1939 to 1945 that country was not an 'occupied' country but a 'liberated' one, see *Seery* v. *United States*.

[3] III, § 690.

[4] The principle of the common law that a conquered country forms immediately part of the King's dominions was asserted as late as 1814, by Sir William Scott in *The Foltina*.

[5] For attempts by an occupant to set up a new independent State, see *Chettiar* v. *Chettiar* (Burma) and *Socony Vacuum Oil Company Claim* (U.S.A.), and Hackworth, *Digest of International Law*, I, p. 146. See also cases cited at p. 387, n. 1 below. The situation in Germany immediately after the War of 1939 to 1945 was in many respects juridically different from, and something more than, belligerent occupation. The Government in Germany had collapsed and the four leading Allied Powers made a Declaration (Cmd. 6648) under which they assumed 'supreme authority with respect to Germany'. The Nuremberg Tribunal's judgment of 30 September and 1 October 1946 (Cmd. 6964), p. 38, contains the following passage: 'The making of the Charter was the exercise of the sovereign legislative power by the countries to which the German Reich unconditionally surrendered; and the undoubted right of these countries to legislate for the occupied territories has been recognised by the civilised world.' See also *R.* v. *Bottrill, ex parte Kuechenmeister*; *In re Altstötter*; *Grahame* v. *Director of Prosecutions*; *Dalldorf* v. *Director of Prosecutions*; Kelsen, 39 *A.J.* (1945), p. 518; Fried, 40 *A.J.* (1946), p. 326; Potter, 43 *A.J.* (1949), p. 323; von Laun, 45 *A.J.* (1951), p. 267.

The distinction between belligerent occupation and sovereignty is exemplified in many decisions (e.g. *Ray Claim* (U.S.A.)); it is well illustrated by a decision of the Philippines Supreme Court that a State can be in belligerent occupation of its own territory in the course of liberating it from enemy occupation: *Tan Tuan et al.* v. *Lucena Food Control Board*. Particular consequences of the continued existence of the occupied State's sovereignty are that treaties between that State and third States will still exist with consequent effect upon rights of individuals in the case of, e.g. consular conventions and civil procedure conventions (see *In re Skewrys' Estate* (U.S.A.), *In re Flaum's Estate* (U.S.A.), and *Occupation of Germany* (*Zurich*) *Case*), and that from the point of view of the occupying State the occupied State remains a foreign State (see *Cobb* v. *United States* (U.S.A.), *Acheson* v. *Wohlmuth* (U.S.A.) (but cf. *Arikawa* v. *Acheson* (U.S.A.)), *In re K.* (*Rhodes Case*) (Greece), and *Compensation (Germany) Case* (Germany, Supreme Court)). The occupying authorities are even restricted in respect of dealings with their own nationals who are resident in the occupied territory: Geneva Civilians Convention, 1949, Article 70.

is entitled to exercise military authority over the territory occupied, but he does not acquire sovereignty unless and until it is ceded to him by a treaty of peace (which is the commonest method), or is simply abandoned in his favour without cession,[1] or is acquired by him by virtue of subjugation, that is, extermination of the local sovereign and annexation of his territory, as happened in the case of the South African Republic and the Orange Free State at the end of the South African War.[2] For the same reason, occupation operates no change of nationality upon the inhabitants and no transfer of allegiance,[3] though the occupant acquires a right against inhabitants who remain that they should obey his lawful regulations for the administration of the territory and the safety of his forces.[4] The occupant's right and duty of administering the occupied territory are governed by international law.[5] It is definitely a military administration and he has no right to make even temporary changes in the law and the administration of the country except in so far as it may be necessary for the maintenance of order, the safety of his forces and the realization of the legitimate purpose of his occupation.[6]

[1] Upon the peculiar case of the acquisition by Italy of Tripoli and Cyrenaica in 1912, see Oppenheim, II, § 273. The general proposition above stated is supported by the Privy Council in *The Gerasimo* (1857) 11 Moore P.C. 88, 105, though for reasons discussed later (at p. 374) certain other aspects of that decision are difficult to reconcile with authority.

[2] A purported incorporation of occupied territory by a military occupant into his own kingdom during the war is illegal and ought not to receive any recognition; e.g. Germany's claim to have annexed Alsace-Lorraine to the Reich during the War of 1939 to 1945 (see *Société au Grand Marché* v. *City of Metz* (France), *In re Wagner and Others*, and *Z. v. K.* (France)). As to the purported German annexation of parts of Belgium, see *Bindels* v. *Administration des Finances, Mommer and Others* v. *Renerken, Bourseaux* v. *Krantz*, and *L.M.* v. *Swiss Banks* (Switzerland); and of Poland, see *In re Greiser* and *In re Will of Josef K.* Article 47 of the 1949 Geneva Civilians Convention expressly provides that the benefits of the Convention relating to inhabitants of occupied territory cannot be taken away by the belligerent trying to take the territory out of the category of occupied territory by annexing it. A Belgian law of 5 May 1944 declared null all decrees, orders, decisions and other acts to the extent that they were based upon the purported annexation of Belgian territory by Germany (although a later law made an exception in respect of certain divorces and annulments of marriages: see *Mommer and Others* v. *Renerken*). See also *In re Goering and Others*.

[3] See Article 45 of the Hague Regulations and Article 68 of the 1949 Geneva Civilians Convention.

[4] See Hall, pp. 553–85; Hyde, III, §§ 697–702; and Oppenheim, II, § 170 and in 33 *L.Q.R.* (1917), pp. 266–86 and 363–70.

[5] An occupant may have wider powers under an armistice agreement: see *Genel and Bussi* v. *Steiner* (Italy, Cour de Cassation), *Ruocco* v. *Fiore* (Italy, Cour de Cassation).

[6] Article 64 of the 1949 Geneva Civilians Convention requires an occupant to leave in force the penal laws of the occupied territory, except that he may suspend or repeal them where they constitute a threat to the occupant's security or an obstacle to the application of the Convention. The occupant may also make new provisions, so long as they are 'essential' (i) to enable him to fulfil his obligations under the Convention, (ii) to maintain the orderly government of the territory, and (iii) to ensure the security of the Occupying Power, of the members and property of the occupying forces or administration, and of the establishments and lines of communication used by them. On 18 September 1944,

Article 43 of the 'Hague Regulations' (that is, the Regulations annexed to Hague Convention IV), which were very widely signed and
ratified and in this respect may be regarded as declaratory of existing
law,[1] obliges the occupant to 'take all steps in his power to re-
establish and ensure, as far as possible, public order and safety, while
respecting, unless absolutely prevented, the laws in force in the
country'.

The provisions of the Hague Regulations are now supplemented
by Articles 27 to 34 and 47 to 78[2] of the 1949 Geneva Convention
Relative to the Protection of Civilian Persons in Time of War.[3]
While these Articles regulate in considerable detail some of the
matters covered by the Hague Regulations, as well as some additional matters, they are based upon the same general view of the
nature of belligerent occupation, and 'reflect the following general
principles:—(a) the limited and temporary nature of occupation,
(b) that sovereignty is not vested in the Occupant, (c) that the prime
duty is the establishment of order in the occupied area, (d) that the
minimum alteration should be made to the existing administration,
economy, legal system, and general life of the occupied community,
and (e) that that minimum is to be determined by the restrictions and
changes properly imposed for the security of the Occupant's armed
forces and civil administration'.[4] It is to be noted that the Convention applies from the outset of any total or partial occupation of the
territory of a Contracting Party, even if the occupation meets with
no armed resistance; and it ceases to apply in the case of occupied
territory one year after the general close of military operations,
although the occupant is bound, for the duration of the occupation
and to the extent that he exercises the functions of government in
the territory, by certain Articles.[5]

In so far as the occupant acts within the scope of the authority
permitted to him by international law, it is customary for the legiti-

---

the Allied Occupation Authorities in Germany, in their first law, prohibited the application of some of the laws of Nazi Germany which were based upon principles contrary to
basic notions of humanity and the rule of law (see Oppenheim, II, pp. 446–7, where this
action is justified on the grounds that in the circumstances the Allies were 'absolutely
prevented' from respecting such laws).

[1] It should be noted that, by Article 2 of the Convention, the Regulations only apply
if all the belligerents are parties to the Convention; but the effect this has in making the
Regulations inapplicable as soon as a non-party to the Convention enters the war (see,
e.g. *Anciens Etablissements Graf Frères* v. *Société La Mure* (France, Cour de Cassation)) is
mitigated to the extent that the rules embodied in the Regulations form part of customary
international law (see Oppenheim, II, pp. 234–6). The 1949 Geneva Civilians Convention
does not require all the belligerents to be parties to the Convention: Article 2.

[2] See also Articles 2, 4, 5 and 6.   [3] T.S. no. 39 (1958).
[4] Draper, *The Red Cross Conventions*, p. 39.   [5] Article 6.

mate government, if and when it reacquires possession of the territory, to recognize his measures and give effect to rights acquired thereunder, while if the occupant acts unlawfully, his measures will not receive that recognition.[1]

Until the War of 1939 to 1945 a long time had elapsed since any British territory was under enemy occupation, though this happened for a short time in the South African War, and there is very little British judicial authority in the matter. It is suggested, however, that since the principles stated above have received general recognition and our Courts apply the generally recognized rules of customary international law[2] except in so far as the United Kingdom has dissented from them, and since, moreover, the United Kingdom has ratified the 'Hague Regulations'[3] and the 1949 Geneva Conventions,[4] the principles stated above would in all probability be adopted by our Courts. It is usual for our Courts to give effect to the acts of foreign Governments within the sphere of their competence, subject to certain exceptions such as penal and revenue laws.[5] But the complementary rule which denies to an English Court any competence to question the validity of the acts of the foreign Government,[6] since it would hardly be proper for a Court to sit in judgment upon the acts of a foreign sovereign within the area of his sovereignty, probably would not apply to the acts of a belligerent occupant who possesses no sovereignty over the occupied territory but certain limited rights only.

The morality or immorality of the occupation is irrelevant. When territory is invaded and held, it must have some kind of government or there will be a state of chaos. The law of belligerent occupation is an attempt to substitute for chaos some kind of order, however harsh it may be. That the power of the occupant affords unique opportunities for the abuse of the law is patent.[7] Similar considerations apply in respect of a belligerent occupation taking place during a war illegally begun by the occupant. In application of the principle *ex iniuria ius non oritur*, the view has sometimes been taken that such an occupation is one to which, to a greater or lesser extent,

---

[1] See further, sections E and F below.

[2] For a recent statement of this principle, see Lord Atkin in *Chung Chi Cheung* v. *The King* [1939] A.C. 160, at p. 168. As to rules created by treaty, see McNair, *Law of Treaties, 1961*, chs. 3 and 4.

[3] It is clear from *Porter* v. *Freudenberg* [1915] 1 K.B. 857, 874, that the Court of Appeal did not doubt that Hague Convention IV is binding upon an English Court.

[4] See the Geneva Conventions Act, 1957.

[5] See further, pp. 384–7 and 428 ff., below.   [6] See below, p. 429.

[7] As to deportations, see Fried, 40 *A.J.* (1946), pp. 303–31, and Article 49 of the 1949 Geneva Civilians Convention.

the rules of belligerent occupation which we are about to discuss do not apply.[1] However, the better view, supported by the bulk of judicial authority, is probably that the law of belligerent occupation applies notwithstanding that the occupant may be an unlawful aggressor.[2]

B. WHAT AMOUNTS TO BELLIGERENT OCCUPATION OF TERRITORY BY THE ENEMY?

We must now consider what facts must be present to convert non-enemy territory into enemy-occupied territory for the purposes of English law, and for what purposes English law assimilates territory thus occupied to enemy territory; for example, for the purposes of trading with the enemy, the effect of war upon contracts,[3] the plea of alien enemy, and the law of prize. We shall consider these matters under the headings of (*a*) common law, (*b*) treaty, and (*c*) statute.

(*a*) At common law (*including the law of prize*)

The abandonment of the early view already referred to, that belligerent occupation operated to transfer sovereignty, and the perception of the distinction between temporary military occupation and permanent conquest, formed a gradual process,[4] and care must be exercised in reading some of the eighteenth and earlier nineteenth century decisions. In some of them the Court in its desire to point out that belligerent occupation does not transfer sovereignty fails to realize that occupied territory might nevertheless acquire enough enemy character to assimilate it to enemy territory for some of the purposes referred to above.

It is believed that the following statement by Marshall C.J. in the *Thirty Hogsheads of Sugar* (*Bentzon* v. *Boyle*)[5] correctly represents the common law as understood by English and American Courts:

---

[1] See *In re Greiser* and *N.* v. *B.*, both decided by the Polish Supreme Court; and *op. cit.* by 'B', 5 *I. and C.L.Q.* (1956), p. 90, n. 14.

[2] H. Lauterpacht, 30 *B.Y.* (1953), pp. 214–17 and 224–33. See also Scelle, 58 *Revue Générale de Droit International Public* (1954), pp. 19–20, for an intermediate solution. In perhaps the most significant decision of the War of 1939 to 1945 in a British jurisdiction in which the issue was raised, the Court of Appeal at Singapore expressly left the issue open: *N.V. Bataafsche Petroleum Maatschappij & Ors.* v. *The War Damage Commission*, 23 I.L.R. (1956), p. 810, at p. 826.

[3] For an instance in which the belligerent occupation by the enemy of the port of delivery under a contract for the sale of goods produced a frustration of the contract, see the *Fibrosa* case; see above, p. 184. For the effect that belligerent occupation can have on a contract of agency, see above, p. 221. [4] See Oppenheim, II, § 166.

[5] (1815) 9 Cranch 191, 195; Prize Cases in U.S. Supreme Court (Carnegie Endowment) 699, now expressly adopted in the House of Lords in the *Sovfracht* case. See also Sir W. Scott in *The Foltina*, where the 'purpose' was purely domestic.

Some doubt has been suggested whether Santa Cruz [a Danish island], while in the possession of Great Britain, could properly be considered as a British island. But for this doubt there can be no foundation. Although acquisitions made during war are not considered as permanent until confirmed by treaty, yet to every commercial and belligerent purpose, they are considered as a part of the domain of the conqueror, so long as he retains the possession and government of them.

The 'purpose' in this case was condemnation in prize as enemy property.

The following English decisions,[1] in greater or less degree, discuss the same point:

Bromley v. *Hesseltine*, where it was suggested that an insurance by a British subject in 1807 upon a voyage to [neutral] Leghorn then in the occupation of French [enemy] troops was illegal and void, but the evidence did not support the plea.

Blackburne v. *Thompson*, where, following *The Manilla* and *The Pelican*, it was held by the King's Bench that when insurgents had successfully ousted French authority from certain ports in the French colony of St Domingo and this fact was recognized by British Orders in Council declaring them to be not hostile, those ports became assimilated to neutral ports and it was lawful for British subjects to trade to them.

Mitsui v. *Mumford*,[2] where Bailhache J. was prepared to assume that Antwerp after 9 October 1914 became for the time being 'alien enemy territory' and that the common law forbade business intercourse with persons there.

But it would be more correct to say that belligerent occupation by the enemy *prima facie* invests the place occupied with enemy character, and that the Crown may by an Order in Council indicate its intention to treat the place as still having neutral character. Thus in *Hagedorn* v. *Bell*,[3] which arose out of the French occupation of Hamburg beginning in 1806, the question arose whether the plaintiff could recover an indemnity upon a policy of marine insurance on behalf of merchants 'domiciled at Hamburg'. Notwithstanding the occupation of Hamburg by a French force 'all the powers of civil government were administered in the same manner as they had formerly been before the arrival of the French'. That Hamburg was, at the time 'when this insurance was effected, under French dominion, and had committed acts to warrant this country to con-

---

[1] For opinions of the Law Officers of the Crown, see McNair, *Opinions*, III, pp. 35 ff.
[2] Upon the insurance point see *Campbell* v. *Evans* and *Moore* v. *Evans*.
[3] (1813) 1 M. & S. 450.

sider her hostile, there can be little doubt' (said Lord Ellenborough C.J. at p. 458). But for reasons of policy the Crown preferred to treat Hamburg as not hostile, and had issued a number of Orders in Council from which it appeared that in the words of Grose J. (at p. 465) 'the trade [with Hamburg] was in some measure made legitimate by this country'. It is for the Crown to decide whether to treat a particular country and its inhabitants as hostile or neutral. Accordingly the plaintiff recovered.

It is difficult to reconcile with these principles the opinion given by the Privy Council in 1857 in *The Gerasimo*, reversing the decision of Dr Lushington. It is to be noted that the great authority of Marshall C.J. in the *Thirty Hogsheads of Sugar* does not appear to have been brought to the attention of the Privy Council, and it is fair to remark that the Privy Council in its desire to establish the rule that belligerent occupation does not transfer sovereignty may not have realized that it was compatible with this doctrine that occupied territory might nevertheless acquire enemy character for the purposes of prize and trading with the enemy.

In *Société Anonyme Belge des Mines d'Aljustrel* (*Portugal*) v. *Anglo-Belgian Agency* the Court of Appeal had to consider the position of the plaintiff company, a Belgian company, registered in Antwerp in 1898, at a time (July 1915) when the greater part of Belgium was under German occupation. It was held that Belgium was not as a whole under enemy occupation, and that the plaintiff company was incorporated in Belgium (not Antwerp) and was not an 'enemy' under the Trading with the Enemy Acts and Proclamations then in force.[1] This is important (though for the purposes of the War of 1939–45 the matter, as we shall see later, is regulated by legislation and orders thereunder) because neither in the case of Belgium, France or Holland was the whole of the national territory occupied by the enemy. It is submitted that any distinction made by the constitutional law of a country between metropolitan and colonial territory is immaterial for this purpose. Unless the whole territory is occupied, it cannot be said that the country is occupied.

In the case of *Re Deutsche Bank* (*London Agency*)[2] Russell J. held for the purpose of subsection (3) of section 1 of the Trading with the Enemy Amendment Act, 1916 (which gave priority of payment of unsecured debts to non-enemy over enemy creditors) that a bank,

---

[1] See *Central India Mining Co.* v. *Société Coloniale Anversoise* for amending Proclamation issued in consequence of this decision.

[2] [1921] 2 Ch. 30, 291. See also *The Leonora*, where the expression 'enemy origin' occurring in one of the retaliatory Orders in Council is discussed.

which was a *société anonyme* constituted according to the laws of Belgium, 'notwithstanding the enemy occupation of the greater part of Belgium...was and remained a subject of an Allied Power, and was not an enemy at common law'. But he expressly pointed out (at p. 300) that this was not equivalent to saying that it would have been lawful to trade with this bank during the war.

The common law position has now been examined and authoritatively established by the House of Lords in what seems likely to rank as the most important of the war decisions given in the War of 1939 to 1945—the *Sovfracht* case.[1] There it became necessary to decide whether the effect of the German occupation of Holland in May 1940 was to convert previously neutral territory into enemy-occupied territory so as to render a shipping company incorporated and domiciled in Holland incapable of continuing in England an arbitration in which it was an *actor*, by reason of the plea of alien enemy. The question arose upon a summons by the Dutch company for the appointment of an umpire as the result of the refusal of the arbitrator appointed by the other party to proceed with the arbitration upon the ground that the Dutch company had become an alien enemy. The Court of Appeal had held that the Dutch company was not an alien enemy, that is to say, an enemy in the territorial sense, at common law, and that the Trading with the Enemy Act, 1939, which defines 'enemy' 'for the purposes of this Act' does not comprise within those purposes that of settling questions of *persona standi in judicio*. The House of Lords reversed this decision, and held that the Dutch company was, as a result of the enemy occupation, an enemy at common law. The following propositions are laid down by Viscount Simon L.C.[2]:

1. The test of 'enemy character' is fundamentally the same whether the question arises over a claim to sue in our courts, or over issues raised in a court of prize, or over a charge of trading with the enemy at common law.

2. The test is an objective test, turning on the relation of the enemy Power to the territory where the individual voluntarily resides or the company is commercially domiciled or controlled. It is not a question of nationality or of patriotic sentiment.

3. If the enemy Power invades and forcibly occupies territory outside his own boundaries, residence in that territory may disqualify from bringing or maintaining suit in the King's courts in the like manner as

---

[1] Considered in *Seethalakshmi Achi et al.* v. *V. T. Veerappa Chettiar* (India), *In re Anglo-International Bank Ltd*, and *Loh Khing Woon* v. *Lai Kong Jin and Another* (Singapore). Upon the position of a London Bank which had carried on business in what became enemy-occupied territory by means of a separate company, see *Isaacs* v. *Barclays Ltd. and Barclays Bank (France) Ltd*.   [2] [1943] A.C. at p. 211.

residence in the enemy Power's own territory would. The same applies to a company commercially domiciled or controlled in occupied territory.[1]

4. But this is not always or absolutely so. It depends on the nature of the occupation and on the facts of each case. If as a result of the occupation the enemy is provisionally in effective control of an area at the material time, and is exercising some kind of government or administration[2] over it, the area acquires 'enemy character'.[3] Local residents cannot sue in our Courts and goods shipped from such an area have enemy origin —see Marshall C.J. in the *Thirty Hogsheads of Sugar, Bentzon* v. *Boyle* (1815), 9 Cranch 191, 195. If, on the other hand, the occupation is of a slighter character, for instance, if it is incidental to military operations and does not result in effective control—the case is different, as in *Cremidi* v. *Powell, The Gerasimo* (1857) 11 Moore P.C. 88. I would adopt the observations of my noble and learned friend Lord Wright on this decision, for I agree that, while Dr Lushington's statement of the law went too far in one direction, Lord Kingsdown (then the Rt Hon. Thomas Pemberton Leigh) in delivering the judgment of the Privy Council reversing the decision of the Prize Court, in one passage went unnecessarily far in the other. In the present case, the occupation of Holland by Germany is plainly, as things stand, of the more absolute kind.[4]

5. It is not irrelevant to bear in mind the reason why a resident in enemy-occupied territory is in certain circumstances subject to the same disability as a resident in enemy territory. 'This law', said Lord Reading C.J. in *Porter* v. *Freudenberg*,[5] referring to the denial to alien enemies of a right to sue, 'was founded in earlier days upon the conception that all subjects owing allegiance to the Crown were at war with subjects of the State at war with the Crown, and later it was grounded upon public policy, which forbids the doing of acts which will be, or may be, to the advantage of the enemy State by increasing its capacity for prolonging hostilities in adding to the credit, money or goods, or other resources available to individuals in the enemy State'. This consideration equally applies to a claim sought to be established in our Courts by a resident in enemy-occupied territory, for if the claimant succeeds an asset in the form of an award or a judgment is created which the occupying power can appropriate and which is calculated to increase the enemy's resources.

[1] Unless of course the company has transferred its domicil to another non-enemy country before the hearing of the action (*Owners of M.V. Lubrafol* v. *Owner of S.S. Pamia*).

[2] An occupation may still be a belligerent occupation notwithstanding that the actual administration is carried out by civilians: see *Soc. Timber et al.* v. *Ministeri Esteri e Tesoro* (Italy, Cour de Cassation).

[3] Upon the degree of enemy control required to constitute enemy occupation, see discussion in *O/Y Wasa Steamship Co.* v. *Newspaper Pulp & Wood Export Ltd.*

[4] See *The Gutenfels*, discussed below on p. 379. See also *The Achaia*. As to the position of Egypt during the War of 1914 to 1918, see also *Commercial and Estates Co. of Egypt* v. *Ball*, and as to the position of several European countries occupied during the War of 1939 to 1945, see *In re Anglo-International Bank Ltd.* For a decision that the Japanese occupation of Burma during the War of 1939 to 1945 did not make Burma into 'occupied enemy territory', see *Seethalakshmi Achi et al.* v. *V.T. Veerappa Chettiar* (India).

[5] [1915] 1 K.B. 857, 867.

6. The common law disability to sue in such cases cannot be regarded as got rid of because Emergency Regulations would prevent the transmission abroad of the sum recovered. The asset would be created, even though it necessarily remained here till the end of the war. Such an asset might well operate as security for an advance to the enemy from a neutral lender.

7. The operation of the rule refusing *persona standi in judicio* is always subject to permission being given by royal licence. In the present case, no application for a royal licence has been made.[1]

These propositions, professedly only a summary, must be studied in the light of the two exhaustive speeches of Lord Wright and Lord Porter. In particular, attention should be directed to the Lord Chancellor's proposition 4. What amounts to enemy occupation is a question of fact, that is, a question of the interpretation which the law will place upon the facts in a given case.[2] In Lord Wright's words:[3]

This enemy character depends on objective facts, not on feeling or sentiment, or birth, or nationality. They [the inhabitants of enemy-occupied countries] have been described as territorial or technical enemies. Their status is based on residence, or, if they are traders, on what has been called commercial domicil, which has the peculiarity that it may be attached to a trader who is not personally present in the occupied territory, but resides, for example, in a neutral country. He is an enemy *vis-à-vis* the other belligerent in respect of the particular affairs of trade in the occupied or conquered territory which gave him a commercial domicil there. The occupied territory may merely be part of a larger territory which, so far as unoccupied, retains its national character.

[1] Viscount Simon L.C. raised the question of a licence to sue in the *Fibrosa* case [1943] A.C. 32, 35, 40, and the party obtained a licence from the Board of Trade which the House of Lords accepted.

[2] The facts might even lead to the conclusion that the enemy is still to be regarded as possessing the powers of a belligerent occupant after the enemy's sovereign has commanded his armed forces to lay down their arms: see *Planters' Loans Board* v. *Managalam* (Malaya); *Cobb* v. *United States* (U.S.A.).

[3] At p. 229. With great respect we venture to express regret that Lord Wright in his most illuminating survey of the law should have used words so strong as 'subjugation' and 'enemy-subjugated' territory, which to the minds of many may suggest a degree of domination more complete and more permanent than is required to constitute enemy occupation. Moreover, in certain quarters 'subjugation' is used in international law to describe the means of terminating a war by exterminating the enemy as a political society and annexing its territory without any treaty of cession, as, for instance, at the end of the South African War (Oppenheim, II, §§ 264, 265). Emphasis on 'subjugation' led an Indian court to the somewhat curious conclusion that the Japanese occupation of Burma was not sufficient to make Burma an enemy-occupied territory: see *Seethalakshmi Achi et al.* v. *V.T. Veerappa Chettiar*.

The National Socialist rulers of Germany invented new ways of controlling the policy and action of other countries without subjecting them to a formal military occupation, and some day it may be necessary for our Courts to consider whether conduct equivalent to the German practice of establishing complete and effective domination over professedly neutral countries by insinuating agents and specialist troops into key positions, while permitting their Governments nominally to continue to exercise their functions, as a prelude to plunging them into war, amounts to enemy occupation or not.

It is true that occupation is a question of fact and of the construction which international law places upon facts.[1] But it must be remembered that 'occupation' is a *terminus technicus* of international law and denotes a state of affairs which, on the one hand, must be distinguished from mere invasion and, on the other, from the rare case of subjugation involving a change of sovereignty without cession by a treaty of peace. There are not two kinds of 'occupation' in the technical sense.

It is clear that the fact of the occupation of territory (either British, allied or neutral) by the enemy places that territory in the position of enemy territory, with the natural consequences both (*a*) upon the procedural capacity in British courts of persons resident or present or carrying on business in the enemy-occupied territory, and (*b*) upon pre-occupation contracts between persons resident, present or carrying on business in British territory on the one hand and persons resident, present or carrying on business in the enemy-occupied territory, and (*c*) for purposes of offences of the trading with the enemy type committed by persons resident, present or carrying on business in British territory. The *Sovfracht* case is authority for this statement. At the same time it is necessary to remember, as was pointed out by Lord Simonds in delivering the opinion of the Judicial Committee of the Privy Council in *Hangkam Kwingtong Woo* v. *Liu Lan Fong*[2] in 1951, that the basic cause of the consequences of enemy occupation referred to above is the need of preventing intercourse with the enemy and of crippling his resources. When, therefore, the matter is looked at from the point of view of the inhabitants and the courts of the occupied territory, it acquires a different complexion. Let us suppose that, as in the last cited case, *X* escapes from the occupied territory—Hong Kong in 1942—during the Japanese occupation after giving a power of attorney to *Y*, who is remaining there, empowering *Y* to sell real or personal property (which *Y* did sell during the war), and *X* lives in Allied territory (China) until the war is over: why should *X* and *Y*, his attorney, be regarded as 'enemies of the King or of each other', and why should the power of attorney be regarded as abrogated because *X* and *Y* were temporarily divided by the line of war? Moreover, it was necessary in an action for specific performance brought against *X* in the courts of Hong Kong after the war to look at the matter from the point of view of the law

---

[1] As to the need for and value of a Foreign Office certificate, see Lord Wright's remarks in the *Sovfracht* case (at p. 229), *Anglo-Czechoslovak & Prague Credit Bank* v. *Jannsen* (Australia), *Yeo How Sam* v. *Chop Bee Huat* (Singapore); and see pp. 401–2 below.

[2] See also the Privy Council's remarks upon this case in *The Chartered Bank of India, Australia and China* v. *Wee Kheng Chiang*.

of Hong Kong, which could not treat as an enemy X who had escaped from enemy-occupied territory to Allied territory and remained there during the war.[1]

At common law the effects of belligerent occupation are believed to be coincident with the area of territory occupied. That is to say, if a country is only occupied in part by the enemy, as Belgium was from 1914 to 1918, it is not, for instance, unlawful to trade with persons in the non-occupied area.[2] But it is for our courts, not for the enemy, to decide whether a particular area is under belligerent occupation or not: thus the mere fact that in the War of 1939 to 1945 it appeared to suit the German Government for more than two years to describe part of France as non-occupied (perhaps in an attempt to reduce geographically the odium attaching to the occupation and to evade the responsibility of feeding and governing a portion of the population) would in no way have disentitled an English Court from deciding whether the so-called non-occupied France was in fact under enemy occupation or not.[3]

(b) By treaty

Article 42 of the Hague Regulations provides that territory is considered occupied when it is actually placed under the authority of the hostile army, and that the occupation extends only to the territory where such authority has been established and can be exercised. Articles 1, 30 and 35 of the unratified Declaration of London of 1909 may be referred to as assimilating enemy-occupied territory to enemy territory for the purposes of blockade and carriage of contraband. In these provisions it is believed to be declaratory of existing law. For the purposes of Hague Convention VI (Status of Merchant Ships in Enemy Ports) it was held by the Privy Council in *The Gutenfels*[4] that Port Said in 1914, when Great Britain was in military, though not belligerent, occupation of Egypt, was as regards German ships an 'enemy port', quoting (at p. 118) the following passage from Hall with approval: 'When a place is militarily occupied by an enemy the fact that it is under his control, and that he consequently can use it for the purposes of his war, outweighs all considerations founded on the bare legal ownership of the soil.'

---

[1] It is easier to visualize this case if one supposes that during either of the two world wars the enemy had occupied the Isle of Man and the owner of the property escaped to Liverpool or to Lisbon during the occupation.   [2] See *Blackburne* v. *Thompson*.

[3] It is clear that the Vichy Government was subordinate to the German Government in the control of the non-occupied area. *Donaldson* v. *Thompson* is an unsatisfactory decision and in our opinion does not militate against the rule suggested in the text.

[4] [1916] 2 A.C. 112.

(c) By statute

By the Trading with the Enemy Act, 1939,[1] section 2, the expression 'enemy' means (among other persons) 'any individual resident in enemy territory', and by section 15 (1) 'enemy territory' means 'any area which is under the sovereignty of, or in the occupation of, a Power with whom His Majesty is at war, not being an area in the occupation of His Majesty or of a Power allied with His Majesty'.

Subsection (2) of section 15 gives power to a Secretary of State to issue a conclusive certificate as to the fact of any territory being or ceasing to be under the sovereignty or occupation of any Power.

In addition to the power thus conferred upon a Secretary of State, the Board of Trade is empowered under section 15 (1 A) of the Act[2] to direct by order that the provisions of the Act shall apply in relation to any territory specified in the order as they apply in relation to enemy territory.

Title by succession

Although in this chapter we are concerned primarily with the rights and duties of private individuals as affected by occupation, it is worth while referring to the principle laid down by our Courts in giving effect to the international rights and liabilities of a Government (or, frequently, a State) which 'succeeds to any other government, whether by revolution or restoration, conquest or reconquest' (which includes the successful termination of a belligerent occupation). In *United States of America* v. *McRae*,[3] Sir W. M. James V.-C. in considering a claim by that country against an agent of the suppressed Confederate Government for an account of his dealings in respect of a Confederate loan raised in this country apprehended 'it to be the clear public universal law that any government which *de facto* succeeds to any other government, whether by revolution or restoration, conquest or reconquest, succeeds to all the public property, to everything in the nature of public property, and to all rights

---

[1] See above, p. 107, and chapter 16 for a general consideration of the Act. As to the effect which insurgency in the course of success, though not formally recognized, may have in changing the national character of territory for purposes of trading in time of war, e.g. from hostile to non-hostile territory from the British point of view, see *The Manilla*; *The Pelican*; and *Blackburne* v. *Thompson*.

[2] See above, p. 352. There are at least three ways in which the Crown may declare territory to have been occupied by the enemy—notification by the Foreign Office or by the Trading with the Enemy Department or an Order by the Board of Trade under section 15 (1 A) of the Trading with the Enemy Act, 1939.

[3] (1869) L.R. 8 Eq. 69, 75.

in respect of the public property of the displaced power, whatever may be the nature or origin of the title of such displaced power'.

An instance of succession to public property on conquest will be found in *Haile Selassie* v. *Cable and Wireless Ltd.* (no. 2)[1] once that case had reached the stage at which the Foreign Office certified that the United Kingdom Government recognized the King of Italy as *de iure* sovereign of Ethiopia and no longer recognized the Emperor Haile Selassie in that capacity.

C. BIRTH IN TERRITORY UNDER BELLIGERENT OCCUPATION

(a) A child born in British territory under enemy occupation

Before the entry into force of the British Nationality Act, 1948, the situation was not entirely clear, turning as it did on whether or not the person concerned was 'born within His Majesty's dominions and allegiance'.[2] Section 4 of the 1948 Act, however, now deals specifically with the question of British territory under enemy occupation by providing that to the general rule that every person born within the United Kingdom and Colonies after 1 January 1949 shall be a citizen of the United Kingdom and Colonies there is an exception if at the time of that person's birth his father[3] is an enemy alien and the birth occurs in a place then under occupation by the enemy. Thus a person born on enemy-occupied territory forming part of the United Kingdom or a Colony nevertheless acquires citizenship of the United Kingdom and Colonies unless his father is an enemy alien. The Act, while stating in section 32 that '"alien" means a person who is not a British subject, a British protected person or a citizen of Eire',[4] does not define 'enemy alien', an expression which usually involves either a national or a territorial test, according to the reason for ascertaining whether a given person is an enemy alien or not. It is believed that it is used in section 4 of the 1948 Act in the national sense. It would certainly be unjust that the child born in, say, the Isle of Wight under enemy occupation to a British father who is resident or detained in enemy territory should not acquire the citizenship of the United Kingdom and Colonies; it would be equally unjust that a child so born to an enemy father who was temporarily in the Isle of Wight, either as a soldier or civilian, should thereby acquire citizenship of the United Kingdom and Colonies.

---

[1] See later, p. 407, n. 2.
[2] British Nationality and Status of Aliens Act, 1914, section 1 (1) (a).
[3] If the child is illegitimate, we suggest that the father's nationality is immaterial.
[4] Parry, *British Nationality*, pp. 125–7.

(*b*) *A child born in non-British territory, whether enemy, allied or neutral, under British occupation*

Such a child born after 1 January 1949 to a father who is a citizen of the United Kingdom and Colonies at the time of the birth would be a citizen of the United Kingdom and Colonies by descent, although if the father himself acquired such citizenship by descent only, the child would only acquire such citizenship by descent if the father fulfilled one of the four conditions set out in section 5 (1) of the 1948 Act.[1] If the circumstances do not bring about the acquisition of citizenship of the United Kingdom and Colonies by descent, we do not consider that it would be acquired *iure soli*: not, even, it is submitted, if his mother were a member of the forces of the Crown serving in the occupied territory, because citizenship of the United Kingdom and Colonies cannot be inherited through a woman; nor even, it is submitted, if the child were born within the lines of the Army. A British army on foreign soil is extraterritorial in the sense that the local foreign jurisdiction is excluded,[2] but that does not mean that the territory occupied by it is deemed to be British territory.[3]

D. MARRIAGE IN TERRITORY UNDER BELLIGERENT OCCUPATION[4]

(*a*) *Where Great Britain is the occupant*

The validity of a marriage, as to matters of form, depends upon the *lex loci celebrationis*, and a marriage in territory occupied by British forces would normally be valid if, and only if, in accordance with that law.[5] There are, however, two exceptions to this rule which are particularly relevant in cases of belligerent occupation. First, section 2 of the Foreign Marriage Act, 1947, replacing section 22 of the Foreign Marriage Act, 1892, provides, in subsection 1, that:

---

[1] It is doubtful whether the first of these four conditions, which requires that the child, or its father, be 'born in...any place in a foreign country where by...lawful means Her Majesty then has or had jurisdiction over British subjects', would apply in respect of a foreign country under belligerent occupation by British forces.

[2] Within the limits explained in Oppenheim, 1, § 445.

[3] In *Wong Man On* v. *The Commonwealth* the High Court of Australia held that a child born of Chinese parents in 1916, on German mandated territory when under belligerent occupation by Australian forces was not born 'within His [Britannic] Majesty's dominions and allegiance' and was therefore an alien; military occupation does not affect nationality. See Goldie, 1 *I. and C.L.Q.* (1952), p. 587, for comment on this decision.

[4] See Brownlie and Webb, 39 *B.T.* (1963), pp. 457–61, and Parry, *British Digest of International Law*, vol. 8, pp. 611–16. As to divorce in occupied territories, see *Del Vecchio* v. *Connio* (Italy); *Mommer and Others* v. *Renerken* (Belgium, Cour de Cassation); *Wandel-Hirschberg* v. *Jacobsfeld-Yakurska* (Israel); *Z.* v. *K.* (France).

[5] See in general, Dicey, Rule 30 and comment.

(1) A marriage solemnised in any foreign territory [as defined in sub-sections 2 and 3] by a chaplain serving with any part of the naval, military or air forces of His Majesty serving in that territory or by a person authorised, either generally or in respect of the particular marriage, by the commanding officer of any part of those forces serving in that territory shall, subject as hereinafter provided, be as valid in law as if the marriage had been solemnised in the United Kingdom with a due observance of all forms required by law...

The Act of 1947 amends the Act of 1892 in several respects. No special form of marriage is required by the section.[1] One at least of the parties to the marriage must be a member of His Majesty's forces or a person employed in the foreign territory in such other capacity as may be prescribed by Order in Council. 'Foreign territory' means territory other than (a) any part of His Majesty's dominions, or (b) a protectorate, or (c) any other country or territory under the protection or suzerainty or jurisdiction of His Majesty, and includes ships in the waters of such foreign territory. The section appears to apply whether the British forces are in peaceful or belligerent occupation of the foreign territory. Hall says that, since an army has no extraterritoriality as against its enemy, it would be too much to expect the local Courts to recognize such a marriage after the end of a belligerent occupation unless it happened also to satisfy the requirements of the local law.[2]

Second, a common law marriage *per verba de praesenti*, such as was valid before the Marriage Act of 1753, taking place within the lines of a British (or other) army of occupation is still valid.[3]

(b) Where British territory is occupied

It is believed that principle requires us to regard a change made in the marriage law by the occupant as outside his competence and invalid,[4] and that a marriage celebrated in accordance with the (British) local form, the other conditions of the validity of a marriage being satisfied, would be valid.[5]

---

[1] Hall, *Foreign Jurisdiction of the British Crown* (1894), pp. 120–1.

[2] *Loc. cit.*, writing of section 22 of the Act of 1892.

[3] *R.* v. *Brampton* (a settlement case, marriage of a soldier, British occupation of San Domingo in 1796); *Burn* v. *Farrar*; *Waldegrave Peerage* case (marriage of an officer within the lines of the army abroad); *Taczanowska (orse. Roth)* v. *Taczanowski*; *Preston* v. *Preston*; *Merker* v. *Merker*; Dicey, Rule 30 and comment.

[4] See below, p. 387.

[5] In *Lee* v. *Lau* the validity of a marriage celebrated in Hong Kong during the Japanese occupation and in accordance with the customary local forms was critically examined, but no objection was taken on the basis that the local forms were inapplicable because of the occupation. See also a German decision, *Army of Occupation (Jurisdiction) Case*: German

E. EFFECTS OF ACTS OF THE AUTHORITIES OF AN
OCCUPYING BELLIGERENT

We shall now consider in their municipal aspect the effects of acts (legislative, executive and judicial) of the occupying authorities,[1,2] whether

(1) enemy authorities in an international war, or

(2) revolutionary authorities in a civil war,

1. *Effects of acts of authorities of enemy occupant in an international war*

By this expression is intended an occupant who is enemy to the local sovereign, whether he be enemy to Great Britain or not. Whether the territory under occupation is British or belongs to a co-belligerent with Great Britain or Great Britain is neutral, the principle is that, the occupant being under a duty to maintain order and to provide for the preservation of the rights of the inhabitants and having a right recognized by international law to impose such regulations and make such changes as may be necessary to secure the safety of his forces[3] and the realization of the legitimate purpose of his occupation, his acts, whether legislative, executive,[4] or judicial,

member of the army of occupation in Russian Poland in 1917 marries a Russian woman, both Catholics. Marriage was valid according to Russian law. On the husband's petition for a declaration of nullity on the ground that it did not accord with the form prescribed by German law it was held by the German Supreme Court in 1924 that the occupied territory must be regarded as foreign territory to which German law does not apply and that the marriage was valid. See also *De Alwis (or Jayatilaka) v. De Alwis and Yeo Giak Choo* (Malaya, Supreme Court); *N. v. Belgian State et al.* (Belgium).

[1] Acts by a local 'puppet' Government in occupied territory may be regarded as acts of the enemy occupant himself: see *In re G.* (Greece) (but cf. *In re Law 900 of 1943* (Greece) and the Note at 15 *A.D.* (1948), p. 562); *Randsfjordsbruket and Jevnaker Kommune v. Viul Tresliperi* (Norway, Supreme Court); *Magnifica Comunità di Fiemme v. Soc. Import. Esport. Legnami* (Italy, Cour de Cassation). But not all acts of administration during a belligerent occupation are acts of the occupant, since they may still be regarded as the acts of the local authorities: *Dickmann v. Federal Ministry of Social Administration* (Austria); *In re Lecoq and Others* (France); *Trost v. Federal Ministry of Finance* (Austria); *Italian State Railways v. Garofalo* (Italy); *Rohde v. Rheden* (Holland); *S.A.C.A. v. Lazzi and the Ministry of the Interior* (Italy, Cour de Cassation).

[2] The forces of the lawful sovereign in reoccupying territory previously occupied by the enemy may still be regarded, at least for some purposes, as subject to the rules relating to belligerent occupation: see *Public Prosecutor v. X* (*Eastern Java*) (Netherlands Indies); *Tan Tuan et al. v. Lucena Food Control Board* (Philippines, Supreme Court).

[3] As to the police powers of an occupant, see *In re Hoffmann* (Holland, Special Cour de Cassation).

[4] As to the right of the lawful sovereign after the occupation to dismiss a public official appointed by the occupant, see *Anastasio v. Ministero dell' Industria e del Commercio* (Italy); as to the right of the occupant to set up a civil administration in the occupied territory, see *Van Creveld v. Onderlinge Oorlog Schadeverzekering-Maatschappij* (*O.O.M.*) (Holland); *K.N.A.C. v. State of the Netherlands* (Holland); *State of the Netherlands v. Jessen* (Holland); as to the duty of the public officials of the occupied country to stay at their posts in the interests of the territory's well-being, see *Schuind v. Belgian State* (Belgium); as to the extent to which the

so long as he does not overstep these limits[1] will be recognized by the British Government and by British Courts of law—during and after the war if Great Britain is neutral, and at least after it if Great Britain is belligerent.[2] However, it is not easy to find British judicial authority for this proposition,[3] for it is only when British territory is under enemy occupation that these questions are likely to arise in British Courts, and that does not often happen. But the following statement by a writer (W. E. Hall) who has always been regarded as most characteristically British and positivist in his exposition of international law, is strong authority. Speaking of the right of *postliminium*, he says:[4]

> Thus judicial acts done under [the control of the occupant], when they are not of a political complexion, administrative acts so done, to the extent that they take effect during the continuance of his control, and the various acts done during the same time by private persons under the sanction of municipal law, remain good. Were it otherwise, the whole social life of a community would be paralysed by an invasion [that is, occupation]; and as between the state and individuals the evil would be scarcely less,—it would be hard for example that payment of taxes made under duress should be ignored, and it would be contrary to the general interest that sentences passed upon criminals should be annulled by the disappearance of the intrusive government.

Similarly Oppenheim[5] in his chapter on *Postliminium* says:

> if the occupant has collected the ordinary taxes, has sold the ordinary fruits of immoveable property, has disposed of such moveable State property as he was competent to appropriate, or has performed other acts in conformity with the laws of war, this may not be ignored by the legitimate

---

acts of a public official during the occupation bind the lawful sovereign after the end of the occupation, see four Dutch cases, *Zeeuwsche Hypotheek-Bank Ltd* v. *State of the Netherlands*, *Triborgh* v. *State of the Netherlands*, *Aniem* v. *State of the Netherlands*, *K.N.A.C.* v. *State of the Netherlands*; as to the extent to which the occupant may succeed to the contractual obligations and rights of the lawful sovereign, see *Société Anonyme du Canal de Blaton à Ath* v. *Germany* (German–Belgian M.A.T.), and *Société des Quais de Smyrna* v. *Greece* (Franco–Greek Arbitral Tribunal); as to the occupant's rights and duties regarding the arrest and detention of private persons, see Schwarzenberger, *International Courts* (2nd ed.), pp. 291–2, 338–9.

[1] *Ochoa* v. *Fernandez* (an American case arising out of the occupation of Porto Rico).

[2] It should be noted that the effect of the existence of an actual state of war upon British territory is to prevent the civil Courts from calling into question acts done by the military authorities, regardless of the question whether there is any enemy occupation or not: *Ex parte Marais*; Halsbury, *Laws of England* (3rd ed. Simonds), vol. 7, § 563.

[3] For an Australian case, see *Anglo-Czechoslovak and Prague Creditbank* v. *Janssen* in which it was observed, *obiter*, that 'such acts of the occupying enemy as are strictly necessary for the protection of inhabitants of that country, and of his own army of occupation, and for the maintenance of order therein may be recognized in the King's Courts as having legal effect there and some operation and effect may be given to them outside the occupied territory'.

[4] *International Law* (8th ed.) (Pearce Higgins), p. 579.   [5] II, § 282.

sovereign after he has again taken possession of the territory. However, this only extends to acts done by or under the authority of the occupant *during the occupation*.

Thus we apprehend that if the enemy were to occupy the Scilly Isles (we refrain from instancing the Channel Islands[1] because they have their own legal system), all the ordinary transactions[2] of private law taking place in accordance with existing English law[3] during the enemy administration, such as contracts, dispositions of movables and immovables, devolution of property by will or upon intestacy,[4] and all normal official transactions such as the collection of ordinary taxes,[5] would, at the end of the occupation, be treated as valid, and all judgments, civil and criminal, given in accordance with English law or with such regulations as the enemy was lawfully entitled to prescribe, would be respected.[6] But if the enemy were to introduce a new system of landholding, for instance, to divide up an estate amongst the tenants and purport to make them freeholders, or a

[1] For a note on the enemy occupation of Jersey, see 31 *Journal of Comparative Legislation* (3rd ser.) (1949), Pt. III, p. 8.

[2] On banking transactions during belligerent occupation, see *Chartered Bank of India* v. *Wee Cheng Chiang*, and see above, p. 227.

[3] As to the continued application, in principle, of the local law, see *Sultan of Johore* v. *Tungku Abubakar* [1952] A.C. 318, 342 (Privy Council); *Hausmann* v. *Koninklijke Rotterdamse Lloyd* (Holland); *Clostermann* v. *Schmidt et al.* (U.S.A.); *Cobb* v. *United States* (U.S.A.); Geneva Civilians Convention, 1949, Article 64. The local law may remain in force as against nationals of the occupying State (see *Auditeur Militaire* v. *Juttens* (Belgium, Cour de Cassation)), members of the occupying forces (*Kauhlen Case* (Belgium, Cour de Cassation)) and the occupying State (*Milaire* v. *Germany* (Belgian–German M.A.T.)).

[4] Thus it was held by a Greek Court (the Court of Appeals in Thrace) in 1925 that a will made on Bulgarian territory under occupation by inter-Allied troops in February 1920 and not in accordance with Bulgarian law was invalid, for during occupation the law of the State owning the territory remains in force: *Thrace (Validity of Wills) Case*. For a Polish decision on a will, see *Stasiuk and Jagnycz* v. *Klewec*, and for a group of Polish decisions on the validity of wills and contracts for the sale of property made during the occupation and the effect of legal changes made by the occupant, see 24 I.L.R. (1957), pp. 960–76, and 26 I.L.R. (1958–II), pp. 716–23.

[5] As to the occupant's power to modify the fiscal system of the occupied territory, see *Ligabue* v. *Finanze* (Italy); as to the continued force during the occupation of the internal revenue laws of the territory, see *Hilado* v. *The Collector of Internal Revenue* (Philippines, Supreme Court). It was held in *United States* v. *Rice* that import duties paid to the British Government while in military occupation of the American State of Maine in 1814–1815 could not be claimed again by the American Government after the occupation had ceased. See also *McLeod* v. *U.S.* (U.S.A. Supreme Court); and Hackworth, *Digest of International Law*, vol. VI, p. 392.

[6] In regard to convictions for offences, it seems necessary to exclude from this statement any unexpired result of convictions for offences against the security of the occupant and his troops and any political offences directed against him (see *Criminal Files (Greece) Case*). But we can see no reason why a conviction for an offence against a rationing system or against a prohibition of profiteering imposed by the occupant in the interest of the community as a whole should not in principle continue to have effect after the end of the occupation: see above, pp. 370–1, and *Re Scarpato* (Italy). The Peace Treaty may, of course, expressly deal with this matter.

new system of local government,[1] or a new marriage law,[2] or were to disestablish and disendow the Church of England, such measures would not be respected.

In considering the occupation of British territory by an enemy we must remark that not only do questions arise in connection with the effects of the occupant's laws and regulations, but the conduct of residents in that territory may also fall to be considered in the light of the English law of treason. So far as our law is concerned, British subjects in British territory under enemy occupation continue, by virtue of their personal allegiance to the Crown, to be amenable to the law of treason, and non-British subjects, whether enemy or otherwise, who were resident before the occupation and therefore owed the Crown local and temporary allegiance, continue to do so, in spite of the occupation. Thus a citizen of the South African Republic resident in Natal who joined the forces of that Republic in 1899 when they invaded and occupied the part of Natal in which he had resided for ten years, was adjudged guilty of high treason and his conviction was later upheld by the Privy Council. It having been contended that his allegiance ceased when the Queen's protection ceased, Lord Loreburn L.C., in delivering the opinion of the Privy Council, said:[3]

The protection of a State does not cease merely because the State forces, for strategical or other reasons, are temporarily withdrawn, so that the enemy for the time being exercises the rights of an army in occupation. On the contrary, when such territory reverts to the control of its rightful Sovereign, wrongs done during the foreign occupation are cognizable by the ordinary Courts. The protection of the Sovereign has not ceased. It is continuous, though the actual redress of what has been done amiss may be necessarily postponed until the enemy forces have been expelled.

---

[1] In the Philippines the Supreme Court has held that the pre-occupation Philippine Constitution was not in force during the Japanese occupation (*Bautista et al.* v. *Hilaria Uy Isabello*), but that the Constitution adopted in 1943 when the Japanese Military Administration purported to give independence was in force (*Rellosa* v. *Gaw Chee Hun*).

[2] See *Listenburg* v. *Rogowska* (Holland); *N.* v. *Belgian State et al.* See, however, the *Slovakia (Occupation) Case* (Supreme Court of Hungary); and also *Krott* v. *Merkens* (Belgium).

[3] *De Jäger* v. *Attorney-General of Natal* [1907] A.C. 326, 328. The occupation lasted for six months and appears to have amounted to more than mere invasion. For an adverse criticism, see Baty in *Law Magazine and Review*, xxxiii (1908), pp. 214–18. For a Malayan case arising out of the War of 1939 to 1945, see *Dominic* v. *Public Prosecutor*. In *In re van Huis* a Dutch court found a Dutch policeman guilty of aiding the German occupation authorities in giving effect to measures against the resistance movements. Dutch courts frequently interpreted the duty of obedience owed to the occupant in a strictly limited way and held it to be subordinate to the inhabitant's duty towards the lawful government and his duty to refrain from helping the enemy: see *In re Contractors Knols*, and *In re Contractor Worp*. See also *In re Mittermaier* (Italy, Cour de Cassation); *Auditeur Général* v. *Bittner* (Belgium); *In re Jutten* (Belgium, Cour de Cassation); cf. *Public Prosecutor* v. *H. and E.* (Luxembourg).

After the Wars of 1914 to 1918 and 1939 to 1945 these general principles were applied in a large number of decisions (which must now be read in the light of the 1949 Geneva Civilians Convention).

(i) *Legislation.*[1] The Brussels Court of Appeal in *City of Malines* v. *Société Centrale pour l'Exploitation de Gaz*[2] upheld certain necessary measures taken by the German authorities during the occupation which resulted in an increase in the cost of supplying gas due to an increase in the cost of materials and the need of ensuring a supply of gas for the population. Similarly, laws concerning the leasing of property,[3] incest,[4] periods of limitation,[5] the surrender of firearms,[6] the prevention of black marketeering[7] and the protection of official secrets[8] have been held to be laws validly made by the occupant within the powers enjoyed by him in international law.[9] While the returning sovereign may, in the exercise of his normal legislative sovereignty, annul with retroactive effect laws which were thus validly made, it is not customary, and it is probably contrary to legal principle,[10] for him to do so. Even the validly made laws do not, of course, necessarily remain part of the law of the land once the occupation has ended: quite apart from action taken by the returning sovereign,[11] some courts have held that certain of the occupant's

[1] Articles 64 ff. of the 1949 Geneva Civilians Convention deal with the occupant's power to make laws (see above, p. 369, n. 6) and the manner of their enforcement in courts of law.

[2] See Oppenheim, II, p. 437, n. 4, for references to the principal Belgian decisions after the War of 1914 to 1918, and also Rankin, 26 *Transactions of the Grotius Society* (1940). As to an occupant's power to change matters of procedure as opposed to substantive laws, see *Marjanoff* v. *Wloclawek* (Poland, Supreme Court). For the situation in the Channel Islands between 1940 and 1945, see Aubin, 31 *Journal of Comparative Legislation* (1949), Pt. III, p. 8.

[3] *In re Law 900 of 1943* (Greece).

[4] *Procurator* v. *X (Incest Case)* (Holland).

[5] *Maung Pa* v. *Daw In* (Burma).

[6] *Re C.* (Belgium); *Public Prosecutor* v. *X (Eastern Java)* (Netherlands East Indies).

[7] *L.* v. *N. (Olive Oil Case)*.

[8] *Attorney-General for Israel* v. *Sylvester* (Israel, Supreme Court).

[9] The fact that a law is validly made by the occupant from the point of view of his powers in international law does not necessarily afford a good defence in municipal law to a charge of having aided the enemy: see *In re Policeman Vollema* (Holland). As to an occupant's powers to enact a retroactive penal law in violation of the Constitution of the occupied territory, see *In re S.* (Germany); the present position is governed by Article 67 of the 1949 Geneva Civilians Convention.

[10] The Dutch Special Cour de Cassation has suggested that a law of the lawful sovereign denying legal validity to laws properly passed by the occupant for the protection of his occupying forces would itself be without binding force as being a municipal act contrary to international law: see *In re Vogt*.

[11] See, e.g. the Proclamation issued on 15 August 1945, by the returning British authorities in Malaya, providing that as from the date of reoccupation the proclamations and legislative enactments issued by the Japanese Military Authority ceased to have any effect: for a general summary of the measures taken by the returning sovereign in Malaya, see Das, *op. cit.* (in the bibliography to this chapter), ch. v. In respect of Holland, the Nether-

laws, at least, cease to be valid as soon as the occupation has ended.[1]

(ii) *Judgments* delivered during the occupation[2] may either be judgments of the normal Courts of the occupied territory[3] or judgments of courts set up by the occupant.[4] In the former case, so long

lands Government in London enacted a Decree on Occupation Measures, dated 17 September 1944, which dealt with the bulk of German occupation legislation by dividing it into four categories, namely (i) those held never to have had any validity, (ii) those inoperative from the date of the liberation, (iii) those maintained in operation for purely practical reasons, and (iv) all others, whose operation was provisionally suspended pending a final decision (see 14 *A.D.* (1947), p. 250). See, in general, Morgenstern, 28 *B.Y.* (1951), pp. 310–15, and cases cited at p. 410, n. 2, below.

[1] See *Re A.* (Greece), to the effect that those of the occupant's laws passed in order to secure the safety of his troops cease their validity at the end of the occupation; *In re G.* (Greece) suggests that all the occupant's laws are to be ignored after the end of the occupation except in so far as they may be ratified by the returning sovereign, and this would appear to be the view taken by the British authorities in relation to the Channel Islands (Aubin, 31 *Journal of Comparative Legislation* (1949), Pt. III, p. 8): see also *Weiss* v. *Weiss* (Luxembourg). See Morgenstern, *op. cit.* p. 312, n. 2, and *Maung Pa* v. *Daw In* (Burma). For the validation of legislative acts of authorities administering any territory under British military occupation during the War of 1914 to 1918, see the Indemnity Act, 1920, section 6.

[2] As to the situation where the occupant's Courts continue to sit after the end of the occupation in order to wind up their business, see *In re Kraussman* (U.S.A.).

[3] The occupant must in general respect the continued existence of the ordinary courts as part of the system of law and administration of the country. Article 64 of the 1949 Geneva Civilians Convention provides that the tribunals of the occupied territory shall continue to function in respect of all offences covered by the penal laws of the territory, unless their continued functioning constitutes an obstacle to the application of the Convention, and subject to the necessity for ensuring the effective administration of justice.

[4] The powers of an occupant in international law include the power to set up his own courts for special purposes connected with the maintenance of the occupation, such as for the trial of offences against the security of his own forces. Article 66 of the 1949 Geneva Civilians Convention recognizes the right of the occupant to try breaches of penal laws properly enacted by him in 'properly constituted, non-political military courts', which must sit in the occupied territory: the procedure to be followed in such proceedings is set out in the following Articles. In appropriate circumstances the occupant may, it is suggested, set up courts to deal with ordinary cases, civil and criminal, not directly concerned with his military requirements, if this is necessary to fulfil his general duty to ensure public order and safety. Courts so established should as far as possible be compatible with the judicial system of the territory and set up in accordance with, and to apply, the laws of the territory (as lawfully amended by the occupant). Courts in this second category are not so much courts of the occupant as courts of the territory, established by the occupant because they were necessary for the life of the community (e.g. if the pre-existing judicial system has disintegrated); it is thus really a matter of the occupant replacing Courts which have disappeared rather than creating new Courts with totally new jurisdictions—to do this would be an unwarranted interference with the legal system of the occupied territory. See in general on the occupant's powers to set up Courts: Oppenheim, II, pp., 445–7; Campbell, 1 *I.L.Q.* (1947), p. 192; Freeman, 41 *A.J.* (1947), p. 579; Wolff, 29 *Transactions of the Grotius Society* (1943), p. 99; Lyons, 30 *B.Y.* (1953), p. 507; *The King* v. *Maung Hmin et al.* (Burma); *Abdul Aziz* v. *The Sooratee Bara Bazaar Co. Ltd* (Burma); *Maung Hli Maung* v. *Ko Maung Maung* (Burma); *In re Dr J. H. Carp* (Holland); *Woo Chan Shi and Pak Chuen Woo* v. *Brown* (Hong Kong); *Endricci* v. *Eisenmayer* (Italy); *L.* v. *N.* (*Bulgarian Occupation of Greece*); *Thrace* (*Notarial Services*) *Case* (Greece); *Mr P.* (*Batavia*) v. *Mrs S.* (*Bandoeng*) (Netherlands East Indies); *United States Military Government* v. *Ybarro*; *United States Military Government* v. *Flamme*; *Re Condarelli* (Italy); *Recognition of Divorce* (*Eastern Germany*) *Case* (Germany, Supreme Court); *Re Cresciani* (Italy, Cour de Cassation). For an Opinion of the Law Officers of the Crown, in 1848, see McNair, *Opinions*, III, p. 38.

as the local courts are functioning more or less normally and freely and are applying the local law (as lawfully amended by the occupant) their decisions have been accepted after the occupation. The Burmese High Court in *The King* v. *Maung Hmin et al.*[1] held that convictions and acquittals during the occupation by a Court applying Burmese municipal law, the Court having existed prior to the occupation and having simply been continued in existence by an Order of the Japanese Occupying Authorities, were binding on the lawful government[2] with the result that pleas of *autrefois convict* or *acquit* based thereon were good and valid defences in subsequent proceedings instituted by the returning British authorities.

Judgments of courts properly set up by the occupant[3] have been treated with greater reserve. In principle judgments of such Courts are accepted as valid in the sense that the occupant was entitled to make them, the parties thereto cannot claim to have been wronged thereby, and they will be regarded as producing legal effects.[4] In *Maung Hli Maung* v. *Ko Maung Maung*[5] the Burmese High Court held that proceedings before the Rangoon City Court set up by the Japanese occupation authorities were valid proceedings so as to bring

[1] See also *U San Wa* v. *U Ba Thin* (Burma); *Laung* v. *Herrman* (France); *Chettiar* v. *Cheng* (Malaya).

[2] As to convictions for political offences or offences against the security of the occupant, see above, p. 386, n. 6.

[3] Where the occupant, in purporting merely to continue in existence the normal local Courts, in fact does so in such a way as to change their character substantially, the Courts are probably to be regarded as courts set up by the occupant. Changes of judges do not necessarily constitute such a change of character: see *The King* v. *Maung Hmin et al.* (Burma) and *Zbigniew G.* v. *Land and Building Company E. in Cracow* (Poland, Supreme Court). As to changes in the status of judges, or measures against them, see Article 54 of the 1949 Geneva Civilians Convention. Where the occupant fails to establish civil courts, the executive act of an occupying military authority in changing a pre-occupation judgment is not entitled to be respected: *Ellin Anak Masing* v. *The King* (Sarawak). In a different category, and outside the scope of this work, are those Courts set up by an occupant which are of an international character, such as the various war crimes tribunals set up at the end of the War of 1939 to 1945: see *In re Flick and Others*.

[4] Of course, even if in principle their judgments may be treated as valid, in any particular case the conduct of the proceedings or the nature of the judgment may justify the court's decision being quashed: see e.g. *In re S.* (Greece).

[5] See also *Abdul Aziz* v. *The Sooratee Bara Bazaar Co. Ltd* (Burma); *Chan Kam Chuen* v. *Leung Ho Wai Chun* (Hong Kong) (suggesting, however, that the validity of such judgments must be considered judgment by judgment, and not on the basis that if the court is validly established all its judgments are therefore valid); *Cheang Sunny* v. *Ramanathan Chettiar and Others* (Singapore); *Madsen* v. *Kinsella* (U.S.A., Supreme Court); *Austrian Amnesty Case* (Austria); *German Military Courts in Greece Case* (Greece); *Cambier* v. *Lebrun* (Belgium, Cour de Cassation). The validity of judgments rendered by tribunals of the occupant may be determined by treaty after the war (see, e.g. Articles 5 (1) and 7 (1) or the Convention on the Settlement of Matters Arising out of the War and the Occupation, 1952 (T.S. no. 13 (1959)) or legislation of the lawful sovereign (e.g. the Japanese Judgments and Civil Proceedings Ordinance, 1946, passed in Malaya (see p. 411, n. 2 below) and the Polish decrees referred to by the Supreme Court of Poland in *In re Will of Jan M.*).

into operation the law preventing a litigant from instituting further proceedings on a cause of action substantially similar to that in earlier proceedings. In some cases however Courts have, while accepting the judgments of such Courts as valid, limited their effects. Thus they have been held to have ceased to have effect at the end of the occupation,[1] not to have the force of *res judicata*,[2] and not to be an adequate basis for a plea of *autrefois convict* or *acquit*.[3] The basis for many of these decisions has been the assimilation of validly set up occupation Courts to foreign Courts.[4]

(iii) *Currency*. It has long been the practice for occupation authorities to introduce their own occupation currency for use in the occupied territory,[5] and, so long as in doing so their action can be justified as being in exercise of the legitimate powers of a belligerent occupant, the practice is not unlawful and the currency itself, as well as transactions conducted in terms of it, should be regarded as valid.[6] Just where lie the limits to the occupant's powers in this matter is, however, not clear. The introduction of an occupation currency with an official rate of exchange damaging to the inhabitants of the occupied territory has been held to be wrongful:[7] clearly such an action can amount to the dispossession of the inhabitants of their assets. Burmese courts have held that by issuing an occupation currency parallel to, and with a fixed value in relation to, the lawful currency of Burma the Japanese occupation authorities had exceeded their powers: they held that Japanese occupation currency notes so issued were not lawful money but 'were no better than tokens, which were given and

---

[1] *Woo Chan Chi and Pak Chuen Woo* v. *Brown* (Hong Kong).   [2] *Re C.* (Belgium).

[3] *Double Jeopardy Case* (Germany, Supreme Court); *Occupation Tribunals Case* (Austria, Supreme Court); *Chin Chi-Huo* v. *Japan* (Japan, Supreme Court); *Re Di Gennaro* (Italy, Cour de Cassation).

[4] See *United States High Commissioner for Germany* v. *Migo and Another* (U.S. Court of Appeals in Occupied Germany); *Recidivist (Military Tribunal of Occupant) Case* (Germany, Supreme Court)—but see the later decision of the same court in *Retrial of Convicted Criminal (Germany) Case*, taking into account the provisions of the 1952 Bonn Convention; *Police Inspector G.* v. *Innsbruck Police Inspectorate* (Austria)—cf. an apparently contradictory decision of the same court at 18 *I.L.R.* (1951), no. 197.

[5] See in general, Oppenheim, II, p. 437, n. 4; Feilchenfeld, *op. cit.* (in bibliography to this chapter), pp. 70–83; Das, *op. cit.* (in bibliography to this chapter), ch. XI; Mann, 26 *B.Y.* (1949), pp. 272–7, and *The Legal Aspect of Money* (1953), pp. 437–44; Nussbaum, *Money in the Law*, pp. 495–501. For the situation in the Channel Islands from 1940 to 1945, see Aubin, 31 *Journal of Comparative Legislation* (1949), Pt. III, pp. 10–11. Much useful historical material is contained in *Haw Pia* v. *The China Banking Corporation* (Philippines, Supreme Court).

[6] *Thorrington* v. *Smith* (U.S. Supreme Court)—a case arising out of the American Civil War; *Aboitiz* v. *Price* (U.S.A.); *Haw Pia* v. *The China Banking Corporation* (Philippines, Supreme Court); *Wladyslaw F. and Others* v. *Panstwowa Fabryka Mebli in Cracow* (Poland, Supreme Court). See also *Eisner* v. *United States* (U.S.A.), asserting the right of an occupant to reorganize the monetary system of the occupied territory.

[7] *G.* v. *H.* (Luxembourg).

had value as media of exchange so long as the occupation lasted '.[1] On the other hand, Japanese occupation currency in the Philippines also issued at par with the local currency, was held to have been lawfully issued.[2]

Particular difficulties arise where the occupation currency depreciates markedly in value in relation to the lawful currency while the occupant maintains an unrealistic rate of exchange. In such circumstances a debtor might be able to discharge debts originally incurred in terms of the lawful currency (particularly pre-occupation debts) by a payment in the much-depreciated occupation currency. It cannot be said that courts have approached this situation with any consistency, some having allowed the settlement of pre-occupation debts in occupation currency,[3] while others have refused to do so.[4] In some countries the uncertainties attending the introduction of an occupation currency have been settled by the introduction of legislation. In Malaya, for example, a Debtor and Creditor (Occupation Period) Ordinance[5] was passed after the occupation: this safeguarded the validity of transactions in the occupation currency, but also laid down a scale of conversion rates for Japanese occupation currency on various dates with reference to which certain debts were to be revalued in such a way as to take account of the depreciation of that currency.

(iv) *Private property*.[6] A belligerent occupant not only has to carry on the government and administration of the occupied territory, but he also performs certain acts directly affecting private rights, especially property rights, and more closely associated with the execution of his war effort: acts of this kind include the sequestration[7] of private

[1] *Dooply* v. *Chan Taik* (Burma, Supreme Court). See also the same case at first instance and *Ko Maung Tin* v. *U Gon Man*.

[2] *Haw Pia* v. *The China Banking Corporation* (Philippines, Supreme Court), as explained by the Supreme Court in *Gibbs et al.* v. *Rodriguez et al.*; *Aboitiz* v. *Price* (U.S.A.).

[3] *Planters' Loans Board* v. *Managalam* (Malaya); *Haw Pia* v. *The China Banking Corporation* (Philippines, Supreme Court); *Madlambayan* v. *Felicidad L. Aquino* (Philippines); *Nicolo* v. *Creni* (Italy, Cour de Cassation)—an unusual case, in that the occupation currency had appreciated rather than depreciated.

[4] *Dooply* v. *Chan Taik* (Burma, Supreme Court); *G.* v. *H.* (Luxembourg). See also *Tse Chung* v. *Lee Yau Chu* (Hong Kong).

[5] Ordinance no. 42 of 1948: see Das, *op. cit.* (in bibliography), ch. XII. Similar Ordinances were passed in Singapore, Hong Kong, Sarawak, North Borneo and Brunei, while in Burma a statute was enacted. The Sarawak Ordinance was considered by the Privy Council in *The Chartered Bank of India, Australia and China* v. *Wee Kheng Chiang*. Provisions relating to occupation currencies will be found in some peace treaties: see Articles 24.4 of the Austrian State Treaty, 1955, and 76.4 of the Treaty of Peace with Italy, 1947.

[6] In addition to works cited in the bibliography, see Downey, 44 *A.J.* (1950), p. 488; Jessup, 38 *A.J.* (1944), p. 457; Robinson, 39 *A.J.* (1945), p. 216.

[7] What is here referred to as 'sequestration' is often referred to by other terms, such as administrative control or the placing of property under custodianship. The essence of these various concepts is that the owner is not deprived of his property, which is merely safe-

property, the making of requisitions, the seizure of war material and the taking of booty of war. The general principle against the background of which these acts have to be seen is that private property in occupied territory must be respected, and may not be confiscated or pillaged.[1]

An occupant's right to sequestrate private enemy property in the occupied territory is generally recognized,[2] so long as what is involved does not amount to a confiscation of the property or a mere cover for some other improper dealing with it.[3] Acts lawfully done by the occupant in exercise of this right to sequestrate private property will generally be accepted as valid after the occupation. Thus Courts have after the occupation held that the occupant may lease premises which he has sequestrated and the tenancy granted by him continues after the end of the occupation,[4] that he may insure sequestrated premises and the policy remains valid after the occupation and premiums must be paid,[5] and that he may appoint a liquidator of a sequestrated company and the payment of a debt to the liquidator is good discharge of the debt.[6]

guarded and conserved on his behalf and will be returned to him in due course when the circumstances giving rise to the sequestration are over (subject to any contrary provisions in, e.g. the peace treaty).

[1] Hague Regulations, Articles 46 and 47; Geneva Civilians Convention, 1949, Article 33. For the rejection of the 'somewhat arresting' proposition that property in some tugs owned by German nationals in a part of Germany occupied by British forces passed by right of conquest, and by reason of the fact of occupation alone, to the Crown, see *Bugsier Reederei-und-Berguns Aktiengesellschaft* v. *Owners of SS. Brighton* (1951) 67 T.L.R., Pt. 2, 409, 411–12. See also *Public Prosecutor* v. *N.* (Holland, Supreme Court). We are not here concerned with ordinary private law transactions, such as sale or gift, whereby an occupant may acquire property, as to which see *Dutch Machines Case*; *Wee Koh Eng* v. *Gan Ah Chang* (Sarawak, Supreme Court); *Randsfjordsbruket and Jevnaker Kommune* v. *Viul Tresliperi* (Norway, Supreme Court); *Beekman* v. *van der Ploeg* (Holland). A fictitious sale is unlikely to be accepted as adequate: see *Delville* v. *Servais* (Belgium).

[2] See *Cohendy* v. *Camilleri* (France); *Scott* v. *Felice* (France); *Haw Pia* v. *The China Banking Corporation* (Philippines, Supreme Court). As to the occupant's right to remove from sequestration property which the lawful sovereign had sequestrated before the occupation, see *Martignoni* v. *Società Job* (Italy).

[3] See *Steinmetz* v. *Société Hoffman & Boss et Epoux Lantin* (Luxembourg).

[4] *Chop Sun Cheong Loong & anor.* v. *Lian Teck Trading Company* (Malaya).

[5] *Christen* v. *Onderlinge Oorlogs-Molestverzekerings-Maatschappij* (Holland). As to the payment of matured life-insurance policies to a sequestrator in the occupied territory, see *D'Escury* v. *Levensverzekerings-Maatschappij Utrecht, Ltd* (Holland) and *Dussourd* v. *'De Nederlanden van 1845' Life Insurance Co.* (Holland).

[6] *Haw Pia* v. *The China Banking Corporation* (Philippines, Supreme Court); *Public Trustee* v. *Chartered Bank of India, Australia and China* (Singapore). It may be necessary to distinguish between a straightforward liquidation of a business in occupied territory, which is probably beyond the powers of the occupant (see *Hong Kong & Shanghai Banking Corporation* v. *Luiz Perez-Samanillo Inc. & Register of Deeds of Manila* (Philippines); Oppenheim, II, 405, n. 2; and pp. 396–8 below) and a liquidation which takes place within the framework of sequestration so that the assets realized by the liquidation remain preserved for eventual return to the owner. Similarly, while an occupant may not require private debts to be paid to him (see the *Hong Kong & Shanghai Banking Corporation* case) if he properly sequest-

The occupant's right to requisition[1] private property[2] is recognized, and also limited, by Article 52 of the Hague Regulations.[3] Requisitions of property may only be demanded for the needs of the army of occupation, and only on the authority of the commander in the locality occupied; they must be in proportion to the resources of the occupied country; they must as far as possible be paid for in cash, but if they are not a receipt must be given and the payment must follow as soon as possible.[4] The legal effect of a valid requisition under Article 52 is usually regarded as being that the occupant may acquire a good title to the requisitioned property.[5] It may be, however, that in those cases where the needs of the army of occupation do not require that the occupant should acquire title (e.g. in requisitions of land and buildings), no title should be considered to have passed: in such a case the payment made by the occupant would be on a different basis from that which would apply if a transfer of title had taken place.[6]

If, however, property in occupied territory constitutes materials of war (*munitions de guerre*)[7] the occupant may, under Article 53[8] of the Hague Regulations, seize it, even if it belongs to private persons,

rates the property of the creditor it would probably be lawful for him to require the debtor to pay the debt to the sequestrator, such payment constituting a valid discharge of the debt (see *Estate of Rohde* v. *Estate of Urquico et al.* (Philippines, Supreme Court)).

[1] As to the legal nature of a requisition, see *Polyxene Plessa* v. *Turkey* (Greco–Turkish M.A.T.), *Leon* v. *Germany* (Germano–Roumanian M.A.T.), and *Poznanski* v. *Germany* (Germano–Polish M.A.T.).

[2] The occupant may also requisition services from the inhabitants. The questions which often arise in this connection concern criminal convictions after the occupation for aiding the enemy in performing the requisitioned service: see *In re Contractors Knols* (Holland) and *In re Contractor Worp* (Holland), holding that the fact that as a matter of international law an occupant is entitled to requisition certain services does not mean that in municipal law the inhabitant is entitled to perform them.

[3] See also Article 55 of the 1949 Geneva Civilians Convention with regard to requisitions of 'foodstuffs, articles or medical supplies': while the meaning of the term 'articles' is not altogether clear, it would seem not to be coterminous with 'property' but to be restricted to the kind of articles associated with food and medical supplies which it is the purpose of the Article to protect.

[4] As to delay in making payments, see *Roumania* v. *Germany* (Special Arbitral Tribunal), *Karmatzucas* v. *Germany* (Germano–Greek M.A.T.), and an unnamed Dutch case referred to in 13 A.D. (1946), p. 381.

[5] See *Potdevin* v. *Monnier* (France); *Re Lepore* (Italy); *Vitse* v. *Brasser and the Dutch State* (Holland); *Giovannini* v. *Renzi* (Italy); *De Riard* v. *Medoro* (Italy, Cour de Cassation). Care should be taken with some reported decisions which refer to 'requisitions' and deny that they operate so as to transfer title, but which are really cases of seizures under Article 53 of the Hague Regulations to which different considerations apply (see below).

[6] See Feilchenfeld, *op. cit.* (in bibliography), pp. 37–8. Even where property is of such a kind that the occupant could have acquired title to it, the facts of a particular transaction may lead to the conclusion that he did not in fact purport to do so: see *Ho Hong Soon* v. *Haji Sahari Bin Haji Su'ut and Another*, 24 I.L.R. (1957), p. 979, and the note at p. 983.

[7] As to the meaning of this term, see E. Lauterpacht, 32 *B.Y.* (1955–6), p. 218.

[8] Article 43 may also permit the seizure of property: see *In re Krupp and Others*.

although any private property so seized must be restored and compensation fixed when peace is made.[1] It is thus clear, and has been so held on many occasions, that even a valid seizure of such private property does not give the occupant a good title to it.[2] Consequently the property, not being owned by the occupant, may not be seized by the opposing belligerent as State-owned property;[3] and a third person to whom the occupant may have transferred the property is usually, in accordance with the applicable system of municipal law, accountable for it to the original owner to whom he may have to return it[4] or to whom he may have to pay damages if the property is damaged while in his possession.[5] Article 53 also covers the seizure of State-owned *munitions de guerre* and the taking possession of State-owned movable property[6] which may be used for the operations of war. Furthermore, any State-owned movable property found on the battlefield by the opposing belligerent may be appropriated by him as booty of war.[7] In both these cases the occupant can acquire a

[1] Although not expressly stated in Article 53, a receipt ought to be given for private property seized under it: see *In re Hinrichsen* (Holland); *N. V. de Bataafsche Petroleum Maatschappij and Others* v. *The War Damage Commission* (Singapore).

[2] But see the German decision reported in 13 *A.D.* (1946), no. 158, holding that a third party can acquire rights in property seized under Article 53 if he believes, in good faith, that the property is owned by the occupying forces alienating it.

[3] See *Bertrand, Mannès and State of Belgium* v. *Bontemps, Camus and Ramelot* (Belgium); *Bilotte* v. *Groos et al.* (Holland); *Statens Jordlovsudvalg* v. *Petersen* (Denmark, Supreme Court). At the end of the War of 1939 to 1945 the Allied Powers issued proclamations or regulations whereby property in the possession of the German forces could be seized as booty, whether or not actually owned by such forces: Courts which were bound by those proclamations and regulations gave effect to them in that sense (see, e.g. *X.* v. *D.*; cf. *Beekman* v. *van der Ploeg* (Holland)). The principle underlying such provisions of those proclamations and regulations is, however, open to criticism, although for practical reasons they may be justifiable. It may be remarked that where the German occupation authorities had looted from occupied France some gold bars belonging to a French company, and those bars were later recovered in Germany by the Allied forces, the Allied Governments concerned did not claim title to the bars: see *Dollfus Mieg et Cie., S.A.* v. *Bank of England* [1950] 1 Ch. 33 (C.A.), and [1952] A.C. 582 (H.L.) (the case was decided on the issue of sovereign immunity).

[4] *Requisitioned Property (Austria) Cases* (Austria, Supreme Court) (cf. *Booty (Requisitioned Car) Case* (Austria, Supreme Court)); *Statens Jordlovsudvalg* v. *Petersen* (Denmark, Supreme Court); *Ransom Philippine Corporation* v. *Puzon and Lao* (Philippines, Supreme Court). Municipal law may even make the third party who had received the lawfully seized property guilty of a criminal offence: see *Bonaventure* v. *Ureel* (Belgium). See also n. 2 above.

[5] *Loss of Requisitioned Motor Car (Germany) Case* (Germany, Supreme Court).

[6] State-owned land and public buildings in occupied territory may only be used by the occupant as an administrator and usufructuary, and may not be seized: Hague Regulations, Article 55. Thus a purported disposition of such property by the occupant has no validity after the occupation: *Hussein Buksh Khan* v. *Mudalia and Another* (Burma, Supreme Court).

[7] See Oppenheim, II, pp. 401–2. Many writers refer to State property seized under Article 53 as having been seized as booty. See in general on seizure of State-owned property, Downey, 44 *A.J.* (1950), p. 488; Freeman, 40 *A.J.* (1946), p. 795; Lew, *ibid.* p. 584; Smith, 23 *B.Y.* (1946), p. 227. For some early Opinions of the Law Officers of the Crown, see McNair, *Opinions*, III, pp. 4 ff.

good title: the occupant may thus transfer title to a third person who will acquire a good title valid even against the original owner.[1]

Where Great Britain is neutral. In the case of a belligerent occupation occurring in a war in which Great Britain is neutral,[2] an English Court will seek and follow the guidance of the Foreign Office as to the fact of the occupation and possibly also as to its territorial extent.[3] Thus in the course of the conquest of Ethiopia by Italy the Chancery Division was called upon in *Bank of Ethiopia* v. *National Bank of Egypt and Liguori*[4] to decide whether the Bank of Ethiopia, a company incorporated by Ethiopian law, had been dissolved or had otherwise ceased to exist by force of a decree promulgated by the Italian Government on 9 May 1936. The relevant facts as found by Clauson J. are as follows:

1 or 2 May. The Emperor of Ethiopia left his capital, Addis Ababa.

5 May. The Italian Army entered the capital.

9 May. The Italian Government issued a Proclamation purporting to annex Ethiopia. As from that date 'it appears as a fact' (said Clauson J.) 'from the evidence before me that the Italian Government, through its officers, exercised effective governmental control over Addis Ababa, the

---

[1] *Andersen* v. *Christensen and the State Committee for Small Allotments* (Denmark); *Austrian Treasury (Postal Administration)* v. *Auer* (Austria, Supreme Court); *French State* v. *Establissements Monmousseau* (France); *Ministero Della Difesa-Esercito* v. *Salamone* (Italy, Cour de Cassation); *Phya Seewikramatit* v. *Ministry of Commerce* (Thailand, Supreme Court); *Ministry of Defence* v. *Ergialli* (Italy). But cf. *Mestre Hospital* v. *Defence Administration* (Italy, Cour de Cassation).

[2] For decisions of other countries in relation to occupations occurring in wars in which, or at a time at which, they were neutrals, see *L.M.* v. *Swiss Banks* (Switzerland); *Occupation of Germany (Zurich) Case* (Switzerland); *P.* v. *A.G.K. and P.* (Switzerland); *Rosenberg* v. *Fischer* (Switzerland); *Amstellbank N.V.* v. *Guaranty Trust Co.* (U.S.A.). In Great Britain, the United States and some other countries the Courts of law look to the Executive for guidance as to the character of our foreign relations with a particular country, and political sympathies may be reflected in the answers given by the Executive. Thus, in the last mentioned case, in relation to the decrees of the German Government during the occupation of Holland, Mr Justice Pecora of the Supreme Court of New York said, at a time before the entry of the U.S.A. into the war: 'The Government of the United States has refused to recognize the German military control of Holland. Any decrees by this unrecognized occupying force would not have "force and effect of mandates of a lawful sovereign"'... In withholding recognition of the Nazi regime in continental Netherlands, the Government of the United States has made a determination of policy which our courts should follow. Therefore, any German decrees promulgated in the Netherlands should be given no force or effect whatever in the determination of questions involving property in this State' (cited by Jessup in 36 *A.J.* (1942), p. 286) and see to the same effect *Koninklijke Lederfabriek 'Oisterwijk', N.V.* v. *Chase National Bank*. It would be difficult to apply this policy to ordinary and lawful routine acts involved in the administration of occupied territory. See also two rather curious decisions of the Austrian Supreme Court, which are based upon Austria not having been a belligerent in the War of 1939 to 1945: *Dralle* v. *Republic of Czechoslovakia* and *Jenaer Glaswerk Schott & Gen.* v. *Waldmuller.*

[3] But see *Yeo How Sam* v. *Chop Bee Huat* (Singapore), suggesting that a Foreign Office certificate on this would not be conclusive.

[4] See *Zarine* v. *Owners of S.S. Ramava: McEvoy* v. *Owners of S.S. Otto.*

"siège social" of the bank, and over a gradually increasing tract of Ethiopian territory'.

20 June. 'A (*semble* Italian) government decree, valid according to the law as recognized and administered by the *de facto* government, placed the bank in liquidation...'

December 1936. At some later date the British Foreign Office issued a certificate to the effect that in December 1936 the United Kingdom Government 'recognized the Italian Government as being in fact (*de facto*) the government of the area of Abyssinia then under Italian control'[1]— which area (said Clauson J.) 'seems to have covered the whole of the portion of Ethiopian territory in which any activities of the bank had ever been carried on'.

28 April 1937. (The day before the trial) the Emperor of Ethiopia, while in England, signed a decree by which he purported to empower all companies incorporated under Ethiopian law to hold valid meetings and to carry on business outside Abyssinia.

The learned judge declined to accept the suggestion that any limitation could be placed upon the full sovereignty of the Italian Government at the material times, either on the ground that it was merely in belligerent occupation of Ethiopian territory and that therefore its decrees were governed by the limits which international law imposes upon the decrees of a belligerent occupant, or on the ground of the continued recognition by the United Kingdom Government of some measure of *de iure* sovereignty in the Emperor of Ethiopia. But he added that if the Italian decrees were limited to the necessity of preserving peace, order, and good government, he would nevertheless uphold the decree in question, having regard to the importance of the Bank of Ethiopia as the only bank of issue in the country acting in close contact with the Minister of Finance.[2] Note that the decree liquidated the bank and did not merely control it.

With great respect, it is submitted that Clauson J. in this judgment has invested a Government in belligerent occupation of the territory of another with a degree of power which it is difficult to reconcile with the rules of international law as accepted by this country. During the past century it was gradually made clear—and very much to the benefit of the inhabitants of territory invaded and occupied— that belligerent occupation is a provisional state of affairs and that it does not transfer sovereignty. That must await either subjugation or cession by treaty of peace. As appears from the Foreign Office

---

[1] Her Majesty's Government recognized the conquest *de jure* on 16 November 1938.

[2] Undoubtedly a belligerent occupant would be entitled in the interests of the welfare of the inhabitants to control the operations of so important a bank, but we cannot see how its liquidation can be reconciled with international law: see also note 6 on p. 393 above.

certificate referred to above, even in December 1936 the Italian Government did not control the whole of Ethiopia, and it is common knowledge that this state of affairs continued for some time later. Nevertheless Clauson J. was prepared to hold that within six weeks of a belligerent occupant's arrival in the enemy capital and before he has brought the whole country under his control he is to be invested with the full panoply of sovereignty—his acts having 'the status of acts of a fully responsible government' and 'the recognized *de facto* government must for all purposes...be treated as a duly recognized foreign sovereign state'.[1]

It is true that—as is shown in *A. M. Luther Co* v. *James Sagor & Co.*—recognition once granted relates back, but it can only relate back to the establishment of the status recognized. In the *National Bank of Egypt* case we suggest that the recognition of *de facto* governmental control certified by the Foreign Office can only relate back to the time at which that control began and did not compel the Court to say that on 9 May 1936, the date of the proclamation of annexation,[2] Italy ceased to be in belligerent occupation of a large part of Ethiopia and became *de facto* sovereign over it. In short, the recognition relates back to the date at which belligerent occupation ceased and merged in *de facto* sovereignty, but it cannot obliterate or curtail the belligerent occupation.[3]

Where Great Britain is a belligerent and questions arise as to the fact of British occupation of enemy territory or enemy occupation of British or allied territory, one would now expect to find English Courts following the practice of consulting some branch of the

---

[1] At p. 522. See Lauterpacht, *Recognition in International Law*, pp. 285–7, 348, 365, 432.

[2] The Italian proclamation of annexation, which was issued four days after the Italian army entered the capital, and while there were still large areas of the country which had not been reduced, was in no way conclusive upon an English Court. A valid annexation involves the transfer of sovereignty, and a purported annexation which precedes subjugation, that is, the virtual annihilation of the enemy forces, is premature and of no effect. Upon the effect of the withdrawal by Great Britain in 1940 of her recognition of the Italian conquest and annexation of Ethiopia, see *Azazh Kebbeda Tesema* v. *Italian Government*. See also Article 35 of the Peace Treaty with Italy, 1947, in which Italy recognized the legality of all measures taken by Ethiopia to annul Italian measures respecting Ethiopia after 3 October 1935, and the effects of such measures.

[3] The decisions in this case and in *The Cristina* (about to be discussed) were subjected to a searching analysis in 19 *B.T.* (1938), p. 236 by an anonymous critic who is known to possess high authority. He said: 'Clauson J. appears to have relied upon the fact that there was no other government in any part of Ethiopia than the *de facto* Italian Government to reject the argument that the Italian Government should only be regarded as in military occupation of enemy territory: but it is submitted that this is the wrong reason for the right conclusion. There was (except in a few square miles) no government in Belgium except the German Government from 1915 to 1918, but the German Government was during these years only in "military occupation". The test is whether the war is over or not and for the court whether the government have recognized that it is over.'

Executive as to the *fact*, including the extent, of the occupation, while reserving for themselves the question of the *effects* of the fact. The practice of consulting the Executive and accepting its reply in regard to matters within the international sphere has developed rapidly in recent years.[1] In the older cases the Courts were more inclined to take judicial notice of such matters or ascertain them by evidence.[2]

2. *Effects of acts of occupying revolutionary authorities in a civil war*[3]

(*a*) When the revolution occurs on the territory of a foreign State.

(*b*) When it occurs on British territory.

(*a*) Here again we shall find that in regard to the preliminary question as to the *fact* of occupation which must precede adjudication upon its *effects*, the recognition of the situation by the British Government is a decisive factor for English Courts. Recognition of belligerency granted by Great Britain, as was granted in the case of the American Civil War, places the revolutionary Government *vis-à-vis* English Courts in substantially the same position as the Government of a belligerent State engaged in a conflict in which Great Britain is neutral. We shall also find that, even when recognition of belligerency is not granted, the recognition by the British Government of certain facts and situations arising out of the hostilities can have important legal consequences.[4] Some of the decisions raise questions of the extra-territorial effect of foreign laws and decrees, and we have found it convenient to defer the treatment of that question to the next chapter.

The American Civil War cases. Although it was necessary for the Federal Government to bring several actions in English Courts for the purposes of liquidating the consequences of the Civil War, we are not aware of any reported action in which an English Court had to consider what effect should be given to the acts of the Confederate Government.

[1] See 3 *A.D.* (1925–26), p. 128. See also p. 37, n. 2, above.

[2] So far as can be ascertained from a perusal of the report of *R.* v. *L. J. de Jäger* in 22 Natal Law Reports (1901), p. 65, and on appeal to the Privy Council [1907] A.C. 326, the Special Court constituted to try this type of case did not consult the Executive as to the extent of the enemy penetration into Natal, but acted upon evidence or its own knowledge.

[3] See H. Lauterpacht, *Recognition in International Law*, chs. xii–xviii, and relevant appendices. Note also the Geneva Civilians Convention of 1949: see above, pp. 31, 33.

[4] The literature upon recognition of new Governments and States, whether arising from revolution or otherwise, is vast and the decisions are numerous. We have tried to avoid referring to them except in so far as they bear upon the strict subject-matter of this chapter. References will be found in Oppenheim, I, § 71–75*g* and notes, and bibliography preceding § 71 and in notes.

Upon the domestic aspect of rebellion on British territory, see numerous cases arising out of the 'troubles' in Ireland in *Irish Reports* from 1921 onwards.

It is instructive in the lack of English authority to note how the American Courts after the Civil War dealt with the governmental acts of the rebel States. An American writer[1] referring to the 'numerous cases which turned upon the validity of decrees of the Confederate States', remarks:

The Supreme Court of the United States sustained numerous acts relating to the creation of domestic corporations, the sale of property, and payment of debts in the specie of the regime. It generally upheld all laws which were necessary to the peace and good order of the realm, such as sanctioning and protecting marriage, determining laws of descent, regulating the transfer of property and providing legal redress for injuries... in each instance the acts, decrees or laws are recognized as valid by the Supreme Court unless public policy and justice required otherwise.

Cases arising out of the Russian Revolution of 1917. The principle to be deduced from these cases is that English Courts must—directly or indirectly—seek and then follow the guidance of the appropriate branch of the Executive, namely, the Foreign Office, as to the status of a revolutionary Government and the date of its effective establishment. For these purposes what is called recognition *de facto*, or more correctly, recognition of a Government as being the *de facto* Government of the territory in question, has the same effect as recognition of the Government as being the Government *de iure*.

Thus in *A. M. Luther Co.* v. *James Sagor & Co.*,[2] once the United Kingdom Government—between the date of the hearing in the King's Bench Division and the date of the hearing of the appeal— had recognized the Soviet Government 'as the *de facto* Government of Russia', and this fact was certified by the Foreign Office, the Court of Appeal was unable to question the validity of the act of that Government in nationalizing *within its own territory* the plaintiff's timber and selling it *in London* to the defendants, the timber being at the time of sale still abroad.[3] Moreover, the effects of the recognition dated back to the time at which the Soviet Government established its power, upon which point the Foreign Office also pronounced.

---

[1] Hervey, *Legal Effects of Recognition* (1928), p. 145, citing a number of cases; and see pp. 405–6 of this chapter. Where insurgents in Mexico, and later in Nicaragua, were in effective control of territory and had exacted payment of certain taxes, the British and American Governments respectively protested when the legitimate government later tried to exact payment of the same taxes: Moore, *Digest of International Law*, i, pp. 49–51.

[2] Approved by the House of Lords in *Russian Commercial and Industrial Bank* v. *Comptoir d'Escompte de Mulhouse and Others* [1925] A.C. 112, 124. See the volumes of the *Annual Digest* for a number of these Russian cases, British and foreign.

[3] An anonymous commentator in 11 *B.Y.* (1930), p. 229, points out that the American decision of *Ricaud* v. *American Metal Co.* applies this principle even to the case where the owner of the property nationalized in the foreign State is an American citizen.

The question of the precise area over which a revolutionary Government exercises authority at a given moment was treated in *The Jupiter* (*No. 3*), another Russian case, as a question of fact to be determined by the Court itself upon evidence and not one to be settled by the certificate of the Foreign Office.[1] In that case, where one of the many questions to be determined was whether two decrees issued by a certain Government in Russia affected a ship registered at Odessa and at the material dates lying at Odessa, Hill J. positively declined to ask the Foreign Office to make inquiries on the question what Government was in power at Odessa at the material dates. 'No,' he said, 'as regards a *de facto* Government it is a question of evidence, and the evidence is closed. I shall not consult the Foreign Office.'[2] In this ruling he was expressly upheld by the Court of Appeal, but when we come to consider the Ethiopian and the Spanish Civil War cases we shall find the question of the local scope of authority treated differently.

The Spanish Civil War of 1936–9. A dispute[3] having arisen as to the power of a group of persons claiming to be the directors of the Banco de Bilbao to determine the agency of the managers of that bank's London branch, it became necessary to decide what system of law prevailed at the material date in the place where the corporate home (*domicilio social*) of the bank was situate, namely Bilbao, for it was that system which governed the interpretation and the operation of the articles of the incorporated bank. 'The question', said Clauson L.J.[4] in delivering the judgment of the Court of Appeal, 'accordingly resolves itself into this: 'What is the Government whose laws govern in such a matter the Banco de Bilbao? The answer would seem necessarily to be: the laws of the Government of the territory in which Bilbao is situate.' If there is any doubt as to what Government that is, the Court must consult the Executive through the appropriate channel. The answer given, in a letter from the British Foreign Office to the solicitors of one of the parties, was that the insurgent Govern-

---

[1] [1927] P. 122, 250.

[2] At p. 126. But, 'the question of what is within the realm of England [*sic*] being one of the matters of which the Court takes judicial notice', two out of three members of the Court of Appeal in *The Fagernes*, considered themselves to be conclusively bound by a statement as to its limits made by the Attorney-General.

The Gagara, in which Hill J. gave effect to the condemnation in prize by the Esthonian Government of a captured ship flying the flag of the Soviet Government, may also be said to arise out of the Russian Revolution, but the Esthonian Government was not regarded as a revolutionary Government. It was probably, for the brief period of its existence, a partial successor of the Imperial Russian Government.

[3] *Banco de Bilbao* v. *Sancha: Same* v. *Rey* [1938] 2 K.B. 176.

[4] At p. 195.

ment set up by General Franco in the Basque country comprising Bilbao since his capture of Bilbao on 19 June 1937, was recognized by His Majesty's Government as the Government which exercised *de facto* administrative control over that portion of the Basque country which comprised Bilbao. Hence it followed that an English Court could not allow the acts of that Government to be impugned as the acts of an usurping Government, 'and conversely the Court must be bound to treat the acts of a rival government claiming jurisdiction over the same area, even if the latter government be recognized by His Majesty's Government as the *de iure* Government of the area, as a mere nullity, and as matters which cannot be taken into account in any way in any of His Majesty's Courts'.[1]

In another case[2] the Spanish Republican Government had requisitioned in 1937 a Spanish ship registered in Bilbao but then outside Spanish waters. In 1938 the Nationalist Government of Spain requisitioned her and obtained possession of her by the consent of her owners and master. While she was lying in the Thames, the Republican Government issued a writ *in rem* to obtain possession. The 'Nationalist Government of Spain' moved to set aside the writ on the ground that it impleaded a foreign sovereign State, being in possession. It thereupon became necessary for the Court to consult the Foreign Office, which replied that 'His Majesty's Government recognizes the Nationalist Government as a Government which at present exercises *de facto* administrative control over the larger portion of Spain...The Nationalist Government is not a Government subordinate to any other Government in Spain...' The letter added that the question whether in these circumstances the Nationalist Government is to be considered 'a foreign sovereign State' appeared to be a question of law for the Court, which answered the question in the affirmative and set aside the writ.

It thus appears from these two decisions that the English Courts accept the view that there can be two Governments recognized by His Majesty for one State, one *de facto* and the other *de iure*, coordinate but not territorially coincident, and with fluctuating frontiers. The recognition of a *de facto* Government which is in control of only part of a State's territory is believed to be an innovation. At any rate we cannot call to mind a former instance (unless it be the almost con-

[1] At p. 196. Following *A. M. Luther Co.* v. *James Sagor & Co.*; *White, Child & Beney* v. *Eagle Star, etc., Insurance Co.*; and *Bank of Ethiopia* v. *National Bank of Egypt*. Note that this important statement of principle applies both to international and to civil war.

[2] *Government of Republic of Spain* v. *S.S. Arantzazu Mendi* [1939] A.C. 256, 258: see note 1 on p. 445 below.

temporaneous case of Ethiopia), and this view may be the product of the highly anomalous political circumstances of the Spanish Civil Wars to be followed in the future with the greatest circumspection.

(*b*) *When the revolution occurs in British territory.* Such revolutions are rare, and judicial authority is scanty: the 1965–6 rebellion in Southern Rhodesia has not yet been directly considered by an English Court.

Holdsworth has described in his *History of English Law*[1] the general outline of the manner in which the legal events occurring during the Commonwealth were dealt with by the early Restoration Parliaments. 'The general principle', he says, 'upon which these Parliaments proceeded was that all the Acts of the Long Parliament which had received the royal assent were valid, and that all other legislation was invalid.' There were exceptions in both directions. 'On grounds of necessity provision was made for the continuance of judicial proceedings begun under the Commonwealth..., for the confirmation of certain judicial proceedings and completed acts in the law which had taken place,[2] and for the validity of marriages celebrated since 1642 under the authority of any Act or Ordinance.'

The American War of Independence gave rise to fewer reported decisions of English Courts than might have been expected.[3] In spite of some wavering the main principle is, we think, clear, namely, that an English Court will not recognize and give effect to the official acts, legislative or otherwise, of a Government in rebellion against His Majesty. Whether this reference would extend to ordinary routine acts such as the granting of probate of wills, or judgments in suits between parties concerning matters not connected with the rebellion, does not appear to have called for decision.

Dudley v. *Folliott* was the case of an action of covenant upon a covenant contained in conveyance of lands in the province or State of New York made in April 1780, that is, during the War of Independence. The plaintiff was evicted by commissioners appointed in pursuance of an Act passed by the State of New York confiscating the land at some date before the date of the conveyance, and the defendant was sued for breach of his warranty that he had full power and authority to grant and convey the premises to the plaintiff's

---

[1] Vol. VI, pp. 165 f.

[2] E.g. 'fines, recoveries, verdicts, judgments, statutes, recognizances, inrolments of deeds and wills, inquisitions,...probates, letters of administration', etc.

[3] It may be useful to the reader to mention some of these cases, though they are not strictly relevant to the matters discussed here: *Kempe* v. *Antill*; *Wright* v. *Nutt*; *Wright* v. *Simpson*; *Peters* v. *Erving*; *Attorney-General* v. *City of London* (affecting William and Mary College in Virginia); *Doe d. Thomas* v. *Acklam*; *Auchmuty* v. *Mulcaster*; *Stansbury* v. *Arkwright*; *Sutton* v. *Sutton*; *In re Bruce*.

26-2

vendor and for quiet enjoyment. On a demurrer the plaintiff made two points:

(i) That by reason of the confiscatory Act the defendant at the time of his covenant had not a good title to the premises which were then vested in the State of New York, and that the recognition of the independence of the United States by the subsequent treaty of peace had retrospective effect (and therefore presumably prevented an English Court from holding that the confiscatory Act was illegal and invalid).

(ii) That the covenant extended even to an eviction by a wrong-doer.

The Court 'having no doubt about the law as it respects the first question, and thinking it would lead to the discussion of improper topics, would not permit it to be argued'. As to the second question, the Court limited the covenant to lawful interruptions and found for the defendant, meaning thereby, we suggest, that they considered the eviction of the plaintiff by the rebel commissioners to be unlawful.

Ogden v. *Folliott*[1] was argued three times—in the Common Pleas, the King's Bench on writ of error, and the House of Lords. Although for a century and a half it has been regarded as a leading authority for the rule that an English Court will not enforce a penal law of a foreign State, it also rests on a preliminary proposition which takes precedence of the rule as to penal laws and which, strictly speaking, rendered unnecessary and irrelevant the application of that rule.[2] *A* and *B* were British subjects in the territory later known as that of the United States of America, when in 1769 *B* made a bond in favour of *A* to secure a loan. In 1776 the revolution broke out. In 1779 both were attainted by the laws of their respective revolutionary States, their property was confiscated, and they fled to England. In 1783 by a treaty of peace Great Britain acknowledged the independence of her revolted colonies. Thereafter *A* brought suit on his bond against *B*.

(*a*) In the Court of Common Pleas Lord Loughborough gave judgment in favour of *B* on the ground that 'the penal laws of foreign countries are strictly local' and seemed to be disposed to admit the validity of the confiscatory Act of the State of New York in other respects. In the words of Lord Kenyon Ch.J., in the King's Bench: 'The Court of Common Pleas...stopped at the plea', considering it to be enough.

---

[1] (1789) 1 H. Bl. 123; (1790) 3 T.R. 726; (1792) 4 Bro. Parl. Cas. 111.
[2] See Dicey, Rule 21.

(*b*) The Court of King's Bench affirmed the judgment, but Lord Kenyon, with the concurrence of Ashhurst J., did so on a different ground, namely, that the confiscatory Act was illegal, having been passed by persons in rebellion against His Majesty, that *A* and *B* came to England with their mutual rights and duties intact, and that whatever retrospective validity the confiscatory Act might acquire their situation as individuals was not affected by it. These two judges at any rate appreciated the distinction between the penal rule and the wider one. Buller J. relied on the rule as to penal laws. So did Grose J., but he also described the confiscatory Act as 'an Act, which at the time it passed was considered as mere waste paper or, if it were of any avail, was an Act of Treason'.

(*c*) The speeches delivered in the House of Lords (which affirmed the judgment) are not reported, but it is relevant to mention that the first of the arguments advanced on behalf of the successful defendant in error was that 'no assumed Act of legislation by the colonies of North America, while in a state of rebellion against His Majesty, can legally affect the rights of any subject of this realm'.

It is unfortunate that the legislation which gave rise to this litigation was of a penal nature. That fact confused the issue.

In *Barclay* v. *Russell* (the Maryland case) Lord Loughborough L.C., after the treaty of peace, had to consider the effect of the successful rebellion upon certain Bank stock in England bought by the Government of Maryland (which was 'a corporation under the Great Seal') before the outbreak of the War of Independence and held in the name of trustees. Before the treaty of peace the new State of Maryland passed a statute purporting to discharge the trustees, to appoint new trustees and to direct a transfer of the Bank stock. After peace had been concluded, Lord Loughborough declined to give effect to this statute in favour of the new State of Maryland or its assignees, and held that the fund, no object of the trust existing, must be at the disposal of the Crown to be dealt with under the treaty and not as a subject of municipal jurisdiction. But the value of the decision lies in the explanation of it which Lord Eldon gave in *Dolder* v. *Lord Huntingfield*[1] as follows:

The Maryland case...does not touch such a case as this; a foreign independent State. That State was only a corporation under the Great Seal, dissolved by means, which a Court of Justice was obliged to consider rebellious; and then the transfer of the title from the State of Maryland to any other State was a question, a Court of Justice could look at, as a

---

[1] (1805) 11 Ves. Jun. 283, 294.

question of law, only in one way; and the principle was, that the Court could not admit, that the title passed to the independent States of America by an act which we were obliged to call 'rebellion'. What national justice was to do, after national policy had arranged the relative situation of the countries, was to be decided, and was decided, elsewhere.

The principle deduced appears to be that an English Court, unless directed to do so by the Legislature, cannot give effect to the acts of a Government which has taken its rise in a rebellion against His Majesty and is still in a condition of rebellion at the date of the act in question.

The American Courts have had more frequent occasion than our own to deal with the legal effects of the acts of revolutionary Governments. The American judicial experience arising out of the American Civil War established[1] the propositions that the territory in revolt was enemy territory and people residing in it were treated as enemies; that no legislation of the revolutionary authority was valid as against the United States or its citizens outside the rebellious territory; that the revolutionary authority was treated simply as the military representatives of the insurrection; that the revolutionary army was accorded such belligerent rights as belonged under international law to the armies of independent States at war; that transactions between persons in the territory dominated by the rebels were not invalid solely because they took place under the sanctions of the rebels' laws; that, within such territory, the preservation of order, the maintenance of police regulations, the prosecution of crimes, the protection of property, the enforcement of contracts, the celebration of marriages, the settlement of estates, the transfer and descent of property, and similar subjects, were, during the war, under the control of the rebel authorities and that what occurred or was done in respect of such matters under the authority of those laws should not be disregarded or held invalid *merely* because the rebels were organized in hostility to the lawful government, since civil government and the regular administration of the laws had to go on, and transactions in the ordinary course of civil society within the enemy's territory were without blame except when proved to have been entered into *with actual intent* to further invasion or insurrection; and that judicial and legislative acts within the rebellious territory should be respected by the Courts of the lawful government unless they were hostile in their

---

[1] See the summaries by the Supreme Court of the United States in *Ford* v. *Surget* (1878) 97 U.S. 594, 604, and *Baldy* v. *Hunter* (1898) 171 U.S. 388, 400 (reproduced in Moore, *Digest of International Law*, § 22) and also *Texas* v. *White* (1868) 7 Wall. 700, 733 (cited in xv *Transactions of Grotius Society* (1929), p. 74, n.).

purpose or mode of enforcement to the authority of the lawful government or impaired the rights of citizens under the Constitution.[1]

De facto *governmental control*. We have mentioned earlier in this chapter a transitional stage of *de facto* governmental control interposed (*a*) in international war, between the stages of belligerent occupation and complete *de iure* conquest either by subjugation or by treaty of cession, and (*b*) in civil war, between the outbreak and the final issue. It would be out of place here to attempt a full examination of the distinction between recognition of *de iure* and recognition of *de facto* situations and Governments, and we must be content to refer the reader to the numerous decisions and the large amount of literature available on this topic.[2] There may be political reasons inducing the British Government for a time to be content with recognition of a *de facto* situation and for not proceeding too rapidly to recognize the same situation *de iure*; for instance, in the case of the Russian Revolution of 1917, the domestic factor of British political feelings and the disapproval which the methods of the Soviet Government incurred in the minds of very large and powerful groups in this country combined to prevent more than recognition of a *de facto* Soviet Government in 1921, which was converted into recognition of a *de iure* Government in 1924. In the case of the conquest of Ethiopia it is probable that our disapproval of the Italian aggression and our membership of the League of Nations were responsible for delaying recognition of the conquest *de iure* until 16 November 1938.

---

[1] Before leaving revolutionary Governments, it is worth while mentioning decisions bearing upon the fate of their property after their collapse: *United States of America* v. *McRae*; *The Same* v. *Prioleau*. Note the distinction between the right of the successful parent Government by virtue of succession and by virtue of its paramount respectively. For two cases arising out of the civil war in Ireland which came to an end in December 1921, see *Fogarty* v. *O'Donoghue* and *Irish Free State* v. *Guaranty Safe Deposit Co.*

[2] See Oppenheim, 1, § 75*f*, and Lauterpacht, *Recognition in International Law*, pp. 329–48. Recognition *de iure* and recognition *de facto* seem to us to be elliptical expressions, and in truth mean recognition of a Government or a situation as complying *de iure* or *de facto* with the conditions which international law requires before a Government is clothed with the normal rights and duties of a Government or before a situation can produce its normal international consequences. It is not the recognition which is *de iure* or *de facto* but the Government or situation. On that understanding we may use the convenient expressions recognition *de iure* and recognition *de facto*. It is not easy to state all the English municipal consequences of the distinction between *de jure* and *de facto* recognition of a foreign sovereign. But one decision arising out of the Italian conquest of Ethiopia, *Haile Selassie* v. *Cable and Wireless (Ltd) (No. 2)*, makes it clear that so long as the Italian Government was recognized by Great Britain as only the Government *de facto* of 'virtually the whole of Ethiopia' and the plaintiff, the Emperor Haile Selassie, was recognized by the British Government as the *de jure* sovereign of Ethiopia, the plaintiff was entitled to recover a sum of money from the defendants, a British company; but from the moment (which occurred between the proceedings in the Chancery Division and the hearing of the appeal) that the British Government recognized the King of Italy as the *de jure* sovereign of Ethiopia, the title of the plaintiff, Haile Selassie, to sue was divested.

In the case of the Spanish Civil War the cause of the delay—we use the word in a morally neutral sense—was probably the Non-Intervention Agreement. Sometimes the reason may be purely prudence and caution lest the *de facto* state of affairs may be provisional and ultimately reversed, as in the case of the recognition *de facto* of the Esthonian National Council in 1919.[1]

But in all these cases[2] it seems that the municipal consequences which were judged to flow from the recognition of the *de facto* situation were the same as if the recognition had been of the corresponding *de iure* situation. So far as the consequences of revolutions and civil wars are concerned, there is nothing new in this distinction. So far as conquests by international war are concerned, we are not aware that an English Court has been called upon to estimate the effect of the distinction until the case of *Bank of Ethiopia* v. *National Bank of Egypt and Liguori*,[3] but we do not suggest that the application of the distinction to this sphere is wrong. What is important is that it should not be allowed to obscure the stage of belligerent occupation and to attach to that status the rights and duties appertaining to conquest recognized as a *de facto* situation. Belligerent occupation creates a well-established status which has been equipped by International Law with rights and duties in the interests of order and the welfare of the inhabitants of the occupied territory.

F. POST-WAR REMEDIES OF INHABITANTS OF OCCUPIED TERRITORY FOR WRONGFUL ACTS OF AN OCCUPYING BELLIGERENT

We have seen that the powers of a belligerent occupant are strictly limited. It is also apparent that a belligerent occupant not infrequently acts in excess of those powers, and we must therefore now consider whether an inhabitant of an occupied territory can, after the occupation has ended,[4] obtain any redress against the conse-

---

[1] *The Gagara.*

[2] As in earlier cases such as *Republic of Peru* v. *Dreyfus Brothers & Co.*

[3] See above, p. 396.

[4] During the occupation the inhabitants' ability to get redress may be severely circumscribed: see for instance, *Booty (Requisitioned Car) Case*, in which the Austrian Supreme Court held that a purported sale by the occupant of property to which it appeared the occupant did not have a good title was 'a sovereign act of the Occupying Power into which the Austrian courts cannot inquire'. See also *Booty (Qualification by the Occupant) Case*; cf. *Billeting of Troops Case*, and *Requisitioned Flat (Austria) Case* (all Austrian cases). But even during the occupation the Courts of the occupied territory have been prepared on occasions to examine acts of the occupant in order to test their legality and to refuse to give legal effect to them if they were obviously unlawful: see *Overland's Case* (Norway); and also *Société des Etablissements Pigeat et Hazard* v. *Cie. de Traction sur les Voies Navigables* (France).

quences of such wrongful acts. It will be convenient to consider the matter under the following heads:

(i) unlawful laws;
(ii) unlawful courts;
(iii) unlawful takings of private property;
(iv) effect of peace treaties.

(i) *Unlawful laws*

Where an occupant has made laws in excess of the powers which he is recognized to have, the general practice has been to regard them, and acts done under them, as invalid.[1] For instance, the German-Belgian Mixed Arbitral Tribunal in 1925, in *City of Antwerp* v. *Germany*, declined to give effect to a modification by the German Governor-General of Antwerp of a pre-war Belgian Decree relating to the responsibilities of municipalities for acts of violence committed by mobs against persons and property, with the result that sums paid under that purported modification had to be refunded by Germany to the City of Antwerp. Similarly, in *Tse Chung* v. *Lee Yau Chu*,[2] the Supreme Court of Hong Kong held that a change made by the occupant to the law of Hong Kong was 'beyond the proper scope of the legislative powers of the Japanese administration' and that it was 'not one that should be treated as valid and effectual by the Courts of the Colony', with the result that a debtor's attempt to discharge a debt by a payment under that invalid change in the law was ineffective.

However, it will frequently happen that the effect to be given to the occupant's unlawful laws will be determined by the lawful sovereign:[3] it would be usual for their nullity to be expressly stipulated.[4] In view, however, of the chaos which might ensue if all transactions entered into under invalid occupation laws by the inhabitants were to be treated as null and void, even though the inhabitants would during the occupation have had little opportunity

---

[1] But see *Wandel-Hirschberg* v. *Jacobsfeld-Yakurska* (Israel), holding a divorce in accordance with an unlawfully introduced law to be valid nevertheless.

[2] See also *Commune of Grace-Berleur* v. *Colliery of Gosson Lagasse and Associates* (Belgium); *Mathot* v. *Longué* (Belgium); *City of Pärnu* case (Esthonia); *Valicelli* v. *Bordese and Ricco* (Italy); *V.* v. *O.* (*Italy in Corfu Case*) (Greece); *In re Foti and Arena* (Italy, Cour de Cassation); *Aboitiz* v. *Price* (U.S.A.); *Listenburg* v. *Rogowska* (Holland); *Lesser* v. *Rotterdamsche Bank and Kling and Others* (Holland).

[3] See the decrees cited by Morgenstern, 28 *B.Y.* (1951), p. 310, n. 2, and the Belgian law of 5 May 1944 (see 20 *I.L.R.* (1953), p. 648). Note also the Indemnity Act, 1920, section 6.

[4] The laws are probably to be regarded as null and void quite apart from any such express annulment: see Morgenstern, *op. cit.* pp. 310–15.

but to comply with them, the returning sovereign may validate other-wise perhaps unlawful laws of the occupant. Thus the Netherlands Decree on Occupation Measures[1] was interpreted[2] as having the effect of declaring certain occupation laws to have had binding force during the occupation period notwithstanding their possible in-validity.

(ii) *Unlawful Courts*

If the establishment or operation of courts by the occupant in the occupied territory is considered to have been illegal, the validity of all convictions and civil judgments issuing from those courts must immediately be in doubt.[3] In principle, one would expect inhabitants who were affected by such decisions to be able to institute proceedings to have them declared a nullity. The lawful sovereign might well think that the matter should be dealt with by special legislation.[4] Thus all convictions by Japanese occupation tribunals in Malaya during the War of 1939 to 1945 were declared void by the British authorities on their return because the procedures adopted in such tribunals were so inconsonant with British conceptions of justice that no convictions resulting from them could be allowed to stand.[5] Such a complete annulment of occupation court decisions is exceptional, and in civil cases probably impossible to apply without causing undue hardship. A Belgian Decree issued in May 1944 declared all de-cisions to be null to the extent that they were based on the purported

---

[1] See above, p. 388, n. 11. See also the Italian Proclamation of 31 December 1945, declaring all proclamations and orders promulgated by the Allied Military Government to be valid for the period when they were carried into effect: notwithstanding this Procla-mation, Italian courts felt able to declare certain laws void because their enactment was in excess of the occupant's lawful powers (see *Vallicelli* v. *Bordese and Ricco*); in *N. V. de Bata-afsche Petroleum Maatschappij and Others* v. *The War Damage Commission*, Whyatt C.J., in the Singapore Court of Appeal, said, *obiter*, that he would be prepared to hold 'that it was contrary to public policy for a British Court to recognize a foreign law which confers validity on illegal acts committed by a belligerent occupant in violation of the Hague Regulations' (23 *I.L.R.* (1956), pp. 810, 831).

[2] Dutch Courts were not altogether consistent in this matter: see *In re van Huis*; *Kloet* v. *Klok* (Supreme Court); *Bedrijfsgroep Bouw- en Aardewer-kambachten The Hague* v. *Vonck* (see particularly the note to this case); *In re Policeman Balster*; *Vakgroep Begrefeniswezen* v. *H.M.C.T.*; and *V.* v. *Ogterop*.

[3] Assistance given by an inhabitant of the occupied territory in operating unlawfully established courts may be made a punishable offence by the lawful sovereign: see *In re Dr Carp* (Holland).

[4] As Taylor J. put it in *Yeap Lean Seng & Ors.* v. *Kok Ho Teik & anor.*, 'No British ter-ritory had ever before been occupied by an enemy and afterwards recovered in comparable circumstances; there was no relevant statute or precedent; in the absence of special legisla-tion, parties would have sued on occupation decrees and their validity would have been challenged; how far the Courts would have had jurisdiction in such matters and many other doubts would have arisen owing to the vagueness of international law.'

[5] See Das, *op. cit.* (in bibliography), ch. VII.

and illegal annexation of Belgian territory by Germany, but it was found necessary to amend this later by a further law in 1953 in connection with, *inter alia*, certain decrees of divorce or nullity of marriage.[1] Perhaps a more usual provision, at least with civil cases, is to provide for the review of judgments of occupation courts so that they can either be adopted or declared invalid according to the circumstances.[2]

In the absence of any such legislative provisions, Courts have held that judgments of unlawful occupation courts were, as judgments, a nullity. In *Ramzan and Others* v. *Ramzan*[3] the Singapore High Court held that as by the laws of the territory (which remained in force during the occupation) certain courts only were established as the courts of the territory, and the Japanese occupation Courts did not comply with the statutory requirements, judgments emanating from such Japanese courts were 'without legal consequences' and a trustee appointed by such a judgment could not derive any right to payment for his services from the bare fact of his appointment in that manner. However, to find that the judgments of unlawful occupation courts were *as judgments* a nullity does not necessarily mean that no legal effect is to be given to the situation which results from them. In the *Ramzan* case the Court, fully recognizing that the trustees appointed by the judgment of a Japanese occupation court had performed valuable services, and while unable to award them any remuneration solely on the basis of their appointment as trustees in that manner, nevertheless found that the benefit derived by the beneficiaries from the services of the 'trustees' created an obligation to give a reasonable remuneration for the services rendered and to indemnify them for expenses incurred. Similarly, in *Z.* v. *K.*,[4] the Court of Appeal of Colmar held that a decree of divorce granted by an illegally constituted German tribunal in a part of France which Germany had

---

[1] See *Mommer and Others* v. *Renerken* (Belgium, Cour de Cassation).

[2] This was broadly the effect in Malaya of the Japanese Judgments and Civil Proceedings Ordinance, 1946 (see Das, *op. cit.* ch. x, and the judgment of the Privy Council in *Sultan of Johore* v. *Abubakar Tunku Aris Bendahar*) and in France of an Ordinance of 15 September 1944, relating to judgments of illegally constituted tribunals in parts of France purportedly annexed by Germany. See also the Polish decrees referred to in *In re Will of Jan M.* (Poland). Note the wide terms in which judgments were validated by the Indemnity Act, 1920, section 5.

[3] Although local legislation had been passed dealing with occupation judgments, the Court considered the question before it on the basis of general principles relating to judgments of occupation courts. See also *In re X.* (France); *City of Antwerp* v. *Germany* (German–Belgian Mixed Arbitral Tribunal); *Re Cresciani* (Italy, Cour de Cassation).

[4] For a Belgian case holding valid a divorce decree granted by a court in Belgian territory purportedly annexed by Germany, see *Mommer and Others* v. *Renerken* (Cour de Cassation).

purported to annex was, while not a legally perfect divorce, still capable as a matter of fact of putting an end to the duty of cohabitation and the other effects of marriage, with the result that a child born to the ex-wife and another man after the decree was not born of an adulterous union.

(iii) *Unlawful takings of private property*

The matters which principally arise in this connection are the possibility of the original owner getting his property returned to him, and the possibility of his getting damages in respect of the wrongful deprivation he has suffered.

The restoration of property primarily turns upon whether or not the occupant in taking it has acquired a good title to it. Private property which constitutes war material may be seized by an occupant but even if validly seized he acquires no good title to it,[1] and *a fortiori* he will not acquire a good title if the seizure is wrongful. In *N.V. Bataafsche Petroleum Maatschappij & Ors.* v. *The War Damage Commission*,[2] the claimants were at the time when Japan occupied Sumatra the holders of the sole concession to explore for and exploit and dispose of petroleum in Sumatra. The Japanese military authorities seized the oil fields and extracted crude oil, some of which was shipped to Singapore, some as refined oil and some as crude oil. In Singapore the oil was kept in storage tanks, and was used by the Japanese occupation authorities for both civilian and military requirements. When the British army returned to Singapore, the British military authorities seized the petroleum as war booty. The claimants contested the legality of this seizure by the British military authorities, contending that the petroleum was still their property and had not become the property of the Japanese occupant and could not therefore be lawfully seized as war booty. The Court of Appeal of Singapore found that the claimants, prior to the Japanese occupation of Sumatra, had title to the crude oil. The Court then found that the Japanese had not, through the process of refining the oil, acquired title by *specificatio*. Nor had they acquired title under Article 53 (2) of the Hague Regulations, for various reasons: (i) the seizure and subsequent exploitation of the oil was, in view of its circumstances and purposes, in violation of the laws and customs of war so as to take it quite outside the scope of Article 53; (ii) in any event crude oil *in situ* was

---

[1] *Supra*, pp. 392–6. As to a wrongful seizure of State property, see *Ministero Difesa* v. *Ambriola* (Italy, Cour de Cassation).

[2] See also a Note by 'B' in 5 *I. and C.L.Q.* (1956), p. 84.

not within the meaning of '*munitions de guerre*' in Article 53; (iii) the failure of the Japanese to provide anything in the nature of a receipt infringed Article 53 and rendered the seizure invalid; (iv) even if the seizure had been valid, Article 53 (2) prevented the acquisition by the belligerent occupant of a good title.

In the case of an improperly made[1] requisition of private property,[2] the prevailing tendency[3] has been to hold the purported requisition to be a nullity and the original owner, not having been deprived of his title by the wrongful requisition, to be entitled, in accordance with the applicable rules of municipal law,[4] to recover it from any third party into whose hands it may have come. As an example we may take the decision of a Norwegian Court of Appeal in 1948 in *Johansen* v. *Gross*.[5] The German occupying authorities in Norway

---

[1] It may be necessary not to regard a requisition as improperly made even if certain peripheral aspects of it are in some ways defective. In all the upheavals associated with a belligerent occupation, particularly at its beginning and end, a strict observance of *minutiae* is not always to be expected. There may thus be, in the circumstances of particular cases, some flexibility in this respect although it must be kept within strict limits. See *Van Dijkhuizen* v. *Van Velsen* (Holland), and comments on *Tesdorpf* v. *German State* in n. 3 below.

[2] As to invalid requisitions of services, see *Iversen* v. *Fallsnes* (Norway), holding that a claim based on a contract ensuing upon such a requisition was unenforceable.

[3] The decision of the Anglo-German Mixed Arbitral Tribunal in *Tesdorpf* v. *German State* would appear to be to the contrary. There the German military occupying authorities in Belgium had requisitioned some coffee, neither giving a receipt nor paying for it (although some steps were taken to this end in that the German authorities later valued the coffee and notified this value to the owner of the warehouse from which it was removed). The coffee was taken to Germany and there distributed. The Tribunal held that although there had been a certain misuse of the right of requisition, the fact that the limits laid down in Article 52 of the Hague Regulations as to requisitions were disregarded did not automatically mean that the requisition was deprived of legal effect: in the particular circumstances of the case the requisition was not to be regarded as void. (See also *Ralli Bros.* v. *German Government*, decided by the same Tribunal.) The Tribunal's remark that the nullity of a wrongful requisition was not provided for in the Hague Regulations, which instead only referred to the payment of damages for infractions of the Regulations, has been taken by some to suggest that the Tribunal considered that the proper remedy for a wrongful requisition is not a declaration of its nullity but the payment of damages (it should be noted that the Tribunal added that the non-mention in the Regulations of nullity as a sanction did not mean that such a sanction was to be excluded—it had to be decided according to the general rules and the spirit of international law having regard to the actual circumstances of each case). The Tribunal's decision is not altogether satisfactory, and other courts have shown no inclination to follow it (see the decisions of the parallel Franco-German Mixed Arbitral Tribunal in *Gros Roman et Cie.* v. *German State*). It may be that it should now be treated as an example of an over-generous interpretation of the kind of details non-compliance with which may nevertheless not make a requisition substantially wrongful so as to deprive it of its character and effects as such (see n. 1 above).

[4] The relevant rules of municipal law may operate so as to prevent the original owner from recovering his property in some circumstances, as where the law acknowledges rights acquired by a *bona fide* purchaser for value in market overt.

[5] See also *Siuta* v. *Guzkowski* (Poland, Supreme Court); *Soubrouillard* v. *Kilbourg* (France); *Maltoni* v. *Companini* (Italy); *Rosenberg* v. *Fischer* (Switzerland); *Kostoris* v. *Meinl* (Italy); *De Rothschild* v. *Teuscher and Société d'Encouragement pour L'Amelioration des Races de Chevaux en France* (Belgium) (recovery of a wrongfully requisitioned mare but not of a filly to which

had acquired possession of a motor belonging to the plaintiff; the motor was installed in a boat belonging to the defendant, which was thereupon requisitioned by the Germans. The Germans did not, however, give the plaintiff a receipt for his motor or make payment for it. The plaintiff sued the defendant for the recovery of the motor. The Court held that Article 53 of the Hague Regulations did not apply, and that for the requisition of the motor to be valid, it must have been in accordance with Article 52. 'Since in the present case no receipt had been given for the motor and nothing had been paid for it, the requisition could not have had the effect of depriving Johansen of his rights in it.' We should note two further consequences of the fact that a wrongful requisition does not deprive the owner of his title in favour of the requisitioning occupant: (i) the occupant himself is in no position to transfer a good title to a third party, and (ii) the opposing belligerent should not be able to seize the property as the State-owned property of the occupying State.[1] It may be that the property wrongfully taken by the occupant did not belong to the person from whose possession it was taken, as where it was merely on loan to him. In such circumstances the original owner has equally been held not to have been deprived of his title.[2]

While wrongful taking by the occupant may consist of a purported but defective seizure under Article 53 or requisition under Article 52 of the Hague Regulations, it may also be that the occupant, in taking private property, has made no attempt to bring his action within the scope of those Articles, as where he has indulged in outright looting and spoliation. Where this has happened, there can be little doubt that he will not thereby be regarded as having deprived the owner of title and acquired it for himself.

The effects of unlawful takings of property and the rights of redress available to the inhabitants of the occupied territory may, of course, be determined by legislation enacted by the lawful sovereign.[3] Thus

the mare later gave birth). Since the consequences of a wrongful requisition and a wrongful seizure under Article 53 are the same in that in neither case is the owner deprived of title, in some cases courts have not considered it necessary to their decision to say under which provision the property was purportedly taken: see *Laurent* v. *Le Jeune* (Belgium, Cour de Cassation).

[1] *Société des Etablissements Pigeat et Hazard* v. *Cie. de Traction sur les Voies Navigables* (France); *Bertrand* v. *Bontemps* (Belgium). But see *Van Dijkhuizen* v. *Van Velsen* and p. 413, n. 1 above.

[2] *Weber* v. *Credito Italiano* (Italy); *Andersen* v. *Christensen et al.* (Denmark); *Levi* v. *Monte Dei Paschi di Siena* (Italy, Cour de Cassation); *Norges Bank* v. *Polski Komitet Azotowy* (Norway, Supreme Court). Cf. *British and Polish Trade Bank A.G.* v. *Handel-Maatschappij Albert de Bary and Co.* (Holland). See also *Kobylinsky* v. *Banco di Chivari* (Italy, Cour de Cassation).

[3] For a summary of the more important legislation passed by several European countries in connection with the War of 1939 to 1945, see Robinson, 39 *A.J.* (1945),

a Belgian Decree-Law of 10 January 1941 rendered null all transfers of property resulting from clear violations of the occupant's powers and duties, and went on to provide that any property affected by a transfer so declared to be null was recoverable from the person in possession thereof.[1]

So far as concerns an inhabitant's right to damages for the wrongful deprivation he has suffered, we shall need to consider in turn his possible right to damages against the occupying power, against the lawful sovereign, and against third parties in possession of his property.

Whether an inhabitant of a lately occupied territory would in practice, in the absence of any special provisions being made in, for example, a treaty of peace, be able to institute proceedings against the ex-occupying State in order to claim damages in respect of wrongful takings of property by the occupying authorities of that State must be extremely doubtful:[2] considerations of sovereign immunity would apply in proceedings outside the territory of that State, while recourse to the courts of that State could well run up against principles akin to the English doctrine of 'act of State'. Although Article 3 of Hague Convention IV (to which the Hague Regulations are annexed) provides that a belligerent who violates the provisions of the Hague Regulations shall, if the case demands, be liable to pay compensation, and also that the belligerent State is responsible for the acts of its occupying forces, this treaty provision should not be taken as giving to private individuals (as opposed to their State) any right to claim damages, although it clearly imposed an international duty upon the belligerent State to pay compensation 'if the case demands'. However, the possibility is not to be entirely excluded that in certain circumstances a claim against the ex-occupying State for damages might lie, particularly in view of the remarks made by the Anglo-German Mixed Arbitral Tribunal in *Tesdorpf* v. *The German State*[3] and the fact that treaties of peace not infrequently waive the claims of nationals of occupied States against the occupying

p. 216; see also Morgenstern, 28 *B.Y.* (1951), pp. 310–15. Much of the legislation was enacted in pursuance of the Inter-Allied Declaration of 5 January 1943 (Cmd. 6418) against Acts of Dispossession committed in Territories under Enemy Occupation or Control (for comment on which see Woolsey, 37 *A.J.* (1943), p. 282, and Drucker, 15 *I. and C.L.Q.* (1966), p. 263).

[1] See *Delville* v. *Servais* (Belgium). See also *Blum* v. *Société d'Injection Rapide et de Conservation des Bois* for the application of a similar French law.

[2] See *Backer* v. *Austrian Federal Treasury* (Austria); *Joint Export–Import Agency (Germany) Case* (Germany, Supreme Court); *Soc. Timber et al.* v. *Ministeri Esteri e Tesoro* (Italy, Cour de Cassation). The position is, however, different where what is involved is an ordinary civil law wrong, such as damage caused in a road accident: see *Personal Injuries (Occupied Germany) Case*; *British Army of Occupation (Road Accident) Case*.

[3] Above, p. 413, n. 3.

State in respect of acts occurring during the occupation (and thereby implying that but for the waiver a claim might be possible).[1]

Although occupation does not transfer sovereignty away from the lawful sovereign, it is not a consequence of this that the lawful sovereign may be held responsible for the acts of the occupant so as to have to pay compensation for wrongful takings of property by the occupant.[2] The lawful sovereign may, however, assume such a responsibility, as by passing legislation to that effect. In particular this may be done where the peace settlement provides for a waiver of claims against the enemy state coupled with the retention of ex-enemy property and assets in payment of reparations, the sums realized by the sale of such property and assets being distributed in settlement of war damage claims. An example of such legislation is the War Damage Ordinance, 1949, enacted in Singapore;[3] this included in the definition of 'war damage' to which the Ordinance applied damage occurring as a direct result of an owner's inability to protect his property for reasons directly connected with the occupation of Malaya, and damage occurring as a direct result of seizure of movable property by enemy forces or individual enemy subjects whether acting under authority or not.

Where the occupant has wrongfully taken property he may have passed it on, perhaps with a purported transfer of title, to a third party. Apart from any question of the original owner's right to recover the property, which we have already considered, can the original owner recover damages from the third party, either for wrongful detention of the property, or for damage to it while in his possession?[4] A Belgian court has held that in the absence of legisla-

[1] Thomson C.J. in *The Chartered Bank of India, Australia and China* v. *The Public Trustee* (Singapore, Court of Appeal) observed that had not the Bank's claim been affected by the waiver clauses of the Peace Treaty with Japan, 'it may have been that the defendant Bank would have had some claim against the Japanese Government in respect of actions of the Japanese occupation authorities'.

[2] *Melkus and Another* v. *Republic of Austria* (Supreme Court of Austria); *De Coene* v. *Town of Courtai and Belgian State* (Belgium); *Soviet Requisition (Austria) Case* (Austria); *Socony Vacuum Oil Company Claim* (U.S.A.).

[3] No. 56 of 1949. See in general, Das, *op. cit.* (in bibliography), ch. XIV. The equivalent British legislation, the War Damage Act, 1943, which is not part of the law of the Channel Islands which have their own legal system, did not apply to a situation of belligerent occupation.

[4] The question also arises whether the third party, who has had to return the property to the original owner and who acquired the property for valuable consideration, is entitled to compensation from any source. The Belgian Decree Law of 10 January 1941 provided that the original owner did not have to compensate the third person from whom he recovered the property: the third person was left to whatever recourse was available to him in the ordinary law against the person who sold him the property: see *Delville* v. *Servais*. See also *Purchase of Dutch Paintings Case* (Austria, Supreme Court); *Mestre Hospital* v. *Defence Administration* (Italy, Cour de Cassation); *Ebrahim* v. *Babu Madan Gopal Bagla* (Burma).

tion[1] the general principles of the law of tort apply, and that the third party is liable in damages for the detention of the property as from the date on which he refused to comply with the original owner's lawful request for its return, it being from that moment that he (as opposed to the occupant) was the cause of the original owner's inability to regain possession.[2] The German Supreme Court has held that where the occupant passes to a third person property to which the occupant has not acquired title, there arises between the third person and the original owner the relationship of bailee-bailor, with the result that the third person is liable in damages to the original owner if he negligently causes damage to the property.[3]

(iv) *Peace treaties*

It is not unusual for peace treaties to contain provisions affecting, directly or indirectly, the remedies available to inhabitants of occupied territories for wrongful acts of the occupying belligerent. Paragraph 1 of the Annex to section IV of part X of the Treaty of Versailles declared void all actions taken in pursuance of war legislation with regard to enemy property, rights or interests, by the German authorities in (*inter alia*) occupied territories. Consequently, requisitions falling within this provision were held not to result in a transfer of title to Germany.[4] The restoration of property taken by the occupant may also be provided for. Article 75 of the Treaty of Peace with Italy, 1947,[5] provided for the return of all identifiable property in Italy which was removed by force or duress by any of the Axis Powers from the territory of any of the United Nations, irrespective of any subsequent transactions by which the present holders of the property had secured possession. The right of inhabitants of occupied territories to bring claims against the occupying State is also likely to be affected. Article 14 (b) of the Japanese Peace Treaty, 1951, for

---

[1] For a case involving a claim for damages under legislation, see *Société Anonyme d'Injection Rapide et de Conservation des Bois* v. *Blum* (France, Cour de Cassation).

[2] *Ledieu, Veuve Vandedaele* v. *Bothilda*. See also *Société au Grand Marché* v. *Ville de Metz* (France); *Jan and Telka S.* v. *Walenty and Katarzyna R.* (Poland, Supreme Court).

[3] *Loss of Requisitioned Motor Car (Germany) Case.*

[4] *Gros Romain et Cie.* v. *German State* (Franco-German Mixed Arbitral Tribunal).

[5] T.S. no. 50 (1948) (and see also the equivalent Articles in the other peace treaties concluded after the War of 1939 to 1945). These provisions reflect the Allied Declaration of 5 January 1943 against Acts of Dispossession committed in Territories under Enemy Occupation or Control: see p. 414, n. 3. See generally, Fitzmaurice, 73 *Hague Receuil* (1948, II) p. 259. The restitution of property from Germany had to be dealt with differently, there being no peace treaty: see Chapter Five of the Convention on the Settlement of Matters Arising Out of the War and Occupation, 1952 (T.S. no. 13 (1959)), and *De Rothschild* v. *Teuscher and Another* (Belgium).

example, provided for the waiver of all 'claims of the Allied Powers and their nationals arising out of any action taken by Japan and its nationals in the course of the prosecution of the war'. So, where a Bank sought a set-off and counter-claim arising out of the actions of the Japanese Custodian of Enemy Property, the Bank's plea was dismissed on the ground that the Peace Treaty negatived any right to claim compensation against the Japanese Custodian or his agent.[1]

G. MILITARY OCCUPATION DURING AN ARMED CONFLICT NOT AMOUNTING TO WAR

During the course of an armed conflict not constituting a war the territory of a State may well be occupied by military forces of the opposing State. There is little direct authority to offer guidance upon the general extent of the occupant's powers, rights and duties in such a case, but there are, we suggest, two basic considerations. First, the military occupation is a fact and the occupant must be admitted to have some powers of government and administration if the occupied territory is to be preserved from chaos and anarchy. Second, it is hardly to be contemplated that the occupant has greater powers than those possessed by a belligerent occupant during a war.

Military occupations taking place otherwise than during a war may occur in a variety of circumstances, of which an actual armed conflict is only one; others may be somewhat more pacific in character.[2] But even the latter are, in view of the scarcity of authority, of some value in considering what régime applies to a military occupation during an armed conflict.

We may mention first those military occupations taking place in pursuance of treaty provisions.[3] Their characteristics will depend upon the terms of the treaty.[4] However, it should be noted that

---

[1] *The Chartered Bank of India, Australia and China* v. *The Public Trustee* (Singapore), affirmed on appeal. In regard to a similar waiver clause in the Italian Peace Treaty, see *German External Debts Agreement Case.*

[2] See Downey, *Proceedings of the American Society of International Law* (1949), p. 103; Jones, 9 *Transactions of the Grotius Society* (1923), p. 149; 23 *Revue Générale de Droit International Public* (1916), p. 84.

[3] We are not here concerned with military occupations pursuant to an armistice agreement, since such occupations still take place while a state of war exists.

[4] While a treaty providing for the occupation of territory on a specific occasion may be expected to set out the occupation régime in some detail, treaties which simply provide a general right of military occupation in certain future eventualities are less likely to do so. For the military occupation of Cuba by the United States of America in 1906 in pursuance of the latter kind of treaty, see Hackworth, *Digest of International Law*, I, pp. 148–50.

Article 47 of the Geneva Civilians Convention, 1949, expressly provides that protected persons in an occupied territory are not to be deprived of the benefits of the Convention by any agreement concluded between the authorities of the occupied territory and the Occupying Power. A leading illustration of a quasi-belligerent military occupation pursuant to a treaty was the occupation of the Rhineland under Article 428 of the Treaty of Versailles, 1919. The régime for this occupation, which was spelt out in detail in the Agreement with regard to the Military Occupation of the Territories of the Rhine, 1919,[1] bore many similarities to the normal régime of belligerent occupation. Thus, the High Commission (which was the supreme representative of the occupying Powers within the occupied territory) was given the power to issue ordinances necessary to secure the maintenance, safety and requirements of the occupying forces, and these ordinances had the force of law when duly published.[2] Although in principle the German courts continued to exercise civil and criminal jurisdiction, the occupying forces and persons accompanying them were exclusively subject to the military law and jurisdiction of those forces, while any person committing an offence against the persons or property of the occupying armed forces was subject to their military jurisdiction.[3] The civil administration of the territory remained in the hands of the German authorities and continued under German law and under the authority of the Central German Government except in so far as it was necessary for the High Commission to adapt that administration to the needs and circumstances of the military occupation.[4] It was also provided expressly that 'the right to requisition in kind and to demand services in the manner laid down in the Hague Convention, 1907, shall be exercised' by the armies of occupation.[5]

In connection with the military occupation of the Rhineland, a Belgian Court, in *Auditeur Militaire* v. *Reinhardt*, had to consider the jurisdiction of a Belgian Military Court in respect of an offence committed in the Belgian area of occupation. In its judgment the Court observed that from a juridical point of view the territory was

---

[1] T.S. no. 7 (1919). See in general Huguet, 31 *Revue Générale de Droit International Public* (1924), p. 554; Ireton, 17 *A.J.* (1923), p. 460.

[2] Article 3 (a). See *Rhineland Ordinances Case* (Germany); *Rhineland (German Legislation) Case* (Germany); *Rhineland Occupation ('Devisen' Legislation) Case* (Germany); *Roucheyrolles* v. *Paris-Orléans Railway Co.* (France); *Borrély* v. *Departmental Administration of the Bouches du Rhône Railway* (France).

[3] Article 3 (c), (d) and (e).

[4] Article 5. The German Authorities were obliged, under penalty of removal, to conform to the ordinances issued by the High Commission.

[5] Article 6.

to be considered an occupied territory according to the definition in paragraph 1 of Article 42 of the Hague Regulations, and added: 'Legally there can be a military occupation even in cases where there is no war properly so-called: there is nevertheless an *occupatio bellica*.' The Court went on to say: 'The jurisdiction of the Occupant comes into force as soon as the occupation is real, effective, and exercised by an army organised on a war footing.'

Situations of military occupation in the course of an armed conflict are unlikely to take place under a treaty, and the nature and effects of the régime of such an occupation have therefore to be determined without the benefit of guidance from specific treaty provisions. Practice in this field has been limited, and it is probably premature to attempt to draw general conclusions. We can, however, indicate how one or two particular points which have arisen have been dealt with.

First, we must draw attention to the Geneva Civilians Convention of 1949.[1] This applies, *inter alia*, to any armed conflict which may arise between two or more of the High Contracting Parties, even if it is not a declared war or if a state of war is not recognized by one of the Parties; it also applies to all cases of partial or total occupation of the territory of a High Contracting Party, even if the occupation meets with no armed resistance.[2] The Convention contains many provisions relating to occupied territory, and it may be regarded as laying down certain basic provisions for a régime of occupation during an armed conflict. It does not, however, cover the whole field of an occupant's activities.

The provisions of section III of the Convention emphasize that a military occupation during an armed conflict does not involve any acquisition by the occupant of sovereignty over the occupied territory. While this is not expressly stated in the Convention, it is the unstated premise underlying its provisions: the exercise in relation to the occupied territory of all those rights which the occupant would normally possess if he were to acquire sovereignty would involve him in violations of the Convention. The non-acquisition of sovereignty by the occupant follows, of course, from the basic consideration, mentioned at the outset, that the occupant can have no greater powers than those possessed by a belligerent occupant during a war. Thus, in 1916, when American military forces occupied the Dominican Republic as a response to repeated violations of a treaty, the American Military Authorities issued a Proclamation which

[1] T.S. no. 39 (1958).   [2] Article 2.

expressly denied any intention of destroying the sovereignty of the Republic.[1]

Turning to more specific matters, the *right to collect dues and taxes* was in issue as a result of the occupation of Veracruz by the United States of America in 1914. During the six-month occupation the American occupation authorities had collected taxes and certain other contributions of a federal character from the inhabitants of Veracruz. Upon the eventual withdrawal of the American forces, it was arranged that persons who had paid such taxes and contributions to the American occupation authorities would not have to pay them again to the returning Mexican authorities.[2] Where the American authorities had collected customs duties which should under Mexican law have been refunded later, the United States-Mexican Claims Commission held, in the *El Emporio del Cafe* case, that the duties ought to be refunded by the United States who were responsible for the administrative acts of the occupying forces.

This case also provides an illustration of the *continued applicability of the local law*, in principle, during the occupation. The American Proclamation at the outset of the American military occupation of the Dominican Republic in 1916 expressly stated that Dominican statutes would continue in effect in so far as they did not conflict with the object of the occupation or necessary regulations established thereunder.[3] The Supreme Court of Peru, in *De Wurts* v. *Wurts*, had to consider the meaning of the term 'the law of the marriage' in relation to a marriage which took place in a part of Peru occupied by Chile. The Court held that the system of law in that place was to be regarded as Peruvian law and not the law of the occupant, Chile. So far as concerns the penal laws of the occupied territory, the Geneva Civilians Convention, 1949, provides that those laws shall remain in force, although they may be repealed or suspended by the occupant where they constitute a threat to his security or an obstacle to the application of the Convention.[4]

The *administration of justice* in the occupied territory is also partially dealt with in that Convention. Article 54 prohibits the occupant from altering the status of judges.[5] Article 64 provides that the

---

[1] Hackworth, *Digest of International Law*, I, p. 155. The United States subsequently took the view that the United States Military Government, as administering the affairs of the Republic, ought to act in accordance with the United States-Dominican Treaty of 1907 in the same way as the Government of the Dominican Republic were thereby obliged to act: *ibid.* p. 158.   [2] *Ibid.* pp. 151–2.

[3] *Ibid.* I, p. 155.   [4] Article 64.

[5] It is noticeable that the second paragraph of that Article, preserving the occupant's right to remove public officials from their posts, would appear not to apply to judges.

tribunals of the occupied territory shall continue to function in respect of all offences covered by the penal laws of that territory, except where that would constitute an obstacle to the application of the Convention and subject to the necessity for ensuring the effective administration of justice. Article 66 allows the occupant, in cases of a breach of any penal laws promulgated by him in accordance with Article 64, to establish properly constituted non-political military courts in the occupied country.[1] This was very much the régime adopted by the United States in 1916 during their military occupation of the Dominican Republic.[2] The ordinary administration of justice through the Dominican Courts was not interfered with, except that cases involving members of the occupying forces, or contempt or defiance of the occupant's authority, were tried by tribunals to be set up by the occupant.

During the French occupation of the Ruhr because of alleged German violations of the Treaty of Versailles,[3] French occupation courts were established. A conviction imposed upon a German subject by the French occupation authorities was, subsequently, disregarded by a German court as having been imposed by a court without jurisdiction.[4] The French Cour de Cassation on the other hand—and perhaps not unexpectedly—concluded that French occupation courts in the Ruhr had jurisdiction to try offences affecting the interests and security of the occupation army.[5] The Japanese occupation of Northern Sakhalin in Russia, after the Russian revolution in 1917, gave rise to a similar case. The plaintiff, a Russian, sued the defendant, a Japanese company, in a Japanese Court in respect of an injury sustained in the occupied territory. The matter was settled by way of compromise and the Court delivered a judgment by consent. After the end of the occupation the plaintiff sued the defendant again in connection with the same cause of action, but this time in a Russian Court. The Supreme Court of the Soviet Union declined to treat the previous judgment as having the force of *res judicata*,

[1] Courts of appeal need not, but preferably should, also sit in the occupied territory.

[2] Hackworth, *op. cit.* I, p. 155.

[3] The legality of the occupation was controversial: see Finch, 17 *A.J.* (1923), p. 724; McNair, 5 *B.Y.* (1924), p. 17; *Schuster*, 18 *A.J.* (1924), p. 407.

[4] *Invasion of the Ruhr District Case.*

[5] *In re Thyssen, In re Krupp.* In the *Casablanca Case* (Scott, *Hague Court Reports*, p. 110) the Permanent Court of Arbitration recognized that the French occupation force in Morocco was entitled to exercise jurisdiction over its members while they were in territory under the immediate, lasting and effective control of French armed forces. On 6 February 1907 the Law Officers advised that the British army occupying Egypt, with which country the United Kingdom was not in a state of war, ought to be treated in accordance with the principles of international law applicable to an army of occupation which entitled the occupying power to constitute military tribunals to deal with offences affecting the safety and position of its forces.

and held that the judgment by consent of the Japanese Court, notwithstanding that it was the court of a State whose forces were in military occupation of the area of jurisdiction, was not binding on Russian nationals and that the plaintiff could therefore bring his new action.[1]

As to *legislation*, Article 64 of the Geneva Civilians Convention allows the occupant to apply to an occupied territory provisions which are essential to enable him to fulfil his obligations under the Convention, to maintain the orderly government of the territory, and to ensure his security and that of the members and property of the occupying forces or administration, their establishments and lines of communication. In *Anglo-Czechoslovak and Prague Credit Bank v. Janssen* the Supreme Court of Victoria had to consider what effect to give in Australia to a decree of the German authorities in occupation of Czechoslovakia, whereby the plaintiff, a company incorporated in Czechoslovakia, was purportedly dissolved. The Court considered it unnecessary to discuss whether the occupation was belligerent or whether, in view of the absence of resistance by Czechoslovakia, it was to be considered a military occupation in time of peace, and was of the opinion that the same rules applied to both situations so far as concerned the consequences flowing from the occupant's control.[2] The powers of the British occupation forces in Persia in 1918 to take certain restrictive measures against the local population were assimilated, in the *Chevreau Case*,[3] to those of a belligerent occupant.

By way of conclusion we may remark that in all the particular matters which we have mentioned there seems to have been a tendency to act upon a basis broadly analogous to that of a belligerent occupation during a war. Thus it is noteworthy that in considering in general the powers possessed by France in respect of the French military occupation of the Ruhr, the United States acknowledged that their extent was to be measured by the powers of a belligerent occupant during a war.[4] Such a tendency will have been reinforced by the extent to which the Geneva Civilians Convention of 1949 applies the same rules to a belligerent occupation taking place during a war and to a military occupation during an armed conflict not constituting a war.

[1] *Komarov* v. *Mitchubisi Gosi Kaisa.*

[2] However, in considering what those consequences were, the Court would, we suggest, seem to have erred in deciding the matter with reference to the effects to be accorded to the legislative acts of a Government recognized as the *de facto* government of a territory rather than in the light of the legitimate legislative powers of the occupant: see below, p. 426.

[3] 27 *A.J.* (1933), pp. 153, 159–60. Note also the opinion of the Rapporteur (Huber) in the *Spanish Zones of Morocco Claims* that the principle established by Article 3 of Hague Convention IV of 1907 (above, p. 415) was applicable to military action outside war *stricto sensu*.   [4] Hackworth, *op. cit.* I, pp. 146–8.

18

ACTS OF GOVERNMENTS DISPOSSESSED BY BELLIGERENT OCCUPATION

BIBLIOGRAPHY

Feilchenfeld, *The International Economic Law of Belligerent Occupation*, §§ 461–72, 481–4.
Oppenheimer, 'Governments and Authorities in Exile', 36 *A.J.I.L.* (1942), 568.
Domke, *Trading with the Enemy in World War II* (1943), ch. 21.
Journal of Comparative Legislation (3rd ser.), vols. 24 (1942), 25 (1943), 26 (1944) and 28 (1946) for articles on the legislation of various European Governments in Exile.
Stein, 46 *Michigan Law Review* (1948), pp. 341–70.

This topic was almost *res integra* in England[1] half a century ago. A number of foreign Allied Governments were accorded the hospitality of a war-time home in London and exercised there in varying degree the functions of government. This novel state of affairs has raised some problems involving fundamental principles. We shall deal with them under the following headings:

1. General principles relating to the exercise of governmental functions in England by a foreign Government.

2. Effects in England of the Decrees and Laws of a Foreign Dispossessed Government.

3. Constitutionality of the legislation or other official acts of a foreign Government.

4. The position of ships.

5. Changes made in the law by the dispossessed Government during the occupation.

---

[1] For some foreign decisions, see the volumes of the *Annual Digest* and International Law Reports under such titles as Jurisdiction, Territorial and Personal, and Extra-territorial Effect of Foreign Legislation, Immunities of Foreign States, and in particular 9 (1938–40), nos. 53–7.

I. GENERAL PRINCIPLES RELATING TO THE EXERCISE OF GOVERNMENTAL FUNCTIONS IN ENGLAND BY A FOREIGN GOVERNMENT

We shall begin by attempting to state what appear to be the underlying principles.

(i) It would be a violation of British sovereignty for a foreign Government to exercise its sovereignty upon British soil without Her Majesty's consent. By exercising its sovereignty is meant the doing of any of the acts normally associated with the carrying on of the business of government, such as the administration of justice,[1] the arrest even of its own nationals,[2] their punishment, the seizure of their property, the recruiting or maintenance of armed forces and, possibly, legislation or the making of executive decrees.

(ii) Consent, express or implied, is frequently given by one Government to the exercise of acts of sovereignty by another upon the territory of the former;[3] for instance, the commanding officers of foreign public ships are habitually allowed by the local sovereign to exercise jurisdiction over members of their crews in accordance with the law of their own country,[4] and a similar jurisdiction is allowed over the members of foreign armed forces, at any rate in respect of offences committed while on duty or within their own lines.[5] In both cases the exercise of this jurisdiction is implied from the permission given by the local sovereign for the entry of the foreign public ships or armed forces.

(iii) The conduct of foreign relations (particularly in time of war and therefore in dealing with allies, for the Crown has a wide prerogative as a belligerent) lies within the prerogative of the Crown, and it may be that there are certain exercises of sovereignty by foreign Governments upon British soil which the Crown could authorize without the sanction of a statute. It is, however, probable that the establishment by a foreign Government of Courts of law on British territory is not legally possible without statutory sanction.[6] At any

---

[1] The *Duc de Sully's* case (1603), Satow, *Diplomatic Practice* (4th ed.), § 357.

[2] *Sun Yat-Sen's* case (1896), *ibid.* § 381; *Vaccaro* v. *Collier* (U.S.A.); *Villareal* v. *Hammond* (U.S.A.) and *In re Jolis* (France); Oppenheim, 1, §§ 125–8, and particularly note 1 on p. 295.

[3] See last case cited in note 1 on p. 443 below.

[4] Oppenheim, 1, § 450; *Chung Chi Cheung* v. *The King*.

[5] Oppenheim, 1, § 445. See *R.* v. *Navratil*, Warwick Winter Assizes, 1942, and a group of cases arising in Egypt during the war of 1939–45, *Ministère Public* v. *Triandafilon*, *Gaitanos* v. *Ministère Public*, and *Stamatopoulos* v. *Ministère Public*.

[6] See Chitty, *Law of the Prerogatives of the Crown*, p. 76, and Viscount Simon, *Journal of Comparative Legislation* (3rd ser.), 24 (1942), p. 3. As to Norwegian Courts in this country in the war of 1939–45, see Jessup, 36 *A.J.* (1942), p. 653.

rate, the jurisdiction of such foreign Courts could not become effective without the aid of a statute, for only in this way would it be possible for their judgments to be enforced by civil execution or by arrest and imprisonment. Otherwise a person affected might invoke the aid of an English Court by means of a writ of *habeas corpus* or of actions of false imprisonment and trespass, and the common law would afford no adequate answer to him.[1]

(iv) The mere fact that a foreign Government has been deprived of the control of a part or the whole of its territory by an enemy in no way invalidates legislation passed, or other acts of sovereignty done, by it outside its normal territory, provided that its constitutional law contains no insuperable obstacle to the validity of such legislation or other sovereign acts,[2] and provided that Her Majesty continues to recognize it as the *de iure* Government and recognizes no other Governments as the *de facto* sovereign. There is a clear legal distinction between the *de facto* Government of a country and a belligerent occupant, and it is inconceivable that any of Her Majesty's Governments would recognize the enemy occupant of British or allied territory as the *de facto* Government of that territory. Even a neutral Government would, we submit, be bound to draw this distinction during the war and could only recognize acts done within the lawful scope of the authority of a belligerent occupant. Moreover,[3] the political sympathies of a technically neutral State may be such that it will readily continue its recognition of an exiled Government and give extra-territorial effect to its decrees.

(v) Most of the official acts of the dispossessed allied Governments, such as the making of decrees, were done on British territory where they had found refuge, though some decrees may have been made in some corner of allied territory still remaining in the control of its proper Government before that Government went into exile. Unless the laws of the allied country limit the validity of governmental acts to those done upon the territory of that country or a particular

---

[1] See the Visiting Forces Act, 1952; Viscount Simon and Dr J. M. de Moor in 58 *L.Q.R.* (1942), pp. 41 ff.; Schwelb in *Czecho-Slovak Year Book of International Law* (1942), pp. 147–71; Kuratowski in 28 *Transactions of Grotius Society* (1943), pp. 1–25; Schwelb in 34 *A.J.* (1945), pp. 330–2 (as to Soviet Forces) and King, 36 *ibid.* (1942), pp. 539–67 and 40 *ibid.* (1946), pp. 257–79. Statutes (now repealed) which arose out of the mutual relations of the United Nations in the Second World War are the Allied Forces Act, 1940, the Allied Powers (Maritime Courts) Act, 1941, the Allied Powers (War Service) Act, 1942, the National Service (Foreign Countries) Act, 1942, and the United States of America (Visiting Forces) Act, 1942; upon the last named, see Schwelb in 38 *A.J.* (1944), pp. 50–73. Upon the deportation of Greek seamen from the U.S.A. to Great Britain, see *Moraitis v. Delany.*

[2] See below, p. 438.   [3] See below, p. 432.

portion of it, it is submitted that it is immaterial in an English Court where the official act is done—be it in the home territory, or be it on British territory whereon Her Majesty has consented to the establishment of the allied Government and the exercise of its governmental functions. There is no principle of international law which says that a Government cannot act validly upon foreign territory with the consent of the local sovereign.[1] Moreover, when a Head of a State is visiting a foreign country, either for the purpose of a holiday or in order to take a cure for gout, it is the regular practice for official decrees and other documents requiring his signature to be sent to him for that purpose. We suggest therefore that the validity of the decree of an allied Government made in London is no greater and no less than if it were made in its own capital, subject to any requirement of its own Constitution as to the locality of governmental acts.[2]

Further, if the allied Government has not been completely ousted from its territory and has non-metropolitan territory of which it is in control and to which it could resort, we do not see why the fact that that Government finds it more convenient to carry on the functions of government from London instead of, say, Curaçao or the Belgian Congo, should alter the legal quality of its acts. Particularly is this true when, as in the case of the Netherlands Government, the Constitution recognizes no distinction between metropolitan and colonial territory and expressly provides that the Kingdom of the Netherlands comprises the territory of Holland, Surinam, and the Netherlands Antilles.

(vi) It may happen that owing to the suddenness of invasion and the exigencies of the ensuing crisis an exiled Government has come into power not strictly in accordance with the terms of the Constitution. Nevertheless, if His Majesty's Government recognizes that Government, a British subject can safely deal with it.[3]

---

[1] In the case of *Re Savini*, the Court of Appeal in Rome had to consider the effect of the acts of the Montenegrin Government when dispossessed and enjoying the hospitality of Italian soil during the occupation of Montenegro by Jugoslavian troops, and held that in order that that Government might exercise, within Italy and without interference by Italian courts, the rights of sovereignty derived from extraterritoriality, it must enjoy full and formal recognition by the Italian Government which was lacking. Baty, *Great Britain and Sea Law*, remarks (p. 83) that 'an act of sovereignty which has no operation except in the realm of ideas [i.e. does not consist of a physical act] may just as well be performed on one part of the earth's surface as another', and states that Mr Asquith became Prime Minister while in the South of France.

[2] See below, p. 438.

[3] *Republic of Peru* v. *Dreyfus Bros.*, an instance of *de facto* recognition; *Guaranty Trust Co. of New York* v. *United States*; and an Award of Chief Justice Taft which goes even further, see *Arbitration between Costa Rica and Great Britain*, 18 *A.J.* (1924), pp. 147–74 and 6 *B.Y.* (1925), pp. 199–204.

2. EFFECTS IN ENGLAND OF THE DECREES AND LAWS OF A FOREIGN DISPOSSESSED GOVERNMENT

The effect given by an English Court to the decrees and laws of a foreign dispossessed Government raises issues closely analogous to, and in many cases identical with, those involved in the general question of the extra-territorial effect of foreign laws and decrees. While a close consideration of this wider field is outside our present scope, it will be necessary to refer to the general principles involved in order the better to understand the position as to the laws of a foreign Government in exile.

A. *As regards property*[1]

First, we may set on one side immovable property. It is governed by the *lex situs* and no foreign law could transfer title to it. We may also disregard the laws of a foreign 'government' which has received no recognition from Her Majesty's Government. The laws of such a 'government' will be given no effect by English Courts, even in respect of happenings within the territory of that 'government' and no matter how effective it might in fact be.[2]

As regards movable property, two distinctions running through the cases (although not always recognized in them as expressly as one could wish) must be noted at the outset.

(i) The first is based upon the *locus* of the debt or other property at the time of the bringing of the action; namely, the difference between the operation of the law of a foreign country upon property in that country and its operation upon property in this country.

(ii) The second depends upon the meaning in which the somewhat ambiguous term 'enforcement' is used; namely, the difference between enabling a party in whom a foreign law purports to vest property to recover as *actor* that property in this country and recognizing and protecting that party's right to the property when another party sues him to recover it in this country.

We shall consider in turn each of the various situations with which an English Court might find itself confronted.

(*a*) The Court might be called upon to recognize and protect in England rights duly acquired in a foreign country under a law or decree (legislative or executive) in respect of property situate in that foreign country at any relevant time (by which expression is meant

---

[1] As regards ships, see later, pp. 441–5. On the *situs* of shares, see above, p. 245, n. 4.
[2] *Carl Zeiss-Stiftung* v. *Rayner* (C.A.).

the date of the coming into force of the law or decree or some later date while it is still effective).[1] In such a situation it would seem that an English court will recognize and protect in England rights duly acquired in a foreign country under the law or decree of that country in respect of property situate there at any relevant time whether or not the law or decree is penal or otherwise objectionable from the English legal point of view.[2] Thus in *A. M. Luther Co.* v. *James Sagor & Co.*[3] a decree of the Russian Soviet Government had already divested from the plaintiffs and vested in that Government the property in certain plywood situate within the jurisdiction of that Government at the time of the decree. By a contract made in London that Government sold the plywood[4] to the defendants, an English firm, who imported it into England. The English Courts recognized and protected the defendants' title by rejecting the plaintiffs' claim for a declaration that the plywood continued to be their property, for an injunction against dealing with it and for damages for conversion. When the Russian Soviet Government had received *de facto* recognition from His Majesty, the Court of Appeal (Bankes, Warrington and Scrutton L.JJ.) declined to question the validity or morality of its acts, whereby property situate within its jurisdiction was vested in that Government. In *Princess Paley Olga* v. *Weisz*[5] the point involved was the

---

[1] See Fachiri, 12 *B.Y.* (1931), 95–106; Mann, 59 *L.Q.R.* (1943), 42–57 and 155–71, and in 70, *L.Q.R.* (1954), 181–202; Cheshire, *Private International Law* (5th ed.), pp. 138–42; Dicey, Rule 130.

[2] It is not entirely clear whether this rule is limited only to the application of foreign laws to the property of nationals of that foreign State. In *Anglo-Iranian Oil Co. Jaffrate (The Rose Mary)*, the Supreme Court of Aden held that *Luther* v. *Sagor* and *Princess Paley Olga* v. *Weisz* (both about to be referred to in the text) only applied to cases where the foreign country's laws affected property in that country belonging to its own nationals, and that consequently a purported deprivation of title of the property of an alien in circumstances which were contrary to international law would not be recognized in an English court, which applies international law as incorporated into English law. The decision is not free from criticism (see *Re Helbert Wagg and Co. Ltd's Claim*; H. Lauterpacht, *C.L.J.* 1954, p. 20; Cheshire, *Private International Law* (5th ed.), p. 140; and Japanese and Italian courts have arrived at the opposite conclusion when faced with the identical situation (*Anglo-Iranian Oil Co.* v. *Idemitsu Kosan Kabushiki Kaisha* (Japan); *The Same* v. *S.U.P.O.R. Company* (Italy)). In 1964 the Supreme Court of the United States, in *Banco Nacional de Cuba* v. *Sabbatino*, recognized the validity of a title to movable property acquired under Cuban law when the property was in Cuba, and refused to deny recognition on the basis of an allegation that the Cuban law was contrary to international law; see also p. 400, n. 3, above.

[3] See also the comments on this case by Bennett J. in *Haile Selassie* v. *Cable and Wireless Ltd (No. 2)* [1939], Ch. 182, 189 and 192.

[4] Being still in Russia: [1921] 3 K.B. at p. 545.

[5] In such a case, namely, one of recognition and protection of rights duly acquired in a foreign country, it is believed that the character of the foreign law or decree under which the right was required is immaterial; in both these Russian cases the issue of the immorality of the Russian confiscatory decrees was discussed and all the members of the two Courts of Appeal were of opinion that an English Court could not—*semble*, when asked to recognize and protect rights acquired under the laws of a foreign State, the

same as in *Luther* v. *Sagor*, and the decision was to the same effect. It will be noted that in both cases the persons whose property was divested were Russians.

Where a territory of the lawful Government is under the occupation of the enemy, it is not to be thought that circumstances will not arise when these principles will apply. We have seen that on occupation the laws of the lawful sovereign continue in principle to apply, and these laws may thus determine questions of title to movable property in the occupied territory (which, of course, is still under the sovereignty of the lawful—though temporarily dispossessed—Government). We shall also see that a Government in exile may continue to make laws applying to its territory even while that territory is under enemy occupation[1] and such laws may also affect the title to movable property situate in that territory. Such a situation arose in *State of the Netherlands* v. *Federal Reserve Bank* where the Court of Appeals of New York had to consider the application of a decree of the Netherlands Government in exile to bearer bonds of certain American corporations, the bonds at the time of the decree being in Holland. The Court held the decree effective to deal with title to the bonds: the Court considered that the bearer bonds could be held to be situated in the United States, but went on to say that, on the basis that the *situs* of the bonds was to be regarded as being where the certificates were, the decree should still be given effect.

(*b*) Now let us consider the case where an English Court is asked actively to enforce the operation of a foreign law upon property now in this country when that property was not within the foreign jurisdiction at any relevant time.

If the foreign law or decree is penal, the answer is clear. Our Courts will not enforce it. If the foreign law or decree is not penal or otherwise obnoxious from the English point of view, the answer was not, until recently, quite so clear.[2]

Generally speaking[3] a State's legislative authority is regarded by

Government of which has been recognized by His Majesty, in regard to property within the jurisdiction of those laws at a relevant date—question the legality of that Government's acts.

[1] Below, p. 445.

[2] For a review of the authorities, see the third edition of this book, pp. 362–6.

[3] An obvious exception is the effect of a foreign bankruptcy in vesting in a trustee the bankrupt's movable property in England if the foreign bankruptcy law provides for extraterritorial effect. See also 9 *B.Y.* (1928), p. 168, where an anonymous writer states the principle as follows: "'A country has no jurisdiction over property situated in another country." As a principle of English Private International Law it may be put thus: (1) The English Courts will not recognize that the legislation of a foreign country, or anything done under such legislation, can affect property not situate in that country. (2) The English Courts will not exercise jurisdiction in respect of property situated in a foreign country, nor

other States and the Courts that represent them as limited territorially to things, events and persons within its territory, and is not extended to things, events or persons (unless they are its subjects) not within its territory. The main difficulty in the way of finding clear English judicial authority for this proposition has lain in the dearth of cases in which the foreign legislation being considered has been free from all taint of penality; much of such authority as there is is *obiter*— although it is pertinent to observe that Lord Mackay, in a Scottish case (the *El Condado*)[1] raising these issues, reviewed these English authorities and remarked that, even though it might be said that much of it was *obiter*, 'a long series of *obiter dicta* of high authority, all in one sense, are a sound foundation for a judgment now'. At the outset of the War of 1939 to 1945 it could only be said that if an English Court were invited to enforce upon property in England rights claimed under a law or decree of a foreign country purporting to have extraterritorial effect, the property not having been situate in that foreign country at any relevant time and the law or decree not being penal or otherwise objectionable, it would *probably* not do so.

Starting from this situation of uncertainty, the first of the wartime decisions which claims our attention is *Anderson v. N. V. Transandine Handelmaatschappij and Others, The State of the Netherlands Intervening*.[2] In that case the Supreme Court of the State of New York (County of New York) had to consider the effect upon Dutch assets in that State of the Royal Netherlands Decree of 24 May 1940, made in London, which purported to nationalize and vest in the State of the Netherlands (*inter alia*) cash and securities which belonged to Dutch individuals and corporations domiciled in occupied Holland and were in the hands of American depositees. The object of the Decree, or at any rate one of its objects, was to prevent Dutch assets in neutral countries from falling into enemy hands as the result of actions brought in neutral Courts. The State Department certified that: 'The Govern-

apply English law to such property. There are exceptions to this principle, no doubt, but this is not the place to discuss them.' See also for a statement of the general principle as understood in the United States, Beale, *Conflict of Laws*, I, pp. 308 and 314, and Moore, *Digest of International Law*, §§ 197–9.

[1] See for a fuller treatment of the case, p. 443 below.

[2] Affirmed by the Appellate Division of the Supreme Court held in and for the First Judicial Department in the County of New York on 14 November 1941, and by the New York Court of Appeals on 29 July 1942. To the same effect are *Grünbaum v. N. V. 'Oxyde' Maatschappij voor Ersten en Metalen*, New York L.J., 27 August 1941, p. 439, *Duesterwald v. Lädwig*, *ibid.* 15 January 1942, p. 215, cited by Jessup in 36 *A.J.* (1942), pp. 282–8, *State of the Netherlands v. Federal Reserve Bank of New York et al.* (1948); and *The State of the Netherlands v. Federal Reserve Bank* (1951). See also *U.S. v. Pink* (1942), and note in 58 *L.Q.R.* (1942), p. 451, and two more American decisions reported in 10 *A.D.* (1941–42), nos. 171 and 172.

ment of the United States continues to recognize as the Government of the Kingdom of the Netherlands the Royal Netherlands Government, which is temporarily residing and exercising its functions in London.' Mr Justice Shientag first held that the fact that the Decree was 'promulgated in London, England, rather than at The Hague, is immaterial, in view of the fact that our government has officially recognized the Netherlands Government since its temporary residence in London'. Moreover, according to the affidavit of the Commercial Counsellor of the Dutch Legation in Washington, 'the British Government has stated that so far as is within their province they recognize the Netherlands Royal Decree of 24 May 1940, as a legitimate exercise of the legislative power of the Netherlands'.[1] Later the learned judge pointed out that the 'Decree is a measure of protection, not of expropriation. Its purpose is to conserve, not to confiscate; to protect the rights of the individual, not to destroy them'. Article 5 of the Decree specifically provides for restitution of the nationalized assets to their owners when the present emergency ceases to exist. The learned judge concluded

that the Decree is a valid exercise of the sovereign power of the Netherlands, that it covers the property here sought to be attached, that as between the Netherlands nationals concerned and the State of the Netherlands it vests title to such assets in the State of the Netherlands, and that, since the public policy of the Decree is in harmony with the public policy of the forum, the Decree should be upheld by our courts under the principles of comity.

This judgment was affirmed by the Appellate Division of the Supreme Court on 14 November 1941; its judgment was in turn affirmed by a judgment given by the New York Court of Appeals given on 29 July 1942[2] (by which date the United States of America had entered the war). The Court of Appeals would appear to have taken the view that the decisions of the lower Courts were in harmony with the policy of the United States thus formulated and communi-

---

[1] Quoted in the Brief for the Netherlands Government.
This practice of the 'recognition' by a Government of the decrees of a foreign Government is, we believe, novel and requires a note. It is clearly a political act. We suggest that there are two ways in which it might affect a judicial decision: (1) as in *Anderson* v. *N.V. Transandine*, where the Court is basing its decision upon the public policy of its own country, of which no clearer evidence could be found; (2) as another illustration of the way in which to an increasing extent our Courts seek and follow the guidance of the Executive in ascertaining or assessing the state of our legal relations with foreign States. (For some instances, see 3 *A.D.* (1925–6), p. 128, note (*d*).) In *Bank voor Handel en Scheepvaart N.V.* v. *Slatford*, [1953] 1 K.B. 248, Devlin J. was unwilling to consider the approval of foreign legislation by the Crown as a relevant factor (see pp. 264–6). There is no evidence that the British Government granted any 'recognition' to the Norwegian decree in the *Lorentzen* case, about to be discussed.   [2] 36 *A.J.* (1942), pp. 701–7.

cated to it, and the Court agreed 'with the Courts below in their determination of the judicial question that the decree of the Government of the Netherlands is valid and bars a levy upon the property'. The Court of Appeals, like Mr Justice Shientag, relied upon the comity of nations, and also drew attention to the non-confiscatory nature of the Decree.

Closely akin to *Anderson* v. *N. V. Transandine*, and directly influenced by it, was the decision in *Lorentzen* v. *Lydden & Co.*[1] There Atkinson J. had to consider the effect of a Norwegian Order in Council made in Norway on 18 May 1940,[2] either before, or in the course of, the establishment of the Norwegian Government in England, which purported to vest in a Norwegian Curator (*inter alia*) rights of action for damages for breach of contract belonging to Norwegian shipowners and enforceable in England against British charterers. The learned judge accepted the opinion of a Norwegian advocate to the effect 'that the Order was properly made in accordance with the Norwegian constitution and was legally binding in Norway and on Norwegian subjects wherever they were', and the Order was not confiscatory but contained a provision for compensation. The learned judge referred to Dicey's statement of principle that a State 'has no authority to legislate for, or adjudicate upon, things or persons (unless they are its subjects) not within its territory'[3] and stressed the proviso 'unless they are its subjects', a point which failed to make any difference in the case of the confiscatory decree under discussion in *Banco de Vizcaya* v. *Don Alfonso de Borbon y Austria*. Upon examining a number of the English decisions relating to the Russian nationalizing decrees he found nothing in them which prevented him from giving extra-territorial effect to this Norwegian Order, and he therefore followed the decision in *Anderson* v. *N. V. Transandine* and upheld the Norwegian Curator's right to enforce the claim of the Norwegian shipowners against the English charterers.[4] 'England and Norway', he said, 'are engaged together in a desperate war for their existence... public policy demands that effect should be given to this decree...It is not confiscatory, it is in the interests of public policy, and it is in accordance with the comity of nations.'

[1] [1942] 2 K.B. 202; an appeal by the defendants was dismissed by consent (*ibid.* 216); see comment by F. A. Mann in 5 *Modern Law Review* (1942), p. 262. See also *O/Y Wasa Steamship Co. Ltd* v. *Newspaper Pulp and Wood Export Ltd* (following *Lorentzen* v. *Lydden & Co.*); and *Frankfurter* v. *Exner*.

[2] For a Swedish decision upon the requisition of a Norwegian ship while in a Swedish port, see *The Rigmor* discussed later, p. 444.

[3] Dicey, *Conflict of Laws* (5th ed.), p. 20.

[4] It does not appear that the learned judge's attention was drawn to *The Navemar* and *The El Condado*, which are referred to later at pp. 441 and 443.

This decision, it will be noticed, ran counter to the tendency which appeared to have been prevailing in English Courts up to 1939. Our next case, however, departed from *Lorentzen* v. *Lydden* and gives direct and explicit authority for the rule that the legislation of a foreign State, even if not penal or otherwise objectionable, will not operate so as to transfer title to movable property in this country. In *Bank voor Handel en Scheepvaart N.V.* v. *Slatford*[1] Devlin J. had to consider the same Dutch Decree as was before the American courts in *Anderson* v. *N. V. Transandine*. A Dutch bank had before the outbreak of the war deposited some gold in a bank in London. The Netherlands became enemy-occupied territory in May 1940 and the bank retained its commercial domicile in the Netherlands. The Dutch Government in exile in London issued their decree purporting to transfer to the State of the Netherlands all property of persons resident in the occupied Netherlands. However, as the Dutch bank had become an enemy for the purposes of the British Trading with the Enemy Act, 1939, the gold was, under certain vesting orders, transferred to the British Custodian of Enemy Property. After the war the Netherlands Government made an order returning the gold to the Dutch bank. The bank brought proceedings against the Custodian on the ground that the vesting orders were invalid since at the time they were made the property in the gold had already vested in the Netherlands Government by virtue of that Government's Decree. There seemed to Devlin J. 'to be every reason, if the authorities permit it, for giving effect to the simple rule that generally property in England is subject to English law and to none other'.[2] After giving full consideration to the two cases just discussed, and to such other authority as was available (including in particular the decision of the Inner House of the Court of Session in the *El Condado*[3]—'of high persuasive authority') he concluded that the authorities permitted him to take such a view, and to hold that the Netherlands decree was ineffective to transfer title to movable property in this country to the Netherlands Government. He further rejected the argument that to the rule he had concluded should prevail there was an exception, based on public policy, which would allow the operation upon movable property in this country of the decree of an ally with whom this country was engaged together in a desperate war for their survival.

(*c*) Lastly an English Court might be invited to enforce upon pro-

---

[1] The further proceedings in this case in the Court of Appeal ([1953] 1 Q.B. 279) and the House of Lords ([1954] A.C. 584) were not concerned with the point decided by Devlin J.

[2] [1953] 1 Q.B. at p. 260.   [3] See below, p. 443.

perty in England rights claimed under a law or decree of a foreign country not purporting to have extraterritorial effect, the property not having been situate in that foreign country at any relevant time. Here, *cadit quaestio*; the law or decree will not be enforced.[1]

B. *As regards persons*

As we have said earlier,[2] a State's legislative authority does not extend to things, events or persons, *unless they are its subjects*, not within its territory. In *Reg. v. Lesley*,[3] where the master of a British merchant ship contracted with the Chilean Government to transport from Chile to Liverpool certain political prisoners banished from Chile, the Court for Crown Cases Reserved held that he was rightly convicted of assault and false imprisonment in respect of his detention of them outside Chilean waters, because 'for an English ship the laws of Chile, out of the state, are powerless, and the lawfulness of the acts must be tried by English law'. Our territorial conception of law is stronger than that of most other countries, and the extent to which British subjects are affected by English law while in foreign countries is small.[4] For instance, there are very few crimes which, when committed abroad by British subjects, are justiciable in this country: treason, murder, manslaughter, bigamy, piracy and a few others.[5] But it would not be right to infer from our restricted views as to the exercise of British control of British subjects abroad that English law would regard as illegal and nugatory foreign legislation purporting to exercise more extensive control over nationals abroad than we should ourselves claim; for upon the question of extraterritorial jurisdiction over nationals abroad great discrepancy exists among States. Moreover, it may well be that, requisitioning being an act of sovereignty and to some extent based upon personal allegiance, an English Court

---

[1] *In re Russian Bank for Foreign Trade*; *The Jupiter (No. 3)*.

[2] Above, p. 431.

[3] See *R. v. Secretary of State for Home Affairs, ex parte Duke of Chateau Thierry*, where however the point involved was different.

[4] Section 18 of the Military Training Act, 1939, empowered the Crown to apply the Act to certain British subjects ordinarily resident outside Great Britain. The National Service (Foreign Countries) Act, 1942, empowered the Crown by Order in Council to impose military service on British subjects in foreign countries, and the Emergency Powers Act, 1939, provided for Defence Regulations made thereunder to have a very extensive extra-territorial application to British subjects. See also Merchant Shipping Act, 1894, s. 687, and the Admiralty jurisdiction in regard to offences on the high seas exercised by the Courts of common law. Observations on the *prima facie* territorial scope of English legislation and of the jurisdiction of English courts will be found in *In re Sawers, ex parte Blain* and *Sirdar Gurdyal Singh v. Rajah of Faridkote*. See, in general, *Craies on Statute Law* (6th ed.), ch. 18.

[5] Upon the exercise of criminal jurisdiction over foreigners, see Beckett in 6 *B.Y.* (1925), pp. 44–60 and 8 *B.Y.* (1927), pp. 108–28.

28-2

might be disposed to give effect to the decree of a foreign State purporting to requisition the movable property of one of its nationals in this country upon the ground of the personal jurisdiction exercisable by his State over him in virtue of his allegiance.[1]

The extent of the control of a foreign State over its nationals in this country was the subject of the *Amand* cases.[2] Amand was a Dutch national who had resided in the United Kingdom for many years, and on or about 20 August 1940, in response to a calling up notice from the Dutch Ministry of Defence based upon a Dutch Decree of 14 August 1940, imposing compulsory military service upon Dutch nationals resident in the United Kingdom, Canada or the United States of America, he reported at Paddington on 20 August and went to a Dutch Army Camp at Porthcawl, after protesting against a refusal to postpone his call for the purpose of attending to his business affairs. He actually served in the Army for some weeks, but, after receiving in February 1941 a week's leave, he declined to return and was soon arrested by the Metropolitan Police in pursuance of a (British) Order in Council made under the (British) Allied Forces Act, 1940, as a deserter from the Dutch Army, and he thereupon applied for a writ of *habeas corpus*.

In the first case the Divisional Court, after holding that he had not become a member of the Dutch Army by voluntary enlistment, decided that his arrest was authorized by the above-mentioned Act and Order in Council and refused his application for the writ. His Majesty's Attorney-General stated to the Court[3]

that the Government of the Netherlands is a Government for the time being allied with His Majesty and established in the United Kingdom; that it is established and exercising its functions in the United Kingdom with the assent and on the invitation of His Majesty's Government in the United Kingdom; and that His Majesty's Government recognize Her Majesty Queen Wilhelmina and her Government as the Sovereign and Government of the Netherlands and as exclusively competent to perform the legislative, administrative and other functions appertaining to the Sovereign and Government of the Netherlands.

The Court received evidence from Dutch lawyers on behalf of the applicant and the Dutch Government respectively, upon (*a*) the con-

---

[1] See Holdsworth in 35 *L.Q.R.* (1919), pp. 12–42.

[2] *In re Amand* [1941] 2 K.B. 239, and *In re Amand (No. 2)* [1942] 1 All E.R. 236 and (on one point only) [1942] 1 K.B. 445; on the question whether an appeal would lie on the refusal of the Divisional Court to grant a writ of *habeas corpus*, see *Amand* v. *Sec. of State for Home Affairs* [1942] 2 K.B. 26; affirmed [1943] A.C. 147. See comment by Hartmann in 5 *Modern Law Review* (July 1942), p. 256. Reference should also be made to a similar South African decision upon a Dutch decree of 28 February 1941; *Haak and Others* v. *Minister of External Affairs*.   [3] [1941] 2 K.B. at p. 250.

stitutional validity of the Dutch Decree[1] and (*b*) if valid, upon the applicability, according to Dutch law, of such a Decree to Dutch subjects resident outside Dutch territory, and decided that 'the Decree was valid according to Netherlands law, and that it applied to the applicant while resident in this country'. The Court pointed out that the Decree could be applicable extraterritorially without being enforceable extraterritorially. Enforceability was supplied by the Allied Forces Act, 1940, and the Order in Council made thereunder, so that the applicant's arrest and detention were authorized. The applicant appealed and gave notice of his desire to cross-examine the deponents to three affidavits filed on behalf of the Dutch Government before the Divisional Court and to adduce further evidence. The appeal was dismissed—apparently not on the merits but on the ground that the proper procedure was a further application for a writ of *habeas corpus*. Accordingly, a second application[2] for the writ was made, and further evidence was adduced by the applicant. It failed, and substantially on the same grounds. Two points require mention. First, the Divisional Court rejected the argument that it was a breach of our constitutional law for the Crown without the assent of Parliament to permit a foreign Government to exercise its functions in this country and pointed out that the Crown had in no way lessened the sovereignty of the Government of this country. Secondly, the Court held that it had both a right and a duty to investigate the validity of the Dutch Decree—a matter which it will be more convenient to discuss separately and later.[3]

The main conclusion relevant to the argument of this chapter which we draw from the *Amand* decisions is this. There is a distinction between recognizing the application of a valid foreign law purporting to have extraterritorial effect upon foreign nationals and enforcing it. The Divisional Court, rightly, it is submitted with respect, recognized that a valid Dutch Decree purporting to have extraterritorial effect upon Dutch nationals could take effect upon a Dutch national in this country; this Decree made Amand a member of the Dutch Army so

---

[1] Justifying the admissibility of such evidence by reference to *A. M. Luther Co.* v. *James Sagor & Co.*; *Princess Paley Olga* v. *Weisz*; and *Russian Commercial and Industrial Bank* v. *Comptoir d'Escompte de Mulhouse*; above, pp. 400, 429–30.

[2] [1942] 1 All E.R. 236; reported in [1942] 1 K.B. 445, on one point only.

[3] In the War of 1914 to 1918 a different practice was adopted as between allies upon the liability of their nationals to military service. By a series of treaties which received the force of statute in the United Kingdom by the Military Service (Conventions with Allied States) Act, 1917, allied nationals were reciprocally compelled to serve in the armed forces of the allied State in whose territory they preferred to remain rather than return to their own. Amand would have been liable to serve in the British forces as a result of this Act if his country had been an allied State entering into such a Convention.

that when he declined to return to it he became a deserter; but it was a British Act of Parliament and an Order in Council thereunder that made him liable to arrest and detention and thus enforced the Dutch Decree.[1]

3. CONSTITUTIONALITY OF THE LEGISLATION OR OTHER OFFICIAL ACTS OF A FOREIGN GOVERNMENT

Let us suppose that by the Constitution of the occupied country whose Government has found a refuge in England a decree purporting to have a particular legal effect can only be made in a particular manner, which has become impossible owing to the dispersal of the organs of Government, for instance, the King and the members of the legislature or the King and his Ministers,[2] or at a particular place, for instance, in the metropolitan territory which is wholly occupied by the enemy. Can this objection be taken in an English Court? Is a statement by the dispossessed Government in England to the effect that in the special circumstances of the emergency the decree is valid, conclusive upon the Court? It is proposed to assume that the refugee Government continues to be recognized by His Majesty as the Government of the State which it represents and as exclusively competent to perform the functions appertaining to the Government of that State. That does not carry us the whole way.

We are aware of no direct and unqualified judicial authority on these points. Let us see how near we can get to it.

(*a*) We submit that the rule illustrated by *A. M. Luther Co.* v. *James Sagor & Co.* and *Princess Paley Olga* v. *Weisz*, which prevents an

---

[1] Note the National Service (Foreign Countries) Act, 1942, which empowered the Crown to impose upon British subjects in foreign countries obligations with respect to service in His Majesty's Forces of the like character as were imposed upon them in Great Britain.

[2] From October 1914 until November 1918 the greater part, but never the whole, of Belgium was under German occupation. The Government was established at Le Havre, the King spent most of the time at his military headquarters in Belgium, and the majority of the members of Parliament remained in their constituencies. The Belgian Congo remained under Belgian control. Though by the Constitution the legislative power was vested in the King, the Senate and the House of Representatives, the Belgian Government in the name of the King issued at Le Havre throughout this period a series of décrêts-lois—a term unknown to the Constitution. The validity of these décrêts-lois was invariably recognized by the executive, the judicial, and (after the war) the constitutional legislative, authorities. They were treated as true laws which could only be modified, when the war was over, by laws passed in accordance with the Constitution. See the following decisions: Cour de Cassation of 11 February 1919, 8 February 1920 (*Pasicrisie*, 1920, 1, p. 62) and 27 April 1920 (*Pasicrisie*, 1920, 1, p. 124). For Dutch and Belgian practice in the 1939–45 war, see *Nederlands Beheersinstituut* v. *Robaver*, 14 *A.D.* (1947), no. 108 (particularly the note at p. 240), 15 *ibid.* (1948), no. 174, and 16 *ibid.* (1949), no. 154 (Holland, Supreme Court); *Damhof* v. *State of the Netherlands* (Holland); *Landelijke Hypotheekbank Ltd* v. *Receiver of Taxes for Amsterdam* (Holland).

English Court from sitting in judgment upon the substantial validity of the acts of a foreign State, done within its own territory, does not mean that it cannot make inquiry as to the formal validity of those acts and their legal nature; the rule relates to the content of the official act rather than to the ascertainment and competence of the organ from which it emanates and the legal form with which it is clothed.

(b) That it is both the right and the duty of an English Court to inform itself, by evidence as on a question of fact, as to the meaning and purported effect of a foreign statute or decree is abundantly clear,[1] and a statement by the representative of a foreign Government as to the meaning and effect is not conclusive.

(c) An English Court is under a duty to decline to give effect to a British Proclamation or Order in Council purporting to do something which can only be done by a statute, and, on principle, it should be under the same duty to examine the competence of the organs of a foreign Government in regard to the official act in question. Do the decisions establish this as the rule? In the Russian cases referred to in this book our Courts have come very near to it and have not hesitated to discuss such questions as whether the body responsible for a particular official act possesses administrative or legislative powers.[2] In one case Hill J. expressly rejected the suggestion that the declaration of the representative of a foreign State as to the effect of the action of his Government within its own territory was binding upon him.[3] Nevertheless, there can be no doubt that an English Court would feel bound to attach great weight to a statement made, say, by or on behalf of the Minister of Justice of a foreign Government, particularly when, as in the case of some countries, it is one of the recognized duties of the Minister of Justice to answer inquiries concerning the law of his country.[4]

(d) Perhaps the nearest approach to a decision upon this matter which our Courts have been compelled to make occurred in the

---

[1] Dicey, Rule 205 and notes: *The Jupiter (No. 3)* [1927] P. 122, 138-40; *Russian Commercial and Industrial Bank* case. In *Lorentzen* v. *Lydden & Co.*, Atkinson J. admitted the evidence of a Norwegian lawyer upon the constitutionality and effect of the Norwegian 'Order in Council'.

[2] See the *Russian Commercial and Industrial Bank* and *Princess Paley Olga* cases.

[3] *The Jupiter (No. 3)* [1927] P. 122, 138-40.

[4] For an instance of an affidavit by a foreign ambassador as to the validity of the requisition of a ship by his Government, see *The Kabalo*; and *The Laurent Meeus*. In *The Cristina* [1938] A.C. 485, 506, Lord Wright said: 'It is unnecessary here to consider whether the Court would act conclusively on a bare assertion by the [foreign] Government that the vessel is in its possession. I should hesitate as at present advised so to hold, but the respondent here has established the necessary facts by evidence.'

second *Amand* case.[1] There the constitutionality of the Dutch Decree imposing compulsory military service upon a Dutch national who had resided in England for thirteen years was challenged by him upon the ground that in six respects[2] it contravened articles of the Constitution of the Netherlands State.[3] The Divisional Court, rejecting the argument of the Dutch Government, which was supported by the English Attorney-General, that these questions could not lawfully be investigated, examined the Decree in relation to each[4] of the articles of the Constitution which it was alleged to contravene and upheld its constitutionality. But the special grounds upon which the Court considered itself to be justified in following this course must be noted. Wrottesley J.'s main ground was that the Decree 'deals with the freedom of a person living in this country within the protection of the Crown'; Croom-Johnson J.'s ground was the same; Cassels J. mentions the same ground and the peculiar fact that the foreign Government was by reason of emergency temporarily established in this country, and was also 'impressed by the fact that the Netherlands courts no longer function'. All three learned judges refer to the absence of express authority.

We submit, therefore, that the decision in the second *Amand* case must be limited to the peculiar facts of that case and is not authority for the general proposition that an English Court must, when called upon to do so, examine the constitutional validity of a foreign decree or other official acts. We suggest, however, that the balance of authority at present is in favour of the existence of such a right and duty, though it must be admitted that there is much to be said for the view that, when the Minister of Justice or other appropriate officer of a duly recognized Government produces an enactment in Court and states that it is formally and constitutionally valid according to the law of his country an English Court ought to accept that statement unless and until the enactment has been pronounced to be invalid by the Courts of that country.

---

[1] *In re Amand* (No. 2) (above, p. 437).

[2] [1942] 1 All E.R. at p. 243, including the point that the Decree was issued outside the Netherlands.

[3] With regard to the objection—perhaps the most difficult—that the Netherlands Constitution contained no provision allowing the imposition of conscription by decree instead of by statute, it is worth mentioning that an English Court would be aware of the facts that in this country the King wages war under the royal prerogative which arms him with exceptional powers and that he has a common law power, not affected by the Bill of Rights, of raising and maintaining an army in time of war. As already mentioned (p. 436) our Government had recognized Queen Wilhelmina and her Government in England as possessing (*inter alia*) the legislative functions of the Sovereign and Government of the Netherlands—which perhaps does not include the power to amend the Constitution.

[4] Except that we do not find any discussion of the point referred to in n. 2 above.

4. THE POSITION OF SHIPS

Merchant ships form so important a part of the resources of maritime countries, particularly in time of war, that their position deserves separate treatment.[1]

Some of the decrees of the allied Governments are concerned with the control and requisitioning of their merchant ships. Apart from the general rules (discussed in the previous section) relating to the control of a Government over the assets of its nationals situated in foreign countries, is there anything peculiar arising from the intrinsic character of merchant ships? Our Courts have not yet said their last word upon this matter, and the available authority, such as it is, must be examined.

There is a considerable amount of authority in favour of the existence of a rule that the essential nature of merchant ships and their peculiar connection with the State whose flag they fly keep them notionally within the territorial jurisdiction of the flag State, wherever physically they may be. (It is unnecessary and, what is more important, erroneous, to call them floating portions of that State's territory.[2] That is a dangerous and misleading metaphor, and, if it corresponded with truth, would exclude foreign merchant ships from the jurisdiction of any State in whose ports they may be.) The following cases may be referred to:

In *The Cristina*,[3] Lord Wright expressly left open the question of the existence of any such rule; it was unnecessary to decide the point because the Spanish Republican Government had obtained possession of the ship—rightly or wrongly—and to have allowed the shipowner's action for the recovery of possession to proceed would have been to allow that Government to be impleaded.[4]

In *The Navemar*[5] the existence of such a rule was plainly asserted by

---

[1] On the requisitioning of ships, see Holdsworth, 35 *L.Q.R.* (1919), pp. 12–42, and McNair, *Journal of Comparative Legislation*, 3rd ser., vol. 27 (1945), pp. 68–78.

[2] Even more so than in the case of public ships. After the opinion of the Privy Council delivered by Lord Atkin in *Chung Chi Cheung* v. *The King*, let us hope that this metaphor is dead.

[3] [1938] A.C. 485, 509, where he said that 'the *Cristina*, even when in Cardiff docks, may have, as being a foreign merchant ship, a different status from an ordinary chattel on land': see 19 *B.Y.* (1938), p. 244, n. 3. See also *The Arraiz* (1938); *The Neptuno* (1938); *The Kabalo* (1940).

[4] *The Cristina* was followed on this point in *Pankos Operating Co.* v. *M. V. Janko* (*otherwise Norsktank*) by the United States District Court for the Eastern District of New York and by the Circuit Court of Appeals.

[5] See note to 9 *A.D.* (1938–40) No. 68; Hyde in 33 *A.J.* (1939), pp. 530–4; and two articles by Preuss, 35 *ibid.* (1941), pp. 263–81 and 36 *ibid.* (1942), pp. 37–55, from which it appears that the U.S.A. Courts incline to the view that, for the purpose of requisitioning,

a United States Circuit Court of Appeals which upheld the operation, upon a Spanish merchant ship in the port of Buenos Aires, of a decree issued by the Spanish Republican Government on 11 October 1936 expropriating merchant ships, with the result that she became a Spanish public ship and acquired immunity from process in the American Courts. The decision is based upon the peculiar character of a ship which is 'considered, constructively at least, as part of the territory of the Sovereign whose flag it flies, and is subject, while on the high seas or in foreign territorial waters, to the jurisdiction of that Sovereign'. No question arose as to the area of Spanish territory then controlled by that Government. The Supreme Court reversed the decision of the Circuit Court of Appeals on the ground that it had not been proved that possession of the ship or the right to it was in the Spanish Republican Government and that she was not as such immune from process, but it also held that the Spanish Ambassador should be permitted to intervene 'for the purpose of asserting the Spanish Republican Government's ownership and right to possession'. Thereupon the case again came before a District Court,[1] which rejected the claim of the Spanish Republican Government on the ground that the decree of expropriation was confiscatory and penal and therefore could not successfully be asserted in an American Court; on appeal from this decision it was held[2] by the same Circuit Court of Appeals that the decree was effective to transfer the title in and right to possession of the vessel to the Spanish Republican Government. After observing that the question whether compensation for the expropriation was payable or not did not matter, the Court said:

In the present case, we are not enforcing claims of another State to property beyond its jurisdiction, as would have been the case if the subject-matter had been a chattel that was within the State of New York when the appropriation became effective. The situation here resembles that of

merchant ships are 'quasi-territorial', so that the requisitioning of a ship outside the territorial waters of the requisitioning State 'is not an extraterritorial exercise of state authority'. In one case it was said that jurisdiction over ships 'partakes more of the characteristics of personal than of territorial sovereignty'—that is, personal allegiance rather than territoriality. And see *Furness, Withy & Co.* v. *Rederiaktiegolabet* (sic) *Banco*; *Belgian Government* v. *The Lubrafol.*

[1] (1938) 62 Ll. L. Rep. 76.

[2] (1939) 64 *ibid.* 220. Note that Augustus N. Hand J., after citing Lord Wright in *The Cristina*, said at p. 225 (col. 1): 'It is not necessary to say that the decree effected an expropriation of the vessel while she was in foreign territorial waters at Buenos Aires, though it was promulgated and notification thereof was given when the ship was at that port. Even if the decree might not be effective while the *Navemar* was at Buenos Aires, nevertheless it was an instrumentality of expropriation that would become operative upon the vessel as soon as she reached the high seas'—meaning, it is suggested, 'operative as a matter of Spanish (Republican) law'.

the appropriation of tangibles within the confines of Spain which afterwards reached our shores. There we should recognize the title acquired
under the laws of the foreign State...In either situation the decree of the
foreign State is recognized as passing title because jurisdiction is held to
exist. When the Spanish decree became effective as to the *Navemar*, she
was on the high seas and recognition of it involved no conflict with our
laws. *Crapo* v. *Kelly*, 16 Wall. 610, 631, 632.[1]

In *The El Condado*[2] the Court of Session had to consider whether a
decree of the Spanish Republican Government of 28 June 1937, purporting to requisition all vessels registered at Bilbao (as the vessel
was), could take effect upon a Spanish merchant ship lying in Scottish
waters. Upon a variety of grounds (to which the following lines do
not attempt to do justice) the Lord Ordinary (Lord Jamieson) and all
the members of the Second Division rejected the argument that the
decree operated upon this ship in Scottish waters, and the variety of
reasons underlying their several judgments on this point must be summarized *only in so far as relevant to our present enquiry*. Lord Jamieson,[3]
apparently treating the Spanish Decree as confiscatory, declined to
give effect to it as regards property situated outside the territory of the
Government issuing the Decree (*semble*, at the time when the Decree
became or remained operative). The Lord Justice-Clerk (Aitchison)
regarded the Decree as 'not confiscatory or penal in the full sense',
and, relying upon *The Jupiter* (*No. 3*),[4] held that the ship 'was moveable property that was outwith the territory and jurisdiction of the
foreign sovereign state, and, having been so at the date of the decree,
it was not capable of being affected by the requisition'.[5] Lord
Mackay[6] referred to 'a most emphatic train of eminent English judges
in favour of the view that such "decrees" of a foreign country as purport to have extraterritorial effect, and to attach property in a subject situated, and at a time when it is situated, within this country or
its territorial waters, will not be recognized by our laws and Courts'.
Lord Pitman[7] refused to recognize the validity of the requisition.
Lord Wark,[8] without referring to the question whether the Decree
was penal and confiscatory or not, stated that the Scots law was the
same as the English law on the matter, held that such a Decree could
have 'no effect whatever upon moveable property, including ships,
outwith the territory' of the Government issuing it.

---

[1] See *The Adriatic*, and *Fields* v. *Predionica I Tkanica*.

[2] *Government of the Republic of Spain and Another* v. *National Bank of Scotland*. See also *The Sendeja*. Volumes 8 and 9 of the *Annual Digest* contain many cases arising out of events in Spain.

[3] [1939] S.C. at p. 421.   [4] [1927] P. 122; *ibid.* 250.   [5] [1939] S.C. at p. 427.

[6] At p. 433.   [7] At p. 436.   [8] At p. 438.

In a case, *The Rigmor*,[1] which concerned a Norwegian tanker, and the parties to which included His Britannic Majesty's Government, the Norwegian Government and the Waages Tankrederei A/S of Oslo, the Supreme Court of Sweden on 17 March 1942, upheld the requisition by the Norwegian Government under a decree of 18 May 1940, of this Norwegian ship then lying in a Swedish port. Upon the requisition being notified to him the Norwegian master of the ship attorned to the Norwegian Government as represented by its Legation in Sweden, so that the Norwegian Government thus acquired possession of the ship in law and in fact. The Norwegian Government later leased the ship to the British Government, represented by the Ministry of War Transport, by means of a demise charter, as the result of which so the Court held, she passed into the possession of the British Government. The Norwegian owners, carrying on business in Oslo and doubtless under constraint by the German occupying Power, instituted these proceedings for the purpose of preventing the British Government from removing the ship from Swedish waters, and the question, not here relevant, was the validity of the claim of State immunity advanced by the British Government upon the basis of its actual and lawful possession. This claim was upheld. In the course of its judgment the Supreme Court upheld the requisition in the following passage:

In the case under consideration the transfer of possession to the Royal Norwegian Government entailed the carrying into effect of a State process of requisitioning. It follows from the nature of such a process that the carrying into effect can occur even without the collaboration of the owner of the requisitioned object, and this will particularly be the case if the owner is in territory occupied by an enemy State. It is true that the carrying into effect within the territory of another State cannot take place under compulsion and be legally binding. But if, as in the present case, it takes place with the consent of the immediate possessor and especially if the latter is a subject of the requisitioning State and holds the position of captain of the vessel affected by the requisitioning, it can only be regarded as not legally binding on the assumption that the decree on which the execution is based is such that because of its departure from the fundamental principles of the law of our country it ought not to be taken into account. This cannot be said to be the case with the Norwegian requisitioning decree.

We may also note the statement, *obiter*, of Hill J. in *The Jupiter* (*No. 3*) that 'If the *Jupiter* was not within the territory of the

---

[1] See also *The Solgry* (1942), and Jägerskiöld, 42 *A.J.* (1948), pp. 601–7, on Swedish practice.

R.S.F.S.R. [at any material date], I do not see how the mere passing of a decree could transfer the property'.[1]

Thus the question of the extraterritorial operation of legislation upon privately-owned merchant ships cannot be regarded as settled. It is clear that for many purposes such a ship carries the law of her flag State with her, and it would not be surprising if this body of law included legislation involving a compulsory change of ownership. So far at any rate as the Crown is concerned, the statutory power of requisitioning ships in times of national emergency is wide,[2] but, of course, that does not involve the proposition that other countries enforce our municipal powers of requisitioning to the full extent or that we enforce theirs. Nevertheless, the requisitioning by a State of merchant ships flying its national flag while in foreign ports is now becoming frequent and widespread, and it would not be surprising if this practice were upheld by British and other Courts.[3]

5. CHANGES MADE IN THE LAW BY THE DISPOSSESSED GOVERNMENT DURING THE OCCUPATION[4]

The question arises whether the sovereign of enemy-occupied territory can effectively make during the occupation changes in that large portion of his law which remains in force therein notwithstanding the occupation. Could the Norwegian Government during the occupation of Norway in the War of 1939 to 1945 make a decree (valid in other respects) changing the law of succession, by will or on intestacy, to movables or immovables in Norway? Supposing during 1914–18 the Belgian Government had changed the law relating to sale of goods, bankruptcy or wills, would that change have operated only in non-occupied Belgium or also in occupied Belgium?

---

[1] In *The Arantzazu Mendi* [1939] A.C. 256 it was unnecessary to decide whether this Spanish ship registered at Bilbao could effectively be requisitioned (1) while outside Spanish territorial waters by the Republic Government after Bilbao had been captured by the Franco Government, or (2) by the Franco Government while lying in a British port. What mattered was that the proceedings instituted by the Republican Government for the purpose of obtaining possession of the ship impleaded the Franco Government and therefore had to be set aside. And see the remarks by Lord Wright and A. N. Hand J. above at pp. 441–2.

[2] Note that section 3 of the Emergency Powers Act, 1939, applied to 'all British ships or aircraft, not being Dominion ships or aircraft, wherever they may be', and see Regulation 53 thereunder.

[3] See above, p. 441, n. 1. For a French decision arising out of the Spanish Civil War, see *Lafuente* v. *Llaguno y Duranona*, and for a Bermuda decision of 1939, *The Cristobal Colon*, see 39 *A.J.* (1945), p. 839.

[4] See Feilchenfeld, *op. cit.* (in bibliography), §§ 461–72; Wolff, 29 *Transactions of the Grotius Society* (1943), pp. 107–10; Schwelb, 30 *ibid.* (1944), p. 239.

We are aware of no British authority, but there is significant foreign authority available which, since the governing principle rests upon a rule of public international law, is relevant to the attitude which might be adopted by an English Court. The conclusion which we may draw from the various foreign decisions—which include not only the decisions of courts of the legislating States[1] but also those of other States[2]—is that a law passed by the dispossessed Government of territory under belligerent occupation will, notwithstanding the absence of any power to make it effective during the occupation, be regarded as part of the law of the occupied territory if the new law is intended to extend to the occupied territory, and if the new law falls within the category of that large portion of national law which persists during the occupation and which the enemy occupant cannot lawfully change or annul.[3] Such a conclusion would seem to be a natural consequence of the retention by the dispossessed State of its sovereignty over the occupied area, and the limitations imposed upon the occupant's powers to introduce new legislation.

[1] *De Nimal* v. *De Nimal* (Belgium); *Auditeur Militaire* v. *Van Dieren* (Belgium); *Kulturas Balss Co-operative Society's Case* (Latvia); *Stasiuk* v. *Klewec* (Poland, Supreme Court); *Public Prosecutor* v. *Reidar Haaland* (Norway, Supreme Court); *Re Hoogeveen et al.* (Belgium, Cour de Cassation); *Ferrovie dello Stato* v. *S.A.G.A.* (Italy); *Agrocide* v. *Arsocid* (Holland); *Nederlands Beheersinstituut* v. *Robaver*, 1947, 1948 and 1950 (Holland); *Damhof* v. *State of the Netherlands*. Greek courts seem to adopt a differing view: see *Occupation of Cavalla Case*, and *Re X.Y.* See also *Herwyn* v. *Muller* in which the Belgian-German M.A.T. held that a Belgian decree, passed at a time when most of Belgian territory was under German occupation during the War of 1914–18, forbidding trade between Belgian and German nationals had no force in the occupied part of Belgium.

[2] *State of the Netherlands* v. *Federal Reserve Bank* (U.S.A.); *Ammon* v. *Royal Dutch Company* (Switzerland).

[3] It may even be that even in respect of those matters for which the occupant may lawfully legislate, the dispossessed Government may still legislate for the occupied territory, unless and until the occupant actually does legislate in respect of them.

19

WHEN THE UNITED KINGDOM IS NEUTRAL: FOREIGN ENLISTMENT, BLOCKADE AND CONTRABAND; NEUTRAL PROPERTY ON BELLIGERENT TERRITORY

BIBLIOGRAPHY

Brownlie, 5 *I. and C.L.Q.* (1956), pp. 570–80.
Hackworth, *Digest of International Law*, vol. VII, §§ 664–6.
Hall, *International Law* (8th ed.), §§ 214–35.
Hyde, III, §§ 867–85.
Oppenheim, II, § 311.
Phillimore, *International Law* (3rd ed.), III, pp. 233–82.
Wheeler, *Foreign Enlistment Acts.*
Pollock, *Principles of Contract* (13th ed. 1950), p. 302.
McNair, *Opinions, sub tit.* 'Foreign Enlistment'.

When Great Britain recognizes the existence of a state of war between two other States, it is necessary for her to define her own position by deciding whether to become a co-belligerent with one of the parties or to remain neutral.[1] It is not uncommon for a State to announce its attitude to the world by means of a proclamation or declaration of neutrality.

Neutrality is defined by Oppenheim[2] as 'the attitude of impartiality adopted by third States towards belligerents and recognized by belligerents, such attitude creating rights and duties between the impartial States and the belligerents'. Rights and duties *between States*. It is thus a matter of public international law. It is, strictly speaking, incorrect to speak of a person being neutral, though loosely the term may be used to denote the subject of a neutral State. Hague Convention XIII is entitled a 'Convention relating to the Rights and Duties of Neutral *Powers* in Maritime War'. Hague Convention V is, not so correctly, entitled a 'Convention respecting the Rights and Duties of Neutral *Powers and Persons* in War on Land'. It is often convenient to speak of a 'neutral' merchant or shipowner, but the expression is truly elliptical.

---

[1] We need hardly say that the terms 'non-belligerent' and 'pre-belligerent' which have become fashionable recently to describe the neutral State which is waiting for a favourable moment to jump into the contest are political and have no legal meaning. When war exists between *A* and *B*, all other States are either belligerent or neutral.　　[2] II, § 293.

The law of neutrality is a law between States. There are, however, three matters which directly affect the private citizen and which require mention: the first concerns the giving of assistance by British subjects to belligerent States,[1] particularly by enlisting in a belligerent's armed forces, and the second concerns the carriage of contraband and blockade running by British subjects; the third concerns the treatment by a belligerent of British property on its territory.

FOREIGN ENLISTMENT

A neutral State is under various obligations designed to secure its impartiality and must control, and sometimes prohibit, certain activities which might take place within its jurisdiction. In the United Kingdom probably the more important of such prohibitions are those now dealt with by the Foreign Enlistment Act, 1870,[2] an Act based upon and expanding the provisions of the Act of 1819[3] which was the first comprehensive British statute dealing with foreign enlistment. Not all of the prohibitions laid down in that Act are required by inter-

---

[1] The Law Officers, in a Report dated 6 April 1904, expressed the opinion that a State which operates a State-owned railway does not violate its duties as a neutral in permitting goods to be carried upon its railway which are intended for the forces of one belligerent if it is prepared to treat goods intended for the other belligerent in the same manner.

[2] The position at common law is unclear. There is some authority for the proposition that it was a misdemeanour at common law for a British subject to enter the service of any foreign State without leave of the Sovereign: and in two cases, *R. v. Rumble* (1864), and *R. v. Corbett* (1865), Cockburn C.J. expressly reserved for further consideration the question whether the offences with which the accused were charged were offences at common law or only under the Foreign Enlistment Act, 1819. But in 1817 the Law Officers seemed to take a different view (McNair, *Opinions*, II, pp. 331–2). For several Law Officers' opinions dealing with the law prior to the first general Foreign Enlistment Act of 1819 see McNair, *loc. cit.* II, pp. 328–36. Statutes dealing with particular aspects of foreign enlistment were passed in 1736 (9 Geo. 2 c. 30) and 1756 (29 Geo. 2 c. 17), and from time to time Royal Proclamations were issued prohibiting foreign enlistment in specific circumstances (e.g. Proclamation of 27 November 1817: 4 *B.F.S.P.* 488). See, in general, on the law prior to the Act of 1870, Wheeler, *Foreign Enlistment Acts*, where the law of the United States of America, and many American cases, are also considered: see also Phillimore's *International law* (3rd ed.), I, pp. 554–9, and III, pp. 233–44 and 274–82, for much useful historical information, and, for views of the Law Officers of the Crown, McNair, *Opinions*, particularly vol. III, section xxv. As to the application of the Foreign Enlistment Acts in Colonies, see Wheeler, *loc. cit.* pp. 66–7, and section 2 of the 1870 Act ('This Act shall extend to all the dominions of Her Majesty...'): see also the British Protectorates Neutrality Order In Council, 1904 (S.R. & O., 1948 Rev. VIII, p. 767) and the Foreign Jurisdiction Neutrality Order in Council, 1904 (*ibid.* p. 777).

[3] See also the Royal Proclamation, 6 June 1823 (10 *B.F.S.P.* 648). In 1867, largely as a result of the events of the American Civil War (and particularly in the light of the Alabama controversy), a Royal Commission was appointed to consider the working of British neutrality laws. This 'Report of the Neutrality Laws Commissioners, 1867–68', formed the basis of the 1870 Act. In many places the language of the 1870 Act is the same as that of the 1819 Act, so that decisions on the terms of the earlier Act are still relevant.

national law.[1] Furthermore, since the Act merely provides the machinery for carrying out the international obligations of Her Majesty's Government, there is no duty upon the Crown to use that Act until those international obligations arise.[2] The Act does not, however, cover all the consequences for the private citizen which flow from the impartiality which international law requires of States in the event of foreign hostilities. Thus in *De Wutz* v. *Hendricks*[3] the raising in England of a loan on behalf of Greek subjects in rebellion against the Government of Greece, with which the British Government was at peace, was held to be contrary to the law of nations with the result that no right of action would arise out of such an illegal transaction.

The principal provision in the 1870 Act relating to foreign enlistment is the prohibition against any British subject accepting, without licence of the Crown,[4] 'any commission or engagement in the military or naval service or any foreign State at war with any foreign State at peace with Her Majesty'[5] (referred to as 'a friendly State'),

[1] See Oppenheim, II, p. 670; McNair, *Opinions*, III, p. 170. Thus the fact that a British subject may be acting in violation of the Act does not necessarily mean that the United Kingdom is violating the duties of a neutral State under international law. See below, p. 450, n. 10.

[2] Law Officers Opinion, 8 March 1895: McNair, *Opinions*, I, p. 61. The Act, however, operates even without any action by the Crown to apply it to a particular outbreak of hostilities. But, particularly in the nineteenth century, a Proclamation has often been issued to bring the operation of the Act to public notice, as in the Ottoman–Greek war in 1825 (12 *B.F.S.P.* 525), the American Civil War in 1861 (51 *B.F.S.P.* 165), the Russo–Turkish War in 1877 (68 *B.F.S.P.* 857), the Greek–Turkish War of 1897 (89 *B.F.S.P.* 451), the Russo–Japanese War of 1904 (97 *B.F.S.P.* 476), the Turkish–Italian War of 1911 (104 *B.F.S.P.* 207) and the Balkan War of 1912 (105 *B.F.S.P.* 163). In 1937 the Act was declared to apply to the Spanish Civil War: see the Foreign Office statement of 10 January 1937 (*The Times*, 11 January 1937). It is probable that no prosecution would now be made under the Act unless the fact that it applied to the hostilities in question had been brought to the notice of the public.

[3] (1824). See also *Yrisarri* v. *Clement* (1826) 3 Bing. 432, 438–40. While a contract such as that considered in *De Wutz* v. *Hendricks* may be unlawful and unenforceable, it is unlikely that any criminal offence is committed by making loans or gifts to one only of the belligerents: see Opinions of the Law Officers in 1823 and 1873, McNair, *Opinions*, III, pp. 362–5.

[4] A licence by the Crown may be under the sign manual, or be signified by Order in Council or by proclamation: section 15. It is thus clear that 'licence' means a document and not merely tacit permission or acquiescence. Licences were given under the Act of 1819 in, for example, 1835 and 1837, permitting enlistment in the military or naval service of Queen Isabella of Spain (23 *B.F.S.P.* p. 738, and 26 *B.F.S.P.* p. 730).

[5] Section 4. As to the possible consequences to which a British subject exposes himself at the hands of the State against which he has enlisted to fight, see McNair, *Opinions*, II, pp. 349, 370–1. British protection may be withdrawn from any person acting in a manner prohibited by the Act and then suffering the consequences at the hands of the party against which he has enlisted: see the final paragraphs of the Proclamations (other than the first) referred to in note 1 above. For the position of British subjects who are compulsorily enlisted in foreign armed forces, see the correspondence in 1821 with the Government of Buenos Aires (8 *B.F.S.P.* pp. 1020–5), and also an Opinion of the Law Officers in 1863 (McNair, *Opinions*, III, p. 183). On the conscription of non-nationals in international law, see Parry, *31 B.Y.* (1954), p. 437.

449

or leaving Her Majesty's dominions with intent to accept any such commission or engagement.[1] It is similarly an offence within Her Majesty's dominions[2] to induce such foreign enlistment on the part of any other person or such departure from Her Majesty's dominions,[3] and also knowingly to take on board ship any illegally enlisted person.[4]

In the case of illegal shipbuilding, the 1870 Act[5] prohibits, without licence of the Crown, any person within Her Majesty's dominions building, equipping or despatching any ship knowing or having reasonable cause to believe that it will be employed in the military or naval service of any foreign State[6] at war with any friendly State,[7] or increasing the warlike equipment of any ship in the military or naval service of such a foreign State.[8] Special provision is made for the building or equipping of a ship in pursuance of a contract made before the commencement of the war.[9] If while the United Kingdom is neutral[10] a ship is illegally built, equipped, commissioned or

[1] Section 5.

[2] As to whether inducing an alien to enlist is an offence where it occurs on board a British ship on the high seas, see *R.* v. *Corbett* (1865), 4 F. & F. 555, 563.

[3] Sections 4 and 5; see also section 6. As to the distinction between inducing a person to enlist and merely facilitating his departure from a country so that he may enlist abroad, see two Opinions by the Law Officers in 1855 (McNair, *Opinions*, III, pp. 188–91).

[4] Section 7. For decisions on the equivalent provisions of the 1819 Act, see *R.* v. *Rumble* (1864); *R.* v. *Jones and Highat* (1864); *R.* v. *Corbett* (1865); and *Burton* v. *Pinkerton* (1867).

[5] The building or equipping of warships without a licence from the Admiralty is also an offence under the Treaties of Washington Act, 1922, by Section 3 of which its provisions are in addition to and not in derogation from the provisions of the Foreign Enlistment Act, 1870. For an opinion concerning illegal shipbuilding given to the House of Lords in 1721 by the Judges, see McNair, *Opinions*, III, p. 162.

[6] On the question whether a ship being built for a foreign State enjoys immunity from jurisdiction so that the Foreign Enlistment Act could not be enforced against her, see an Opinion of the Law Officers in 1866 (McNair, *Opinions*, I, p. 103), and Foreign Enlistment Act, 1870, section 32.

[7] Section 8. The *cause célébre* in this connection, although occurring while the 1819 Act was in force, was the *Alabama* case, which resulted in an international arbitration between the United Kingdom and the United States (see Pitt Cobbett, II, pp. 377–403): for Opinions given by the Law Officers during this controversy, see McNair, *Opinions*, III, pp. 171–87. As to illegal equipment, see *R.* v. *Rumble* (1864); *R.* v. *Granatelli* (1849); *A.-G.* v. *Sillem* (1864); *Re Grazebrook, Ex parte Chavasse* (1865); all these are decisions under the equivalent provisions of the 1819 Act. It is thus illegal in the circumstances envisaged in the 1870 Act for a British ship to supply a belligerent fleet with coal: Holland, *Letters on War and Neutrality*, pp. 92–5. *Quaere* whether the mere entering into a contract for equipping a vessel is contrary to the Act; see McNair, *Opinions*, III, p. 163. As to illegal despatching (a new offence under the 1870 Act), see *Dyke* v. *Elliott, The Gauntlett* (1872); *United States of America* v. *Pelly* (1899); *The International* (1871). [8] Section 10.

[9] Section 8 proviso. As to a contract of service on board a foreign vessel becoming illegal on the outbreak of war, see *Burton* v. *Pinkerton* (1867); see also an opinion of the Law Officers in 1829, McNair, *Opinions*, III, p. 163.

[10] The Law Officers on 13 June 1904 advised that the sale of a British merchant ship to a Russian subject—Russia and Japan being at war—would not in the circumstances constitute a breach of British neutrality towards Japan, that the sale would in the circumstances amount to a breach of section 8 (4) of the Foreign Enlistment Act, 1870,

despatched or its force illegally augmented contrary to the Act, and such ship captures any other ship or goods as prize and that prize comes within the territorial jurisdiction of the Crown, the owner may apply for their restoration.[1]

In respect of illegal expeditions, it is an offence for any person within the limits of Her Majesty's dominions and without licence of the Crown to prepare or fit out any naval or military expedition to proceed against the dominions of any friendly State.[2] Any act of preparation within Her Majesty's dominions is sufficient to constitute an offence, it not being necessary that the expedition be completely fitted out therein.[3] Furthermore, if an expedition is prepared therein, any British subject who assists, even if he is outside Her Majesty's dominions, commits an offence under this provision.[4]

The principal provisions of the 1870 Act are dependent upon the existence of a 'war' and also upon there being a 'foreign State' at war with another 'foreign State' which is at peace with Her Majesty. While the Act does not define 'war', it does provide that '"foreign State" *includes* (our italics) any foreign prince, colony, province or part of any province or people, or any person or persons exercising or assuming to exercise the powers of government in or over any foreign country, colony, province, or part of any province or people'.[5] The Law Officers of the Crown have advised that a Protectorate may be a 'friendly State' within the meaning of the Act,[6] and it would also seem that that term includes mere insurgents or rebels to whom recognition of belligerency has not been accorded.[7] But it would seem probable that the rebels must have a certain modicum of quasi-governmental

and that, although there is no international obligations to enforce the Foreign Enlistment Act so far as it is in excess of the requirements of international law, the failure to do so would probably lead to remonstrances from Japan. See also an opinion of 4 March 1909 on the same sub-section of the Act.

[1] Section 14. For similar cases in the United States see: *The Estrella* (1819); *The Santissima Trinidad* (1822); *The Gran Para* (1822). Section 14 also applies to ships or goods captured as prize within the territorial jurisdiction of the Crown, in violation of the neutrality of the United Kingdom.

[2] Section 11. This offence is not dependent upon the existence of a war: see *R. v. Sandoval* (1887). As to the impossibility of indicting a corporation under the equivalent section of the 1819 Act, see *The King of the Two Sicilies* v. *Willcox* (1851) 1 Sim. (N.S.) 301, 335. The Terceira Affair in 1828–29 during the Portuguese Civil War was an early *cause célèbre* involving a hostile expedition from the United Kingdom: see McNair, *Opinions*, II, pp. 340–9, and 16 *B.F.S.P.* pp. 417–69. In that incident a British naval force was despatched to prevent the expedition from landing in the foreign territory for which it was destined.

[3] *R. v. Sandoval* (1887); *The Harrier* (1921).   [4] *R. v. Jameson* (1896).

[5] Section 30.   [6] McNair, *Opinions*, I, pp. 60–1.

[7] Law Officers Opinions, 10 October 1876 (McNair, *Opinions*, II, pp. 368–9); *R. v. Carlin, The Salvador* (1870) (a decision under the Act of 1819); Law Officers Opinion, 7 December 1877; H. Lauterpacht, *Recognition in International Law*, pp. 266–8.

organization in order to be considered a 'foreign State' within the definition in the Act.

The meaning to be given to the term 'war' would seem clearly not to be limited to war in the strict technical sense referred to in chapter 1.[1] This would follow from the wide definition of 'foreign State' as a possible participant in the war. The term certainly covers civil war, to which the Act has been applied on several occasions,[2] but it would not seem that actual recognition of belligerency by the United Kingdom is necessary.[3] Similarly, the requirement that the foreign State in the forces opposing which enlistment takes place must be 'at peace' with Her Majesty is not to be interpreted in terms of the technical legal state of peace.

It is not clear to what extent the Act applies to an armed conflict in which the United Nations is engaged. Enlistment in the military service of the State against which the United Nations is acting raises two points in particular. First, much depends on whether or not the United Kingdom is participating in the conflict as a contributory of part of the United Nations forces. If so, the situation would hardly be one to which the Foreign Enlistment Act was designed to apply: the Act was primarily intended to apply to conflicts in which the United Kingdom was not involved, and not to those in which the United Kingdom was a participant. In such circumstances enlistment in the forces of the 'foreign State' against which the United Nations is taking action would seem to be more appropriately dealt with in terms of the law of treason.[4] Second, we have seen that there must be a 'foreign State' at war with another 'foreign State' which is at peace with the United Kingdom. Where the situation is one in which two States, or two factions within a State, are engaged in hostilities and the United Nations forces are aiding one of the parties against the other, the necessary two 'foreign States' will exist.[5] But should the situation be one where the conflict is solely between a foreign State and the United Nations forces, the question would then arise whether

[1] Where no formal state of war exists between two States the Act might apply if those States were actually engaged in an armed conflict.

[2] The 1870 Act (or its 1819 predecessor) has, for example, been declared to be applicable in respect of the American Civil War (51 *B.F.S.P.* p. 165) and the Spanish Civil War (Foreign Office statement, 10 January 1937).

[3] See n. 7, p. 451 above. Thus in 1937 the Act was declared applicable in respect of the Spanish Civil War, even though there was no recognition of belligerency: H. Lauterpacht, *Recognition in International Law*, p. 273, n. 7.

[4] The law of treason applied during the Korean conflict: see above, p. 52.

[5] Provided, of course, that in the case of two factions within a State, each faction satisfies the very wide definition in the Act of 'foreign State'. Since the Act contains its own definition of 'foreign State', the decision in *Re Harshaw Chemical Co.'s Patent* (see above, p. 296, n. 5), concerning the Korean conflict, is distinguishable.

the United Nations could be regarded as constituting a 'foreign State' within the meaning given to that term in the Act. This might present some difficulty.[1] Enlistment in the United Nations forces, or in the forces of the 'foreign State' which the United Nations is assisting, is not necessarily free from the sanctions of the Act. If the State against which those forces are fighting remains for purposes of the Act a 'foreign state at peace with Her Majesty', enlistment in such forces would seem to be capable of constituting an offence under the Act.[2]

In connection with the United Nations actions in Korea and the Congo no clear authoritative view has been expressed whether the Act applied. In relation to the Congo, where many foreign mercenaries, including some British subjects, enlisted with the forces opposing the United Nations forces, the British Government did not invoke the Foreign Enlistment Act but 'decided that the passport of any United Kingdom national who takes up a military engagement in the Congo other than under United Nations Command will be invalidated or withdrawn'.[3]

BREACH OF BLOCKADE: CARRIAGE OF CONTRABAND

International law does not require a neutral State to prohibit its nationals or others within its territory from carrying contraband or attempting to run a blockade[4] on any similar activities, but it permits it to do so provided that the prohibition applies to shipments to all the belligerents alike.[5] English law allows them to engage upon these activities at their own peril:[6] 'carriage of contraband, though hazardous, is not an unlawful or an unneutral trade' (*per* Lord Sumner in delivering the judgment of the Privy Council in *The*

---

[1] It should be noted that the definition of 'foreign State' is not in terms exhaustive. Furthermore, the United Nations, while not a State in the modern acceptance of that term, is an international organization and enjoys a certain degree of international personality (see the Advisory opinion in the *Reparations for Injuries* case, I.C.J. Reports, 1949, p. 174). Circumstances could arise in which persons appointed by some appropriate organ of the United Nations to carry out a mission in territory which is foreign to the United Kingdom could be regarded as 'persons exercising or assuming to exercise the powers of government in or over any foreign country, colony, province, or part of any province or people'.

[2] Subject to the point already made as to whether the United Nations could be a 'foreign State'.

[3] *Parliamentary Debates* (5th series) (Commons), vol. 638 (1960–1), cols. *27–8*; see also *ibid.* cols. *105–6*, and vol. 631 (1960–1), cols. *113–14*.

[4] Upon the meaning of 'blockade' occurring in a charterparty, see *Spanish Government* v. *North of England Steamship Co.*: see above, p. 53.

[5] Oppenheim, II, § 350.

[6] As to the effect of such activities upon contracts of affreightment, see above, p. 215; upon insurance, see above, p. 267; upon Seamen's Contracts, see above, ch. 10.

Rannveig).[1] Internationally, the British Government will not protect them against the penalties which international law permits a belligerent to inflict upon the owners of property so engaged.[2] Municipally, English law does not normally prohibit them, though if their activities seemed likely to cause grave embarrassment to the British Government Parliament might be asked to pass prohibitive legislation.[3] Thus, when it is said that the carriage of contraband and blockade-running and similar unneutral services are 'illegal', it is (or should be) meant that they expose the property involved in them to the penalties which international law permits a belligerent to inflict and in the lawful infliction of which it compels the neutral Government representing the owners to acquiesce. It does not mean—so far as English law is concerned—that they are criminal or even illegal.

Exposition of these principles will be found in judgments by Story J. (a great authority) in *The Santissima Trinidad*[4] (contraband), by Parsons C.J. in *Richardson v. Maine Fire and Marine Insurance Company* (contraband), by Lord Westbury L.C. in *Ex Parte Chavasse, in re Grazebrook*[5] (where a partnership for blockade-running was declared to be not illegal), and by Kent J. in *Seton, Maitland & Co.* v. *Low* (contraband), and, above all, in an admirable judgment by Dr Lushington in *The Helen*[6] (a wages suit in respect of a voyage designed to run the blockade of the Confederate ports in 1864). 'The fact is' (said Dr Lushington in that case, at p. 4), 'the law of nations has never declared that a neutral state is bound to impede or diminish its own trade by municipal restriction', and again (at p. 7): 'It appears that principle, authority, and usage unite in calling on me to reject the new doctrine that to carry on trade with a blockaded port is or ought to be a municipal offence by the law of nations.' It is a case of a collision of rights. As it was put by Parsons C.J. in *Richardson v. Maine Fire and Marine Insurance Co.*: 'It is one of the cases where two conflicting rights exist, which either party [the neutral merchant or shipowner and the belligerent State affected] may exercise without

---

[1] [1922] 1 A.C. 97, 99. See also McNair, *Opinions*, III, pp. 249–53.

[2] The unlawful exercise of alleged belligerent rights relating to contraband and blockade may, of course, cause the British Government to protest to the State exercising or claiming such rights: see, for example, the Note sent by the British Government on 11 July 1951 to the Egyptian Government in connection with the SS. 'Empire Roach' (Bloomfield, *Egypt, Israel and the Gulf of Aqaba*, p. 12).

[3] For instance, in the case of a civil war, the Merchant Shipping (Carriage of Munitions to Spain) Act, 1936.

[4] (1822).

[5] (1865).

[6] (1865). 1 L.R. Adm. and Ecc. Cas. 1. But references in some of these cases to the fitting out of armed ships for a belligerent must be read by British readers subject to the Foreign Enlistment Act, 1870.

charging the other with doing wrong.' Or in the words of Lord Westbury L.C. in *Ex parte Chavasse*: 'Their conflicting rights are co-existent, and the right of the one party does not render the act of the other party wrongful or illegal.' Modern decisions have not disturbed these principles and they may be regarded as well settled.[1]

NEUTRAL PROPERTY ON BELLIGERENT TERRITORY

Where foreign-owned property is within the territory of a State with some degree of permanence or may reasonably be regarded as belonging there, as where it is the property of an alien resident, in general it enjoys the resultant benefits and protection and is subject to the incidental liabilities falling upon property in that country.[2] Thus where a State adopts special laws and regulations to secure the effective prosecution of a war, neutral property in that State will in principle be subject thereto like any other property. Furthermore, just as the property in a State of a national thereof is in time of emergency liable to be requisitioned in order to meet the needs of the emergency, so too is neutral property, in accordance with whatever powers of requisition at the time exist. This is in accordance with international law so long as compensation is paid.[3]

It may, however, happen that neutral property is in time of war within a State only temporarily or by accident. There is, at least in English law, a limit to the extent to which war-time Regulations and powers of requisition will be regarded as applying to such property. Thus where some neutral timber was on a British ship in Finland, and that ship was requisitioned by the British Government and returned to the United Kingdom bringing with it, without the consent of the neutral owner, its cargo of timber the Court of Appeal held[4] that Defence of the Realm Regulations conferring a power to requisition which, taken literally, was wide enough to cover this property, could not be held applicable to it. Atkin L.J. said: 'Neutrals who have not sought the protection of this country, even temporarily, either for themselves or their goods, have no particular interest in the defence of this realm; and I cannot think that it was within the power of the authority making regulations under the

---

[1] We should note that a blockade or embargo imposed under Chapter vii of the U.N. Charter is subject to different considerations.

[2] See Schwarzenberger, *International Courts* (2nd ed.), pp. 339–41.

[3] See Oppenheim, ii, § 367; Hyde, iii, § 632; H. Lauterpacht, 27 *B.Y.* (1950), p. 455. The right of requisition in an emergency is, of course, available to a State even if no state of war exists and there is merely an armed conflict not constituting a war.

[4] *Commercial and Estates Company of Egypt* v. *The Board of Trade* [1925] 1 K.B. 271.

Defence of the Realm Act to make regulations which affected such neutrals.'[1] In earlier proceedings[2] arising out of the requisition of this timber, Bailhache J., while also holding the Regulations inapplicable, did not exclude the possibility that such a vital change in the neutral's position could be made by a Regulation, although it would need perfectly clear, express words, and not general words, to do so.

Property present only temporarily or accidentally—even property in the custody of a Prize Court[3]—may nevertheless be requisitioned. International law recognizes a belligerent's right of angary, and English Courts have accepted this.[4] In its modern form this right has been described, so far as concerns us here, as 'a right of belligerents to destroy, or use, in case of necessity, for the purpose of offence and defence, neutral property on their territory...All sorts of neutral property, whether it consists of vessels or other means of transport, or arms, ammunition, provisions, or other personal property, may be the object of the right of angary, provided it is serviceable to military ends and wants.'[5] The exercise of the right of angary is to be accompanied by the payment of *full* compensation. While the right of angary is not limited to property which is only temporarily or accidentally present in this country but also applies to neutral property here on a more permanent basis, it is to be expected that, since the latter may lawfully be requisitioned in the ordinary way without any requirement for the payment of full compensation the use of the right of angary will in practice be limited to the former situation.[6]

The right of angary forms part of English law: it is a prerogative right of the Crown, and the right of redress to which it gives rise is one which before the Crown Proceedings Act, 1947 was enforceable by petition of right.[7]

---

[1] At p. 293.

[2] *Commercial and Estates Company of Egypt* v. *Ball* (1920).

[3] *The Zamora*; *The Canton.*

[4] *The Zamora*; *Commercial and Estates Company of Egypt* v. *The Board of Trade.*

[5] Oppenheim, II, § 365. See also Hyde, III, §§ 633–4; Bullock, 3 *B.Y.* (1922–3), pp. 99–129; McNair, *Opinions*, III, pp. 398–401; H. Lauterpacht, 27 *B.Y.* (1950), pp. 455–9; Hackworth, *Digest of International Law*, vol. VI, pp. 638–55; Schwarzenberger, *International Courts* (2nd ed.), pp. 360–2. A full examination of the right of angary in international law was made by the Supreme Court of Chile in 1956 in *Lauritzen et al.* v. *Government of Chile.* As to the nature of the requisitioning State's rights over requisitioned neutral ships, see Schwarzenberger, *op. cit.* pp. 303–4, and 3rd ed. of this book, p. 434, n. 4.

[6] See H. Lauterpacht, 27 *B.Y.* (1950), pp. 455–9.

[7] See note 4 above. As to the right of an alien to proceed by way of petition of right, see Street, *Governmental Liability*, p. 49.

APPENDIX

NOTE ON INDO-PAKISTAN HOSTILITIES, 1965

Although the fighting (involving extensive action by land and air forces and minor naval action) between India and Pakistan in September 1965 was fully reported in the press, we may mention certain features of the conflict significant in the context of this book, and particularly of chapter 1.

The fighting on both sides of the cease-fire line in Kashmir was not accompanied by any declaration of war, nor was there any such declaration by India when India attacked into Pakistan territory on 6 September. The President of Pakistan, however, thereupon stated that Pakistan was 'at war' with India. The Prime Minister of India referred to the situation as 'full-scale war', but an Indian official spokesman stated on 6 September that India was not at war with either the State or people of Pakistan, and this was repeated later by the President of India.

Both States took restrictive measures against the other's nationals and their property, of which a custodian was appointed; trade between the two countries was prohibited. Ships of the other country were impounded; contraband lists were published (and were finally abolished by both sides early in December 1965); many neutral vessels and cargoes were interfered with in the waters and ports of the two States; and Pakistan (but apparently not India) established a Prize Court which *inter alia* condemned as prize certain neutral-owned property. On 26 March 1966 the Government of India announced that cargoes detained in India and belonging to third countries would be returned to them, and stated that 'prize court action is contrary to the international law as at present established under the regime of the United Nations Charter. It is well known that the United Nations Charter has banned war and no country can, therefore, legally declare a war. Without such declaration of war, prize court action is illegal. If any country declares a war, it establishes its naked aggression. In the circumstances, contraband control and prize court action stand illegal.'

Diplomatic relations were not formally broken off. However, in practice the diplomatic activities of the respective diplomatic missions seem to have been more or less suspended, and members of the missions were placed under certain physical restrictions.

Both States apparently regarded the existing 1965 Kutch Arbitration Agreement between them as continuing in force, taking action under it in connection with the appointment of arbitrators.

No other State appears publicly to have made any formal statement as to the existence or otherwise of a state of war, although several (including the United Kingdom) took action to suspend military assistance and to establish an attitude of impartiality. Much foreign-owned property (including British property, and also British insurance interests) was affected (see *The Times*, 4 October 1965, p. 10; *Parliamentary Debates* (Commons), vol. 720, col. 59 and vol. 722, col. 326). At the time of going to press we are not aware that any court of a third State has considered the legal nature and effects of the conflict, although two actions begun in the English courts (*State Bank of Pakistan* v. *State Bank of India, Custodian of Enemy Property for India, Third Party*, and *Custodian of Enemy Property in Pakistan* v. *The Same*) might occasion such consideration in due course.

INDEX

abrogation of contracts, *see under* contracts
Abyssinia, Italian annexation of, *see* Italy
Act of Settlement, 1700..., 36 n.
act of State, 95
  friendly alien resident and, 73
acts of war, 3, 218
  abstention from, whether ending state of war, 12
actual military service, 342
administration of estates
  debts to territorial enemies, 337 n.
  enemy deceased, 339
Administrator of Enemy Property, 336
affreightment, contracts of, 203–19
  abandonment of venture, 212–14
  abrogation, 203–9, 362 n.
  armed conflict, effect of, 217
  contraband, carriage of, legality, 215
  United Kingdom belligerent, frustration, 209–14; legality, 203–9
  United Kingdom neutral, legality, 214–17
  unneutral service, 215
agency, 220–3
  abrogation, 220
  company directors, 246
  enemy principal, licence to continue agency, 221, 360–1; power to bind, 222, 361; transfer of property on behalf of, 338–9
  internment of agent, 252
  irrevocable power of sale, 99, 135, 222, 339, 349 n.
  partnership, 234
  profits in war, accountability for, 220–1
  ratification of acts done in war, 222
  territorial enemy, contract with, 126
  third parties, 221–3
Alabama arbitration, 450 n.
alien enemies
  Defence Regulations, 76
  definition, 77
  effect of outbreak of war, 76–7
  enemy 'in protection', 78–81
alien enemies, procedural status, 78–116
  'actor' in proceedings, 82 n., 105, 113
  appellant, 113
  bankruptcy, 114
  cessation of hostilities, effect, 109
  claimant in prize proceedings, 105
  controller under Trading with Enemy Act, powers, 131
  co-plaintiff, 86
  corporations, 102–4

defendant, 110–13, 361
enemy by adherence or assistance, 100–2
enemy resident in foreign non-enemy territory, 88
enemy suing for non-enemy, 86
holder of licence to trade, 110, 361–2
interned civilians, 96–8
internment for hostile act, 97
interpleader, plaintiff in, 104
non-enemy plaintiff in enemy territory, 89–91
non-enemy plaintiff in enemy-occupied territory, 91
non-enemy plaintiff suing for enemy, 87
pending action, plaintiff in, 84–6
prisoners of war and internees, 92–100
  repatriation, effect of, 99
statutes of limitation, 114–16
statutory enemy, 106–8
suing by licence, 108–9, 362
alien enemy, plea of, 82–4
  legal character, 82–4, 140
  procedural or substantive, 79 n., 140
alien friends, 75
  military service obligations, 75 n.
alien status, 71–7
see also alien enemies
aliens
  effect of outbreak of war, 75–7
  European Human Rights Convention, effect of, 73
  expulsion of, 71–3
Aliens Order, 1953..., 81 n.
allies
  distinguished from co-belligerents, 148 n.
  trading with the enemy by, 349
American Civil War, decisions on acts of Confederate Government, 399–400, 406
angary, right of, 455–6
appellant, enemy, 113
Arab States, relations with Israel, *see* Israel *and* United Arab Republic
arbitration, continuation when one party becomes enemy, 321 n., 375
armed conflicts not amounting to war, 15–23, 45–50
  ad hoc legislation, 50, 51, 365
  affreightment, contracts of, 217–19
  contracts, 155
  frustration of contract, 192–9
  insurance, 275–6, 287 n.
  legal effects, 19, 45–50
  military occupation in, 418–23

459